The Condition of Education 2020

Bill Hussar
National Center for Education Statistics

Jijun Zhang
Sarah Hein
Ke Wang
Ashley Roberts
Jiashan Cui
Mary Smith
American Institutes for Research

Farrah Bullock Mann
Amy Barmer
Rita Dilig
RTI International

Thomas Nachazel
Senior Editor
Megan Barnett
Stephen Purcell
Editors
American Institutes for Research

U.S. Department of Education
Betsy DeVos
Secretary

Institute of Education Sciences
Mark Schneider
Director

National Center for Education Statistics
James L. Woodworth
Commissioner

The National Center for Education Statistics (NCES) is the primary federal entity for collecting, analyzing, and reporting data related to education in the United States and other nations. It fulfills a congressional mandate to collect, collate, analyze, and report full and complete statistics on the condition of education in the United States; conduct and publish reports and specialized analyses of the meaning and significance of such statistics; assist state and local education agencies in improving their statistical systems; and review and report on education activities in foreign countries.

NCES activities are designed to address high-priority education data needs; provide consistent, reliable, complete, and accurate indicators of education status and trends; and report timely, useful, and high-quality data to the U.S. Department of Education, Congress, the states, other education policymakers, practitioners, data users, and the general public. Unless specifically noted, all information contained herein is in the public domain.

Suggested Citation
Hussar, B., Zhang, J., Hein, S., Wang, K., Roberts, A., Cui, J., Smith, M., Bullock Mann, F., Barmer, A., and Dilig, R. (2020). *The Condition of Education 2020* (NCES 2020-144). U.S. Department of Education. Washington, DC: National Center for Education Statistics. Retrieved [date] from https://nces.ed.gov/pubsearch/pubsinfo.asp?pubid=2020144.

ISBN: 978-1-63671-012-9

A Letter from the

Commissioner of the National Center for Education Statistics
May 2020

On behalf of the National Center for Education Statistics (NCES), I am pleased to present *The Condition of Education 2020*, an annual report mandated by the U.S. Congress that summarizes the latest data on education in the United States. This report uses data from across the center and from other sources and is designed to help policymakers and the public monitor educational progress. This year's report includes 47 indicators on topics ranging from prekindergarten through postsecondary education, as well as labor force outcomes and international comparisons.

The data show that 50.7 million students were enrolled in public elementary and secondary schools (prekindergarten through grade 12) and approximately 5.7 million students were enrolled in private elementary and secondary schools in fall 2017, the most recent year for which data were available at the time this report was written. In school year 2017–18, some 85 percent of public high school students graduated on time with a regular diploma. This rate was similar to the previous year's rate. About 2.2 million, or 69 percent, of those who completed high school in 2018, enrolled in college that fall. Meanwhile, the status dropout rate, or the percentage of 16- to 24-year-olds who were not enrolled in school and did not have a high school diploma or its equivalent, was 5.3 percent in 2018.

Total undergraduate enrollment in degree-granting postsecondary institutions in 2018 stood at 16.6 million students. The average net price of college for first-time, full-time undergraduates attending 4-year institutions was $13,700 at public institutions, $27,000 at private nonprofit institutions, and $22,100 at private for-profit institutions (in constant 2018–19 dollars). In the same year, institutions awarded 1.0 million associate's degrees, 2.0 million bachelor's degrees, 820,000 master's degrees, and 184,000 doctor's degrees.

Ninety-two percent of 25- to 34-year-olds in the United States had a high school diploma or its equivalent in 2018. In comparison, the average rate for the Organization for Economic Cooperation and Development (OECD) member countries was 85 percent. Some 49 percent of these individuals in the United States had obtained a postsecondary degree, compared with the OECD average of 44 percent. Similar to previous years, annual median earnings in 2018 were higher for 25- to 34-year-olds with higher levels of education. In 2018, U.S. 25- to 34-year-olds with a bachelor's or higher degree earned 66 percent more than those with a high school diploma or equivalent.

The Condition of Education includes an Executive Summary, an At a Glance section, a Reader's Guide, a Glossary, and a Guide to Sources, all of which provide additional background information. Each indicator includes references to the source data tables used to produce the indicator.

As new data are released throughout the year, indicators will be updated and made available on *The Condition of Education* website.

In addition to publishing *The Condition of Education*, NCES produces a wide range of other reports and datasets designed to help inform policymakers and the public about significant trends and topics in education. More information about the latest activities and releases at NCES may be found on our website or at our social media sites on Twitter, Facebook, and LinkedIn.

James L. Woodworth
Commissioner National Center for Education Statistics

Executive Summary

The Condition of Education is a congressionally mandated compendium of education indicators that is updated yearly. Using the most recent data available (at the time this report was written) from the National Center for Education Statistics and other sources, the indicators show the enrollment levels, academic progress, educational attainment, financial status, and other characteristics of those people and institutions involved in the American educational endeavor. There are core indicators that are updated every year and other indicators that introduce new topics of interest to education systems, policymakers, researchers, and the public. The indicators are organized into four sections: preprimary, elementary, and secondary education; postsecondary education; population characteristics and economic outcomes; and international comparisons. Some of the key findings from selected indicators are summarized below.

In fall 2017, some 50.7 million students were enrolled in public elementary and secondary schools (prekindergarten [preK] through grade 12). Total public school enrollment in preK through grade 12 is projected to increase to 51.1 million students (a 1 percent increase) by 2029, with changes across states ranging from an increase of 16 percent in North Dakota to a decrease of 12 percent in New Mexico. See Public School Enrollment.

A public charter school is a publicly funded school that is typically governed under a legislative contract—a charter—with the state, the district, or another entity. Between fall 2000 and fall 2017, overall public charter school enrollment increased from 0.4 million to 3.1 million. During this period, the percentage of public school students who attended charter schools increased from 1 to 6 percent. See Public Charter School Enrollment.

In fall 2017, some 5.7 million students were enrolled in private elementary and secondary schools. Private schools are generally supported with private funds. The percentage of elementary and secondary students who were enrolled in private schools decreased from 11 percent (6.0 million) in fall 1999 to 10 percent (5.7 million) in fall 2017. See Private School Enrollment.

The percentage of public school students eligible for free or reduced-price lunch (FRPL) under the National School Lunch Program serves as a proxy measure for the concentration of low-income students within a school. In fall 2017, the percentages of students who attended high-poverty public schools were highest for Black and Hispanic students (45 percent each), followed by American Indian/Alaska Native students (41 percent). The percentage of

students who attended high-poverty public schools was lowest for White students (8 percent). See Concentration of Public School Students Eligible for Free or Reduced-Price Lunch.

It has become increasingly important for students of all ages to be able to access and use the Internet for learning. This topic became especially salient as schools moved to remote learning in response to COVID-19 concerns at the start of 2020. In 2018, some 94 percent of 3- to 18-year-olds had home internet access: 88 percent had access through a computer, and 6 percent had access only through a smartphone. The remaining 6 percent had no internet access at home. See Children's Internet Access at Home.

The National Assessment of Educational Progress (NAEP) assesses U.S. public and private school student performance in a variety of subjects, including reading, mathematics, and science, at grades 4, 8, and 12. Reading and mathematics NAEP assessments at grades 4 and 8 are legislatively mandated to occur every 2 years. At grade 4, the average NAEP reading score in 2019 (220) was lower than the score in 2017 (222), when the assessment was last administered, but it was higher than the score in 1992 (217). Similarly, at grade 8, the average reading score in 2019 (263) was lower than the score in 2017 (267), but it was higher than the score in 1992 (260). See Reading Performance.

At grade 4, the average NAEP mathematics score in 2019 (241) was higher than the scores in both 2017 (240), when the assessment was last administered, and 1990 (213). At grade 8, the average mathematics score in 2019 (282) was lower than the score in 2017 (283), but it was higher than the score in 1990 (263). See Mathematics Performance. Data for grade 12 in 2019 were not available in time for publication.

In addition to NAEP, the United States participates at the national level in several international assessment programs. The Program for International Student Assessment (PISA), which is coordinated by the Organization for Economic Cooperation and Development (OECD), measures the performance of 15-year-old students in reading, mathematics, and science literacy and provides an opportunity to compare U.S. students' performance with that of their international peers. In 2018, there were 8 education systems with higher average reading literacy scores for 15-year-olds than the United States, 30 with higher mathematics literacy scores, and 11 with higher science literacy scores. The U.S. average reading score (505) and average science score (502) were higher than the

OECD average scores of 487 and 489, respectively. The U.S. average mathematics score (478) was lower than the OECD average score (489). See International Comparisons: Reading, Mathematics, and Science Literacy of 15-Year-Old Students.

Another critical outcome measure of interest is graduation rates for K–12 students. *The Condition of Education* reports the percentage of U.S. public high school students who graduate on time, as measured by the adjusted cohort graduation rate (ACGR). State education agencies identify the "cohort" of first-time ninth graders in a particular school year, and this cohort is then adjusted by adding or subtracting students who transfer in or out. The ACGR is the percentage of students in this adjusted cohort who graduate within 4 years with a regular high school diploma. In 2017–18, the U.S. average ACGR for public high school students was 85 percent; this rate was unchanged from the prior school year, and the rate for both school years was the highest rate since ACGR was first measured in 2010–11. See Public High School Graduation Rates. *The Condition of Education* also contains information on dropouts in the United States. The overall status dropout rate decreased from 9.7 percent in 2006 to 5.3 percent in 2018. See Status Dropout Rates.

One of the paths high school graduates may take to prepare for their future is to enroll in some form of postsecondary education. The overall college enrollment rate for 18- to 24-year-olds at undergraduate or graduate institutions increased from 35 percent in 2000 to 41 percent in 2018. In 2018, the college enrollment rate was higher for 18- to 24-year-olds who were Asian (59 percent) than for those who were White (42 percent), Black (37 percent), and Hispanic (36 percent). See College Enrollment Rates.

Postsecondary educational activities can have strong relationships with long-term life outcomes. For 25- to 34-year-olds who worked full time, year round in 2018, higher educational attainment was associated with higher median earnings. This pattern was consistent from 2000 through 2018. In 2018, the median earnings of 25- to 34-year-olds with a master's or higher degree ($65,000) were 19 percent higher than the earnings of those with a bachelor's degree ($54,700), and the median earnings of those with a bachelor's degree were 57 percent higher than the earnings of high school completers ($34,900). See Annual Earnings. Similar to the earnings pattern, the employment rate in 2019 was higher for 25- to 34-year-olds with higher levels of educational attainment than for those with lower levels of educational attainment. See Employment and Unemployment Rates by Educational Attainment.

In 2017–18, the average net price of attendance (total cost minus grant and scholarship aid) for first-time, full-time undergraduate students attending 4-year institutions was $13,700 at public institutions, compared with $27,000 at private nonprofit institutions and $22,100 at private for-profit institutions (in constant 2018–19 dollars). See Price of Attending an Undergraduate Institution.

In 2017–18, degree-granting postsecondary institutions in the United States spent $604 billion (in current dollars). In 2017–18, instruction expenses per full-time-equivalent (FTE) student (in constant 2018–19 dollars) was the largest expense category at public institutions ($10,870) and private nonprofit institutions ($18,710). At private for-profit institutions, the combined category of academic support, student services, and institutional support expenses was the largest category of expenses per FTE student ($10,480). See Postsecondary Institution Expenses.

The Condition of Education also reports on the operational activities of education systems by providing financial information such as education revenue sources and educational expenditures. In 2016–17, elementary and secondary public school revenues totaled $736 billion (in constant 2018–19 dollars). Since 2000–01, public school revenues have increased by 27 percent, while public school enrollment has increased by 7 percent. The majority of these revenues come from state and local sources. Of the total elementary and secondary public school revenues, states provided $346 billion (47 percent), local sources provided $330 billion (45 percent), and federal sources provided $60 billion (8 percent). While these numbers represent the national averages, revenue and source distribution varied by state. See Public School Revenue Sources.

The other side of the education finance system is expenditures. In 2016–17, public schools spent $12,794 per pupil on current expenditures (in constant 2018–19 dollars), a category that includes salaries, employee benefits, purchased services, and supplies. Current expenditures per pupil were 20 percent higher in 2016–17 than in 2000–01, after adjusting for inflation. On a national basis in 2016–17, approximately 80 percent of current expenditures for public elementary and secondary schools were for salaries and benefits for staff. See Public School Expenditures.

This summary highlights some of the interesting findings within *The Condition of Education 2020*. The report includes more detail and additional topics. The content of the report can be found on *The Condition of Education* website.

Reader's Guide

The Condition of Education contains indicators on the state of education in the United States, from prekindergarten through postsecondary education, as well as labor force outcomes and international comparisons. Each indicator uses both text and figures to present a narrative that highlights key findings and significant patterns in the data. It is important to note that all data from the figures may not be described in the text and all data in the text may not be presented in the figures. The data source(s) for the indicator can be found in the reference tables section at the end of the indicator. For more information about data sources, see the Data Sources and Estimates section below.

Readers can browse the full report online through the HTML site or download PDFs of the full report or individual indicators. In both the PDF and HTML versions, indicators are hyperlinked to tables in the *Digest of Education Statistics*. These tables contain the source data used in the most recent edition of *The Condition of Education*.

Data Sources and Estimates

The data in these indicators were obtained from many different sources—including students and teachers, state education agencies, elementary and secondary schools, and colleges and universities—using surveys and compilations of administrative records. Users should be cautious when comparing data from different sources. Differences in aspects such as procedures, timing, question phrasing, and interviewer training can affect the comparability of results across data sources.

Most indicators in *The Condition of Education* summarize data from surveys conducted by the National Center for Education Statistics (NCES) or by the U.S. Census Bureau with support from NCES. Brief descriptions of the major NCES surveys used in these indicators can be found in the Guide to Sources. More detailed descriptions can be obtained on the NCES website under "Surveys and Programs."

The Guide to Sources also includes information on non-NCES sources used to develop indicators, such as the Census Bureau's American Community Survey (ACS) and Current Population Survey (CPS). For details on the ACS, see https://www.census.gov/programs-surveys/acs. For details on the CPS, see https://www.census.gov/cps.

Data for *The Condition of Education* indicators are obtained from two types of surveys: universe surveys and sample surveys. In universe surveys, information is collected from every member of the population. For example, in a survey regarding expenditures of public elementary and secondary schools, data would be obtained from each school district in the United States. When data from an entire population are available, estimates of the total population or a subpopulation are made by simply summing the units in the population or subpopulation. As a result, there is no sampling error, and observed differences are reported as true.

Since universe surveys are often expensive and time consuming, many surveys collect data from a sample of the population of interest (sample surveys). For example, the National Assessment of Educational Progress (NAEP) assesses a representative sample of students rather than the entire population of students. When a sample survey is used, statistical uncertainty is introduced because the data come from only a portion of the entire population. This statistical uncertainty must be considered when reporting estimates and making comparisons. For more information, please see the section on standard errors below.

Various types of statistics derived from universe and sample surveys are reported in *The Condition of Education*. Many indicators report the size of a population or subpopulation, and the size of a subpopulation is often expressed as a percentage of the total population. In addition, the average (or *mean*) value of some characteristic of the population or subpopulation may be reported. The average is obtained by summing the values for all members of the population and dividing the sum by the size of the population. An example is the annual average salaries of full-time instructional faculty at degree-granting postsecondary institutions. Another measure that is sometimes used is the *median*. The median is the midpoint value of a characteristic at or above which 50 percent of the population is estimated to fall and at or below which 50 percent of the population is estimated to fall. An example is the median annual earnings of young adults who are full-time, full-year wage and salary workers.

Standard Errors

Using estimates calculated from data based on a sample of the population requires consideration of several factors before the estimates become meaningful. When using data from a sample, some *margin of error* will always be present in estimations of characteristics of the total population or subpopulation because the data are available from only a portion of the total population. Consequently, data from samples can provide only an approximation of the true or actual value. The margin of error of an estimate—i.e., the range of potential true or actual values—depends on several factors, such as the amount of variation in the responses, the size and representativeness of the sample, and the size of the subgroup for which the estimate is computed. The magnitude of this margin of error is measured by what statisticians call the *standard error* of an estimate. A larger standard error typically indicates that the estimate is less precise, while a smaller standard error typically indicates that the estimate is more precise.

When data from sample surveys are reported, the standard error is calculated for each estimate. The standard errors for all estimated totals, means, medians, or percentages are reported in the reference tables.

In order to caution the reader when interpreting findings in the indicators, estimates from sample surveys are flagged with a "!" when the standard error is between 30 and 50 percent of the estimate, and estimates are suppressed and replaced with a "‡" when the standard error is 50 percent of the estimate or greater.

Data Analysis and Interpretation

When estimates are from a sample, caution is warranted when drawing conclusions about whether one estimate is different in comparison to another; whether a time series of estimates is increasing, decreasing, or staying the same; or whether two variables are associated. Although one estimate may appear to be larger than another, a statistical test may find that the apparent difference between them is not measurable due to the uncertainty around the estimates. In this case, the estimates are described as having *no measurable difference*, meaning the difference between them is not statistically significant.

Whether differences in means or percentages are statistically significant can be determined using the standard errors of the estimates. In the indicators in *The Condition of Education* and other NCES reports, when differences are statistically significant, the probability that the difference occurred by chance is less than 5 percent, according to NCES standards.

For all indicators that report estimates based on samples, differences between estimates (including increases and decreases) are stated only when they are statistically significant. To determine whether differences are statistically significant, most indicators use two-tailed t tests at the .05 level. The t test formula for determining statistical significance is adjusted when the samples being compared are dependent. The analyses are not adjusted for multiple comparisons, with the exception of indicators that use NAEP data. All analyses in NAEP indicators are conducted using the NAEP Data Explorer, which makes adjustments for comparisons involving a variable with more than two categories. The NAEP Data Explorer makes such adjustments using the Benjamini-Hochberg False Discovery Rate. When the variables to be tested are postulated to form a trend over time, the relationship may be tested using linear regression or ANOVA trend analyses instead of a series of t tests. Indicators that use other methods of statistical comparison include a separate technical notes section. For more information on data analysis, see the NCES Statistical Standards, Standard 5-1.

Multivariate analyses, such as ordinary least squares (OLS) regression models, provide information on whether the relationship between an independent variable and an outcome measure (such as group differences in the outcome measure) persists after taking into account other variables (such as student, family, and school characteristics). For indicators that include a regression analysis, multiple categorical or continuous independent variables are entered simultaneously. A significant regression coefficient indicates an association between the dependent (outcome) variable and the independent variable, after controlling for other independent variables included in the regression analysis.

Data presented in the indicators typically do not investigate more complex hypotheses or support causal inferences. We encourage readers who are interested in more complex questions and in-depth analyses to explore other NCES resources, including publications, online data tools, and public- and restricted-use datasets at https://nces.ed.gov/.

A number of considerations influence the ultimate selection of the data years to feature in the indicators. To make analyses as timely as possible, the latest year of available data is shown. The choice of comparison years is often based on the need to show the earliest available survey year, as in the case of the NAEP and the international assessment surveys. In the case of surveys with long time frames, such as surveys measuring enrollment, a decade's beginning year (e.g., 1990 or 2000) often starts the trend line. In the figures and tables of the indicators, intervening years are selected in increments in order to show the general trend. The narrative for the indicators typically compares the most current year's data with those from the initial year and then with those from a more recent year. Where applicable, the narrative may also note years in which the data begin to diverge from previous trends.

Rounding and Other Considerations

All calculations within the indicators in this report are based on unrounded estimates. Therefore, the reader may find that a calculation cited in the text or figure, such as a difference or a percentage change, may not be identical to the calculation obtained by using the rounded values shown in the accompanying tables. Although values reported in the reference tables are generally rounded to one decimal place (e.g., 76.5 percent), values reported in each indicator are generally rounded to whole numbers (with any value of 0.50 or above rounded to the next highest whole number). Due to rounding, cumulative percentages may sometimes equal 99 or 101 percent rather than 100 percent. While the data labels on the figures have been rounded to whole numbers, the graphical presentation of these data is based on the unrounded estimates.

Race and Ethnicity

The Office of Management and Budget (OMB) is responsible for the standards that govern the categories used to collect and present federal data on race and ethnicity. The OMB revised the guidelines on racial/ethnic categories used by the federal government in October 1997, with a January 2003 deadline for implementation. The revised standards require a minimum of these five categories for data on race: American Indian or Alaska Native, Asian, Black or African American, Native Hawaiian or Other Pacific Islander, and White. The standards also require the collection of data on ethnicity categories: at a minimum, Hispanic or Latino and Not Hispanic or Latino. It is important to note that Hispanic origin is an ethnicity rather than a race, and, therefore, persons of Hispanic origin may be of any race. Origin can be viewed as the heritage, nationality group, lineage, or country of birth of the person or the person's parents or ancestors before their arrival in the United States. The race categories White, Black, Asian, Native Hawaiian or Other Pacific Islander, and American Indian or Alaska Native, as presented in these indicators, exclude persons of Hispanic origin unless noted otherwise.

The categories are defined as follows:

American Indian or Alaska Native: A person having origins in any of the original peoples of North and South America (including Central America) and maintaining tribal affiliation or community attachment.

Asian: A person having origins in any of the original peoples of the Far East, Southeast Asia, or the Indian subcontinent, including Cambodia, China, India, Japan, Korea, Malaysia, Pakistan, the Philippine Islands, Thailand, and Vietnam.

Black or African American: A person having origins in any of the black racial groups of Africa.

Native Hawaiian or Other Pacific Islander: A person having origins in any of the original peoples of Hawaii, Guam, Samoa, or other Pacific Islands.

White: A person having origins in any of the original peoples of Europe, the Middle East, or North Africa.

Hispanic or Latino: A person of Mexican, Puerto Rican, Cuban, South or Central American, or other Spanish culture or origin, regardless of race.

Within these indicators, some of the category labels have been shortened in the text, tables, and figures for ease of reference. American Indian or Alaska Native is denoted as American Indian/Alaska Native (except when separate estimates are available for American Indians alone or Alaska Natives alone); Black or African American is

shortened to Black; Native Hawaiian or Other Pacific Islander is shortened to Pacific Islander; and Hispanic or Latino is shortened to Hispanic.

The indicators in this report draw from a number of different data sources. Many are federal surveys that collect data using the OMB standards for racial/ethnic classification described above; however, some sources have not fully adopted the standards, and some indicators include data collected prior to the adoption of the standards. This report focuses on the six categories that are the most common among the various data sources used: White, Black, Hispanic, Asian, Pacific Islander, and American Indian/Alaska Native. Asians and Pacific Islanders are combined into one category in indicators for which the data were not collected separately for the two groups.

Some of the surveys from which data are presented in these indicators give respondents the option of selecting either an "other" race category, a "Two or more races" or "multiracial" category, or both. Where possible, indicators present data on the "Two or more races" category; in some cases, however, this category may not be separately shown because the information was not collected or because of other data issues. In general, the "other" category is not separately shown. Any comparisons made between persons of one racial/ethnic group to "all other racial/ethnic groups" include only the racial/ethnic groups shown in the indicator. In some surveys, respondents are not given the option to select more than one race. In these surveys, respondents of Two or more races must select a single race category. Any comparisons between data from surveys that offer the option to select more than one race and surveys that do not offer such an option should take into account the fact that there is a potential for bias if members of one racial group are more likely than members of other racial groups to identify themselves as "Two or more races."[1] For postsecondary data, foreign students are counted separately and are therefore not included in any racial/ethnic category.

More detailed information on racial/ethnic groups, including data for specific Asian and Hispanic ancestry subgroups (such as Mexican, Puerto Rican, Chinese, or Vietnamese) can be found in the *Status and Trends in the Education of Racial and Ethnic Groups* report.

Limitations of the Data

The relatively small sizes of the American Indian/Alaska Native and Pacific Islander populations pose many

---

[1] See Parker, J.D., Schenker, N., Ingram, D.D., Weed, J.A., Heck, K.E., and Madans, J.H. (2004). Bridging Between Two Standards for Collecting Information on Race and Ethnicity: An Application to Census 2000 and Vital Rates. *Public Health Reports, 119*(2): 192–205. Retrieved April 25, 2017, from https://journals.sagepub.com/doi/pdf/10.1177/003335490411900213.

measurement difficulties when conducting statistical analyses. Even in larger surveys, the numbers of American Indians/Alaska Natives and Pacific Islanders included in a sample are often small. Researchers studying data on these two populations often face small sample sizes that reduce the reliability of results. Survey data for American Indians/Alaska Natives and Pacific Islanders often have somewhat higher standard errors than data for other racial/ethnic groups. Due to large standard errors, differences that seem substantial are often not statistically significant and, therefore, are not cited in the text.

Data on American Indians/Alaska Natives are often subject to inconsistencies in how respondents identify their race/ethnicity. According to research on the collection of race/ethnicity data conducted by the Bureau of Labor Statistics in 1995, the categorization of American Indian and Alaska Native is the least stable self-identification. The racial/ethnic categories presented to a respondent, and the way in which the question is asked, can influence the response, especially for individuals who consider themselves as being of mixed race or ethnicity.

As mentioned above, Asians and Pacific Islanders are combined into one category in indicators for which the data were not collected separately for the two groups. The combined category can sometimes mask significant differences between subgroups. For example, prior to 2011, NAEP collected data that did not allow for separate reporting of estimates for Asians and Pacific Islanders. Information from the *Digest of Education Statistics 2019* (table 101.20), based on the Census Bureau's Current Population Reports, indicates that 96 percent of all Asian/Pacific Islander 5- to 24-year-olds are Asian. This combined category for Asians/Pacific Islanders is more representative of Asians than Pacific Islanders.

Symbols

In accordance with the NCES Statistical Standards, many tables in this volume use special symbols to alert the reader to various statistical notes. These symbols and their meanings are as follows:

— Not available.

† Not applicable.

Rounds to zero.

! Interpret data with caution. The coefficient of variation (CV) for this estimate is between 30 and 50 percent.

‡ Reporting standards not met. Either there are too few cases for a reliable estimate or the coefficient of variation (CV) for this estimate is 50 percent or greater.

* $p < .05$ significance level.

Contents

Teachers and Staff

Assessments

High School Completion

Postsecondary Institutions

Programs, Courses, and Completions

Finances and Resources

Enrollment and Attainment

The Condition of Education 2020 **At a Glance**

More information is available at nces.ed.gov/programs/coe.

Preprimary, Elementary, and Secondary Education

Characteristics of Children's Families	2017	2018	Change between years
Percentage of children under age 18 whose parents' highest level of education was less than high school	9.7%	9.4%	▼
Percentage of children under age 18 whose parents' highest level of education was a bachelor's or higher degree	41.0%	41.8%	▲
Percentage of children under age 18 living in mother-only households	26.3%	26.4%	
Percentage of children under age 18 in families living in poverty	18.0%	17.5%	▼

Children's Internet Access at Home	2016	2018	
Percentage of 3- to 18-year-olds who had home internet access	92%	94%	▲
Percentage of 3- to 18-year-olds who had home internet access only through smartphone	5%	6%	▲

Preschool and Kindergarten Enrollment	2017	2018	
Percentage of 3- to 5-year-olds enrolled in preprimary education			
3-year-olds	40%	40%	
4-year-olds	68%	68%	
5-year-olds	86%	84%	

Public School Enrollment	Fall 2016	Fall 2017	
Number of students enrolled in public schools	50.62 million	50.69 million	▲
Prekindergarten through 8th grade	35.48 million	35.50 million	▲
9th through 12th grade	15.14 million	15.19 million	▲

Public Charter School Enrollment	Fall 2016	Fall 2017	
Number of students enrolled in public charter schools	3.0 million	3.1 million	▲
Percentage of public school students enrolled in charter schools	6.0%	6.2%	▲
Number of public charter schools	7,010	7,190	▲
Percentage of public schools that are charter schools	7.1%	7.3%	▲

Private School Enrollment	Fall 2015	Fall 2017	
Number of students enrolled in private schools	5.8 million	5.7 million	
Percentage of all students enrolled in private schools	10.2%	10.1%	▼

Racial/Ethnic Enrollment in Public Schools	Fall 2016	Fall 2017	
Percentage of public school students			
White	48.23%	47.60%	▼
Black	15.34%	15.21%	▼
Hispanic	26.33%	26.77%	▲
Asian/Pacific Islander	5.44%	5.57%	▲
American Indian/Alaska Native	1.01%	0.98%	▼
Two or more races	3.64%	3.86%	▲

English Language Learners in Public Schools	Fall 2016	Fall 2017	
Percentage of public school students who were English language learners	9.9%	10.1%	▲

See notes at end of table.

LEGEND: ▲ = Higher, ▼ = Lower, Blank = Not measurably different

Students With Disabilities	2017–18	2018–19	Change between years
Number of public school students ages 3–21 receiving special education services	7.0 million	7.1 million	▲
Percentage of public school students ages 3–21 receiving special education services	13.7%	14.1%	▲

Characteristics of Elementary and Secondary Schools	2016–17	2017–18	
Total number of traditional public schools	91,150	91,280	▲
Total number of public charter schools	7,010	7,190	▲
	Fall 2015	Fall 2017	
Total number of private schools	34,580	32,460	

Concentration of Public School Students Eligible for Free or Reduced-Price Lunch	2016–17	2017–18	
Percentage of students attending public low-poverty schools[1]	21.2%	21.0%	▼
Percentage of students attending public high-poverty schools[1]	24.2%	24.8%	▲

School Crime and Safety	2017	2018	
Nonfatal victimization rate per 1,000 students			
Victimization occurred at school	33	33	
Victimization occurred away from school	20	16	

Characteristics of Public School Teachers	1999–2000	2017–18	
Total number of public school teachers	3.0 million	3.5 million	▲
In elementary schools	1.6 million	1.8 million	▲
In secondary schools	1.4 million	1.8 million	▲
Percentage of public school teachers			
Who are female	75%	76%	▲
Who are male	25%	24%	▼
Who held a postbaccalaureate degree	47%	58%	▲
Who held a regular teaching certificate	87%	90%	▲
	2011–12	2017–18	
Annual base salary of public school teachers[2]	$59,060	$59,150	

Characteristics of Public School Principals	2015–16	2017–18	
Total number of public school principals	90,400	90,900	
In elementary schools	62,100	62,000	
In secondary schools	20,300	20,200	
Percentage of public school principals			
Who are male	46%	46%	
Who are female	54%	54%	
Annual base salary of public school principals[2]	$101,740	$100,340	▼

See notes at end of table.

LEGEND: ▲ = Higher,   ▼ = Lower,   Blank = Not measurably different

			Change between years
Reading Performance	2017	2019	
Percentage of students who scored at or above *NAEP Proficient*[3]			
4th-grade students	37%	35%	▼
8th-grade students	36%	34%	▼
	2013	2015	
12th-grade students	38%	37%	
Mathematics Performance	2017	2019	
Percentage of students who scored at or above *NAEP Proficient*[3]			
4th-grade students	40%	41%	
8th-grade students	34%	34%	
	2013	2015	
12th-grade students	26%	25%	
Science Performance	2009	2015	
Percentage of students who scored at or above *NAEP Proficient*[3]			
4th-grade students	34%	38%	▲
12th-grade students	21%	22%	
	2011	2015	
8th-grade students	32%	34%	
Public High School Graduation Rates	2016–17	2017–18	
Adjusted cohort graduation rate (ACGR)[4]	84.6%	85.3%	▲
Status Dropout Rates	2017	2018	
Percentage of 16- to 24-year-olds not enrolled in school who had not completed high school	5.4%	5.3%	
Male	6.4%	6.2%	
Female	4.4%	4.4%	
White	4.3%	4.2%	
Black	6.5%	6.4%	
Hispanic	8.2%	8.0%	
Asian	2.1%	1.9%	
Pacific Islander	3.9%	8.1%	▲
American Indian/ Alaska Native	10.1%	9.5%	
Two or more races	4.5%	5.2%	
Public School Revenue Sources[2]	2015–16	2016–17	
Total	$719.8 billion	$736.1 billion	▲
Federal	$59.5 billion	$59.8 billion	▲
State	$337.7 billion	$345.8 billion	▲
Local	$322.7 billion	$330.5 billion	▲
Public School Expenditures[2]	2015–16	2016–17	
Total	$720.2 billion	$738.5 billion	▲
Total expenditures per pupil (in fall enrollment)	$14,136	$14,439	▲

See notes at end of table.

LEGEND: ▲ = Higher, ▼ = Lower, Blank = Not measurably different

Postsecondary Education

Immediate College Enrollment Rate	2017	2018	Change between years
Immediate college enrollment rate of high school completers	67%	69%	
2-year institutions	23%	26%	
4-year institutions	44%	44%	

College Enrollment Rates	2017	2018	
College enrollment rates of 18- to 24-year-olds			
Total, all students	40%	41%	
Male	37%	38%	
Female	44%	44%	
White	41%	42%	
Black	36%	37%	
Hispanic	36%	36%	
Asian	65%	59%	
Pacific Islander	33%	24%	
American Indian/Alaska Native	20%	24%	
Two or more races	41%	44%	

Undergraduate Enrollment	Fall 2017	Fall 2018	
Total enrollment	16.77 million	16.61 million	▼
Full-time enrollment	10.37 million	10.27 million	▼
Part-time enrollment	6.40 million	6.34 million	▼
Percentage enrolled in any distance education course	33%	34%	▲
Percentage enrolled exclusively in distance education	13%	14%	▲

Postbaccalaureate Enrollment	Fall 2017	Fall 2018	
Total enrollment	3.01 million	3.04 million	▲
Full-time enrollment	1.70 million	1.72 million	▲
Part-time enrollment	1.30 million	1.31 million	▲
Percentage enrolled in any distance education course	38%	40%	▲
Percentage enrolled exclusively in distance education	29%	31%	▲

Characteristics of Postsecondary Students	Fall 2017	Fall 2018	
Total enrollment	19.77 million	19.65 million	▼
Undergraduate	16.76 million	16.61 million	▼
White	8.88 million	8.66 million	▼
Black	2.18 million	2.13 million	▼
Hispanic	3.27 million	3.35 million	▲
Asian	1.07 million	1.09 million	▲
Pacific Islander	46,100	44,700	▼
American Indian/Alaska Native	124,000	120,200	▼
Two or more races	623,400	646,500	▲
Nonresident alien	575,000	566,600	▼

See notes at end of table.

LEGEND: ▲ = Higher, ▼ = Lower, Blank = Not measurably different

			Change between years
Postbaccalaureate	3.01 million	3.04 million	▲
White	1.63 million	1.64 million	▲
Black	365,400	365,400	▼
Hispanic	275,000	292,400	▲
Asian	208,900	215,000	▲
Pacific Islander	5,900	5,800	▼
American Indian/Alaska Native	13,600	13,600	▼
Two or more races	76,800	81,300	▲
Nonresident alien	425,700	425,400	▼

Characteristics of Degree-Granting Postsecondary Institutions	2017–18	2018–19	
Total number of degree-granting institutions with first-year undergraduates	3,883	3,652	▼
Number of 4-year institutions with first-year undergraduates	2,407	2,323	▼
Number of 2-year institutions with first-year undergraduates	1,476	1,329	▼

Characteristics of Postsecondary Faculty	Fall 2017	Fall 2018	
Number of full-time instructional faculty[5]	823,000	832,000	▲
Number of part-time instructional faculty	723,000	710,000	▼

Undergraduate Degree Fields	2016–17	2017–18	
Number of bachelor's degrees conferred (top three bachelor's programs)			
Business	381,100	386,200	▲
Health professions and related programs	238,000	244,900	▲
Social sciences and history	159,100	160,000	▲

Graduate Degree Fields	2016–17	2017–18	
Number of master's degrees conferred (top three master's programs)			
Business	187,400	192,200	▲
Education	145,600	146,400	▲
Health professions and related programs	119,200	125,200	▲

Undergraduate Retention and Graduation Rates	2016–17	2017–18	
4-year institutions			
Retention rate of first-time undergraduates	81.0%	81.0%	▲
Graduation rate (within 6 years of starting program) of first-time, full-time undergraduates	60.4%	62.4%	▲
2-year institutions			
Retention rate of first-time undergraduates	62.4%	62.3%	▼
Graduation rate (within 150% of normal time for degree completion) of first-time, full-time undergraduates	31.6%	32.6%	▲

See notes at end of table.

LEGEND: ▲ = Higher, ▼ = Lower, Blank = Not measurably different

Postsecondary Certificates and Degrees Conferred	2016–17	2017–18	Change between years
Number of degrees/certificates conferred by postsecondary institutions			
Certificates below associate's degrees	946,000	955,000	▲
Associate's degrees	1,006,000	1,011,000	▲
Bachelor's degrees	1,956,000	1,981,000	▲
Master's degrees	805,000	820,000	▲
Doctor's degrees	181,000	184,000	▲

Price of Attending an Undergraduate Institution[2]	2016–17	2017–18	
Average net price at 4-year institutions for first-time, full-time undergraduate students			
Public, in-state or in-district[6]	$14,000	$13,700	▼
Private nonprofit	$27,300	$27,000	▼
Private for-profit	$22,300	$22,100	▼

Loans for Undergraduate Students	2016–17	2017–18	
Percentage of undergraduates with student loans	46.1%	44.4%	▼
Average student loan amount[2]	$7,390	$7,230	▼

Sources of Financial Aid	2016–17	2017–18	
Percentage of students receiving any financial aid at 4-year institutions	85.0%	85.7%	▲
Percentage of students receiving any financial aid at 2-year institutions	77.8%	78.1%	▲

Postsecondary Institution Revenues[2]	2016–17	2017–18	
Revenue from tuition and fees per full-time-equivalent (FTE) student			
Public institutions	$7,660	$7,690	▲
Private nonprofit institutions	$22,330	$22,350	▲
Private for-profit institutions	$16,810	$16,820	▲

Postsecondary Institution Expenses[2]	2016–17	2017–18	
Instruction expenses per full-time-equivalent (FTE) student			
Public institutions	$11,040	$10,870	▼
Private nonprofit institutions	$18,770	$18,710	▼
Private for-profit institutions	$4,570	$4,490	▼

Population Characteristics and Economic Outcomes

Educational Attainment of Young Adults	2018	2019	Change between years
Percentage of 25- to 29-year-olds with selected levels of educational attainment			
High school completion or higher	93%	94%	
Associate's or higher degree	47%	49%	▲
Bachelor's or higher degree	37%	39%	
Master's or higher degree	9%	9%	

See notes at end of table.

LEGEND: ▲ = Higher, ▼ = Lower, Blank = Not measurably different

Young Adults Neither Enrolled in School nor Working	2017	2018	Change between years
Percentage of 18- to 24-year-olds who were neither enrolled in school nor working			
Total 18- to 24-year-olds	13.9%	13.5%	▼
18- and 19-year-olds	10.8%	10.8%	
20- to 24-year-olds	15.1%	14.5%	▼
White	11.3%	11.0%	
Black	21.6%	21.0%	
Hispanic	16.1%	15.5%	▼
Asian	7.4%	6.9%	
Pacific Islander	19.8%	20.8%	
American Indian/Alaska Native	29.2%	28.7%	
Two or more races	14.4%	14.0%	

Annual Earnings	2017	2018	
Median annual earnings for 25- to 34-year-olds[2]			
Total	$42,900	$44,900	
With less than high school completion	$26,600	$27,900	
Who completed high school as highest level	$32,800	$34,900	▲
Who completed some college but did not attain a degree	$35,900	$36,300	
Who attained an associate's degree	$39,800	$40,000	
Who attained a bachelor's or higher degree	$56,300	$57,900	
Who attained a bachelor's degree	$53,000	$54,700	
Who attained a master's or higher degree	$66,600	$65,000	

Employment and Unemployment Rates by Educational Attainment	2018	2019	
Employment rates of 25- to 34-year-old			
Total	79%	79%	
With less than high school completion	59%	57%	
Who completed high school as highest level	72%	74%	
Who attained a bachelor's or higher degree	86%	87%	
Unemployment rates of 25- to 34-year-olds			
Total	4%	4%	
With less than high school completion	9%	10%	
Who completed high school as highest level	6%	6%	
Who attained a bachelor's or higher degree	2%	2%	

See notes at end of table.

LEGEND: ▲ = Higher, ▼ = Lower, Blank = Not measurably different

International Comparisons

International Comparisons: Reading Literacy at Grade 4 (2016)	U.S. average score	International average score	Difference between U.S. average and international average
Progress in International Reading Literacy Study (PIRLS)			
Average reading literacy scores of 4th-grade students	549	500	▲
Average online informational reading score of 4th-grade students	557	500	▲

International Comparisons: U.S. 4th-, 8th-, and 12th-Graders' Mathematics and Science Achievement (2015)	U.S. average score	TIMSS scale center-point	Difference between U.S. average and TIMSS scale center-point
Trends in International Mathematics and Science Study (TIMSS)			
Mathematics scores of 4th-grade students	539	500	▲
Mathematics scores of 8th-grade students	518	500	▲
Science scores of 4th-grade students	546	500	▲
Science scores of 8th-grade students	530	500	▲
TIMSS Advanced			
Advanced mathematics scores of 12th-grade students	485	500	▼
Physics scores of 12th-grade students	437	500	▼

International Comparisons: Reading, Mathematics, and Science Literacy of 15-Year-Old Students (2018)	U.S. average score	OECD average score	Difference between U.S. average and OECD average
Program for International Student Assessment (PISA)			
Reading literacy scores of 15-year-old students	505	487	▲
Mathematics literacy scores of 15-year-old students	478	489	▼
Science literacy scores of 15-year-old students	502	489	▲

Enrollment Rates by Country	2016	2017	Change between years
Percentage of 3- and 4-year-olds enrolled in school at any level			
United States	52.7%	53.8%	▲
Organization for Economic Cooperation and Development (OECD) countries	80.4%	82.8%	▲
Percentage of 5- to 14-year-olds enrolled in school at any level			
United States	99.2%	99.8%	▲
OECD countries	97.9%	98.1%	▲

See notes at end of table.

LEGEND: ▲ = Higher, ▼ = Lower, Blank = Not measurably different

			Change between years
Percentage of 15- to 19-year-olds enrolled in school at any level			
United States	82.5%	82.9%	▲
OECD countries	84.9%	84.5%	▼
Percentage of 20- to 29-year-olds enrolled in school at any level			
United States	24.5%	24.6%	▲
OECD countries	28.6%	28.2%	▼

International Educational Attainment	2017	2018	
Percentage of the population 25 to 34 years old who completed high school			
United States	92.1%	92.4%	
Organization for Economic Cooperation and Development (OECD) countries	84.4%	84.7%	▲
Percentage of the population 25 to 34 years old who attained a postsecondary degree			
United States	47.8%	49.4%	▲
OECD countries	43.7%	44.5%	▲

Education Expenditures by Country (2016)[7]	U.S.	OECD	Difference between U.S. and OECD
Expenditures per full-time-equivalent (FTE) student			
Elementary and secondary education	$13,600	$9,800	▲
Postsecondary education	$31,600	$16,200	▲

[1] Low-poverty schools are defined as public schools where 25 percent or less of the students are eligible for free or reduced-price lunch (FRPL). High-poverty schools are defined as public schools where more than 75 percent of the students are eligible for FRPL.
[2] Data are reported in constant 2018–19 dollars, based on the Consumer Price Index (CPI).
[3] *NAEP Proficient* demonstrates solid academic performance and competency over challenging subject matter.
[4] The adjusted cohort graduation rate (ACGR) is the number of students who graduate in 4 years with a regular high school diploma divided by the number of students who form the adjusted cohort for the graduating class. From the beginning of 9th grade (or the earliest high school grade), students who enter that grade for the first time form a cohort that is "adjusted" by adding any students who subsequently transfer into the cohort and subtracting any students who subsequently transfer out, emigrate to another country, or die.
[5] Data are for full-time instructional faculty on 9-month contracts at degree-granting postsecondary institutions.
[6] The average net price at public 4-year institutions uses the lower of in-district or in-state average net price.
[7] Data are reported in constant 2018 dollars based on the OECD's National Consumer Price Index.
NOTE: All calculations within the At a Glance are based on unrounded numbers. Race categories exclude persons of Hispanic ethnicity.
SOURCE: *The Condition of Education 2020.*

LEGEND: ▲ = Higher, ▼ = Lower, Blank = Not measurably different

The indicators in this chapter of *The Condition of Education* describe aspects of preprimary, elementary, and secondary education in the United States. The indicators examine enrollment, school characteristics and climate; principals, teachers, and staff; school financial resources; student assessments; and other measures of students' progress as they move through the education system, such as graduation rates. In addition, this chapter contains indicators on key demographic characteristics, such as poverty and access to the Internet.

This chapter gives particular attention to how various subgroups in the population proceed through school and attain different levels of education. The indicators on student achievement illustrate how students perform on assessments in reading, mathematics, and science. Other indicators describe aspects of the context of learning in elementary and secondary schools.

Chapter 1

Preprimary, Elementary, and Secondary Education

Characteristics of Children's Families

In 2018, some 9 percent of children under the age of 18 lived in households where no parent had completed high school, 26 percent lived in mother-only households, 8 percent lived in father-only households, and 18 percent were in families living in poverty.

Characteristics of children's families are associated with children's educational experiences and their academic achievement. Prior research has found that the risk factors of living in a household without a parent who has completed high school, living in a single-parent household, and living in poverty are associated with poor educational outcomes—including receiving low achievement scores, having to repeat a grade, and dropping out of high school.[1,2] This indicator examines

the prevalence of these risk factors among racial/ethnic groups and, for poverty status, among states. For more information on the relationship between family socioeconomic status and later postsecondary and employment outcomes, please see *The Condition of Education 2019* Spotlight indicator Young Adult Educational and Employment Outcomes by Family Socioeconomic Status.

Figure 1. Percentage distribution of children under age 18, by child's race/ethnicity and parents' highest level of educational attainment: 2018

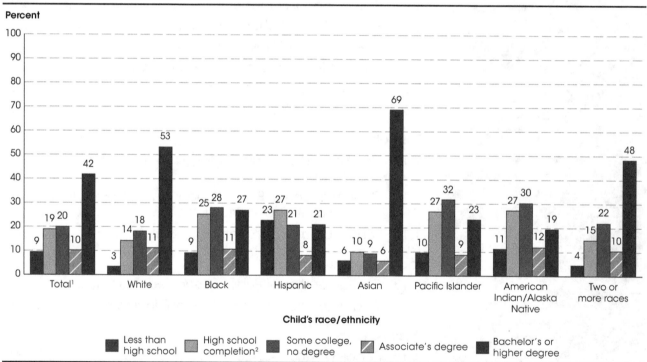

[1] Includes respondents who wrote in some other race that was not included as an option on the questionnaire.
[2] Includes parents who completed high school through equivalency programs, such as a GED program.
NOTE: Includes only children under age 18 who resided with at least one of their parents (including an adoptive or stepparent; excluding a foster parent). Parents' highest level of educational attainment is the highest level of education attained by any parent residing in the same household as the child. Parents include adoptive and stepparents but exclude parents not residing in the same household as their child. Race categories exclude persons of Hispanic ethnicity. Detail may not sum to totals because of rounding. Although rounded numbers are displayed, the figures are based on unrounded data.
SOURCE: U.S. Department of Commerce, Census Bureau, American Community Survey (ACS), 2018. See *Digest of Education Statistics 2019*, table 104.70.

In 2018, some 9 percent of children under age 18 lived in households where no parent had completed high school. Nineteen percent lived in households where the highest level of education attained by either parent was high school completion.[3] Twenty percent lived in households where the highest level of education attained by either parent was some college attendance but no degree. Ten percent lived in households where the highest level of education attained by either parent was an associate's degree. Forty-two percent of children lived in households where the highest level of education attained by either parent was a bachelor's or higher degree: 22 percent lived in households where this level was a bachelor's degree, 14 percent lived in households where this level was a master's degree, and 6 percent lived in households where this level was a doctor's degree.[4]

Lower percentages of children under age 18 in 2018 than in 2010 lived in households where no parent had completed high school (9 vs. 12 percent), in households where the highest level of education attained by either parent was high school completion (19 vs. 20 percent), and in households where the highest level of education attained by either parent was some college attendance but no degree (20 vs. 23 percent). Meanwhile, a higher percentage of children in 2018 than in 2010 lived in households where the highest level of parental education was a bachelor's or higher degree (42 vs. 35 percent).[5]

The percentage distribution of children under age 18 by the highest level of education either parent in their household attained varied across racial/ethnic groups in 2018. For example, the percentage of children who lived in households where the highest level of education attained by either parent was a bachelor's or higher degree was higher for Asian children (69 percent) than for children of other racial/ethnic groups: White (53 percent), Two or more races (48 percent), Black (27 percent), Pacific Islander (23 percent), Hispanic (21 percent), and American Indian/Alaska Native (19 percent).

In contrast, in 2018, the percentage of children under age 18 who lived in households where no parent had completed high school was higher for Hispanic children (23 percent) than for children of other racial/ethnic groups: American Indian/Alaska Native (11 percent), Pacific Islander (10 percent), Black (9 percent), Asian (6 percent), Two or more races (4 percent), and White (3 percent). The percentage of children who lived in households without a parent who had completed high school was lower for White children than for children of any other racial/ethnic group.

Figure 2. Percentage of children under age 18, by child's race/ethnicity and family structure: 2018

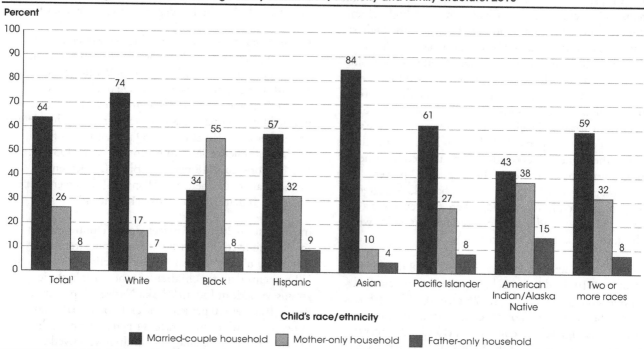

Percent

Married-couple household   Mother-only household   Father-only household

Child's race/ethnicity

[1] Includes respondents who wrote in some other race that was not included as an option on the questionnaire.
NOTE: Data do not include foster children, children in unrelated subfamilies, children living in group quarters, and children who were reported as the householder or spouse of the householder. A "mother-only household" has a female householder, with no spouse present (i.e., the householder is unmarried or the spouse is not in the household), while a "father-only household" has a male householder, with no spouse present. Includes all children who live either with their parent(s) or with a householder to whom they are related by birth, marriage, or adoption (except a child who is the spouse of the householder). Children are classified by their parents' marital status or, if no parents are present in the household, by the marital status of the householder who is related to the children. The householder is the person (or one of the people) who owns or rents (maintains) the housing unit. Race categories exclude persons of Hispanic ethnicity. Although rounded numbers are displayed, the figures are based on unrounded data.
SOURCE: U.S. Department of Commerce, Census Bureau, American Community Survey (ACS), 2018. See *Digest of Education Statistics 2019*, table 102.20.

In 2018, some 64 percent of children under age 18 lived in married-couple households, 26 percent lived in mother-only households, and 8 percent lived in father-only households.[6] This pattern of a higher percentage of children living in married-couple households than in mother- and father-only households was observed for children across all racial/ethnic groups, except for Black children. Fifty-five percent of Black children lived in mother-only households, compared with 34 percent who lived in married-couple households and 8 percent who lived in father-only households.

Figure 3.   Percentage of children under age 18 in families living in poverty, by child's race/ethnicity: 2010 and 2018

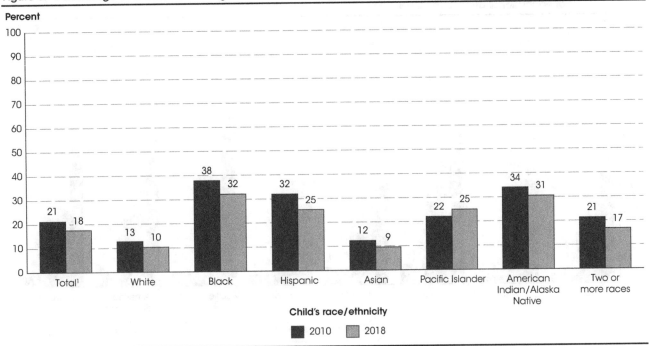

¹ Includes respondents who wrote in some other race that was not included as an option on the questionnaire.
NOTE: The measure of child poverty includes all children who are related to the householder by birth, marriage, or adoption (except a child who is the spouse of the householder). The householder is the person (or one of the people) who owns or rents (maintains) the housing unit. For additional information about poverty status, see https://www.census.gov/topics/income-poverty/poverty/guidance/poverty-measures.html. Race categories exclude persons of Hispanic ethnicity. Although rounded numbers are displayed, the figures are based on unrounded data.
SOURCE: U.S. Department of Commerce, Census Bureau, American Community Survey (ACS), 2010 and 2018. See *Digest of Education Statistics 2019*, table 102.60.

In 2018, approximately 12.6 million children under age 18 were in families living in poverty.[7] The poverty rate for children in 2018 (18 percent) was lower than in 2010 (21 percent). This pattern was observed for children across all racial/ethnic groups, except for Pacific Islander children. For example, 25 percent of Hispanic children lived in poverty in 2018, compared with 32 percent in 2010, and 32 percent of Black children lived in poverty in 2018, compared with 38 percent in 2010. The 2018 poverty rate for Pacific Islander children was not measurably different from the rate in 2010.

The poverty rate for children under age 18 varied across racial/ethnic groups in 2018. The poverty rates were highest for Black (32 percent) and American

Indian/Alaska Native children (31 percent), followed by Hispanic and Pacific Islander children (25 percent each). Additionally, the poverty rate for children of Two or more races (17 percent) was higher than the rates for White (10 percent) and Asian (9 percent) children. Black, American Indian/Alaska Native, Hispanic, and Pacific Islander children had poverty rates higher than the national average (18 percent), while White and Asian children had rates lower than the national average. The poverty rate for children of Two or more races was not measurably different from the national average. For additional information about poverty rates and racial/ethnic subgroups, please refer to the *Status and Trends in the Education of Racial and Ethnic Groups* report.

Figure 4. Percentage of children under age 18 in families living in poverty, by child's race/ethnicity and parents' highest level of educational attainment: 2018

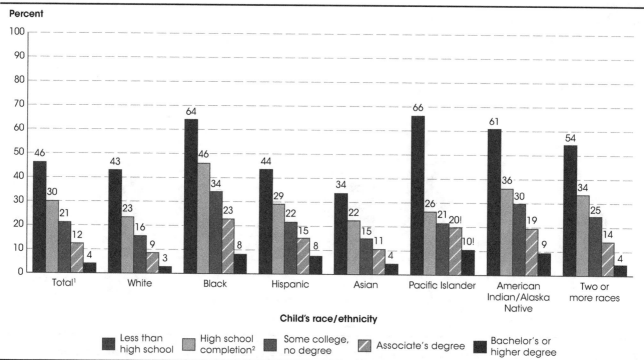

! Interpret data with caution. The coefficient of variation (CV) for this estimate is between 30 and 50 percent.
[1] Includes respondents who wrote in some other race that was not included as an option on the questionnaire.
[2] Includes parents who completed high school through equivalency programs, such as a GED program.
NOTE: Includes only children under age 18 who resided with at least one of their parents (including an adoptive or stepparent; excluding a foster parent). Parents' highest level of educational attainment is the highest level of education attained by any parent residing in the same household as the child. Parents include adoptive and stepparents but exclude parents not residing in the same household as their child. The measure of child poverty includes children who are related to the householder by birth, marriage, or adoption (except a child who is the spouse of the householder). The householder is the person (or one of the people) who owns or rents (maintains) the housing unit. For additional information about poverty status, see https://www.census.gov/topics/income-poverty/poverty/guidance/poverty-measures.html. Race categories exclude persons of Hispanic ethnicity. Although rounded numbers are displayed, the figures are based on unrounded data.
SOURCE: U.S. Department of Commerce, Census Bureau, American Community Survey (ACS), 2018. See *Digest of Education Statistics 2019*, table 102.62.

In 2018, the poverty rate for children under age 18 was highest for those in households where no parent had completed high school and lowest for those in households where the highest level of education attained by either parent was a bachelor's or higher degree, both overall (46 vs. 4 percent) and within all racial/ethnic groups.

Figure 5. Percentage of children under age 18 in families living in poverty, by child's race/ethnicity and family structure: 2018

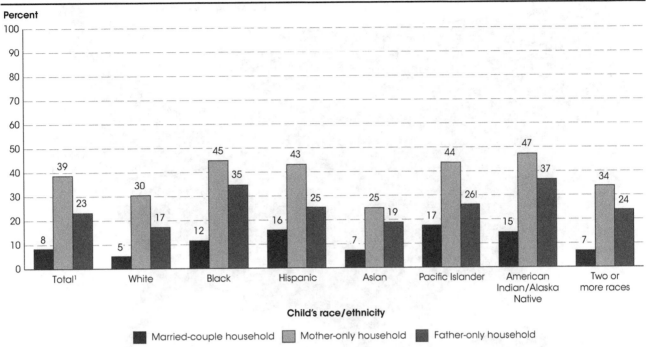

Percent

! Interpret data with caution. The coefficient of variation (CV) for this estimate is between 30 and 50 percent.
[1] Includes respondents who wrote in some other race that was not included as an option on the questionnaire.
NOTE: A "mother-only household" has a female householder, with no spouse present (i.e., the householder is unmarried or their spouse is not in the household), while a "father-only household" has a male householder, with no spouse present. Includes all children who live either with their parent(s) or with a householder to whom they are related by birth, marriage, or adoption (except a child who is the spouse of the householder). Children are classified by their parents' marital status or, if no parents are present in the household, by the marital status of the householder who is related to the children. The householder is the person (or one of the people) who owns or rents (maintains) the housing unit. For additional information about poverty status, see https://www.census.gov/topics/income-poverty/poverty/guidance/poverty-measures.html. Race categories exclude persons of Hispanic ethnicity. Although rounded numbers are displayed, the figures are based on unrounded data.
SOURCE: U.S. Department of Commerce, Census Bureau, American Community Survey (ACS), 2018. See *Digest of Education Statistics 2019*, table 102.60.

In 2018, the poverty rate for children under age 18 was highest for those living in mother-only households (39 percent), followed by those living in father-only households (23 percent). Children living in married-couple households had the lowest poverty rate (8 percent). This pattern of children living in married-couple households having the lowest poverty rate was generally observed across most racial/ethnic groups. For example, among Black children, the poverty rates were 45 percent for those living in mother-only households, 35 percent for those living in father-only households, and 12 percent for those living in married-couple households.

Figure 6. Percentage of children under age 18 in families living in poverty, by state: 2018

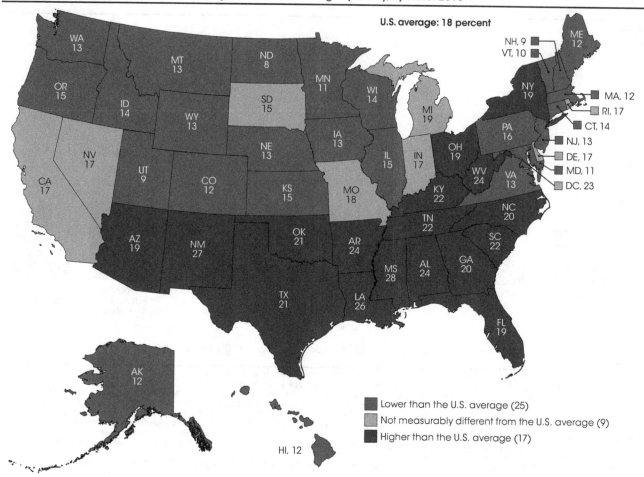

NOTE: The measure of child poverty includes all children who are related to the householder by birth, marriage, or adoption (except a child who is the spouse of the householder). The householder is the person (or one of the people) who owns or rents (maintains) the housing unit. For additional information about poverty status, see https://www.census.gov/topics/income-poverty/poverty/guidance/poverty-measures.html.
SOURCE: U.S. Department of Commerce, Census Bureau, American Community Survey (ACS), 2018. See *Digest of Education Statistics 2019*, table 102.40.

While the national average poverty rate for children under age 18 was 18 percent in 2018, the rates among states ranged from 8 percent in North Dakota to 28 percent in Mississippi. Twenty-five states had poverty rates for children that were lower than the national average, 17 states had rates that were higher than the national average, and 8 states and the District of Columbia had rates that were not measurably different from the national average. Of the 17 states that had poverty rates higher than the national average, the majority (13) were located in the South. In 37 states, the poverty rates were lower in 2018 than in 2010. In the remaining 13 states and the District of Columbia, there was no measurable difference between the poverty rates in 2010 and 2018.

Endnotes:

[1] Pungello, E.P., Kainz, K., Burchinal, M., Wasik, B.H., Sparling, J.J., Ramey, C.T., and Campbell, F.A. (2010, February). Early Educational Intervention, Early Cumulative Risk, and the Early Home Environment as Predictors of Young Adult Outcomes Within a High-Risk Sample. *Child Development, 81*(1): 410–426. Retrieved February 7, 2020, from http://onlinelibrary.wiley.com/doi/10.1111/j.1467-8624.2009.01403.x/full.

[2] Ross, T., Kena, G., Rathbun, A., KewalRamani, A., Zhang, J., Kristapovich, P., and Manning, E. (2012). *Higher Education: Gaps in Access and Persistence Study* (NCES 2012-046). U.S. Department of Education. Washington, DC: National Center for Education Statistics. Retrieved February 7, 2020, from https://nces.ed.gov/pubsearch/pubsinfo.asp?pubid=2012046.

[3] Includes parents who completed high school through equivalency programs, such as a GED program.

[4] Includes parents who had completed professional degrees.

[5] Although the percentage of children living in households where the highest level of education attained by either parent was an associate's degree was also higher in 2018 than in 2010 (10.1 vs. 9.7 percent), both percentages round to 10 percent.

[6] A "mother-only household" has a female householder, with no spouse present (i.e., the householder is unmarried or the spouse is not in the household), while a "father-only household" has a male householder, with no spouse present. Includes all children who live either with their parent(s) or with a householder to whom they are related by birth, marriage, or adoption (except a child who is the spouse of the householder). Children are classified by their parents' marital status or, if no parents are present in the household, by the marital status of the householder who is related to the children. The householder is the person (or one of the people) who owns or rents (maintains) the housing unit. Foster children, children in unrelated subfamilies, children living in group quarters, and children who were reported as the householder or spouse of the householder are not included in this analysis.

[7] In this indicator, data on household income and the number of people living in the household are combined with the poverty threshold, published by the Census Bureau, to determine the poverty status of children. A household includes all families in which children are related to the householder by birth or adoption, or through marriage. The householder is the person (or one of the people) who owns or rents (maintains) the housing unit. In 2018, the poverty threshold for a family of four with two related children under 18 years old was $25,465. For a more detailed breakdown of the 2018 poverty rate, refer to this table.

Reference tables: *Digest of Education Statistics 2019*, tables 102.20, 102.40, 102.60, 102.62, and 104.70

Related indicators and resources: Children Living in Poverty [*Status and Trends in the Education of Racial and Ethnic Groups*]; Children's Living Arrangements [*Status and Trends in the Education of Racial and Ethnic Groups*]; Concentration of Public School Students Eligible for Free or Reduced-Price Lunch; Disparities in Educational Outcomes Among Male Youth [*The Condition of Education 2015 Spotlight*]; Risk Factors and Academic Outcomes in Kindergarten Through Third Grade [*The Condition of Education 2017 Spotlight*]; Snapshot: Children Living in Poverty for Racial/Ethnic Subgroups [*Status and Trends in the Education of Racial and Ethnic Groups*]; Young Adult Educational and Employment Outcomes by Family Socioeconomic Status [*The Condition of Education 2019 Spotlight*]

Glossary: Associate's degree; Bachelor's degree; College; Doctor's degree; Educational attainment; Geographic region; High school completer; Household; Master's degree; Poverty (official measure); Racial/ethnic group

Children's Internet Access at Home

In 2018, some 94 percent of 3- to 18-year-olds had home internet access: 88 percent had access through a computer, and 6 percent had access only through a smartphone. The remaining 6 percent had no internet access at home.

This indicator uses data from the American Community Survey (ACS) to describe the percentage of 3- to 18-year-olds with home internet access and the percentage with home internet access only through a smartphone in 2018. This indicator also uses data from the Current Population Survey (CPS) to examine the main reasons reported for not having access in 2017, which is the most recent year such data were collected by CPS.

In 2018, some 94 percent of 3- to 18-year-olds had home internet access: 88 percent had access through a computer,[1] and 6 percent had access only through a smartphone.[2] The remaining 6 percent had no internet access at home. Compared with 2018, the percentages with home internet access through a computer and with access only through a smartphone were lower in 2016 (87 and 5 percent, respectively). 2016 was the first year data on internet access through smartphones were collected by ACS.

Figure 1.   Percentage of 3- to 18-year-olds who had home internet access, by child's race/ethnicity: 2018

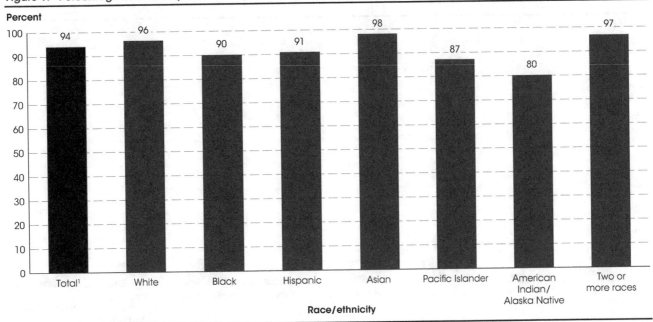

¹ Total includes other racial/ethnic groups not shown separately.
NOTE: Includes only 3- to 18-year-olds living in households (respondents living in group quarters such as shelters, healthcare facilities, or correctional facilities were not asked about internet access). Race categories exclude persons of Hispanic ethnicity. Although rounded numbers are displayed, the figures are based on unrounded data.
SOURCE: U.S. Department of Commerce, Census Bureau, American Community Survey (ACS), 2018. See *Digest of Education Statistics 2019*, table 702.12.

The percentage of 3- to 18-year-olds with home internet access varied across racial/ethnic groups. For instance, in 2018, the percentage with home internet access was highest for those who were Asian (98 percent) and lowest for those who were American Indian/Alaska Native (80 percent). In addition, the percentages with home internet access were higher for those who were of Two or more races (97 percent) and White (96 percent) than for those who were Hispanic (91 percent), Black (90 percent), and Pacific Islander (87 percent).

The percentages of 3- to 18-year-olds with home internet access were higher for those whose parents had attained higher levels of education. For instance, in 2018, the percentage with home internet access was highest for those

whose parents had attained a bachelor's or higher degree (99 percent), followed by those whose parents had an associate's degree (96 percent), some college but no degree (94 percent), a high school credential[3] (90 percent), and less than a high school credential (82 percent).

The percentage of 3- to 18-year-olds with home internet access was higher for those in higher income families. In 2018, some 99 percent of those in families in the highest family income quarter and 97 percent of those in families in the middle-high quarter had home internet access, compared with 94 percent and 87 percent of those in families in the middle-low and lowest quarters, respectively.[4]

Figure 2. Percentage of 3- to 18-year-olds who had home internet access only through a smartphone, by child's race/ethnicity: 2018

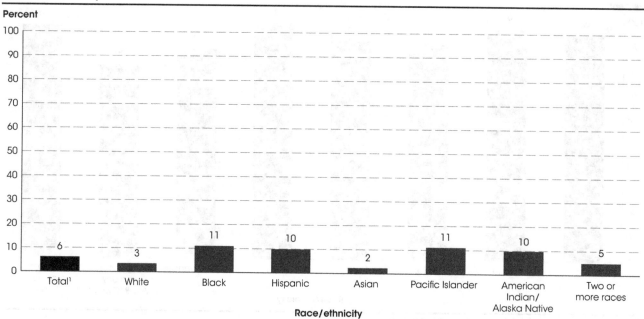

¹ Total includes other racial/ethnic groups not shown separately.
NOTE: Includes only 3- to 18-year-olds living in households (respondents living in group quarters such as shelters, healthcare facilities, or correctional facilities were not asked about internet access). Includes 3- to 18-year-olds who had home internet access only through a smartphone but did not have any of the following types of computers: desktop or laptop, tablet or other portable wireless computer, or "some other type of computer." Race categories exclude persons of Hispanic ethnicity. Although rounded numbers are displayed, the figures are based on unrounded data.
SOURCE: U.S. Department of Commerce, Census Bureau, American Community Survey (ACS), 2018. See *Digest of Education Statistics 2019*, table 702.12.

The percentage of 3- to 18-year-olds with home internet access only through a smartphone varied by race and ethnicity and was lower for those who were Asian (2 percent), White (3 percent), and of Two or more races (5 percent) than for those who were American Indian/Alaska Native (10 percent), Hispanic (10 percent), Black (11 percent), and Pacific Islander (11 percent).

Figure 3.   Percentage of 3- to 18-year-olds who had home internet access only through a smartphone, by parental education and family income quarter: 2018

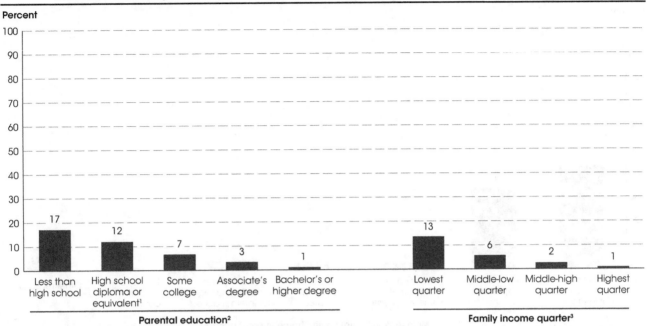

[1] Includes those who completed high school through equivalency credentials, such as the GED.
[2] Highest education level of any parent residing with the 3- to 18-year-olds (including an adoptive or stepparent). Includes only 3- to 18-year-olds who resided with at least one of their parents.
[3] The lowest quarter refers to the bottom 25 percent of all family incomes; the middle-low quarter refers to the 26th through the 50th percentile of all family incomes; the middle-high quarter refers to the 51st through the 75th percentile of all family incomes; and the highest quarter refers to the top 25 percent of all family incomes.
NOTE: Includes only 3- to 18-year-olds living in households (respondents living in group quarters such as shelters, healthcare facilities, or correctional facilities were not asked about internet access). Includes 3- to 18-year-olds who had home internet access only through a smartphone but did not have any of the following types of computers: desktop or laptop, tablet or other portable wireless computer, or "some other type of computer." Although rounded numbers are displayed, the figures are based on unrounded data.
SOURCE: U.S. Department of Commerce, Census Bureau, American Community Survey (ACS), 2018. See *Digest of Education Statistics 2019*, table 702.12.

In addition, the percentage of 3- to 18-year-olds with home internet access only through a smartphone was lower for those whose parents had attained higher levels of education. For instance, in 2018, the percentage with home internet access only through a smartphone was lowest for those whose parents had attained a bachelor's or higher degree (1 percent), followed by those whose parents had an associate's degree (3 percent), some college but no degree (7 percent), a high school credential (12 percent), and less than a high school credential (17 percent).

Similarly, the percentage of 3- to 18-year-olds with home internet access only through a smartphone was lower for those in higher income families. In 2018, some 1 percent of those in families in the highest family income quarter and 2 percent of those in families in the middle-high quarter had home internet access only through a smartphone, compared with 6 percent and 13 percent of those in families in the middle-low and lowest quarters, respectively.

Figure 4. Percentage distribution of 3- to 18-year-olds with no internet access at home, by main reason for not having access: 2017

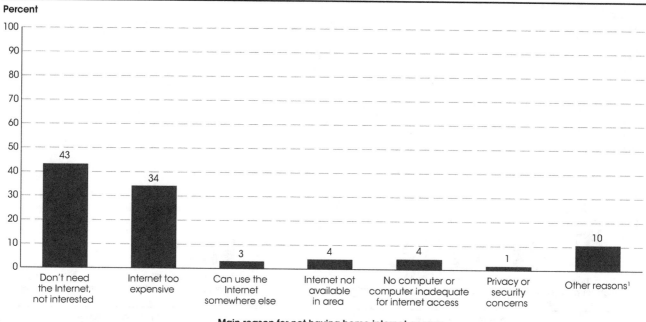

¹ Respondents could specify "other" reasons. Examples of other reasons were not provided to respondents.
NOTE: Includes only 3- to 18-year-olds living in homes with no internet access. Data are based on sample surveys of the civilian noninstitutionalized population, which excludes persons in the military and persons living in institutions (e.g., prisons or nursing facilities). The survey respondent usually is the person who either owns or rents the housing unit. Detail may not sum to totals because of rounding. Although rounded numbers are displayed, the figures are based on unrounded data.
SOURCE: U.S. Department of Commerce, Census Bureau, Current Population Survey (CPS), November 2017. See *Digest of Education Statistics 2018*, table 702.40.

In 2017, the two most commonly cited main reasons that 3- to 18-year-olds did not have home internet access were that the family did not need it or was not interested in having it (43 percent) and that it was too expensive (34 percent). Other main reasons cited for not having home internet access included the following: the home either had no computer or had a computer inadequate for internet use (4 percent), internet service was not available in the area (4 percent), the Internet could be used somewhere else (3 percent), and the existence of privacy or security concerns (1 percent).

In 2017, the percentage of 3- to 18-year-olds whose main barrier to home internet access was that it was too expensive was higher for those who were Hispanic (45 percent) than for those who were of Two or more races (30 percent), White (25 percent), and American Indian/Alaska Native (24 percent). The percentage whose main barrier to home internet access was that it was too expensive was also higher for those who were Black (39 percent) than for those who were White. In addition, the percentages whose main barrier to home internet access was that it was too expensive were higher for those whose parents had less than a high school credential (46 percent) and a high school credential (39 percent) than for those whose parents had attained a bachelor's or higher degree (25 percent) in 2017. Similarly, the percentage whose main barrier to home internet access was that it was too expensive was higher for those with family income levels of less than $40,000 than for those with family income levels of $50,000 or more in 2017.

Endnotes:

¹ Refers to the percentage of 3- to 18-year-olds with home internet access through one or more of the following types of computers: desktop or laptop, tablet or other portable wireless computer, or "some other type of computer." Includes homes having both smartphones and any of these types of computers.
² Refers to the percentage of 3- to 18-year-olds with home internet access only through a smartphone but did not have any of the types of computers listed in endnote 1.

³ Includes those who completed high school through equivalency credentials, such as the GED.
⁴ The highest quarter refers to the top 25 percent of all family incomes; the middle-high quarter refers to the 51st through the 75th percentile of all family incomes; the middle-low quarter refers to the 26th through the 50th percentile of all family incomes; and the lowest quarter refers to the bottom 25 percent of all family incomes.

Reference tables: *Digest of Education Statistics 2019*, table 702.12; *Digest of Education Statistics 2018*, table 702.40
Related indicators and resources: *Student Access to Digital Learning Resources Outside of the Classroom*; Technology and Engineering Literacy [*web-only*]

Glossary: Bachelor's degree; College; Educational attainment; Educational attainment (Current Population Survey); Gap; High school completer; Racial/ethnic group

Preschool and Kindergarten Enrollment

In 2018, 3- to 5-year-olds whose parents' highest level of education was less than a high school credential (19 vs. 11 percent) or high school credential (19 vs. 13 percent) were more likely to be enrolled in full-day preschool than in part-day preschool. Among the remaining groups, there were no measurable differences between the percentages enrolled in full-day preschool programs versus the percentages enrolled in part-day programs.

Preprimary programs, which include preschool[1] and kindergarten programs, are groups or classes that are organized to provide educational experiences for children. Preprimary programs include both full-day and part-day programs. Child care programs that are not primarily designed to provide educational experiences, such as daycare programs, are not included in preprimary programs.

Figure 1.   Percentage of 3-, 4-, and 5-year-olds enrolled in preprimary programs: 2000 through 2018

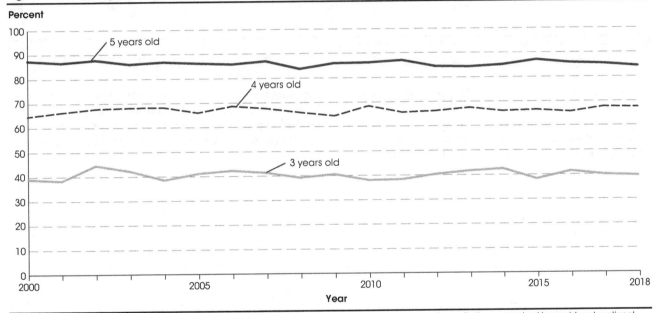

NOTE: Includes enrollment in both full-day and part-day programs. "Preprimary programs" are groups or classes that are organized to provide educational experiences for children and include kindergarten, preschool, and nursery school programs. Data are based on sample surveys of the civilian noninstitutionalized population.
SOURCE: U.S. Department of Commerce, Census Bureau, Current Population Survey (CPS), October 2000 through 2018. See *Digest of Education Statistics 2006*, table 41; *Digest of Education Statistics 2009*, table 43; and *Digest of Education Statistics 2013, 2017,* and *2019*, table 202.10.

In 2018, the preprimary program enrollment rate was higher for 5-year-olds (84 percent) than for 4-year-olds (68 percent) and higher for 4-year-olds than for 3-year-olds (40 percent). The percentage of 5-year-olds enrolled in preprimary programs was lower in 2018 than in 2000 (84 vs. 88 percent). For both 3-year-olds and 4-year-olds, however, there was no measurable difference between the percentage enrolled in preprimary programs in 2018 and the percentage enrolled in preprimary programs in 2000.

Enrollment in full-day preprimary programs varied. In 2018, among those enrolled in preprimary programs, the percentage of 5-year-olds attending full-day programs (77 percent) was higher than the percentage of 3- to 4-year-olds attending full-day programs (55 percent).

Figure 2. Percentage of 3- to 5-year-olds in preschool and kindergarten programs attending full-day programs: 2000 through 2018

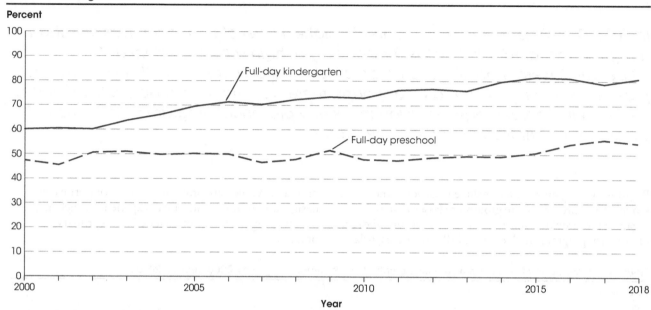

NOTE: Data are based on sample surveys of the civilian noninstitutionalized population.
SOURCE: U.S. Department of Commerce, Census Bureau, Current Population Survey (CPS), October 2000 through 2018. See *Digest of Education Statistics 2006,* table 41; *Digest of Education Statistics 2009,* table 43; and *Digest of Education Statistics 2013, 2017,* and *2019,* table 202.10.

In every year from 2000 to 2018, the percentage of 3- to 5-year-old *kindergarten* students enrolled in full-day programs was higher than the percentage of 3- to 5-year-old *preschool* students enrolled in full-day programs. Among those attending kindergarten, the percentage attending full-day programs increased from 60 percent in 2000 to 81 percent in 2018. Similarly, of those who were enrolled in preschool programs, the percentage attending full-day programs increased from 47 percent in 2000 to 54 percent in 2018.

Figure 3. Percentage of 3- to 5-year-olds enrolled in preschool programs, by race/ethnicity and attendance status: October 2018

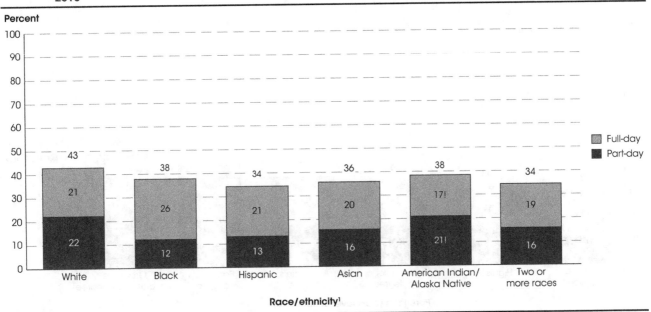

! Interpret data with caution. The coefficient of variation (CV) for this estimate is between 30 and 50 percent.
[1] Reporting standards for Pacific Islander 3- to 5-year-olds were not met; therefore, data for this group are not shown in the figure. Race categories exclude persons of Hispanic ethnicity.
NOTE: Enrollment data include only those 3- to 5-year-olds in preschool programs and do not include those enrolled in kindergarten or primary programs. Data are based on sample surveys of the civilian noninstitutionalized population. Although rounded numbers are displayed, the figures are based on unrounded data. Detail may not sum to totals because of rounding.
SOURCE: U.S. Department of Commerce, Census Bureau, Current Population Survey (CPS), October 2018. See *Digest of Education Statistics 2019*, table 202.20.

The rest of this indicator focuses on enrollment in preschool programs only. In 2018, the percentage of 3- to 5-year-olds enrolled in preschool programs was higher for those who were White (43 percent) than for those who were of Two or more races and Hispanic (34 percent each). The preschool enrollment rates of 3- to 5-year-olds who were American Indian/Alaska Native (38 percent), Black (38 percent), and Asian (36 percent) were not measurably different from the preschool enrollment rates of 3- to 5-year-olds from other racial/ethnic groups.

Comparing full-day versus part-day attendance status, a higher percentage of Black 3- to 5-year-olds (26 vs. 12 percent) and Hispanic 3- to 5-year-olds (21 vs. 13 percent) attended full-day preschool programs than part-day programs. For 3- to 5-year-olds in the other racial/ethnic groups, there were no measurable differences between the percentages enrolled in full-day programs and part-day programs.

Figure 4. Percentage of 3- to 5-year-olds enrolled in preschool programs, by parents' highest level of education and preschoolers' attendance status: October 2018

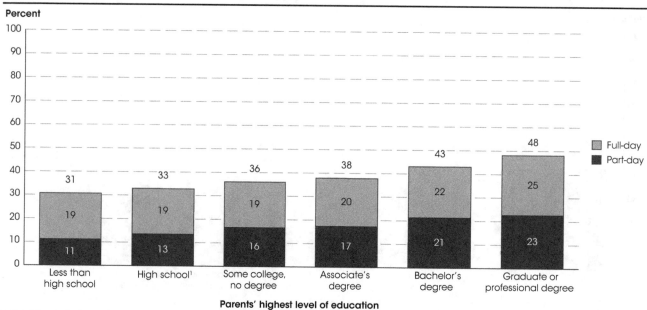

[1] Includes completing high school through equivalency credentials, such as the GED.
NOTE: Enrollment data include only those 3- to 5-year-olds in preschool programs and do not include those enrolled in kindergarten or primary programs. "Parents' highest level of education" is defined as the highest level of education attained by either parent in the child's household. Data are based on sample surveys of the civilian noninstitutionalized population. Although rounded numbers are displayed, the figures are based on unrounded data. Detail may not sum to totals because of rounding.
SOURCE: U.S. Department of Commerce, Census Bureau, Current Population Survey (CPS), October 2018. See *Digest of Education Statistics 2019*, table 202.20.

Enrollment in preschool programs varied by parents' highest level of education, defined as the highest level of education attained by either parent in the child's household. In 2018, the percentage of 3- to 5-year-olds enrolled in preschool programs was higher for those whose parents' highest level of education was a graduate or professional degree (48 percent) or a bachelor's degree (43 percent) than for those whose parents' highest level of education was some college but no degree (36 percent), a high school credential[2] (33 percent), or less than a high school credential (31 percent). The preschool enrollment rate was also higher for 3- to 5-year-olds whose parents' highest level of education was a graduate or professional degree than for those whose parents' highest level of education was an associate's degree (38 percent).

In 2018, the percentage of 3- to 5-year-olds enrolled in full-day preschool programs was higher for those whose parents' highest level of education was a graduate or professional degree (25 percent) than for those whose parents' highest level of education was some college but no degree or a high school credential (19 percent each).

In 2018, 3- to 5-year-olds whose parents' highest level of education was less than a high school credential (19 vs. 11 percent) or high school credential (19 vs. 13 percent) were more likely to be enrolled in full-day preschool than in part-day preschool. Among the remaining groups, there were no measurable differences between the percentages enrolled in full-day preschool programs versus the percentages enrolled in part-day programs.

Endnotes:

[1] Preschool programs are also known as nursery school programs and are defined as a group or class that provides educational experiences for children during the year or years preceding kindergarten. Private homes in which essentially custodial care is provided are not considered preschool programs. For a complete definition, see https://www.census.gov/programs-surveys/cps/technical-documentation/subject-definitions.html#nurseryschool.

[2] Includes completion of high school through equivalency programs, such as a GED program.

Reference tables: *Digest of Education Statistics 2019*, tables 202.10 and 202.20; *Digest of Education Statistics 2017*, table 202.10; *Digest of Education Statistics 2013*, table 202.10; *Digest of Education Statistics 2009*, table 43; *Digest of Education Statistics 2006*, table 41

Related indicators and resources: Early Childcare and Education Arrangements [*Status and Trends in the Education of Racial and Ethnic Groups*]; Early Childhood Care Arrangements: Choices and Costs [*The Condition of Education 2018 Spotlight*]; Kindergarten Entry Status: On-Time, Delayed-Entry, and Repeating Kindergartners [*The Condition of Education 2013 Spotlight*]; Kindergartners' Approaches to Learning Behaviors and Academic Outcomes [*The Condition of Education 2015 Spotlight*]; Kindergartners' Approaches to Learning, Family Socioeconomic Status, and Early Academic Gains [*The Condition of Education 2016 Spotlight*]; Private School Enrollment; Public School Enrollment; Risk Factors and Academic Outcomes in Kindergarten Through Third Grade [*The Condition of Education 2017 Spotlight*]

Glossary terms: Associate's degree; Bachelor's degree; College; Educational attainment (Current Population Survey); Enrollment; High school completer; Preschool; Racial/ethnic group

Public School Enrollment

Between fall 2017 and fall 2029, total public school enrollment in prekindergarten through grade 12 is projected to increase by 1 percent (from 50.7 million to 51.1 million students), with changes across states ranging from an increase of 16 percent in North Dakota to a decrease of 12 percent in New Mexico.

This indicator discusses overall changes in the number of students enrolled in public schools (including both traditional public schools and public charter schools), as well as changes by grade level and by state. In fall 2017, some 50.7 million students were enrolled in public elementary and secondary schools (prekindergarten [preK] through grade 12).[1,2] Of these students, 70 percent were enrolled in preK through grade 8, and the remaining 30 percent were enrolled in grades 9 through 12.

Figure 1. Actual and projected public school enrollment, by level: Fall 2000 through fall 2029

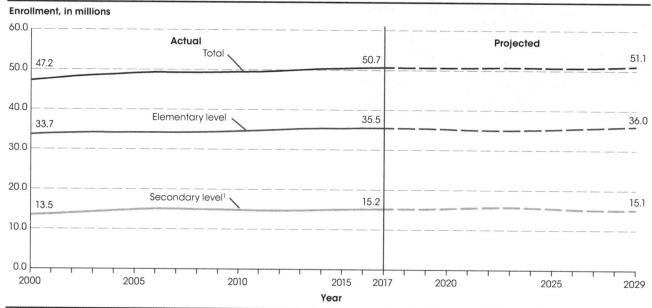

¹ Includes students reported as being enrolled in grade 13.
NOTE: The total ungraded counts of students were prorated to the elementary level (prekindergarten through grade 8) and the secondary level (grades 9 through 12). Prekindergarten enrollments for California and Oregon were imputed for fall 2015 and fall 2017; prekindergarten enrollment for California was imputed for fall 2016. Detail may not sum to totals because of rounding. Some data have been revised from previously published figures.
SOURCE: U.S. Department of Education, National Center for Education Statistics, Common Core of Data (CCD), "State Nonfiscal Survey of Public Elementary/Secondary Education," 2000–01 through 2017–18; and National Elementary and Secondary Enrollment Projection Model, 1972 through 2029. See *Digest of Education Statistics 2019*, table 203.10.

Between fall 2000 and fall 2017, total public elementary and secondary school enrollment increased by 7 percent, reaching 50.7 million students in fall 2017. During the same period, enrollment in preK through grade 8 increased by 5 percent, reaching 35.5 million students in fall 2017. Enrollment in grades 9 through 12 increased by 12 percent between fall 2000 and fall 2007, to 15.1 million students; enrollment then decreased by 2 percent between fall 2007 and fall 2011 before increasing by 3 percent between fall 2011 and fall 2017, when it reached 15.2 million students.

Total public school enrollment is projected to continue increasing through fall 2029 (the last year for which projected data are available). From fall 2017 to fall 2029, total enrollment is projected to increase by 1 percent to 51.1 million students. Enrollment in preK through grade 8 is projected to decrease by 1 percent, to 35.0 million students, between fall 2017 and fall 2022 and then increase by 3 percent, to 36.0 million students, between fall 2022 and fall 2029. Enrollment in grades 9 through 12 is projected to increase by 4 percent, to 15.7 million students, between fall 2017 and fall 2023 and then decrease by 4 percent, to 15.1 million students, between fall 2023 and fall 2029.

Figure 2.   Percentage change in public elementary and secondary school enrollment, by state: Fall 2000 to fall 2017

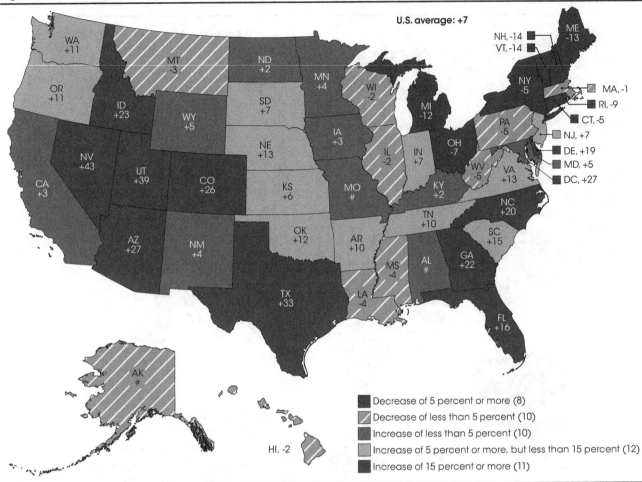

U.S. average: +7

Legend:
- Decrease of 5 percent or more (8)
- Decrease of less than 5 percent (10)
- Increase of less than 5 percent (10)
- Increase of 5 percent or more, but less than 15 percent (12)
- Increase of 15 percent or more (11)

Rounds to zero.
NOTE: Categorizations are based on unrounded percentages. Prekindergarten enrollments for California and Oregon were imputed for fall 2017.
SOURCE: U.S. Department of Education, National Center for Education Statistics, Common Core of Data (CCD), "State Nonfiscal Survey of Public Elementary/Secondary Education," 2000–01 and 2017–18. See *Digest of Education Statistics 2019*, table 203.20.

Changes in public elementary and secondary school enrollment varied by state. Total enrollment in preK through grade 12 was higher in fall 2017 than in fall 2000 for 32 states and the District of Columbia, with increases of 15 percent or more occurring in the District of Columbia and 10 states (Florida, Delaware, North Carolina, Georgia, Idaho, Colorado, Arizona, Texas, Utah, and Nevada). Total enrollment in preK through grade 12 was lower in fall 2017 than in fall 2000 for the other 18 states, with decreases of 10 percent or more occurring in 4 states (Michigan, Maine, Vermont, and New Hampshire).

Figure 3.   Projected percentage change in public elementary and secondary school enrollment, by state: Fall 2017 to fall 2029

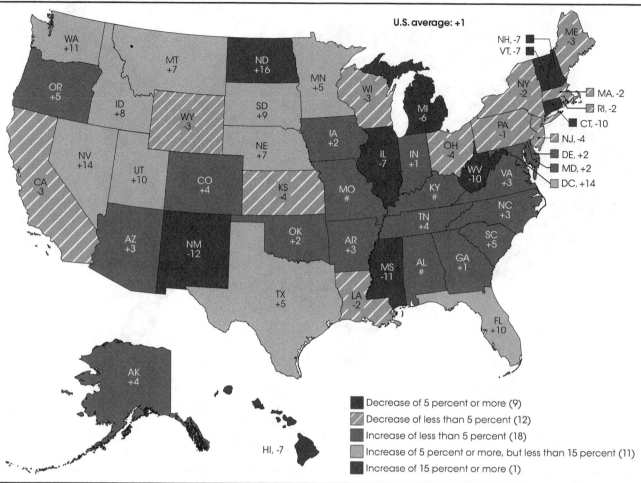

Rounds to zero.
NOTE: Categorizations are based on unrounded percentages. Prekindergarten enrollments for California and Oregon were imputed for fall 2017.
SOURCE: U.S. Department of Education, National Center for Education Statistics, Common Core of Data (CCD), "State Nonfiscal Survey of Public Elementary/ Secondary Education," 2017–18; and State Public Elementary and Secondary Enrollment Projection Model, 1980 through 2029. See *Digest of Education Statistics 2019*, table 203.20.

Total public elementary and secondary school enrollment is projected to be higher in fall 2029 than in fall 2017 in the District of Columbia and 29 states, all of which are located in the South, the West, or the Midwest. Total enrollment is projected to be lower in fall 2029 than in fall 2017 in the other 21 states: 9 of these states are located in the Northeast, 5 states are located in the Midwest, 4 states are located in the West, and 3 states are located in the South. During this period, North Dakota is projected to have the largest percentage increase in total enrollment (16 percent), followed by the District of Columbia and Nevada (14 percent each). In contrast, New Mexico and Mississippi are projected to have the largest percentage decreases in total enrollment (12 and 11 percent, respectively). In fall 2017, total enrollment ranged from fewer than 100,000 students in the District of Columbia (87,300 students), Vermont (88,000 students), and Wyoming (94,300 students) to 5.4 million students in Texas and 6.3 million students in California. In fall 2029, Vermont (82,000 students), Wyoming (91,500 students), and the District of Columbia (99,800 students) are projected to still have fewer than 100,000 students. California is projected to have the largest total enrollment

in fall 2029 (6.1 million students), followed by Texas (5.7 million students).

Between fall 2017 and fall 2029, some 22 states and the District of Columbia are projected to have public school enrollment increases in both preK through grade 8 and grades 9 through 12. In contrast, 21 other states are projected to have enrollment decreases in both grade ranges. Alabama, Georgia, Indiana, Kentucky, Missouri, North Carolina, and Tennessee are projected to have enrollment increases in preK through grade 8 but enrollment decreases in grades 9 through 12. For preK through grade 8, enrollment is projected to be at least 15 percent higher in fall 2029 than in fall 2017 in North Dakota (15 percent), while enrollment is projected to be at least 10 percent lower in fall 2029 than in fall 2017 in New Mexico (12 percent). For grades 9 through 12, enrollment is projected to be at least 15 percent higher in fall 2029 than in fall 2017 in Nevada, North Dakota, and the District of Columbia, while enrollment is projected to be at least 10 percent lower in fall 2029 than in fall 2017 in New Hampshire, Michigan, New Mexico, Mississippi, West Virginia, and Connecticut.

Endnotes:

[1] In this indicator, public elementary and secondary school enrollment includes ungraded students for all years. This also includes a small number of students reported as being enrolled in grade 13, who were counted as enrolled in grades 9 through 12. Prekindergarten enrollments for California and Oregon were imputed for fall 2015 and fall 2017; prekindergarten enrollment

for California was imputed for fall 2016.

[2] This indicator includes public elementary and secondary school enrollment in the United States, defined as including the 50 states and the District of Columbia.

Reference tables: *Digest of Education Statistics 2019,* tables 203.10, 203.20, 203.25, and 203.30

Related indicators and resources: Characteristics of Elementary and Secondary Schools; Elementary and Secondary Enrollment [*Status and Trends in the Education of Racial and Ethnic Groups*]; English Language Learners in Public Schools; Homeless Children and Youth in Public Schools [*The Condition of Education 2017 Spotlight*]; Private School Enrollment; Public Charter School Enrollment; Students With Disabilities

Glossary: Elementary school; Enrollment; Geographic region; Prekindergarten; Public school or institution; Secondary school

Public Charter School Enrollment

Between fall 2000 and fall 2017, overall public charter school enrollment increased from 0.4 million to 3.1 million. During this period, the percentage of public school students who attended charter schools increased from 1 to 6 percent.

A *public charter school* is a publicly funded school that is typically governed by a group or organization under a legislative contract—a charter—with the state, the district, or another entity. The charter exempts the school from certain state or local rules and regulations. In return for flexibility and autonomy, the charter school must meet the accountability standards outlined in its charter. A school's charter is reviewed periodically by the entity that granted it, and can be revoked if guidelines on curriculum and management are not followed or if the accountability standards are not met.[1] Between school years 2000–01 and 2017–18, the percentage of all public schools in the United States (defined in this indicator as the 50 states and the District of Columbia) that were charter schools increased from 2 to 7 percent, and the total number of charter schools increased from approximately 2,000 to 7,200.

Figure 1.   Public charter school enrollment, by school level: Selected years, fall 2000 through fall 2017

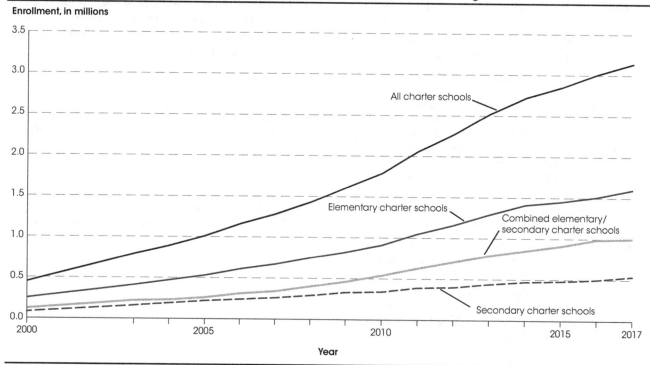

NOTE: "Elementary" includes schools beginning with grade 6 or below and with no grade higher than 8. "Secondary" includes schools with no grade lower than 7. "Combined elementary/secondary" includes schools beginning with grade 6 or below and ending with grade 9 or above. Other schools not classified by grade span are included in the "All charter schools" count but are not presented separately in the figure.
SOURCE: U.S. Department of Education, National Center for Education Statistics, Common Core of Data (CCD), "Public Elementary/Secondary School Universe Survey," 2000–01 through 2017–18. See *Digest of Education Statistics 2014, 2015, 2016, 2017, 2018,* and *2019,* table 216.20.

The percentage of all public school students who attended public charter schools increased from 1 to 6 percent between fall 2000 and fall 2017. During this period, public charter school enrollment increased steadily, from 0.4 million students in fall 2000 to 3.1 million students in fall 2017—an overall increase of 2.7 million students. In contrast, the number of students attending traditional public schools increased by 1.3 million between fall 2000 and fall 2005, and then decreased by 0.7 million between fall 2005 and fall 2017, for a net increase of 0.6 million students. In each year from fall 2000 to fall 2017, larger numbers of public charter school students were enrolled in elementary schools than in any of the other three levels of charter schools: secondary schools, combined schools, and other levels of schools that were not classified by grade span.

Figure 2.   Percentage of all public school students enrolled in public charter schools, by state: Fall 2017

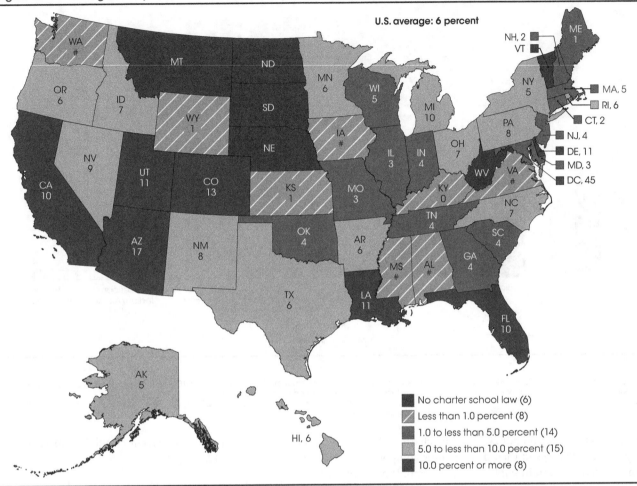

U.S. average: 6 percent

Legend:
- No charter school law (6)
- Less than 1.0 percent (8)
- 1.0 to less than 5.0 percent (14)
- 5.0 to less than 10.0 percent (15)
- 10.0 percent or more (8)

#Rounds to zero.
NOTE: Categorizations are based on unrounded percentages.
SOURCE: U.S. Department of Education, National Center for Education Statistics, Common Core of Data (CCD), "Public Elementary/Secondary School Universe Survey," 2017-18. See *Digest of Education Statistics 2019*, table 216.90.

The first law allowing the establishment of public charter schools was passed in Minnesota in 1991.[2] As of fall 2017, charter school legislation had been passed in 44 states and the District of Columbia.[3,4] The states in which public charter school legislation had not been passed by that time were Montana, Nebraska, North Dakota, South Dakota, Vermont, and West Virginia.

Of the 45 jurisdictions with legislative approval for public charter schools as of fall 2017, California had the largest number of students enrolled in charter schools (approximately 627,000 students, representing 10 percent of all public school students in the state), and the District of Columbia had the highest percentage of public school students enrolled in charter schools (45 percent, or approximately 38,700 students). After the District of Columbia, Arizona had the next highest percentage of public school students enrolled in charter schools (17 percent, or approximately 189,700 students). Eight states, however, had less than 1 percent of their public school students enrolled in public charter schools in fall 2017: Alabama, Iowa, Kansas, Kentucky, Mississippi, Virginia, Washington, and Wyoming.

Figure 3. Percentage distribution of public charter school students, by race/ethnicity: Fall 2000 and fall 2017

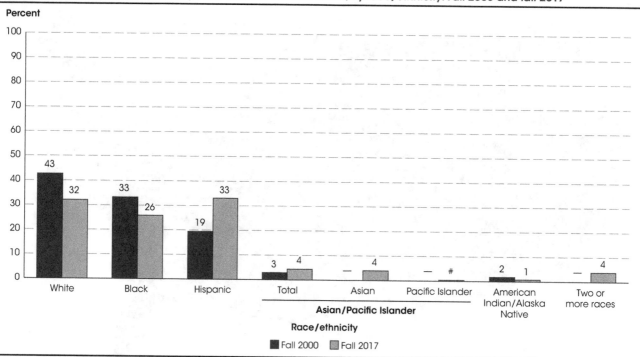

— Not available.
Rounds to zero.
NOTE: Data for the "Asian," "Pacific Islander," and "Two or more races" categories were not available prior to 2009–10. Race categories exclude persons of Hispanic ethnicity. Although rounded numbers are displayed, the figures are based on unrounded data.
SOURCE: U.S. Department of Education, National Center for Education Statistics, Common Core of Data (CCD), "Public Elementary/Secondary School Universe Survey," 2000–01 and 2017–18. See *Digest of Education Statistics 2019*, table 216.30.

Between fall 2000 and fall 2017, public charter schools experienced changes in their demographic composition similar to those seen in public schools overall. (For more information on racial/ethnic enrollment in public schools, please see the report *Status and Trends in the Education of Racial and Ethnic Groups*.) The percentage of public charter school students who were Hispanic increased (from 19 to 33 percent), as did the percentage who were Asian/Pacific Islander[5] (from 3 to 4 percent). In contrast, the percentage of public charter school students who were White decreased (from 43 to 32 percent), as did the percentages who were Black (from 33 to 26 percent) and American Indian/Alaska Native (from 2 to 1 percent). Beginning in fall 2009, data were collected on students of Two or more races attending public charter schools; students of Two or

more races accounted for 4 percent of public charter school students in fall 2017.

Schools in which more than 75 percent of students qualify for free or reduced-price lunch (FRPL) under the National School Lunch Program are considered high-poverty schools.[6] Those in which 25 percent or less of students qualify for FRPL are considered low-poverty schools. In fall 2017, some 35 percent of public charter school students attended high-poverty schools, which was higher than the percentage of traditional public school students who attended high-poverty schools (24 percent). The percentage of students attending low-poverty schools was lower for public charter school students (18 percent) than for traditional public school students (21 percent).[7]

Figure 4. Percentage distribution of public charter schools, by enrollment size: School years 2000–01 and 2017–18

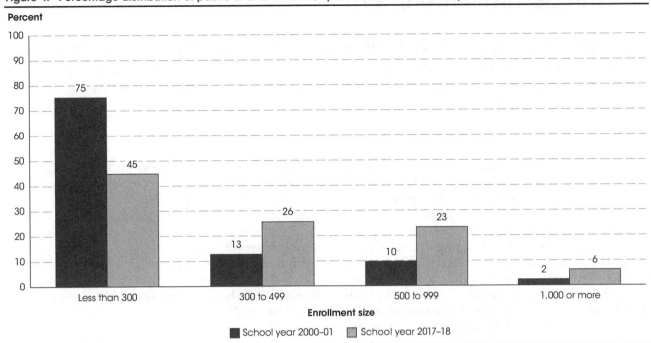

SOURCE: U.S. Department of Education, National Center for Education Statistics, Common Core of Data (CCD), "Public Elementary/Secondary School Universe Survey," 2000–01 and 2017–18. See *Digest of Education Statistics 2019*, table 216.30.

The average enrollment size of public charter schools increased between 2000–01 and 2017–18. The percentages of public charter schools with 300–499, 500–999, and 1,000 or more students each increased, while the percentage of public charter schools with fewer than 300 students decreased.

Endnotes:

[1] Wixom, M.A. (2018). *50-State Comparison: Charter School Policies.* Denver, CO: Education Commission of the States. Retrieved January 9, 2020, from http://www.ecs.org/charter-school-policies/.

[2] Finnigan, K., Adelman, N., Anderson, L., Cotton, L., Donnelly, M.B., and Price, T. (2004). *Evaluation of the Public Charter Schools Program: Final Report.* U.S. Department of Education, Office of the Deputy Secretary. Washington, DC: Policy and Program Studies Service. Retrieved January 9, 2020, from https://www2.ed.gov/rschstat/eval/choice/pcsp-final/finalreport.pdf.

[3] Wixom, M.A. (2018). *50-State Comparison: Charter School Policies.* Denver, CO: Education Commission of the States. Retrieved January 9, 2020, from http://www.ecs.org/charter-school-policies/.

[4] Foster, K. (2019). *Charter Schools.* Frankfort, KY: Kentucky Department of Education. Retrieved January 9, 2020, from https://education.ky.gov/CommOfEd/chartsch/Pages/default.aspx.

[5] Separate data on students who were Asian and Pacific Islander were not available in fall 2000. In fall 2000, data for students who were Asian included students who were Pacific Islander.

[6] Includes students whose National School Lunch Program (NSLP) eligibility has been determined through direct certification.

[7] In fall 2017, some 6 percent of public charter school students and less than 1 percent of traditional public school students attended schools that did not participate in FRPL or had missing data.

Reference tables: *Digest of Education Statistics 2019*, tables 216.20, 216.30, and 216.90

Related indicators and resources: Characteristics of Elementary and Secondary Schools; Elementary and Secondary Enrollment [*Status and Trends in the Education of Racial and Ethnic Groups*]; Private School Enrollment; Public School Enrollment

Glossary: Combined school; Elementary school; Enrollment; Free or reduced-price lunch; National School Lunch Program; Public charter school; Public school or institution; Racial/ethnic group; Secondary school; Student membership; Traditional public school

Private School Enrollment

In fall 2017, some 5.7 million students were enrolled in private elementary and secondary schools. The percentage of elementary and secondary students who were enrolled in private schools decreased from 11 percent in fall 1999 to 10 percent in fall 2017.

Private elementary and secondary schools are educational institutions that are not primarily supported by public funds.[1] In this indicator, private schools are grouped into the following categories by school orientation: Catholic, other religious, and nonsectarian (not religiously affiliated). Catholic schools include parochial, diocesan, and private Catholic schools. The other religious category includes conservative Christian schools, schools that are affiliated with other denominations, and religious schools that are not affiliated with any specific denomination. In addition, private school enrollment totals for elementary

or elementary and secondary grades in this indicator include prekindergarten students enrolled in schools that provide instruction in kindergarten or a higher grade, whereas other National Center for Education Statistics (NCES) analyses from the same source data (the Private School Universe Survey) do not include prekindergarten in private elementary and secondary school enrollment. Therefore, private school enrollment data in this indicator are not comparable to estimates published by the Private School Survey Program.

Figure 1. Private school enrollment in elementary and secondary schools, by school orientation: Fall 1999 through fall 2017

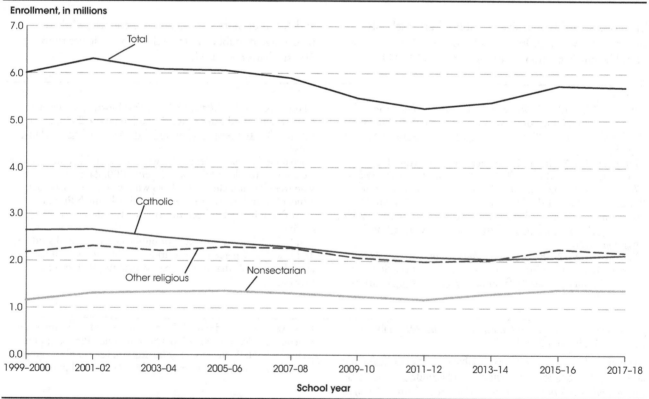

NOTE: Excludes prekindergarten students not enrolled in schools that offer kindergarten or higher grades.
SOURCE: U.S. Department of Education, National Center for Education Statistics, Private School Universe Survey (PSS), 1999–2000 through 2017–18. See *Digest of Education Statistics 2019*, table 205.20.

The number of private school students decreased from 6.0 million in fall 1999 to 5.7 million in fall 2017. The number of private school students enrolled in Catholic schools decreased from 2.7 million in fall 1999 to 2.1 million in fall 2017. The number of students enrolled in other religious schools in fall 2017 was not

measurably different from the number enrolled in fall 1999 (2.2 million students each). The number of students enrolled in nonsectarian schools was higher in fall 2017 (1.4 million students) than in fall 1999 (1.2 million students).

Figure 2. Percentage of elementary and secondary students enrolled in private schools: Fall 1999 through fall 2017

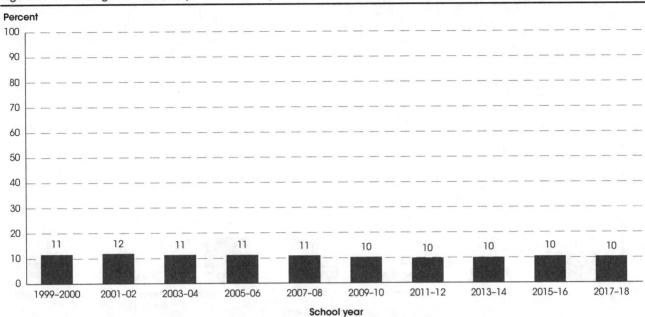

NOTE: Excludes prekindergarten students not enrolled in schools that offer kindergarten or higher grades. Although rounded numbers are displayed, the figures are based on unrounded data.
SOURCE: U.S. Department of Education, National Center for Education Statistics, Private School Universe Survey (PSS), 1999–2000 through 2017–18; Common Core of Data (CCD), "State Nonfiscal Survey of Public Elementary/Secondary Education," 1999–2000 through 2017–18. See *Digest of Education Statistics 2019*, tables 203.65 and 205.20.

The percentage of elementary and secondary students who were enrolled in private schools decreased from 11 percent in fall 1999 to 10 percent in fall 2017.

Figure 3. Percentage of elementary and secondary students enrolled in private schools, by race/ethnicity: Fall 2017

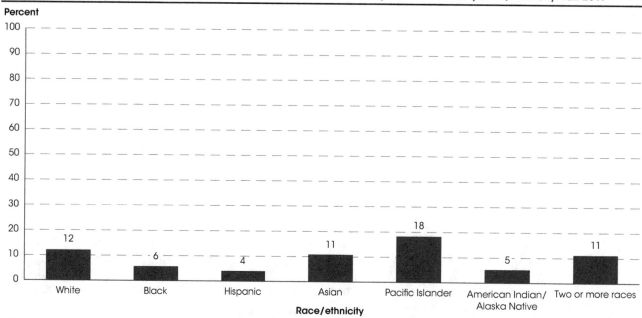

NOTE: Excludes prekindergarten students not enrolled in schools that offer kindergarten or higher grades. Ungraded students are prorated into prekindergarten through grade 8 and grades 9 through 12. Race categories exclude persons of Hispanic ethnicity. Race/ethnicity data were not collected for prekindergarten students who were enrolled in private schools (821,800 out of 5,719,990 students in 2017). Percentages in this figure are based on the students for whom race/ethnicity was reported. Although rounded numbers are displayed, the figures are based on unrounded data.
SOURCE: U.S. Department of Education, National Center for Education Statistics, Private School Universe Survey (PSS), 2017–18; Common Core of Data (CCD), "State Nonfiscal Survey of Public Elementary/Secondary Education," 2017–18. See *Digest of Education Statistics 2019*, tables 203.65, 205.20, and 205.30.

The percentage of elementary and secondary students who were enrolled in private schools varied by race/ethnicity. In fall 2017, about 18 percent of Pacific Islander students,[2] 12 percent of White students, 11 percent of students of Two or more races, and 11 percent of Asian students were enrolled in private schools, compared with 6 percent of Black students, 5 percent of American Indian/Alaska Native students, and 4 percent of Hispanic students in private schools.

Figure 4. Percentage distribution of private elementary and secondary school enrollment, by school orientation and race/ethnicity: Fall 2017

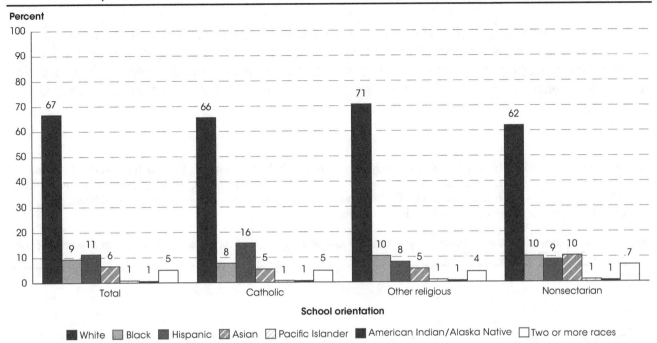

NOTE: Excludes prekindergarten students not enrolled in schools that offer kindergarten or higher grades. Race categories exclude persons of Hispanic ethnicity. Percentage distribution is based on the students for whom race/ethnicity was reported. Although rounded numbers are displayed, the figures are based on unrounded data. Detail may not sum to totals because of rounding.
SOURCE: U.S. Department of Education, National Center for Education Statistics, Private School Universe Survey (PSS), 2017–18. See *Digest of Education Statistics 2019*, table 205.30.

In fall 2017, about 5.7 million students were enrolled in private schools. Sixty-seven percent of private elementary and secondary school students were White, 11 percent were Hispanic, 9 percent were Black, 6 percent were Asian, and 5 percent were students of Two or more races. Pacific Islander and American Indian/Alaska Native students each constituted 1 percent of private school enrollment in 2017. Among students enrolled in the various categories of private schools, Black students made up the second-largest share of enrollment in other

religious schools (10 percent), and Hispanic students made up the second-largest share of enrollment at Catholic schools (16 percent).

In fall 2017, the poverty rate for private school students was 9 percent. Some 43 percent of all private school students were enrolled in schools in cities and 40 percent were enrolled in schools in suburban areas, while 11 percent were enrolled in schools in rural areas and 6 percent were enrolled in schools in towns.

Endnotes:
[1] For the purposes of this indicator, private schools exclude organizations or institutions that provide support for home-schooling. This indicator includes elementary and secondary enrollment in the United States, defined as including the 50 states and the District of Columbia.

[2] Race/ethnicity data were not collected for prekindergarten students who were enrolled in private schools (821,800 out of 5,719,990 students in 2017). Percentages in this indicator are based on the students for whom race/ethnicity was reported.

Reference tables: *Digest of Education Statistics 2019*, tables 102.70, 203.65, 205.20 and 205.30
Related indicators and resources: Characteristics of Elementary and Secondary Schools; Elementary and Secondary Enrollment [*Status and Trends in the Education of Racial and Ethnic Groups*]; Public Charter School Enrollment; Public School Enrollment; *School Choice in the United States: 2019*

Glossary: Catholic school; Combined school; Elementary school; Enrollment; Nonsectarian school; Other religious school; Prekindergarten; Private school; Racial/ethnic group; Secondary school

Racial/Ethnic Enrollment in Public Schools

Between fall 2000 and fall 2017, the percentage of public school students who were White decreased from 61 to 48 percent, and the percentage of students who were Black decreased from 17 to 15 percent. In contrast, the percentage of public school students who were Hispanic increased from 16 to 27 percent during the same period.

Total enrollment in public elementary and secondary schools increased from 47.2 million students to 50.7 million students between fall 2000 and fall 2017, and is projected to continue increasing to 51.1 million students in fall 2029 (the last year for which projected data are available). In addition, racial/ethnic distributions of public school students across the country have shifted.

Figure 1. Percentage distribution of students enrolled in public elementary and secondary schools, by race/ethnicity: Fall 2000, fall 2017, and fall 2029

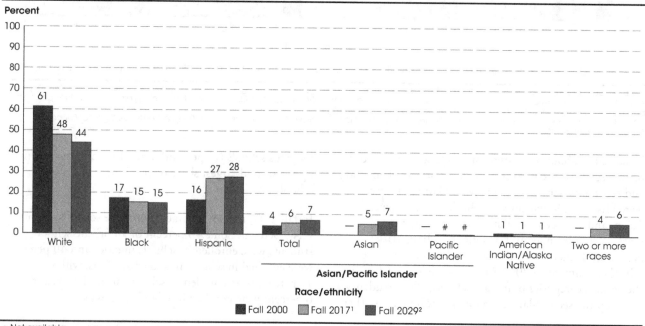

— Not available.
Rounds to zero.
[1] Includes imputations for prekindergarten enrollment in California and Oregon.
[2] Data for fall 2029 are projected.
NOTE: Prior to 2008, separate data on students who were Asian, Pacific Islander, and of Two or more races were not collected; data for students who were Asian included students who were Pacific Islander, and students of Two or more races were required to select a single category from among the offered race/ethnicity categories (White, Black, Hispanic, Asian, and American Indian/Alaska Native). Race categories exclude persons of Hispanic ethnicity. Detail may not sum to totals because of rounding. Although rounded numbers are displayed, the figures are based on unrounded data.
SOURCE: U.S. Department of Education, National Center for Education Statistics, Common Core of Data (CCD), "State Nonfiscal Survey of Public Elementary and Secondary Education," 2000–01 and 2017–18; and National Elementary and Secondary Enrollment by Race/Ethnicity Projection Model, 1972 through 2029. See *Digest of Education Statistics 2019*, table 203.50.

In fall 2017, of the 50.7 million students enrolled in public elementary and secondary schools, 24.1 million were White, 7.7 million were Black, 13.6 million were Hispanic, 2.8 million were Asian/Pacific Islander (2.6 million were Asian and 185,000 were Pacific Islander), half a million were American Indian/Alaska Native, and 2 million were of Two or more races. Between fall 2000 and fall 2017, the percentage of students who were White decreased from 61 to 48 percent, and the number of White students decreased from 28.9 million to 24.1 million. Similarly, the percentage of students who were Black decreased from 17 to 15 percent, and the number of Black students decreased from 8.1 million to 7.7 million. In contrast, the percentage of students who were Hispanic increased from 16 to 27 percent during the same period, and the percentage of students who were Asian/Pacific Islander[1] increased from 4 to 6 percent. In both fall 2000 and fall 2017, American Indian/Alaska Native students accounted for 1 percent of public elementary and secondary enrollment. Between fall 2008 (the first year data on students of Two or more races were collected)[2] and fall 2017, the percentage of students who were of Two or more races increased from 1 to 4 percent.

Between fall 2017 and fall 2029, the percentage of public elementary and secondary students who were White is projected to continue decreasing (from 48 to 44 percent). In contrast, the percentage of students who were Asian/Pacific Islander is projected to continue increasing (from 6 to 7 percent), as is the percentage of students who were of Two or more races (from 4 to 6 percent). Additionally, the percentage of students who were Hispanic is projected to be higher in fall 2029 than in fall 2017 (28 vs. 27 percent). The percentage of students who were Black is projected to remain at 15 percent in fall 2029. Similar to fall 2017, American Indian/Alaska Native students are projected to account for 1 percent of public elementary and secondary enrollment in fall 2029.

Changes in the racial/ethnic distribution of public school enrollment between fall 2000 and fall 2017 differed by state. In all 50 states, the percentage of students enrolled who were White was lower in fall 2017 than in fall 2000, with the difference ranging from 24 percentage points in Nevada to 3 percentage points in Mississippi. However, in the District of Columbia, the percentage of public school students who were White was 7 percentage points higher in fall 2017 than in fall 2000. Across all 50 states and the District of Columbia, the percentage of students who were Hispanic was higher in fall 2017 than in fall 2000; the difference was largest in Nevada (17 percentage points) and smallest in Vermont and West Virginia (1 percentage point each). The percentage of public school students who were Black was higher in fall 2017 than in fall 2000 in 17 states; all differences were 4 percentage points or less. In the remaining 33 states and the District of Columbia, the percentage of public school students who were Black was lower in fall 2017 than in fall 2000; the largest difference occurred in the District of Columbia (16 percentage points).

Figure 2. Percentage of public elementary and secondary school students enrolled in schools with at least 75 percent minority enrollment, by student's race/ethnicity: Fall 2000 and fall 2017

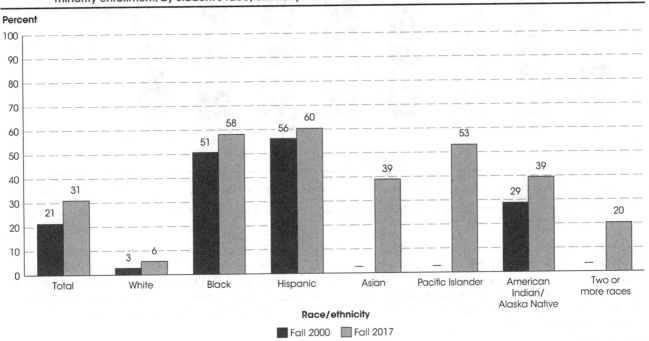

— Not available.
NOTE: Minority students include students who were Black, Hispanic, Asian, Pacific Islander, American Indian/Alaska Native, and of Two or more races. Prior to 2008, separate data on students who were Asian, Pacific Islander, and of Two or more races were not collected; data for students who were Asian included students who were Pacific Islander, and students of Two or more races were required to select a single category from among the offered race/ethnicity categories (White, Black, Hispanic, Asian, and American Indian/Alaska Native). Data reflect racial/ethnic data reported by schools. Excludes 2000 data for Tennessee because racial/ethnic data were not reported. Race categories exclude persons of Hispanic ethnicity. Although rounded numbers are displayed, the figures are based on unrounded data.
SOURCE: U.S. Department of Education, National Center for Education Statistics, Common Core of Data (CCD), "Public Elementary/Secondary School Universe Survey," 2000–01 and 2017–18. See *Digest of Education Statistics 2019*, table 216.50.

The extent to which minority students attend public schools with nonminority students has changed over time. In fall 2017, about 31 percent of all public school students were enrolled in schools where minority students[3] comprised at least 75 percent of the student population; this was higher than the corresponding percentage in fall 2000 (21 percent). The percentages of White, Black, Hispanic, and American Indian/Alaska Native students enrolled in these schools increased from fall 2000 to fall 2017.[4] The percentage of American Indian/Alaska Native students in such schools increased by 11 percentage points, from 29 percent in fall 2000 to 39 percent in fall 2017. Increases in enrollments in these schools for the remaining racial/ethnic groups ranged from 3 percentage points for White students to 7 percentage points for Black students.

Figure 3. Percentage distribution of public elementary and secondary school students, by student's race/ethnicity and percentage of minority enrollment in school: Fall 2017

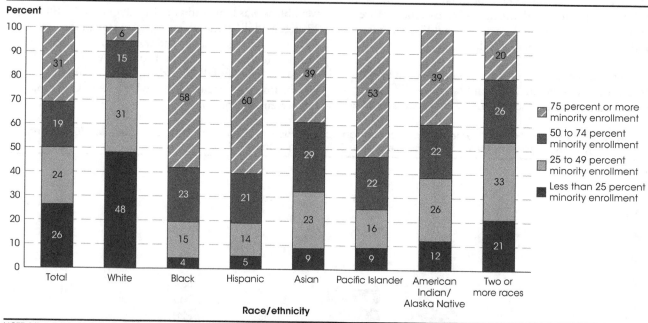

NOTE: Minority students include students who were Black, Hispanic, Asian, Pacific Islander, American Indian/Alaska Native, and of Two or more races. Data reflect racial/ethnic data reported by schools. Race categories exclude persons of Hispanic ethnicity. Detail may not sum to totals because of rounding. Although rounded numbers are displayed, the figures are based on unrounded data.
SOURCE: U.S. Department of Education, National Center for Education Statistics, Common Core of Data (CCD), "Public Elementary/Secondary School Universe Survey," 2017–18. See *Digest of Education Statistics 2019*, table 216.50.

As noted in the preceding paragraph, in fall 2017, approximately 31 percent of public elementary and secondary students attended public schools in which the combined enrollment of minority students was at least 75 percent of total enrollment. More than half of Hispanic (60 percent), Black (58 percent), and Pacific Islander (53 percent) students attended such schools. In contrast, less than half of American Indian/Alaska Native students (39 percent), Asian students (39 percent), students of Two or more races (20 percent), and White students (6 percent) attended such schools.

Figure 4. Percentage distribution of public elementary and secondary school students, by student's race/ethnicity and percentage of own racial/ethnic group enrolled in the school: Fall 2017

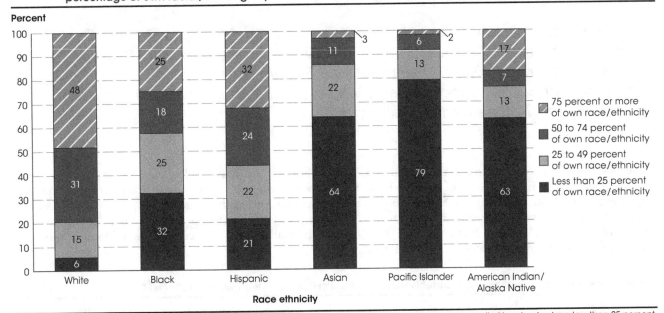

NOTE: Data for Two or more races are omitted from this figure; 99 percent of students of Two or more races were enrolled in schools where less than 25 percent of the students were of their own race. Data reflect racial/ethnic data reported by schools. Race categories exclude persons of Hispanic ethnicity. Detail may not sum to totals because of rounding. Although rounded numbers are displayed, the figures are based on unrounded data.
SOURCE: U.S. Department of Education, National Center for Education Statistics, Common Core of Data (CCD), "Public Elementary/Secondary School Universe Survey," 2017–18. See *Digest of Education Statistics 2019*, table 216.55.

Examining the enrollment data for individual racial/ethnic groups can yield more detailed insights on school enrollment patterns. These data show the extent to which students attend public schools with peers of the same racial/ethnic group. In fall 2017, some 48 percent of White students were enrolled in public schools that were predominantly composed of students of their own race (i.e., 75 percent or more of enrollment was White), while 6 percent of White students were enrolled in schools in which less than a quarter of the students were White. About 25 percent of Black students were enrolled in public schools that were predominantly Black, while 32 percent of Black students were enrolled in schools

in which less than a quarter of the students were Black. Similarly, 32 percent of Hispanic students were enrolled in public schools that were predominantly Hispanic, while 21 percent were enrolled in schools in which less than a quarter were Hispanic. In comparison, lower percentages of students who were of Two or more races (less than 1 percent), Pacific Islander (2 percent), Asian (3 percent), and American Indian/Alaska Native (17 percent) were enrolled in public schools that were predominantly composed of students of their own racial/ethnic group. Instead, more than half of students of these races were enrolled in public schools in which less than a quarter of the students were of their own race.

Endnotes:

[1] Separate data on students who were Asian and Pacific Islander were not available in fall 2000. Prior to 2008, data for students who were Asian included students who were Pacific Islander.
[2] Prior to 2008, separate data on students of Two or more races were not collected; these students were required to select a single category from among the offered race/ethnicity categories (White, Black, Hispanic, Asian, and American Indian/Alaska Native).

[3] Minority students include students who were Black, Hispanic, Asian, Pacific Islander, American Indian/Alaska Native, and of Two or more races.
[4] Students who were Asian, Pacific Islander, and of Two of more races are not included in the trend analysis since prior to 2008 separate data on these racial/ethnic groups were not collected.

Reference tables: *Digest of Education Statistics 2019*, tables 203.50, 203.70, 216.50, and 216.55

Related indicators and resources: Characteristics of Elementary and Secondary Schools; Public Charter School Enrollment; Public School Enrollment; *Status and Trends in the Education of Racial and Ethnic Groups*

Glossary: Elementary school; Enrollment; Public school or institution; Racial/ethnic group; Secondary school

English Language Learners in Public Schools

The percentage of public school students in the United States who were English language learners (ELLs) was higher in fall 2017 (10.1 percent, or 5.0 million students) than in fall 2000 (8.1 percent, or 3.8 million students). In fall 2017, the percentage of public school students who were ELLs ranged from 0.8 percent in West Virginia to 19.2 percent in California.

Students who are identified as English language learners (ELLs) can participate in language assistance programs to help ensure that they attain English proficiency and meet the academic content and achievement standards that all students are expected to meet. Participation in these types of programs can improve students' English language proficiency, which in turn has been associated with improved educational outcomes.[1] The percentage of public school students in the United States who were ELLs was higher in fall 2017 (10.1 percent, or 5.0 million students) than in fall 2000 (8.1 percent, or 3.8 million students).[2]

Figure 1. Percentage of public school students who were English language learners, by state: Fall 2017

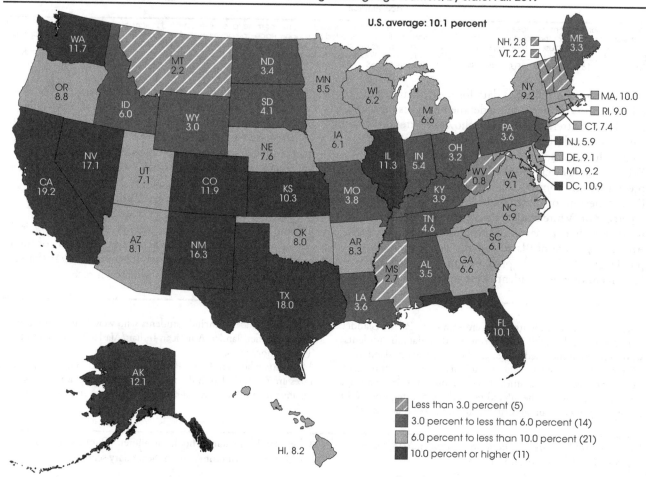

NOTE: Categorizations are based on unrounded percentages.
SOURCE: U.S. Department of Education, National Center for Education Statistics, Common Core of Data (CCD), "Local Education Agency Universe Survey," 2017–18. See *Digest of Education Statistics 2019*, table 204.20.

In fall 2017, the percentage of public school students who were ELLs was 10.0 percent or more in 10 states, most of which were located in the West, and the District of Columbia.[3] The states were Alaska, California, Colorado, Florida, Illinois, Kansas, Nevada, New Mexico, Texas, and Washington. California reported the highest percentage of ELLs among its public school students, at 19.2 percent, followed by Texas (18.0 percent) and Nevada (17.1 percent). Twenty-one states had percentages of ELL students that were 6.0 percent or higher but less than 10.0 percent, and 14 states had percentages that were 3.0 percent or higher but less than 6.0 percent. The percentage of students who were ELLs was less than 3.0 percent in five states, with Vermont (2.2 percent), Montana (2.2 percent), and West Virginia (0.8 percent) having the lowest percentages.

Reflecting the national change, the percentage of public school students who were ELLs was higher in fall 2017 than in fall 2000 for all but seven states and the District of Columbia. The largest percentage point increase occurred in Delaware (7.3 percentage points) and the largest percentage point decrease occurred in Arizona (7.0 percentage points). More recently, the percentage of public school students who were ELLs was higher in fall 2017 than in fall 2010 in 40 states and the District of Columbia, with the largest increase occurring in Massachusetts (4.3 percentage points). In contrast, the percentage of public school students who were ELLs was lower in fall 2017 than in fall 2010 in 10 states, with the largest decrease occurring in California (4.1 percentage points).

Figure 2. Percentage of public school students who were English language learners, by locale: Fall 2017

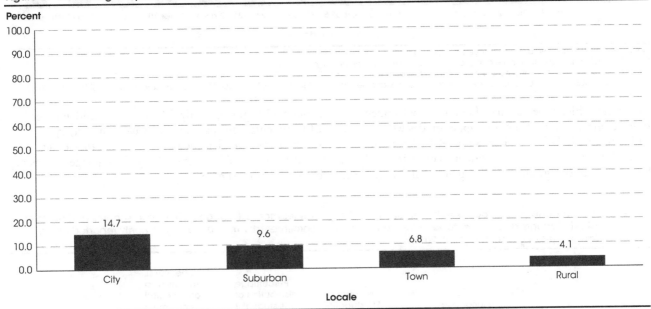

NOTE: Data are based on locales of school districts.
SOURCE: U.S. Department of Education, National Center for Education Statistics, Common Core of Data (CCD), "Local Education Agency Universe Survey," 2017–18. See *Digest of Education Statistics 2019*, table 214.40.

In fall 2017, the percentage of students who were ELLs was higher for school districts in more urbanized areas than for those in less urbanized areas. ELL students constituted an average of 14.7 percent of total public school enrollment in cities, 9.6 percent in suburban areas, 6.8 percent in towns, and 4.1 percent in rural areas.

Figure 3. Percentage of public school students who were English language learners, by grade level: Fall 2017

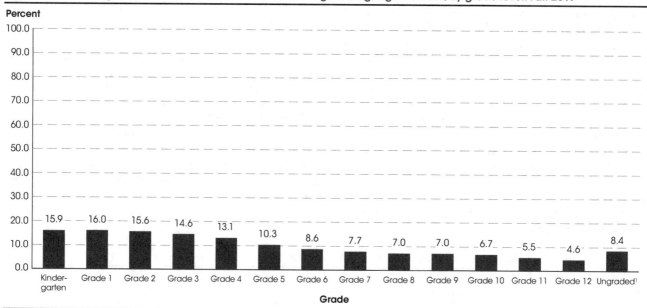

¹ Includes students reported as being enrolled in grade 13.
NOTE: Although rounded numbers are displayed, the figures are based on unrounded data.
SOURCE: U.S. Department of Education, National Center for Education Statistics, ED*Facts* file 141, Data Group 678, extracted August 30, 2019; and Common Core of Data (CCD), "State Nonfiscal Survey of Public Elementary and Secondary Education," 2017–18. See *Digest of Education Statistics 2019*, table 204.27.

In general, a higher percentage of public school students in lower grades than of those in upper grades were ELL students in fall 2017. For example, 15.9 percent of kindergarteners were ELL students, compared with 8.6 percent of 6th-graders and 7.0 percent of 8th-graders.

Among 12th-graders, only 4.6 percent of students were ELL students. This pattern was driven, in part, by students who are identified as ELLs when they enter elementary school but obtain English language proficiency before reaching the upper grades.[4]

Table 1. Number and percentage distribution of English language learner (ELL) students in public schools and number of ELL students as a percentage of total public school enrollment, by the 10 most commonly reported home languages of ELL students: Fall 2017

Home language	Number of ELL students	Percentage distribution of ELL students¹	Number of ELL students as a percent of total enrollment
Spanish, Castilian	3,749,314	74.8	7.6
Arabic	136,531	2.7	0.3
Chinese	106,516	2.1	0.2
English²	94,910	1.9	0.2
Vietnamese	77,765	1.6	0.2
Somali	41,264	0.8	0.1
Russian	36,809	0.7	0.1
Portuguese	33,252	0.7	0.1
Haitian, Haitian Creole	32,655	0.7	0.1
Hmong	32,174	0.6	0.1

¹ Detail does not sum to 100 percent because not all categories are reported.
² Examples of situations in which English might be reported as an ELL student's home language include students who live in multilingual households and students adopted from other countries who speak English at home but also have been raised speaking another language.
SOURCE: U.S. Department of Education, National Center for Education Statistics, ED*Facts* file 141, Data Group 678, extracted August 30, 2019; and Common Core of Data (CCD), "State Nonfiscal Survey of Public Elementary and Secondary Education," 2017–18. See *Digest of Education Statistics 2019*, table 204.27.

Spanish was the home language of 3.7 million ELL public school students in fall 2017, representing 74.8 percent of all ELL students and 7.6 percent of all public K–12 students. Arabic and Chinese were the next most commonly reported home languages (spoken by 136,500 and 106,500 students, respectively). English was the fourth most common home language for ELL students (94,900 students), which may reflect students who live in multilingual households or students adopted from other countries who were raised speaking another language but currently live in households where English is spoken. Vietnamese (77,800 students), Somali (41,300 students), Russian (36,800 students), Portuguese (33,300 students), Haitian (32,700 students), and Hmong (32,200 students) were the next most commonly reported home languages of ELL students in fall 2017. The 30 most commonly reported home languages also include several whose prevalence has increased rapidly in recent years. For example, the number of ELLs who reported that their home language was Swahili, Nepali, or a Karen language[5] more than quadrupled between school year 2008–09 and fall 2017 (the increases were from 3,500 to 16,100 for students who reported that Swahili was their home language, from 3,200 to 14,100 for students who reported that Nepali was their home language, and from 3,000 to 12,800 for students who reported that a Karen language was their home language).[6]

In fall 2017, there were about 3.8 million Hispanic ELL public school students, constituting over three-quarters (76.5 percent) of ELL student enrollment overall.[7] Asian students were the next largest racial/ethnic group among ELLs, with 530,900 students (10.7 percent of ELL students). In addition, there were 327,300 White ELL students (6.6 percent of ELL students) and 211,000 Black ELL students (4.3 percent of ELL students). In each of the other racial/ethnic groups for which data were collected (Pacific Islanders, American Indians/Alaska Natives, and individuals of Two or more races), fewer than 40,000 students were identified as ELLs. In addition, some 718,400 ELL students were identified as students with disabilities, representing 14.3 percent of the total ELL population enrolled in U.S. public elementary and secondary schools.

Endnotes:

[1] Genesee, F., Lindholm-Leary, K., Saunders, W., and Christian, D. (2005). English Language Learners in U.S. Schools: An Overview of Research Findings. *Journal of Education for Students Placed at Risk, 10*(4): 363–385. Retrieved November 25, 2019, from https://doi.org/10.1207/s15327671espr1004_2.

[2] For 2014 and earlier years, data on the total number of ELLs enrolled in public schools and on the percentage of public school students who were ELLs include only those ELL students who participated in ELL programs. Starting with 2015, data include all ELL students, regardless of program participation. Due to this change in definition, comparisons between 2017 and earlier years should be interpreted with caution. For all years, data do not include students who were formerly identified as ELLs but later obtained English language proficiency.

[3] Categorizations are based on unrounded percentages.

[4] Saunders, W.M., and Marcelletti, D.J. (2013). The Gap That Can't Go Away: The Catch-22 of Reclassification in Monitoring the Progress of English Learners. *Educational Evaluation and Policy Analysis, 35*(2): 139–156. Retrieved November 25, 2019, from http://journals.sagepub.com/doi/full/10.3102/0162373712461849.

[5] Includes several languages spoken by the Karen ethnic groups of Burma and by individuals of Karen descent in the United States.

[6] School year 2008–09 data include all ELL students enrolled at any time during the 2008–09 school year, except data for California which reflect ELL students enrolled on a single date. All other data in this indicator include only ELL students enrolled on October 1 of the corresponding year.

[7] The number of Hispanic ELL students is larger than the number of ELL students who speak Spanish. Home language data may be missing for some Hispanic ELL students. In addition, some Hispanic ELL students may report that they speak a language other than Spanish at home (such as a language that is indigenous to Latin America).

Reference tables: *Digest of Education Statistics 2019*, tables 204.20, 204.27, and 214.40

Related indicators and resources: English Language Learners in Public Schools [*Status and Trends in the Education of Racial and Ethnic Groups*]; Mathematics Performance; *Programs and Services for High School English Learners in Public School Districts: 2015–16*; Public School Enrollment; Reading Performance; Science Performance; Students With Disabilities; Technology and Engineering Literacy [*web-only*]

Glossary: Disabilities, children with; English language learner (ELL); Enrollment; Geographic region; Household; Locale codes; Public school or institution; Racial/ethnic group; School district

Students With Disabilities

In 2018–19, the number of students ages 3–21 who received special education services under the Individuals with Disabilities Education Act (IDEA) was 7.1 million, or 14 percent of all public school students. Among students receiving special education services, 33 percent had specific learning disabilities.

Enacted in 1975, the Individuals with Disabilities Education Act (IDEA), formerly known as the Education for All Handicapped Children Act, mandates the provision of a free and appropriate public school education for eligible students ages 3–21. Eligible students are those identified by a team of professionals as having a disability that adversely affects academic performance and as being in need of special education and related services. Data collection activities to monitor compliance with IDEA began in 1976.

From school year 2000–01 through 2004–05, the number of students ages 3–21 who received special education services under IDEA increased from 6.3 million, or 13 percent of total public school enrollment, to 6.7 million, or 14 percent of total public school enrollment.[1] Both the number and the percentage of students served under IDEA declined from 2004–05 through 2011–12. Between 2011–12 and 2018–19, the number of students served increased from 6.4 million to 7.1 million and the percentage served increased from 13 percent of total public school enrollment to 14 percent of total public school enrollment.

Figure 1. Percentage distribution of students ages 3–21 served under the Individuals with Disabilities Education Act (IDEA), by disability type: School year 2018–19

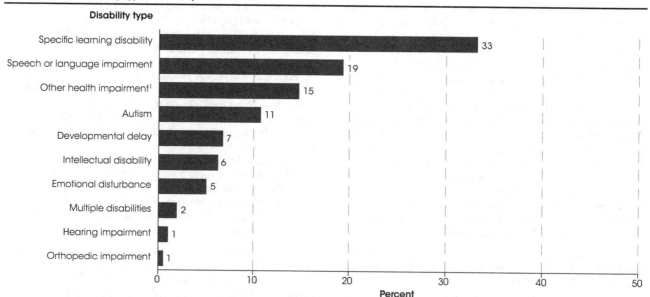

[1] Other health impairments include having limited strength, vitality, or alertness due to chronic or acute health problems such as a heart condition, tuberculosis, rheumatic fever, nephritis, asthma, sickle cell anemia, hemophilia, epilepsy, lead poisoning, leukemia, or diabetes.
NOTE: Data are for the 50 states and the District of Columbia only. Includes 2015–16 data for 3- to 21-year-olds in Wisconsin due to unavailability of more recent data for children served in Wisconsin. Visual impairment, traumatic brain injury, and deaf-blindness are not shown because they each account for less than 0.5 percent of students served under IDEA. Due to categories not shown, detail does not sum to 100 percent. Although rounded numbers are displayed, the figures are based on unrounded data.
SOURCE: U.S. Department of Education, Office of Special Education Programs, Individuals with Disabilities Education Act (IDEA) database, retrieved February 20, 2020, from https://www2.ed.gov/programs/osepidea/618-data/state-level-data-files/index.html#bcc; and National Center for Education Statistics, National Elementary and Secondary Enrollment Projection Model, 1972 through 2029. See *Digest of Education Statistics 2019*, table 204.30.

In school year 2018–19, a higher percentage of students ages 3–21 received special education services under IDEA for specific learning disabilities than for any other type of disability. A specific learning disability is a disorder in one or more of the basic psychological processes involved in understanding or using language, spoken or written, that may manifest itself in an imperfect ability to listen, think, speak, read, write, spell, or do mathematical calculations. In 2018–19, some 33 percent of all students who received special education services had specific learning disabilities, 19 percent had speech or language impairments, and 15 percent had other health impairments (including

having limited strength, vitality, or alertness due to chronic or acute health problems such as a heart condition, tuberculosis, rheumatic fever, nephritis, asthma, sickle cell anemia, hemophilia, epilepsy, lead poisoning, leukemia, or diabetes). Students with autism, developmental delays, intellectual disabilities, and emotional disturbances each accounted for between 5 and 11 percent of students served under IDEA. Students with multiple disabilities, hearing impairments, orthopedic impairments, visual impairments, traumatic brain injuries, and deaf-blindness each accounted for 2 percent or less of those served under IDEA.

Figure 2. Percentage of students ages 3–21 served under the Individuals with Disabilities Education Act (IDEA), by race/ethnicity: School year 2018–19

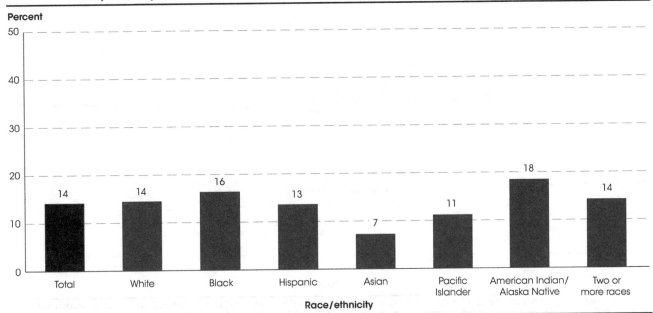

NOTE: Based on the total public school enrollment in prekindergarten through grade 12 by race/ethnicity. Although data are for the 50 states and the District of Columbia, data limitations result in inclusion of a small (but unknown) number of students from other jurisdictions. Includes 2015–16 data for 3- to 21-year-olds in Wisconsin due to unavailability of more recent data for children served in Wisconsin. Race categories exclude persons of Hispanic ethnicity. Although rounded numbers are displayed, the figures are based on unrounded data.
SOURCE: U.S. Department of Education, Office of Special Education Programs, Individuals with Disabilities Education Act (IDEA) database, retrieved February 20, 2020, from https://www2.ed.gov/programs/osepidea/618-data/state-level-data-files/index.html#bcc; and National Center for Education Statistics, National Elementary and Secondary Enrollment Projection Model, 1972 through 2029. See *Digest of Education Statistics 2019*, table 204.50.

In school year 2018–19, the percentage (out of total public school enrollment) of students ages 3–21 who received special education services under IDEA differed by race/ethnicity. The percentage of students served under IDEA was highest for American Indian/Alaska Native students (18 percent), followed by Black students (16 percent), White students and students of Two or more races (14 percent each), Hispanic students (13 percent), Pacific Islander students (11 percent), and Asian students (7 percent).

Among Hispanic, American Indian/Alaska Native, Pacific Islander, and White students ages 3–21, the percentage of students who received special education services in 2018–19 for specific learning disabilities combined with the percentage who received services for speech or

language impairments accounted for 50 percent or more of students served under IDEA. Among their peers who were Black, of Two or more races, and Asian, the percentage accounted for between 40 and 50 percent of students served under IDEA. The percentage distribution of various types of special education services received by students differed by race/ethnicity. For example, the percentage of students with disabilities who received services under IDEA for specific learning disabilities was lower for Asian students (19 percent), students of Two or more races (29 percent), and White students (29 percent) than for students overall (33 percent). However, the percentage of students with disabilities who received services under IDEA for autism was higher for Asian students (25 percent) and students of Two or more races (12 percent) than for students overall (11 percent).[2]

Additionally, among students served under IDEA, 7 percent each of Black students and students of Two or more races received services for emotional disturbances. In comparison, 5 percent of all students served under IDEA received services for emotional disturbances.

Separate data on special education services for males and females are available only for students ages 6–21, rather than ages 3–21. Among those 6- to 21-year-old students enrolled in public schools in 2018–19, a higher percentage of male students (18 percent) than of female students (10 percent) received special education services under IDEA. In addition, the percentage distribution of 6- to 21-year-old students who received various types of special education services in 2018–19 differed by sex. For example, the percentage of students served under IDEA who received services for specific learning disabilities was higher for female students (44 percent) than for male students (34 percent), while the percentage served under IDEA who received services for autism was higher for male students (13 percent) than for female students (5 percent).

Figure 3. Among students ages 6–21 served under the Individuals with Disabilities Education Act (IDEA), percentage who spent various amounts of time inside general classes: Fall 2000 through fall 2018

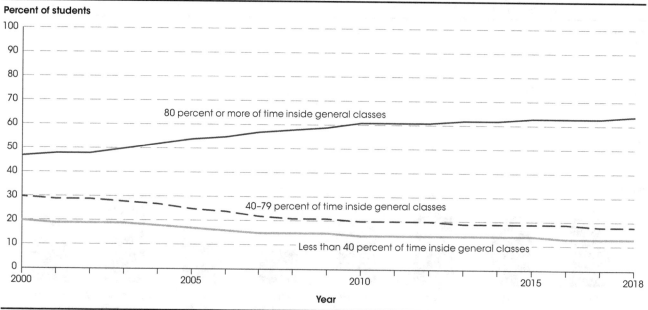

NOTE: Data are for the 50 states and the District of Columbia only. Fall 2016, 2017, and 2018 include fall 2015 data for 6- to 21-year-olds in Wisconsin due to unavailability of fall 2016, 2017, and 2018 data for children served in Wisconsin. Fall 2017 also includes fall 2016 data for 6- to 21-year-olds in Maine and Vermont due to unavailability of fall 2017 data for children in that age group served in those states.
SOURCE: U.S. Department of Education, Office of Special Education Programs, Individuals with Disabilities Education Act (IDEA) database, retrieved February 20, 2020, from https://www2.ed.gov/programs/osepidea/618-data/state-level-data-files/index.html#bcc. See Digest of Education Statistics 2019, table 204.60.

Educational environment data are also available for students ages 6–21 served under IDEA. About 95 percent of students ages 6–21 served under IDEA in fall 2018 were enrolled in regular schools. Three percent of students served under IDEA were enrolled in separate schools (public or private) for students with disabilities; 1 percent were placed by their parents in regular private schools;[3] and less than 1 percent each were homebound or in hospitals, in separate residential facilities (public or private), or in correctional facilities. Among all students ages 6–21 served under IDEA, the percentage who spent most of the school day (i.e., 80 percent or more of their time) inside general classes in regular schools increased from 47 percent in fall 2000 to 64 percent in fall 2018. In contrast, during the same period, the percentage of students who spent 40 to 79 percent of the school day inside general classes decreased from 30 to 18 percent, and the percentage of students who spent less than 40 percent of their time inside general classes decreased from 20 to 13 percent. In fall 2018, the percentage of students served under IDEA who spent most of the school day inside general classes was highest for students with speech or language impairments (88 percent). Approximately two-thirds of students with specific learning disabilities (72 percent), visual impairments (68 percent), other health impairments (67 percent), developmental delays (66 percent), and hearing impairments (63 percent) spent most of the school day inside general classes. In contrast, 17 percent of students with intellectual disabilities and 14 percent of students with multiple disabilities spent most of the school day inside general classes.

Data are also available for students ages 14–21 served under IDEA who exited school during school year 2017–18, including exit reason.[4] Approximately 414,000 students ages 14–21 served under IDEA exited school in 2017–18: over two-thirds (73 percent) graduated with a regular high school diploma, 16 percent dropped out, 10 percent received an alternative certificate,[5] 1 percent reached the maximum age[6] to receive special education services, and less than one-half of 1 percent died.

Figure 4. Among students ages 14–21 served under the Individuals with Disabilities Education Act (IDEA) who exited school, percentage who exited for selected reasons, by race/ethnicity: School year 2017–18

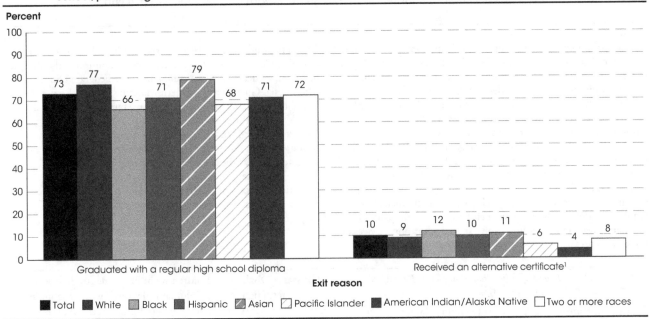

Percent

Exit reason

■ Total ■ White ▨ Black ▨ Hispanic ▧ Asian ☐ Pacific Islander ■ American Indian/Alaska Native ☐ Two or more races

[1] Received a certificate of completion, modified diploma, or some similar document, but did not meet the same standards for graduation as those for students without disabilities.
NOTE: Data in this figure are for the 50 states, the District of Columbia, the Bureau of Indian Education, American Samoa, the Federated States of Micronesia, Guam, the Northern Marianas, Puerto Rico, the Republic of Palau, the Republic of the Marshall Islands, and the U.S. Virgin Islands. Data for all other figures in this indicator are for the 50 states and the District of Columbia only. Includes imputations for missing or unavailable data from Vermont. Race categories exclude persons of Hispanic ethnicity. Although rounded numbers are displayed, the figures are based on unrounded data.
SOURCE: U.S. Department of Education, Office of Special Education Programs, Individuals with Disabilities Education Act (IDEA) Section 618 Data Products: State Level Data Files. Retrieved February 20, 2020, from https://www2.ed.gov/programs/osepidea/618-data/state-level-data-files/index.html. See *Digest of Education Statistics 2019*, table 219.90.

Among students ages 14–21 served under IDEA who exited school in school year 2017–18, the percentages who graduated with a regular high school diploma, received an alternative certificate, and dropped out differed by race/ethnicity. The percentage of exiting students who graduated with a regular high school diploma was highest for Asian students (79 percent) and lowest for Black students (66 percent). The percentage of exiting students who received an alternative certificate was highest for Black students (12 percent) and lowest for American Indian/Alaska Native students (4 percent). The percentage of exiting students who dropped out in 2017–18 was highest for American Indian/Alaska Native students (24 percent) and lowest for Asian students (7 percent).

Among students ages 14–21 served under IDEA who exited school in school year 2017–18, the percentages who graduated with a regular high school diploma, received an alternative certificate, and dropped out also differed by type of disability. The percentage of exiting students who graduated with a regular high school diploma was highest for students with speech or language impairments (86 percent) and lowest for students with multiple disabilities (47 percent). The percentage of exiting students who received an alternative certificate was highest for students with intellectual disabilities (32 percent) and lowest for students with speech or language impairments (3 percent). The percentage of exiting students who dropped out in 2017–18 was highest for students with emotional disturbances (32 percent) and lowest for students with deaf-blindness (5 percent).

Endnotes:

[1] Totals presented in this indicator include imputations for states for which data were unavailable. See reference tables in the *Digest of Education Statistics* for more information. Data for students ages 3–21 and 6–21 served under IDEA are for the 50 states and the District of Columbia only. Number of children served as a percent of total enrollment is based on total public school enrollment in prekindergarten through grade 12.

[2] In 2018–19, the unrounded percentage of White students with disabilities who received services under IDEA for autism was also higher than the percentage for students overall, but both rounded to 11 percent.

[3] Students who are enrolled by their parents or guardians in regular private schools and have their basic education paid for through private resources but receive special education services at public expense.

[4] Data for students ages 14–21 served under IDEA who exited school are for the 50 states, the District of Columbia, the Bureau of Indian Education, American Samoa, the Federated States of Micronesia, Guam, the Northern Marianas, Puerto Rico, the Republic of Palau, the Republic of the Marshall Islands, and the U.S. Virgin Islands.

[5] Received a certificate of completion, modified diploma, or some similar document but did not meet the same standards for graduation as those for students without disabilities.

[6] Each state determines its maximum age to receive special education services. At the time these data were collected, the maximum age across states generally ranged from 20 to 22 years old.

Reference tables: *Digest of Education Statistics 2019*, tables 204.30, 204.50, 204.60, and 219.90

Related indicators and resources: Disability Rates and Employment Status by Educational Attainment [*The Condition of Education 2017 Spotlight*]; English Language Learners in Public Schools; Students With Disabilities [*Status and Trends in the Education of Racial and Ethnic Groups*]

Glossary: Disabilities, children with; Enrollment; High school completer; High school diploma; Individuals with Disabilities Education Act (IDEA); Private school; Public school or institution; Racial/ethnic group; Regular school

Characteristics of Elementary and Secondary Schools

In school year 2017–18, some 57 percent of traditional public schools had more than 50 percent White enrollment, compared with 32 percent of public charter schools and 72 percent of private schools.

In school year 2017–18, there were approximately 98,500 public schools in the United States (in this indicator, the United States refers to the 50 states and the District of Columbia), consisting of about 91,300 traditional public schools and 7,200 public charter schools. The total number of public schools was higher in 2017–18 than in 1999–2000, when there was a total of approximately 92,000 public schools—90,500 traditional public schools and 1,500 public charter schools. Between school years 1999–2000 and 2017–18, the percentage of all public

schools that were traditional public schools decreased from 98 to 93 percent, while the percentage that were charter schools increased from 2 to 7 percent. See indicator Public Charter School Enrollment for additional information about charter schools and charter school legislation. In school year 2017–18, there were also about 32,500 private schools in the United States, which was not measurably different from the number of private schools in 1999–2000.

Figure 1. Percentage distribution of traditional public schools, public charter schools, and private schools, by school level: School year 2017–18

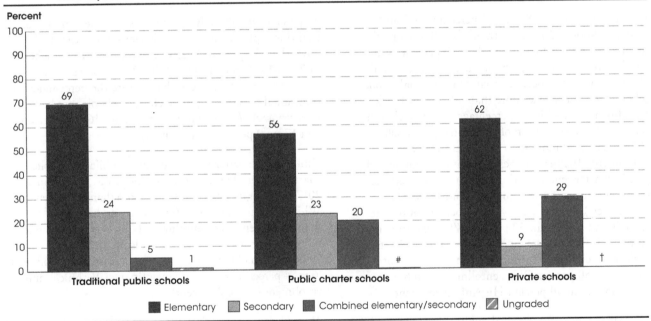

† Not applicable.
# Rounds to zero.
NOTE: "Elementary" comprises public and private schools beginning with grade 6 or below and with no grade higher than 8. "Secondary" comprises public and private schools with no grade lower than 7. "Combined elementary/secondary" comprises public and private schools beginning with grade 6 or below and ending with grade 9 or above, as well as private schools that do not classify students by grade level. "Ungraded" comprises public schools not classified by grade span. Detail may not sum to totals because of rounding.
SOURCE: U.S. Department of Education, National Center for Education Statistics, Common Core of Data (CCD), "Public Elementary/Secondary School Universe Survey," 2017–18; Private School Universe Survey (PSS), 2017–18. See *Digest of Education Statistics 2019*, tables 205.40 and 216.30.

In school year 2017–18, more than two-thirds of traditional public schools (69 percent) were elementary schools, compared with 56 percent of public charter schools. The percentages of traditional public and public charter schools that were secondary schools were similar (24 and 23 percent, respectively). In contrast, 5 percent

of traditional public schools were combined elementary/secondary schools,[1] compared with 20 percent of public charter schools. In that same year, 62 percent of private schools were elementary schools, 9 percent were secondary schools, and 29 percent were combined elementary/secondary schools.

Figure 2. Percentage of traditional public schools, public charter schools, and private schools, by selected racial/ethnic concentration: School years 1999-2000 and 2017-18

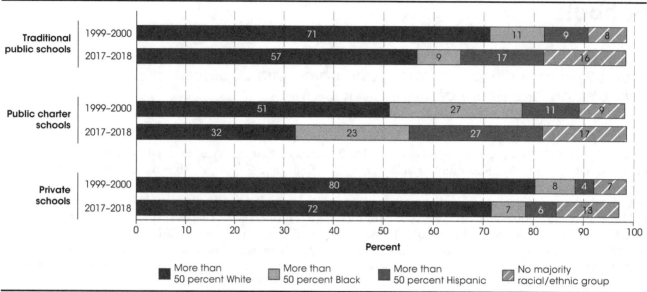

NOTE: Race categories exclude persons of Hispanic ethnicity. Schools with other racial/ethnic concentrations, such those with enrollment that is more than 50 percent of students who were Asian, Pacific Islander, American Indian/Alaska Native, or of Two or more races, are not included in this figure; thus, the sum of the racial/ethnic concentration categories does not equal 100 percent. Although rounded numbers are displayed, the figures are based on unrounded data. SOURCE: U.S. Department of Education, National Center for Education Statistics, Common Core of Data (CCD), "Public Elementary/Secondary School Universe Survey," 1999–2000 and 2017–18; Private School Universe Survey (PSS), 1999–2000 and 2017–18. See *Digest of Education Statistics 2019*, tables 205.40 and 216.30.

In school year 2017–18, a lower percentage of public charter schools (32 percent) than of traditional public schools (57 percent) had more than 50 percent White enrollment. In contrast, a higher percentage of public charter schools (23 percent) than of traditional public schools (9 percent) had more than 50 percent Black enrollment, and a higher percentage of public charter schools (27 percent) than of traditional public schools (17 percent) had more than 50 percent Hispanic enrollment. The percentages of traditional public and public charter schools with no majority racial/ethnic group enrollment were similar (16 and 17 percent, respectively). In that same year, 72 percent of private schools had more than 50 percent White enrollment, compared with 13 percent of private schools with no majority racial/ethnic group enrollment, 7 percent with more than 50 percent Black enrollment, and 6 percent with more than 50 percent Hispanic enrollment.

The percentages of traditional public schools and public charter schools that had more than 50 percent White enrollment were lower in 2017–18 than in 1999–2000 (57 vs. 71 percent and 32 vs. 51 percent, respectively). A similar pattern was observed for traditional public schools and public charter schools that had more than 50 percent Black enrollment (9 vs. 11 percent and 23 vs.

27 percent, respectively). In contrast, the percentages of traditional public and public charter schools that had more than 50 percent Hispanic enrollment were higher in 2017–18 than in 1999–2000 (17 vs. 9 percent and 27 vs. 11 percent, respectively), as were the percentages of traditional public and public charter schools that had no majority racial/ethnic group enrollment (16 vs. 8 percent and 17 vs. 9 percent, respectively).

Similar to the patterns for traditional public and public charter schools, lower percentages of private schools in 2017–18 than in 1999–2000 had more than 50 percent White enrollment (72 vs. 80 percent) and had more than 50 percent Black enrollment (7 vs. 8 percent), while higher percentages of private schools in 2017–18 than in 1999–2000 had more than 50 percent Hispanic enrollment (6 vs. 4 percent) and had no majority racial/ethnic group enrollment (13 vs. 7 percent).

These shifts in the racial/ethnic concentration of schools reflect, in part, general changes in the school-age population. Between 2000 and 2018, the percentage of children ages 5 to 17 who were White decreased from 62 to 51 percent, the percentage who were Black decreased from 15 to 14 percent, and the percentage who were Hispanic increased from 16 to 25 percent.

Figure 3. Percentage distribution of traditional public schools, public charter schools, and private schools, by school locale: School year 2017–18

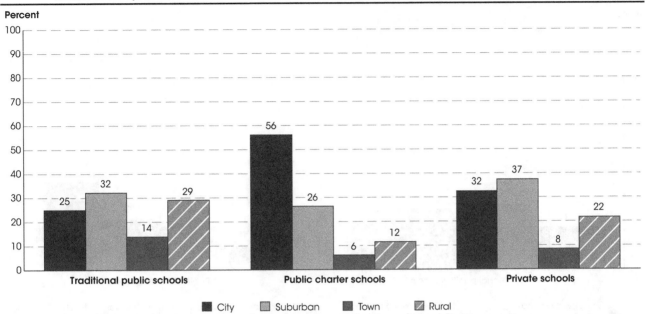

NOTE: Detail may not sum to totals because of rounding. Although rounded numbers are displayed, the figures are based on unrounded data.
SOURCE: U.S. Department of Education, National Center for Education Statistics, Common Core of Data (CCD), "Public Elementary/Secondary School Universe Survey," 2017–18; Education Demographic and Geographic Estimates (EDGE), "Public School File," 2017–18; Private School Universe Survey (PSS), 2017–18. See *Digest of Education Statistics 2019*, tables 205.40 and 216.30.

Compared with traditional public schools, a higher percentage of public charter schools were located in cities and lower percentages were located in all other locales in school year 2017–18. For example, some 56 percent of public charter schools were located in cities, compared with 25 percent of traditional public schools. In contrast, 12 percent of public charter schools were located in rural areas, compared with 29 percent of traditional public schools. In that same year among private schools, a higher percentage of schools were located in suburban areas (37 percent) than in cities (32 percent), rural areas (22 percent), and towns (8 percent).

Figure 4. Percentage of traditional public schools and public charter schools, by percentage of students eligible for free or reduced-price lunch: School year 2017–18

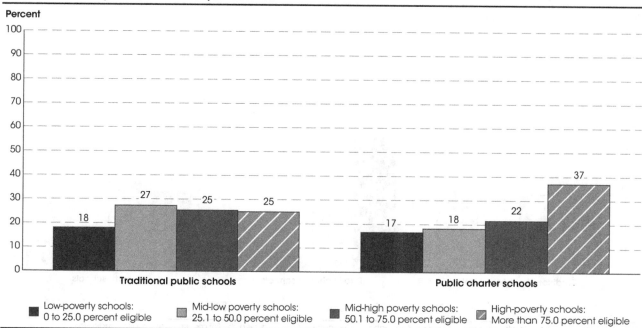

NOTE: Students with household incomes under 185 percent of the poverty threshold are eligible for free or reduced-price lunch under the National School Lunch Program (NSLP). In addition, some groups of children—such as foster children, children participating in the Head Start and Migrant Education programs, and children receiving services under the Runaway and Homeless Youth Act—are assumed to be categorically eligible to participate in the NSLP. Data include students whose NSLP eligibility has been determined through direct certification, which is a "process conducted by the states and by local educational agencies (LEAs) to certify eligible children for free meals without the need for household applications" (https://www.fns.usda.gov/direct-certification-national-school-lunch-program-report-congress-state-implementation-progress-1). Also, under the Community Eligibility option, some nonpoor children who attend school in a low-income area may participate if the district decides that it would be more efficient to provide free lunch to all children in the school. For more information, see http://www.fns.usda.gov/nslp/national-school-lunch-program-nslp. The category "Missing/school does not participate" is not included in this figure; thus, the sum of the free or reduced-price lunch (FRPL) eligibility categories does not equal 100 percent. Although rounded numbers are displayed, the figures are based on unrounded data.
SOURCE: U.S. Department of Education, National Center for Education Statistics, Common Core of Data (CCD), "Public Elementary/Secondary School Universe Survey," 2017–18. See *Digest of Education Statistics 2019*, table 216.30.

In this indicator, low-poverty schools are defined as public schools where 25.0 percent or less of the students are eligible for free or reduced-price lunch (FRPL); mid-low poverty schools are defined as those where 25.1 to 50.0 percent of the students are eligible for FRPL; mid-high poverty schools are defined as those where 50.1 to 75.0 percent of the students are eligible for FRPL; and high-poverty schools are defined as those where more than 75.0 percent of the students are eligible for FRPL.[2]

In school year 2017–18, about 37 percent of public charter schools were high-poverty schools, compared with 25 percent of traditional public schools. In contrast, the percentages of schools that were low-poverty, mid-low poverty, and mid-high poverty were higher among traditional public schools (18 percent, 27 percent, and 25 percent, respectively) than among public charter schools (17 percent, 18 percent, and 22 percent, respectively).[3]

Figure 5. Percentage distribution of private schools, by school orientation: School year 2017–18

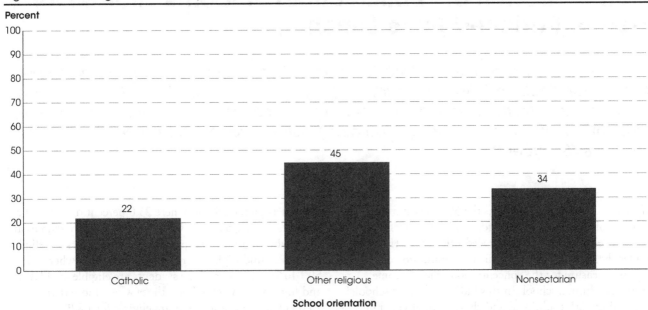

NOTE: Detail may not sum to totals because of rounding.
SOURCE: U.S. Department of Education, National Center for Education Statistics, Private School Universe Survey (PSS), 2017–18. See *Digest of Education Statistics 2019*, table 205.40.

In this indicator, private schools are grouped into the following categories: Catholic, other religious, and nonsectarian (i.e., not religiously affiliated). In school year 2017–18, some 22 percent of private schools were Catholic, 45 percent had another religious affiliation, and 34 percent were nonsectarian. The size of private schools varied by religious orientation. For example, a lower percentage of Catholic schools (3 percent) than of nonsectarian schools (39 percent) and other religious schools (40 percent) were very small (i.e., had 50 or fewer students). In addition, a higher percentage of Catholic schools (5 percent) than of nonsectarian schools and other religious schools (2 percent each) were very large (i.e., had 750 or more students).

Endnotes:

[1] Combined elementary/secondary schools include public and private schools beginning with grade 6 or below and ending with grade 9 or above, as well as private schools that do not classify students by grade level.

[2] Students with household incomes under 185 percent of the poverty threshold are eligible for free or reduced-price lunch under the National School Lunch Program (NSLP). In addition, some groups of children—such as foster children, children participating in the Head Start and Migrant Education programs, and children receiving services under the Runaway and Homeless Youth Act—are assumed to be categorically eligible to participate in the NSLP. Data include students whose NSLP eligibility has been determined through direct certification, which is a "process conducted by the states and by local educational agencies (LEAs) to certify eligible children for free meals without the need for household applications" (https://www.fns.usda.gov/direct-certification-national-school-lunch-program-report-congress-state-implementation-progress-1). Also, under the Community Eligibility option, some nonpoor children who attend school in a low-income area may participate if the district decides that it would be more efficient to provide free lunch to all children in the school. For more information, see http://www.fns.usda.gov/nslp/national-school-lunch-program-nslp.

[3] In school year 2017–18, some 6 percent of public charter school students and less than 1 percent of traditional public school students attended schools that did not participate in FRPL or had missing data. No data on the percentage of students eligible for FRPL were collected for private schools in school year 2017–18.

Reference tables: *Digest of Education Statistics 2019*, tables 101.20, 205.40, and 216.30

Related indicators and resources: Concentration of Public School Students Eligible for Free or Reduced-Price Lunch; Private School Enrollment; Public Charter School Enrollment; Public School Enrollment

Glossary: Catholic school; Combined school; Elementary school; Enrollment; Free or reduced-price lunch; Locale codes; National School Lunch Program; Public charter school; Public school or institution; Racial/ethnic group; Secondary school; Traditional public school

Concentration of Public School Students Eligible for Free or Reduced-Price Lunch

In fall 2017, the percentages of students who attended high-poverty schools were highest for Black and Hispanic students (45 percent each), followed by American Indian/Alaska Native students (41 percent), Pacific Islander students (24 percent), students of Two or more races (18 percent), Asian students (15 percent), and White students (8 percent).

In the United States (defined as the 50 states and the District of Columbia in this indicator), the percentage of students eligible for free or reduced-price lunch (FRPL) under the National School Lunch Program provides a proxy measure for the concentration of low-income students within a school. In this indicator, public schools[1] (including both traditional and charter) are divided into categories by FRPL eligibility.[2] Low-poverty schools are

defined as public schools where 25.0 percent or less of the students are eligible for FRPL; mid-low poverty schools are those where 25.1 to 50.0 percent of the students are eligible for FRPL; mid-high poverty schools are those where 50.1 to 75.0 percent of the students are eligible for FRPL; and high-poverty schools are those where more than 75.0 percent of the students are eligible for FRPL.

Figure 1. Percentage distribution of public school students, for each racial and ethnic group, by school poverty level: Fall 2017

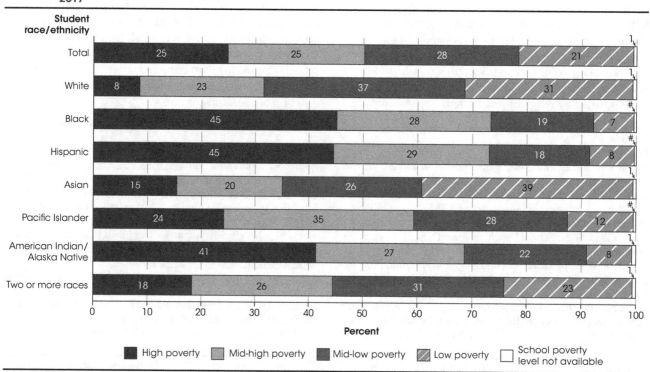

Rounds to zero.
NOTE: High-poverty schools are defined as public schools where more than 75.0 percent of the students are eligible for free or reduced-price lunch (FRPL); mid-high poverty schools are those where 50.1 to 75.0 percent of the students are eligible for FRPL; mid-low poverty schools are those where 25.1 to 50.0 percent of the students are eligible for FRPL; and low-poverty schools are those where 25.0 percent or less of the students are eligible for FRPL. "School poverty level not available" includes schools for which information on FRPL is missing and schools that did not participate in the National School Lunch Program (NSLP). Data include students whose NSLP eligibility has been determined through direct certification, which is a "process conducted by the states and by local educational agencies (LEAs) to certify eligible children for free meals without the need for household applications" (https://www.fns.usda.gov/direct-certification-national-school-lunch-program-report-congress-state-implementation-progress-1). For more information on eligibility for FRPL and its relationship to poverty, see the NCES blog post "Free or reduced price lunch: A proxy for poverty?" Race categories exclude persons of Hispanic ethnicity. Detail may not sum to totals because of rounding. Although rounded numbers are displayed, the figures are based on unrounded data.
SOURCE: U.S. Department of Education, National Center for Education Statistics, Common Core of Data (CCD), "Public Elementary/Secondary School Universe Survey," 2017–18; and Education Demographic and Geographic Estimates (EDGE), "Public School File," 2017–18. See *Digest of Education Statistics 2019*, table 216.60.

In fall 2017, the percentage of public school students in high-poverty schools was higher than the percentage in low-poverty schools (25 vs. 21 percent), and both percentages varied by race/ethnicity. The percentages of students who attended high-poverty schools were highest for Black and Hispanic students (45 percent each), followed by American Indian/Alaska Native students (41 percent), Pacific Islander students (24 percent), students of Two or

more races (18 percent), Asian students (15 percent), and White students (8 percent). In contrast, the percentages of students who attended low-poverty schools were higher for Asian students (39 percent), White students (31 percent), and students of Two or more races (23 percent) than for Pacific Islander students (12 percent), American Indian/Alaska Native students (8 percent), Hispanic students (8 percent), and Black students (7 percent).

Figure 2.   Percentage distribution of public school students, for each school locale, by school poverty level: Fall 2017

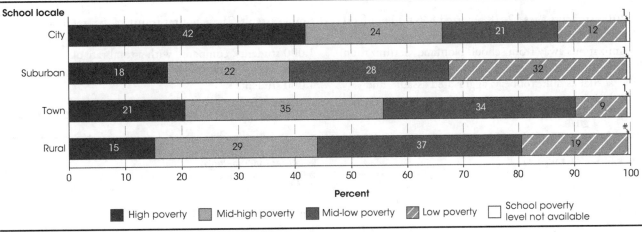

Rounds to zero.
NOTE: High-poverty schools are defined as public schools where more than 75.0 percent of the students are eligible for free or reduced-price lunch (FRPL); mid-high poverty schools are those where 50.1 to 75.0 percent of the students are eligible for FRPL; mid-low poverty schools are those where 25.1 to 50.0 percent of the students are eligible for FRPL; and low-poverty schools are those where 25.0 percent or less of the students are eligible for FRPL. "School poverty level not available" includes schools for which information on FRPL is missing and schools that did not participate in the National School Lunch Program (NSLP). Data include students whose NSLP eligibility has been determined through direct certification, which is a "process conducted by the states and by local educational agencies (LEAs) to certify eligible children for free meals without the need for household applications" (https://www.fns.usda.gov/direct-certification-national-school-lunch-program-report-congress-state-implementation-progress-1). For more information on eligibility for FRPL and its relationship to poverty, see the NCES blog post "Free or reduced price lunch: A proxy for poverty?" Race categories exclude persons of Hispanic ethnicity. Detail may not sum to totals because of rounding. Although rounded numbers are displayed, the figures are based on unrounded data.
SOURCE: U.S. Department of Education, National Center for Education Statistics, Common Core of Data (CCD), "Public Elementary/Secondary School Universe Survey," 2017–18; and Education Demographic and Geographic Estimates (EDGE), "Public School File," 2017–18. See *Digest of Education Statistics 2019*, table 216.60.

The percentage of students attending public schools with different poverty concentrations varied by school locale (i.e., city, suburban, town, or rural). In fall 2017, about 42 percent of students who attended city schools were in high-poverty schools, compared with 21 percent of students who attended town schools, 18 percent of students who attended suburban schools, and 15 percent of students who attended rural schools. In contrast, 32 percent of

students who attended suburban schools were in low-poverty schools, which was more than three times as large as the percentage of students in town schools who attended low-poverty schools (9 percent). The percentage of students who attended low-poverty schools was higher among suburban schools (32 percent) than among rural schools and city schools (19 and 12 percent, respectively).

Endnotes:

[1] In fall 2017, information on school poverty level was not available for 1 percent of public school students. This included schools for which information on FRPL was missing and schools that did not participate in the National School Lunch Program (NSLP).
[2] Students with household incomes under 185 percent of the poverty threshold are eligible for free or reduced-price lunch under the NSLP. In addition, some groups of children—such as foster children, children participating in the Head Start and Migrant Education programs, and children receiving services under the Runaway and Homeless Youth Act—are assumed to be categorically eligible to participate in the NSLP. Data

include students whose NSLP eligibility has been determined through direct certification, which is a "process conducted by the states and by local educational agencies (LEAs) to certify eligible children for free meals without the need for household applications" (https://www.fns.usda.gov/certification-national-school-lunch-program-report-congress-state-implementation-progress-1). Also, under the Community Eligibility option, some nonpoor children who attend school in a low-income area may participate if the district decides that it would be more efficient to provide free lunch to all children in the school. For more information, see https://www.fns.usda.gov/nslp.

Reference tables: *Digest of Education Statistics 2019*, table 216.60.
Related indicators and resources: Characteristics of Children's Families; Characteristics of Elementary and Secondary Schools; Mathematics Performance; Reading Performance

Glossary: Free or reduced-price lunch; Locale codes; National School Lunch Program; Public school or institution; Racial/ethnic group

School Crime and Safety

Between 2000 and 2018, the rates of nonfatal victimization both at school and away from school declined for students ages 12–18. The rate of victimization at school declined 61 percent, and the rate of victimization away from school declined 81 percent.

In 2018, students ages 12–18 reported 836,000 nonfatal victimizations at school[1] and 410,000 nonfatal victimizations away from school. Nonfatal victimizations include theft and all violent crime. Violent crime includes rape, sexual assault, robbery, aggravated assault, and simple assault. These figures translate to a total rate of victimization at school of 33 victimizations per 1,000 students, compared with a total rate of victimization away from school of 16 victimizations per 1,000 students.

Figure 1. Rate of nonfatal victimization per 1,000 students ages 12–18, by type of victimization and location: 2000 through 2018

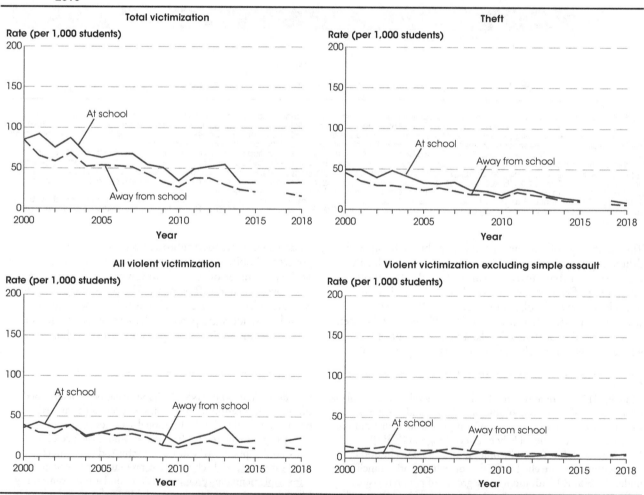

NOTE: "Total victimization" includes theft and violent crimes. "Theft" includes attempted and completed purse-snatching, completed pickpocketing, and all attempted and completed thefts, with the exception of motor vehicle thefts. Theft does not include robbery, which involves the threat or use of force and is classified as a violent crime. "All violent victimization" includes the crimes of rape, sexual assault, robbery, aggravated assault, and simple assault. "At school" includes in the school building, on school property, on a school bus, and going to or from school. The survey sample was redesigned in 2006 and 2016 to reflect changes in the population. Due to the sample redesign and other methodological changes implemented in 2006, use caution when comparing 2006 estimates to other years. Due to a sample increase and redesign in 2016, victimization estimates among students ages 12–18 in 2016 were not comparable to estimates for other years and thus were excluded from the figures.
SOURCE: U.S. Department of Justice, Bureau of Justice Statistics, National Crime Victimization Survey (NCVS), 2000 through 2018. See *Digest of Education Statistics 2019*, table 228.20.

Between 2000 and 2018, the total rates of nonfatal victimization both at school and away from school declined for 12- to 18-year-old students.[2] The total rate of victimization at school declined 61 percent, and the total rate of victimization away from school declined 81 percent. In terms of specific types of victimization, the rates of theft and violent victimization—both at school and away from school—declined between 2000 and 2018. The rate of violent victimization excluding simple assault[3] at school was not measurably different between 2000 and 2018, while the rate of violent victimization excluding simple assault away from school declined during this period.

Figure 2. Percentage of public schools that used selected safety and security measures: School years 1999–2000, 2015–16, and 2017–18

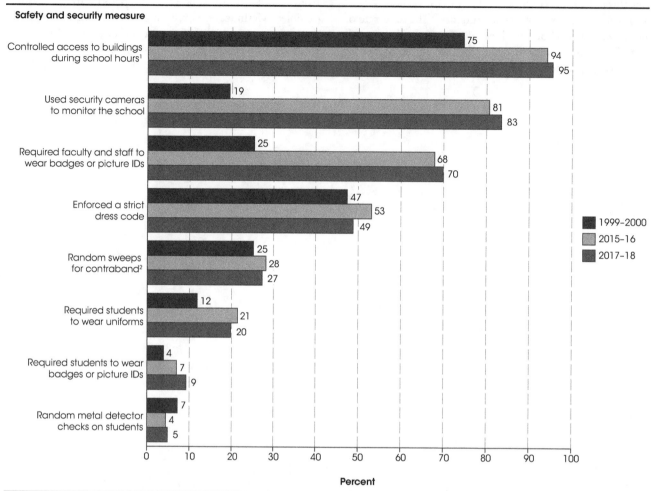

Safety and security measure

[Controlled access to buildings during school hours[1]: 75, 94, 95]
[Used security cameras to monitor the school: 19, 81, 83]
[Required faculty and staff to wear badges or picture IDs: 25, 68, 70]
[Enforced a strict dress code: 47, 53, 49]
[Random sweeps for contraband[2]: 25, 28, 27]
[Required students to wear uniforms: 12, 21, 20]
[Required students to wear badges or picture IDs: 4, 7, 9]
[Random metal detector checks on students: 7, 4, 5]

Legend: 1999–2000, 2015–16, 2017–18

Percent

[1] Prior to 2017–18, the examples of controlled access to buildings included only "locked or monitored doors" and did not include loading docks.
[2] The 2017–18 questionnaire included only a single item about random sweeps for contraband, and it provided locker checks and dog sniffs as examples of types of sweeps. Prior to 2017–18, the questionnaire included one item about dog sniffs for drugs, followed by a separate item about sweeps not including dog sniffs. For years prior to 2017–18, schools are treated as using random sweeps for contraband if they answered "yes" to either or both of these items; each school is counted only once, even if it answered "yes" to both items.
NOTE: Responses were provided by the principal or the person most knowledgeable about crime and safety issues at the school. Although rounded numbers are displayed, the figures are based on unrounded data.
SOURCE: U.S. Department of Education, National Center for Education Statistics, 1999–2000, 2015–16, and 2017–18 School Survey on Crime and Safety (SSOCS), 2000, 2016, and 2018. See *Digest of Education Statistics 2019*, table 233.50.

Some security practices, such as locking or monitoring doors and gates, are intended to limit or control access to school campuses, while others, such as the use of metal detectors and security cameras, are intended to monitor or restrict students' and visitors' behavior on campus. The percentage of public schools reporting the use of safety and security measures was higher in 2017–18 than in most prior years for several categories of measures. For example, the percentage of public schools reporting the use of security cameras increased from 19 percent in 1999–2000 to 83 percent in 2017–18. The percentage of public schools reporting the use of the following safety and security

measures also increased during this time: controlling access to school buildings (from 75 to 95 percent), requiring faculty and staff to wear badges or picture IDs (from 25 to 70 percent), requiring school uniforms (from 12 to 20 percent), and requiring students to wear badges or picture IDs (from 4 to 9 percent). Conversely, the percentage of schools that reported using random metal detector checks on students decreased from 7 percent in 1999–2000 to 5 percent in 2017–18. There were no measurable differences between 1999–2000 and 2017–18 in the percentages of public schools that reported enforcing a strict dress code or using random sweeps for contraband.[4]

Figure 3. Percentage of public schools with one or more security staff present at least once a week, by school level: School years 2005–06 and 2017–18

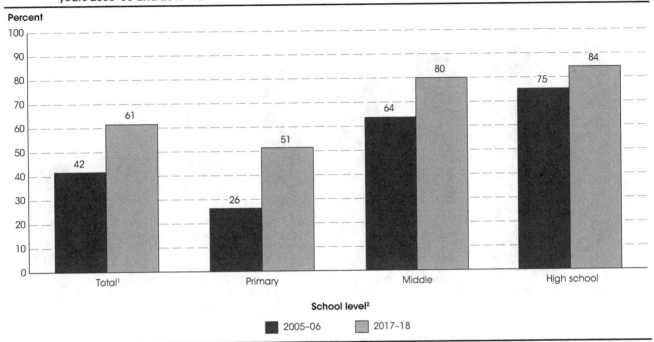

[1] Total includes combined schools, which are not shown separately in this figure.
[2] Primary schools are defined as schools in which the lowest grade is not higher than grade 3 and the highest grade is not higher than grade 8. Middle schools are defined as schools in which the lowest grade is not lower than grade 4 and the highest grade is not higher than grade 9. High schools are defined as schools in which the lowest grade is not lower than grade 9.
NOTE: Security staff include security guards, security personnel, school resource officers (SROs), and sworn law enforcement officers who are not SROs. SROs include all career law enforcement officers with arrest authority who have specialized training and are assigned to work in collaboration with school organizations. Responses were provided by the principal or the person most knowledgeable about crime and safety issues at the school.
SOURCE: U.S. Department of Education, National Center for Education Statistics, 2005–06 and 2017–18 School Survey on Crime and Safety (SSOCS), 2006 and 2018. See *Digest of Education Statistics 2019*, table 233.70.

In the 2017–18 school year, 61 percent of public schools reported the presence of one or more security staff at their school at least once a week during the school year.[5] The percentage of public schools reporting the presence of any security staff was higher in 2017–18 than in 2005–06 (42 percent). This same pattern of a higher percentage of public schools overall reporting the presence of any security staff in 2017–18 than in 2005–06 was observed for primary, middle, and high schools. The

percentage point change from 2005–06 to 2017–18 was larger for primary schools (25 percentage points) than for middle schools (16 percentage points) and high schools (9 percentage points). Despite these changes, the percentage of primary schools reporting the presence of any security staff in 2017–18 (51 percent) remained lower than the corresponding percentages of middle schools (80 percent) and high schools (84 percent).

Figure 4. Percentage of public schools with a written plan for procedures to be performed in selected scenarios: School year 2017–18

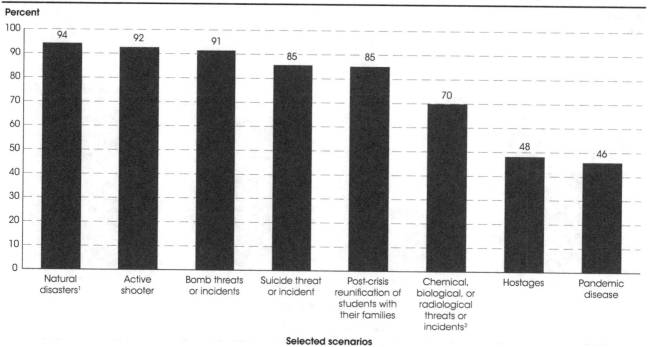

¹ For example, earthquakes or tornadoes.
² For example, release of mustard gas, anthrax, smallpox, or radioactive materials.
NOTE: Responses were provided by the principal or the person most knowledgeable about crime and safety issues at the school. Although rounded numbers are displayed, the figures are based on unrounded data.
SOURCE: U.S. Department of Education, National Center for Education Statistics, 2017–18 School Survey on Crime and Safety (SSOCS), 2018. See *Digest of Education Statistics 2019,* table 233.65.

Schools use a variety of practices and procedures to promote the safety of students, faculty, and staff. One aspect of school safety and security is ensuring that plans are in place to be carried out in the event of specific scenarios. In 2017–18, about 94 percent of public schools reported they had a written plan for procedures to be performed in the event of a natural disaster, 92 percent reported they had a written plan for procedures to be performed in the event of an active shooter, and 91 percent reported they had a written plan for procedures to be performed in the event of bomb threats or incidents. The percentage of schools reporting that they had a written plan for procedures to be performed in response to other events included in the survey questionnaire ranged from 85 percent each for suicide threat or incident and post-crisis reunification of students with their families to 46 percent for a pandemic disease.

Endnotes:
[1] "At school" includes in the school building, on school property, on a school bus, and going to or from school.
[2] Due to a sample increase and redesign of the National Crime Victimization Survey in 2016, victimization estimates among students ages 12–18 in 2016 were not comparable to estimates for other years and were thus excluded from this analysis.
[3] "Violent victimization excluding simple assault" includes the crimes of rape, sexual assault, robbery, and aggravated assault. In prior versions of this indicator, this was labeled as "serious violent victimization."
[4] The 2017–18 School Survey on Crime and Safety (SSOCS) questionnaire included only a single item about random sweeps for contraband, and it provided locker checks and dog sniffs as examples of types of sweeps. Prior to 2017–18, the SSOCS questionnaire included one item about dog sniffs for drugs, followed by a separate item about sweeps not including dog sniffs. For years prior to 2017–18, schools are treated as using random sweeps for contraband if they answered "yes" to either or both of these items; each school is counted only once, even if it answered "yes" to both items.
[5] Security staff include security guards, security personnel, School Resource Officers (SROs), and sworn law enforcement officers who are not SROs. "Security guards" and "security personnel" do not include law enforcement. SROs include all career law enforcement officers with arrest authority who have specialized training and are assigned to work in collaboration with school organizations.

Reference tables: *Digest of Education Statistics 2019,* tables 228.20, 233.50, 233.65, and 233.70
Related indicators and resources: *Indicators of School Crime and Safety; Safety at School* [*Status and Trends in the Education of Racial and Ethnic Groups*]

Glossary: Public school or institution

Characteristics of Public School Teachers

The percentage of public school teachers who held a postbaccalaureate degree (i.e., a master's, education specialist, or doctor's degree) was higher in 2017–18 (58 percent) than in 1999–2000 (47 percent). In both school years, a lower percentage of elementary school teachers than secondary school teachers held a postbaccalaureate degree.

In the 2017–18 school year, there were 3.5 million full- and part-time public school teachers, including 1.8 million elementary school teachers and 1.8 million secondary school teachers.[1] Overall, the number of public school teachers in 2017–18 was 18 percent higher than in 1999–2000 (3.0 million). These changes were accompanied by an 8 percent increase in public school enrollment in kindergarten through 12th grade, from 45.5 million students in fall 1999 to 49.1 million students in fall 2017. At the elementary school level, the number of teachers was 11 percent higher in 2017–18 than in 1999–2000 (1.6 million), while at the secondary school level the number of teachers was 26 percent higher in 2017–18 than in 1999–2000 (1.4 million).

Figure 1. Percentage distribution of teachers in public elementary and secondary schools, by instructional level and sex: School years 1999–2000 and 2017–18

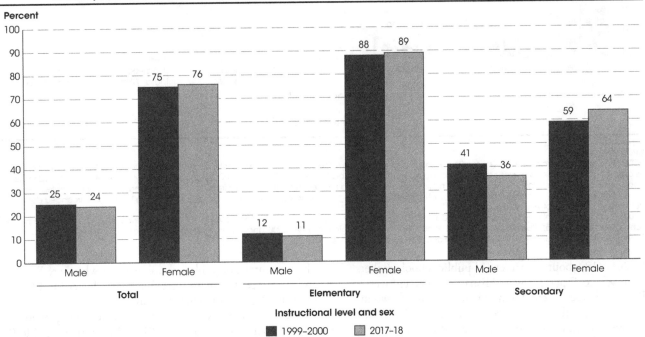

NOTE: Data are based on a head count of full-time and part-time teachers rather than on the number of full-time-equivalent teachers. Teachers were classified as elementary or secondary on the basis of the grades they taught, rather than on the level of the school in which they taught. In general, elementary teachers include those teaching prekindergarten through grade 6 and those teaching multiple grades, with a preponderance of grades taught being kindergarten through grade 6. In general, secondary teachers include those teaching any of grades 7 through 12 and those teaching multiple grades, with a preponderance of grades taught being grades 7 through 12 and usually with no grade taught being lower than grade 5.
SOURCE: U.S. Department of Education, National Center for Education Statistics, Schools and Staffing Survey (SASS), "Public School Teacher Data File," "Charter School Teacher Data File," "Public School Data File," and "Charter School Data File," 1999–2000; and National Teacher and Principal Survey (NTPS), "Public School Teacher Data File," 2017–18. See *Digest of Education Statistics 2019*, table 209.22.

About 76 percent of public school teachers were female and 24 percent were male in 2017–18, with a lower percentage of male teachers at the elementary school level (11 percent) than at the secondary school level (36 percent). Overall, the percentage of public school teachers who were male was 2 percentage points lower in 2017–18 than in 1999–2000. At the elementary school level, the percentage of male teachers was not measurably different between 2017–18 and 1999–2000. By comparison, at the secondary school level, the percentage of male teachers was 5 percentage points lower in 2017–18 than in 1999–2000.

Figure 2. Percentage distribution of teachers in public elementary and secondary schools, by race/ethnicity: School years 1999–2000 and 2017–18

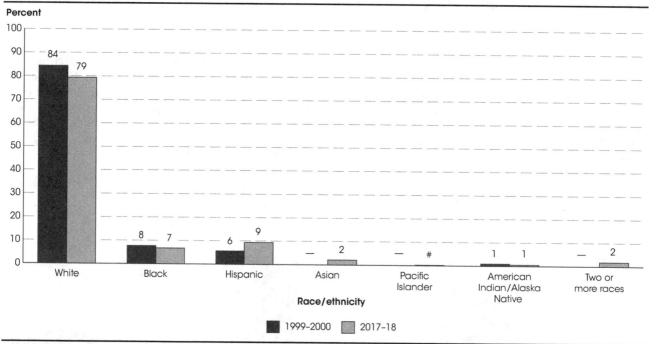

— Not available.
Rounds to zero.
NOTE: Data are based on a head count of full-time and part-time teachers rather than on the number of full-time-equivalent teachers. Separate data on Asians, Pacific Islanders, and persons of Two or more races were not available in 1999–2000. In 1999–2000, data for teachers who were Asian included those who were Pacific Islander, and teachers of Two or more races were required to select a single category from among the offered race/ethnicity categories (White, Black, Hispanic, Asian, and American Indian/Alaska Native). Although rounded numbers are displayed, the figures are based on unrounded data. Detail may not sum to totals due to rounding.
SOURCE: U.S. Department of Education, National Center for Education Statistics, Schools and Staffing Survey (SASS), "Public School Teacher Data File," "Charter School Teacher Data File," "Public School Data File," and "Charter School Data File," 1999–2000; and National Teacher and Principal Survey (NTPS), "Public School Teacher Data File," 2017–18. See *Digest of Education Statistics 2019*, table 209.22.

In 2017–18, about 79 percent of public school teachers were White, 9 percent were Hispanic, 7 percent were Black, 2 percent were Asian, 2 percent were of Two or more races, and 1 percent were American Indian/Alaska Native; additionally, those who were Pacific Islander made up less than 1 percent of public school teachers.

The percentage of public school teachers who were White and the percentage who were Black were lower in 2017–18 than in 1999–2000, when 84 percent were White and 8 percent were Black.[2] In contrast, the percentage who were Hispanic was higher in 2017–18 than in 1999–2000, when 6 percent were Hispanic.

Figure 3. Percentage of public school teachers who held a postbaccalaureate degree and percentage who held a regular or standard state teaching certificate or advanced professional certificate, by instructional level: School years 1999–2000 and 2017–18

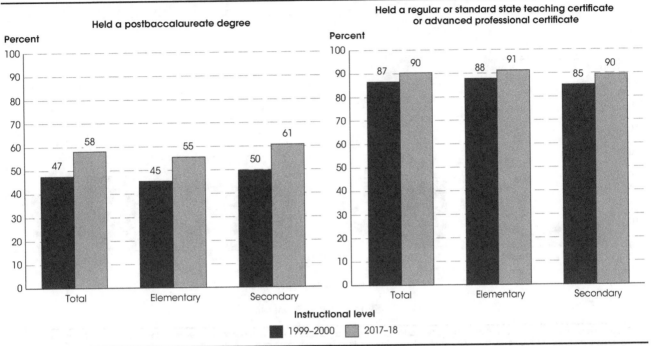

NOTE: Data are based on a head count of full-time and part-time teachers rather than on the number of full-time-equivalent teachers. Postbaccalaureate degree recipients include teachers who held a master's, education specialist, or doctor's degree. Education specialist degrees or certificates are generally awarded for 1 year's work beyond the master's level, including a certificate of advanced graduate studies. Doctor's degrees include Ph.D., Ed.D., and comparable degrees at the doctoral level, as well as first-professional degrees, such as M.D., D.D.S., and J.D. degrees. Teachers were classified as elementary or secondary on the basis of the grades they taught, rather than on the level of the school in which they taught. In general, elementary teachers include those teaching prekindergarten through grade 6 and those teaching multiple grades, with a preponderance of grades taught being kindergarten through grade 6. In general, secondary teachers include those teaching any of grades 7 through 12 and those teaching multiple grades, with a preponderance of grades taught being grades 7 through 12 and usually with no grade taught being lower than grade 5.
SOURCE: U.S. Department of Education, National Center for Education Statistics, Schools and Staffing Survey (SASS), "Public School Teacher Data File," "Charter School Teacher Data File," "Public School Data File," and "Charter School Data File," 1999–2000; and National Teacher and Principal Survey (NTPS), "Public School Teacher Data File," 2017–18. See *Digest of Education Statistics 2019*, table 209.22.

The percentage of public school teachers who held a postbaccalaureate degree (a master's, education specialist, or doctor's degree)[3] was higher in 2017–18 (58 percent) than in 1999–2000 (47 percent). This pattern was observed at both the elementary and secondary levels. Some 55 percent of elementary school teachers and 61 percent of secondary school teachers held a postbaccalaureate degree in 2017–18, whereas 45 and 50 percent, respectively, held a postbaccalaureate degree in 1999–2000. In both school years, a lower percentage of elementary school teachers than secondary school teachers held a postbaccalaureate degree.

In 2017–18, some 90 percent of public school teachers held a regular or standard state teaching certificate or advanced professional certificate, 4 percent held a provisional or temporary certificate, 3 percent held a probationary certificate, 2 percent held no certification, and 1 percent held a waiver or emergency certificate. A higher percentage of teachers in 2017–18 than in 1999–2000 held a regular certificate (90 vs. 87 percent). In both school years, a higher percentage of elementary than secondary school teachers held a regular certificate (88 vs. 85 percent in 1999–2000; 91 vs. 90 percent in 2017–18).

Figure 4. Percentage distribution of teachers in public elementary and secondary schools, by years of teaching experience: School years 1999–2000 and 2017–18

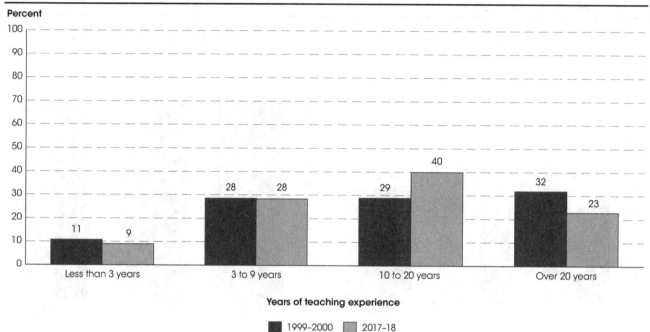

NOTE: Data are based on a head count of full-time and part-time teachers rather than on the number of full-time-equivalent teachers. Although rounded numbers are displayed, the figures are based on unrounded data. Detail may not sum to totals due to rounding.
SOURCE: U.S. Department of Education, National Center for Education Statistics, Schools and Staffing Survey (SASS), "Public School Teacher Data File," "Charter School Teacher Data File," "Public School Data File," and "Charter School Data File," 1999–2000; and National Teacher and Principal Survey (NTPS), "Public School Teacher Data File," 2017–18. See *Digest of Education Statistics 2019*, table 209.22.

In 2017–18, about 9 percent of public school teachers had less than 3 years of teaching experience, 28 percent had 3 to 9 years of experience, 40 percent had 10 to 20 years of experience, and 23 percent had more than 20 years of experience. Lower percentages of teachers in 2017–18 than in 1999–2000 had less than 3 years of experience (9 vs. 11 percent) and over 20 years of experience (23 vs. 32 percent). At the same time, the percentage who had 10 to 20 years of experience was higher in 2017–18 than in 1999–2000 (40 vs. 29 percent). There was no measurable difference between 1999–2000 and 2017–18 in the percentage of teachers with 3 to 9 years of experience.

Figure 5. Average base salary for full-time teachers in public elementary and secondary schools, by years of full- and part-time teaching experience: 2017–18

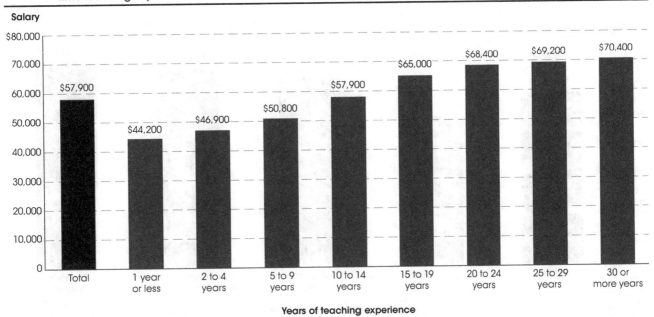

NOTE: Amounts presented in current 2017–18 dollars. Estimates are for regular full-time teachers only; they exclude other staff even when they have full-time teaching duties (regular part-time teachers, itinerant teachers, long-term substitutes, administrators, library media specialists, other professional staff, and support staff).
SOURCE: U.S. Department of Education, National Center for Education Statistics, National Teacher and Principal Survey (NTPS), "Public School Teacher Data File," 2017–18. See *Digest of Education Statistics 2019*, table 211.10.

Earlier sections of this indicator explore characteristics of all full-time and part-time public school teachers. Teacher salary information is also available, but is presented only for regular full-time teachers in public schools.[4] In 2017–18, the average base salary (in current 2017–18 dollars) for full-time public school teachers was $57,900. Average salaries for full-time public school teachers in 2017–18 tended to increase with years of full- and part-time teaching experience, with the exception that average salaries for teachers with 25 to 29 years of experience were not measurably different from those for teachers with 20 to 24 years of experience or those for teachers with 30 or more years of experience. Average base salaries, in current 2017–18 dollars, ranged from $44,200 for teachers with 1 year or less of experience to $70,400 for teachers with 30 or more years of experience.

Figure 6. Average base salary for full-time teachers in public elementary and secondary schools, by highest degree earned: 2017–18

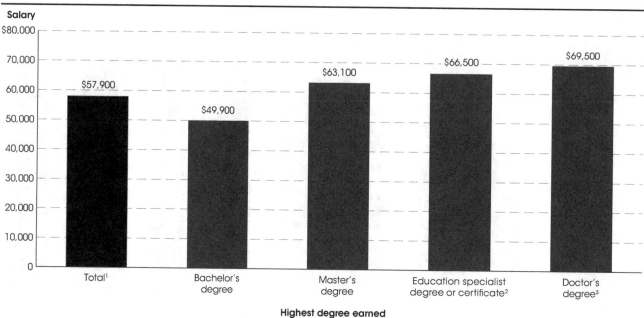

[1] Includes teachers with levels of education below the bachelor's degree (not shown separately).
[2] Education specialist degrees or certificates are generally awarded for 1 year's work beyond the master's level, including a certificate of advanced graduate studies.
[3] Doctor's degrees include Ph.D., Ed.D., and comparable degrees at the doctoral level, as well as first-professional degrees, such as M.D., D.D.S., and J.D. degrees.
NOTE: Amounts presented in current 2017–18 dollars. Estimates are for regular full-time teachers only; they exclude other staff even when they have full-time teaching duties (regular part-time teachers, itinerant teachers, long-term substitutes, administrators, library media specialists, other professional staff, and support staff).
SOURCE: U.S. Department of Education, National Center for Education Statistics, National Teacher and Principal Survey (NTPS), "Public School Teacher Data File," 2017–18. See *Digest of Education Statistics 2019*, table 211.10

Higher educational attainment was associated with higher average base salaries for full-time public school teachers who held at least a bachelor's degree. For example, in 2017–18 the average salary, in current 2017–18 dollars, for teachers with a doctor's degree ($69,500) was 39 percent higher than the salary of teachers with a bachelor's degree ($49,900), 10 percent higher than the salary of teachers with a master's degree ($63,100), and 5 percent higher than the salary of teachers with an education specialist degree or certificate ($66,500).

In 2017–18, the average base salary (in current 2017–18 dollars) for full-time public school teachers was lower for elementary school teachers ($56,600) than for secondary school teachers ($59,200). Female teachers had a lower average base salary than male teachers ($57,500 vs. $59,400). The average base salary for Asian teachers ($65,200) was higher than the average salaries for teachers of all other racial/ethnic groups except the average salary

for Pacific Islander teachers ($63,000), which was not measurably different from the average salary for Asian teachers. In addition, the average salaries for Hispanic ($58,300) and White ($57,900) teachers were higher than those for Black teachers ($56,500). The average base salary for teachers of Two or more races ($56,800) was not measurably different from that of Black teachers. The average base salary for American Indian/Alaska Native teachers ($49,000) was lower than the average salary for all other racial/ethnic groups.

The average base salary for full-time public school teachers in 2017–18 can be compared to average salaries in previous years using constant 2018–19 dollars. In terms of constant 2018–19 dollars,[5] for instance, the average salary for full-time public school teachers was lower in 2017–18 than in 1999–2000 ($59,100 vs. $59,700) but not measurably different in 2017–18 than in 2011–12 ($59,000).

Endnotes:

[1] All data except those on school enrollment are based on a head count of full-time and part-time teachers rather than on the number of full-time equivalent teachers.

[2] In 1999–2000, data for teachers who were Asian included those who were Pacific Islander, and teachers of Two or more races were required to select a single category from among the offered race/ethnicity categories (White, Black, Hispanic, Asian, and American Indian/Alaska Native).

[3] Education specialist degrees or certificates are generally awarded for 1 year's work beyond the master's level, including a certificate of advanced graduate studies. Doctor's degrees include Ph.D., Ed.D., and comparable degrees at the doctoral level, as well as first-professional degrees, such as M.D., D.D.S., and J.D. degrees.

[4] Salary data are presented for regular, full-time public school teachers only; the data exclude other staff even when they have full-time teaching duties (regular part-time teachers, itinerant teachers, long-term substitutes, administrators, library media specialists, other professional staff, and support staff).

[5] Constant dollar estimates are based on the Consumer Price Index, prepared by the Bureau of Labor Statistics, U.S. Department of Labor, adjusted to a school-year basis.

Reference tables: *Digest of Education Statistics 2019*, tables 203.40, 209.22, 211.10, and 211.20; *Digest of Education Statistics 2018*, table 203.10

Related indicators and resources: Characteristics of Public School Principals; Characteristics of Public School Teachers Who Completed Alternative Route to Certification Programs [*The Condition of Education 2018 Spotlight*]; Spotlight A: Characteristics of Public School Teachers by Race/Ethnicity [*Status and Trends in the Education of Racial and Ethnic Groups*]; Teacher Turnover: Stayers, Movers, and Leavers [*web-only*]

Glossary: Doctor's degree; Education specialist/professional diploma; Elementary school; Master's degree; Public school; Secondary school

Characteristics of Public School Principals

The percentage of public school principals who were female in 2017–18 (54 percent) was 10 percentage points higher than in 1999–2000 (44 percent). The percentage of public school principals who were White was lower in 2017–18 than in 1999–2000 (78 vs. 82 percent). In contrast, the percentage who were Hispanic was higher in 2017–18 than in 1999–2000 (9 vs. 5 percent).

During the 2017–18 school year, public schools in the United States employed 90,900 principals: 68 percent were elementary school principals, 22 percent were secondary school principals, and 9 percent were principals at combined elementary and secondary schools. The number of public school principals in 2017–18 was about 8 percent higher than in 1999–2000 (83,800), while the number of public schools in 2017–18 (98,500) was 7 percent higher than in 1999–2000 (92,000).

Figure 1. Percentage distribution of public school principals, by sex and race/ethnicity: 1999–2000 and 2017–18

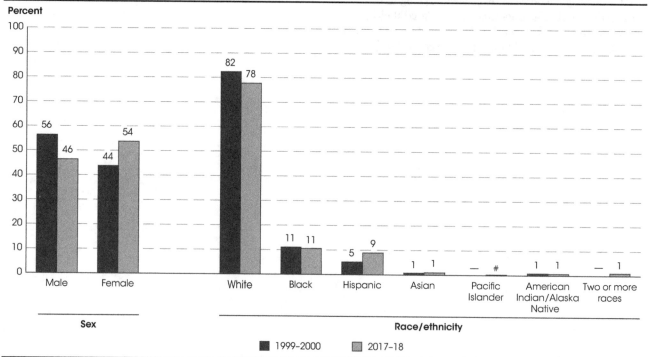

— Not available.
Rounds to zero.
NOTE: Data are based on a head count of full-time and part-time principals rather than on the number of full-time-equivalent principals. Separate data on principals who were Asian, Pacific Islander, and of Two or more races were not available in 1999–2000. In 1999–2000, data for principals who were Asian included principals who were Pacific Islander, and principals of Two or more races were required to select a single category from among the offered race/ethnicity categories (White, Black, Hispanic, Asian, and American Indian/Alaska Native). Although rounded numbers are displayed, the figures are based on unrounded data. Race categories exclude persons of Hispanic ethnicity. Detail may not sum to totals because of rounding.
SOURCE: U.S. Department of Education, National Center for Education Statistics, Schools and Staffing Survey (SASS), "Public School Principal Data File," 1999–2000; and National Teacher and Principal Survey (NTPS), "Public School Principal Data File," 2017–18. See *Digest of Education Statistics 2019*, table 212.08.

Forty-six percent of public school principals were male and 54 percent were female in 2017–18 . The percentage of public school principals who were female was 10 percentage points higher in 2017–18 than in 1999–2000 (54 vs. 44 percent).

In 2017–18, about 78 percent of public school principals were White, 11 percent were Black, and 9 percent were Hispanic. Those who were of Two or more races, Asian, and American Indian/Alaska Native each made up

1 percent of public school principals, and those who were Pacific Islander made up less than 1 percent of public school principals. The percentage of public school principals who were White was lower in 2017–18 than in 1999–2000 (78 vs. 82 percent).[1] In contrast, the percentage who were Hispanic was higher in 2017–18 than in 1999–2000 (9 vs. 5 percent). The percentages of principals who were Black were not measurably different across these two school years.

Figure 2. Percentage distribution of public school principals, by years of experience as a principal: 1999–2000 and 2017–18

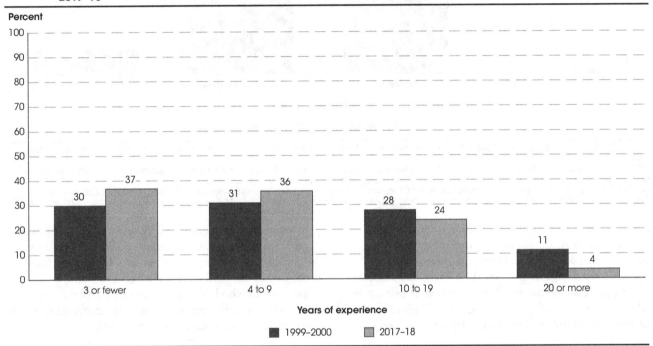

NOTE: Data are based on a head count of full-time and part-time principals rather than on the number of full-time-equivalent principals. Detail may not sum to totals because of rounding.
SOURCE: U.S. Department of Education, National Center for Education Statistics, Schools and Staffing Survey (SASS), "Public School Principal Data File," 1999–2000; and National Teacher and Principal Survey (NTPS), "Public School Principal Data File," 2017–18. See *Digest of Education Statistics 2019*, table 212.08.

In 2017–18, about 37 percent of public school principals had 3 or fewer years of experience as a principal, 36 percent had 4 to 9 years of experience, 24 percent had 10 to 19 years of experience, and 4 percent had 20 or more years of experience. Higher percentages of principals in 2017–18 than in 1999–2000 had 3 or fewer years of experience as a principal (37 vs. 30 percent) and 4 to 9 years of experience as a principal (36 vs. 31 percent). In contrast, lower percentages of principals in 2017–18 than in 1999–2000 had 10 to 19 years of experience as

a principal (24 vs. 28 percent) and 20 or more years of experience as a principal (4 vs. 11 percent). Also, higher percentages of principals in 2017–18 than in 1999–2000 were under 40 years of age (17 vs. 10 percent) and 40 to 44 years of age (20 vs. 13 percent), and a lower percentage of principals in 2017–18 than in 1999–2000 were 50 to 54 years of age (18 vs. 32 percent). The percentages of principals in 2017–18 who were 45 to 49 (23 percent) and 55 or over (22 percent) were not measurably different from the corresponding percentages in 1999–2000.

Figure 3. Percentage distribution of public school principals, by highest degree earned: 1999–2000 and 2017–18

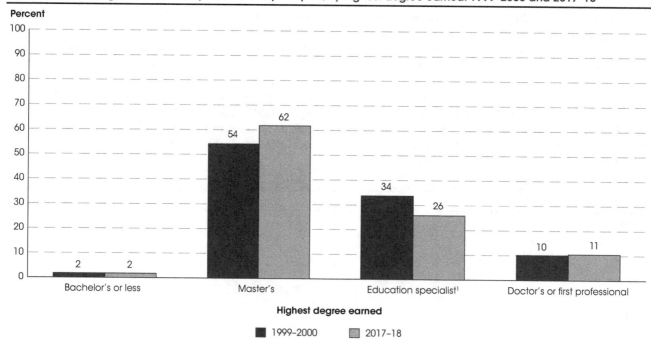

[1] Education specialist degrees or certificates are generally awarded for 1 year's work beyond the master's level. Includes certificate of advanced graduate studies.

NOTE: Data are based on a head count of full-time and part-time principals rather than on the number of full-time-equivalent principals. Although rounded numbers are displayed, the figures are based on unrounded data. Detail may not sum to totals because of rounding.

SOURCE: U.S. Department of Education, National Center for Education Statistics, Schools and Staffing Survey (SASS), "Public School Principal Data File," 1999–2000; and National Teacher and Principal Survey (NTPS), "Public School Principal Data File," 2017–18. See *Digest of Education Statistics 2019*, table 212.08.

Most public school principals in 2017–18 had a postbaccalaureate degree as their highest degree: 62 percent had a master's degree, 26 percent had an education specialist degree, and 11 percent had a doctor's or first-professional degree. The percentage of principals who had a master's degree was higher in 2017–18 than in 1999–2000 (62 vs. 54 percent). In contrast, the percentage of principals who had an education specialist degree was lower in 2017–18 than in 1999–2000 (26 vs. 34 percent). However, the percentages of public school principals in 2017–18 who had a bachelor's or lower degree (2 percent) or who had a doctor's or first-professional degree (11 percent) were not measurably different from the corresponding percentages in 1999–2000.

Figure 4. Principals' average annual salary at public schools, by school level and locale: 2017–18

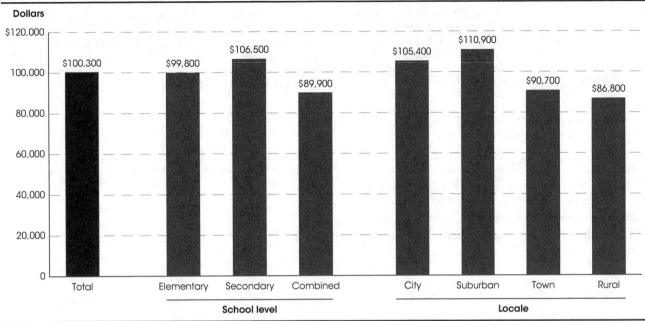

NOTE: Average annual salaries are reported in constant 2018–19 dollars based on the Consumer Price Index, prepared by the Bureau of Labor Statistics, U.S. Department of Labor, adjusted to a school-year basis.
SOURCE: U.S. Department of Education, National Center for Education Statistics, National Teacher and Principal Survey (NTPS), "Public School Principal Data File," 2017–18. See *Digest of Education Statistics 2019*, table 212.10.

The average annual salary of public school principals (in constant 2018–19 dollars)[2] was higher in 2017–18 ($100,300) than in 1999–2000 ($99,500). The 2017–18 average salary for secondary school principals ($106,500) was higher than the salaries for principals at elementary schools ($99,800) and combined schools ($89,900). The average annual salary of public school principals also varied by school locale. In 2017–18, it was highest in suburban areas ($110,900), followed by cities ($105,400) and towns ($90,700), and lowest in rural areas ($86,800).

In 2017–18, average salaries were lower for public school principals who were under 40 years of age ($92,300) and from 40 to 44 years of age ($99,200) than for principals in older age groups. Specifically, the average salaries for those who were either 45 to 49 or 50 to 54 were both $102,400, and the average salary was $103,600 for those who were 55 or over.

The average salary for public school principals also varied by sex and race/ethnicity. In 2017–18, female principals earned lower salaries than their male counterparts

($98,300 vs. $102,700). Average salaries were higher for Asian ($125,400) and Hispanic ($105,100) principals than for Black ($101,100), White ($99,400), and American Indian/Alaska Native ($86,700) principals. In addition, average salaries were higher for Asian principals than for Hispanic principals and principals of Two or more races ($103,000).

In 2017–18, the differences observed in average principal salaries by sex and race/ethnicity were correlated with other related variables. For example, compared with male principals, a higher percentage of female principals were in elementary schools. As noted earlier, elementary school principals had lower average salaries than secondary school principals. Compared with Hispanic principals, a higher percentage of White principals were in rural schools. Average principal salaries were lower in rural areas than in other areas. After controlling for these and other principal characteristics, the male-female salary difference remained significant, while the White-Hispanic salary difference was no longer significant.[3]

Endnotes:

[1] Separate data on principals who were Asian, Pacific Islander, and of Two or more races were not available in 1999–2000. In 1999–2000, data for principals who were Asian included principals who were Pacific Islander, and principals of Two or more races were required to select a single category from among the offered race/ethnicity categories (White, Black, Hispanic, Asian, and American Indian/Alaska Native).

[2] Constant dollar estimates are based on the Consumer Price Index, prepared by the Bureau of Labor Statistics, U.S. Department of Labor, adjusted to a school-year basis.

[3] A regression analysis was run using the National Teacher and Principal Survey Public School Principal Data File. The dependent variable was the average principal salary; the independent variables were school locale and level and principal's highest level of educational attainment, years of experience as a principal, sex, and race/ethnicity.

Reference tables: *Digest of Education Statistics 2019*, tables 212.08, 212.10, and 214.40; *Digest of Education Statistics 2017*, table 214.10; *Digest of Education Statistics 2005*, table 83

Related indicators and resources: Characteristics of Public School Teachers; Principal Turnover: Stayers, Movers, and Leavers [*web-only*]

Glossary: Elementary school; Public school or institution; Secondary school

Reading Performance

At grade 4, the average reading score in 2019 (220) was lower than the score in 2017 (222), when the assessment was last administered, but it was higher than the score in 1992 (217). Similarly, at grade 8 the average reading score in 2019 (263) was lower than the score in 2017 (267), but it was higher than the score in 1992 (260).

The National Assessment of Educational Progress (NAEP) assesses student performance in reading at grades 4, 8, and 12 in both public and private schools across the nation. NAEP reading scale scores range from 0 to 500 for all grade levels.[1] NAEP achievement levels define what students should know and be able to do: *NAEP Basic* indicates partial mastery of fundamental skills, *NAEP Proficient* indicates solid academic performance and demonstrated competency over challenging subject matter, and *NAEP Advanced* indicates superior performance beyond proficient.[2] NAEP reading assessments have been administered periodically since 1992. Beginning in 2003, assessments have been administered every four years at

grade 12 and every two years at grades 4 and 8. The grade 4 and grade 8 assessments are also administered at the state and selected district levels.[3] The most recent reading assessments were conducted in 2019 for grades 4, 8, and 12; however, data for grade 12 in 2019 were not available in time for publication. In this indicator, data for grade 12 comes from the 2015 assessment, the most recent NAEP assessment year with available data.[4] Throughout this indicator, reading scores from the most recent assessment year with available data will be compared with scores from the immediate prior assessment year and the first assessment year.

Figure 1. Average National Assessment of Educational Progress (NAEP) reading scale scores of 4th-, 8th-, and 12th-grade students: Selected years, 1992–2019

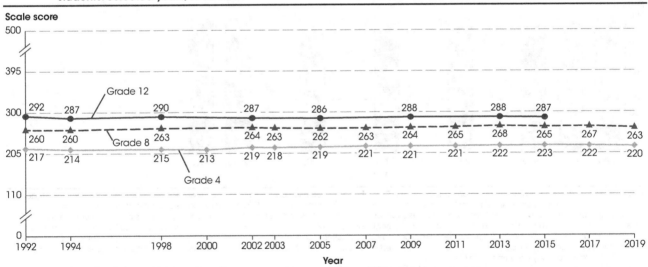

NOTE: Includes public, private, Bureau of Indian Education, and Department of Defense Education Activity schools. The reading scale scores range from 0 to 500. Although average scores are reported on a 0–500 scale at grades 4, 8, and 12, the scale scores were derived separately and therefore scores cannot be compared across grades. Assessment was not conducted for grade 8 in 2000 or for grade 12 in 2000, 2003, 2007, 2011, and 2017. Data for grade 12 in 2019 were not available in time for publication. Testing accommodations (e.g., extended time, small-group testing) for children with disabilities and English language learners were not permitted in 1992 and 1994. Although rounded numbers are displayed, the figures are based on unrounded data.
SOURCE: U.S. Department of Education, National Center for Education Statistics, National Assessment of Educational Progress (NAEP), selected years, 1992–2019 Reading Assessments, NAEP Data Explorer. See *Digest of Education Statistics 2019*, table 221.10.

The average reading score for 4th-grade students in 2019 (220) was lower than the score in 2017 (222), but it was higher than the score in 1992 (217). For 8th-grade students, the reading score in 2019 (263) was lower than

the score in 2017 (267), but it was higher than the score in 1992 (260). The reading score for 12th-grade students in 2015 (287) was not measurably different from the score in 2013, but it was lower than the score in 1992 (292).

Figure 2. Percentage distribution of 4th-, 8th-, and 12th-grade students, by National Assessment of Educational Progress (NAEP) reading achievement level: Selected years, 1992–2019

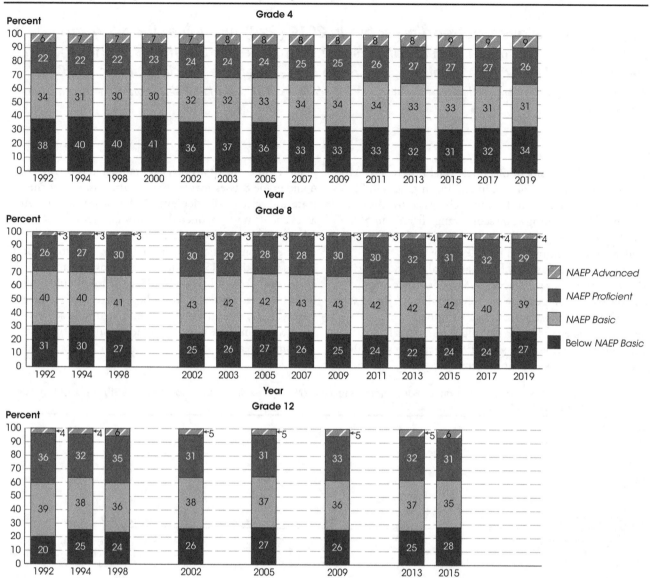

NOTE: Includes public, private, Bureau of Indian Education, and Department of Defense Education Activity schools. Achievement levels define what students should know and be able to do: *NAEP Basic* indicates partial mastery of fundamental skills, *NAEP Proficient* indicates demonstrated competency over challenging subject matter, and *NAEP Advanced* indicates superior performance beyond proficient. NAEP achievement levels are to be used on a trial basis and should be interpreted and used with caution. Assessment was not conducted for grade 8 in 2000 or for grade 12 in 2000, 2003, 2007, 2011, and 2017. Data for grade 12 in 2019 were not available in time for publication. Testing accommodations (e.g., extended time, small-group testing) for children with disabilities and English language learners were not permitted in 1992 and 1994. Although rounded numbers are displayed, the figures are based on unrounded data. Detail may not sum to totals because of rounding.
SOURCE: U.S. Department of Education, National Center for Education Statistics, National Assessment of Educational Progress (NAEP), selected years, 1992–2019 Reading Assessments, NAEP Data Explorer. See *Digest of Education Statistics 2019*, table 221.12.

In 2019, some 66 percent of 4th-grade students performed at or above the *NAEP Basic* achievement level in reading, 35 percent performed at or above *NAEP Proficient*, and 9 percent performed at *NAEP Advanced*. The percentage of 4th-grade students who performed at or above *NAEP Basic* in 2019 was lower than the percentage in 2017 (68 percent), but it was higher than the percentage in 1992 (62 percent). In addition, the percentage of 4th-grade students who performed at or above *NAEP Proficient* in 2019 was lower than the percentage in 2017 (37 percent), but it was higher than the percentage in 1992 (29 percent). The percentage of 4th-grade students who performed at *NAEP Advanced* in 2019 was not measurably different from the percentage in 2017, but it was higher than the percentage in 1992 (6 percent).

In 2019, some 73 percent of 8th-grade students performed at or above the *NAEP Basic* achievement level in reading, 34 percent performed at or above *NAEP Proficient*, and 4 percent performed at *NAEP Advanced*. The percentage of 8th-grade students who performed at or above *NAEP Basic* in 2019 was lower than the percentage in 2017 (76 percent), but it was higher than the percentage in 1992 (69 percent). Similarly, a lower percentage of 8th-grade students performed at or above *NAEP Proficient* in 2019 than in 2017 (36 percent), but the percentage in 2019 was higher than the percentage in 1992 (29 percent). The percentage of 8th-grade students who performed at *NAEP Advanced* was higher in 2019 than in 1992 (3 percent), but the percentage in 2019 was not measurably different from the percentage in 2017.

In 2015, some 72 percent of 12th-grade students performed at or above the *NAEP Basic* achievement level in reading, 37 percent performed at or above *NAEP Proficient*, and 6 percent performed at *NAEP Advanced*. A lower percentage of 12th-grade students performed at or above *NAEP Basic* in 2015 than in 2013 (75 percent) and 1992 (80 percent). The percentage of 12th-graders who performed at or above *NAEP Proficient* in 2015 was not measurably different from the percentage in 2013, but it was lower than the percentage in 1992 (40 percent). A higher percentage of 12th-grade students performed at *NAEP Advanced* in 2015 than in 2013 (5 percent) and 1992 (4 percent).

Figure 3. Average National Assessment of Educational Progress (NAEP) reading scale scores of 4th-grade students, by selected characteristics: Selected years, 1992–2019

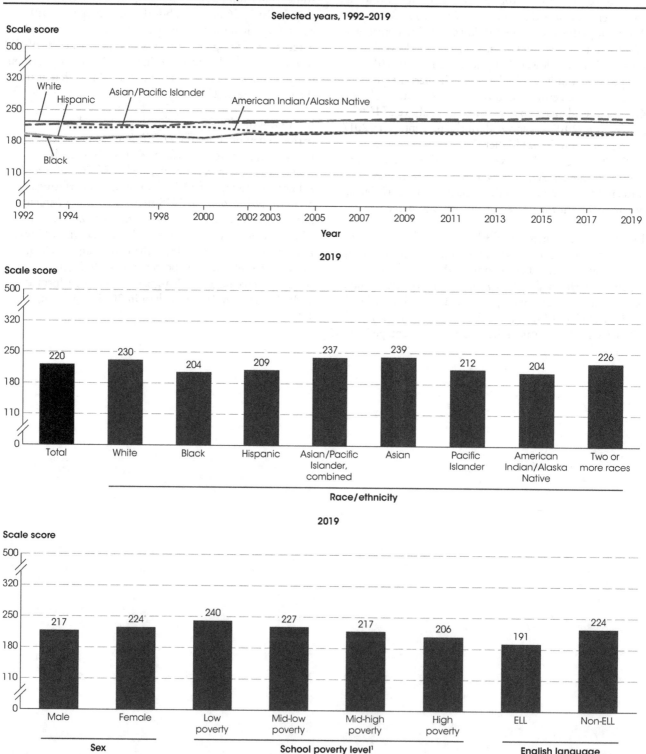

[1] High-poverty schools are defined as schools where 76 to 100 percent of the students are eligible for free or reduced-price lunch (FRPL); mid-high poverty schools are schools where 51 to 75 percent of the students are eligible for FRPL; mid-low poverty schools are schools where 26 to 50 percent of the students are eligible for FRPL; and low-poverty schools are schools where 25 percent or less of the students are eligible for FRPL. For more information on eligibility for FRPL and its relationship to poverty, see the NCES blog post "Free or reduced price lunch: A proxy for poverty?" The nonresponse rate for FRPL was greater than 15 percent but not greater than 50 percent.
NOTE: Includes public, private, Bureau of Indian Education, and Department of Defense Education Activity schools. The reading scale scores range from 0 to 500. Scale scores for American Indian/Alaska Native students were suppressed in 1992 and 1998 because reporting standards were not met (too few cases for a reliable estimate). Testing accommodations (e.g., extended time, small-group testing) for children with disabilities and English language learners were not permitted in 1992 and 1994. Race categories exclude persons of Hispanic ethnicity.
SOURCE: U.S. Department of Education, National Center for Education Statistics, National Assessment of Educational Progress (NAEP), selected years, 1992–2019 Reading Assessments, NAEP Data Explorer. See *Digest of Education Statistics 2019*, tables 221.10 and 221.12.

At grade 4, the average 2019 reading scores for White (230) and Black (204) students were lower than the corresponding scores in 2017 (232 and 206, respectively), but the scores for both groups were higher in 2019 than in 1992 (224 and 192, respectively). In 2019, the reading scores for Hispanic (209) and Asian/Pacific Islander students (237) were not measurably different from the corresponding scores in 2017, but the scores for both groups were higher in 2019 than in 1992 (197 and 216, respectively). In 2019, the reading score for American Indian/Alaska Native 4th-graders (204) was not measurably different from the scores in 2017 and 1994 (1994 was the first year data were available for 4th-grade American Indian/Alaska Native students). In 2011, NAEP began reporting separate data for Asian students, Pacific Islander students, and students of Two or more races.[5] The 2019 4th-grade reading scores for Asian students (239), Pacific Islander students (212), and students of Two or more races (226) were not measurably different from the corresponding scores in 2017 and 2011.

From 1992 through 2019, the average reading scores for White 4th-graders were higher than those of their Black and Hispanic peers. Although the White-Black achievement gap did not change measurably from 2017 to 2019, the achievement gap narrowed from 32 points in 1992 to 27 points in 2019. The White-Hispanic achievement gap in 2019 (21 points) was smaller than the achievement gap in 2017 (23 points), but it was not measurably different from the achievement gap in 1992.

At grade 4, the average reading score for male students in 2019 (217) was lower than the score in 2017 (219) but higher than the score in 1992 (213). The reading score for female students in 2019 (224) was not measurably different from the score in 2017, but it was higher than the score in 1992 (221). In each assessment year since 1992, female students have scored higher than male students at grade 4. The 2019 achievement gap between male and female 4th-grade students (7 points) was larger than the male-female achievement gap in 2017 (6 points), but it was not measurably different from the achievement gap in 1992.

NAEP scores can also be disaggregated by the poverty level of the school students attended and by students' English language learner (ELL) status. In 2019, the average reading score for 4th-grade students in high-poverty schools (206) was lower than the scores for 4th-grade students in mid-high poverty schools (217), mid-low poverty schools (227), and low-poverty schools (240).[6,7] In 2019, the reading score for 4th-grade ELL students (191) was 33 points lower than the score for their non-ELL peers (224).

Figure 4. Average National Assessment of Educational Progress (NAEP) reading scale scores of 8th-grade students, by selected characteristics: Selected years, 1992–2019

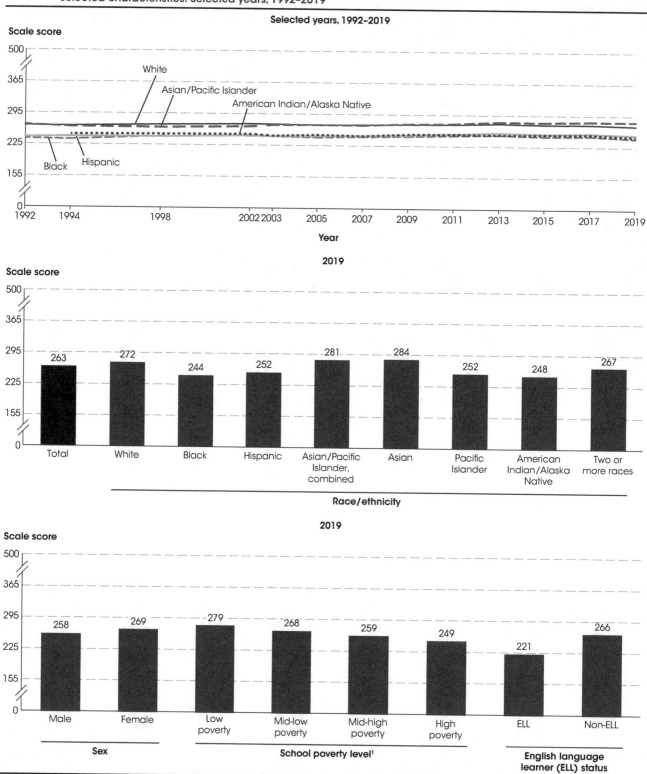

¹ High-poverty schools are defined as schools where 76 to 100 percent of the students are eligible for free or reduced-price lunch (FRPL); mid-high poverty schools are schools where 51 to 75 percent of the students are eligible for FRPL; mid-low poverty schools are schools where 26 to 50 percent of the students are eligible for FRPL; and low-poverty schools are schools where 25 percent or less of the students are eligible for FRPL. For more information on eligibility for FRPL and its relationship to poverty, see the NCES blog post "Free or reduced price lunch: A proxy for poverty?" The nonresponse rate for FRPL was greater than 15 percent but not greater than 50 percent.
NOTE: Includes public, private, Bureau of Indian Education, and Department of Defense Education Activity schools. The reading scale scores range from 0 to 500. Scale scores for American Indian/Alaska Native students were suppressed in 1992 and 1998 because reporting standards were not met (too few cases for a reliable estimate). Testing accommodations (e.g., extended time, small-group testing) for children with disabilities and English language learners were not permitted in 1992 and 1994. Race categories exclude persons of Hispanic ethnicity.
SOURCE: U.S. Department of Education, National Center for Education Statistics, National Assessment of Educational Progress (NAEP), selected years, 1992–2019 Reading Assessments, NAEP Data Explorer. See *Digest of Education Statistics 2019*, tables 221.10 and 221.12.

The Condition of Education 2020 | **74**

At grade 8, the average reading scores for White (272), Black (244), and Hispanic (252) students in 2019 were lower than the corresponding scores in 2017 (275, 249, and 255, respectively), but the score for each group was higher in 2019 than in 1992 (267, 237, and 241, respectively). In 2019, the reading score for 8th-grade Asian/Pacific Islander students (281) was not measurably different from the score in 2017, but it was higher than the score in 1992 (268). The reading score for 8th-grade American Indian/Alaska Native students (248) was lower than the score in 2017 (253), but it was not measurably different from the score in 1994 (1994 was the first year data were available for 8th-grade American Indian/Alaska Native students). In 2011, NAEP began reporting separate data for Asian students, Pacific Islander students, and students of Two or more races. At grade 8, the 2019 reading score for Asian students (284) was not measurably different from the score in 2017, but it was higher than the score in 2011 (277). The 2019 reading score for Pacific Islander 8th-graders (252) was not measurably different from the scores in 2017 and 2011. While the 2019 reading score for 8th-graders of Two or more races (267) was lower than the score in 2017 (272), it was not measurably different from the score in 2011.

From 1992 through 2019, the average reading score for White 8th-graders was higher than the scores of their Black and Hispanic peers. The White-Black achievement gap in 2019 (28 points) was larger than the White-Black achievement gap in 2017 (25 points), but it was not measurably different from the achievement gap in 1992. Although the White-Hispanic achievement gap at grade 8 did not change measurably from 2017 to 2019, the White-Hispanic achievement gap narrowed from 26 points in 1992 to 20 points in 2019.

At grade 8, the average reading scores in 2019 for both male (258) and female students (269) were lower than the corresponding scores in 2017 (262 and 272, respectively), but they were higher than the scores in 1992 (254 and 267, respectively). In each year since 1992, female students have scored higher than male students at grade 8. The 2019 achievement gap between male and female 8th-grade students (11 points) was not measurably different from the male-female achievement gaps in 2017 and 1992.

In 2019, the average reading score for 8th-grade students in high-poverty schools (249) was lower than the scores for 8th-grade students in mid-high poverty schools (259), mid-low poverty schools (268), and low-poverty schools (279).[8] The 2019 reading score for 8th-grade ELL students (221) was 45 points lower than the score for their non-ELL peers (266).

Figure 5. Average National Assessment of Educational Progress (NAEP) reading scale scores of 12th-grade students, by selected characteristics: Selected years, 1992–2015

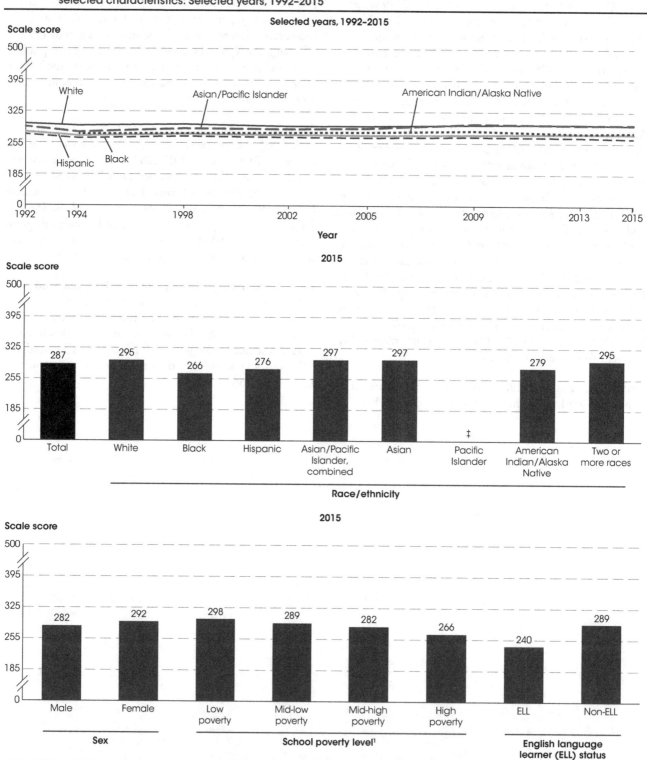

‡ Reporting standards not met. There were too few cases for a reliable estimate.
[1] High-poverty schools are defined as schools where 76 to 100 percent of the students are eligible for free or reduced-price lunch (FRPL); mid-high poverty schools are schools where 51 to 75 percent of the students are eligible for FRPL; mid-low poverty schools are schools where 26 to 50 percent of the students are eligible for FRPL; and low-poverty schools are schools where 25 percent or less of the students are eligible for FRPL. For more information on eligibility for FRPL and its relationship to poverty, see the NCES blog post "Free or reduced price lunch: A proxy for poverty?"
NOTE: Includes public, private, Bureau of Indian Education, and Department of Defense Education Activity schools. The reading scale scores range from 0 to 500. Assessment was not conducted for grade 12 in 2017, and data for the 2019 assessment were not available in time for publication. Scale scores for American Indian/Alaska Native students were suppressed in 1992, 1998, and 2002 because reporting standards were not met (too few cases for a reliable estimate). Testing accommodations (e.g., extended time, small-group testing) for children with disabilities and English language learners were not permitted in 1992 and 1994. Race categories exclude persons of Hispanic ethnicity.
SOURCE: U.S. Department of Education, National Center for Education Statistics, National Assessment of Educational Progress (NAEP), selected years, 1992–2015 Reading Assessments, NAEP Data Explorer. See Digest of Education Statistics 2019, tables 221.10 and 221.12.

At grade 12, the average reading scores in 2015 for White (295), Hispanic (276), and Asian/Pacific Islander students (297) were not measurably different from the scores in 2013 and 1992. For Black students, the 2015 reading score (266) was lower than the 1992 score (273), but it was not measurably different from the 2013 score. The reading score for American Indian/Alaska Native students in 2015 (279) was not measurably different from the scores in 2013 and 1994 (1994 was the first year data were available for 12th-grade American Indian/Alaska Native students). In 2013, NAEP began reporting separate data at the 12th-grade level for Asian students, Pacific Islander students, and students of Two or more races. The 2015 reading scores for Asian students (297) and students of Two or more races (295) were not measurably different from the scores in 2013. The reading score for Pacific Islander students was 289 in 2013, but it was suppressed in 2015 because reporting standards were not met. The White-Black achievement gap for 12th-grade students was larger in 2015 (30 points) than in 1992 (24 points), while the White-Hispanic achievement gap in 2015 (20 points) was not measurably different from the achievement gap in any previous assessment year.

The 2015 average reading scores for male (282) and female (292) 12th-grade students were not measurably different from the scores in 2013, but they were lower than the scores in 1992 (287 and 297, respectively). The achievement gap between male and female 12th-grade students in 2015 (10 points) was not measurably different from the male-female achievement gaps in 2013 and 1992.

In 2015, the reading score for 12th-grade students in high-poverty schools (266) was lower than the scores for 12th-grade students in mid-high poverty schools (282), mid-low poverty schools (289), and low-poverty schools (298). In addition, the average reading score for 12th-grade ELL students (240) was 49 points lower than the score for their non-ELL peers (289).

Figure 6. Change in average National Assessment of Educational Progress (NAEP) reading scale scores of 4th- and 8th-grade public school students, by state: 2017 to 2019

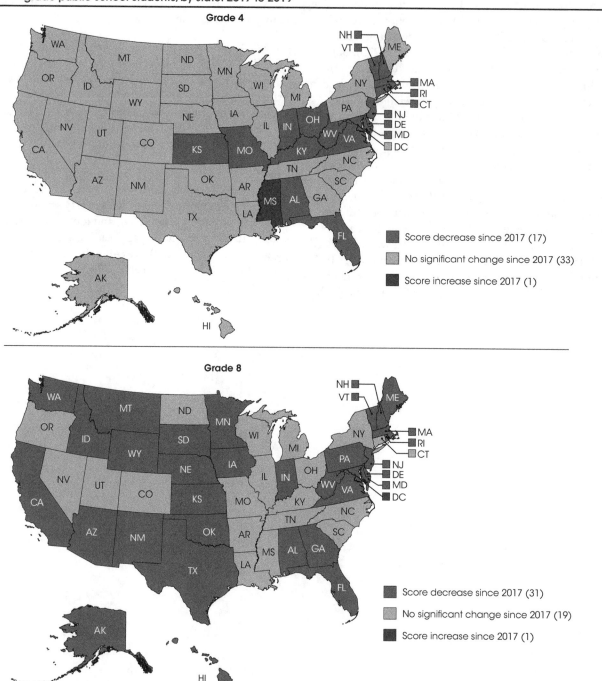

NOTE: The reading scale scores range from 0 to 500.
SOURCE: U.S. Department of Education, National Center for Education Statistics, National Assessment of Educational Progress (NAEP), 2017 and 2019 Reading Assessments, The Nation's Report Card (https://www.nationsreportcard.gov/). See *Digest of Education Statistics 2019*, tables 221.40 and 221.60.

NAEP results also permit state-level comparisons of the reading achievement of 4th- and 8th-grade students in public schools.[9] The national average reading score for 4th-grade public school students decreased from 221 in 2017 to 219 in 2019, and scores across states ranged from 204 to 231. In 16 states, reading scores for 4th-grade public school students were higher than the national average score for public school students, and in 23 states, public school students had scores that were not measurably different from the national average score. Reading scores in the District of Columbia and the remaining 11 states were lower than the national average score for 4th-grade students in public schools. Reading scores were lower in 2019 than in 2017 in 17 states and higher in 2019 than in 2017 in one state (Mississippi). The reading scores in the remaining 32 states and the District of Columbia showed no measurable change from 2017 to 2019.

At grade 8, the national average reading score for public school students in 2019 was 262, and scores across states ranged from 250 to 273. In 17 states, reading scores for public school students in 2019 were higher than the national average score for 8th-grade students in public schools, and in 19 states, public school students had scores that were not measurably different from the national average score. Reading scores in the District of Columbia

and the remaining 14 states were lower than the national average score for 8th-grade students in public schools. Reading scores were also lower in 2019 than in 2017 in 31 states; however, the score was higher in 2019 than in 2017 in the District of Columbia. In the remaining 19 states, the reading score for 8th-grade students in public schools showed no measurable change from 2017 to 2019.

Endnotes:

[1] Although average scores are reported on a 0–500 scale at grades 4, 8, and 12, the scale scores were derived separately and therefore scores cannot be compared across grades. For more information on NAEP including the history of the assessment, sampling procedures, and the transition from paper-based assessments to digitally based assessments, please see https://nces. ed.gov/nationsreportcard/.

[2] NAEP achievement-level setting is based on the judgments of a broadly representative panel of teachers, education specialists, and members of the general public. The authorizing legislation for NAEP requires that the achievement levels be used on a trial basis until the Commissioner of the National Center for Education Statistics (NCES) determines that the achievement levels are reasonable, valid, and informative to the public (20 USC § 9622(e)(2)(C)). The NCES Commissioner's determination is to be based on a congressionally mandated, rigorous, and independent evaluation. The latest evaluation of the achievement levels was conducted by a committee convened by the National Academies of Sciences, Engineering, and Medicine in 2016. The evaluation concluded that further evidence should be gathered to determine whether the achievement levels are reasonable, valid, and informative. Accordingly, the NCES Commissioner determined that the trial status of the achievement levels should be maintained at this time. Read more about the NAEP reading achievement levels by grade.

[3] This indicator presents data from the Main NAEP reading assessment, which is not comparable to the Long-Term Trend NAEP reading assessment. The Main NAEP reading assessment

was first administered in 1992 and assesses student performance at grades 4, 8, and 12, while the Long-Term Trend NAEP reading assessment was first administered in 1971 and assesses student performance at ages 9, 13, and 17. In addition, the two assessments differ in the content assessed, how often the assessment is administered, and how the results are reported.

[4] NAEP reading scores for 4th-grade students in 2019 had a mean of 220 and a standard deviation (SD) of 39. NAEP reading scores for 8th-grade students in 2019 had a mean of 263 and an SD of 38. NAEP reading scores for 12th-grade students in 2015 had a mean of 287 and an SD of 41 (retrieved December 10, 2019, from the Main NAEP Data Explorer).

[5] While NAEP reported some data on students of Two or more races for earlier years, the reporting standards changed in 2011.

[6] High-poverty schools are defined as schools where 76 to 100 percent of the students are eligible for free or reduced-price lunch (FRPL); mid-high poverty schools are schools where 51 to 75 percent of the students are eligible for FRPL; mid-low poverty schools are schools where 26 to 50 percent of the students are eligible for FRPL; and low-poverty schools are schools where 25 percent or less of the students are eligible for FRPL.

[7] Nonresponse for this variable was greater than 15 percent but not greater than 50 percent.

[8] Nonresponse for this variable was greater than 15 percent but not greater than 50 percent.

[9] NAEP results serve as a common metric for all states and are not comparable to results from assessments administered by state education agencies.

Reference tables: *Digest of Education Statistics 2019,* tables 221.10, 221.12, 221.40, 221.60, and 221.75

Related indicators and resources: Absenteeism and Achievement [*Status and Trends in the Education of Racial and Ethnic Groups*]; International Comparisons: Reading Literacy at Grade 4; International Comparisons: Reading, Mathematics, and Science Literacy of 15-Year-Old Students; Mathematics Performance; Reading Achievement [*Status and Trends in the Education of Racial and Ethnic Groups*]; Reading and Mathematics Score Trends [*web-only*]; Science Performance; Technology and Engineering Literacy [*web-only*]

Glossary: Achievement gap; Achievement levels, NAEP; English language learner (ELL); Public school or institution; Racial/ethnic group

Mathematics Performance

At grade 4, the average mathematics score in 2019 (241) was higher than the scores in both 2017 (240), when the assessment was last administered, and 1990 (213). At grade 8, the mathematics score in 2019 (282) was lower than the score in 2017 (283), but it was higher than the score in 1990 (263). There was no measurable difference between average math scores for males and females at grade 8 in 2019.

The National Assessment of Educational Progress (NAEP) assesses student performance in mathematics at grades 4, 8, and 12 in both public and private schools across the nation. NAEP mathematics scale scores range from 0 to 500 for grades 4 and 8 and from 0 to 300 for grade 12.[1] NAEP achievement levels define what students should know and be able to do: *NAEP Basic* indicates partial mastery of fundamental skills, *NAEP Proficient* indicates solid academic performance and demonstrated competency over challenging subject matter, and

NAEP Advanced indicates superior performance beyond proficient.[2] NAEP mathematics assessments have been administered periodically since 1990, more frequently in grades 4 and 8 than in grade 12.[3] The most recent mathematics assessments were conducted in 2019 for grades 4, 8, and 12; however, data for grade 12 in 2019 were not available in time for publication. In this indicator, data for grade 12 come from the 2015 assessment, the most recent NAEP assessment year with available data.[4]

Figure 1. Average National Assessment of Educational Progress (NAEP) mathematics scale scores of 4th- and 8th-grade students: Selected years, 1990–2019

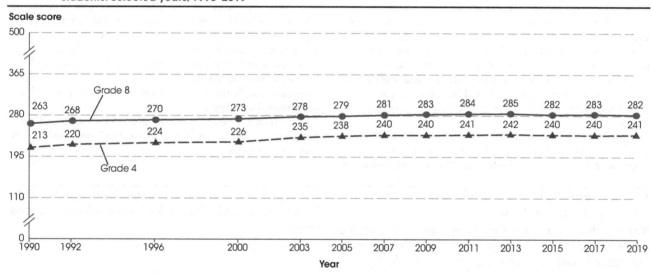

NOTE: Includes public and private schools. Average scores are reported on a 0–500 scale at grades 4 and 8; however, the scale scores were derived separately and therefore scores cannot be compared across grades. Grade 12 mathematics scores are not shown because they are reported on a scale of 0 to 300. Testing accommodations (e.g., extended time, small-group testing) for children with disabilities and English language learners were not permitted in 1990 and 1992.
SOURCE: U.S. Department of Education, National Center for Education Statistics, National Assessment of Educational Progress (NAEP), selected years, 1990–2019 Mathematics Assessments, NAEP Data Explorer. See *Digest of Education Statistics 2019*, table 222.10.

The average mathematics score for 4th-grade students in 2019 (241) was higher than the scores in both 2017 (240) and 1990 (213). For 8th-grade students, the mathematics score in 2019 (282) was lower than the score in 2017 (283), but it was higher than the score in 1990 (263). The

mathematics score for 12th-grade students in 2015 (152) was lower than the score in 2013 (153), but it was not measurably different from the score in 2005, the earliest year with comparable data.[5]

Figure 2.   Percentage distribution of 4th-, 8th-, and 12th-grade students, by National Assessment of Educational Progress (NAEP) mathematics achievement levels: Selected years, 1990–2019

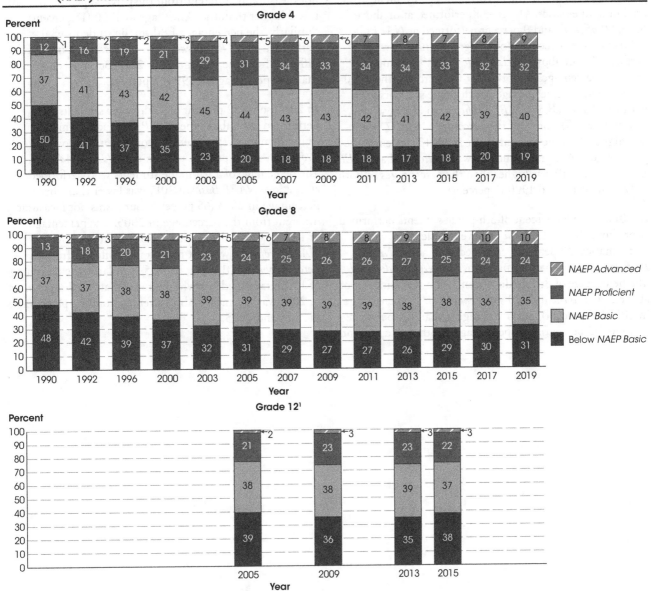

¹ In 2005, there were major changes to the framework and content of the grade 12 assessment, and, as a result, scores from 2005 and later assessment years cannot be compared with scores and results from earlier assessment years. Assessment was not conducted for grade 12 in 2007, 2011, and 2017. Data for grade 12 in 2019 were not available in time for publication.
NOTE: Includes public and private schools. Achievement levels define what students should know and be able to do: *NAEP Basic* indicates partial mastery of fundamental skills, *NAEP Proficient* indicates demonstrated competency over challenging subject matter, and *NAEP Advanced* indicates superior performance beyond proficient. Testing accommodations (e.g., extended time, small-group testing) for children with disabilities and English language learners were not permitted in 1990 and 1992. Although rounded numbers are displayed, the figures are based on unrounded data. Detail may not sum to totals because of rounding.
SOURCE: U.S. Department of Education, National Center for Education Statistics, National Assessment of Educational Progress (NAEP), selected years, 1990–2019 Mathematics Assessments, NAEP Data Explorer. See *Digest of Education Statistics 2019*, table 222.12.

In 2019, some 81 percent of 4th-grade students performed at or above the *NAEP Basic* achievement level in mathematics, 41 percent performed at or above *NAEP Proficient*, and 9 percent performed at *NAEP Advanced*. The percentage of 4th-grade students who performed at or above *NAEP Basic* in 2019 was higher than the percentages in both 2017 (80 percent) and 1990 (50 percent). The percentage of 4th-grade students who performed at or above *NAEP Proficient* in 2019 was not measurably different from the percentage in 2017, but it was higher than the percentage in 1990 (13 percent). The percentage of 4th-grade students who performed at *NAEP Advanced* in 2019 was higher than the percentages in both 2017 (8 percent) and 1990 (1 percent).

In 2019, some 69 percent of 8th-grade students performed at or above the *NAEP Basic* achievement level in mathematics, 34 percent performed at or above *NAEP Proficient*, and 10 percent performed at *NAEP Advanced*. The percentage of 8th-grade students who performed at or above *NAEP Basic* in 2019 was lower than the percentage in 2017 (70 percent), but it was higher than the percentage in 1990 (52 percent). The percentage of 8th-grade students who performed at or above *NAEP Proficient* in 2019 was not measurably different from the percentage in 2017, but it was higher than the percentage in 1990 (15 percent). Similarly, the percentage of 8th-grade students who performed at *NAEP Advanced* in 2019 was not measurably different from the percentage in 2017, but it was higher than the percentage in 1990 (2 percent).

In 2015, some 62 percent of 12th-grade students performed at or above the *NAEP Basic* achievement level in mathematics, 25 percent performed at or above *NAEP Proficient*, and 3 percent performed at *NAEP Advanced*. The percentage of 12th-grade students who performed at or above *NAEP Basic* in 2015 was lower than the percentage in 2013 (65 percent), but it was not measurably different from the percentage in 2005. The percentage of 12th-grade students who performed at or above *NAEP Proficient* was not measurably different from the percentages in 2013 and in 2005. Similarly, the percentage of 12th-grade students who performed at *NAEP Advanced* in 2015 was not measurably different from the percentages in 2013 and 2005.

Figure 3. Average National Assessment of Educational Progress (NAEP) mathematics scale scores of 4th-grade students, by selected characteristics: Selected years, 1990–2019

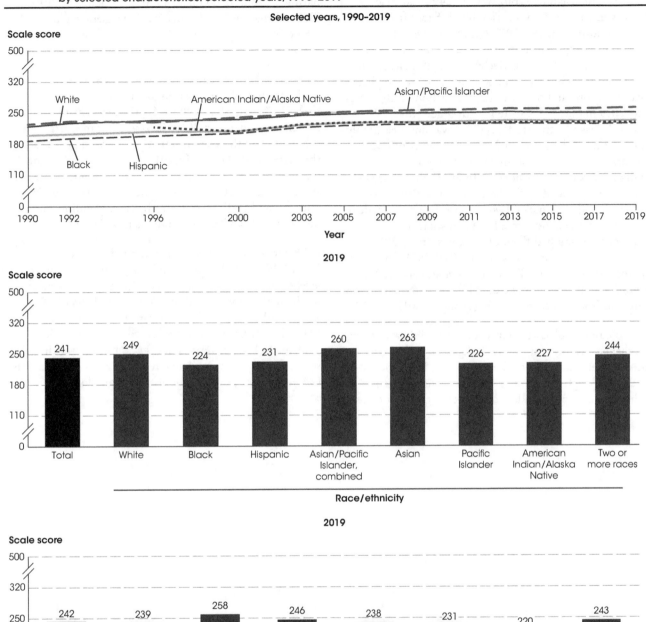

[1] High-poverty schools are defined as schools where 76 to 100 percent of the students are eligible for free or reduced-price lunch (FRPL); mid-high poverty schools are schools where 51 to 75 percent of the students are eligible for FRPL; mid-low poverty schools are schools where 26 to 50 percent of the students are eligible for FRPL; and low-poverty schools are schools where 25 percent or less of the students are eligible for FRPL. For more information on eligibility for FRPL and its relationship to poverty, see the NCES blog post "Free or reduced price lunch: A proxy for poverty?" The nonresponse rate for FRPL was greater than 15 percent but not greater than 50 percent.
NOTE: Includes public and private schools. The mathematics scale scores range from 0 to 500. Scale scores for American Indian/Alaska Native students were suppressed in 1990 and 1992 and for Asian/Pacific Islander students in 2000 because reporting standards were not met (too few cases for a reliable estimate). Testing accommodations (e.g., extended time, small-group testing) for children with disabilities and English language learners were not permitted in 1990 and 1992. Race categories exclude persons of Hispanic ethnicity. Although rounded numbers are displayed, the figures are based on unrounded data.
SOURCE: U.S. Department of Education, National Center for Education Statistics, National Assessment of Educational Progress (NAEP), selected years, 1990–2019 Mathematics Assessments, NAEP Data Explorer. See *Digest of Education Statistics 2019*, tables 222.10 and 222.12.

At grade 4, the average mathematics scores in 2019 for Asian/Pacific Islander (260), White (249), and Black (224) students were not measurably different from the corresponding scores in 2017, but the mathematics score for each group was higher in 2019 than in 1990 (225, 220, and 188, respectively). The 2019 mathematics score for 4th-grade Hispanic students (231) was higher than the scores in both 2017 (229) and 1990 (200). The 2019 mathematics score for 4th-grade American Indian/Alaska Native students (227) was not measurably different from the scores in 2017 and 1996 (1996 was the first year data were available for 4th-grade American Indian/Alaska Native students). In 2011, NAEP began reporting separate data for Asian students, Pacific Islander students, and students of Two or more races.[6] At grade 4, the 2019 mathematics score for Asian students (263) was not measurably different from the score in 2017, but it was higher than the score in 2011 (257). The 2019 mathematics scores for Pacific Islander students (226) and students of Two or more races (244) were not measurably different from the corresponding scores in 2017 and 2011.

In 2019 and in all assessment years since 1990, the average mathematics scores for White students in grade 4 have been higher than those of their Black and Hispanic peers. Although the White-Black and White-Hispanic achievement gaps at grade 4 did not change measurably from 2017 to 2019, the White-Black achievement gap narrowed from 32 points in 1990 to 25 points in 2019. The 4th-grade White-Hispanic achievement gap in 2019 (18 points) was not measurably different from the gap in 1990.

At grade 4, the average mathematics score for male students in 2019 (242) was higher than the scores in both 2017 (241) and 1990 (214). The mathematics score for female students in 2019 (239) was not measurably different from the score in 2017, but it was higher than the score in 1990 (213). In 2019, the mathematics score for 4th-grade male students was 3 points higher than the score for 4th-grade female students; this 3-point gap was not measurably different from the corresponding gaps between male and female students in 2017 and 1990.

NAEP scores can also be disaggregated by students' English language learner (ELL) status and by the poverty level of the school they attended.[7] In 2019, the average mathematics score for 4th-grade ELL students (220) was 24 points lower than the score for their non-ELL peers (243). In 2019, the mathematics score for 4th-grade students in high-poverty schools (231) was lower than the scores for 4th-grade students in mid-high poverty schools (238), mid-low poverty schools (246), and low-poverty schools (258).[8]

Figure 4. Average National Assessment of Educational Progress (NAEP) mathematics scale scores of 8th-grade students, by selected characteristics: Selected years, 1990–2019

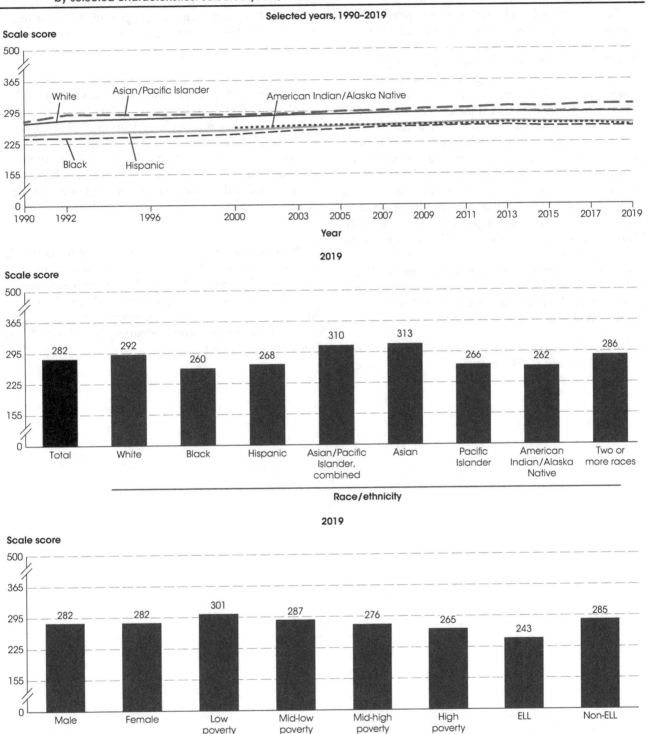

Selected years, 1990–2019

2019

Race/ethnicity

2019

[1] High-poverty schools are defined as schools where 76 to 100 percent of the students are eligible for free or reduced-price lunch (FRPL); mid-high poverty schools are schools where 51 to 75 percent of the students are eligible for FRPL; mid-low poverty schools are schools where 26 to 50 percent of the students are eligible for FRPL; and low-poverty schools are schools where 25 percent or less of the students are eligible for FRPL. For more information on eligibility for FRPL and its relationship to poverty, see the NCES blog post "Free or reduced price lunch: A proxy for poverty?" The nonresponse rate for FRPL was greater than 15 percent but not greater than 50 percent.

NOTE: Includes public and private schools. The mathematics scale scores range from 0 to 500. Scale scores for Asian/Pacific Islander students in 1996 and for American Indian/Alaska Native students in 1990, 1992, and 1996 were suppressed because reporting standards were not met (too few cases for a reliable estimate). Testing accommodations (e.g., extended time, small-group testing) for children with disabilities and English language learners were not permitted in 1990 and 1992. Race categories exclude persons of Hispanic ethnicity. Although rounded numbers are displayed, the figures are based on unrounded data.

SOURCE: U.S. Department of Education, National Center for Education Statistics, National Assessment of Educational Progress (NAEP), selected years, 1990–2019 Mathematics Assessments, NAEP Data Explorer. See *Digest of Education Statistics 2019*, tables 222.10 and 222.12.

At grade 8, the average mathematics scores for Asian/Pacific Islander (310), White (292), Hispanic (268), and Black (260) students in 2019 were not measurably different from the corresponding scores in 2017, but the score for each group was higher in 2019 than in 1990 (275, 270, 246, and 237, respectively). In 2019, the mathematics score for 8th-grade American Indian/Alaska Native students (262) was lower than the score in 2017 (267), but it was not measurably different from the score in 2000 (2000 was the first year data were available for 8th-grade American Indian/Alaska Native students). In 2011, NAEP began reporting separate data for Asian students, Pacific Islander students, and students of Two or more races. At grade 8, the 2019 mathematics score for Asian students (313) was not measurably different from the score in 2017, but it was higher than the score in 2011 (305). The mathematics score for Pacific Islander students (266) in 2019 was lower than the score in 2017 (274), but it was not measurably different from the score in 2011. The 2019 grade 8 mathematics score for students of Two or more races (286) was not measurably different from the scores in 2017 and 2011.

In 2019 and in all assessment years since 1990, the average mathematics scores for White students in grade 8 have been higher than the scores for their Black and Hispanic peers. At grade 8, the White-Black (32 points) and White-Hispanic (24 points) achievement gaps in 2019 were not measurably different from the corresponding gaps in 2017 and 1990.

At grade 8, the average mathematics score for male students in 2019 (282) was lower than the score in 2017 (283) and higher than the score in 1990 (263). The mathematics score for female students in 2019 (282) was not measurably different from the score in 2017, but it was higher than the score in 1990 (262). In 2019 and 1990, the mathematics scores for male and female students were not measurably different from each other; however, male students scored 1 point higher than female students in 2017.

In 2019, the average mathematics score for 8th-grade ELL students (243) was 42 points lower than the score for their non-ELL peers (285). The 2019 mathematics score for 8th-grade students in high-poverty schools (265) was lower than the scores for 8th-grade students in mid-high poverty schools (276), mid-low poverty schools (287), and low-poverty schools (301).[9]

Figure 5. Average National Assessment of Educational Progress (NAEP) mathematics scale scores of 12th-grade students, by selected characteristics: Selected years, 2005–2015

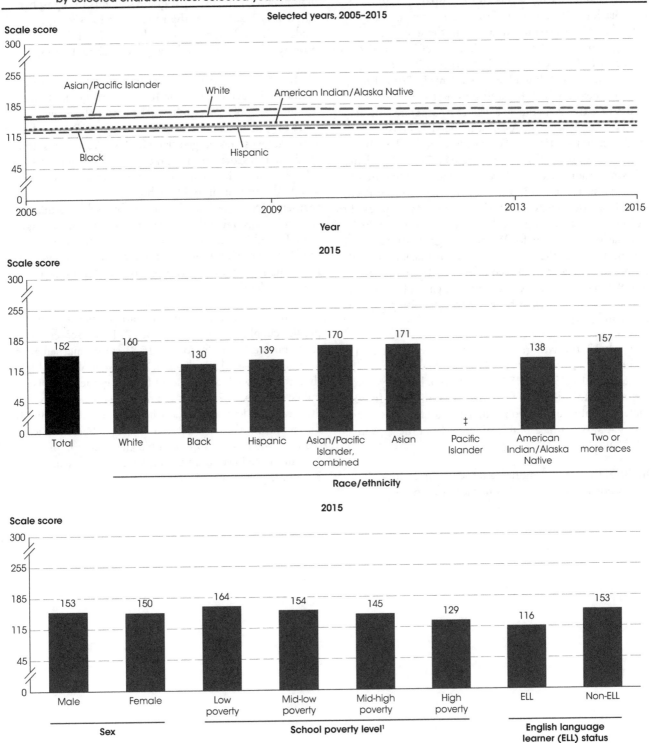

‡ Reporting standards not met. There were too few cases for a reliable estimate.
[1] High-poverty schools are defined as schools where 76 to 100 percent of the students are eligible for free or reduced-price lunch (FRPL); mid-high poverty schools are schools where 51 to 75 percent of the students are eligible for FRPL; mid-low poverty schools are schools where 26 to 50 percent of the students are eligible for FRPL; and low-poverty schools are schools where 25 percent or less of the students are eligible for FRPL. For more information on eligibility for FRPL and its relationship to poverty, see the NCES blog post "Free or reduced price lunch: A proxy for poverty?"
NOTE: Includes public and private schools. The mathematics scale scores range from 0 to 300. Assessment was not conducted for grade 12 in 2007, 2011, and 2017. The most recent mathematics assessment for grade 12 was conducted in 2019; however, data for grade 12 in 2019 were not available in time for publication. In this figure, data for grade 12 come from the 2015 assessment, the most recent NAEP assessment year with available data. Because of major changes to the framework and content of the grade 12 assessment, scores from 2005 and later assessment years cannot be compared with scores from earlier assessment years. Race categories exclude persons of Hispanic ethnicity. Although rounded numbers are displayed, the figures are based on unrounded data.
SOURCE: U.S. Department of Education, National Center for Education Statistics, National Assessment of Educational Progress (NAEP), selected years, 2005–2015 Mathematics Assessments, NAEP Data Explorer. See *Digest of Education Statistics 2019*, tables 222.10 and 222.12.

At grade 12, the average mathematics scores for Asian/ Pacific Islander (170), White (160), Hispanic (139), and Black (130) students in 2015 were not measurably different from the scores in 2013, but the score for each group was higher in 2015 than in 2005 (163, 157, 133, and 127, respectively). The mathematics score for American Indian/Alaska Native students in 2015 (138) was not measurably different from the scores in 2013 and 2005. In 2013, NAEP began reporting separate data at the 12th-grade level for Asian students, Pacific Islander students, and students of Two or more races. The 2015 mathematics scores for Asian students (171) and students of Two or more races (157) were not measurably different from the scores in 2013. The mathematics score for Pacific Islander students was 151 in 2013, but it was suppressed in 2015 because reporting standards were not met. In 2015, the mathematics score for White 12th-grade students was 30 points higher than the score for their Black peers and 22 points higher than the score for their Hispanic peers. The White-Black and White-Hispanic gaps in 2015 were not measurably different from the corresponding gaps in 2005 and 2013.

At grade 12, the average mathematics scores for male (153) and female (150) students in 2015 were lower than the scores in 2013 (155 and 152, respectively), but they were not measurably different from the scores in 2005. In 2015, male students scored 3 points higher than female students. This gap was not measurably different from the gaps in 2005 and 2013.

In 2015, the average mathematics score for 12th-grade ELL students (115) was 37 points lower than the

average score for their non-ELL peers (153). In 2015, the mathematics score for 12th-grade students in high-poverty schools (129) was lower than the scores for 12th-grade students in mid-high poverty schools (145), mid-low poverty schools (154), and low-poverty schools (164).

NAEP results also permit state-level comparisons of the mathematics achievement of 4th- and 8th-grade students in public schools.[10] At grade 4, the national average score for public school students in 2019 was 240, and scores across states ranged from 230 to 248. In 14 states, mathematics scores for 4th-grade students in public schools were higher than the national average score for 4th-grade students in public schools. In 20 states, the mathematics scores for 4th-grade public school students were not measurably different from the national average score for public school students. Mathematics scores in the District of Columbia and the remaining 16 states were lower than the national average score for 4th-grade public school students.

At grade 8, the national average mathematics score for public school students in 2019 was 281, and scores across states ranged from 269 to 294. In 21 states, mathematics scores for 8th-grade students in public schools were higher than the national average score for 8th-grade students in public schools. In 14 states the mathematics scores for 8th-grade students in public schools were not measurably different from the national average score. Mathematics scores in the District of Columbia and the remaining 15 states were lower than the national average score for 8th-grade public school students.

Figure 6. Change in average National Assessment of Educational Progress (NAEP) mathematics scale scores of 4th- and 8th-grade public school students, by state: 2017 to 2019

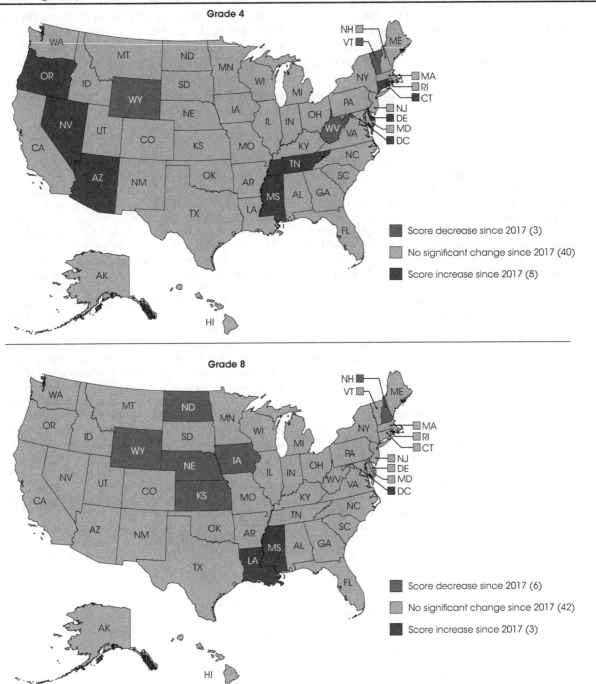

Grade 4

- Score decrease since 2017 (3)
- No significant change since 2017 (40)
- Score increase since 2017 (8)

Grade 8

- Score decrease since 2017 (6)
- No significant change since 2017 (42)
- Score increase since 2017 (3)

NOTE: At grades 4 and 8, the National Assessment of Educational Progress (NAEP) mathematics scale ranges from 0 to 500.
SOURCE: U.S. Department of Education, National Center for Education Statistics, National Assessment of Educational Progress (NAEP), 2017 and 2019 Mathematics Assessments, NAEP Data Explorer. See *Digest of Education Statistics 2019*, tables 222.50 and 222.60.

The average mathematics score for 4th-grade public school students nationally was higher in 2019 than in 2017 (239). Similarly, the mathematics score was higher in 2019 than in 2017 in seven states and the District of Columbia. Grade 4 mathematics scores for public school students were lower in 2019 than in 2017 in three states—Vermont, West Virginia, and Wyoming. For the remaining 40 states, mathematics scores in 2019 were not measurably different from the scores in 2017. At grade 8, the national average mathematics score for public school students in 2019 was lower than the score in 2017 (282). In two states (Louisiana and Mississippi) and the District of Columbia, the mathematics scores for 8th-grade public school students were higher in 2019 than in 2017. In six states, the mathematics scores for 8th-grade public school students were lower in 2019 than in 2017. Mathematics scores in the remaining 42 states showed no measurable change between 2017 and 2019.

Endnotes:

[1] Average scores are reported on a 0–500 scale at grades 4 and 8; however, the scale scores were derived separately and therefore scores cannot be compared across grades.

[2] NAEP achievement-level setting is based on the judgments of a broadly representative panel of teachers, education specialists, and members of the general public. The authorizing legislation for NAEP requires that the achievement levels be used on a trial basis until the Commissioner of the National Center for Education Statistics (NCES) determines that the achievement levels are reasonable, valid, and informative to the public (20 USC § 9622(e)(2)(C)). The NCES Commissioner's determination is to be based on a congressionally mandated, rigorous, and independent evaluation. The latest evaluation of the achievement levels was conducted by a committee convened by the National Academies of Sciences, Engineering, and Medicine in 2016. The evaluation concluded that further evidence should be gathered to determine whether the achievement levels are reasonable, valid, and informative. Accordingly, the NCES Commissioner determined that the trial status of the achievement levels should be maintained at this time. Read more about the NAEP mathematics achievement levels by grade.

[3] This indicator presents data from the Main NAEP mathematics assessment, which is not comparable to the Long-Term Trend NAEP mathematics assessment. The Main NAEP mathematics assessment was first administered in 1990 and assesses student performance at grades 4, 8, and 12, while the Long-Term Trend NAEP mathematics assessment was first administered in 1973 and assesses student performance at ages 9, 13, and 17. In addition, the two assessments differ in the content assessed, how often the assessment is administered, and how the results are reported.

[4] NAEP mathematics scores for 4th-grade students in 2019 had a mean of 241 and a standard deviation (SD) of 32. NAEP mathematics scores for 8th-grade students in 2019 had a mean of 282 and an SD of 40. NAEP mathematics scores for 12th-grade students in 2015 had a mean of 152 and an SD of 34 (retrieved December 20, 2019, from the Main NAEP Data Explorer).

[5] The 2005 mathematics framework for grade 12 introduced changes from the previous framework in order to reflect adjustments in curricular emphases and to ensure an appropriate balance of content. Consequently, the 12th-grade mathematics results in 2005 and subsequent years could not be compared to previous assessments, and a new trend line was established beginning in 2005.

[6] While NAEP reported some data on students of Two or more races for earlier years, the reporting standards changed in 2011.

[7] High-poverty schools are defined as schools where 76 to 100 percent of the students are eligible for free or reduced-price lunch (FRPL); mid-high poverty schools are schools where 51 to 75 percent of the students are eligible for FRPL; mid-low poverty schools are schools where 26 to 50 percent of the students are eligible for FRPL; and low-poverty schools are schools where 25 percent or less of the students are eligible for FRPL.

[8] Nonresponse rate for this variable was greater than 15 percent but not greater than 50 percent.

[9] Nonresponse rate for this variable was greater than 15 percent but not greater than 50 percent.

[10] NAEP results serve as a common metric for all states and selected urban districts and are not comparable to results from assessments administered by state education agencies.

Reference tables: *Digest of Education Statistics 2019,* tables 222.10, 222.12, 222.50, 222.60, and 222.77

Related indicators and resources: Absenteeism and Achievement [*Status and Trends in the Education of Racial and Ethnic Groups*]; International Comparisons: Reading, Mathematics, and Science Literacy of 15-Year-Old Students; International Comparisons: U.S. 4th-, 8th-, and 12th-Graders' Mathematics and Science Achievement; Mathematics Achievement [*Status and Trends in the Education of Racial and Ethnic Groups*]; Reading and Mathematics Score Trends [*web-only*]; Reading Performance; Science Performance; Technology and Engineering Literacy [*web-only*]

Glossary: Achievement gap; Achievement levels, NAEP; English language learner (ELL); Public school or institution; Racial/ethnic group

Science Performance

The percentage of 4th-grade students scoring at or above the Proficient *level was higher in 2015 (38 percent) than in 2009 (34 percent), according to data from the National Assessment of Educational Progress. In addition, the percentage of 8th-grade students scoring at or above the* Proficient *level was higher in 2015 (34 percent) than in 2009 (30 percent). The percentage of 12th-grade students scoring at or above the* Proficient *level in 2015 (22 percent) was not measurably different from the percentage in 2009.*

The National Assessment of Educational Progress (NAEP) assesses student performance in science at grades 4, 8, and 12 in both public and private schools across the nation. The NAEP science assessment was designed to measure students' knowledge of three content areas: physical science, life science, and Earth and space sciences. NAEP science scores range from 0 to 300 for all three grades. NAEP achievement levels define what students should know and be able to do: *Basic* indicates partial mastery of fundamental skills, and *Proficient* indicates solid academic performance and competency over challenging subject matter. The most recent science assessments were conducted in 2015 for grades 4, 8, and 12. Prior to 2015, grades 4 and 12 were last assessed in 2009 while grade 8 was assessed in 2011 and 2009.[1]

Figure 1. Average National Assessment of Educational Progress (NAEP) science scale scores of 4th-, 8th-, and 12th-grade students: 2009, 2011, and 2015

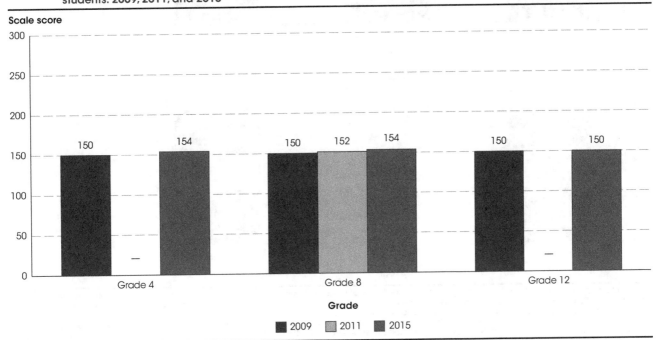

Scale score

— Not available.
NOTE: Includes public and private schools. Scale ranges from 0 to 300 for all grades, but scores cannot be compared across grades. Assessment was not conducted for grades 4 and 12 in 2011.
SOURCE: U.S. Department of Education, National Center for Education Statistics, National Assessment of Educational Progress (NAEP), 2009, 2011, and 2015 Science Assessment, NAEP Data Explorer. See *Digest of Education Statistics 2016*, table 223.10.

In 2015, the average 4th-grade science score (154) was higher than the score in 2009 (150). The average 8th-grade science score in 2015 (154) was higher than the scores in both 2009 (150) and 2011 (152). The average 12th-grade science score in 2015 (150) was not measurably different from the score in 2009.

Figure 2. Percentage distribution of 4th-, 8th-, and 12th-grade students across National Assessment of Educational Progress (NAEP) science achievement levels: 2009, 2011, and 2015

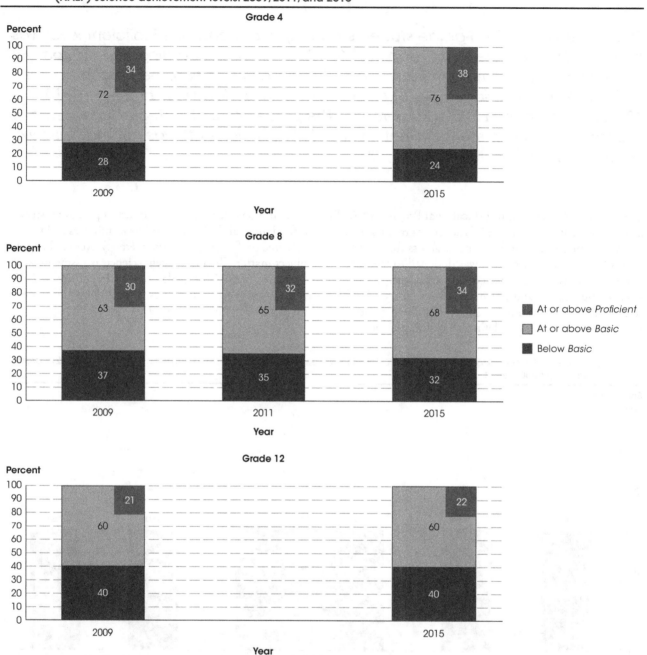

NOTE: Includes public and private schools. Achievement levels define what students should know and be able to do: *Basic* indicates partial mastery of fundamental skills, and *Proficient* indicates solid academic performance and competency over challenging subject matter. Assessment was not conducted for grades 4 and 12 in 2011. Detail may not sum to totals because of rounding.
SOURCE: U.S. Department of Education, National Center for Education Statistics, National Assessment of Educational Progress (NAEP), 2009, 2011, and 2015 Science Assessment, NAEP Data Explorer. See *Digest of Education Statistics 2016*, table 223.10.

In 2015, about 76 percent of 4th-grade students performed at or above the *Basic* achievement level in science, and 38 percent performed at or above the *Proficient* level. These percentages were higher than the corresponding 2009 percentages for at or above *Basic* (72 percent) and at or above *Proficient* (34 percent). Among 8th-grade students in 2015, about 68 percent performed at or above *Basic* in science, and 34 percent performed at or above *Proficient*. The percentage performing at or above *Basic*

was higher in 2015 than in both 2009 (63 percent) and 2011 (65 percent), and the percentage performing at or above *Proficient* was also higher in 2015 than in 2009 (30 percent) and 2011 (32 percent). The percentages of 12th-grade students in 2015 performing at or above *Basic* (60 percent) and at or above *Proficient* (22 percent) were not measurably different from the corresponding percentages in 2009.

Figure 3. Average National Assessment of Educational Progress (NAEP) science scale scores of 4th-, 8th-, and 12th-grade students, by race/ethnicity: 2009, 2011, and 2015

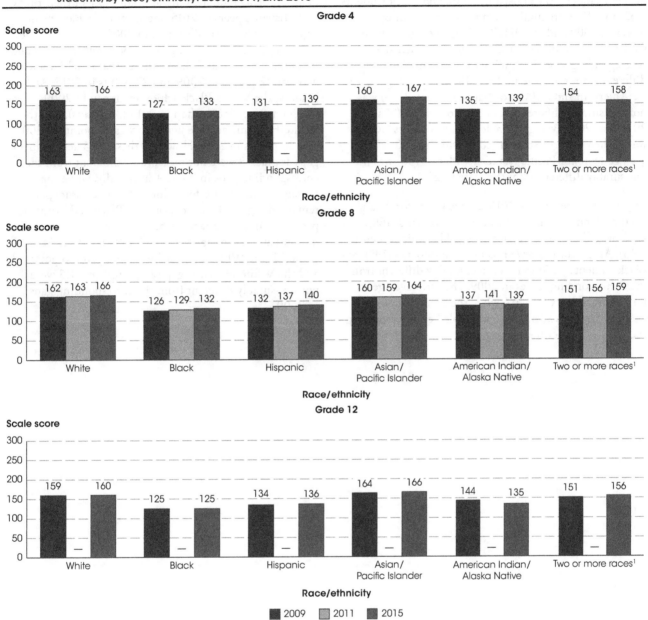

— Not available.
[1] In 2009, students in the "Two or more races" category were categorized as "Unclassified."
NOTE: Includes public and private schools. Scale ranges from 0 to 300 for all grades, but scores cannot be compared across grades. Assessment was not conducted for grades 4 and 12 in 2011. Race categories exclude persons of Hispanic ethnicity.
SOURCE: U.S. Department of Education, National Center for Education Statistics, National Assessment of Educational Progress (NAEP), 2009, 2011, and 2015 Science Assessment, NAEP Data Explorer. See *Digest of Education Statistics 2016*, table 223.10.

At grade 4, the average scores for Asian/Pacific Islander students (167), White students (166), students of Two or more races[2] (158), Hispanic students (139), American Indian/Alaska Native students (139), and Black students (133) in 2015 were higher than the corresponding scores in 2009. Starting in 2011, separate data for Asian and Pacific Islander students were collected. In 2015, the first year that data for these students were available at grade 4, the average score was 169 for Asian students and 143 for Pacific Islander students.

At grade 8, the average scores for White (166), Asian/Pacific Islander (164), Hispanic (140), and Black students (132) in 2015 were higher than the corresponding scores in 2009 and in 2011. The 2015 average score for students of Two or more races (159) was higher than the corresponding score in 2009 but was not measurably different from the score in 2011. The 2015 average score for American Indian/Alaska Native students (139) was not measurably different from the scores in 2009 and 2011. The 2015 average score for Asian students (166) was higher than the score in 2011, while the 2015 average score for Pacific Islander students (138) was not measurably different from the score in 2011.

At grade 12, the average 2015 science scores for Asian/Pacific Islander students (166), White students (160), students of Two or more races (156), Hispanic students (136), American Indian/Alaska Native students (135), and Black students (125) were not measurably different from the corresponding scores in 2009. The 2015 average score for Asian students was 167, while the average score for Pacific Islander students is unavailable because reporting standards were not met.

While the average science scores for White 4th- and 8th-grade students remained higher than those of their Black and Hispanic peers in 2015, racial/ethnic achievement gaps in 2015 were smaller than in 2009. At grade 4, the White-Black achievement gap was 36 points in 2009 and 33 points in 2015, and the White-Hispanic achievement gap was 32 points in 2009 and 27 points in 2015. At grade 8, the White-Black achievement gap in 2009 (36 points) was larger than in 2015 (34 points), and the White-Hispanic achievement gap was 30 points in 2009 and 26 points in 2015. However, these 2015 achievement gaps at grade 8 were not measurably different from the corresponding gaps in 2011. Additionally, while the average science scores for White 12th-grade students remained higher than those of their Black and Hispanic peers in 2015, these racial/ethnic achievement gaps did not measurably change between 2009 and 2015. At grade 12, the White-Black achievement gap (36 points) and the White-Hispanic gap (24 points) in 2015 were not measurably different from the corresponding gaps in 2009.

Figure 4. Average National Assessment of Educational Progress (NAEP) science scale scores of 4th-, 8th-, and 12th-grade students, by sex: 2009, 2011, and 2015

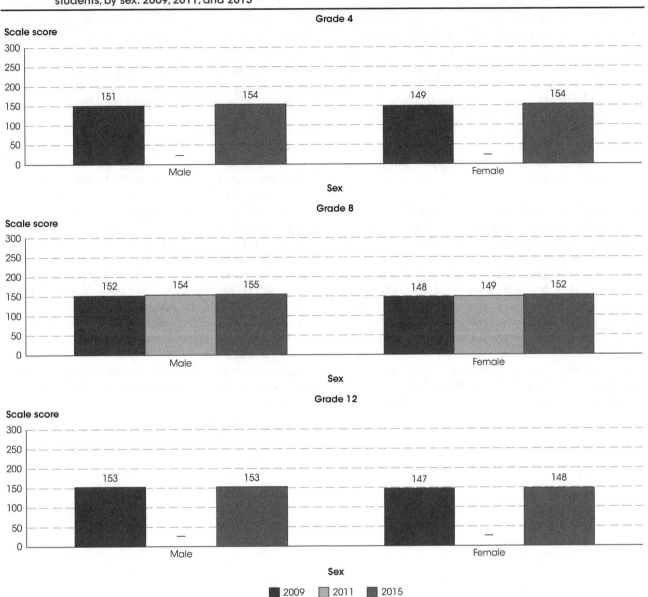

— Not available.
NOTE: Includes public and private schools. Scale ranges from 0 to 300 for all grades, but scores cannot be compared across grades. Assessment was not conducted for grades 4 and 12 in 2011.
SOURCE: U.S. Department of Education, National Center for Education Statistics, National Assessment of Educational Progress (NAEP), 2009, 2011, and 2015 Science Assessment, NAEP Data Explorer. See *Digest of Education Statistics 2016*, table 223.10.

The average science score for male 4th-grade students in 2015 (154) was higher than the score in 2009 (151). The average score for female 4th-grade students was also higher in 2015 (154) than in 2009 (149). While there was a 1-point gap between male and female 4th-grade students in 2009, there was no measurable gender gap in 2015. The average science score for male 8th-grade students in 2015 (155) was higher than the scores in 2009 (152) and 2011 (154). Similarly, for female 8th-grade students, the average score in 2015 (152) was higher than the scores in 2009 (148) and 2011 (149). In 2015, 2011,

and 2009, the average science score for male 8th-grade students was higher than that of their female peers. The 3-point score gap between male and female 8th-graders in 2015 was smaller than the gap in 2011 (5 points) but not measurably different from the gap in 2009. Average science scores in 2015 for 12th-grade male (153) and female (148) students were not measurably different from the corresponding scores in 2009. In addition, the 5-point gender gap among 12th-grade students in 2015 was not measurably different from the gap in 2009.

Since 2009, the average science scores for English language learner (ELL) 4th- and 8th-grade students were lower than their non-ELL peers' scores. At grade 4, the achievement gap between non-ELL and ELL students was larger in 2009 (39 points) than in 2015 (36 points). At grade 8, the 2015 achievement gap (46 points) was not measurably different from the gaps in 2009 and 2011. At grade 12, the average scores for non-ELL students in 2015 (152) and 2009 (151) were higher than their ELL peers' scores in those years (105 and 104, respectively). The 47-point achievement gap between non-ELL and ELL 12th-grade students in 2015 was not measurably different from the gap in 2009.

In 2015, the average science score for 4th-grade students in high-poverty schools (134) was lower than the average scores for 4th-grade students in mid-high poverty schools (151), mid-low poverty schools (161), and low-poverty schools (172).[3] At grade 8, the average 2015 science score for students in high-poverty schools (134) was lower than the average scores for students in mid-high poverty schools (150), mid-low poverty schools (161), and low-poverty schools (170). At grade 4, the 2015 achievement gap between students at high-poverty schools and low-poverty schools (38 points) was lower than the gap in 2009 (41 points). At grade 8, the 2015 achievement gap (36 points) was lower than the gap in 2009 (41 points)

but was not measurably different from the gap in 2011. At grade 12 in 2015, the average science score for students in high-poverty schools (126) was lower than the average scores for those in mid-high poverty schools (143), mid-low poverty schools (154), and low-poverty schools (165). The achievement gap between students at high-poverty schools and low-poverty schools was 39 points in 2015, which was not measurably different from the gap in 2009.

NAEP results also permit state-level comparisons of the science performance of 4th- and 8th-grade students in public schools. Forty-six states[4] participated in the NAEP science assessment in 2015, and average scores varied across the states for both grades. At grade 4, the national public school average score was 153, and state average scores ranged from 140 to 165. Twenty-two states had average scores that were higher than the national average, 15 states had average scores that were not measurably different from the national average, and 9 states had average scores that were lower than the national average. At grade 8, the 2015 national public school average score was also 153, and state average scores ranged from 140 to 166. Twenty-six states had average scores that were higher than the national average, 6 states had average scores that were not measurably different from the national average, and 14 states had scores that were lower than the national average.

Figure 5. Change in average National Assessment of Educational Progress (NAEP) science scale scores of 4th- and 8th-grade public school students, by state: 2009 and 2015

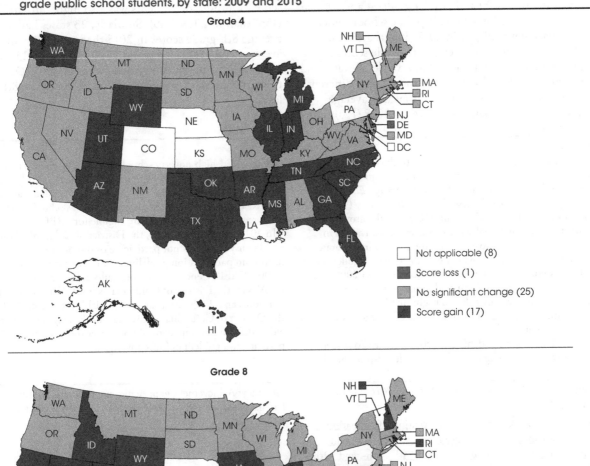

Grade 4

Not applicable (8)
Score loss (1)
No significant change (25)
Score gain (17)

Grade 8

Not applicable (8)
Score loss (0)
No significant change (20)
Score gain (23)

NOTE: Scale ranges from 0 to 300 for all grades, but scores cannot be compared across grades. "Gain" is defined as a significant increase from 2009 to 2015, "no change" is defined as no significant change from 2009 to 2015, and "loss" is defined as a significant decrease from 2009 to 2015.
SOURCE: U.S. Department of Education, National Center for Education Statistics, National Assessment of Educational Progress (NAEP), 2009 and 2015 Science Assessment, NAEP Data Explorer. See *Digest of Education Statistics 2016*, table 223.20.

Forty-three states participated in the NAEP science assessment in both 2009 and 2015 at grades 4 and 8.[5] The average science score for 4th-grade public school students across the nation was higher in 2015 (153) than in 2009 (149). Seventeen states had average 4th-grade scores that were also higher in 2015 than in 2009, while 25 states had average scores in 2015 that were not measurably different from their average scores in 2009. Delaware's average score for 4th-grade students was lower in 2015 (150) than in 2009 (153). The national public school average science score for 8th-grade students was also higher in 2015 (153) than in 2009 (149). Similarly, 23 states had higher average 8th-grade scores in 2015 than in 2009, while average scores for the remaining 20 states in 2015 were not measurably different from their scores in 2009. During this time, no state experienced a score loss at the 8th-grade level.

Endnotes:

[1] In 2009, a new science framework was introduced at all grade levels. A variety of factors made it necessary to create a new framework: the publication of *National Science Education Standards* (1996) and *Benchmarks for Scientific Literacy* (1993), advances in both science and cognitive research, the growth in national and international science assessments, advances in innovative assessment approaches, and the need to incorporate accommodations so that the widest possible range of students can be fairly assessed. Consequently, the science results in 2009 and subsequent years cannot be compared to previous assessments, and a new trend line was established beginning in 2009.

[2] In 2009, students in the "Two or more races" category were categorized as "Unclassified."

[3] High-poverty schools are defined as schools where 76 percent or more of students are eligible for free or reduced-price lunch (FRPL). Mid-high poverty schools are schools where 51 to 75 percent of students are eligible for FRPL, and mid-low poverty schools are schools where 26 to 50 percent of students are eligible for FRPL. Low-poverty schools are defined as schools where 25 percent or less of students are eligible for FRPL.

[4] In 2015, Alaska, Colorado, the District of Columbia, Louisiana, and Pennsylvania did not participate or did not meet the minimum participation guidelines for reporting at grades 4 and 8.

[5] 2009 NAEP science assessment results are not available for Alaska, the District of Columbia, Kansas, Nebraska, and Vermont, and 2015 results are not available for Alaska, Colorado, the District of Columbia, Louisiana, and Pennsylvania. States either did not participate or did not meet the minimum participation guidelines for reporting.

Reference tables: *Digest of Education Statistics 2016*, tables 223.10 and 223.20

Related indicators and resources: International Comparisons: Reading, Mathematics, and Science Literacy of 15-Year-Old Students; International Comparisons: U.S. 4th-, 8th-, and 12th-Graders' Mathematics and Science Achievement; Mathematics Performance; Reading Performance; Technology and Engineering Literacy [*web-only*]

Glossary: Achievement gap; Achievement levels, NAEP; English language learners (ELL); Public school or institution; Racial/ethnic group

Public High School Graduation Rates

In school year 2017–18, the national adjusted cohort graduation rate (ACGR) for public high school students was 85 percent, the highest it has been since the rate was first measured in 2010–11. Asian/Pacific Islander students had the highest ACGR (92 percent), followed by White (89 percent), Hispanic (81 percent), Black (79 percent), and American Indian/Alaska Native (74 percent) students.

This indicator examines the percentage of U.S. public high school students who graduate on time, as measured by the adjusted cohort graduation rate (ACGR). In this indicator, the United States includes public schools in the 50 states and the District of Columbia, except for the Bureau of Indian Education schools. State education agencies calculate the ACGR by identifying the "cohort" of first-time ninth-graders in a particular school year.

The cohort is then adjusted by adding any students who immigrate from another country or transfer into the cohort after 9th grade and subtracting any students who transfer out, emigrate to another country, or die. The ACGR is the percentage of students in this adjusted cohort who graduate within 4 years with a regular high school diploma. The U.S. Department of Education first collected the ACGR in 2010–11.

Figure 1. Adjusted cohort graduation rate (ACGR) for public high school students, by state: 2017–18

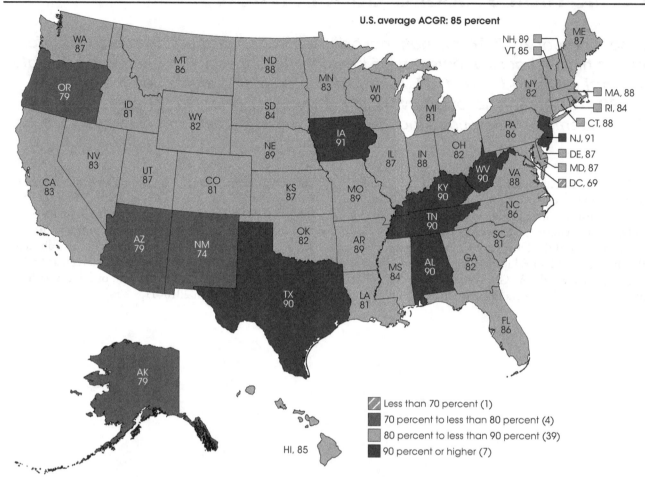

NOTE: The ACGR is the percentage of public high school freshmen who graduate with a regular diploma within 4 years of starting ninth grade. The Bureau of Indian Education and Puerto Rico are not included in the U.S. average ACGR. The graduation rates displayed above have been rounded to whole numbers. Categorizations are based on unrounded percentages.
SOURCE: U.S. Department of Education, Office of Elementary and Secondary Education, Consolidated State Performance Report, 2017–18. See *Digest of Education Statistics 2019*, table 219.46.

The U.S. average ACGR for public high school students increased over the first 8 years it was collected, from 79 percent in 2010–11 to 85 percent in 2017–18. In 2017–18, the ACGR ranged from 69 percent in the District of Columbia to 91 percent in Iowa. More than three-quarters of the states (39) reported ACGRs from 80 percent to less than 90 percent.[1]

Figure 2. Adjusted cohort graduation rate (ACGR) for public high school students, by race/ethnicity: 2017–18

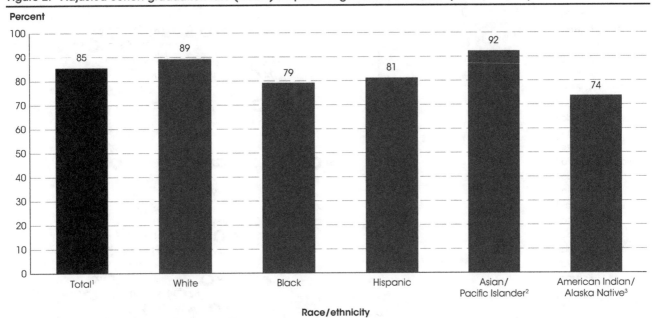

In 2017–18, the ACGRs for American Indian/Alaska Native² (74 percent), Black (79 percent), and Hispanic (81 percent) public high school students were below the U.S. average of 85 percent. The ACGRs for White (89 percent) and Asian/Pacific Islander³ (92 percent) students were above the U.S. average. Across states, the ACGRs for White students ranged from 79 percent in New Mexico to 95 percent in New Jersey, and were higher than the U.S. average ACGR of 85 percent in 39 states and the District of Columbia. The rates for Black students ranged from 67 percent in the District of Columbia to 88 percent in Alabama. Arkansas, West Virginia, Texas, and Alabama were the only four states in which the rates for Black students were higher than the U.S. average ACGR. The ACGRs for Hispanic students ranged from 65 percent in the District of Columbia to 92 percent in West Virginia, and they were higher than the U.S. average ACGR in five states (Florida, Arkansas, Alabama, Texas, and West Virginia). For Asian/Pacific Islander students, ACGRs ranged from 72 percent in Vermont to 95 percent or higher in Delaware, Indiana, Kentucky, Tennessee, Florida, West Virginia, Connecticut, Texas, Maryland, and New Jersey, and they were higher than the U.S. average ACGR in 45 states and the District of Columbia. The ACGRs for American Indian/Alaska Native students ranged from 50 percent in South Dakota to 90 percent in Alabama, Maryland, and Tennessee, and were higher than the U.S. average ACGR in nine states (Mississippi, Missouri, New Jersey, West Virginia, Kentucky, Louisiana, Alabama, Maryland, and Tennessee).[4]

Figure 3. Adjusted cohort graduation rate (ACGR) of White and Black public high school students, by state: 2017–18

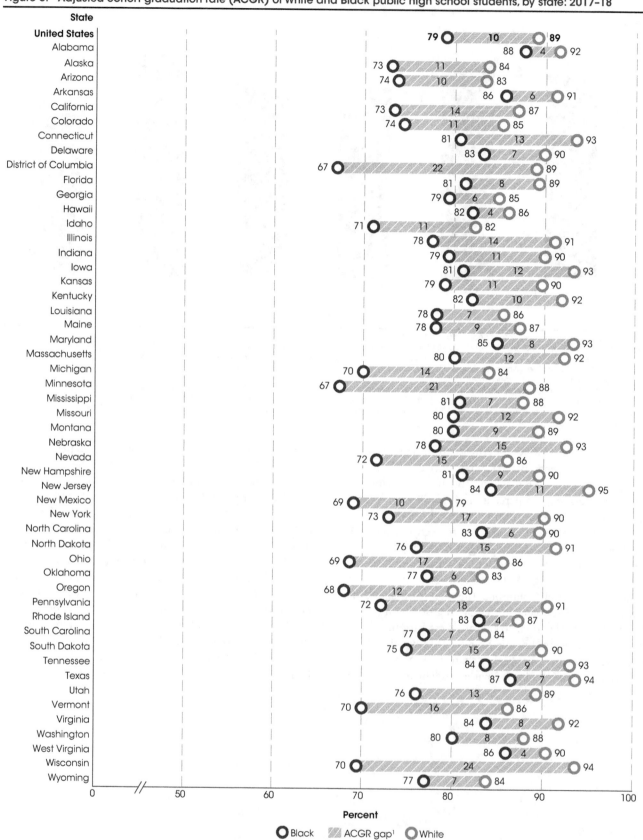

[1] The graduation rate gaps are calculated using the most precise graduation rates available for public use, which include some rates rounded to one decimal place and some rates rounded to whole numbers. These gaps may vary slightly from those that would be calculated using unrounded rates.
NOTE: The ACGR is the percentage of public high school freshmen who graduate with a regular diploma within 4 years of starting ninth grade. The Bureau of Indian Education and Puerto Rico are not included in the U.S. average ACGR. Race categories exclude persons of Hispanic ethnicity.
SOURCE: U.S. Department of Education, Office of Elementary and Secondary Education, Consolidated State Performance Report, 2017–18. See *Digest of Education Statistics 2019*, table 219.46.

The Condition of Education 2020 | **102**

The U.S. average ACGR for White public high school students (89 percent) was 10 percentage points higher than the U.S. average ACGR for their Black peers (79 percent) in 2017–18.[5] White students had higher ACGRs than Black students in every state and the District of Columbia. Minnesota, the District of Columbia, and Wisconsin reported the largest gaps between the ACGRs for White and Black students (21 percentage points, 22 percentage points, and 24 percentage points, respectively).

Figure 4. Adjusted cohort graduation rate (ACGR) of White and Hispanic public high school students, by state: 2017-18

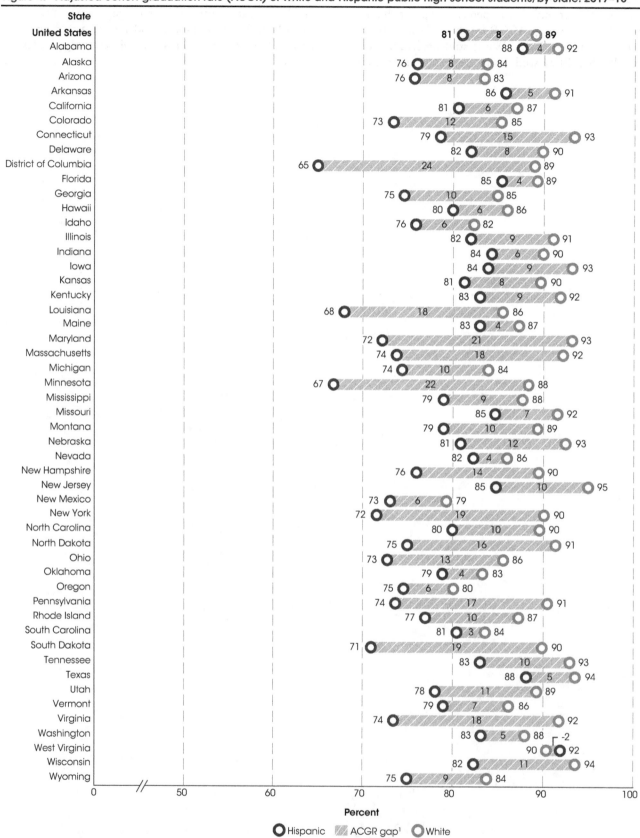

¹ The graduation rate gaps are calculated using the most precise graduation rates available for public use, which include some rates rounded to one decimal place and some rates rounded to whole numbers. These gaps may vary slightly from those that would be calculated using unrounded rates.
NOTE: The ACGR is the percentage of public high school freshmen who graduate with a regular diploma within 4 years of starting ninth grade. The Bureau of Indian Education and Puerto Rico are not included in the U.S. average ACGR. Race categories exclude persons of Hispanic ethnicity.
SOURCE: U.S. Department of Education, Office of Elementary and Secondary Education, Consolidated State Performance Report, 2017-18. See *Digest of Education Statistics 2019*, table 219.46.

The U.S. average ACGR for White students (89 percent) was 8 percentage points higher than the U.S. average ACGR for Hispanic students (81 percent) in 2017–18. The ACGRs for White students were higher than the ACGRs for Hispanic students in every state and the District of Columbia except for West Virginia, where the ACGR for Hispanic students was higher than the ACGR for White students (92 vs. 90 percent). The District of Columbia reported the largest gap between the ACGRs for White and Hispanic students (24 percentage points).

Endnotes:

[1] Based on unrounded graduation rates.

[2] Estimated assuming a count of zero American Indian/Alaska Native students for Hawaii.

[3] Reporting practices for data on Asian and Pacific Islander students vary by state. Asian/Pacific Islander data in this indicator represent either the value reported by the state for the "Asian/Pacific Islander" group or an aggregation of separate values reported by the state for "Asian" and "Pacific Islander." "Asian/Pacific Islander" includes the "Filipino" group, which only California and Hawaii report separately.

[4] Discussion of ACGRs for American Indian/Alaska Native students excludes data for the District of Columbia, Hawaii, and Vermont. The American Indian/Alaska Native data are suppressed for the District of Columbia and Vermont to protect student privacy and are unavailable for Hawaii.

[5] Percentage point gaps are calculated using the most precise graduation rates available for public use, which include some rates rounded to one decimal place and some rates rounded to whole numbers to protect student privacy. These gaps may vary slightly from those that would be calculated using unrounded rates.

Reference tables: *Digest of Education Statistics 2019*, table 219.46

Related indicators and resources: Educational Attainment of Young Adults; High School Status Completion Rates [*Status and Trends in the Education of Racial and Ethnic Groups*]; Status Dropout Rates; *Trends in High School Dropout and Completion Rates in the United States*

Glossary: Adjusted Cohort Graduation Rate (ACGR); Gap; High school completer; High school diploma; Public school or institution; Racial/ethnic group

Status Dropout Rates

The overall status dropout rate decreased from 9.7 percent in 2006 to 5.3 percent in 2018. During this time, the Hispanic status dropout rate decreased from 21.0 to 8.0 percent, the Black status dropout rate decreased from 11.5 to 6.4 percent, and the White status dropout rate decreased from 6.4 to 4.2 percent. Nevertheless, in 2018, the Hispanic (8.0 percent) and Black (6.4 percent) status dropout rates remained higher than the White (4.2 percent) status dropout rate.

The *status dropout rate* represents the percentage of 16- to 24-year-olds who are not enrolled in school and have not earned a high school credential (either a diploma or an equivalency credential such as a GED certificate). In this indicator, status dropout rates are based on data from the American Community Survey (ACS). The ACS is an annual survey that covers a broad population, including individuals living in households as well as individuals living in *noninstitutionalized group quarters* (such as college or military housing) and *institutionalized group quarters* (such as correctional or health care facilities).[1] In 2018, there were 2.1 million status dropouts between the ages of 16 and 24, and the overall status dropout rate was 5.3 percent.

Figure 1. Status dropout rates of 16- to 24-year-olds, by race/ethnicity: 2006 through 2018

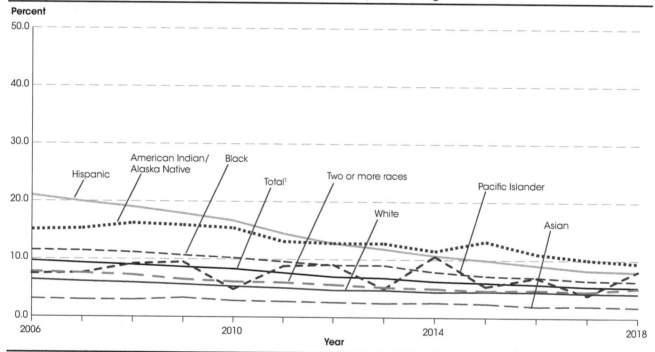

[1] Includes other racial/ethnic categories not separately shown.
NOTE: The status dropout rate is the percentage of 16- to 24-year-olds who are not enrolled in school and have not earned a high school credential (either a diploma or an equivalency credential such as a GED certificate). Data are based on sample surveys of persons living in households, noninstitutionalized group quarters (including college and university housing, military quarters, facilities for workers and religious groups, and temporary shelters for the homeless), and institutionalized group quarters (including adult and juvenile correctional facilities, nursing facilities, and other health care facilities). Race categories exclude persons of Hispanic ethnicity.
SOURCE: U.S. Department of Commerce, Census Bureau, American Community Survey (ACS), 2006 through 2018. See *Digest of Education Statistics 2019*, table 219.80.

The status dropout rate varied by race/ethnicity in 2018. The status dropout rate for Asian 16- to 24-year-olds (1.9 percent) was lower than the rates for their peers who were White (4.2 percent), of Two or more races (5.2 percent), Black (6.4 percent), Hispanic (8.0 percent), Pacific Islander (8.1 percent), and American Indian/Alaska Native (9.5 percent). In addition, the status dropout rate for those who were White was lower than that of every other racial/ethnic group except those who were Asian. The status dropout rate for those who were Hispanic was higher than that of most racial/ethnic groups, but was not measurably different from the rates for those who were Pacific Islander and American Indian/Alaska Native.

The overall status dropout rate decreased from 9.7 percent in 2006 to 5.3 percent in 2018. During this time, the status dropout rate declined for 16- to 24-year-olds who were Hispanic (from 21.0 to 8.0 percent), American Indian/Alaska Native (from 15.1 to 9.5 percent), Black (from 11.5 to 6.4 percent), of Two or more races (from 7.8 to 5.2 percent), White (from 6.4 to 4.2 percent), and Asian (from 3.1 to 1.9 percent). In contrast, there was no measurable difference between the status dropout rate in 2006 and 2018 for those who were Pacific Islander.

In each year from 2006 to 2018, the status dropout rate for Hispanic 16- to 24-year-olds was higher than the rate for those who were Black, and the rates for both groups were higher than the rate for those who were White. Between 2006 and 2018, the gap in status dropout rates between those who were Hispanic and those who were White decreased from 14.6 percentage points to 3.8 percentage points and the gap between those who were Black and those who were White decreased from 5.2 percentage points to 2.1 percentage points. During the same period, the gap between those who were Hispanic and those who were Black decreased from 9.5 percentage points to 1.7 percentage points.

Figure 2. Status dropout rates of 16- to 24-year-olds, by race/ethnicity and sex: 2018

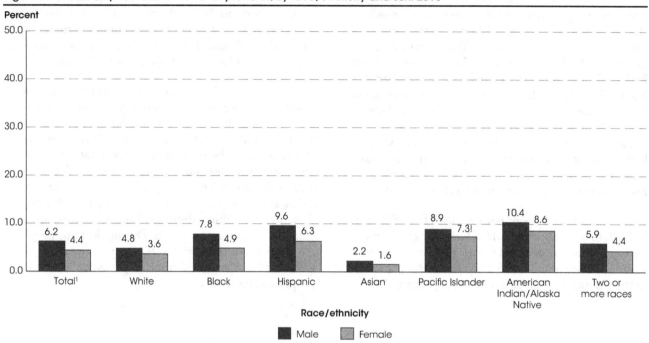

! Interpret data with caution. The coefficient of variation (CV) for this estimate is between 30 and 50 percent.
[1] Includes respondents who wrote in some other race that was not included as an option on the questionnaire.
NOTE: The status dropout rate is the percentage of 16- to 24-year-olds who are not enrolled in school and have not earned a high school credential (either a diploma or an equivalency credential such as a GED certificate). Data are based on sample surveys of persons living in households, noninstitutionalized group quarters (including college and university housing, military quarters, facilities for workers and religious groups, and temporary shelters for the homeless), and institutionalized group quarters (including adult and juvenile correctional facilities, nursing facilities, and other health care facilities). Race categories exclude persons of Hispanic ethnicity. Although rounded numbers are displayed, the figures are based on unrounded data.
SOURCE: U.S. Department of Commerce, Census Bureau, American Community Survey (ACS), 2018. See *Digest of Education Statistics 2019*, table 219.80.

The status dropout rate was higher for male 16- to 24-year-olds than for female 16- to 24-year-olds overall (6.2 vs. 4.4 percent) and within most racial/ethnic groups in 2018. Status dropout rates were higher for males than for females among those who were White (4.8 vs. 3.6 percent), Black (7.8 vs. 4.9 percent), Hispanic (9.6 vs. 6.3 percent), Asian (2.3 vs. 1.6 percent), and of Two or more races (5.9 vs. 4.4 percent). However, there were no measurable differences in status dropout rates between males and females for those who were Pacific Islander or American Indian/Alaska Native. The size of the male-female gap also differed by race/ethnicity. The male-female gaps for those who were Hispanic (3.3 percentage points) and Black (2.9 percentage points) were higher than the male-female gaps for those who were of Two or more races (1.6 percentage points), White (1.1 percentage points), and Asian (0.7 percentage points).

Figure 3. Status dropout rates of U.S.-born and foreign-born 16- to 24-year-olds, by race/ethnicity: 2018

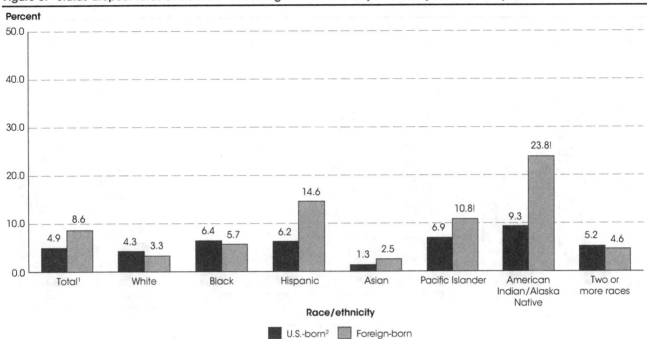

! Interpret data with caution. The coefficient of variation (CV) for this estimate is between 30 and 50 percent.
[1] Includes respondents who wrote in some other race that was not included as an option on the questionnaire.
[2] Includes those born in the 50 states, the District of Columbia, Puerto Rico, American Samoa, Guam, the U.S. Virgin Islands, and the Northern Marianas, as well as those born abroad to U.S.-citizen parents.
NOTE: The status dropout rate is the percentage of 16- to 24-year-olds who are not enrolled in school and have not earned a high school credential (either a diploma or an equivalency credential such as a GED certificate). Data are based on sample surveys of persons living in households, noninstitutionalized group quarters (including college and university housing, military quarters, facilities for workers and religious groups, and temporary shelters for the homeless), and institutionalized group quarters (including adult and juvenile correctional facilities, nursing facilities, and other health care facilities). Race categories exclude persons of Hispanic ethnicity.
SOURCE: U.S. Department of Commerce, Census Bureau, American Community Survey (ACS), 2018. See *Digest of Education Statistics 2019*, table 219.80.

Overall, U.S.-born 16- to 24-year-olds[2] had a lower status dropout rate in 2018 than their foreign-born peers (4.9 vs. 8.6 percent). Differences in status dropout rates between U.S.- and foreign-born individuals varied by race/ethnicity. The status dropout rate for Hispanic individuals born in the United States was 8.3 percentage points lower than the rate for their peers born outside of the United States (6.2 and 14.6 percent, respectively). The status dropout rate for Asian individuals born in the United States was 1.2 percentage points lower than the rate for their peers

born outside of the United States (1.3 and 2.5 percent, respectively). However, White individuals born in the United States had a higher status dropout rate (4.3 percent) than did their peers born outside of the United States (3.3 percent). The status dropout rates for U.S.-born individuals who were Black, Pacific Islander, American Indian/Alaska Native, and of Two or more races were not measurably different from the rates for their foreign-born peers.

Figure 4. Status dropout rates of 16- to 24-year-olds, by race/ethnicity and noninstitutionalized or institutionalized status: 2018

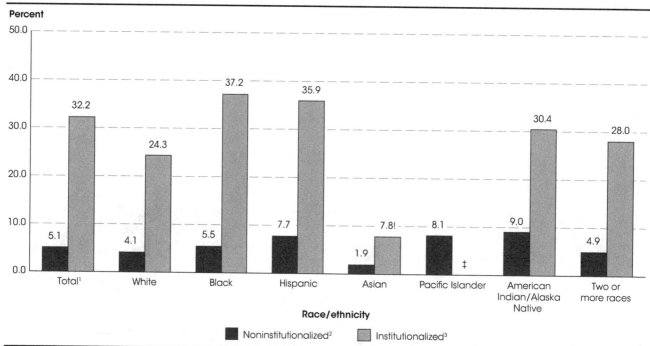

! Interpret data with caution. The coefficient of variation (CV) for this estimate is between 30 and 50 percent.
‡ Reporting standards not met. Either there are too few cases for a reliable estimate or the coefficient of variation (CV) is 50 percent or greater.
[1] Includes respondents who wrote in some other race that was not included as an option on the questionnaire.
[2] Includes persons living in households as well as persons living in noninstitutionalized group quarters. Noninstitutionalized group quarters include college and university housing, military quarters, facilities for workers and religious groups, and temporary shelters for the homeless.
[3] Includes persons living in institutionalized group quarters, including adult and juvenile correctional facilities, nursing facilities, and other health care facilities.
NOTE: The status dropout rate is the percentage of 16- to 24-year-olds who are not enrolled in school and have not earned a high school credential (either a diploma or an equivalency credential such as a GED certificate). Data are based on sample surveys of persons living in households, noninstitutionalized group quarters, and institutionalized group quarters. Race categories exclude persons of Hispanic ethnicity.
SOURCE: U.S. Department of Commerce, Census Bureau, American Community Survey (ACS), 2018. See *Digest of Education Statistics 2019*, table 219.80.

In 2018, the status dropout rate was lower for 16- to 24-year-olds living in households and noninstitutionalized group quarters such as college or military housing (5.1 percent) than for those living in institutionalized group quarters such as correctional or health care facilities (32.2 percent). The status dropout rate was also lower for noninstitutionalized individuals than for institutionalized individuals in the following racial/ethnic groups: White (4.1 vs. 24.3 percent), Black (5.5 vs. 37.2 percent), Hispanic

(7.7 vs. 35.9 percent), American Indian/Alaska Native (9.0 vs. 30.4 percent), and of Two or more races (4.9 vs. 28.0 percent).

The status dropout rate also differed by disability status[3] in 2018. The status dropout rate was 11.7 percent for 16- to 24-year-olds with a disability compared with 4.9 percent for 16- to 24-year-olds without a disability.

Endnotes:

[1] More specifically, institutionalized group quarters include adult and juvenile correctional facilities, nursing facilities, and other health care facilities. Noninstitutionalized group quarters include college and university housing, military quarters, facilities for workers and religious groups, and temporary shelters for the homeless.

[2] U.S.-born 16- to 24-year-olds include those born in the 50 states, the District of Columbia, Puerto Rico, American Samoa, Guam, the U.S. Virgin Islands, and the Northern Marianas, as well as those born abroad to U.S.-citizen parents.

[3] In this indicator, a disability is a long-lasting physical, mental, or emotional condition that can make it difficult for a person to do activities such as walking, climbing stairs, dressing, bathing, learning, or remembering. The condition can also impede a person from being able to go outside the home alone or to work at a job or business. For more details, see https://www.census.gov/topics/health/disability/about/glossary.html.

Reference tables: *Digest of Education Statistics 2019*, table 219.80

Related indicators and resources: Educational Attainment of Young Adults; High School Status Dropout Rates [*Status and Trends in the Education of Racial and Ethnic Groups*]; Public High School Graduation Rates; Snapshot: High School Status Dropout Rates for Racial/Ethnic Subgroups [*Status and Trends in the Education of Racial and Ethnic Groups*]; *Trends in High School Dropout and Completion Rates in the United States*

Glossary: Gap; High school diploma; Household; Racial/ethnic group; Status dropout rate (American Community Survey)

Public School Revenue Sources

Since 2000–01, public school revenues have increased by 27 percent in constant dollars, and public school enrollment increased by 7 percent.

In school year 2016–17, elementary and secondary public school revenues totaled $736 billion in constant 2018–19 dollars.[1] Of this total, 8 percent, or $60 billion, were from federal sources; 47 percent, or $346 billion, were from state sources; and 45 percent, or $330 billion, were from local sources.[2] In 2016–17, the percentages from each source differed across the 50 states and the District of Columbia. For example, the percentages of total revenues coming from federal, state, and local sources in New Hampshire were 6 percent, 32 percent, and 62 percent, respectively, while the corresponding percentages in Vermont were 7 percent, 90 percent, and 4 percent.

Total public school revenues were 27 percent higher in school year 2016–17 than in 2000–01 ($736 billion vs. $581 billion, in constant 2018–19 dollars). During this time, total revenues rose from $581 billion in 2000–01 to $699 billion in 2007–08, decreased to $661 billion in 2012–13, and then increased to $736 billion in 2016–17. These changes were accompanied by a 7 percent increase in total elementary and secondary public school enrollment, from 47 million students in 2000–01 to 51 million students in 2016–17 (see indicator Public School Enrollment).

Figure 1. Revenues for public elementary and secondary schools, by revenue source: School years 2000–01 through 2016–17

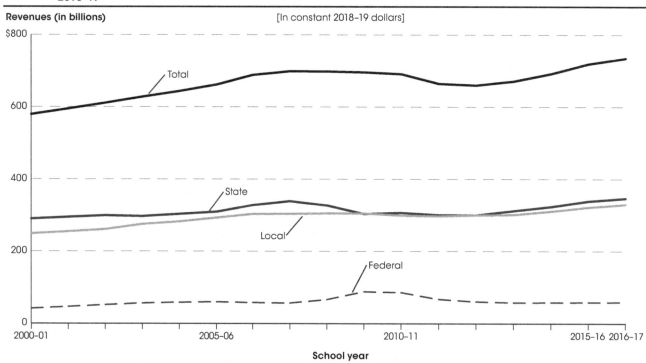

NOTE: Revenues are in constant 2018–19 dollars, adjusted using the Consumer Price Index (CPI). See *Digest of Education Statistics 2019*, table 106.70.
SOURCE: U.S. Department of Education, National Center for Education Statistics, Common Core of Data (CCD), "National Public Education Financial Survey," 2000–01 through 2016–17. See *Digest of Education Statistics 2019*, table 235.10.

All revenue streams provided higher revenues in 2016–17 than in 2000–01: federal was higher by 42 percent, state increased by 20 percent, and local increased by 32 percent. However, the revenue streams have progressed differently over time. Federal revenues for public schools were 111 percent higher in school year 2009–10, the year after the passage of the American Recovery and Reinvestment Act of 2009, than in 2000–01 ($89 billion vs. $42 billion, in constant 2018–19 dollars). Federal revenues have since decreased 33 percent from the 2009–10 high to $60 billion in 2016–17. State revenues increased 17 percent from 2000–01 to 2007–08 ($289 billion to $338 billion), decreased 12 percent from 2007–08 to 2012–13 ($299 billion), and then increased 16 percent from 2012–13 to a high of $346 billion in 2016–17. Local revenues increased steadily, from $250 billion to $330 billion, from 2000–01 through 2016–17.

More recently, total revenues for public schools were $16 billion (2 percent) higher in school year 2016–17 ($736 billion) than in 2015–16 ($720 billion), in constant 2018–19 dollars. Federal revenues were $0.3 billion (1 percent) higher in 2016–17 than in 2015–16. State revenues were $8.2 billion (2 percent) higher in 2016–17 than in 2015–16. Local revenues were $7.8 billion (2 percent) higher in 2016–17 than in 2015–16, reflecting revenues from local property taxes that were $6.9 billion (3 percent) higher and revenues from other local government sources that were $1.0 billion (2 percent) higher. Local revenues from private sources were $0.1 billion (1 percent) lower in 2016–17 than in 2015–16.[3]

Between school years 2000–01 and 2016–17, the percentage of total revenues for public schools coming from federal sources fluctuated between 7 and 13 percent, accounting for 7 percent of total revenues in 2000–01, for 13 percent in 2009–10 and 2010–11 following the American Recovery and Reinvestment Act of 2009, and for 8 percent in 2016–17. Local sources accounted for 45 percent of total revenues from 2011–12 through 2016–17, which was higher than the percentages between 2000–01 and 2010–11. The percentage of total revenues coming from state sources decreased 3 percentage points between 2000–01 and 2016–17 (50 to 47 percent). Within the 2000–01 to 2016–17 period, the percentage of revenues coming from state sources was highest in 2000–01 (50 percent) and lowest in 2009–10 (43 percent).

In school year 2016–17, there were substantial variations across the states in the percentages of public school revenues coming from state, local, and federal sources. In 22 states, more than half of all revenues came from state governments, while in 16 states and the District of Columbia, more than half of all revenue came from local governments. In the remaining 12 states, no single revenue source comprised more than half of all revenues.

Figure 2. State revenues for public elementary and secondary schools as a percentage of total public school revenues, by state: School year 2016–17

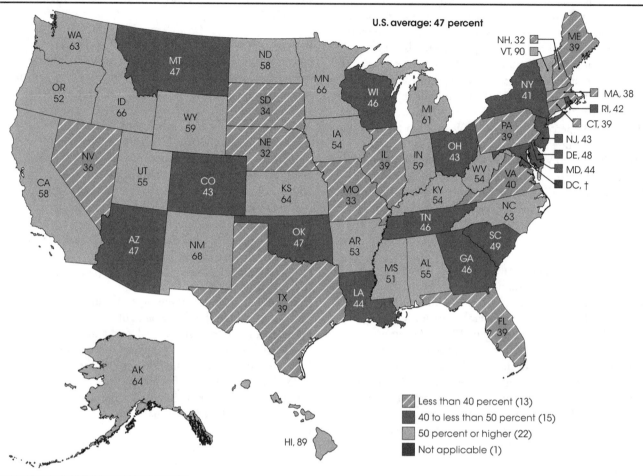

U.S. average: 47 percent

Legend:
- Less than 40 percent (13)
- 40 to less than 50 percent (15)
- 50 percent or higher (22)
- Not applicable (1)

† Not applicable.
NOTE: All 50 states and the District of Columbia are included in the U.S. average, even though the District of Columbia does not receive any state revenue. The District of Columbia and Hawaii have only one school district each; therefore, the distinction between state and local revenue sources is not comparable to other states. Categorizations are based on unrounded percentages. Excludes revenues for state education agencies.
SOURCE: U.S. Department of Education, National Center for Education Statistics, Common Core of Data (CCD), "National Public Education Financial Survey," 2016–17. See *Digest of Education Statistics 2019*, table 235.20.

In school year 2016–17, the percentages of public school revenues coming from state sources were highest in Vermont and Hawaii (90 and 89 percent, respectively) and lowest in Missouri (33 percent) and Nebraska and New Hampshire (32 percent each). The percentages of revenues coming from federal sources were highest in New Mexico (15 percent) and Mississippi and Alaska (14 percent each) and lowest in Connecticut and New Jersey (4 percent

each). The percentages of revenues coming from local sources were highest in New Hampshire and Nebraska (62 and 60 percent, respectively) and lowest in Vermont and Hawaii (4 and 2 percent, respectively). Ninety-one percent of all revenues for the District of Columbia were from local sources, and the remaining 9 percent were from federal sources.

Figure 3. Property tax revenues for public elementary and secondary schools as a percentage of total public school revenues, by state: School year 2016–17

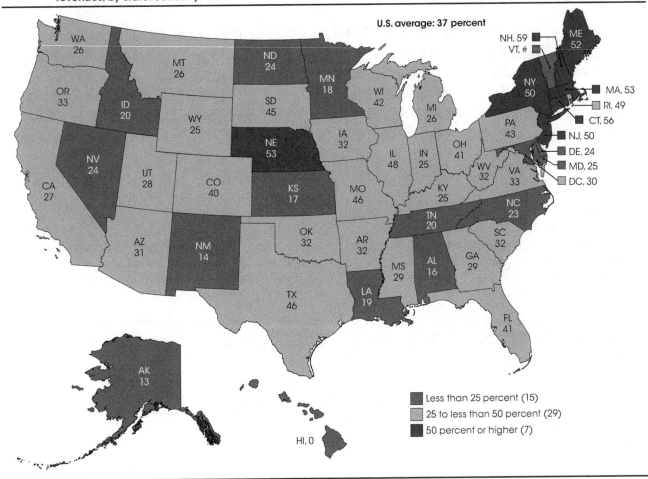

NOTE: All 50 states and the District of Columbia are included in the U.S. average. Categorizations are based on unrounded percentages.
SOURCE: U.S. Department of Education, National Center for Education Statistics, Common Core of Data (CCD), "National Public Education Financial Survey," 2016–17. See *Digest of Education Statistics 2019*, table 235.20.

On a national basis in 2016–17, some $269 billion,[4] or 82 percent, of local revenues for public school districts were derived from local property taxes. Connecticut and Rhode Island had the highest percentages of *local* revenues from property taxes (98 and 97 percent, respectively). The percentages of total revenues from local property taxes differed by state. In 2016–17, New Hampshire and Connecticut had the highest percentages of *total* revenues from property taxes (59 and 56 percent, respectively). In Vermont, the percentage of revenues from local property taxes rounded to zero. Hawaii has only one school district, which received no funding from property taxes.

Endnotes:
[1] Revenues in this indicator are adjusted for inflation using the Consumer Price Index, or CPI. For this indicator, the CPI is adjusted to a school-year basis. The CPI is prepared by the Bureau of Labor Statistics, U.S. Department of Labor.
[2] Local revenues include revenues from such sources as local property and nonproperty taxes, investments, and student activities such as textbook sales, transportation and tuition fees, and food service revenues. Local revenues also include revenues from intermediate sources (education agencies with fundraising capabilities that operate between the state and local government levels).
[3] Private revenues consist of tuition and fees from patrons and revenues from gifts.
[4] In constant 2018–19 dollars.

Reference tables: *Digest of Education Statistics 2019*, tables 235.10 and 235.20; *Digest of Education Statistics 2018*, table 105.30
Related indicators and resources: Public School Expenditures

Glossary: Constant dollars; Consumer Price Index (CPI); Elementary school; Property tax; Public school or institution; Revenue; School district; Secondary school

Public School Expenditures

In 2016–17, public schools spent $12,794 per pupil on current expenditures (in constant 2018–19 dollars), a category that includes salaries, employee benefits, purchased services, and supplies. Current expenditures per pupil were 20 percent higher in 2016–17 than in 2000–01, after adjusting for inflation. During this period, current expenditures per student increased from $10,675 in 2000–01 to $12,435 in 2008–09, decreased between 2008–09 and 2012–13 to $11,791, and then reached $12,794 in 2016–17.

Total expenditures for public elementary and secondary schools in the United States in 2016–17 amounted to $739 billion, or $14,439 per public school student enrolled in the fall (in constant 2018–19 dollars).[1] Total expenditures included $12,794 per pupil in current expenditures, which include salaries, employee benefits, purchased services, tuition, and supplies. Total expenditures per pupil also included $1,266 in capital outlay (expenditures for property and for buildings and alterations completed by school district staff or contractors) and $379 for interest on school debt.

Figure 1. Current expenditures, capital outlay, and interest on school debt per student in fall enrollment in public elementary and secondary schools: Selected years, 2000–01 through 2016–17

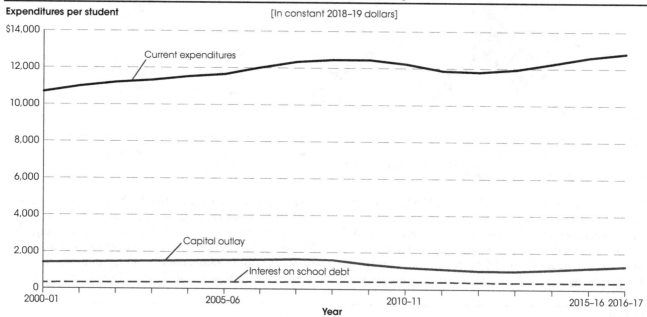

NOTE: "Current expenditures," "Capital outlay," and "Interest on school debt" are subcategories of total expenditures. Current expenditures include instruction, support services, food services, and enterprise operations (expenditures for operations funded by sales of products and services). Capital outlay includes expenditures for property and for buildings and alterations completed by school district staff or contractors. Expenditures are reported in constant 2018–19 dollars, based on the Consumer Price Index (CPI). Some data have been revised from previous figures. Excludes expenditures for state education agencies.
SOURCE: U.S. Department of Education, National Center for Education Statistics, Common Core of Data (CCD), "National Public Education Financial Survey," 2000–01 through 2016–17; CCD, "State Nonfiscal Survey of Public Elementary/Secondary Education," 2000–01 through 2016–17. See *Digest of Education Statistics 2018*, table 105.30, and *Digest of Education Statistics 2019*, tables 236.10, 236.55, and 236.60.

Current expenditures per pupil enrolled in the fall in public elementary and secondary schools were 20 percent higher in 2016–17 than in 2000–01 ($12,794 vs. $10,675, both in constant 2018–19 dollars). Current expenditures per pupil increased from $10,675 in 2000–01 to $12,435 in 2008–09, decreased between 2008–09 and 2012–13 to $11,791, and then increased to $12,794 in 2016–17.

Capital outlay expenditures per pupil in 2016–17 ($1,266) were 10 percent lower than in 2000–01 ($1,412). Interest payments on public elementary and secondary school debt per pupil were 22 percent higher in 2016–17 than in 2000–01. During this period, interest payments per pupil increased from $312 in 2000–01 to $415 in 2010–11, before declining to $379 in 2016–17 (all in constant 2018–19 dollars).

Figure 2. Percentage of current expenditures per student in fall enrollment in public elementary and secondary schools, by type of expenditure: 2000–01, 2010–11, and 2016–17

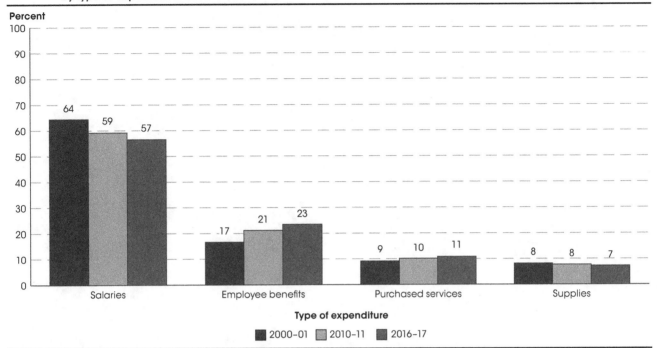

NOTE: "Salaries," "Employee benefits," "Purchased services," and "Supplies" are subcategories of current expenditures. Purchased services include expenditures for contracts for food, transportation, and janitorial services and professional development for teachers. Supplies include expenditures for items ranging from books to heating oil. Two additional subcategories of expenditures, "Tuition" and "Other," are not included in this figure. Excludes expenditures for state education agencies. Although rounded numbers are displayed, the figures are based on unrounded data.
SOURCE: U.S. Department of Education, National Center for Education Statistics, Common Core of Data (CCD), "National Public Education Financial Survey," 2000–01, 2010–11, and 2016–17. See *Digest of Education Statistics 2019*, table 236.60.

Current expenditures for education can be expressed in terms of the percentage of funds going toward salaries, employee benefits, purchased services, tuition, supplies, or other expenditures. On a national basis in 2016–17, approximately 80 percent of current expenditures for public elementary and secondary schools were for salaries and benefits for staff, compared with 81 percent in 2000–01. As the proportion of current expenditures for staff salaries decreased from 64 percent in 2000–01 to 57 percent in 2016–17, the proportion of current expenditures for employee benefits increased from 17 to 23 percent. Eleven percent of current expenditures in

2016–17 were for purchased services, which include a variety of items, such as contracts for food, transportation, janitorial services, and professional development for teachers. The percentage of the current expenditure distribution going toward purchased services increased from 9 percent in 2000–01 to 11 percent in 2016–17. Seven percent of current expenditures in 2016–17 were for supplies, ranging from books to heating oil. The percentage of current expenditures for supplies decreased about 1 percentage point from 2000–01 to 2016–17. Tuition and other expenditures accounted for 2 percent of current expenditures in both 2000–01 and 2016–17.

Endnotes:
[1] Expenditures in this indicator are adjusted for inflation using the Consumer Price Index, or CPI. For this indicator, the CPI is adjusted to a school-year basis. The CPI is prepared by the Bureau of Labor Statistics, U.S. Department of Labor.

Reference tables: *Digest of Education Statistics 2019*, tables 236.10, 236.55, and 236.60; *Digest of Education Statistics 2018*, table 105.30

Related indicators and resources: Education Expenditures by Country; Public School Revenue Sources

Glossary: Capital outlay; Constant dollars; Consumer Price Index (CPI); Current expenditures (elementary/secondary); Elementary school; Expenditures per pupil; Expenditures, total; Interest on debt; Public school or institution; Salary; Secondary school

The indicators in this chapter of *The Condition of Education* examine features of postsecondary education, many of which parallel those presented in the previous chapter on elementary and secondary education. The indicators describe enrollment, student characteristics, programs and courses of study, institutional financial resources, student costs, and degrees conferred.

Postsecondary education is characterized by diversity in both institutional and student characteristics. Postsecondary institutions vary by the types of degrees awarded, control (public or private), and whether they are operated on a nonprofit or for-profit basis. In addition, postsecondary institutions have distinctly different missions and provide students with a wide range of learning environments.

This chapter's indicators, as well as additional indicators on postsecondary education, are available at *The Condition of Education* website: http://nces.ed.gov/programs/coe.

Chapter 2

Postsecondary Education

Immediate College Enrollment Rate

The immediate college enrollment rate for high school completers increased from 63 percent in 2000 to 69 percent in 2018. In 2018, about 44 percent of high school completers immediately enrolled in 4-year institutions and 26 percent immediately enrolled in 2-year institutions.

Of the 3.2 million 16- to 24-year-olds who completed high school in the first 9 months of 2018, some 2.2 million, or 69 percent, were enrolled in college in October 2018. In this indicator, high school completers include those who graduated with a high school diploma as well as those who completed a GED or other high school equivalency credential. This annual percentage

of high school completers who are enrolled in 2- or 4-year institutions within the specified time frame is known as the *immediate college enrollment rate*. The overall immediate college enrollment rate increased from 63 percent in 2000 to 69 percent in 2018, though the 2018 rate was not measurably different from the rate in 2010.

Figure 1. Immediate college enrollment rate of high school completers, by level of institution: 2000 through 2018

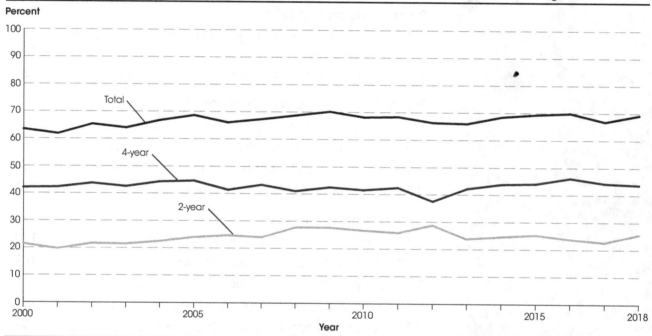

NOTE: *Immediate college enrollment rate* is defined as the annual percentage of high school completers who are enrolled in 2- or 4-year institutions in the October immediately following high school completion. High school completers include those who graduated with a high school diploma as well as those who completed a GED or other high school equivalency credential.
SOURCE: U.S. Department of Commerce, Census Bureau, Current Population Survey (CPS), October Supplement, 2000 through 2018. See *Digest of Education Statistics 2019*, table 302.10.

In every year from 2000 to 2018, higher percentages of high school completers immediately enrolled in 4-year institutions than in 2-year institutions. In 2018, about 44 percent of high school completers immediately enrolled in 4-year institutions and 26 percent immediately enrolled

in 2-year institutions. The immediate college enrollment rate for 4-year institutions in 2018 was not measurably different from the rate in 2000. The rate for 2-year institutions was higher in 2018 (26 percent) than in 2000 (21 percent).

Figure 2.   Immediate college enrollment rate of high school completers, by sex: 2000 through 2018

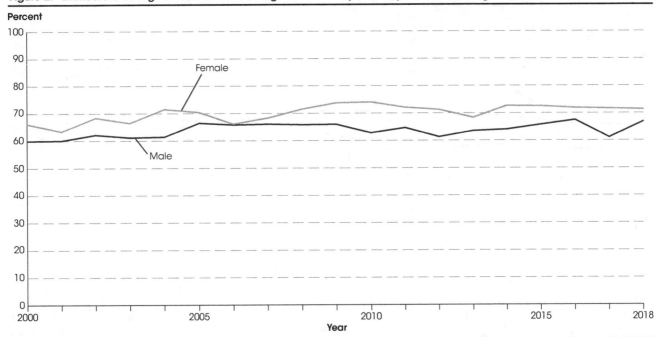

NOTE: *Immediate college enrollment rate* is defined as the annual percentage of high school completers who are enrolled in 2- or 4-year institutions in the October immediately following high school completion. High school completers include those who graduated with a high school diploma as well as those who completed a GED or other high school equivalency credential.
SOURCE: U.S. Department of Commerce, Census Bureau, Current Population Survey (CPS), October Supplement, 2000 through 2018. See *Digest of Education Statistics 2019*, table 302.10.

The immediate college enrollment rate for male students[1] increased from 60 percent in 2000 to 67 percent in 2018, while the rate for female students did not change measurably between these two years. As a result, the overall immediate college enrollment rate for male students was not measurably different from the rate for female students (71 percent) in 2018. Similarly, there were no measurable male-female differences in the immediate college enrollment rate at either 2-year institutions or 4-year institutions in 2018.

Figure 3.   Immediate college enrollment rate of high school completers, by race/ethnicity: 2000 through 2018

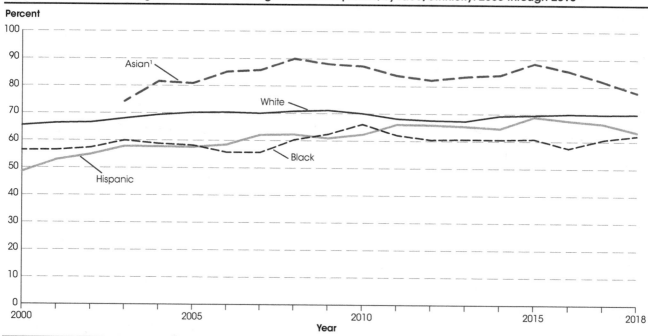

Percent

[1] The separate collection of data on Asian high school completers did not begin until 2003.
NOTE: *Immediate college enrollment rate* is defined as the annual percentage of high school completers who are enrolled in 2- or 4-year institutions in the October immediately following high school completion. High school completers include those who graduated with a high school diploma as well as those who completed a GED or other high school equivalency credential. Due to some short-term data fluctuations associated with small sample sizes, percentages for racial/ethnic groups were calculated based on 3-year moving averages, with the following exceptions: the percentages for 2018 were calculated based on a 2-year moving average (an average of 2017 and 2018), and the 2003 percentage for Asian high school completers was based on a 2-year moving average (an average of 2003 and 2004). From 2003 onward, data for White, Black, and Asian high school completers exclude persons identifying themselves as of Two or more races. Race categories exclude persons of Hispanic ethnicity.
SOURCE: U.S. Department of Commerce, Census Bureau, Current Population Survey (CPS), October Supplement, 2000 through 2018. See *Digest of Education Statistics 2019*, table 302.20.

The immediate college enrollment rate for White students[2] was higher in 2018 (70 percent) than in 2000 (65 percent), as was the rate for Hispanic students (63 percent in 2018 vs. 49 percent in 2000). The immediate college enrollment rate for Black students in 2018 (62 percent) was not measurably different from the rate in 2000. The immediate college enrollment rate for Asian students in 2018 (78 percent) was not measurably different from the rate in 2003, when the collection of separate data on Asian students began.[3]

The immediate college enrollment rate for White students was higher than the rate for Black students in every year since 2000 except for 2010, when there was no measurable difference between the two rates. The immediate college enrollment rate for White students was higher than the rate for Hispanic students in every year

from 2000 through 2010 but not measurably different every year between 2011 and 2017; however, the gap became significant again in 2018. The immediate college enrollment rate for Black students was higher than the rate for Hispanic students in 2000, but lower than the rate for Hispanic students in 2015 and 2016. In the rest of the years between 2000 and 2018, there was no measurable difference between the immediate college enrollment rates for Black and Hispanic students. The immediate college enrollment rate for Asian students was higher than the rates for Black and Hispanic students in every year since 2003. In addition, the immediate college enrollment rate for Asian students was higher than the rate for White students in every year since 2004, although the rates between these two groups were not measurably different in 2003.

Endnotes:

[1] The terms "high school completers" and "students" are used interchangeably throughout the indicator.

[2] Due to some short-term data fluctuations associated with small sample sizes, estimates for the racial/ethnic groups were calculated based on 3-year moving averages, with the following exceptions: the percentages for 2018 were calculated based on a 2-year moving average (an average of 2017 and 2018), and the 2003 percentage for Asians was based on a 2-year moving average (an average of 2003 and 2004).

[3] Prior to 2003, data were collected for the combined race category of Asian/Pacific Islander.

Reference tables: *Digest of Education Statistics 2019,* tables 302.10 and 302.20

Related indicators and resources: College Enrollment Rates; College Participation Rates [*Status and Trends in the Education of Racial and Ethnic Groups*]; Public High School Graduation Rates; Snapshot: College Participation Rates for Racial/Ethnic Subgroups [*Status and Trends in the Education of Racial and Ethnic Groups*]; Status Dropout Rates; Undergraduate Enrollment; Young Adult Educational and Employment Outcomes by Family Socioeconomic Status [*The Condition of Education 2019 Spotlight*]

Glossary: College; Enrollment; Gap; High school completer; Postsecondary institutions (basic classification by level); Racial/ethnic group

College Enrollment Rates

The overall college enrollment rate for 18- to 24-year-olds increased from 35 percent in 2000 to 41 percent in 2018. In 2018, the college enrollment rate was higher for 18- to 24-year-olds who were Asian (59 percent) than for 18- to 24-year-olds who were White (42 percent), Black (37 percent), and Hispanic (36 percent).

The overall college enrollment rate has increased since 2000. Different factors, such as changes in the labor market and the economy, may have contributed to this increase.[1,2] In this indicator, *college enrollment rate* is defined as the percentage of 18- to 24-year-olds enrolled as undergraduate or graduate students in 2- or 4-year institutions. The Immediate College Enrollment Rate indicator, in contrast, presents data on the percentage of high school completers who enroll in 2- or 4-year institutions in the fall immediately following high school.

Figure 1. College enrollment rates of 18- to 24-year-olds, by level of institution: 2000 through 2018

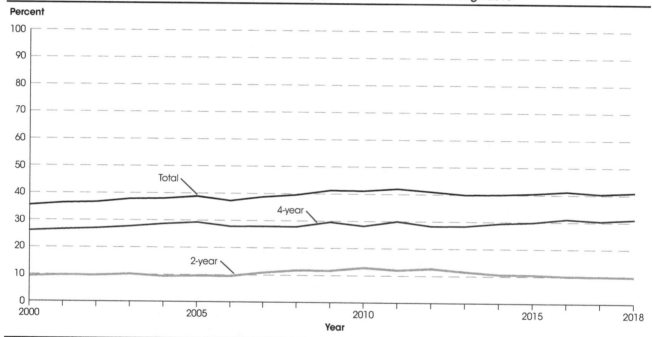

NOTE: Data are based on sample surveys of the civilian noninstitutionalized population.
SOURCE: U.S. Department of Commerce, Census Bureau, Current Population Survey (CPS), October Supplement, 2000 through 2018. See *Digest of Education Statistics 2019*, table 302.60.

The overall college enrollment rate increased from 2000 to 2010. Similarly, the college enrollment rate increased at both 2-year institutions and 4-year institutions during this period. Over a more recent time period, the overall college enrollment rate in 2018 was not measurably different from the rate in 2010, but the rate at 2-year institutions decreased from 2010 (13 percent) to 2018 (10 percent), and the rate at 4-year institutions increased from 28 percent to 31 percent during this period.

Figure 2.   College enrollment rates of 18- to 24-year-olds, by race/ethnicity: 2000, 2010, and 2018

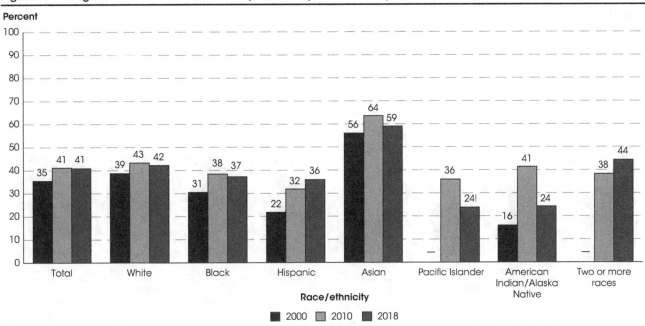

— Not available.
! Interpret data with caution. The coefficient of variation (CV) for this estimate is between 30 and 50 percent.
NOTE: Data are based on sample surveys of the civilian noninstitutionalized population. Separate data for 18- to 24-year-olds who were Pacific Islander and of Two or more races were not available in 2000. In 2000, respondents of Two or more races were required to select a single race category. Prior to 2003, data for Asian 18- to 24-year-olds include Pacific Islander 18- to 24-year-olds. Race categories exclude persons of Hispanic ethnicity. Although rounded numbers are displayed, the figures are based on unrounded data.
SOURCE: U.S. Department of Commerce, Census Bureau, Current Population Survey (CPS), October Supplement, 2000, 2010, and 2018. See *Digest of Education Statistics 2019*, table 302.60.

From 2000 to 2018, college enrollment rates among 18- to 24-year-olds increased for those who were Black (from 31 to 37 percent) and Hispanic (from 22 to 36 percent). The college enrollment rate in 2018 was also higher than in 2000 for those who were White (42 vs. 39 percent). The college enrollment rate was not measurably different between 2000 and 2018 for those who were Asian[3] and American Indian/Alaska Native. More recently, the college enrollment rate was higher in 2018 than in 2010 for those who were Hispanic (36 vs. 32 percent) and lower in 2018 than in 2010 for those who were American Indian/Alaska Native (24 vs. 41 percent). There was no measurable difference between the 2010 and 2018 college enrollment rates for those who were White, Black, Asian, Pacific Islander, and of Two or more races.

In 2018, the college enrollment rate among 18- to 24-year-olds was higher for those who were Asian (59 percent) than for those of other reported racial and ethnic groups. In every year between 2000 and 2018, the college enrollment rate for those who were Asian was higher than the rates for those who were White, Black, and Hispanic, and the rate for those who were White was higher than the rate for those who were Black. The college enrollment rate for those who were White was also higher than the rate for those who were Hispanic in every year between 2000 and 2018, except 2016, when the rates were not measurably different.

Figure 3. College enrollment rates of 18- to 24-year-olds, by sex and race/ethnicity: 2000 and 2018

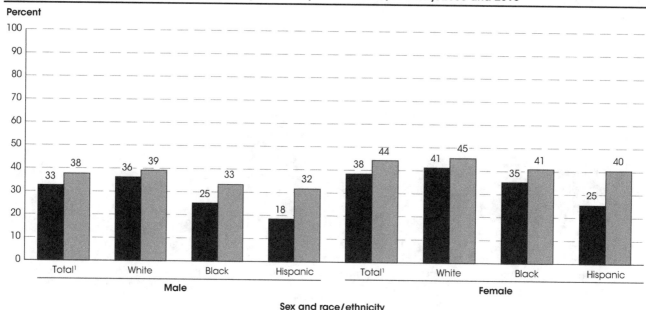

Percent

¹ Includes other racial/ethnic groups not shown separately.
NOTE: Data are based on sample surveys of the civilian noninstitutionalized population. In 2000, respondents of Two or more races were required to select a single race category. Race categories exclude persons of Hispanic ethnicity. Although rounded numbers are displayed, the figures are based on unrounded data.
SOURCE: U.S. Department of Commerce, Census Bureau, Current Population Survey (CPS), October Supplement, 2000 and 2018. See *Digest of Education Statistics 2019*, table 302.60.

Between 2000 and 2018, overall college enrollment rates increased for both 18- to 24-year-old males (from 33 to 38 percent) and females (from 38 to 44 percent). Among males, college enrollment rates were higher in 2018 than in 2000 for those who were White (39 vs. 36 percent), Black (33 vs. 25 percent), and Hispanic (32 vs. 18 percent). Among females, college enrollment rates were also higher in 2018 than in 2000 for those who were White (45 vs. 41 percent) and Hispanic (40 vs. 25 percent). The rate in 2018 was not measurably different from the rate in 2000 for females who were Black.

In every year since 2000, the college enrollment rate for 18- to 24-year-olds overall was higher for females than for males. This pattern was also observed for both White and Hispanic 18- to 24-year-olds. For example, in 2018 the female-male gap in college enrollment rates was 7 percentage points for this age group overall, 6 percentage points for those who were White, and 9 percentage points for those who were Hispanic. Among those who were Black, the college enrollment rate was higher for females than for males in most years since 2000, except in 2007, 2012, 2015, and 2016, when the rates were not measurably different. In 2018, the female-male gap in college enrollment rates for those who were Black was 8 percentage points.

Endnotes:

[1] Fry, R. (2009). *College Enrollment Hits All-Time High, Fueled by Community College Surge.* Washington, DC: Pew Research Center. Retrieved May 3, 2017, from http://www.pewsocialtrends.org/2009/10/29/college-enrollment-hits-all-time-high-fueled-by-community-college-surge/.
[2] Brown, J.R., and Hoxby, C.M. (Eds.). (2014). *How the Financial Crisis and Great Recession Affected Higher Education.* Chicago: University of Chicago Press.

[3] Separate data for 18- to 24-year-olds who were Pacific Islander or of Two or more races were not available in 2000. Prior to 2003, data for Asian 18- to 24-year-olds included Pacific Islander 18- to 24-year-olds. Information from *Digest of Education Statistics 2018*, table 101.20, based on the Census Bureau Current Population Reports, indicates that 97 percent of all Asian/Pacific Islander 18- to 24-year-olds in 2018 were Asian.

Reference tables: *Digest of Education Statistics 2019*, table 302.60; *Digest of Education Statistics 2018*, table 101.20
Related indicators and resources: College Participation Rates [*Status and Trends in the Education of Racial and Ethnic Groups*]; Immediate College Enrollment Rate; Snapshot: College Participation Rates for Racial/Ethnic Subgroups [*Status and Trends in the Education of Racial and Ethnic Groups*]; Undergraduate Enrollment; Young Adult Educational and Employment Outcomes by Family Socioeconomic Status [*The Condition of Education 2019 Spotlight*]

Glossary: College; Enrollment; Gap; Racial/ethnic group

Undergraduate Enrollment

Between 2000 and 2018, total undergraduate enrollment in degree-granting postsecondary institutions increased by 26 percent (from 13.2 million to 16.6 million students). By 2029, total undergraduate enrollment is projected to increase to 17.0 million students.

In fall 2018, total undergraduate enrollment in degree-granting postsecondary institutions was 16.6 million students, an increase of 26 percent from 2000, when enrollment was 13.2 million students. Total undergraduate enrollment increased by 37 percent (from 13.2 million to 18.1 million students) between 2000 and 2010, but decreased by 8 percent (from 18.1 million to 16.6 million students) between 2010 and 2018. Total undergraduate enrollment is projected to increase by 2 percent (from 16.6 million to 17.0 million students) between 2018 and 2029.

Figure 1. Actual and projected undergraduate enrollment in degree-granting postsecondary institutions, by sex: Fall 2000 through 2029

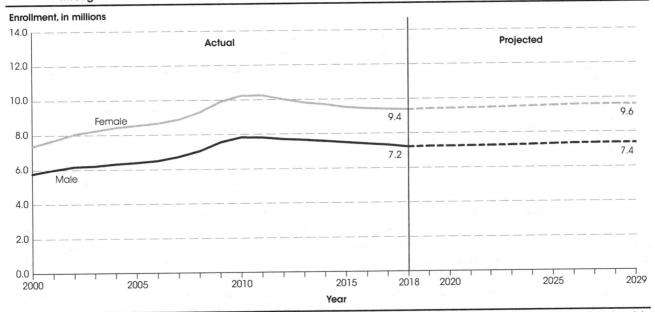

NOTE: Degree-granting institutions grant associate's or higher degrees and participate in Title IV federal financial aid programs. Projections are based on data through 2018. Some data have been revised from previously published figures.
SOURCE: U.S. Department of Education, National Center for Education Statistics, Integrated Postsecondary Education Data System (IPEDS), Spring 2001 through Spring 2019, Fall Enrollment component; and Enrollment in Degree-Granting Institutions Projection Model, 2000 through 2029. See *Digest of Education Statistics 2019*, table 303.70.

In fall 2018, female students made up 56 percent of total undergraduate enrollment (9.4 million students), and male students made up 44 percent (7.2 million students). Enrollment patterns for female and male students exhibited similar trends between 2000 and 2018. Between 2000 and 2010, female and male enrollments increased by 39 percent and 36 percent, respectively; between 2010 and 2018, female and male enrollments both decreased by 8 percent. Between 2018 and 2029, female and male enrollments are projected to increase by 2 percent each (from 9.4 million to 9.6 million students and from 7.2 million to 7.4 million students, respectively).

Figure 2. Undergraduate enrollment in degree-granting postsecondary institutions, by race/ethnicity and nonresident alien status: Fall 2000, 2010, and 2018

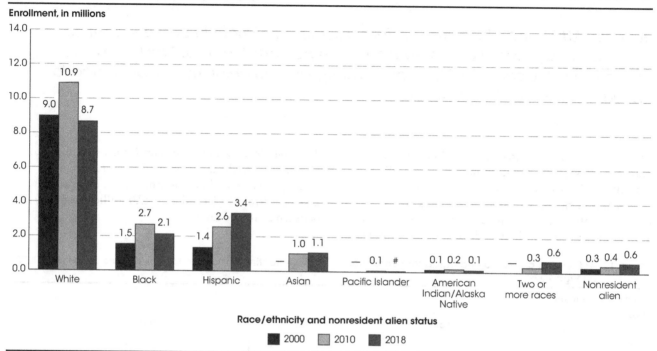

— Not available.
Rounds to zero.
NOTE: Prior to 2010, separate data on Asian students, Pacific Islander students, and students of Two or more races were not available. Race categories exclude persons of Hispanic ethnicity. Race/ethnicity categories exclude nonresident aliens. Degree-granting institutions grant associate's or higher degrees and participate in Title IV federal financial aid programs. Some data have been revised from previously published figures. Although rounded numbers are displayed, the figures are based on unrounded data.
SOURCE: U.S. Department of Education, National Center for Education Statistics, Integrated Postsecondary Education Data System (IPEDS), Spring 2001, Spring 2011, and Spring 2019, Fall Enrollment component. See *Digest of Education Statistics 2019*, table 306.10.

Of the 16.6 million undergraduate students enrolled in fall 2018, some 8.7 million were White, 3.4 million were Hispanic, 2.1 million were Black, 1.1 million were Asian, 647,000 were of Two or more races, 120,000 were American Indian/Alaska Native, and 45,000 were Pacific Islander. Hispanic enrollment increased in each year between 2000 and 2018, increasing by 148 percent during this period (from 1.4 million to 3.4 million students). Enrollment trends for other racial/ethnic groups with available data varied from 2000 to 2018.[1] Between 2000 and 2010, White enrollment increased by 21 percent (from 9.0 million to 10.9 million students), Black enrollment increased by 73 percent (from 1.5 million to 2.7 million students), and American Indian/Alaska Native enrollment increased by 29 percent (from 139,000 to 179,000 students). However, between 2010 and 2018, White enrollment decreased by 20 percent (from 10.9 million to

8.7 million students), Black enrollment decreased by 21 percent (from 2.7 million to 2.1 million students), and American Indian/Alaska Native enrollment decreased by 33 percent (from 179,000 to 120,000 students). Similarly, between 2010 and 2018, Pacific Islander enrollment decreased by 22 percent (from 58,000 to 45,000 students). In contrast, between 2010 and 2018, the enrollment of individuals who were of Two or more races increased by 120 percent (from 294,000 to 647,000 students), and Asian enrollment increased by 6 percent (from 1.0 million to 1.1 million students). In fall 2018, degree-granting postsecondary institutions enrolled 567,000 nonresident alien[2] undergraduate students. The number of nonresident alien undergraduate students increased by 38 percent (from 288,000 to 398,000 students) between 2000 and 2010 and increased by 42 percent (from 398,000 to 567,000 students) between 2010 and 2018.

Figure 3. Actual and projected undergraduate enrollment in degree-granting postsecondary institutions, by attendance status: Fall 2000 through 2029

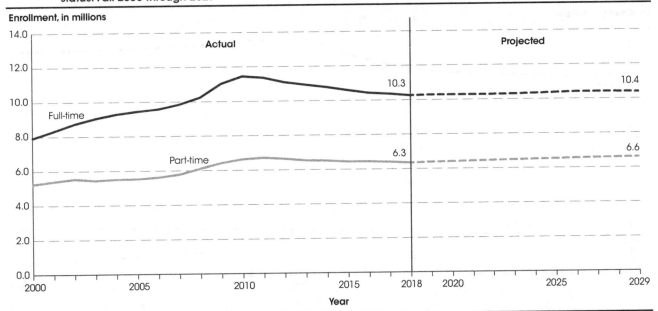

NOTE: Degree-granting institutions grant associate's or higher degrees and participate in Title IV federal financial aid programs. Projections are based on data through 2018. Some data have been revised from previously published figures.
SOURCE: U.S. Department of Education, National Center for Education Statistics, Integrated Postsecondary Education Data System (IPEDS), Spring 2001 through Spring 2019, Fall Enrollment component; and Enrollment in Degree-Granting Institutions Projection Model, 2000 through 2029. See *Digest of Education Statistics 2019*, table 303.70.

In fall 2018, degree-granting postsecondary institutions enrolled 10.3 million full-time and 6.3 million part-time undergraduate students. Between 2000 and 2018, both full- and part-time enrollment increased overall, most notably between 2000 and 2010. Between 2000 and 2010, full-time enrollment increased by 45 percent (from 7.9 million to 11.5 million students) and part-time enrollment increased by 27 percent (from 5.2 million to 6.6 million students). More recently, between 2010

and 2018, full-time enrollment decreased by 10 percent (from 11.5 million to 10.3 million students) and part-time enrollment decreased by 4 percent (from 6.6 million to 6.3 million students). Between 2018 and 2029, full-time enrollment is projected to increase by 1 percent (from 10.3 million to 10.4 million students) and part-time enrollment is projected to increase by 4 percent (from 6.3 million to 6.6 million students).

Figure 4.   Undergraduate enrollment in degree-granting postsecondary institutions, by control of institution: Fall 2000 through 2018

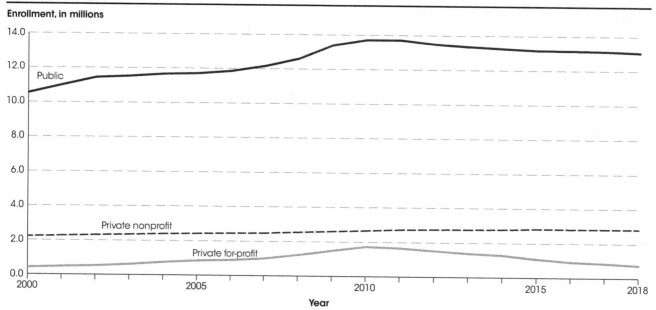

NOTE: Degree-granting institutions grant associate's or higher degrees and participate in Title IV federal financial aid programs. Some data have been revised from previously published figures.
SOURCE: U.S. Department of Education, National Center for Education Statistics, Integrated Postsecondary Education Data System (IPEDS), Spring 2001 through Spring 2019, Fall Enrollment component. See *Digest of Education Statistics 2019*, table 303.70.

Between fall 2000 and fall 2018, undergraduate enrollment increased by 83 percent (from 403,000 to 739,000 students) at private for-profit institutions, compared with increases of 27 percent (from 2.2 million to 2.8 million students) at private nonprofit institutions and 24 percent (from 10.5 million to 13.0 million students) at public institutions. Between 2000 and 2010, enrollment in private for-profit institutions increased by 329 percent (from 403,000 to 1.7 million students). In comparison, enrollment increased by 30 percent at public institutions (from 10.5 million to 13.7 million students)

and by 20 percent at private nonprofit institutions (from 2.2 million to 2.7 million students) during this period. Enrollment in private for-profit institutions peaked in 2010 and then decreased by 57 percent (from 1.7 million to 739,000 students) between 2010 and 2018. During this period, enrollment in public institutions decreased by 5 percent (from 13.7 million to 13.0 million students), whereas enrollment in private nonprofit institutions increased by 6 percent (from 2.7 million to 2.8 million students).[3]

Figure 5. Actual and projected undergraduate enrollment in degree-granting postsecondary institutions, by level of institution: Fall 2000 through 2029

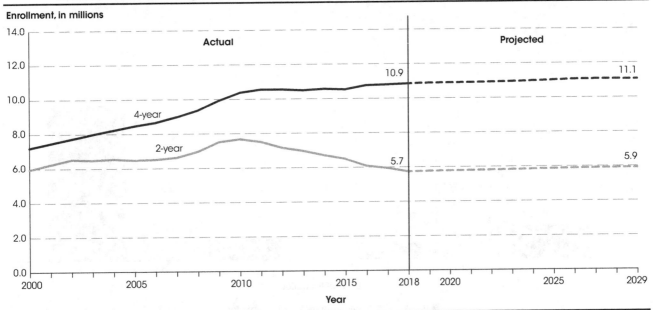

NOTE: Degree-granting institutions grant associate's or higher degrees and participate in Title IV federal financial aid programs. Projections are based on data through 2018. Some data have been revised from previously published figures.
SOURCE: U.S. Department of Education, National Center for Education Statistics, Integrated Postsecondary Education Data System (IPEDS), Spring 2001 through Spring 2019, Fall Enrollment component; and Enrollment in Degree-Granting Institutions Projection Model, 2000 through 2029. See *Digest of Education Statistics 2019*, table 303.70.

In fall 2018, the 10.9 million students at 4-year institutions made up 65 percent of total undergraduate enrollment; the remaining 35 percent (5.7 million students) were enrolled in 2-year institutions. Between 2000 and 2010, enrollment increased by 44 percent at 4-year institutions (from 7.2 million to 10.4 million students) and by 29 percent at 2-year institutions (from 5.9 million to 7.7 million students). However, between 2010 and 2018, enrollment increased by 4 percent at 4-year institutions (from 10.4 million to 10.9 million students) and decreased by 25 percent at 2-year institutions (from 7.7 million to 5.7 million

students). Some of the shift in enrollment patterns for 2-year and 4-year institutions during this period is likely explained by 2-year institutions' beginning to offer 4-year degree programs, which caused their classification to change. In 2018, some 695,000 undergraduate students were enrolled in 4-year institutions that were classified as 2-year institutions in 2010. Between 2018 and 2029, undergraduate enrollment in 4-year institutions is projected to increase by 2 percent (from 10.9 to 11.1 million students) and enrollment in 2-year institutions is projected to increase by 3 percent (from 5.7 million to 5.9 million students).

Figure 6. Percentage of undergraduate students at degree-granting postsecondary institutions who enrolled exclusively in distance education courses, by level and control of institution: Fall 2018

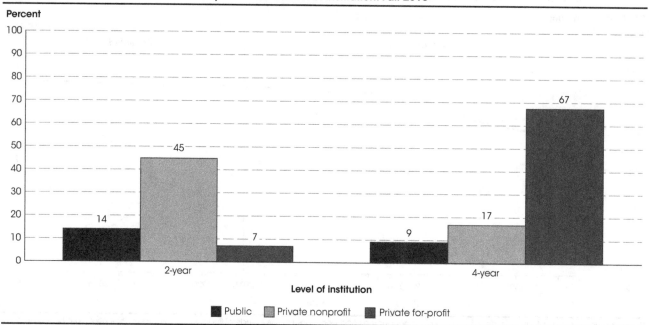

NOTE: Degree-granting institutions grant associate's or higher degrees and participate in Title IV federal financial aid programs. Distance education uses one or more technologies to deliver instruction to students who are separated from the instructor and to support regular and substantive interaction between the student and the instructor synchronously or asynchronously. Technologies used for instruction may include the following: the Internet; one-way and two-way transmissions through open broadcasts, closed circuit, cable, microwave, broadband lines, fiber optics, satellite, or wireless communication devices; audio conferencing; and videocassettes, DVDs, and CD-ROMs, only if the videocassettes, DVDs, and CD-ROMs are used in a course in conjunction with the technologies listed above.
SOURCE: U.S. Department of Education, National Center for Education Statistics, Integrated Postsecondary Education Data System (IPEDS), Spring 2019, Fall Enrollment component. See *Digest of Education Statistics 2019*, table 311.15.

Distance education[4] courses and programs provide students with flexible learning opportunities. In fall 2018, some 34 percent (5.7 million) of all undergraduate students participated in distance education. Some 2.3 million students, or 14 percent of total undergraduate enrollment, exclusively took distance education courses. Among undergraduate students who took distance education courses exclusively, 1.5 million were enrolled in institutions located in the same state in which they resided, and 799,000 were enrolled in institutions in a different state.[5]

In fall 2018, the percentage of students at private for-profit institutions who took distance education courses exclusively (55 percent) was more than three times that of students at private nonprofit institutions (17 percent) and five times that of students at public institutions (11 percent). In particular, the percentage of students at private for-profit 4-year institutions who took distance education courses exclusively (67 percent) was larger than the percentages of students at 2-year institutions who took distance education courses exclusively (percentages at these institutions ranged from 7 percent at private for-profit 2-year institutions to 45 percent at private nonprofit 2-year institutions) and also larger than the percentages of students at public 4-year institutions (9 percent) and private nonprofit 4-year institutions (17 percent) who took distance education courses exclusively.

Endnotes:

[1] Prior to 2010, separate data on Asian students, Pacific Islander students, and students of Two or more races were not available.

[2] In the Integrated Postsecondary Education Data System (IPEDS), racial/ethnic data were not collected for nonresident alien students, and their data were compiled as a separate group.

[3] In addition, in 2018, some 55,000 undergraduate students were enrolled in nonprofit institutions that were classified as for-profit institutions in 2010.

[4] Distance education uses one or more technologies to deliver instruction to students who are separated from the instructor and to support regular and substantive interaction between the student and the instructor synchronously or asynchronously.

Technologies used for instruction may include the following: the Internet; one-way and two-way transmissions through open broadcasts, closed circuit, cable, microwave, broadband lines, fiber optics, satellite, or wireless communication devices; audio conferencing; and videocassettes, DVDs, and CD-ROMs, only if the videocassettes, DVDs, and CD-ROMs are used in a course in conjunction with the technologies listed above.

[5] Not all students taking distance education courses exclusively are specified separately in this comparison; for instance, students residing outside the United States or those whose location is unknown are not specified separately.

Reference tables: *Digest of Education Statistics 2019*, tables 303.70, 306.10, and 311.15

Related indicators and resources: Characteristics of Degree-Granting Postsecondary Institutions; College Enrollment Rates; Differences in Postsecondary Enrollment Among Recent High School Completers [*The Condition of Education 2016 Spotlight*]; Immediate College Enrollment Rate; Postbaccalaureate Enrollment; STEM Degrees [*Status and Trends in the Education of Racial and Ethnic Groups*]; Undergraduate Enrollment [*Status and Trends in the Education of Racial and Ethnic Groups*]; Young Adult Educational and Employment Outcomes by Family Socioeconomic Status [*The Condition of Education 2019 Spotlight*]

Glossary: Control of institutions; Degree-granting institutions; Distance education; Enrollment; Full-time enrollment; Part-time enrollment; Postsecondary institutions (basic classification by level); Private institution; Public school or institution; Racial/ethnic group; Undergraduate students

Postbaccalaureate Enrollment

Between 2000 and 2018, total postbaccalaureate enrollment increased by 41 percent (from 2.2 million to 3.0 million students). By 2029, postbaccalaureate enrollment is projected to increase to 3.1 million students.

In fall 2018, some 3.0 million students were enrolled in postbaccalaureate degree programs. Postbaccalaureate degree programs include master's and doctoral programs, as well as professional doctoral programs such as law, medicine, and dentistry. Total postbaccalaureate enrollment increased by 36 percent between 2000 and 2010 (from 2.2 million to 2.9 million students), and by 3 percent between 2010 and 2018 (from 2.9 million to 3.0 million students). Between 2018 and 2029, postbaccalaureate enrollment is projected to increase by 3 percent (from 3.0 million to 3.1 million students).

Figure 1. Actual and projected postbaccalaureate enrollment in degree-granting postsecondary institutions, by sex: Fall 2000 through 2029

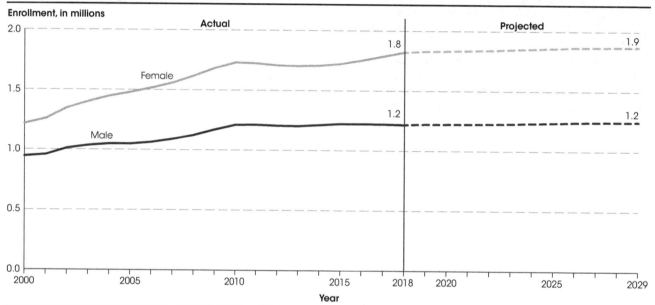

NOTE: Postbaccalaureate degree programs include master's and doctoral programs, as well as professional doctoral programs such as law, medicine, and dentistry. Degree-granting institutions grant associate's or higher degrees and participate in Title IV federal financial aid programs. Projections are based on data through 2018. Some data have been revised from previously published figures.
SOURCE: U.S. Department of Education, National Center for Education Statistics, Integrated Postsecondary Education Data System (IPEDS), Spring 2001 through Spring 2019, Fall Enrollment component; and Enrollment in Degree-Granting Institutions Projection Model, 2000 through 2029. See *Digest of Education Statistics 2019*, table 303.80.

In fall 2018, female students made up 60 percent of total postbaccalaureate enrollment (1.8 million students), and male students made up 40 percent (1.2 million students). Between 2000 and 2010, female enrollment increased by 42 percent, a larger percentage increase than that observed for male enrollment (28 percent). In addition, female enrollment increased by 5 percent between 2010 and 2018 (from 1.7 million to 1.8 million students), whereas male enrollment was 1 percent higher in 2018 than in 2010 (1.22 million vs. 1.21 million students). Between 2018 and 2029, female enrollment is projected to increase by 3 percent (from 1.8 million to 1.9 million students), and male enrollment is projected to increase by 2 percent (from 1.22 million to 1.25 million students).

Figure 2. Postbaccalaureate enrollment in degree-granting postsecondary institutions, by race/ethnicity and nonresident alien status: Fall 2000 through 2018

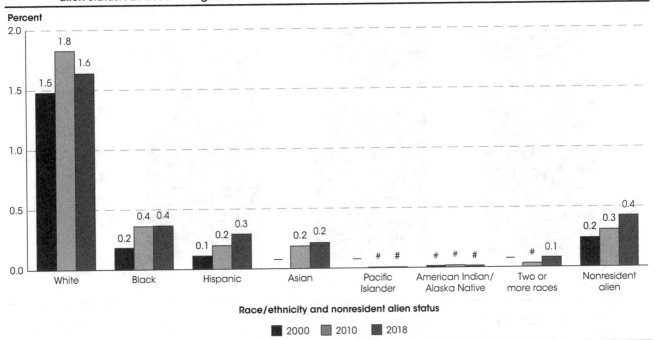

— Not available.
Rounds to zero.
NOTE: Postbaccalaureate degree programs include master's and doctoral programs, as well as professional doctoral programs such as law, medicine, and dentistry. Prior to 2010, separate data on Asian students, Pacific Islander students, and students of Two or more races were not available. Race categories exclude persons of Hispanic ethnicity. Race/ethnicity categories exclude nonresident aliens. Degree-granting institutions grant associate's or higher degrees and participate in Title IV federal financial aid programs. Some data have been revised from previously published figures. Although rounded numbers are displayed, the figures are based on unrounded data.
SOURCE: U.S. Department of Education, National Center for Education Statistics, Integrated Postsecondary Education Data System (IPEDS), Spring 2001 through Spring 2019, Fall Enrollment component. See *Digest of Education Statistics 2019*, table 306.10.

Of the 3.0 million postbaccalaureate students enrolled in fall 2018, some 1.6 million were White, 365,000 were Black, 292,000 were Hispanic, 215,000 were Asian, 81,300 were of Two or more races, 13,600 were American Indian/Alaska Native, and 5,800 were Pacific Islander. Overall, postbaccalaureate enrollment for each racial/ethnic group with available data[1] was higher in 2018 than in 2000. For example, between 2000 and 2018, Hispanic enrollment increased by 164 percent (from 111,000 to 292,000 students), and Black enrollment increased by 101 percent (from 181,000 to 365,000 students). Between 2000 and 2010, enrollment increased for all racial/ethnic groups with available data: Black enrollment increased by 99 percent (from 181,000 to 362,000 students), Hispanic enrollment increased by 79 percent (from 111,000 to 198,000 students), American Indian/Alaska Native enrollment increased by 36 percent (from 12,600 to 17,100 students), and White enrollment increased by 23 percent (from 1.5 million to 1.8 million students). However, between 2010 and 2018, changes in enrollment varied by racial/ethnic group. During this period, American Indian/Alaska Native enrollment decreased by 21 percent (from 17,100 to 13,600 students), White enrollment decreased by 10 percent (from 1.8 million to 1.6 million students), and Pacific Islander enrollment decreased by 10 percent (from 6,500 to 5,800 students). Enrollment of postbaccalaureate students of Two or more races increased by 156 percent (from 31,700 to 81,300 students), Hispanic enrollment increased by 48 percent (from 198,000 to 292,000 students), and Asian enrollment increased by 14 percent (from 188,000 to 215,000 students) between 2010 and 2018. Black enrollment was 1 percent higher in 2018 than in 2010 (365,000 vs. 362,000 students). In fall 2018, degree-granting postsecondary institutions enrolled 425,000 nonresident alien postbaccalaureate students.[2] Enrollment of nonresident alien postbaccalaureate students increased by 28 percent between 2000 and 2010 (from 241,000 to 309,000 students) and increased by 38 percent between 2010 and 2018 (from 309,000 to 425,000 students).

Figure 3. Percentage distribution of postbaccalaureate enrollment in degree-granting postsecondary institutions, by race/ethnicity: Fall 2000, fall 2010, and fall 2018

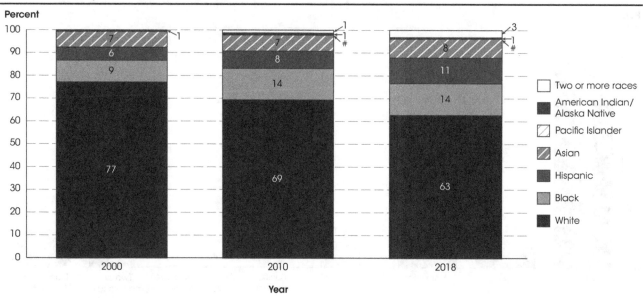

Rounds to zero.
NOTE: Postbaccalaureate degree programs include master's and doctoral programs, as well as professional doctoral programs such as law, medicine, and dentistry. Separate data on those who were Asian and Pacific Islander were unavailable in 2000. In 2000, individuals of Two or more races were required to select a single race category. Race categories exclude persons of Hispanic ethnicity. Race/ethnicity categories exclude nonresident aliens. Degree-granting institutions grant associate's or higher degrees and participate in Title IV federal financial aid programs. Although rounded numbers are displayed, the figures are based on unrounded data.
SOURCE: U.S. Department of Education, National Center for Education Statistics, Integrated Postsecondary Education Data System (IPEDS), Spring 2001, 2011, and 2019, Fall Enrollment component. See *Digest of Education Statistics 2019,* table 306.10.

Of the 2.6 million U.S. resident postbaccalaureate students (excludes enrollment of nonresident alien postbaccalaureate students), the percentage of postbaccalaureate students who were White was lower in fall 2018 (63 percent) than in 2010 (69 percent) and 2000 (77 percent). By contrast, the percentage of postbaccalaureate students who were Black was higher in 2010 and 2018 (14 percent in both years) than in 2000 (9 percent), and the percentage who were Hispanic was higher in 2018 (11 percent) than in 2010 (8 percent) and

2000 (6 percent). In all three years, the percentage of postbaccalaureate students who were American Indian/Alaska Native was 1 percent. In addition, the percentage who were Asian was higher in 2018 (8 percent) than in 2010 (7 percent), the first year for which separate data on individuals who were Asian, Pacific Islander, and of Two or more races were available. The percentage who were of Two or more races was higher in 2018 (3 percent) than in 2010 (1 percent), and the percentage who were Pacific Islander was less than one-half of 1 percent in both years.

Figure 4. Actual and projected postbaccalaureate enrollment in degree-granting postsecondary institutions, by attendance status: Fall 2000 through 2029

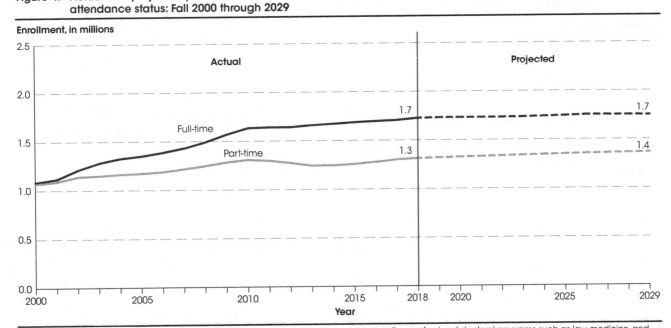

NOTE: Postbaccalaureate degree programs include master's and doctoral programs, as well as professional doctoral programs such as law, medicine, and dentistry. Degree-granting institutions grant associate's or higher degrees and participate in Title IV federal financial aid programs. Projections are based on data through 2018. Some data have been revised from previously published figures.
SOURCE: U.S. Department of Education, National Center for Education Statistics, Integrated Postsecondary Education Data System (IPEDS), Spring 2001 through Spring 2019, Fall Enrollment component; and Enrollment in Degree-Granting Institutions Projection Model, 2000 through 2029. See *Digest of Education Statistics 2019*, table 303.80.

In fall 2018, there were 1.7 million full-time postbaccalaureate students and 1.3 million part-time postbaccalaureate students. Between 2000 and 2018, full-time enrollment had a larger percentage increase (59 percent, from 1.1 million to 1.7 million students) than part-time enrollment (23 percent, from 1.1 million to 1.3 million students). Between 2000 and 2010, full-time enrollment increased by 50 percent (from 1.1 million to 1.6 million students), while part-time enrollment increased by 22 percent (from 1.1 million to 1.3 million

students). More recently, between 2010 and 2018, full-time enrollment increased by 6 percent (from 1.6 million to 1.7 million students), while part-time enrollment remained steady (at 1.3 million students). Between 2018 and 2029, however, part-time enrollment is projected to increase by 4 percent (from 1.3 million to 1.4 million students), whereas full-time enrollment is projected to increase by 1 percent (from 1.72 million to 1.75 million students).

Figure 5. Postbaccalaureate enrollment in degree-granting postsecondary institutions, by control of institution: Fall 2000 through 2018

Enrollment, in millions

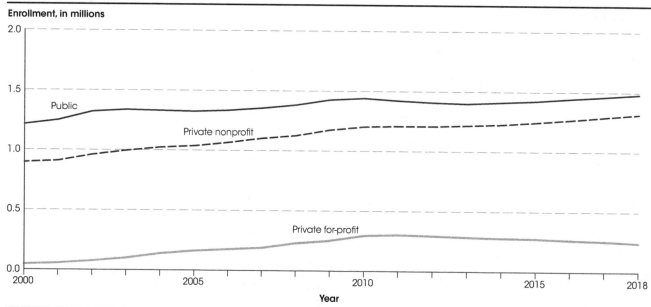

NOTE: Postbaccalaureate degree programs include master's and doctoral programs, as well as professional doctoral programs such as law, medicine, and dentistry. Degree-granting institutions grant associate's or higher degrees and participate in Title IV federal financial aid programs. Some data have been revised from previously published figures.
SOURCE: U.S. Department of Education, National Center for Education Statistics, Integrated Postsecondary Education Data System (IPEDS), Spring 2001 through Spring 2019, Fall Enrollment component. See *Digest of Education Statistics 2019*, table 303.80.

From fall 2000 to fall 2018, postbaccalaureate enrollment had a larger percentage increase at private for-profit institutions (415 percent, from 47,200 to 243,000 students) than at private nonprofit institutions (46 percent, from 896,000 to 1.3 million students) and public institutions (22 percent, from 1.2 million to 1.5 million students). Between 2000 and 2010, postbaccalaureate enrollment increased by 528 percent (from 47,200 to 296,000 students) at private for-profit institutions, compared with increases of 34 percent (from 896,000 to 1.2 million students) at private nonprofit institutions and 19 percent (from 1.2 million to 1.4 million students) at public institutions. More recently, however, between 2010 and 2018, enrollment at private for-profit institutions decreased by 18 percent (from 296,000 to 243,000 students), while enrollment at private nonprofit institutions increased by 9 percent (from 1.2 million to 1.3 million students). Enrollment at public institutions was 3 percent higher in 2018 than in 2010 (1.5 million vs. 1.4 million students).

Figure 6. Percentage of postbaccalaureate students enrolled in degree-granting postsecondary institutions, by participation in distance education and control of institution: Fall 2018

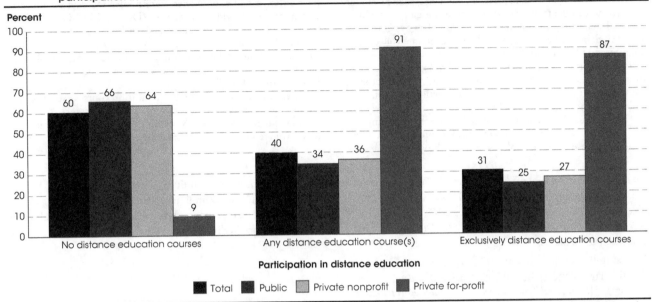

NOTE: Postbaccalaureate degree programs include master's and doctoral programs, as well as professional doctoral programs such as law, medicine, and dentistry. Distance education uses one or more technologies to deliver instruction to students who are separated from the instructor and to support regular and substantive interaction between the student and the instructor synchronously or asynchronously. Technologies used for instruction may include the following: the Internet; one-way and two-way transmissions through open broadcasts, closed circuit, cable, microwave, broadband lines, fiber optics, satellite, or wireless communication devices; audio conferencing; and videocassettes, DVDs, and CD-ROMs, only if the videocassettes, DVDs, and CD-ROMs are used in a course in conjunction with the technologies listed above. Degree-granting institutions grant associate's or higher degrees and participate in Title IV federal financial aid programs.
SOURCE: U.S. Department of Education, National Center for Education Statistics, Integrated Postsecondary Education Data System (IPEDS), Spring 2019, Fall Enrollment component. See *Digest of Education Statistics 2019*, table 311.15.

Distance education[3] courses and programs provide flexible learning opportunities to postbaccalaureate students. In fall 2018, more than one-third (1.2 million) of all postbaccalaureate students participated in distance education. Some 933,000 students, or 31 percent of total postbaccalaureate enrollment, took distance education courses exclusively.[4] Among students who took distance education courses exclusively, 406,000 were enrolled at institutions located in the same state in which they resided, and 495,000 were enrolled at institutions in a different state.[5]

The percentage of postbaccalaureate students enrolled exclusively in distance education courses varied by institutional control (i.e., public, private nonprofit, or private for-profit). In fall 2018, the percentage of students at private for-profit institutions who took distance education courses exclusively (87 percent) was more than three times higher than that of students at private nonprofit (27 percent) and public (25 percent) institutions. The percentage of students who did not take any distance education courses was higher for those enrolled at public (66 percent) and private nonprofit (64 percent) institutions than for those at private for-profit institutions (9 percent).

Endnotes:

[1] Prior to 2010, separate data on Asian students, Pacific Islander students, and students of Two or more races were not available.

[2] In the Integrated Postsecondary Education Data System (IPEDS), data for the nonresident alien category are collected alongside data for racial/ethnic categories.

[3] Distance education uses one or more technologies to deliver instruction to students who are separated from the instructor and to support regular and substantive interaction between the student and the instructor synchronously or asynchronously. Technologies used for instruction may include the following: the Internet; one-way and two-way transmissions through open broadcasts, closed circuit, cable, microwave, broadband lines, fiber optics, satellite, or wireless communication devices; audio conferencing; and videocassettes, DVDs, and CD-ROMs, only if the videocassettes, DVDs, and CD-ROMs are used in a course in conjunction with the technologies listed above.

[4] In comparison, 14 percent of undergraduate students took distance education courses exclusively. See indicator on Undergraduate Enrollment.

[5] Not all students taking distance education courses exclusively are specified separately in this comparison; for instance, students residing outside the United States or those whose location is unknown are not specified separately.

Reference tables: *Digest of Education Statistics 2019*, tables 303.80, 306.10, and 311.15; *Digest of Education Statistics 2017*, table 306.10; *Digest of Education Statistics 2015*, table 306.10; *Digest of Education Statistics 2009*, table 226; *Digest of Education Statistics 2005*, table 205

Related indicators and resources: Characteristics of Degree-Granting Postsecondary Institutions; Postbaccalaureate Enrollment [*Status and Trends in the Education of Racial and Ethnic Groups*]; Trends in Student Loan Debt for Graduate School Completers [*The Condition of Education 2018 Spotlight*]; Undergraduate Enrollment; Undergraduate Enrollment [*Status and Trends in the Education of Racial and Ethnic Groups*]

Glossary: Control of institutions; Distance education; Enrollment; Full-time enrollment; Part-time enrollment; Postbaccalaureate enrollment; Private institution; Public school or institution; Racial/ethnic group

Characteristics of Postsecondary Students

In fall 2018, some 75 percent of the 10.9 million undergraduate students at 4-year institutions were enrolled full time, compared with 37 percent of the 5.7 million undergraduate students at 2-year institutions.

In fall 2018, there were 16.6 million undergraduate students and 3.0 million postbaccalaureate (graduate) students attending degree-granting postsecondary institutions in the United States.[1] Unless otherwise noted, enrollment includes both U.S. resident students and nonresident alien students. The characteristics of students, such as their age and race or ethnicity, varied among public, private nonprofit, and private for-profit 2- and 4-year institutions.

Approximately 10.9 million (65 percent) undergraduate students attended 4-year institutions, and 5.7 million (35 percent) attended 2-year institutions in fall 2018. Of the undergraduate students at 4-year institutions, 8.2 million (75 percent) attended full time and 2.7 million (25 percent) attended part time. Of the undergraduate students at 2-year institutions, 2.1 million (37 percent) attended full time and 3.6 million (63 percent) attended part time.

Figure 1. Percentage distribution of U.S. resident undergraduate enrollment in degree-granting postsecondary institutions, by level and control of institution and student race/ethnicity: Fall 2018

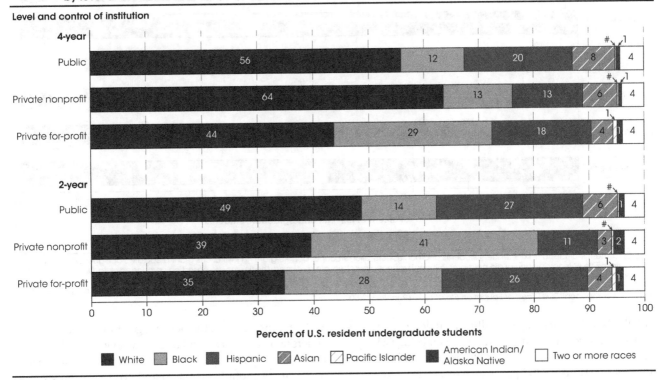

Level and control of institution

Percent of U.S. resident undergraduate students

Legend: White, Black, Hispanic, Asian, Pacific Islander, American Indian/Alaska Native, Two or more races

Rounds to zero.
NOTE: Degree-granting institutions grant associate's or higher degrees and participate in Title IV federal financial aid programs. Race categories exclude persons of Hispanic ethnicity. Although rounded numbers are displayed, the figures are based on unrounded data. Detail may not sum to totals because of rounding.
SOURCE: U.S. Department of Education, National Center for Education Statistics, Integrated Postsecondary Education Data System (IPEDS), Spring 2019, Fall Enrollment component. See *Digest of Education Statistics 2019*, table 306.50.

In fall 2018,[2] the distribution of U.S. resident undergraduates (full- and part-time) by racial or ethnic groups varied among public, private nonprofit, and private for-profit institutions and between 2- and 4-year institutions.[3] Sixty-four percent of undergraduate students at private nonprofit 4-year institutions in fall 2018 were White, which was higher than the percentages of

undergraduate students at public (56 percent) and private for-profit (44 percent) 4-year institutions who were White. The percentage of undergraduate students at private for-profit 4-year institutions who were Black (29 percent) was more than double the percentages at private nonprofit (13 percent) and public (12 percent) 4-year institutions. The percentage of undergraduate students who were

Hispanic was higher at public 4-year institutions (20 percent) than at private for-profit 4-year institutions (18 percent), which in turn was higher than the percentage at private nonprofit 4-year institutions (13 percent). The percentages of undergraduate students at public and private nonprofit 4-year institutions who were Asian (8 and 6 percent, respectively) were higher than the percentage at private for-profit 4-year institutions (4 percent).

The percentages of U.S. resident undergraduate students at public 2-year institutions in fall 2018 who were White or Asian (49 and 6 percent, respectively) were higher than

the corresponding percentages at private nonprofit (39 and 3 percent, respectively) and private for-profit (35 and 4 percent, respectively) 2-year institutions. In contrast, the percentage of undergraduate students at private nonprofit 2-year institutions who were Black (41 percent) was higher than the corresponding percentages at private for-profit and public 2-year institutions (28 and 14 percent, respectively). Higher percentages of undergraduate students at public and private for-profit 2-year institutions (27 and 26 percent, respectively) were Hispanic than at private nonprofit 2-year institutions (11 percent).

Figure 2. Percentage distribution of full-time undergraduate enrollment in degree-granting postsecondary institutions, by level and control of institution and student age: Fall 2017

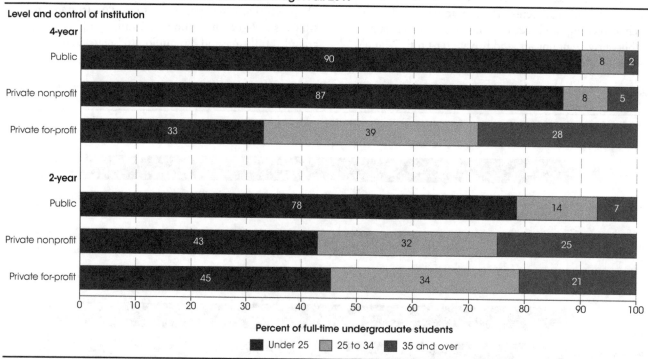

NOTE: Enrollment includes both U.S. resident students and nonresident alien students. Degree-granting institutions grant associate's or higher degrees and participate in Title IV federal financial aid programs. Although rounded numbers are displayed, the figures are based on unrounded data. Detail may not sum to totals because of rounding. Percentage distributions exclude students whose age is unknown.
SOURCE: U.S. Department of Education, National Center for Education Statistics, Integrated Postsecondary Education Data System (IPEDS), Spring 2018, Fall Enrollment component. See *Digest of Education Statistics 2019*, table 303.50.

In fall 2017, the percentage of full-time undergraduate students at 4-year institutions who were under age 25 was higher at public institutions (90 percent) and private nonprofit institutions (87 percent) than at private for-profit institutions (33 percent).[4] At public and private nonprofit 4-year institutions, the percentages of full-time undergraduate students ages 25 to 34 were each 8 percent. In contrast, at private for-profit 4-year institutions, undergraduate students ages 25 to 34 made up the largest age group of those enrolled full time (39 percent).

At 2-year institutions, the percentage of full-time undergraduate students in fall 2017 who were under age 25 was higher at public institutions (78 percent) than at private for-profit (45 percent) and private nonprofit (43 percent) institutions. In contrast, lower percentages of full-time undergraduate students were age 35 and over at public 2-year institutions (7 percent) compared with private for-profit (21 percent) and private nonprofit (25 percent) 2-year institutions.

Figure 3. Percentage distribution of part-time undergraduate enrollment in degree-granting postsecondary institutions, by level and control of institution and student age: Fall 2017

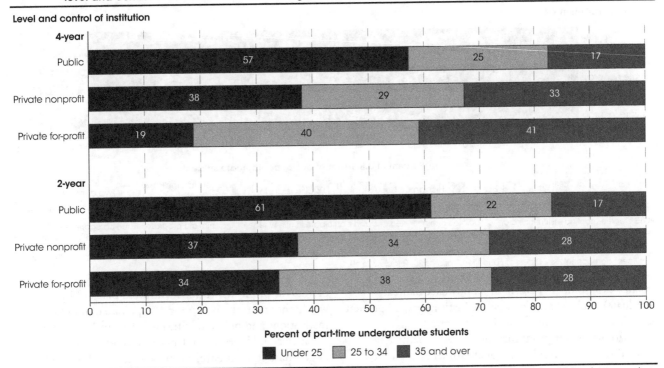

Level and control of institution

NOTE: Enrollment includes both U.S. resident students and nonresident alien students. Degree-granting institutions grant associate's or higher degrees and participate in Title IV federal financial aid programs. Although rounded numbers are displayed, the figures are based on unrounded data. Detail may not sum to totals because of rounding. Percentage distributions exclude students whose age is unknown.
SOURCE: U.S. Department of Education, National Center for Education Statistics, Integrated Postsecondary Education Data System (IPEDS), Spring 2018, Fall Enrollment component. See *Digest of Education Statistics 2019*, table 303.50.

In fall 2017, the percentage of part-time undergraduate students at public 4-year institutions who were under age 25 (57 percent) was higher than the percentages at private nonprofit (38 percent) and private for-profit (19 percent) 4-year institutions. The percentage of part-time undergraduate students who were ages 25 to 34 was lower at public (25 percent) and private nonprofit (29 percent) 4-year institutions than at private for-profit (40 percent) 4-year institutions. The percentage of part-time undergraduate students who were age 35 and over was lower at public 4-year institutions (17 percent) than at private nonprofit (33 percent) and private for-profit (41 percent) 4-year institutions.

At public 2-year institutions, the percentage of part-time undergraduate students who were under age 25 (61 percent) in fall 2017 was higher than at private nonprofit (37 percent) and private for-profit (34 percent) 2-year institutions. The percentage of part-time undergraduate students who were ages 25 to 34 was lower at public institutions (22 percent) than at private nonprofit (34 percent) and private for-profit (38 percent) 2-year institutions. Similarly, the percentage of part-time undergraduate students who were age 35 and over was lower at public institutions (17 percent) than at private nonprofit and private for-profit 2-year institutions (28 percent each).

Figure 4. Percentage distribution of U.S. resident postbaccalaureate enrollment in degree-granting postsecondary institutions, by control of institution and student race/ethnicity: Fall 2018

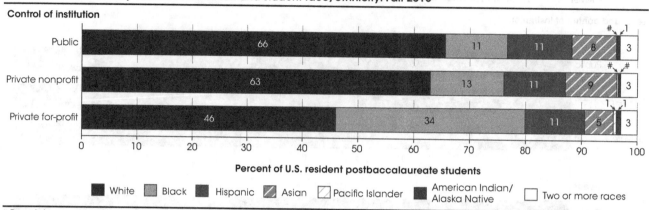

Rounds to zero.
NOTE: Degree-granting institutions grant associate's or higher degrees and participate in Title IV federal financial aid programs. Race categories exclude persons of Hispanic ethnicity. Although rounded numbers are displayed, the figures are based on unrounded data. Detail may not sum to totals because of rounding.
SOURCE: U.S. Department of Education, National Center for Education Statistics, Integrated Postsecondary Education Data System (IPEDS), Spring 2019, Fall Enrollment component. See *Digest of Education Statistics 2019*, table 306.50.

In fall 2018, some 49 percent of all postbaccalaureate (graduate) students attended public institutions, 43 percent attended private nonprofit institutions, and 8 percent attended private for-profit institutions. Approximately two-thirds of U.S. resident graduate students at public institutions and private nonprofit institutions were White (66 and 63 percent, respectively), compared with less than one-half of students at private for-profit institutions (46 percent). The percentage of graduate students at private for-profit institutions who were Black (34 percent) was higher than the percentages at private nonprofit institutions and public institutions (13 and 11 percent, respectively). Hispanic students accounted for 11 percent of graduate student enrollment each at public, private nonprofit, and private for-profit institutions. Asian students accounted for 9 percent of graduate student enrollment at private nonprofit institutions, 8 percent at public institutions, and 5 percent at private for-profit institutions.

Figure 5. Percentage distribution of full-time and part-time postbaccalaureate enrollment in degree-granting postsecondary institutions, by control of institution and student age: Fall 2017

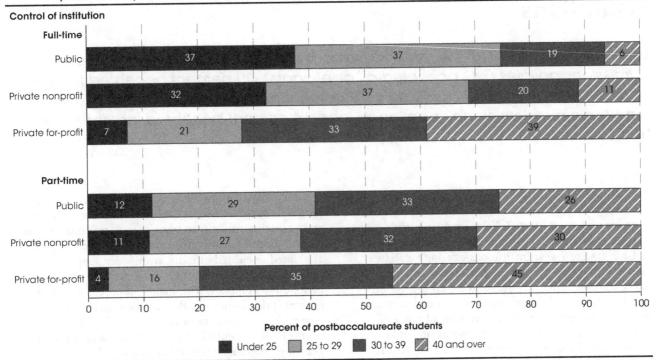

NOTE: Enrollment includes both U.S. resident students and nonresident alien students. Degree-granting institutions grant associate's or higher degrees and participate in Title IV federal financial aid programs. Although rounded numbers are displayed, the figures are based on unrounded data. Detail may not sum to totals because of rounding. Percentage distributions exclude students whose age is unknown.
SOURCE: U.S. Department of Education, National Center for Education Statistics, Integrated Postsecondary Education Data System (IPEDS), Spring 2018, Fall Enrollment component. See *Digest of Education Statistics 2019*, table 303.50.

In fall 2017, approximately three-quarters of full-time postbaccalaureate students at public institutions were under age 30, with 37 percent under age 25 and 37 percent ages 25 to 29. At private nonprofit institutions, the majority (69 percent) of full-time graduate students were under age 30, with 32 percent under age 25 and 37 percent ages 25 to 29. In contrast, the majority (72 percent) of full-time graduate students at private for-profit institutions were age 30 and over, with 33 percent ages 30 to 39 and 39 percent age 40 and over. Among part-time graduate students, 80 percent were age 30 and over at private for-profit institutions, as were 62 percent at private nonprofit institutions and 59 percent at public institutions.

Endnotes:
[1] For more information on how postsecondary enrollment has changed over time, see indicators Undergraduate Enrollment and Postbaccalaureate Enrollment.
[2] The most recent year available for enrollment data by age group is 2017. The most recent year available for enrollment data by racial/ethnic group is 2018.

[3] Throughout this indicator, comparisons by race/ethnicity exclude nonresident alien students.
[4] Throughout this indicator, students of unknown ages are excluded from the age analysis.

Reference tables: *Digest of Education Statistics 2019*, tables 303.50, 303.60, and 306.50; *Digest of Education Statistics 2018*, table 306.50
Related indicators and resources: Characteristics of Degree-Granting Postsecondary Institutions; Characteristics of Postsecondary Faculty; Postbaccalaureate Enrollment; Spotlight B: Characteristics of Postsecondary Institutions Serving Specific Minority Racial/Ethnic Groups [*Status and Trends in the Education of Racial and Ethnic Groups*]; Undergraduate Enrollment

Glossary: College; Control of institutions; Enrollment; Full-time enrollment; Nonresident alien; Part-time enrollment; Postbaccalaureate enrollment; Postsecondary institutions (basic classification by level); Private institution; Public school or institution; Racial/ethnic group; Undergraduate students; U.S. resident

Characteristics of Degree-Granting Postsecondary Institutions

In academic year 2018–19, some 25 percent of 4-year institutions had open admissions policies (i.e., accepted all applicants), 30 percent accepted three-quarters or more of their applicants, 30 percent accepted from one-half to less than three-quarters of their applicants, and 14 percent accepted less than one-half of their applicants.

In academic year 2018–19, there were approximately 3,700 degree-granting institutions in the United States[1] with first-year undergraduates: 2,300 were 4-year institutions offering programs at the bachelor's or higher degree level and 1,300 were 2-year institutions offering associate's degrees and other certificates. Some of the differences in the characteristics of 4-year and 2-year institutions may be related to their differing institutional missions. Four-year institutions tend to have a broad range of instructional programs at the undergraduate and graduate levels. Some 4-year institutions have a strong research focus. The instructional missions of 2-year institutions

generally focus on providing a range of career-oriented programs at the certificate and associate's degree levels and preparing students to transfer to 4-year institutions. Degree-granting institutions may be governed by publicly appointed or elected officials, with major support from public funds (public control), or by privately elected or appointed officials, with major support from private sources (private control). Private institutions may be operated on a nonprofit or for-profit basis. All institutions in this indicator enroll first-year undergraduates in degree-granting programs unless otherwise noted.

Figure 1. Number of degree-granting institutions with first-year undergraduates, by level and control of institution: Academic years 2000–01, 2012–13, and 2018–19

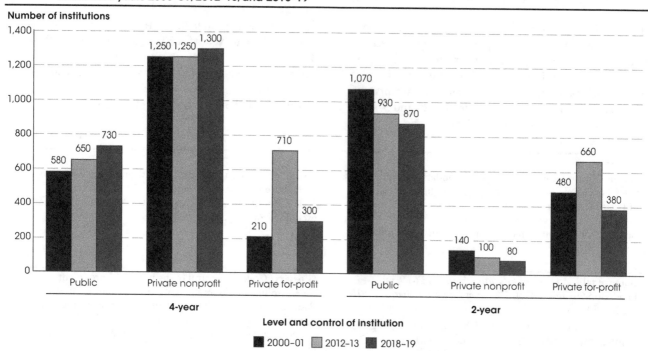

NOTE: Degree-granting institutions grant associate's or higher degrees and participate in Title IV federal financial aid programs. Excludes institutions not enrolling any first-time degree/certificate-seeking undergraduates. Although rounded numbers are displayed, the figures are based on unrounded data.
SOURCE: U.S. Department of Education, National Center for Education Statistics, Integrated Postsecondary Education Data System (IPEDS), Fall 2000 and Fall 2012, Institutional Characteristics component; and Winter 2018–19, Admissions component. See *Digest of Education Statistics 2013*, table 305.30; and *Digest of Education Statistics 2019*, table 305.30.

In academic year 2018–19, the number of public 4-year institutions (730) was 25 percent higher than in 2000–01 (580), and the number of private nonprofit 4-year institutions (1,300) was 4 percent higher than in 2000–01 (1,250). In contrast, the number of private for-profit 4-year institutions fluctuated. Between 2000–01 and 2012–13, the number of private for-profit 4-year institutions more than tripled, from 210 to 710. After peaking in 2012–13, the number of private for-profit 4-year institutions declined to 300 in 2018–19, which was 45 percent higher than the number of such institutions in 2000–01.

The number of public 2-year institutions declined 13 percent from 1,100 in 2000–01 to 930 in 2012–13

and subsequently 7 percent to 870 in 2018–19 for a total decline of 19 percent from 2000-01 to 2018–19. The number of private nonprofit 2-year institutions decreased 30 percent from 140 in 2000–01 to 100 in 2012–13 and was 80 in 2018–19. The number of private for-profit 2-year institutions fluctuated during this period, but not as widely as the number of private for-profit 4-year institutions. Between 2000–01 and 2012–13, the number of private for-profit 2-year institutions increased by 37 percent, from 480 to 660, and then declined by 42 percent to 380 in 2018–19. Overall, the number of private for-profit 2-year institutions was 21 percent lower in 2018–19 than in 2000–01.

Figure 2. Percentage distribution of application acceptance rates at degree-granting institutions with first-year undergraduates, by level and control of institution: Fall 2018

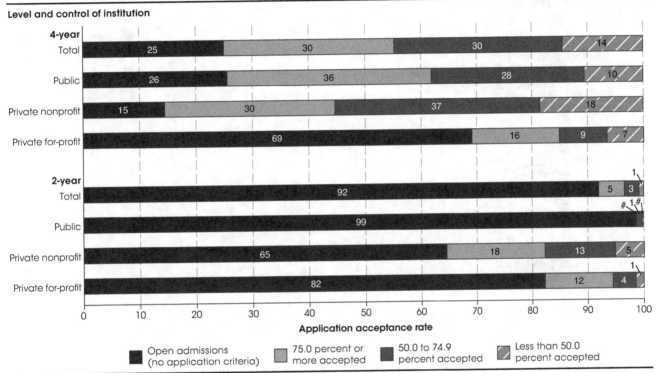

Rounds to zero.
NOTE: Degree-granting institutions grant associate's or higher degrees and participate in Title IV federal financial aid programs. Excludes institutions not enrolling any first-time degree/certificate-seeking undergraduates. Although rounded numbers are displayed, the figures are based on unrounded data. Detail may not sum to totals because of rounding.
SOURCE: U.S. Department of Education, National Center for Education Statistics, Integrated Postsecondary Education Data System (IPEDS), Winter 2018–19, Admissions component. See *Digest of Education Statistics 2019*, table 305.40.

Admissions policies varied among public, private nonprofit, and private for-profit institutions at both the 4-year and the 2-year levels in fall 2018. For example, the percentage of 4-year institutions that had open admissions policies (i.e., accepted all applicants) was 69 percent at private for-profit institutions, 26 percent at public institutions, and 15 percent at private nonprofit institutions. Accordingly, a lower percentage of private for-profit 4-year institutions (7 percent) accepted less than one-half of their applicants than did public (10 percent) and private nonprofit (18 percent) 4-year institutions.

Most 2-year institutions (92 percent) had open admissions policies in 2018–19. Some 99 percent of public 2-year institutions and 82 percent of private for-profit 2-year institutions had open admissions policies, compared with 65 percent of private nonprofit 2-year institutions. Five percent of private nonprofit 2-year institutions accepted less than one-half of their applicants, compared with 1 percent of private for-profit 2-year institutions and less than 1 percent of public 2-year institutions.

Figure 3. Number of degree-granting institutions, by level and control of institution and enrollment size: Fall 2018

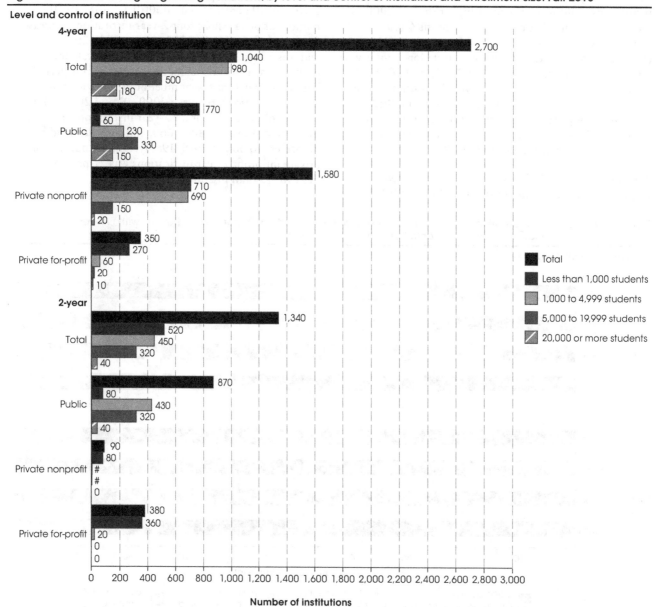

Level and control of institution

Number of institutions

Rounds to zero.
NOTE: Degree-granting institutions grant associate's or higher degrees and participate in Title IV federal financial aid programs. Excludes institutions with no enrollment reported separately from the enrollment of an associated main campus. Although rounded numbers are displayed, the figures are based on unrounded data.
SOURCE: U.S. Department of Education, National Center for Education Statistics, Integrated Postsecondary Education Data System (IPEDS), Spring 2019, Fall Enrollment component. See *Digest of Education Statistics 2019*, table 317.40.

In fall 2018, the approximately 4,000 degree-granting institutions that enrolled both undergraduate and graduate students varied in enrollment size, from institutions enrolling fewer than 200 students to institutions enrolling more than 30,000 students. Despite the sizable number of small degree-granting colleges and universities, most students attended larger colleges and universities. Some 39 percent of institutions (1,600 institutions) had an enrollment size of fewer than 1,000 students, yet these institutions enrolled 3 percent

of all students. Conversely, institutions with 20,000 or more students made up 6 percent of institutions (220 institutions) yet enrolled 38 percent of all students. Midsized institutions that enrolled between 1,000 and 4,999 students made up 35 percent of all institutions and enrolled 18 percent of all students, while those that enrolled between 5,000 and 19,999 students made up 20 percent of all institutions and enrolled 41 percent of all students.

Historically Black colleges and universities (HBCUs) are degree-granting institutions established prior to 1964 with the principal mission of educating Black Americans. In fall 2018, there were 101 degree-granting 4-year and 2-year HBCUs in operation—51 were public institutions and 50 were private nonprofit institutions.

In addition, for fiscal year 2016 (the most current year for which data were available at time of release) the U.S. Department of Education categorized 415 institutions as eligible Hispanic-Serving Institutions. These institutions are eligible to apply for a number of grant programs through the Hispanic-Serving Institutions Division in the Department's Office of Postsecondary Education. Eligible institutions meet various program criteria and have at least 25 percent Hispanic student enrollment.[2]

In fall 2018, thirty-four tribal colleges were members of the American Indian Higher Education Consortium. With few exceptions, tribal colleges are tribally controlled and located on reservations. Seventy-nine percent of the 34 tribally controlled institutions in operation in 2018–19 were public institutions.

Other institutions serving specific populations in fall 2018 included 36 colleges and universities identified by the Women's College Coalition as women's colleges.

Endnotes:
[1] Includes the 50 states and the District of Columbia.
[2] For more information on Hispanic-Serving Institutions, including a list of eligible Hispanic-Serving Institutions for fiscal year 2016, please see https://www2.ed.gov/about/offices/list/ope/idues/hsidivision.html.

Reference tables: *Digest of Education Statistics 2019*; tables 305.30, 305.40, 312.30, 312.50, 313.10, and 317.40; *Digest of Education Statistics 2018*, table 305.30; *Digest of Education Statistics 2013*, table 305.30

Related indicators and resources: Characteristics of Postsecondary Faculty; Characteristics of Postsecondary Students; Postbaccalaureate Enrollment; Postsecondary Institution Expenses; Postsecondary Institution Revenues; Spotlight B: Characteristics of Postsecondary Institutions Serving Specific Minority Racial/Ethnic Groups [*Status and Trends in the Education of Racial and Ethnic Groups*]; Undergraduate Enrollment

Glossary: Associate's degree; Bachelor's degree; Control of institutions; Degree-granting institution; Doctor's degree; Historically Black colleges and universities; Master's degree; Postsecondary education; Postsecondary institutions (basic classification by level); Private institution; Public school or institution; Tribal colleges and universities; Undergraduate students; Women's colleges

Characteristics of Postsecondary Faculty

From fall 1999 to fall 2018, the total number of faculty in degree-granting postsecondary institutions increased by 49 percent (from 1.0 to 1.5 million). While the number of full-time faculty increased by 40 percent over this period, the number of part-time faculty increased by 72 percent between 1999 and 2011 and then decreased by 7 percent between 2011 and 2018.

In fall 2018, of the 1.5 million faculty in degree-granting postsecondary institutions, 54 percent were full time and 46 percent were part time. Faculty include professors, associate professors, assistant professors, instructors, lecturers, assisting professors, adjunct professors, and interim professors.

Figure 1. Number of faculty in degree-granting postsecondary institutions, by employment status: Selected years, fall 1999 through fall 2018

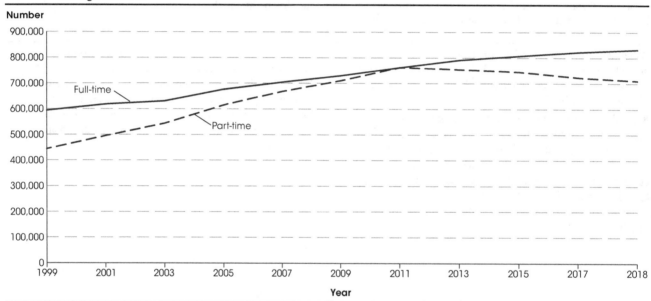

NOTE: Includes faculty members with the title of professor, associate professor, assistant professor, instructor, lecturer, assisting professor, adjunct professor, or interim professor (or the equivalent). Excludes graduate students with titles such as graduate or teaching fellows who assist senior faculty. Degree-granting institutions grant associate's or higher degrees and participate in Title IV federal financial aid programs. Data prior to 2007 exclude institutions with fewer than 15 full-time employees. Some data have been revised from previously published figures.
SOURCE: U.S. Department of Education, National Center for Education Statistics, Integrated Postsecondary Education Data System (IPEDS), "Fall Staff Survey" (IPEDS-S:99); IPEDS Winter 2001–02 through Winter 2004–05, Fall Staff survey; IPEDS Winter 2005–06 through Winter 2011–12, Human Resources component, Fall Staff section; and IPEDS Spring 2014 and Spring 2016 through Spring 2019, Human Resources component. See *Digest of Education Statistics 2019,* table 315.10.

From fall 1999 to fall 2018, the total number of faculty in degree-granting postsecondary institutions increased by 49 percent (from 1.0 to 1.5 million). The number of full-time faculty increased by 40 percent (from 593,400 to 832,100) from fall 1999 to fall 2018—an increase of 28 percent from fall 1999 to fall 2011 and 9 percent from fall 2011 to fall 2018. In comparison, the number of part-time faculty increased by 72 percent (from 444,200 to 762,400) between 1999 and 2011 and then decreased by 7 percent (from 762,400 to 710,500) between 2011 and 2018. As a result of the faster increase in the number of part-time faculty during the first part of this time period, the percentage of all faculty who were part time was still higher in 2018 (46 percent) than in 1999 (43 percent).

Also between 1999 and 2018, the percentage of faculty who were female increased from 41 to 50 percent.

Although the number of faculty in degree-granting public, private nonprofit, and private for-profit postsecondary institutions was higher in 2018 than in 1999, the percentage changes in the number of faculty were much smaller in public institutions and private nonprofit institutions than in private for-profit institutions. The number of faculty in 2018 compared to 1999 was 36 percent higher in public institutions (980,800 vs. 718,600), 70 percent higher in private nonprofit institutions (491,000 vs. 288,700), and 134 percent higher in private for-profit institutions (70,800 vs. 30,300).

Despite the larger change in the number of faculty in private for-profit institutions between 1999 and 2018, only 5 percent of all faculty were employed by private for-profit institutions in 2018, while 64 percent were employed by public institutions and 32 percent were employed by private nonprofit institutions.

The ratio of full-time-equivalent (FTE) students to FTE faculty in degree-granting postsecondary institutions

was 14:1 in fall 2018, a lower ratio than in both fall 1999 (15:1) and fall 2009 (16:1). The FTE student-to-faculty ratio in 2018 was higher in private for-profit institutions (22:1) and public 2-year institutions (18:1) than in public 4-year institutions (14:1) and private nonprofit 4-year institutions (10:1).[1] For more information about how student enrollments have changed over time, see the indicator Undergraduate Enrollment.

Figure 2. For each academic rank, percentage distribution of full-time faculty in degree-granting postsecondary institutions, by race/ethnicity and sex: Fall 2018

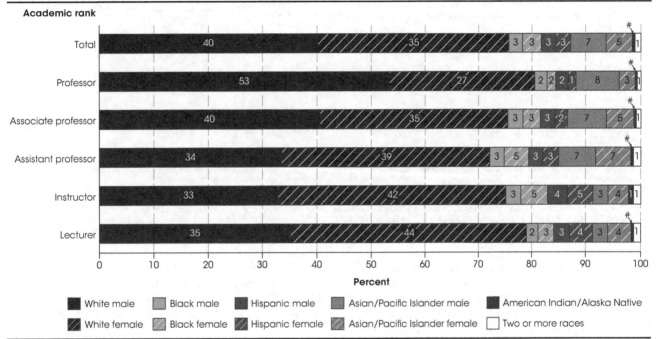

Rounds to zero.
NOTE: Sex breakouts excluded for faculty who were American Indian/Alaska Native and of Two or more races because the percentages were 1 percent or less. Degree-granting institutions grant associate's or higher degrees and participate in Title IV federal financial aid programs. Race categories exclude persons of Hispanic ethnicity. Percentages are based on full-time faculty whose race/ethnicity was known. Detail may not sum to 100 percent due to rounding. Although rounded numbers are displayed, the figures are based on unrounded data.
SOURCE: U.S. Department of Education, National Center for Education Statistics, Integrated Postsecondary Education Data System (IPEDS), IPEDS Spring 2019, Human Resources component. See *Digest of Education Statistics 2019*, table 315.20.

Of all full-time faculty in degree-granting postsecondary institutions in fall 2018, some 40 percent were White males; 35 percent were White females; 7 percent were Asian/Pacific Islander males; 5 percent were Asian/Pacific Islander females; and 3 percent each were Black males, Black females, Hispanic males, and Hispanic females.[2] Those who were American Indian/Alaska Native and those who were of Two or more races each made up 1 percent or less of full-time faculty.

The racial/ethnic and sex distribution of faculty varied by academic rank at degree-granting postsecondary institutions in fall 2018. For example, among full-time professors, 53 percent were White males, 27 percent were White females, 8 percent were Asian/Pacific Islander

males, and 3 percent were Asian/Pacific Islander females. Black males, Black females, and Hispanic males each accounted for 2 percent of full-time professors. The following groups each made up 1 percent or less of full-time professors: Hispanic females, American Indian/ Alaska Native individuals, and individuals of Two or more races. In comparison, among full-time assistant professors, 34 percent were White males, 39 percent were White females, 7 percent each were Asian/Pacific Islander males and Asian/Pacific Islander females, and 5 percent were Black females. Black males, Hispanic males, and Hispanic females each accounted for 3 percent of full-time assistant professors, while American Indian/Alaska Native individuals and individuals of Two or more races each made up 1 percent or less of full-time assistant professors.

Figure 3. Average salary of full-time instructional faculty on 9-month contracts in degree-granting postsecondary institutions, by academic rank: Selected years, 1999–2000 through 2018–19

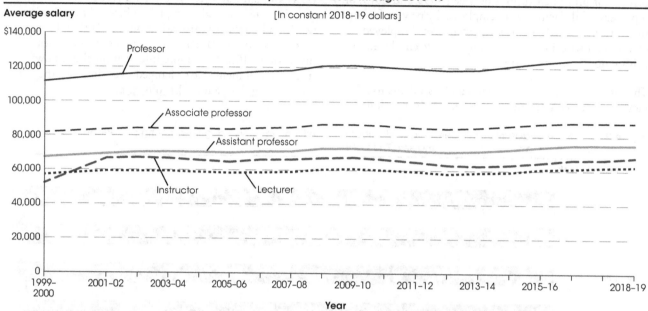

NOTE: Data for academic year 2000–01 are not available. Degree-granting institutions grant associate's or higher degrees and participate in Title IV federal financial aid programs. Data prior to 2007 exclude institutions with fewer than 15 full-time employees. Data exclude instructional faculty at medical schools. Data include imputations for nonrespondent institutions. Salaries are reported in constant 2018–19 dollars, based on the Consumer Price Index (CPI). Some data have been revised from previously published figures.
SOURCE: U.S. Department of Education, National Center for Education Statistics, Integrated Postsecondary Education Data System (IPEDS), "Salaries, Tenure, and Fringe Benefits of Full-Time Instructional Faculty Survey" (IPEDS-SA:1999–2000); IPEDS Winter 2001–02 through Winter 2004–05, Salaries survey; IPEDS Winter 2005–06 through Winter 2011–12, Human Resources component, Salaries section; and IPEDS Spring 2013 through Spring 2019, Human Resources component. See *Digest of Education Statistics 2019*, table 316.10.

In academic year 2018–19, the average salary for full-time instructional faculty on 9-month contracts in degree-granting postsecondary institutions was $88,700. Average salaries ranged from $62,500 for lecturers to $124,700 for professors. The average salary (expressed in constant 2018–19 dollars) for all full-time instructional faculty increased by 4 percent between 1999–2000 and 2009–10 (from $83,600 to $87,200) and was 2 percent higher in 2018–19 than in 2009–10 ($88,700 vs. $87,200). A similar pattern was observed for faculty at most individual academic ranks. The increase in average salary between 1999–2000 and 2009–10 was 9 percent for professors (from $111,300 to $121,200), 6 percent for associate professors (from $81,600 to $86,600), 8 percent for assistant professors (from $67,300 to $72,700), and 7 percent for lecturers (from $57,100 to $61,000). The average salary for most academic ranks showed smaller changes between 2009–10 and 2018–19 than between 1999–2000 and 2009–10. The average salary was 3 percent higher for professors, assistant professors, and lecturers and 1 percent higher for associate professors

in 2018–19 than in 2009–10. The average salary for instructors was 28 percent higher in 2001–02 than in 1999–2000, but there was no measurable change in average salary for instructors from 2001–02 to 2018–19.

Average faculty salaries also varied by sex. The average salary for all full-time instructional faculty in degree-granting postsecondary institutions was higher for males than for females in every academic year from 1999–2000 to 2018–19. In 2018–19, the average salary was $96,400 for males and $80,000 for females. In 2018–19, the male-female gap in average salaries ranged from $3,800 for instructors to $19,500 for professors. Between 1999–2000 and 2018–19, the male-female salary gap (in constant 2018–19 dollars) increased by 38 percent for professors (from $14,100 to $19,500), 8 percent for associate professors (from $5,800 to $6,200), 47 percent for assistant professors (from $4,600 to $6,700), and 56 percent for instructors (from $2,400 to $3,800). In contrast, the gap decreased by 1 percent for lecturers during this time period (from $5,400 to $5,300).

Figure 4. Average salary of full-time instructional faculty on 9-month contracts in degree-granting postsecondary institutions, by control and level of institution: 2018–19

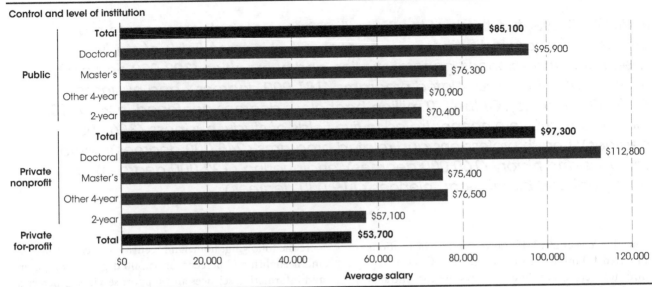

NOTE: Doctoral institutions include institutions that awarded 20 or more doctor's degrees during the previous academic year. Master's institutions include institutions that awarded 20 or more master's degrees, but less than 20 doctor's degrees, during the previous academic year. Data exclude instructional faculty at medical schools. Degree-granting postsecondary institutions grant associate's or higher degrees and participate in Title IV federal financial aid programs. Salaries are reported in constant 2018–19 dollars, based on the Consumer Price Index (CPI).
SOURCE: U.S. Department of Education, National Center for Education Statistics, Integrated Postsecondary Education Data System (IPEDS), IPEDS Spring 2019, Human Resources component. See *Digest of Education Statistics 2019*, table 316.20.

Faculty salaries also varied according to control (i.e., public, private nonprofit, or private for-profit) and level (i.e., 2-year or 4-year) of degree-granting postsecondary institutions. In academic year 2018–19, the average salary (in constant 2018–19 dollars) for full-time instructional faculty in private nonprofit institutions ($97,300) was higher than the average salaries in public institutions ($85,100) and in private for-profit institutions ($53,700). Among the specific types of private nonprofit institutions and public institutions, average salaries for instructional faculty were highest in private nonprofit doctoral institutions ($112,800) and public doctoral institutions ($95,900). Average salaries were lowest for instructional faculty in private nonprofit 2-year institutions ($57,100), public 2-year institutions ($70,400), and public 4-year institutions other than doctoral and master's degree-granting institutions ($70,900). Average salaries for instructional faculty were 3 percent higher in 2018–19 than in 1999–2000 in public institutions ($85,100 vs. $82,300), 12 percent higher in private nonprofit

institutions ($97,300 vs. $87,000), and 21 percent higher in private for-profit institutions ($53,700 vs. $44,200).

In academic year 2018–19, approximately 57 percent of degree-granting postsecondary institutions had tenure systems. A tenure system guarantees that, after completing a probationary period, a professor will not be terminated without just cause. The percentage of institutions with tenure systems ranged from 1 percent at private for-profit institutions to 99 percent at public doctoral institutions. Of full-time faculty at institutions with tenure systems, 45 percent had tenure in 2018–19, down from 54 percent in 1999–2000. At public institutions with tenure systems, the percentage of full-time faculty with tenure decreased by 9 percentage points over this period; at private nonprofit institutions, the percentage decreased by 7 percentage points; and at private for-profit institutions, the percentage decreased by 65 percentage points. At institutions with tenure systems, the percentage of full-time instructional faculty with tenure in 2018–19 was higher for males than for females (54 vs. 40 percent).

Endnotes:
[1] The ratios are calculated by dividing the number of FTE undergraduate and graduate students by the number of FTE faculty (full-time faculty plus the FTE of part-time faculty, including instructional, research, and public service faculty).

[2] Percentages are based on full-time faculty whose race/ethnicity was known. Race/ethnicity was not collected for nonresident aliens.

Reference tables: *Digest of Education Statistics 2019*, tables 314.10, 314.50, 314.60, 315.10, 315.20, 316.10, 316.20, and 316.80

Related indicators and resources: <u>Characteristics of Degree-Granting Postsecondary Institutions</u>; <u>Characteristics of Postsecondary Students</u>; <u>Undergraduate Enrollment</u>

Glossary: Constant dollars; Control of institutions; Degree-granting institution; Doctor's degree; Gap; Postsecondary education; Postsecondary institutions (basic classification by level); Private institution; Public school or institution; Racial/ethnic group; Salary

Undergraduate Degree Fields

In 2017–18, over two-thirds of the 1.0 million associate's degrees conferred by postsecondary institutions were concentrated in three fields of study: liberal arts and sciences, general studies, and humanities (398,000 degrees); health professions and related programs (181,000 degrees); and business (118,000 degrees). Of the 2.0 million bachelor's degrees conferred in 2017–18, more than half were concentrated in five fields of study: business (386,000 degrees); health professions and related programs (245,000 degrees); social sciences and history (160,000 degrees); engineering (122,000 degrees); and biological and biomedical sciences (119,000 degrees).

In academic year 2017–18, postsecondary institutions conferred 1.0 million associate's degrees. Over two-thirds (69 percent) of these degrees were concentrated in three fields of study: liberal arts and sciences, general studies, and humanities (39 percent, or 398,000 degrees); health professions and related programs (18 percent, or 181,000 degrees); and business[1] (12 percent, or 118,000 degrees). The three fields that constituted the next largest percentages of associate's degrees conferred in 2017–18

were the following: homeland security, law enforcement, and firefighting (3 percent, or 35,300 degrees); computer and information sciences and support services (3 percent, or 31,500 degrees); and multi/interdisciplinary studies[2] (3 percent, or 31,100 degrees). Overall, 85,300 associate's degrees or certificates (8 percent) were conferred in science, technology, engineering, and mathematics (STEM)[3] fields in 2017–18.

Figure 1. Number of associate's degrees conferred by postsecondary institutions in selected fields of study: Academic years 2000–01 through 2017–18

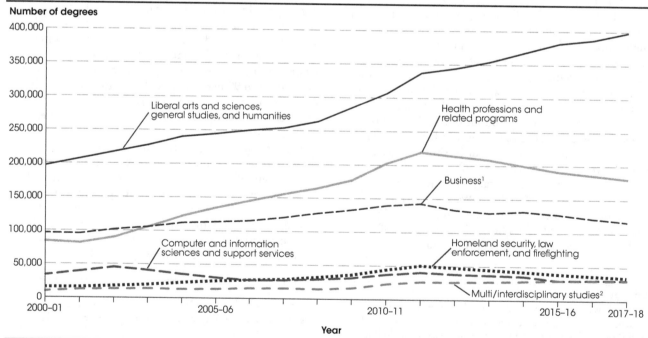

[1] In order to be consistent with the definition of "business" for bachelor's degree data, "business" is defined as business, management, marketing, and related support services, as well as personal and culinary services.
[2] Multi/interdisciplinary studies are instructional programs that derive from two or more distinct programs to provide a cross-cutting focus on a subject concentration that is not subsumed under a single discipline or occupational field. Examples include biological and physical sciences; peace studies and conflict resolution; systems science and theory; and mathematics and computer science.
NOTE: The fields shown are the six programs in which the largest number of associate's degrees were conferred in 2017–18. Data are for postsecondary institutions participating in Title IV federal financial aid programs. Data have been adjusted where necessary to conform to the 2009–10 Classification of Instructional Programs. Some data have been revised from previously published figures.
SOURCE: U.S. Department of Education, National Center for Education Statistics, Integrated Postsecondary Education Data System (IPEDS), Fall 2001 through Fall 2018, Completions component. See *Digest of Education Statistics 2019*, table 321.10; and *Digest of Education Statistics 2012*, table 312.

Between 2000–01 and 2017–18, the number of associate's degrees conferred increased by 75 percent, from 579,000 degrees to 1.0 million degrees. Over this time period, the number of associate's degrees conferred in liberal arts and sciences, general studies, and humanities increased by 102 percent, from 197,000 degrees in 2000–01 to 398,000 degrees in 2017–18. The number of associate's degrees conferred in health professions and related programs increased by 159 percent between 2000–01 and 2011–12, from 84,700 to 219,000 degrees, and then decreased by 18 percent, to 181,000 associate's degrees, between 2011–12 and 2017–18. The number of associate's degrees conferred in business increased by 48 percent between 2000–01 and 2011–12, from 96,800 to 143,000 degrees, and then

decreased by 18 percent, to 118,000 associate's degrees, between 2011–12 and 2017–18. Among other fields in which at least 10,000 associate's degrees were conferred in 2017–18, the number of degrees conferred more than doubled between 2000–01 and 2017–18 in the following fields: homeland security, law enforcement, and firefighting (from 16,400 to 35,300 degrees, an increase of 115 percent); multi/interdisciplinary studies (from 10,400 to 31,100 degrees, an increase of 198 percent); social sciences and history (from 5,100 to 23,700 degrees, an increase of 361 percent); psychology (from 1,600 to 12,500 degrees, an increase of 704 percent); and physical sciences and science technologies (from 2,400 to 10,100 degrees, an increase of 330 percent).

Figure 2. Percentage of associate's degrees conferred in science, technology, engineering, and mathematics (STEM) fields, by race/ethnicity and nonresident status: Academic year 2017–18

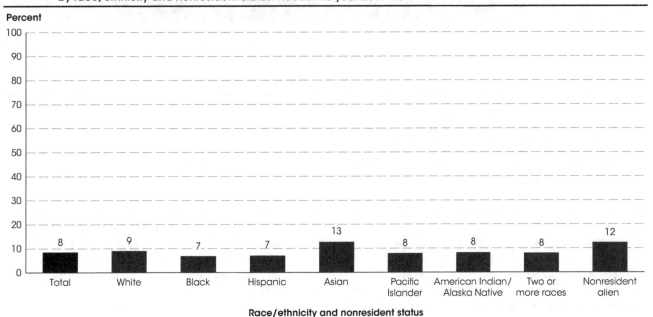

NOTE: STEM fields include biological and biomedical sciences, computer and information sciences, engineering and engineering technologies, mathematics and statistics, and physical sciences and science technologies. Data are for postsecondary institutions participating in Title IV federal financial aid programs. Race categories exclude persons of Hispanic ethnicity. Race/ethnicity categories exclude nonresident aliens. Although rounded numbers are displayed, the figures are based on unrounded data.
SOURCE: U.S. Department of Education, National Center for Education Statistics, IPEDS, Fall 2018, Completions component. See *Digest of Education Statistics 2019*, tables 318.45 and 321.30.

Liberal arts and sciences, general studies, and humanities; health professions and related programs; and business were the top three associate's degree fields of study for all racial/ethnic groups and for nonresident alien graduates in 2017–18. The percentage of associate's degrees conferred in a STEM field varied by race/ethnicity. Thirteen percent of associate's degrees conferred to Asian graduates were

in a STEM field, which was higher than the percentage conferred to nonresident alien[4] graduates (12 percent) and to graduates who were White (9 percent), American Indian/Alaska Native (8 percent), of Two or more races (8 percent), Pacific Islander (8 percent), Black (7 percent), and Hispanic (7 percent).

Figure 3. Percentage distribution of associate's degrees conferred by postsecondary institutions in selected fields of study, by sex: Academic year 2017–18

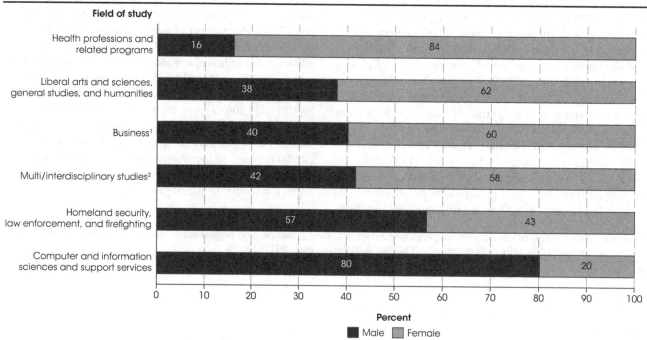

¹ In order to be consistent with the definition of "business" for bachelor's degree data, "business" is defined as business, management, marketing, and related support services, as well as personal and culinary services.
² Multi/interdisciplinary studies are instructional programs that derive from two or more distinct programs to provide a cross-cutting focus on a subject concentration that is not subsumed under a single discipline or occupational field. Examples include biological and physical sciences; peace studies and conflict resolution; systems science and theory; and mathematics and computer science.
NOTE: The fields shown are the six programs in which the largest number of associate's degrees were conferred in 2017–18. Data are for postsecondary institutions participating in Title IV federal financial aid programs. Detail may not sum to totals because of rounding.
SOURCE: U.S. Department of Education, National Center for Education Statistics, Integrated Postsecondary Education Data System (IPEDS), Fall 2018, Completions component. See *Digest of Education Statistics 2019*, table 321.10.

In 2017–18, females earned 61 percent (613,000 degrees) and males earned 39 percent (399,000 degrees) of all associate's degrees conferred. Of the six fields in which the most associate's degrees were conferred in 2017–18, females were conferred the majority of degrees in four: health professions and related programs (84 percent); liberal arts and sciences, general studies, and humanities (62 percent); business (60 percent); and multi/interdisciplinary studies (58 percent). Males were conferred the majority of associate's degrees in homeland security, law enforcement, and firefighting (57 percent) and in computer and information sciences and support services (80 percent).

Figure 4. Number of bachelor's degrees conferred by postsecondary institutions in selected fields of study: Academic years 2000–01 through 2017–18

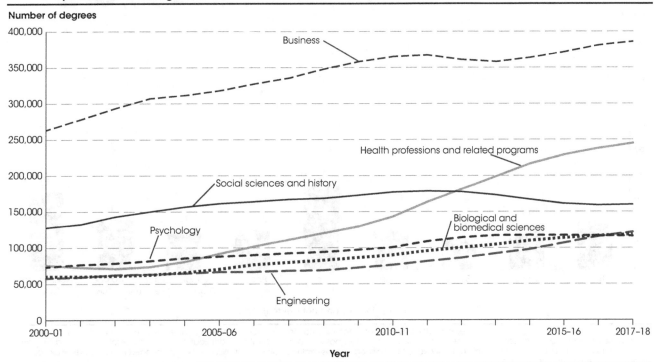

NOTE: The fields shown are the six programs in which the largest number of bachelor's degrees were conferred in 2017–18. Data are for postsecondary institutions participating in Title IV federal financial aid programs. Data have been adjusted where necessary to conform to the 2009–10 Classification of Instructional Programs. Some data have been revised from previously published figures.
SOURCE: U.S. Department of Education, National Center for Education Statistics, Integrated Postsecondary Education Data System (IPEDS), Fall 2001 through Fall 2018, Completions component. See *Digest of Education Statistics 2019*, table 322.10; and *Digest of Education Statistics 2012*, table 313.

Postsecondary institutions conferred 2.0 million bachelor's degrees in 2017–18. More than half were concentrated in five fields of study: business (19 percent, or 386,000 degrees); health professions and related programs (12 percent, or 245,000 degrees); social sciences and history (8 percent, or 160,000 degrees); engineering (6 percent, or 122,000 degrees); and biological and biomedical sciences (6 percent, or 119,000 degrees). The fields in which the next largest percentages of bachelor's degrees were conferred in 2017–18 were psychology (6 percent, or 116,000 degrees); communication, journalism, and related programs (5 percent, or 92,300 degrees); visual and performing arts (4 percent, or 88,600 degrees); education (4 percent, or 82,600 degrees); and computer and information sciences (4 percent, or 79,600 degrees). Overall, 395,000 bachelor's degrees (20 percent) were conferred in a STEM field.

Between 2000–01 and 2017–18, the number of bachelor's degrees conferred increased by 59 percent, from 1.2 million degrees to 2.0 million degrees. Between 2000–01 and 2017–18, the number of bachelor's degrees conferred in business increased by 47 percent, from 264,000 to 386,000 degrees. The number of bachelor's degrees conferred in health professions and related programs increased by 223 percent between 2000–01 and 2017–18, from 75,900 to 245,000 degrees. The number of bachelor's degrees conferred in social sciences and history increased by 39 percent between 2000–01 and 2011–12, from 128,000 to 179,000 degrees, and then decreased by 10 percent to 160,000 degrees in 2017–18. Among other fields in which more than 10,000 bachelor's degrees were conferred in 2017–18, the number of degrees conferred more than doubled between 2000–01 and 2017–18 in each of the following fields: engineering (from 58,200 to 122,000 degrees, an increase of 110 percent); homeland security, law enforcement, and firefighting (from 25,200 to 58,100 degrees, an increase of 131 percent); parks, recreation, leisure, and fitness studies (from 17,900 to 53,900 degrees, an increase of 200 percent); and mathematics and statistics (from 11,200 to 25,300 degrees, an increase of 126 percent).

Figure 5. Percentage of bachelor's degrees conferred in science, technology, engineering, and mathematics (STEM) fields, by race/ethnicity and nonresident status: Academic year 2017–18

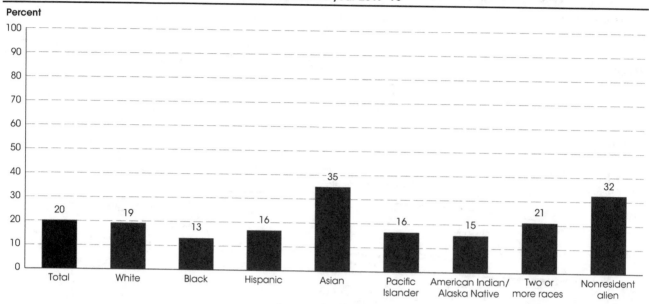

NOTE: STEM fields include biological and biomedical sciences, computer and information sciences, engineering and engineering technologies, mathematics and statistics, and physical sciences and science technologies. Data are for postsecondary institutions participating in Title IV federal financial aid programs. Race categories exclude persons of Hispanic ethnicity. Race/ethnicity categories exclude nonresident aliens. Although rounded numbers are displayed, the figures are based on unrounded data.
SOURCE: U.S. Department of Education, National Center for Education Statistics, IPEDS, Fall 2018, Completions component. See *Digest of Education Statistics 2019*, tables 318.45 and 322.30.

Business was the most common field of study for bachelor's degrees conferred in 2017–18 within each racial/ethnic group and for nonresident alien graduates. As with associate's degrees, the percentage of bachelor's degrees that were conferred in a STEM field varied by race/ethnicity. Over one-third (35 percent) of bachelor's degrees conferred to Asian graduates were in a STEM field, which was higher than the percentage conferred to graduates in all other racial/ethnic groups. Also, the percentage of nonresident aliens (32 percent) receiving bachelor's degrees in a STEM field was higher than that for students who were of Two or more races (21 percent), White (19 percent), Hispanic (16 percent), Pacific Islander (16 percent), American Indian/Alaska Native (15 percent), and Black (13 percent).

Figure 6. Percentage distribution of bachelor's degrees conferred by postsecondary institutions in selected fields of study, by sex: Academic year 2017–18

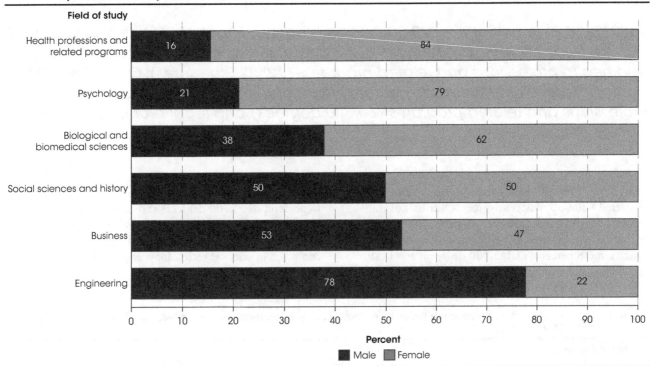

NOTE: The fields shown are the six programs in which the largest number of bachelor's degrees were conferred in 2017–18. Data are for postsecondary institutions participating in Title IV federal financial aid programs. Detail may not sum to totals because of rounding. Although rounded numbers are displayed, the figures are based on unrounded data.
SOURCE: U.S. Department of Education, National Center for Education Statistics, Integrated Postsecondary Education Data System (IPEDS), Fall 2018, Completions component. See *Digest of Education Statistics 2019*, tables 322.40 and 322.50.

In 2017–18, females earned 57 percent (1.1 million degrees) and males earned 43 percent (845,000 degrees) of all bachelor's degrees conferred. Of the six fields in which the most bachelor's degrees were conferred in 2017–18, females earned the majority of degrees in three: health professions and related programs (84 percent); psychology (79 percent); and biological and biomedical sciences (62 percent). Bachelor's degrees conferred in social sciences and history were equally divided between males and females (50 percent each). Males earned the majority of degrees conferred in business (53 percent) and engineering (78 percent).

Endnotes:
[1] Personal and culinary services have been added to the definition of "business" for associate's degree data in order to be consistent with the definition of "business" for bachelor's degree data. Thus, for all data in this indicator, "business" is defined as business, management, marketing, and related support services, as well as personal and culinary services.
[2] Multi/interdisciplinary studies are instructional programs that derive from two or more distinct programs to provide a cross-cutting focus on a subject concentration that is not subsumed under a single discipline or occupational field. Examples include biological and physical sciences; peace studies and conflict resolution; systems science and theory; and mathematics and computer science.

[3] STEM fields include biological and biomedical sciences; computer and information sciences; engineering and engineering technologies; mathematics and statistics; and physical sciences and science technologies. Construction trades and mechanic and repair technologies/technicians are categorized as engineering technologies in some tables to faciliate trend comparisons but are not included as STEM fields in this indicator.
[4] In the Integrated Postsecondary Education Data System (IPEDS), racial/ethnic data were not collected for nonresident alien students, and their data were compiled as a separate group.

Reference tables: *Digest of Education Statistics 2019*, tables 318.45, 321.10, 321.30, 322.10, 322.30, 322.40, and 322.50; *Digest of Education Statistics 2012*, tables 312 and 313
Related indicators and resources: Employment Outcomes of Bachelor's Degree Holders; Graduate Degree Fields; Post-Bachelor's Employment Outcomes by Sex and Race/Ethnicity [*The Condition of Education 2016 Spotlight*]; Postsecondary Certificates and Degrees Conferred; Undergraduate and Graduate Degree Fields [*Status and Trends in the Education of Racial and Ethnic Groups*]

Glossary: Associate's degree; Bachelor's degree; Classification of Instructional Programs (CIP); Racial/ethnic group; STEM fields

Graduate Degree Fields

In 2017–18, over half of the 820,000 master's degrees conferred were concentrated in three fields of study: business (192,000 degrees), education (146,000 degrees), and health professions and related programs (125,000 degrees). Of the 184,000 doctor's degrees conferred, 62 percent were concentrated in two fields: health professions and related programs (80,300 degrees) and legal professions and studies (34,500 degrees).

In academic year 2017–18, postsecondary institutions conferred 820,000 master's degrees. Over half of the master's degrees conferred were concentrated in three fields of study: business (23 percent, or 192,000 degrees), education (18 percent, or 146,000 degrees), and health professions and related programs (15 percent, or 125,000 degrees). The fields in which the next largest percentages

of master's degrees were conferred were engineering (6 percent, or 51,700 degrees) and computer and information sciences (6 percent, or 46,500 degrees). Overall, 140,000 master's degrees (17 percent) were conferred in science, technology, engineering, and mathematics (STEM)[1] fields.

Figure 1. Number of master's degrees conferred by postsecondary institutions in selected fields of study: Academic years 2000–01 through 2017–18

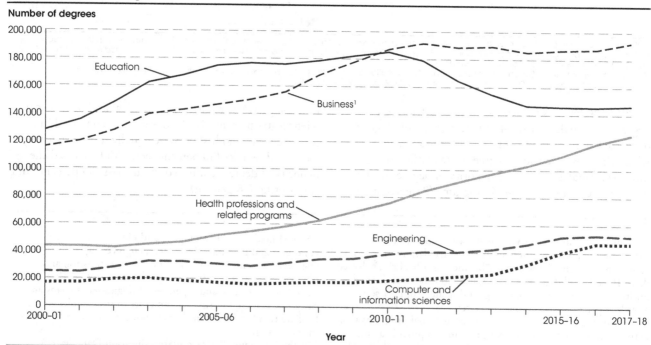

[1] In order to be consistent with the definition of "business" for bachelor's degree data, "business" is defined as business, management, marketing, and related support services, as well as personal and culinary services.
NOTE: The fields shown are the five programs in which the largest numbers of master's degrees were conferred in 2017–18. Data are for postsecondary institutions participating in Title IV federal financial aid programs. Data have been adjusted where necessary to conform to the 2009–10 Classification of Instructional Programs. Some data have been revised from previously published figures.
SOURCE: U.S. Department of Education, National Center for Education Statistics, Integrated Postsecondary Education Data System (IPEDS), Fall 2001 through Fall 2018, Completions component. See *Digest of Education Statistics 2019*, table 323.10; *Digest of Education Statistics 2012*, table 314.

Between 2000–01 and 2017–18, the number of master's degrees conferred increased by 73 percent, from 474,000 to 820,000 degrees. Between 2000–01 and 2011–12, the number of master's degrees conferred in business rose by 66 percent, from 116,000 to 192,000 degrees, but there was no clear trend between 2011–12 and 2017–18 (192,000 degrees were conferred in business in 2017–18). In 2010–11, business surpassed education as the field in which the largest number of master's degrees were conferred and has remained the largest field in each subsequent year. Between 2000–01 and 2010–11, the number of master's degrees conferred in education rose by 45 percent, from 128,000 to 185,000 degrees. The number of degrees then fell 21 percent to 147,000 degrees in 2014–15 and remained flat through 2017–18. Between 2000–01 and 2017–18, the number of master's degrees conferred increased in each of the three next largest

fields: health professions and related programs (from 43,600 to 125,000 degrees, an increase of 187 percent), engineering (from 25,200 to 51,700 degrees, an increase of 105 percent), and computer and information sciences (from 16,900 to 46,500 degrees, an increase of 175 percent). Among other fields in which at least 10,000 master's degrees were conferred in 2017–18, the number of degrees conferred more than doubled between 2000–01 and 2017–18 in biological and biomedical sciences (from 7,000 to 17,200 degrees, an increase of 145 percent), mathematics and statistics (from 3,200 to 10,400 degrees, an increase of 225 percent), homeland security, law enforcement, and firefighting (from 2,500 to 10,300 degrees, an increase of 309 percent), and multi/interdisciplinary studies[2] (from 3,400 to 10,200 degrees, an increase of 198 percent).

Figure 2.   Percentage of master's degrees conferred in science, technology, engineering, and mathematics (STEM) fields, by race/ethnicity and nonresident status: Academic year 2017–18

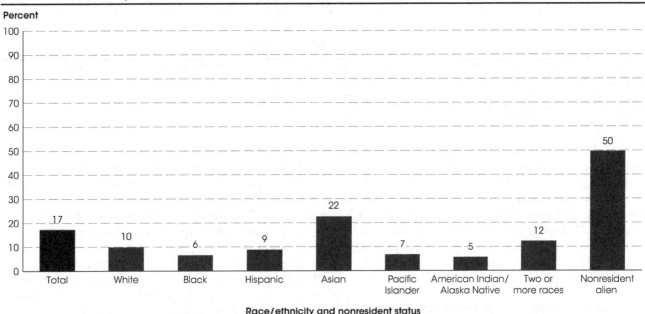

NOTE: STEM fields include biological and biomedical sciences, computer and information sciences, engineering, engineering technologies, mathematics and statistics, and physical sciences and science technologies. Data are for postsecondary institutions participating in Title IV federal financial aid programs. Race categories exclude persons of Hispanic ethnicity. Race/ethnicity categories exclude nonresident alien students.
SOURCE: U.S. Department of Education, National Center for Education Statistics, IPEDS, Fall 2018, Completions component. See Digest of Education Statistics 2019, table 323.30.

In 2017–18, the three fields in which the most master's degrees were conferred—business, education, and health professions and related programs—were the same for all racial/ethnic groups, although the rank order of these fields differed across groups. Business was the top field for all but White students, for whom education was the top field. For nonresident alien[3] students, the three fields in which the most master's degrees were conferred were business, computer and information sciences, and engineering. The percentage of master's degrees conferred

in a STEM field varied by race/ethnicity. Twenty-two percent of master's degrees conferred to Asian students were in a STEM field, which was higher than the percentages for students who were of Two or more races (12 percent), White (10 percent), Hispanic (9 percent), Pacific Islander (7 percent), Black (6 percent), and American Indian/Alaska Native (5 percent). Notably, 50 percent of master's degrees conferred to nonresident alien students were in a STEM field.

Figure 3. Percentage distribution of master's degrees conferred by postsecondary institutions in selected fields of study, by sex: Academic year 2017–18

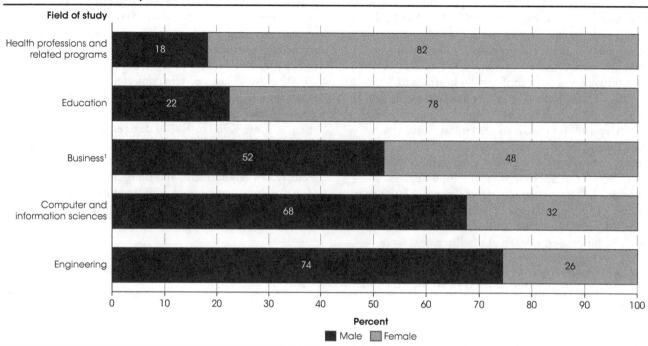

Percent

■ Male ■ Female

[1] In order to be consistent with the definition of "business" for bachelor's degree data, "business" is defined as business, management, marketing, and related support services, as well as personal and culinary services.
NOTE: The fields shown are the five programs in which the largest numbers of master's degrees were conferred in 2017–18. Data are for postsecondary institutions participating in Title IV federal financial aid programs. Detail may not sum to totals because of rounding.
SOURCE: U.S. Department of Education, National Center for Education Statistics, Integrated Postsecondary Education Data System (IPEDS), Fall 2018, Completions component. See *Digest of Education Statistics 2019*, tables 323.40 and 323.50.

In 2017–18, females earned 60 percent (493,000 degrees) and males earned 40 percent (327,000 degrees) of all master's degrees conferred. Of the five fields in which the most master's degrees were conferred, females earned the majority of degrees in health professions and related programs (82 percent) and education (78 percent). Males earned the majority of degrees in business (52 percent), computer and information sciences (68 percent), and engineering (74 percent).

Two fields accounted for 62 percent of the 184,000 doctor's degrees conferred in 2017–18: health professions and related programs (44 percent, or 80,300 degrees) and legal professions and studies (19 percent, or 34,500 degrees). The three fields in which the next largest percentages of doctor's degrees were conferred were education (7 percent, or 12,800 degrees), engineering (6 percent, or 10,800 degrees), and biological and biomedical sciences (4 percent, or 8,200 degrees). For the purposes of this analysis, doctor's degrees include Ph.D., Ed.D., and comparable degrees at the doctoral level, as well as such degrees as M.D., D.D.S., and J.D. that were previously classified as first-professional degrees.[4]

Figure 4. Number of doctor's degrees conferred by postsecondary institutions in selected fields of study: Academic years 2000–01 through 2017–18

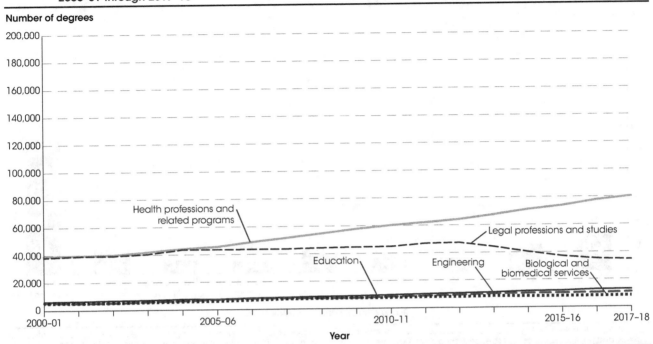

NOTE: Doctor's degrees include Ph.D., Ed.D., and comparable degrees at the doctoral level, as well as such degrees as M.D., D.D.S., and J.D. that were formerly classified as first-professional degrees. The fields shown are the five programs in which the largest numbers of doctor's degrees were conferred in 2017–18. Data are for postsecondary institutions participating in Title IV federal financial aid programs. Data have been adjusted where necessary to conform to the 2009–10 Classification of Instructional Programs. 2010–11 was the last year the classification of first-professional degrees was used. Some data have been revised from previously published figures.
SOURCE: U.S. Department of Education, National Center for Education Statistics, Integrated Postsecondary Education Data System (IPEDS), Fall 2001 through Fall 2018, Completions component. See *Digest of Education Statistics 2019*, table 324.10; *Digest of Education Statistics 2012*, table 315.

Between 2000–01 and 2017–18, the number of doctor's degrees conferred increased by 54 percent, from 120,000 to 184,000 degrees. Over this time period, the number of doctor's degrees conferred in health professions and related programs increased by 106 percent, from 39,000 degrees in 2000–01 to 80,300 degrees in 2017–18. Between 2000–01 and 2012–13, the number of doctor's degrees conferred in legal professions and studies increased by 24 percent, from 38,200 to 47,200 degrees;

the number of degrees then fell to 34,500 degrees in 2017–18 (a decrease of 27 percent). Between 2000–01 and 2017–18, the number of doctor's degrees conferred increased in each of the next three largest fields: education (from 6,300 to 12,800 degrees, an increase of 103 percent), engineering (from 5,500 to 10,800 degrees, an increase of 97 percent), and biological and biomedical sciences (from 5,200 to 8,200 degrees, an increase of 57 percent).

Figure 5. Percentage of doctor's degrees conferred in science, technology, engineering, and mathematics (STEM) fields, by race/ethnicity and nonresident status: Academic year 2017–18

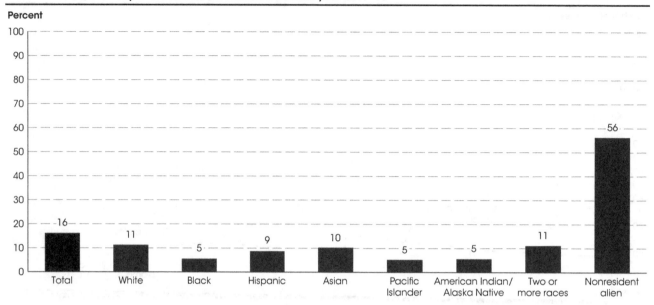

NOTE: STEM fields include biological and biomedical sciences, computer and information sciences, engineering, engineering technologies, mathematics and statistics, and physical sciences and science technologies. Data are for postsecondary institutions participating in Title IV federal financial aid programs. Race categories exclude persons of Hispanic ethnicity. Race/ethnicity categories exclude nonresident aliens. Although rounded numbers are displayed, the figures are based on unrounded data.
SOURCE: U.S. Department of Education, National Center for Education Statistics, IPEDS, Fall 2018, Completions component. See *Digest of Education Statistics 2019*, tables 318.45 and 324.25.

In 2017–18, the two fields in which the most doctor's degrees were conferred—health professions and related programs and legal professions and studies—were the same for all racial/ethnic groups. For nonresident alien students, the two fields in which the most doctor's degrees were conferred were engineering and health professions and related programs. The percentage of doctor's degrees conferred in a STEM field varied among racial/ethnic groups. The percentage of doctor's degrees conferred in a STEM field was highest for nonresident alien students (56 percent). Eleven percent of doctor's degrees conferred to White students and students of Two or more races were in a STEM field, which was higher than the percentages for Asian (10 percent), Hispanic (9 percent), American Indian/Alaska Native (5 percent), Black (5 percent), and Pacific Islander (5 percent) students.

Figure 6. Percentage distribution of doctor's degrees conferred by postsecondary institutions in selected fields of study, by sex: Academic year 2017–18

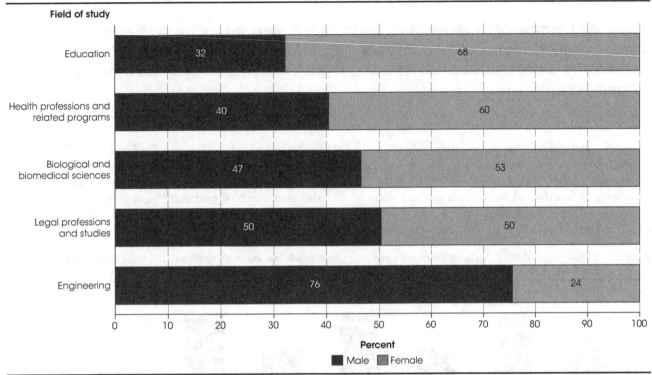

NOTE: The fields shown are the five programs in which the largest numbers of doctor's degrees were conferred in 2017–18. Doctor's degrees include Ph.D., Ed.D., and comparable degrees at the doctoral level, as well as such degrees as M.D., D.D.S., and J.D. that were formerly classified as first-professional degrees. Data are for postsecondary institutions participating in Title IV federal financial aid programs. 2010–11 was the last year the classification of first-professional degrees was used. Detail may not sum to totals because of rounding. Although rounded numbers are displayed, the figures are based on unrounded data.
SOURCE: U.S. Department of Education, National Center for Education Statistics, Integrated Postsecondary Education Data System (IPEDS), Fall 2018, Completions component. See *Digest of Education Statistics 2019*, tables 324.30 and 324.35.

In 2017–18, females earned 54 percent (98,500 degrees) and males earned 46 percent (85,600 degrees) of all doctor's degrees conferred. Of the five fields in which the most doctor's degrees were conferred, females earned the majority of degrees in education (68 percent), health professions and related programs (60 percent), and biological and biomedical sciences (53 percent).

Doctor's degrees in legal professions and studies were split evenly between males and females (50 percent each). Of the five fields in which the most doctor's degrees were conferred, females earned the fewest in engineering (24 percent). In contrast, of the five fields in which the most doctor's degrees were conferred, males earn the most in engineering (76 percent).

Endnotes:
[1] STEM fields include biological and biomedical sciences, computer and information sciences, engineering, engineering technologies, mathematics and statistics, and physical sciences and science technologies.
[2] Multi/interdisciplinary studies are instructional programs that derive from two or more distinct programs to provide a cross-cutting focus on a subject concentration that is not subsumed under a single discipline or occupational field. Examples include biological and physical sciences; peace studies and conflict resolution; systems science and theory; and mathematics and computer science.
[3] In the Integrated Postsecondary Education Data System (IPEDS), racial/ethnic data were not collected for nonresident alien students, and their data were compiled as a separate group.
[4] 2010–11 was the last year the classification of first-professional degrees was used.

Reference tables: *Digest of Education Statistics 2019*, tables 318.45, 323.10, 323.20, 323.30, 323.40, 323.50, 324.10, 324.20, 324.25, 324.30, and 324.35; *Digest of Education Statistics 2012*, tables 314 and 315

Related indicators and resources: Postsecondary Certificates and Degrees Conferred; Trends in Student Loan Debt for Graduate School Completers [*The Condition of Education 2018 Spotlight*]; Undergraduate and Graduate Degree Fields [*Status and Trends in the Education of Racial and Ethnic Groups*]; Undergraduate Degree Fields

Glossary: Classification of Instructional Programs (CIP); Doctor's degree; Master's degree; Racial/ethnic group; STEM fields

Undergraduate Retention and Graduation Rates

About 62 percent of students who began seeking a bachelor's degree at a 4-year institution in fall 2012 completed that degree at the same institution within 6 years; the 6-year graduation rate was higher for females than for males (65 vs. 59 percent).

Retention rates measure the percentage of first-time undergraduate students who return to the same institution the following fall, and graduation rates measure the percentage of first-time undergraduate students who complete their program at the same institution within a specified period of time. This indicator examines how retention and graduation rates for first-time, full-time degree/certificate-seeking undergraduate students vary among different types of postsecondary institutions. It also examines how graduation rates have changed over time and how they differ between male and female students.

Figure 1. Percentage of first-time, full-time degree-seeking undergraduate students retained at 4-year degree-granting institutions, by control of institution and percentage of applications accepted: 2017 to 2018

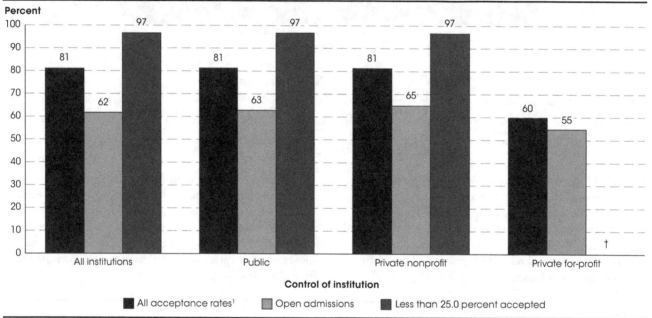

† Not applicable.
[1] Includes institutions that have an open admissions policy, institutions that have various applicant acceptance rates, and institutions for which no acceptance rate information is available.
NOTE: Data are for 4-year degree-granting postsecondary institutions participating in Title IV federal financial aid programs. Retained first-time undergraduate students are those who returned to the institutions to continue their studies the following fall. Although rounded numbers are displayed, the figures are based on unrounded data.
SOURCE: U.S. Department of Education, National Center for Education Statistics, Integrated Postsecondary Education Data System (IPEDS), Spring 2019, Fall Enrollment component; and Fall 2017, Institutional Characteristics component. See *Digest of Education Statistics 2019*, table 326.30.

For first-time, full-time degree-seeking undergraduate students who enrolled in 4-year degree-granting institutions in fall 2017, the overall retention rate was 81 percent. Retention rates were highest at the most selective institutions (i.e., those with acceptance rates of less than 25 percent) for both public and private nonprofit institutions. At public 4-year institutions, the retention rate was 81 percent overall. At the least selective public institutions (i.e., those with an open admissions policy), the retention rate was 63 percent, and at the most selective public institutions (i.e., those with acceptance rates of less than 25 percent), the retention rate was 97 percent. Similarly, the retention rate for private nonprofit 4-year institutions was 81 percent overall and ranged from 65 percent at institutions with an open admissions policy to 97 percent at institutions with acceptance rates of less than 25 percent. The retention rate for private for-profit 4-year institutions was 60 percent overall.

Figure 2. Percentage of first-time, full-time degree-seeking undergraduate students retained at 2-year degree-granting institutions, by control of institution: 2017 to 2018

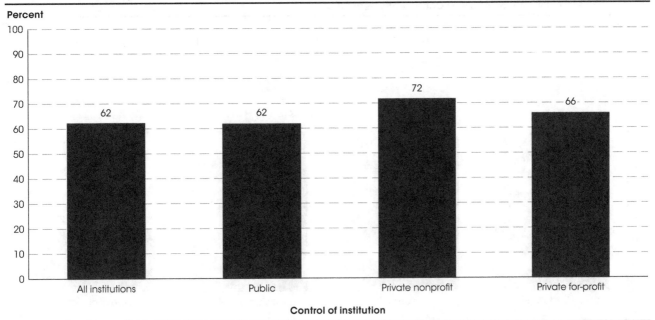

Percent

NOTE: Data are for 2-year degree-granting postsecondary institutions participating in Title IV federal financial aid programs. Returning students data for 2-year institutions include returning students, plus students who completed their program. Although rounded numbers are displayed, the figures are based on unrounded data.
SOURCE: U.S. Department of Education, National Center for Education Statistics, Integrated Postsecondary Education Data System (IPEDS), Spring 2019, Fall Enrollment component. See *Digest of Education Statistics 2019*, table 326.30.

At 2-year degree-granting institutions, the overall retention rate for first-time, full-time degree-seeking undergraduate students who enrolled in fall 2017 was 62 percent. The retention rate for public 2-year institutions (62 percent) was lower than the retention rates for private nonprofit (72 percent) and private for-profit (66 percent) 2-year institutions.

The 1990 Student Right-to-Know Act requires postsecondary institutions to report the percentage of students who complete their program within 150 percent of the normal time for completion (e.g., within 6 years for students seeking a bachelor's degree). The graduation rates in this indicator are based on this measure. Students who transfer without completing a degree are counted as noncompleters in the calculation of these rates, regardless of whether they complete a degree at another institution. In addition to graduation rates, this indicator presents information on transfer rates at 2-year institutions.

Figure 3. Graduation rate within 150 percent of normal time (within 6 years) for degree completion from first institution attended for first-time, full-time bachelor's degree-seeking students at 4-year postsecondary institutions, by control of institution and sex: Cohort entry year 2012

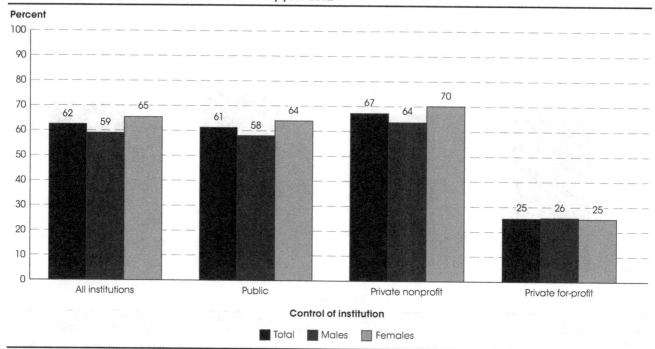

NOTE: Data are for 4-year degree-granting postsecondary institutions participating in Title IV federal financial aid programs. Graduation rates include students receiving bachelor's degrees from their initial institution of attendance only. Although rounded numbers are displayed, the figures are based on unrounded data.
SOURCE: U.S. Department of Education, National Center for Education Statistics, Integrated Postsecondary Education Data System (IPEDS), Winter 2018–19, Graduation Rates component. See *Digest of Education Statistics 2019*, table 326.10.

The overall 6-year graduation rate for first-time, full-time undergraduate students who began seeking a bachelor's degree at 4-year degree-granting institutions in fall 2012 was 62 percent. That is, by 2018 some 62 percent of students had completed a bachelor's degree at the same institution where they started in 2012. The 6-year graduation rate was 61 percent at public institutions, 67 percent at private nonprofit institutions, and 25 percent at private for-profit institutions. The overall 6-year graduation rate was 65 percent for females and 59 percent for males; it was higher for females than for males at both public (64 vs. 58 percent) and private nonprofit (70 vs. 64 percent) institutions. However, at private for-profit institutions, males had a higher 6-year graduation rate than females (26 vs. 25 percent).

Six-year graduation rates for first-time, full-time undergraduate students who began seeking a bachelor's degree at 4-year degree-granting institutions in fall 2012 varied according to institutional selectivity. In particular, 6-year graduation rates were highest at institutions that were the most selective (i.e., those with acceptance rates of less than 25 percent) and were lowest at institutions

that were the least selective (i.e., those with an open admissions policy). For example, at 4-year institutions with an open admissions policy, 34 percent of students completed a bachelor's degree within 6 years. At 4-year institutions with acceptance rates of less than 25 percent, the 6-year graduation rate was 90 percent.

Between 2010 and 2018, the overall 6-year graduation rate for first-time, full-time undergraduate students who began seeking a bachelor's degree at 4-year degree-granting institutions increased by 4 percentage points, from 58 percent (for students who began their studies in 2004 and graduated within 6 years) to 62 percent (for students who began their studies in 2012 and graduated within 6 years). During this period, 6-year graduation rates increased by 5 percentage points at public institutions (from 56 to 61 percent) and by 2 percentage points at private nonprofit institutions (from 65 to 67 percent) but decreased by 3 percentage points at private for-profit institutions (from 29 to 25 percent). Also from 2010 to 2018, the 6-year graduation rate for males increased from 56 to 59 percent and the rate for females increased from 61 to 65 percent.

Figure 4. Graduation rate within 150 percent of normal time for degree completion from first institution attended for first-time, full-time degree/certificate-seeking students at 2-year postsecondary institutions, by control of institution and sex: Cohort entry year 2015

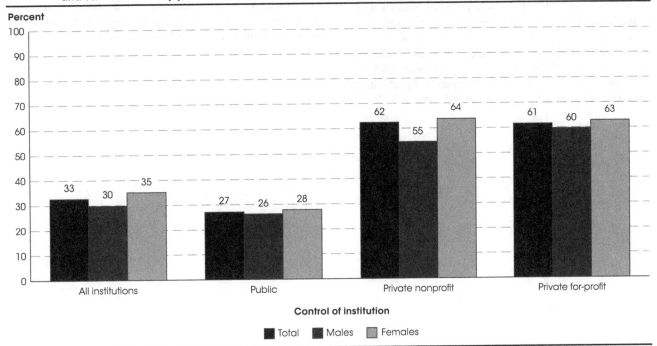

NOTE: Data are for 2-year degree-granting postsecondary institutions participating in Title IV federal financial aid programs. Graduation rates include students receiving associate's degrees or certificates from their initial institution of attendance only. An example of completing a credential within 150 percent of the normal time is completing a 2-year degree within 3 years.
SOURCE: U.S. Department of Education, National Center for Education Statistics, Integrated Postsecondary Education Data System (IPEDS), Winter 2018–19, Graduation Rates component. See *Digest of Education Statistics 2019*, table 326.20.

At 2-year degree-granting institutions overall, 33 percent of first-time, full-time undergraduate students who began seeking a certificate or associate's degree in fall 2015 attained it within 150 percent of the normal time required for completion of these programs (an example of completing a credential within 150 percent of the normal time is completing a 2-year degree within 3 years). In addition, after 150 percent of the normal time required for the completion of a program at a 2-year degree-granting institution, 15 percent of students had transferred to another institution, 11 percent remained enrolled in their first institution, and 41 percent were no longer enrolled in their first institution and had not been reported as a transfer at a different institution.

For first-time, full-time undergraduate students who began seeking a certificate or associate's degree at 2-year degree-granting institutions in fall 2015, the graduation rate within 150 percent of the normal time required for the completion of a program was 27 percent at public institutions, 62 percent at private nonprofit institutions, and 61 percent at private for-profit institutions. In addition, 17 percent of students at public 2-year

institutions had transferred to a different institution, compared with 3 percent at private nonprofit 2-year institutions and 1 percent at private for-profit 2-year institutions. The percentage of students who remained enrolled in their first institution was 13 percent at public 2-year institutions, 1 percent at private nonprofit 2-year institutions, and 2 percent at private for-profit 2-year institutions. The percentage of students who had not graduated from their first institution, were no longer enrolled in their first institution, and had not been reported as a transfer at a different institution was 42 percent for public 2-year institutions, 34 percent for private nonprofit 2-year institutions, and 36 percent for private for-profit 2-year institutions.

At 2-year degree-granting institutions overall, as well as at public, private nonprofit, and private for-profit 2-year institutions, the 150 percent graduation rates were higher for females than for males. For example, at private for-profit 2-year institutions, 63 percent of females versus 60 percent of males who began seeking a certificate or associate's degree in 2015 completed it within 150 percent of the normal time required for completion.

Reference tables: *Digest of Education Statistics 2019*, tables 326.10, 326.20, 326.25, and 326.30

Related indicators and resources: Educational Attainment of Young Adults; First-Time Postsecondary Students' Persistence After 3 Years [*The Condition of Education 2017 Spotlight*]; Postsecondary Certificates and Degrees Conferred; Postsecondary Graduation Rates [*Status and Trends in the Education of Racial and Ethnic Groups*]; Postsecondary Outcomes for Nontraditional Undergraduate Students [*The Condition of Education 2019 Spotlight*]

Glossary: Associate's degree; Bachelor's degree; Certificate; Degree-granting institution; Full-time enrollment; Open admissions; Postsecondary education; Postsecondary institutions (basic classification by level); Private institution; Public school or institution; Retention rate; Undergraduate students

Postsecondary Certificates and Degrees Conferred

While the public sector confers far more degrees than the private for-profit sector, from 2000–01 to 2017–18 the private for-profit sector increased the number of bachelor's degrees conferred by 328 percent, number of master's degrees by 451 percent, and the number of doctorates by 603 percent. In contrast, public institutions increased their numbers of degrees by 61 percent for bachelor's, 56 percent for master's, and 53 percent for doctorates.

In academic year 2017–18, postsecondary institutions conferred 955,000 certificates[1] below the associate's level, 1.0 million associate's degrees, 2.0 million bachelor's degrees, 820,000 master's degrees, and 184,000 doctor's degrees. The number of postsecondary certificates and degrees conferred at each award level increased between 2000–01 and 2017–18.

Figure 1. Number of certificates and degrees conferred by postsecondary institutions: Academic years 2000–01 through 2017–18

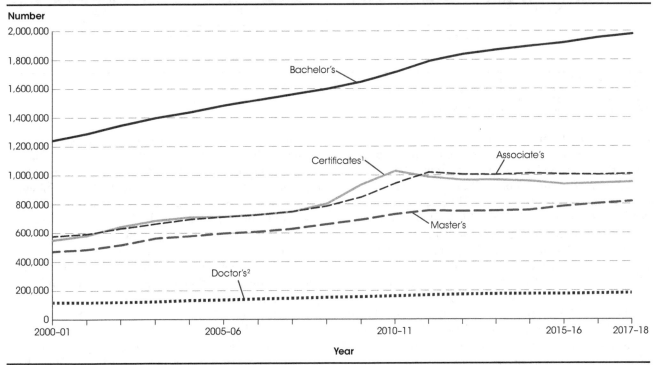

[1] Data are for certificates below the associate's degree level.
[2] Includes Ph.D., Ed.D., and comparable degrees at the doctoral levels. Includes most degrees formerly classified as first-professional, such as M.D., D.D.S., and law degrees.
NOTE: Data are for postsecondary institutions participating in Title IV federal financial aid programs. Some data have been revised from previously published figures.
SOURCE: U.S. Department of Education, National Center for Education Statistics, Integrated Postsecondary Education Data System (IPEDS), Fall 2001 through Fall 2018, Completions component. See *Digest of Education Statistics 2019,* table 318.40.

The number of certificates conferred below the associate's level increased by 87 percent between 2000–01 and 2010–11, from 553,000 to a peak of 1.0 million. Between 2010–11 and 2017–18, the number of certificates conferred decreased by 7 percent (from 1.0 million to 955,000). The number of associate's degrees conferred peaked in 2011–12, which was 1 year later than the peak in the number of certificates conferred. Between 2000–01 and 2011–12 the number of associate's degrees conferred increased by 77 percent, from 579,000 to 1.0 million. The number of associate's degrees conferred has fluctuated since 2011 with single year changes of 1 percent or less from 2011–12 to 2017–18. The number of bachelor's degrees conferred increased by 59 percent (from 1.2 million to 2.0 million) between 2000–01 and 2017–18.

Between 2000–01 and 2011–12, the number of master's degrees conferred increased by 60 percent (from 474,000 to 756,000), but the number has increased by only 8 percent (from 756,000 to 820,000) between 2011–12

and 2017–18. The number of doctor's degrees conferred increased by 54 percent (from 120,000 to 184,000) between 2000–01 and 2017–18.

Figure 2. Percentage distribution of certificates and associate's degrees conferred by postsecondary institutions, by control of institution: Academic years 2000–01 and 2017–18

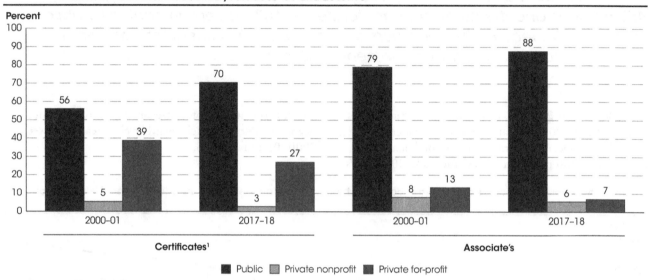

[1] Data are for certificates below the associate's degree level.
NOTE: Data are for postsecondary institutions participating in Title IV federal financial aid programs. Detail may not sum to totals because of rounding.
SOURCE: U.S. Department of Education, National Center for Education Statistics, Integrated Postsecondary Education Data System (IPEDS), Fall 2001 and Fall 2018, Completions component. See *Digest of Education Statistics 2019*, table 318.40.

Between 2000–01 and 2017–18, the number of certificates below the associate's level conferred by public institutions increased by 117 percent (from 310,000 to 672,000). The number of certificates conferred by private nonprofit institutions was 12 percent lower in 2017–18 (26,000) than in 2000–01 (29,000) but showed no consistent trend during this period. The number of certificates conferred by private for-profit institutions increased by 122 percent between 2000–01 and 2010–11 (from 214,000 to 474,000) and then decreased by 46 percent between 2010–11 and 2017–18 (from 474,000 to 257,000). Between 2000–01 and 2017–18, the proportion of certificates conferred by public institutions increased from 56 to 70 percent, the proportion conferred by private nonprofit institutions decreased from 5 to 3 percent, and the proportion conferred by private for-profit institutions decreased from 39 to 27 percent.

The number of associate's degrees conferred increased between 2000–01 and 2017–18 by 94 percent at public institutions (from 456,000 to 886,000) and by 23 percent at private nonprofit institutions (from 46,000 to 56,000). The number of associate's degrees conferred by private for-profit institutions increased by 175 percent between 2000–01 and 2011–12 (from 77,000 to 211,000) and then decreased by 67 percent between 2011–12 and 2017–18 (from 211,000 to 69,000), reaching its lowest point since 2000–01. The proportion of associate's degrees conferred by public institutions was higher in 2017–18 (88 percent) than in 2000–01 (79 percent). By contrast, the proportion of associate's degrees conferred by private nonprofit institutions was lower in 2017–18 (6 percent) than in 2000–01 (8 percent), as was the proportion conferred by private for-profit institutions (7 percent in 2017–18 vs. 13 percent in 2000–01).

Figure 3. Percentage distribution of bachelor's, master's, and doctor's degrees conferred by postsecondary institutions, by control of institution: Academic years 2000–01 and 2017–18

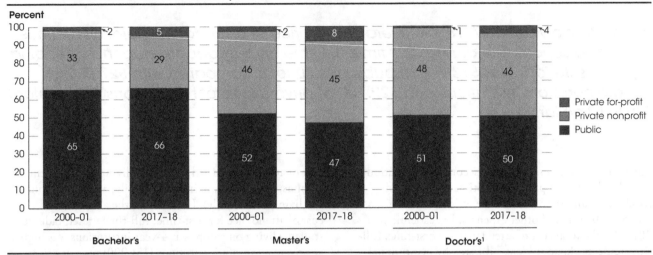

[1] Includes Ph.D., Ed.D., and comparable degrees at the doctoral level. Includes most degrees formerly classified as first-professional, such as M.D., D.D.S., and law degrees.
NOTE: Data are for degree-granting postsecondary institutions participating in Title IV federal financial aid programs. Detail may not sum to totals because of rounding. Although rounded numbers are displayed, the figures are based on unrounded data.
SOURCE: U.S. Department of Education, National Center for Education Statistics, Integrated Postsecondary Education Data System (IPEDS), Fall 2001 and Fall 2018, Completions component. *See Digest of Education Statistics 2019*, table 318.40.

Between 2000–01 and 2017–18, the number of bachelor's degrees conferred by public institutions increased by 61 percent (from 812,000 to 1.3 million), the number conferred by private nonprofit institutions increased by 40 percent (from 409,000 to 571,000), and the number conferred by private for-profit institutions increased by 328 percent (from 23,000 to 99,000). The proportion of bachelor's degrees conferred by private nonprofit institutions decreased (from 33 to 29 percent), and the proportion conferred by private for-profit institutions increased (from 2 to 5 percent). The proportion conferred by public institutions changed very little between 2000–01 and 2017–18.

The number of master's degrees conferred between 2000–01 and 2017–18 increased by 56 percent at public institutions (from 246,000 to 384,000), by 72 percent at private nonprofit institutions (from 216,000 to 372,000),

and by 451 percent at private for-profit institutions (from 12,000 to 64,000). Over this period, the proportion of master's degrees conferred by public institutions (from 52 to 47 percent) and private nonprofit institutions (from 46 to 45 percent) decreased. The difference was made up by private for-profit institutions which increased their proportion of master's degrees between 2000–01 and 2017–18 (from 2 to 8 percent).

Between 2000–01 and 2017–18, the number of doctor's degrees conferred increased by 53 percent at public institutions (from 61,000 to 93,000), by 45 percent at private nonprofit institutions (from 58,000 to 84,000), and by 603 percent at private for-profit institutions (from 1,000 to 7,000). There were small shifts in the proportion of doctor's degrees conferred with the proportion conferred by private for-profit institutions increasing from 1 to 4 percent.

Endnotes:
[1] A certificate is a recognized postsecondary credential certifying the satisfactory completion of a postsecondary education program.

Reference tables: *Digest of Education Statistics 2019*, table 318.40
Related indicators and resources: Degrees Awarded [*Status and Trends in the Education of Racial and Ethnic Groups*]; Graduate Degree Fields; Postsecondary Outcomes for Nontraditional Undergraduate Students [*The Condition of Education 2019 Spotlight*]; Trends in Student Loan Debt for Graduate School Completers [*The Condition of Education 2018 Spotlight*]; Undergraduate Degree Fields; Undergraduate Retention and Graduation Rates

Glossary: Associate's degree; Bachelor's degree; Certificate; Control of institutions; Doctor's degree; Master's degree; Private institution; Public school or institution

Price of Attending an Undergraduate Institution

In academic year 2017–18, the average net price of attendance (total cost minus grant and scholarship aid) for first-time, full-time undergraduate students attending 4-year institutions was $13,700 at public institutions, compared with $27,000 at private nonprofit institutions and $22,100 at private for-profit institutions (in constant 2018–19 dollars).

The total cost of attending a postsecondary institution includes the sum of published tuition and required fees,[1] books and supplies, and the weighted average cost for room, board, and other expenses. In academic year 2018–19, the total cost of attendance for first-time, full-time undergraduate students[2] differed by institutional control (public,[3] private nonprofit, or private for-profit) and institutional level (4-year or 2-year). In addition, the total

cost of attendance varied by student living arrangement (on campus; off campus, living with family; and off campus, not living with family). In 2018–19, the average total cost of attendance for first-time, full-time undergraduate students living on campus at 4-year institutions was higher at private nonprofit institutions ($51,900) than at private for-profit institutions ($33,200) and public institutions ($24,900).

Figure 1. Average total cost of attending degree-granting institutions for first-time, full-time undergraduate students, by level and control of institution and student living arrangement: Academic year 2018–19

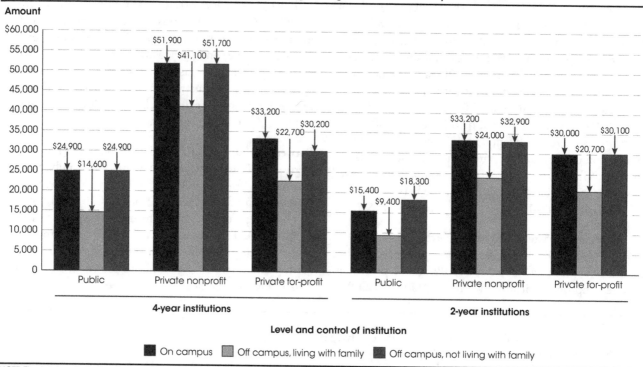

NOTE: The total cost of attending a postsecondary institution includes tuition and required fees, books and supplies, and the average cost for room, board, and other expenses. Tuition and fees at public institutions are the lower of either in-district or in-state tuition and fees. Excludes students who have already attended another postsecondary institution or who began their studies on a part-time basis. Data are weighted by the number of students at the institution who were awarded Title IV aid. Title IV aid includes grant aid, work-study aid, and loan aid. Although rounded numbers are displayed, the figures are based on unrounded data.
SOURCE: U.S. Department of Education, National Center for Education Statistics, Integrated Postsecondary Education Data System (IPEDS), Winter 2018–19, Student Financial Aid component; and Fall 2018, Institutional Characteristics component. See *Digest of Education Statistics 2019*, table 330.40.

Among first-time, full-time undergraduate students in academic year 2018–19, the average total cost of attendance at 4-year institutions was similar for those living on campus and those living off campus but not with family. In comparison, the average total cost of attendance was lower for those living off campus with family. This pattern in the total cost of attendance was observed for public, private nonprofit, and private for-profit institutions. For example, at public 4-year institutions, the average total cost of attendance was $24,900 for both students living on campus and students living off campus but not with family, compared with $14,600 for students living off campus with family.

At 2-year institutions, the average total cost of attendance for first-time, full-time undergraduate students in academic year 2018–19 was higher for students living on campus and those living off campus but not with family than for those living off campus with family. This pattern was observed for public, private nonprofit, and private for-profit institutions. For example, at public 2-year institutions, the average total cost of attendance for students living off campus but not with family ($18,300) was higher than for students living on campus ($15,400); both groups had a higher average total cost of attendance than students living off campus with family ($9,400).

Figure 2. Average tuition and fees of degree-granting institutions for first-time, full-time undergraduate students, by level and control of institution: Academic years 2010–11 and 2018–19

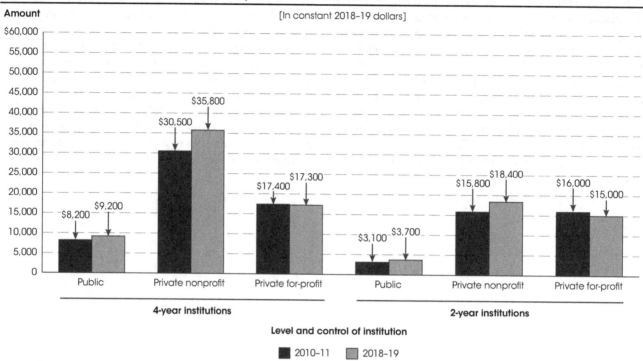

NOTE: Tuition and fees at public institutions are the lower of either in-district or in-state tuition and fees. Excludes students who have already attended another postsecondary institution or who began their studies on a part-time basis. Data are weighted by the number of students at the institution who were awarded Title IV aid. Title IV aid includes grant aid, work-study aid, and loan aid. Constant dollars based on the Consumer Price Index, prepared by the Bureau of Labor Statistics, U.S. Department of Labor, adjusted to an academic-year basis.
SOURCE: U.S. Department of Education, National Center for Education Statistics, Integrated Postsecondary Education Data System (IPEDS), Spring 2011 and Winter 2018–19, Student Financial Aid component; and Fall 2010 and Fall 2018, Institutional Characteristics component. See *Digest of Education Statistics 2019*, table 330.40.

Average tuition and fees were higher in academic year 2018–19 than in academic year 2010–11 for first-time, full-time undergraduate students at public and private nonprofit 4-year institutions (in constant 2018–19 dollars). At public 4-year institutions, average tuition and fees were $9,200 in 2018–19, about 12 percent higher than they were in 2010–11 ($8,200). At private nonprofit 4-year institutions, average tuition and fees were $35,800 in 2018–19, about 17 percent higher than they were in 2010–11 ($30,500). At private for-profit 4-year institutions, in contrast, average tuition and fees in 2018–19 ($17,300) were similar to those in 2010–11 ($17,400).

The pattern of average tuition and fees at 2-year institutions by academic year and institutional control (in constant 2018–19 dollars) was generally similar to the pattern at 4-year institutions. Average tuition and fees were 19 percent higher in academic year 2018–19 than in academic year 2010–11 at public 2-year institutions ($3,700 vs. $3,100) and 16 percent higher in 2018–19 than in 2010–11 at private nonprofit 2-year institutions ($18,400 vs. $15,800). In contrast, average tuition and fees were 6 percent lower in 2018–19 than in 2010–11 at private for-profit 2-year institutions ($15,000 vs. $16,000).

Many students and their families pay less than the full price of attendance because they receive financial aid to help cover expenses. The primary types of financial aid are grant and scholarship aid, which do not have to be repaid, and loans, which must be repaid. Grant and scholarship aid may be awarded based on financial need, merit, or both and may include tuition aid from employers. In academic year 2017–18, the average amount of grant and scholarship aid[4] (in constant 2018–19 dollars) for first-time, full-time undergraduate students awarded Title IV aid[5] was higher for students at private nonprofit institutions than for those at public and private for-profit institutions. Students at private nonprofit 4-year institutions received an average of $23,700 in grant and scholarship aid, compared with $8,100 at public institutions and $6,600 at private for-profit institutions.

The net price of attendance is the estimate of the actual amount of money that students and their families need to pay in a given year to cover educational expenses. Net price is calculated here as the total cost of attendance minus grant and scholarship aid. Net price provides an indication of what the total financial burden is on students and their families, since it also includes loans.

In academic year 2017–18, among 4-year institutions, the average net price of attendance (in constant 2018–19 dollars) for first-time, full-time undergraduate students awarded Title IV aid was lower for students at public institutions ($13,700) than for those at both private for-profit institutions ($22,100) and private nonprofit institutions ($27,000). Similarly, the average net price at 2-year institutions in 2017–18 was lowest at public institutions ($7,200) and higher at private nonprofit institutions ($18,800) and private for-profit institutions ($21,600).

Figure 3. Average total cost, grant and scholarship aid, and net price for first-time, full-time degree/certificate-seeking undergraduate students paying in-state tuition and awarded Title IV aid at public 4-year institutions, by family income level: Academic year 2017–18

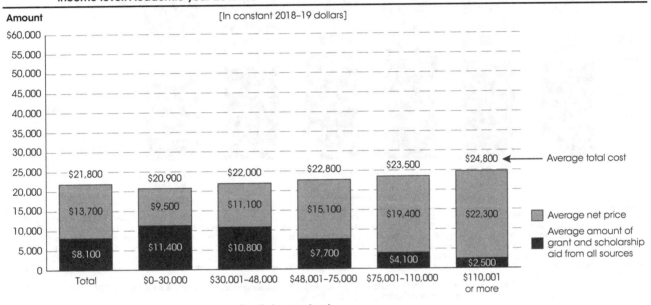

NOTE: Excludes students who previously attended another postsecondary institution or who began their studies on a part-time basis. Net price is calculated here as the average total cost of attendance minus average grant and scholarship aid. Includes only first-time, full-time students who paid the in-district or in-state tuition rate and who were awarded Title IV aid. Excludes students who were not awarded any Title IV aid. Title IV aid includes grant aid, work-study aid, and loan aid. Grant and scholarship aid consists of federal Title IV grants, as well as other grant or scholarship aid from the federal government, state or local governments, or institutional sources. Data are weighted by the number of students at the institution who were awarded Title IV aid. Totals include students for whom income data were not available. Constant dollars based on the Consumer Price Index, prepared by the Bureau of Labor Statistics, U.S. Department of Labor, adjusted to an academic-year basis. Detail may not sum to totals because of rounding.
SOURCE: U.S. Department of Education, National Center for Education Statistics, Integrated Postsecondary Education Data System (IPEDS), Winter 2018–19, Student Financial Aid component. See *Digest of Education Statistics 2019*, table 331.30.

In academic year 2017–18, the average amount of grant and scholarship aid awarded and the net price paid (in constant 2018–19 dollars) differed by students' family income level. In general, the lower the income, the greater the average amount of grant and scholarship aid awarded. For example, at public 4-year institutions, the average amount of grant and scholarship aid awarded to first-time, full-time undergraduate students paying in-state tuition in 2017–18 was highest for those with family incomes of $30,000 or less ($11,400 in aid) and lowest for those with family incomes of $110,001 or more ($2,500 in aid). Accordingly, at public 4-year institutions, the lowest average net price ($9,500) was paid by students with family incomes of $30,000 or less, and the highest average net price ($22,300) was paid by those with family incomes of $110,001 or more.

Figure 4. Average total cost, grant and scholarship aid, and net price for first-time, full-time degree/certificate-seeking undergraduate students awarded Title IV aid at private nonprofit 4-year institutions, by family income level: Academic year 2017–18

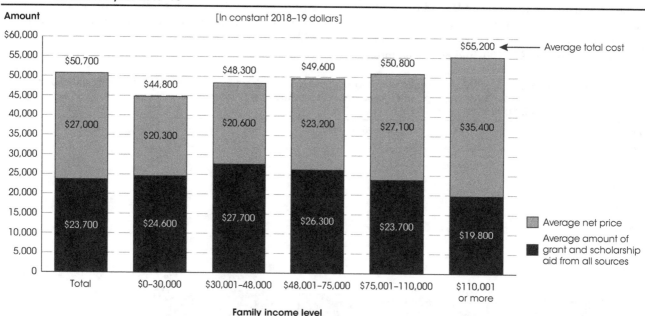

NOTE: Excludes students who previously attended another postsecondary institution or who began their studies on a part-time basis. Net price is calculated here as the average total cost of attendance minus average grant and scholarship aid. Includes only first-time, full-time students who were awarded Title IV aid. Excludes students who were not awarded any Title IV aid. Title IV aid includes grant aid, work-study aid, and loan aid. Grant and scholarship aid consists of federal Title IV grants, as well as other grant or scholarship aid from the federal government, state or local governments, or institutional sources. Data are weighted by the number of students at the institution who were awarded Title IV aid. Totals include students for whom income data were not available. Constant dollars based on the Consumer Price Index, prepared by the Bureau of Labor Statistics, U.S. Department of Labor, adjusted to an academic-year basis. Detail may not sum to totals because of rounding.
SOURCE: U.S. Department of Education, National Center for Education Statistics, Integrated Postsecondary Education Data System (IPEDS), Winter 2018–19, Student Financial Aid component. See *Digest of Education Statistics 2019*, table 331.30.

The pattern of average net price increasing with family income was also observed at private nonprofit 4-year institutions in academic year 2017–18. However, the average amount of grant and scholarship aid awarded at these institutions (in constant 2018–19 dollars) was highest for first-time, full-time undergraduate students with family incomes between $30,001 and $48,000 ($27,700 in aid), followed by those with family incomes between $48,001 and $75,000 ($26,300 in aid), those with family incomes of $30,000 or less ($24,600 in aid), those with family incomes between $75,001 and $110,000 ($23,700 in aid), and those with family incomes of $110,001 or more ($19,800 in aid). The lowest average net price ($20,300) was paid by students with family incomes of $30,000 or less, and the highest average net price ($35,400) was paid by those with family incomes of $110,001 or more.

Figure 5. Average total cost, grant and scholarship aid, and net price for first-time, full-time degree/certificate-seeking undergraduate students awarded Title IV aid at private for-profit 4-year institutions, by family income level: Academic year 2017–18

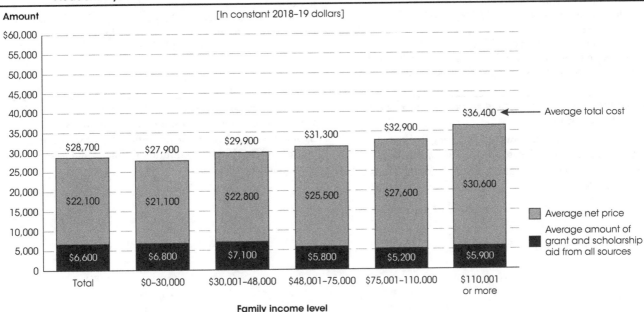

NOTE: Excludes students who previously attended another postsecondary institution or who began their studies on a part-time basis. Net price is calculated here as the average total cost of attendance minus average grant and scholarship aid. Includes only first-time, full-time students who were awarded Title IV aid. Excludes students who were not awarded any Title IV aid. Title IV aid includes grant aid, work-study aid, and loan aid. Grant and scholarship aid consists of federal Title IV grants, as well as other grant or scholarship aid from the federal government, state or local governments, or institutional sources. Data are weighted by the number of students at the institution who were awarded Title IV aid. Totals include students for whom income data were not available. Constant dollars based on the Consumer Price Index, prepared by the Bureau of Labor Statistics, U.S. Department of Labor, adjusted to an academic-year basis. Detail may not sum to totals because of rounding.
SOURCE: U.S. Department of Education, National Center for Education Statistics, Integrated Postsecondary Education Data System (IPEDS), Winter 2018–19, Student Financial Aid component. See *Digest of Education Statistics 2019*, table 331.30.

At private for-profit 4-year institutions, the average amount of grant and scholarship aid awarded to first-time, full-time undergraduate students in academic year 2017–18 (in constant 2018–19 dollars) was highest for those with family incomes between $30,001 and $48,000 ($7,100 in aid) and lowest for those with family incomes between $75,001 and $110,000 ($5,200 in aid). The lowest average net price ($21,100) was paid by students with family incomes of $30,000 or less, and the highest average net price ($30,600) was paid by those with family incomes of $110,001 or more.

In academic year 2017–18, at most family income levels, the average amount of grant and scholarship aid at 4-year institutions (in constant 2018–19 dollars) was highest for first-time, full-time undergraduate students at private

nonprofit 4-year institutions and lowest for students at private for-profit 4-year institutions. Additionally, at each family income level except the highest level ($110,001 or more), the average net price was highest for students attending private for-profit 4-year institutions and lowest for students attending public 4-year institutions. For example, the average amount of grant and scholarship aid awarded to students with family incomes between $30,001 and $48,000 who attended 4-year institutions was highest at private nonprofit institutions ($27,700), followed by public institutions ($10,800) and then private for-profit institutions ($7,100). The average net price of attending a private for-profit 4-year institution ($22,800) at this family income level was higher than the price of attending a private nonprofit institution ($20,600) or a public institution ($11,100).

Endnotes:

[1] For public institutions, this is the lower of in-district or in-state published tuition and required fees.

[2] Includes only students who are seeking a degree or certificate.

[3] Data for public institutions only include students who paid the in-district or in-state tuition and fees.

[4] Average amounts of grant and scholarship aid include federal Title IV grants, as well as other grant or scholarship aid from the federal government, state or local governments, or institutional sources.

[5] Title IV aid includes grant aid, work-study aid, and loan aid. Data for net price and grant and scholarship aid only include students who were awarded Title IV aid.

Reference tables: *Digest of Education Statistics 2019,* tables 330.40 and 331.30

Related indicators and resources: Financing Postsecondary Education in the United States [*The Condition of Education 2013 Spotlight*]; Loans for Undergraduate Students; Sources of Financial Aid

Glossary: Constant dollars; Control of institutions; Financial aid; Full-time enrollment; Postsecondary institutions (basic classification by level); Private institution; Public school or institution; Title IV eligible institution; Tuition and fees; Undergraduate students

Loans for Undergraduate Students

In 2017–18, some 44 percent of first-time, full-time degree/certificate-seeking undergraduate students were awarded loan aid, a 6 percentage point decrease from 2010–11 (50 percent). Between 2010–11 and 2017–18, the average annual undergraduate student loan amount decreased by 5 percent, from $7,600 to $7,200 (in constant 2018–19 dollars).

To help offset the cost of attending a postsecondary institution, Title IV of the Higher Education Act of 1965 authorized several student financial assistance programs—namely, federal grants, loans, and the Federal Work-Study Program. The largest federal loan program is the William D. Ford Federal Direct Loan Program, established in 2010, for which the federal government is the lender. Interest on the loans provided under the Direct Loan

Program may be subsidized, based on need, while the recipient is in school. Other types of student loans include institutional loans and private loans. The standard loan repayment plan is designed so that loans are payable within 10 years, beginning 6 months after the student graduates, drops below half-time enrollment, or withdraws from the academic program.

Figure 1. Average annual undergraduate tuition and fees for full-time students at degree-granting postsecondary institutions, by level and control of institution: Academic years 2010–11 through 2018–19

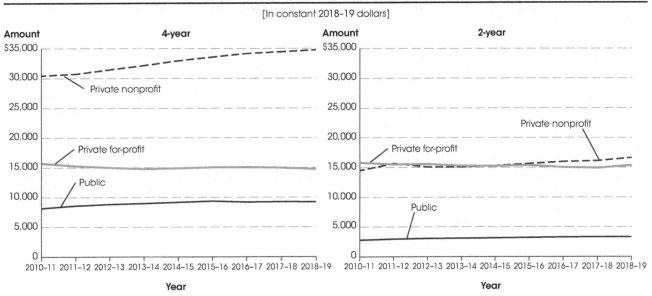

NOTE: Degree-granting institutions grant associate's or higher degrees and participate in Title IV federal financial aid programs. Some data have been revised from previously published figures. For public institutions, in-state tuition and required fees are used. Tuition and fees are weighted by the number of full-time-equivalent undergraduates. Constant dollars are based on the Consumer Price Index, prepared by the Bureau of Labor Statistics, U.S. Department of Labor, adjusted to an academic-year basis.
SOURCE: U.S. Department of Education, National Center for Education Statistics, Integrated Postsecondary Education Data System (IPEDS), Spring 2011 through Spring 2019, Fall Enrollment component, and Fall 2010 through Fall 2018, Institutional Characteristics component. See *Digest of Education Statistics 2019*, table 330.10.

Between academic years 2010–11 and 2018–19, average annual undergraduate tuition and fees for full-time students across all degree-granting postsecondary institutions increased by 19 percent, from $11,000 to $13,000.[1] Among 4-year institutions, tuition and fees increased by 13 percent between 2010–11 and 2018–19 at public institutions (from $8,200 to $9,200) and by 14 percent at private nonprofit institutions (from $30,500 to $34,800). In contrast, during this period, tuition and fees at private for-profit 4-year institutions decreased by 6 percent (from $15,700 to $14,700).

At 2-year institutions, the largest percentage increase in tuition and fees from 2010–11 to 2018–19 was at public institutions (18 percent, from $2,800 to $3,300). Tuition and fees at private nonprofit 2-year institutions increased by 15 percent, from $14,500 in 2010–11 to $16,600 in 2018–19. In contrast, tuition and fees at private for-profit 2-year institutions decreased by 3 percent between 2010–11 and 2018–19 (from $15,800 to $15,400).

Figure 2. Percentage of first-time, full-time degree/certificate-seeking undergraduates who were awarded loan aid at degree-granting postsecondary institutions, by level and control of institution: Academic years 2010–11 through 2017–18

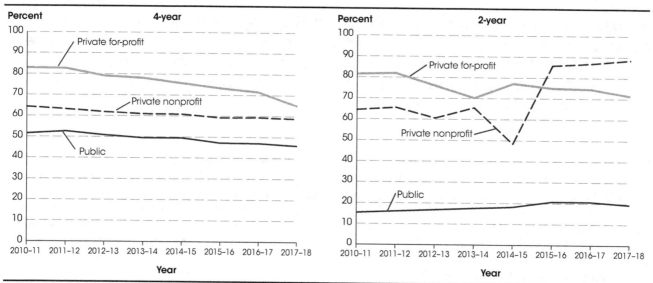

NOTE: Degree-granting institutions grant associate's or higher degrees and participate in Title IV federal financial aid programs. Some data have been revised from previously published figures. Data for public 2-year institutions exclude 2011–12 and 2012–13. Includes only loans made directly to students; does not include Parent PLUS Loans or other loans made directly to parents.
SOURCE: U.S. Department of Education, National Center for Education Statistics, Integrated Postsecondary Education Data System (IPEDS), Winter 2011–12 through Winter 2018–19, Student Financial Aid component. See *Digest of Education Statistics 2019*, table 331.20; *Digest of Education Statistics 2018*, table 331.20; and *Digest of Education Statistics 2017*, table 331.20.

Some 44 percent of first-time, full-time degree/certificate-seeking undergraduate students were awarded loan aid in 2017–18, a 6 percentage point decrease from 2010–11 (50 percent).[2] At public 4-year institutions, the percentage of undergraduates who were awarded loans decreased by 5 percentage points, from 51 percent in 2010–11 to 46 percent in 2017–18. Likewise, at private nonprofit 4-year institutions, the percentage of undergraduates who were awarded loans decreased by 6 percentage points, from 64 percent in 2010–11 to 59 percent in 2017–18. Among 4-year institutions, the largest decrease in the percentage of students who were awarded loans was at private for-profit institutions (18 percentage points), from 83 percent in 2010–11 to 65 percent in 2017–18.

Among public 2-year institutions, the percentage of students who were awarded loans was 4 percentage points higher in 2017–18 (19 percent) than in 2010–11 (15 percent). The percentage of undergraduates who were awarded loans at private nonprofit 2-year institutions was 24 percentage points higher in 2017–18 (88 percent) than in 2010–11 (64 percent), with most of the change occurring between 2013–14 and 2015–16. At private for-profit 2-year institutions, however, the percentage of undergraduates who were awarded loans was 10 percentage points lower in 2017–18 (71 percent) than in 2010–11 (82 percent).

Figure 3. Average annual loan amounts for first-time, full-time degree/certificate-seeking undergraduates who were awarded loan aid at degree-granting postsecondary institutions, by level and control of institution: Academic years 2010–11 through 2017–18

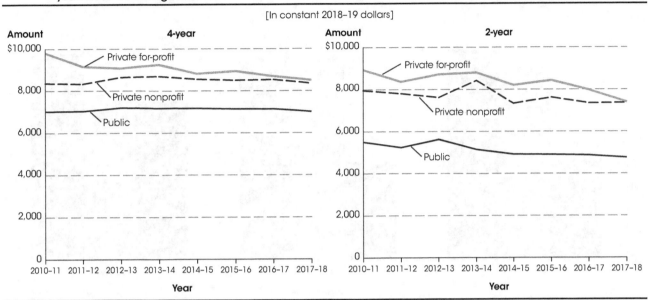

[In constant 2018–19 dollars]

NOTE: Degree-granting institutions grant associate's or higher degrees and participate in Title IV federal financial aid programs. Some data have been revised from previously published figures. Data for public 2-year institutions exclude 2011–12 and 2012–13. Includes only loans made directly to students; does not include Parent PLUS Loans or other loans made directly to parents. Constant dollars are based on the Consumer Price Index, prepared by the Bureau of Labor Statistics, U.S. Department of Labor, adjusted to an academic-year basis.
SOURCE: U.S. Department of Education, National Center for Education Statistics, Integrated Postsecondary Education Data System (IPEDS), Winter 2011–12 through Winter 2018–19, Student Financial Aid component. See *Digest of Education Statistics 2019*, table 331.20; *Digest of Education Statistics 2018*, table 331.20; and *Digest of Education Statistics 2017*, table 331.20.

Overall, the average annual loan amount that first-time, full-time degree/certificate-seeking undergraduate students were awarded decreased by 5 percent between 2010–11 and 2017–18 (from $7,600 to $7,200). At public 4-year and private nonprofit 4-year institutions, loan amounts were similar in 2017–18 and 2010–11 ($7,000 in both years at public 4-year institutions and $8,400 in both years at private nonprofit 4-year institutions). In contrast, at private for-profit 4-year institutions, the loan amount was 13 percent lower in 2017–18 ($8,500) than it was in 2010–11 ($9,800).

At public 2-year institutions, the loan amount was 14 percent lower in 2017–18 ($4,800) than it was in

2010–11 ($5,500). The loan amount was 7 percent lower at private nonprofit 2-year institutions in 2017–18 ($7,400) than it was in 2010–11 ($8,000) and 17 percent lower at private for-profit 2-year institutions in 2017–18 ($7,400) than it was in 2010–11 ($8,900).

In 2017–18, the loan amount for students at private for-profit 4-year institutions ($8,500) was higher than the amount for students at all other categories of institutions (public, private nonprofit, and private for-profit 2-year institutions and public and private nonprofit 4-year institutions).

Figure 4. Percentage of undergraduate degree/certificate completers who ever received loans, by degree type and control of institution: Academic year 2015–16

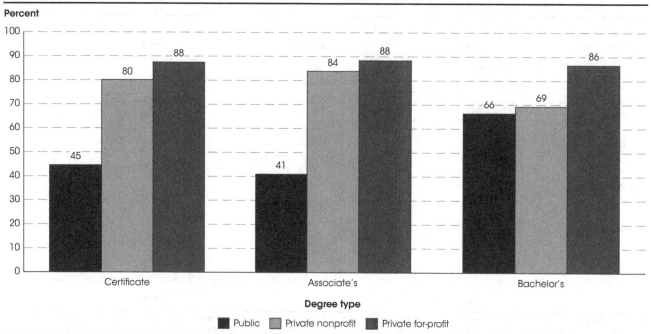

NOTE: Degree-granting institutions grant associate's or higher degrees and participate in Title IV federal financial aid programs. Includes only loans made directly to students; does not include Parent PLUS Loans or other loans made directly to parents. Although rounded numbers are displayed, the figures are based on unrounded data.
SOURCE: U.S. Department of Education, National Center for Education Statistics, 2015–16 National Postsecondary Student Aid Study (NPSAS:16). See *Digest of Education Statistics 2019*, table 331.95.

Among undergraduate students who completed an undergraduate degree or certificate in the 2015–16 academic year, 62 percent ever received at least one loan. The percentage who ever received loans was lowest among those who attended public institutions. Among certificate completers, 45 percent of those who attended public institutions, 80 percent of those who attended private nonprofit institutions, and 88 percent of those who attended private for-profit institutions ever received loans.

Among associate's degree completers, 41 percent of those who attended public institutions, 84 percent of those who attended private nonprofit institutions, and 88 percent of those who attended private for-profit institutions ever received loans. Among bachelor's degree completers, 66 percent of those who attended public institutions, 69 percent of those who attended private nonprofit institutions, and 86 percent of those who attended private for-profit institutions ever received loans.

Figure 5. Average cumulative loan amount for undergraduate degree/certificate completers who ever received loans, by degree type and control of institution: Academic year 2015–16

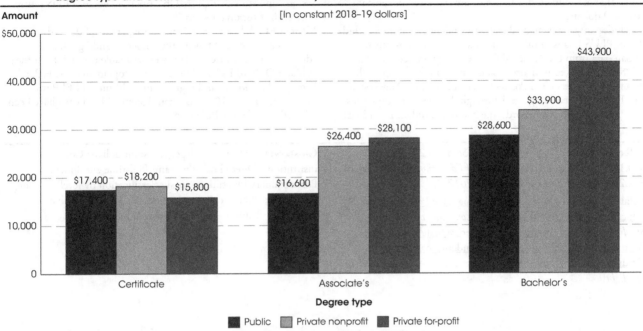

NOTE: Degree-granting institutions grant associate's or higher degrees and participate in Title IV federal financial aid programs. Includes only loans made directly to students; does not include Parent PLUS Loans or other loans made directly to parents. Constant dollars are based on the Consumer Price Index, prepared by the Bureau of Labor Statistics, U.S. Department of Labor, adjusted to an academic-year basis. Averages exclude students with no student loans. SOURCE: U.S. Department of Education, National Center for Education Statistics, 2015–16 National Postsecondary Student Aid Study (NPSAS:16). See *Digest of Education Statistics 2019*, table 331.95.

The average cumulative loan amount borrowed (not shown) among 2015–16 undergraduate degree/certificate completers who ever received loans was lowest among certificate completers ($16,500), followed by associate's degree completers ($19,700) and bachelor's degree completers ($31,800).[3] Among bachelor's degree completers, those who attended public institutions received the lowest cumulative loan amount ($28,600), followed by those who attended private nonprofit institutions ($33,900) and those who attended private for-profit institutions ($43,900). Among associate's degree completers, those who attended public institutions received a lower cumulative loan amount ($16,600) than those who attended private nonprofit institutions ($26,400) and those who attended private for-profit institutions ($28,100). Among certificate completers, however, there were no measurable differences in cumulative loan amounts between those who attended public, private nonprofit, or private for-profit institutions.

Ten percent of 2015–16 undergraduate degree/certificate completers had parents who received PLUS loans.[4] A lower percentage of associate's degree completers had parents who received PLUS loans (5 percent) than did certificate completers (7 percent) and bachelor's degree completers (15 percent). Among bachelor's degree completers, 17 percent of those who attended private nonprofit institutions had parents who received PLUS loans, compared with 14 percent of those who attended public institutions and 13 percent of those who attended private for-profit institutions.

The average PLUS loan amount for the parents of bachelor's degree completers ($34,700) was higher than for parents of certificate completers ($13,700) and of associate's degree completers ($13,800). Average PLUS loan amounts among parents of bachelor's degree completers varied by institutional control, with parents of those who attended private nonprofit institutions borrowing the most ($44,600), compared with those who attended public institutions ($29,300) and private for-profit institutions ($33,900).

Endnotes:

[1] All dollar amounts in this indicator are expressed in constant 2018–19 dollars.

[2] Includes only loans made directly to students. Does not include Parent PLUS Loans or other loans made directly to parents.

[3] Loan data from the National Postsecondary Student Aid Study (NPSAS) presented in figures 4 and 5 may not be comparable to data from the Integrated Postsecondary Education Data System (IPEDS) presented in figures 1 through 3. NPSAS incorporates data from institutional records, the National Student Loan Data System, and student-reported information, while IPEDS relies only on institutional records.

[4] Parent PLUS Loans are taken out by parents of dependent students and are used toward the students' undergraduate education. Parent PLUS Loans were available through both the William D. Ford Federal Direct Loan Program and the Federal Family Education Loan Program (FFELP) until FFELP was discontinued in 2010. Since then, Parent PLUS Loans have been referred to as Direct PLUS Loans.

Reference tables: *Digest of Education Statistics 2019*, tables 330.10, 331.20, and 331.95; *Digest of Education Statistics 2018*, 331.20; *Digest of Education Statistics 2017*, 331.20

Related indicators and resources: Financing Postsecondary Education in the United States [*The Condition of Education 2013 Spotlight*]; Price of Attending an Undergraduate Institution; Sources of Financial Aid; Trends in Student Loan Debt for Graduate School Completers [*The Condition of Education 2018 Spotlight*]

Glossary: Certificate; College; Constant dollars; Control of institutions; Direct Loan Program; Full-time enrollment; Postsecondary institutions (basic classification by level); Private institution; Public school or institution; Title IV eligible institution; Tuition and fees; Undergraduate students

Sources of Financial Aid

The percentage of first-time, full-time degree/certificate-seeking undergraduate students at 4-year degree-granting postsecondary institutions who were awarded financial aid was higher in academic year 2017–18 (86 percent) than in 2000–01 (75 percent).

Grants and loans are the major forms of federal financial aid for first-time, full-time degree/certificate-seeking undergraduate students. The largest federal grant program available to undergraduate students is the Pell Grant program. In order to qualify for a Pell Grant, a student must demonstrate financial need. Some federal loan programs are available to all students and some are based on financial need. Other sources of financial aid include state and local governments, institutions, and private sources, as well as private loans. The forms of financial aid discussed in this indicator are only those provided directly to students. For example, student loans include only loans made directly to students; they do not include Parent Loans for Undergraduate Students (PLUS) and other loans made directly to parents.

Figure 1. Percentage of first-time, full-time undergraduate students awarded financial aid at 4-year degree-granting postsecondary institutions, by control of institution: Academic years 2000–01, 2005–06, 2010–11, and 2017–18

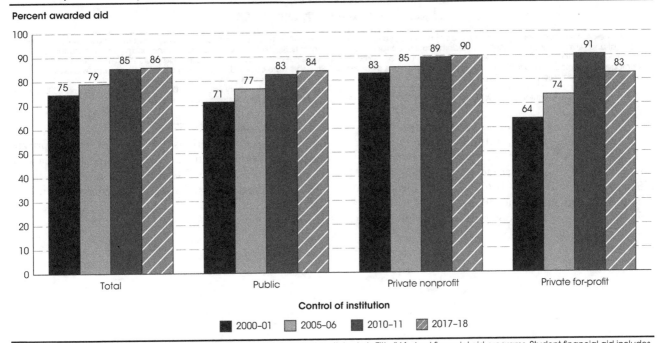

Percent awarded aid

	2000–01	2005–06	2010–11	2017–18
Total	75	79	85	86
Public	71	77	83	84
Private nonprofit	83	85	89	90
Private for-profit	64	74	91	83

Control of institution

NOTE: Degree-granting institutions grant associate's or higher degrees and participate in Title IV federal financial aid programs. Student financial aid includes any federal and private loans to students and federal, state/local, and institutional grants. Student loans include only loans made directly to students; they do not include Parent Loans for Undergraduate Students (PLUS) and other loans made directly to parents. For academic years 2000–01 and 2005–06, the percentage represents students receiving aid rather than students awarded aid. Students were counted as receiving aid only if they were awarded and accepted aid and their aid was also disbursed. Although rounded numbers are displayed, the figures are based on unrounded data.
SOURCE: U.S. Department of Education, National Center for Education Statistics, Integrated Postsecondary Education Data System (IPEDS), Spring 2002, Spring 2007, Winter 2011–12, and Winter 2018–19, Student Financial Aid component. See *Digest of Education Statistics 2019*, table 331.20.

At 4-year degree-granting postsecondary institutions, the percentage of first-time, full-time degree/certificate-seeking undergraduate students who were awarded financial aid was higher in academic year 2017–18 (86 percent) than in 2000–01 (75 percent).[1] The pattern of higher percentages of students being awarded aid in 2017–18 than in 2000–01 was observed for public (84 vs. 71 percent), private nonprofit (90 vs. 83 percent), and private for-profit (83 vs. 64 percent) 4-year institutions.

Over a more recent time period, the percentage of students overall at 4-year institutions awarded aid in 2017–18 was 1 percentage point higher than in 2010–11 (86 vs. 85 percent). This pattern was also observed for students at public (84 vs. 83 percent) and private nonprofit (90 vs. 89 percent) 4-year institutions. In contrast, at private for-profit 4-year institutions, the percentage of students awarded financial aid was lower in 2017–18 (83 percent) than in 2010–11 (91 percent).

Figure 2. Percentage of first-time, full-time undergraduate students awarded financial aid at 2-year degree-granting postsecondary institutions, by control of institution: Academic years 2000–01, 2005–06, 2010–11, and 2017–18

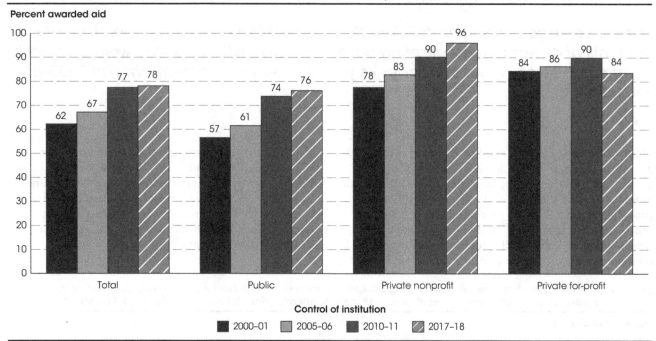

Percent awarded aid

Control of institution

■ 2000–01 ▨ 2005–06 ■ 2010–11 ▨ 2017–18

NOTE: Degree-granting institutions grant associate's or higher degrees and participate in Title IV federal financial aid programs. Student financial aid includes any federal and private loans to students and federal, state/local, and institutional grants. Student loans include only loans made directly to students; they do not include Parent Loans for Undergraduate Students (PLUS) and other loans made directly to parents. For academic years 2000–01 and 2005–06, the percentage represents students receiving aid rather than students awarded aid. Students were counted as receiving aid only if they were awarded and accepted aid and their aid was also disbursed. Although rounded numbers are displayed, the figures are based on unrounded data.
SOURCE: U.S. Department of Education, National Center for Education Statistics, Integrated Postsecondary Education Data System (IPEDS), Spring 2002, Spring 2007, Winter 2011–12, and Winter 2018–19, Student Financial Aid component. See *Digest of Education Statistics 2019*, table 331.20.

At 2-year degree-granting postsecondary institutions, the percentage of first-time, full-time degree/certificate-seeking undergraduate students who were awarded financial aid was higher in academic year 2017–18 (78 percent) than in 2000–01 (62 percent). This pattern of higher percentages of students awarded aid in 2017–18 than in 2000–01 was also observed for students at public

2-year institutions (76 vs. 57 percent) and at private nonprofit 2-year institutions (96 vs. 78 percent). At private for-profit 2-year institutions, the percentage of students awarded aid in 2017–18 (84 percent) was lower than in 2010–11 (90 percent) but similar to the percentage in 2000–01 (84 percent).

Figure 3. Percentage of first-time, full-time undergraduate students awarded financial aid at 4-year degree-granting postsecondary institutions, by type of financial aid and control of institution: Academic year 2017–18

Percent awarded aid

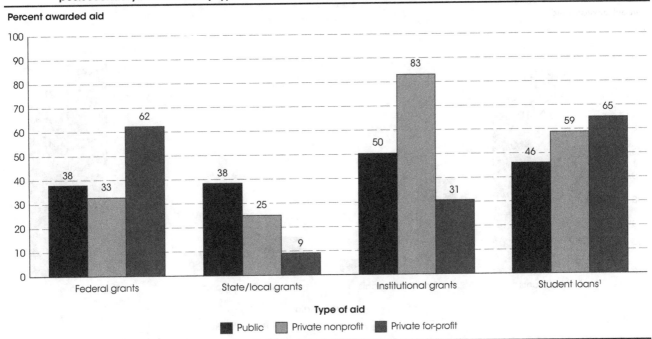

Type of aid

█ Public ▨ Private nonprofit ▨ Private for-profit

[1] Student loans include only loans made directly to students; they do not include Parent Loans for Undergraduate Students (PLUS) and other loans made directly to parents.
NOTE: Degree-granting institutions grant associate's or higher degrees and participate in Title IV federal financial aid programs. Student financial aid includes any federal and private loans to students and federal, state/local, and institutional grants. Although rounded numbers are displayed, the figures are based on unrounded data.
SOURCE: U.S. Department of Education, National Center for Education Statistics, Integrated Postsecondary Education Data System (IPEDS), Winter 2018–19, Student Financial Aid component. See *Digest of Education Statistics 2019*, table 331.20.

The percentage of first-time, full-time degree/certificate-seeking undergraduate students at 4-year institutions who were awarded specific types of financial aid varied according to institutional control (i.e., public, private nonprofit, or private for-profit). In academic year 2017–18, the percentage of students at 4-year institutions awarded federal grants was higher at private for-profit institutions (62 percent) than at public institutions (38 percent) and private nonprofit institutions (33 percent). The percentage of students at 4-year institutions awarded state or local grants was higher at public institutions (38 percent) than at private nonprofit institutions (25 percent) and private for-profit institutions (9 percent). The percentage of students at 4-year institutions awarded institutional grants was higher at private nonprofit institutions (83 percent) than at public institutions (50 percent) and private for-profit institutions (31 percent). The percentage of students at 4-year institutions awarded student loans was higher at private for-profit institutions (65 percent) than at private nonprofit institutions (59 percent) and at public institutions (46 percent).

Figure 4. Percentage of first-time, full-time undergraduate students awarded financial aid at 2-year degree-granting postsecondary institutions, by type of financial aid and control of institution: Academic year 2017–18

Percent awarded aid

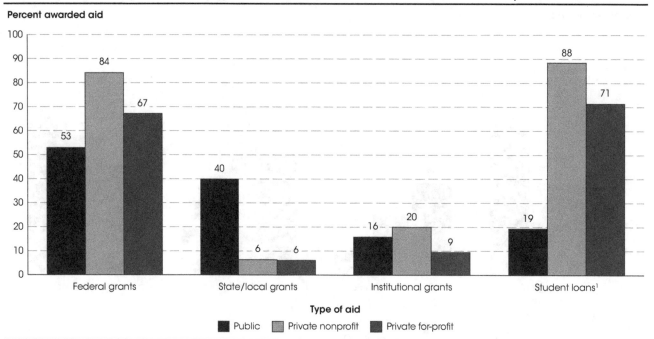

[1] Student loans include only loans made directly to students; they do not include Parent Loans for Undergraduate Students (PLUS) and other loans made directly to parents.
NOTE: Degree-granting institutions grant associate's or higher degrees and participate in Title IV federal financial aid programs. Student financial aid includes any federal and private loans to students and federal, state/local, and institutional grants. Although rounded numbers are displayed, the figures are based on unrounded data.
SOURCE: U.S. Department of Education, National Center for Education Statistics, Integrated Postsecondary Education Data System (IPEDS), Winter 2018–19, Student Financial Aid component. See *Digest of Education Statistics 2019*, table 331.20.

The percentage of first-time, full-time degree/certificate-seeking undergraduate students at 2-year institutions who were awarded specific types of financial aid also varied according to institutional control. In academic year 2017–18, the percentage of students at 2-year institutions awarded federal grants was higher at private nonprofit institutions (84 percent) than at private for-profit institutions (67 percent) and public institutions (53 percent). The percentage of students at 2-year institutions who were awarded state or local grants was over six times higher at public institutions (40 percent)

than at private nonprofit and private for-profit 2-year institutions (6 percent each). The percentage of students at 2-year institutions awarded institutional grants was higher at private nonprofit institutions (20 percent) than at public institutions (16 percent) and private for-profit institutions (9 percent). The percentages of students at 2-year institutions awarded student loans were higher at private nonprofit institutions (88 percent) and private for-profit institutions (71 percent) than at public institutions (19 percent).

Figure 5. Average amount of financial aid awarded to first-time, full-time undergraduate students at 4-year degree-granting postsecondary institutions, by type of financial aid and control of institution: Academic year 2017–18

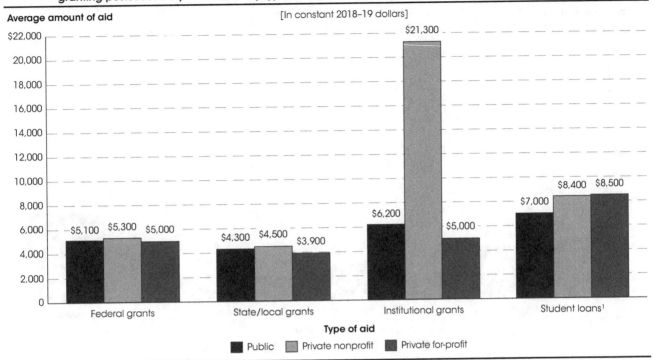

Average amount of aid

[In constant 2018–19 dollars]

Type of aid

■ Public ■ Private nonprofit ■ Private for-profit

[1] Student loans include only loans made directly to students; they do not include Parent Loans for Undergraduate Students (PLUS) and other loans made directly to parents.
NOTE: Degree-granting institutions grant associate's or higher degrees and participate in Title IV federal financial aid programs. Student financial aid includes any federal and private loans to students and federal, state/local, and institutional grants. Award amounts are in constant 2018–19 dollars, based on the Consumer Price Index (CPI). Averages exclude students who were not awarded financial aid. Although rounded numbers are displayed, the figures are based on unrounded data.
SOURCE: U.S. Department of Education, National Center for Education Statistics, Integrated Postsecondary Education Data System (IPEDS), Winter 2018–19, Student Financial Aid component. See *Digest of Education Statistics 2019*, table 331.20.

Across 4-year institutions, the average federal grant award in academic year 2017–18 ranged from $5,000 at private for-profit institutions to $5,300 at private nonprofit institutions (reported in constant 2018–19 dollars). The average state or local grant award ranged from $3,900 at private for-profit institutions to $4,500 at private nonprofit institutions. There were larger differences by institutional control in average institutional grant awards. The average institutional grant award at private nonprofit institutions ($21,300) was more than three times higher than at public institutions ($6,200) and more than four times higher than at private for-profit institutions ($5,000). The average student loan amount was higher at private for-profit institutions ($8,500) and private nonprofit institutions ($8,400) than at public institutions ($7,000).

Figure 6. Average amount of financial aid awarded to first-time, full-time undergraduate students at 2-year degree-granting postsecondary institutions, by type of financial aid and control of institution: Academic year 2017–18

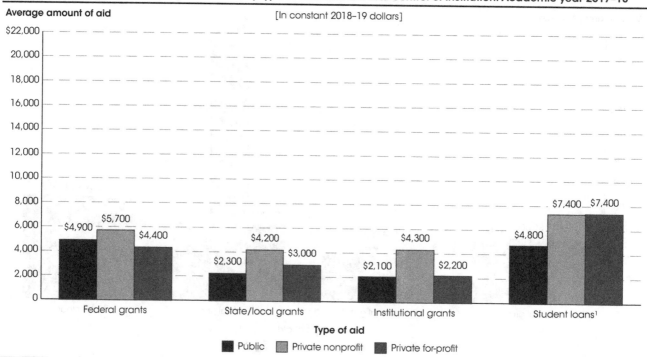

¹ Student loans include only loans made directly to students; they do not include Parent Loans for Undergraduate Students (PLUS) and other loans made directly to parents.
NOTE: Degree-granting institutions grant associate's or higher degrees and participate in Title IV federal financial aid programs. Student financial aid includes any federal and private loans to students and federal, state/local, and institutional grants. Award amounts are in constant 2018–19 dollars, based on the Consumer Price Index (CPI). Averages exclude students who were not awarded financial aid. Although rounded numbers are displayed, the figures are based on unrounded data.
SOURCE: U.S. Department of Education, National Center for Education Statistics, Integrated Postsecondary Education Data System (IPEDS), Winter 2018–19, Student Financial Aid component. See *Digest of Education Statistics 2019*, table 331.20.

Across 2-year institutions, the average federal grant award in academic year 2017–18 ranged from $4,400 at private for-profit institutions to $5,700 at private nonprofit institutions (reported in constant 2018–19 dollars). There were larger differences by institutional control among the other award types. The average state or local grant award was higher at private nonprofit institutions ($4,200) than at private for-profit institutions ($3,000) and public institutions ($2,300). The average institutional grant award was higher at private nonprofit institutions ($4,300) than at private for-profit institutions ($2,200) and public institutions ($2,100). The average student loan amount was higher at private for-profit institutions and private nonprofit institutions ($7,400 each) than at public institutions ($4,800).

Endnotes:

¹ Student financial aid includes any federal and private loans to students and federal, state/local, and institutional grants. For academic years 2000–01 and 2005–06, the percentage of students with financial aid was reported as the percentage of students who "received aid." Starting with academic year 2010–11, postsecondary institutions reported the same data as the percentage of students who "were awarded aid" to better reflect that some students were awarded aid but did not receive it.

Reference tables: *Digest of Education Statistics 2019*, table 331.20

Related indicators and resources: Financial Aid [*Status and Trends in the Education of Racial and Ethnic Groups*]; Financing Postsecondary Education in the United States [*The Condition of Education 2013 Spotlight*]; Loans for Undergraduate Students; Price of Attending an Undergraduate Institution; Trends in Student Loan Debt for Graduate School Completers [*The Condition of Education 2018 Spotlight*]

Glossary: Certificate; Constant dollars; Control of institutions; Degree-granting institutions; Financial aid; Full-time enrollment; Postsecondary institutions (basic classification by level); Private institution; Public school or institution; Undergraduate students

Postsecondary Institution Revenues

Revenues from tuition and fees per full-time-equivalent (FTE) student were 25 percent higher in 2017–18 than in 2010–11 at public institutions ($7,700 vs. $6,100 in constant 2018–19 dollars) and 7 percent higher at private nonprofit institutions ($22,400 vs. $20,900). At private for-profit institutions, revenues from tuition and fees per FTE student were 3 percent lower in 2017–18 than in 2010–11 ($16,800 vs. $17,400).

In 2017–18, total revenues at degree-granting postsecondary institutions in the United States were $671 billion (in current dollars). Total revenues were $409 billion at public institutions, $248 billion at private nonprofit institutions, and $13 billion at private for-profit institutions.

Figure 1. Percentage distribution of total revenues for degree-granting postsecondary institutions, by control of institution and source of funds: 2017–18

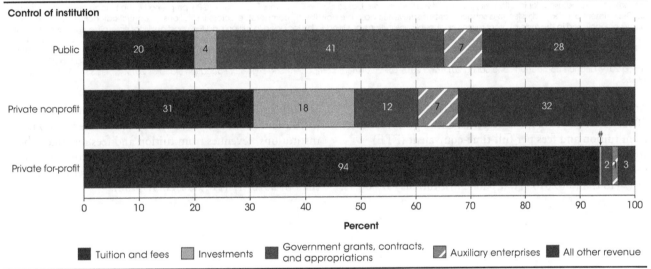

Control of institution

Rounds to zero.
NOTE: Government grants, contracts, and appropriations include revenues from federal, state, and local governments. Private grants and contracts are included in the local government revenue category at public institutions. All other revenue includes gifts, capital or private grants and contracts, hospital revenue, sales and services of educational activities, and other revenue. Revenue data are not directly comparable across institutions by control categories because Pell Grants are included in the federal grant revenues at public institutions but tend to be included in tuition and fees and auxiliary enterprise revenues at private nonprofit and private for-profit institutions. Revenues from tuition and fees are net of discounts and allowances. Degree-granting institutions grant associate's or higher degrees and participate in Title IV federal financial aid programs. Detail may not sum to totals because of rounding. Although rounded numbers are displayed, figures are based on unrounded data.
SOURCE: U.S. Department of Education, National Center for Education Statistics, Integrated Postsecondary Education Data System (IPEDS), Spring 2019, Finance component. See *Digest of Education Statistics 2019*, tables 333.10, 333.40, and 333.55.

The primary[1] sources of revenue for degree-granting institutions in 2017–18 were tuition and fees; investments;[2] and government grants, contracts, and appropriations. The percentages from these revenue sources varied by control of institution (i.e., public, private nonprofit, or private for-profit). Public institutions received the largest proportion of their revenues from government sources (including federal, state, and local government[3] grants, contracts, and appropriations), which constituted 41 percent of their overall revenues, while student tuition and fees constituted the largest primary source of revenue at private for-profit institutions (94 percent). At private nonprofit institutions, all other revenue sources (including gifts, capital or private grants and contracts, hospital revenue, sales and services of educational activities, and other revenue) constituted

32 percent of overall revenues, and student tuition and fees constituted 31 percent of overall revenues.

It is important to note that data may not be comparable across institutions by control categories (i.e., public, private nonprofit, and private for-profit) because of differences in accounting standards that pertain to the type of institution. For example, Pell Grants are included in revenues from federal grants at public institutions but tend to be included in revenues from tuition and fees and auxiliary enterprises at private nonprofit and private for-profit institutions. Thus, some categories of revenue data are not directly comparable across public, private nonprofit, and private for-profit institutions.

Figure 2. Revenues from tuition and fees per full-time-equivalent (FTE) student for degree-granting postsecondary institutions, by control of institution: 2010–11 and 2017–18

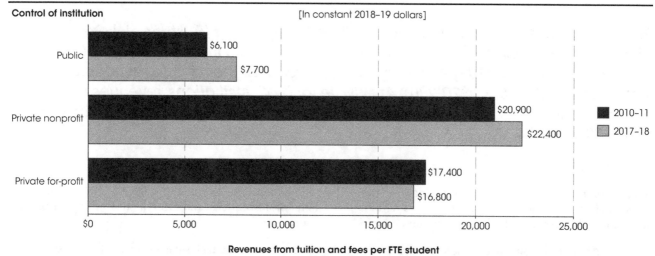

NOTE: Full-time-equivalent (FTE) student enrollment includes full-time students plus the full-time equivalent of part-time students. Revenues per FTE student in this indicator are adjusted for inflation using constant 2018-19 dollars, based on the Consumer Price Index (CPI), prepared by the Bureau of Labor Statistics, U.S. Department of Labor, adjusted to a school-year basis. Revenue data are not directly comparable across institutions by control categories because Pell Grants are included in the federal grant revenues at public institutions but tend to be included in tuition and fees and auxiliary enterprise revenues at private nonprofit and private for-profit institutions. Revenues from tuition and fees are net of discounts and allowances. Degree-granting institutions grant associate's or higher degrees and participate in Title IV federal financial aid programs. Although rounded numbers are displayed, figures are based on unrounded data. SOURCE: U.S. Department of Education, National Center for Education Statistics, Integrated Postsecondary Education Data System (IPEDS), Spring 2012 and Spring 2019, Finance component; and Spring 2011 and 2018, Fall Enrollment component. See *Digest of Education Statistics 2019*, tables 333.10, 333.40, and 333.55.

At degree-granting postsecondary institutions between 2010–11 and 2017–18, the percentage change in revenues from tuition and fees per full-time-equivalent (FTE) student[4] varied by control of institution. Revenues from tuition and fees per FTE student were 25 percent higher in 2017–18 than in 2010–11 at public institutions ($7,700 vs.

$6,100) and 7 percent higher at private nonprofit institutions ($22,400 vs. $20,900). At private for-profit institutions, revenues from tuition and fees remained the primary revenue source; however, revenues from tuition and fees per FTE student were 3 percent lower in 2017–18 than in 2010–11 ($16,800 vs. $17,400).

Figure 3. Revenues from government grants, contracts, and appropriations per full-time-equivalent (FTE) student for degree-granting postsecondary institutions, by source of funds and control of institution: 2010–11 and 2017–18

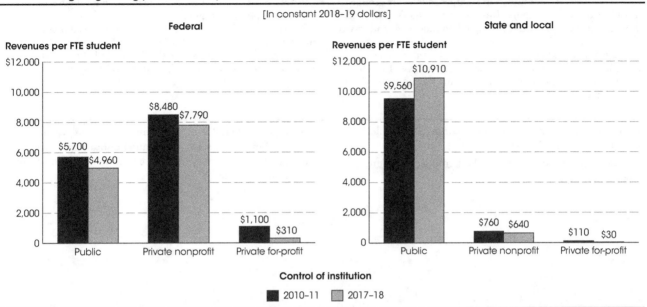

[In constant 2018–19 dollars]

NOTE: Full-time-equivalent (FTE) student enrollment includes full-time students plus the full-time equivalent of part-time students. Revenues per FTE student in this indicator are adjusted for inflation using constant 2018–19 dollars, based on the Consumer Price Index (CPI), prepared by the Bureau of Labor Statistics, U.S. Department of Labor, adjusted to a school-year basis. Private grants and contracts are included in the local government revenue category at public institutions. Revenue data are not directly comparable across institutions by control categories because Pell Grants are included in the federal grant revenues at public institutions but tend to be included in tuition and fees and auxiliary enterprise revenues at private nonprofit and private for-profit institutions. Degree-granting institutions grant associate's or higher degrees and participate in Title IV federal financial aid programs. Although rounded numbers are displayed, figures are based on unrounded data.
SOURCE: U.S. Department of Education, National Center for Education Statistics, Integrated Postsecondary Education Data System (IPEDS), Spring 2012 and Spring 2019, Finance component; and Spring 2011 and 2018, Fall Enrollment component. See *Digest of Education Statistics 2019*, tables 333.10, 333.40, and 333.55.

Revenues from government sources per FTE student were 4 percent higher in 2017–18 than in 2010–11 ($15,880 vs. $15,260) at public institutions, driven by higher revenues from state and local government sources. In contrast, revenues per FTE student from government sources were 72 percent lower in 2017–18 than in 2010–11 ($340 vs. $1,210) at private for-profit institutions and 9 percent lower in 2017–18 than in 2010–11 ($8,430 vs. $9,240) at private nonprofit institutions.

Revenues from federal government sources per FTE student were lower in 2017–18 than in 2010–11 across all control categories. The largest percentage change was at private for-profit institutions, where federal revenues per FTE student were 72 percent lower in 2017–18 than in 2010–11 ($310 vs. $1,100). Federal revenues per FTE student were 13 percent lower in 2017–18 than in 2010–11

($4,960 vs. $5,700) at public institutions and 8 percent lower in 2017–18 than in 2010–11 ($7,790 vs. $8,480) at private nonprofit institutions.

The percentage change in state and local government revenues per FTE student varied by control of institution. Revenues from state and local government sources per FTE student were 14 percent higher in 2017–18 than in 2010–11 ($10,910 vs. $9,560) at public institutions but 16 percent lower in 2017–18 than in 2010–11 ($640 vs. $760) at private nonprofit institutions. At private for-profit institutions, revenues from state and local government sources per FTE student were 73 percent lower in 2017–18 than in 2010–11 ($30 vs. $110) but constituted only a small percentage (less than 1 percent) of total revenues in both years.

Endnotes:

[1] For this indicator, revenues from all other sources are grouped into a broad "other" category. This category includes gifts, capital or private grants and contracts, hospital revenue, sales and services of educational activities, and other revenue.

[2] Investments/investment returns are aggregate amounts of dividends, interest, royalties, rent, and gains or losses from both fair value adjustments and trades of institutions' investments and/or endowments.

[3] Private grants and contracts are included in local government revenues at public institutions.

[4] Revenues per FTE student in this indicator are adjusted for inflation using constant 2018–19 dollars, based on the Consumer Price Index (CPI), prepared by the Bureau of Labor Statistics, U.S. Department of Labor, adjusted to a school-year basis.

Reference tables: *Digest of Education Statistics 2019*, tables 333.10, 333.40, and 333.55

Related indicators and resources: Postsecondary Institution Expenses

Glossary: Constant dollars; Consumer Price Index (CPI); Control of institutions; Degree-granting institutions; Full-time-equivalent (FTE) enrollment; Private institution; Public school or institution; Revenue; Tuition and fees

Postsecondary Institution Expenses

In 2017–18, instruction expenses per full-time-equivalent (FTE) student (in constant 2018–19 dollars) was the largest expense category at public institutions ($10,870) and private nonprofit institutions ($18,710). At private for-profit institutions, the combined category of academic support, student services, and institutional support expenses was the largest category of expenses per FTE student ($10,480).

In 2017–18, degree-granting postsecondary institutions in the United States spent $604 billion (in current dollars). Total expenses were $385 billion at public institutions, $207 billion at private nonprofit institutions, and $12 billion at private for-profit institutions. Some data may not be comparable across institutions by control categories (i.e., public, private nonprofit, or private for-profit) because of differences in accounting standards. Comparisons by institutional level (i.e., between 2-year and 4-year institutions) may also be limited because of different institutional missions. The missions of 2-year institutions generally focus on providing student instruction and related activities through a range of career-oriented programs at the certificate and associate's

degree levels and preparing students to transfer to 4-year institutions. Four-year institutions tend to have a broad range of instructional programs at the undergraduate level, leading to bachelor's degrees, and many offer graduate-level programs as well. Research activities, on-campus student housing, teaching hospitals, and auxiliary enterprises can also have a substantial impact on the financial structure of 4-year institutions. In this indicator, expenses are grouped into the following broad categories: instruction; research and public service; academic support, student services, and institutional support; net grant aid to students;[1] auxiliary enterprises; hospitals; independent operations and other.[2]

Figure 1. Percentage distribution of total expenses for degree-granting postsecondary institutions, by level and control of institution and expense categories: 2017–18

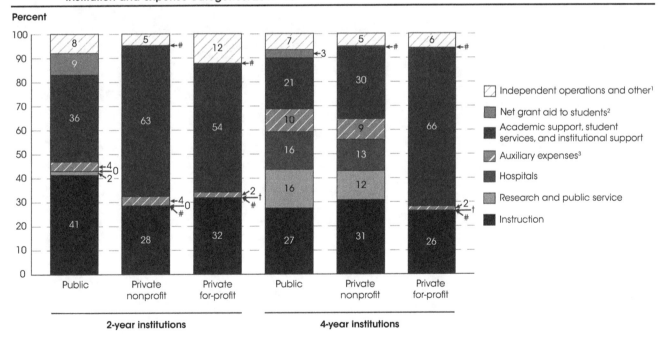

Percent

Legend:
- Independent operations and other[1]
- Net grant aid to students[2]
- Academic support, student services, and institutional support
- Auxiliary expenses[3]
- Hospitals
- Research and public service
- Instruction

2-year institutions: Public, Private nonprofit, Private for-profit
4-year institutions: Public, Private nonprofit, Private for-profit

Level and control of institution

† Not applicable.
# Rounds to zero.
[1] For private for-profit institutions, hospital expenses are included in the "other" category. Expenses for independent operations are not applicable for for-profit institutions.
[2] For public institutions, includes scholarship and fellowship expenses, net of discounts and allowances. Excludes the amount of discounts and allowances that were recorded as a reduction to revenues from tuition, fees, and auxiliary enterprises, such as room, board, and books. For private nonprofit and private for-profit institutions, excludes tuition, fee, and auxiliary enterprise allowances and agency transactions, such as student awards made from contributed funds or grant funds. These exclusions account for the majority of total student grants.
[3] Essentially self-supporting operations of institutions that furnish a service to students, faculty, or staff, such as residence halls and food services.
NOTE: Degree-granting institutions grant associate's or higher degrees and participate in Title IV federal financial aid programs. Although rounded numbers are displayed, the figures are based on unrounded data. Detail may not sum to totals because of rounding.
SOURCE: U.S. Department of Education, National Center for Education Statistics, Integrated Postsecondary Education Data System (IPEDS), Spring 2019, Finance component. See *Digest of Education Statistics 2019*, tables 334.10, 334.30, and 334.50.

Instruction, including faculty salaries and benefits, was the largest single expense category at public 2-year (41 percent), public 4-year (27 percent), and private nonprofit 4-year (31 percent) degree-granting postsecondary institutions in 2017–18. At private nonprofit 2-year institutions and private for-profit 2- and 4-year institutions, the largest expense category was the combined category of academic support, student services, and institutional support, which includes expenses associated with noninstructional activities, such as admissions, student activities, libraries, and administrative and executive activities. These expenses constituted 63 percent of total expenses at private nonprofit 2-year institutions, 54 percent of total expenses at private for-profit 2-year institutions, and 66 percent of total expenses at private for-profit 4-year institutions.

In 2017–18, combined expenses for research and public service (such as expenses for public broadcasting and community services) constituted 16 percent of total expenses at public 4-year institutions and 12 percent of total expenses at private nonprofit 4-year institutions.

Combined expenses for research and public service were 2 percent of total expenses at public 2-year institutions and less than one-half of 1 percent of total expenses at private nonprofit 2-year institutions, private for-profit 2-year institutions, and private for-profit 4-year institutions.

In 2017–18, net grant aid to students constituted 9 percent of total expenses at public 2-year institutions and 3 percent of total expenses at public 4-year institutions. Net grant aid to students was less than one-half of 1 percent of total expenses for all other categories of institutional control and level. Hospital expenses were 16 percent of total expenses at public 4-year institutions, 13 percent of total expenses at private nonprofit 4-year institutions, and were zero percent at both public and private nonprofit 2-year institutions. For private for-profit institutions, hospital expenses are included in the "other" category. Auxiliary expenses ranged from 2 percent of total expenses at private for-profit 2- and 4-year institutions to 10 percent at public 4-year institutions.

Figure 2. Expenses per full-time-equivalent (FTE) student at 4-year degree-granting postsecondary institutions, by control of institution and expense categories: 2017–18

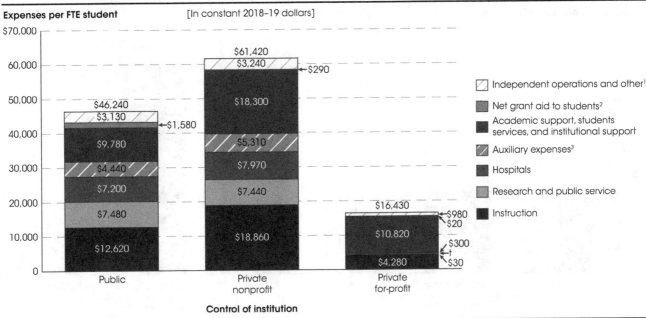

Expenses per FTE student   [In constant 2018–19 dollars]

† Not applicable.
[1] For private for-profit institutions, hospital expenses are included in the "other" category. Expenses for independent operations are not applicable for for-profit institutions.
[2] For public institutions, includes scholarship and fellowship expenses, net of discounts and allowances. Excludes the amount of discounts and allowances that were recorded as a reduction to revenues from tuition, fees, and auxiliary enterprises, such as room, board, and books. For private nonprofit and private for-profit institutions, excludes tuition, fee, and auxiliary enterprise allowances and agency transactions, such as student awards made from contributed funds or grant funds. These exclusions account for the majority of total student grants.
[3] Essentially self-supporting operations of institutions that furnish a service to students, faculty, or staff, such as residence halls and food services.
NOTE: Full-time-equivalent (FTE) students include full-time students plus the full-time equivalent of part-time students. Expenses per FTE student in this indicator are adjusted for inflation using constant 2018–19 dollars, based on the Consumer Price Index (CPI), prepared by the Bureau of Labor Statistics, U.S. Department of Labor, adjusted to a school-year basis. Degree-granting institutions grant associate's or higher degrees and participate in Title IV federal financial aid programs. Detail may not sum to totals because of rounding.
SOURCE: U.S. Department of Education, National Center for Education Statistics, Integrated Postsecondary Education Data System (IPEDS), Spring 2019, Finance component; and Spring 2018, Fall Enrollment component. See *Digest of Education Statistics 2019*, tables 334.10, 334.30, and 334.50.

In 2017–18, total expenses per full-time-equivalent (FTE) student[3] at degree-granting postsecondary institutions were higher at private nonprofit 4-year institutions ($61,420) than at public 4-year institutions ($46,240) and private for-profit 4-year institutions ($16,430). For instruction expenses, private nonprofit 4-year institutions spent 50 percent more per FTE student ($18,860) than did public 4-year institutions ($12,620) and 341 percent more than did private for-profit 4-year institutions ($4,280). Similarly, for the combined category of academic support, student services, and institutional support, private nonprofit 4-year institutions spent

87 percent more per FTE student ($18,300) than did public 4-year institutions ($9,780) and 69 percent more than did private for-profit 4-year institutions ($10,820). Expenses per FTE student for the combined category of research and public service were much higher at public 4-year institutions ($7,480) and private nonprofit 4-year institutions ($7,440) than at private for-profit 4-year institutions ($30). Among 2-year institutions, public institutions spent more per FTE student on instruction expenses ($6,950) than did private nonprofit institutions and private for-profit institutions ($5,480 and $5,380, respectively).

Figure 3. Instruction expenses per full-time-equivalent (FTE) student at degree-granting postsecondary institutions, by level and control of institution: 2010–11 and 2017–18

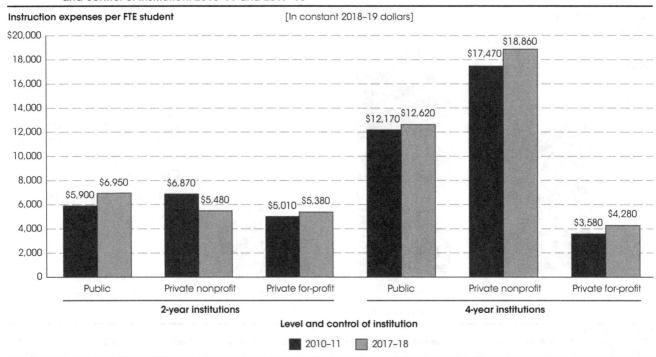

Instruction expenses per FTE student   [In constant 2018–19 dollars]

NOTE: Full-time-equivalent (FTE) students include full-time students plus the full-time equivalent of part-time students. Expenses per FTE student in this indicator are adjusted for inflation using constant 2018–19 dollars, based on the Consumer Price Index (CPI), prepared by the Bureau of Labor Statistics, U.S. Department of Labor, adjusted to a school-year basis. Degree-granting institutions grant associate's or higher degrees and participate in Title IV federal financial aid programs.
SOURCE: U.S. Department of Education, National Center for Education Statistics, Integrated Postsecondary Education Data System (IPEDS), Spring 2012 and Spring 2019, Finance component; and Spring 2011 and Spring 2018, Fall Enrollment component. See *Digest of Education Statistics 2019*, tables 334.10, 334.30, and 334.50.

Between 2010–11 and 2017–18, the percentage change in inflation-adjusted instruction expenses per FTE student at degree-granting postsecondary institutions varied by level and control of institution. Among 2-year institutions, instruction expenses per FTE student were 18 percent higher in 2017–18 than in 2010–11 at public institutions ($6,950 vs. $5,900) and 7 percent higher at private for-profit institutions ($5,380 vs. $5,010). In contrast, at private nonprofit 2-year institutions, instruction expenses per FTE student were 20 percent lower in 2017–18 than in 2010–11 ($5,480 vs. $6,870). Among 4-year institutions, instruction expenses per FTE student were 4 percent higher in 2017–18 than in 2010–11 at public institutions ($12,620 vs. $12,170), 8 percent higher at private nonprofit institutions ($18,860 vs. $17,470), and 20 percent higher at private for-profit institutions ($4,280 vs. $3,580).

Endnotes:
[1] For public institutions, includes scholarship and fellowship expenses, net of discounts and allowances. Excludes the amount of discounts and allowances that were recorded as a reduction to revenues from tuition, fees, and auxiliary enterprises, such as room, board, and books. For private nonprofit and private for-profit institutions, excludes tuition, fees, and auxiliary enterprise allowances and agency transactions, such as student awards made from contributed funds or grant funds. These exclusions account for the majority of total student grants.

[2] For private for-profit institutions, hospital expenses are included in the "other" category. Expenses for independent operations are not applicable for for-profit institutions.
[3] Expenses per FTE student in this indicator are adjusted for inflation using constant 2018–19 dollars, based on the Consumer Price Index (CPI), prepared by the Bureau of Labor Statistics, U.S. Department of Labor, adjusted to a school-year basis.

Reference tables: *Digest of Education Statistics 2019*, tables 334.10, 334.30, and 334.50
Related indicators and resources: Education Expenditures by Country; Postsecondary Institution Revenues

Glossary: Constant dollars; Consumer Price Index (CPI); Control of institutions; Full-time-equivalent (FTE) enrollment; Postsecondary education; Postsecondary institutions (basic classification by level); Private institution; Public school or institution

The indicators in this chapter of *The Condition of Education* describe population characteristics and economic outcomes for the United States. Individuals' levels of educational attainment are related to median earnings and other labor outcomes, such as unemployment rates.

Chapter 3

Population Characteristics and Economic Outcomes

Population Characteristics

Economic Outcomes

Educational Attainment of Young Adults

The gender gap in the percentage of 25- to 29-year-olds who had attained a bachelor's or higher degree widened from 2 percentage points in 2000 to 6 percentage points in 2019 with a higher percentage of females obtaining bachelor's or higher degrees than males.

Educational attainment refers to the level of education completed (reported here as high school completion or higher,[1] an associate's or higher degree, a bachelor's or higher degree, or a master's or higher degree). Between 2000 and 2019, educational attainment rates among 25- to 29-year-olds increased at each attainment level. During this time, the percentage with high school completion or higher increased from 88 to 94 percent, the percentage with an associate's or higher degree increased from 38 to 49 percent, the percentage with a bachelor's or higher degree increased from 29 to 39 percent, and the percentage with a master's or higher degree increased from 5 to 9 percent.

Figure 1. Percentage of 25- to 29-year-olds, by educational attainment and sex: 2000 and 2019

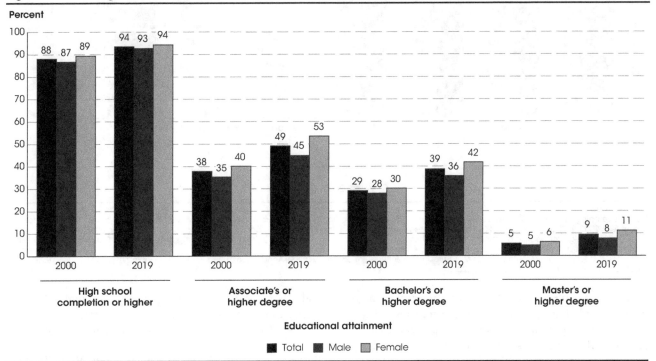

NOTE: High school completion includes those who graduated from high school with a diploma as well as those who completed high school through equivalency programs, such as a GED program. Although rounded numbers are displayed, the figures are based on unrounded data.
SOURCE: U.S. Department of Commerce, Census Bureau, Current Population Survey (CPS), Annual Social and Economic Supplement, 2000 and 2019. See *Digest of Education Statistics 2019*, table 104.20.

Between 2000 and 2019, educational attainment rates increased for both female and male 25- to 29-year-olds across all attainment levels. During this period, attainment rates for this age group were generally higher for females than for males, and the difference between the attainment rates for females and males (also referred to in this indicator as the gender gap) widened at all attainment levels except for the high school completion or higher level. For example, at the bachelor's or higher degree level, the gender gap widened from 2 percentage points in 2000 to 6 percentage points in 2019. Similarly, at the master's or higher degree level, the gender gap widened from 1 percentage point in 2000 to 3 percentage points in 2019. However, the gender gap at the high school completion or higher level in 2019 (2 percentage points) was not measurably different from the gap in 2000.

Gender gaps in educational attainment rates were observed across racial/ethnic groups in 2019. For White and Hispanic 25- to 29-year-olds, attainment rates were higher for females than for males at most attainment levels in 2019. For example, the Hispanic gender gap was 9 percentage points at the associate's or higher degree level and 5 percentage points at the bachelor's or higher degree level. The only exception was that there was no measurable gender gap at the high school completion or higher level for White 25- to 29-year-olds. In addition, the Black attainment rates were 5 percentage points higher for females than for males in 2019 at the master's or higher degree level, and for those who were American Indian/Alaska Native, attainment rates were 14 percentage points higher for females than males at the bachelor's or higher degree level.[2] There was no measurable gender gap at any attainment level in 2019 for those who were Asian and for those of Two or more races.[3]

Figure 2.   Percentage of 25- to 29-year-olds with high school completion or higher, by race/ethnicity: 2000 and 2019

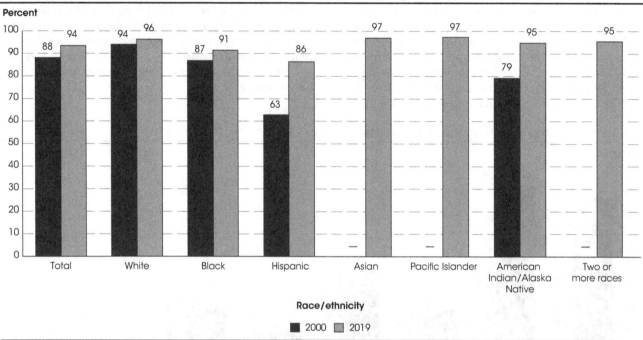

— Not available.
NOTE: Race categories exclude persons of Hispanic ethnicity. Separate data on those who were Asian, Pacific Islander, and of Two or more races were not available in 2000. In 2000, individuals of Two or more races were required to select a single race category. High school completion includes those who graduated from high school with a diploma as well as those who completed high school through equivalency programs, such as a GED program. Although rounded numbers are displayed, the figures are based on unrounded data.
SOURCE: U.S. Department of Commerce, Census Bureau, Current Population Survey (CPS), Annual Social and Economic Supplement, 2000 and 2019. See *Digest of Education Statistics 2019*, table 104.20.

In 2019, the percentage of 25- to 29-year-olds with high school completion or higher was higher for those who were Asian (97 percent) and White (96 percent) than for those who were Black (91 percent) and Hispanic (86 percent). Between 2000 and 2019, the percentages with high school completion or higher increased for those who were White (from 94 to 96 percent), Black (from 87 to 91 percent), Hispanic (from 63 to 86 percent), and American Indian/Alaska Native (from 79 to 95 percent). In addition, the percentage of Pacific Islander 25- to 29-year-olds with high school completion or higher was higher in 2019 (97 percent) than in 2003 (82 percent), the first year for which separate data on individuals who were Pacific Islander, Asian, and of Two or more races were available. The percentages who were Asian (97 percent)

and of Two or more races (95 percent) with high school completion or higher in 2019 were not measurably different from the corresponding percentages in 2003.

Between 2000 and 2019, the percentage of White 25- to 29-year-olds with high school completion or higher remained higher than the percentages of Black and Hispanic 25- to 29-year-olds who had attained this educational attainment level. The White-Black attainment gap at this level in 2019 (5 percentage points) was not measurably different from the corresponding gap in 2000. However, the White-Hispanic gap at this level narrowed from 31 to 10 percentage points, primarily due to the increase in the percentage of Hispanic 25- to 29-year-olds with high school completion or higher.

Figure 3.   Percentage of 25- to 29-year-olds with an associate's or higher degree, by race/ethnicity: 2000 and 2019

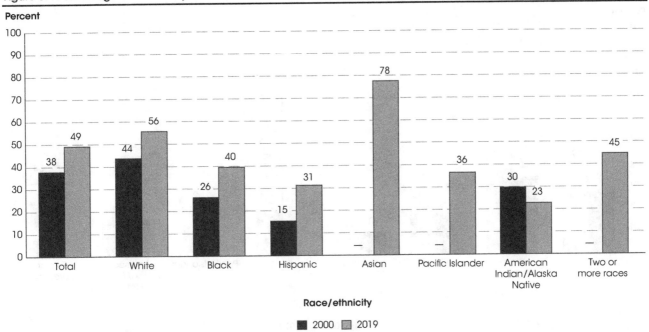

— Not available.
NOTE: Race categories exclude persons of Hispanic ethnicity. Separate data on those who were Asian, Pacific Islander, and of Two or more races were not available in 2000. In 2000, individuals of Two or more races were required to select a single race category.
SOURCE: U.S. Department of Commerce, Census Bureau, Current Population Survey (CPS), Annual Social and Economic Supplement, 2000 and 2019. See *Digest of Education Statistics 2019*, table 104.20.

Similar to the pattern observed at the high school completion or higher level, the percentage of 25- to 29-year-olds who had attained an associate's or higher degree was higher for those who were Asian (78 percent) and White (56 percent) than for those of any other racial/ethnic group in 2019. In addition, the percentage was higher for those who were Black (40 percent) than for those who were Hispanic (31 percent) and American Indian/Alaska Native (23 percent). From 2000 to 2019, the percentages who had attained an associate's or higher degree increased for those who were White (from 44 to 56 percent), Black (from 26 to 40 percent), and Hispanic (from 15 to 31 percent). In addition, the percentage of Asian 25- to 29-year-olds who had attained an associate's or higher degree increased from 2003 to 2019 (from 67 to 78 percent). The percentage of American Indian/Alaska Native 25- to 29-year-olds (23 percent) who had attained

an associate's or higher degree in 2019 was not measurably different from the percentage in 2000. Similarly, for those who were Pacific Islander or of Two or more races, the percentages with an associate's or higher degree in 2019 (36 percent and 45 percent, respectively) were not measurably different from the corresponding percentages in 2003.

The gap between the percentages of White and Black 25- to 29-year-olds who had attained an associate's or higher degree in 2019 (16 percentage points) was not measurably different from the corresponding gap in 2000, while the gap between the percentages of White and Hispanic 25- to 29-year-olds with an associate's or higher degree in 2019 (24 percentage points) was smaller than the corresponding gap in 2000 (28 percentage points).

Figure 4.   Percentage of 25- to 29-year-olds with a bachelor's or higher degree, by race/ethnicity: 2000 and 2019

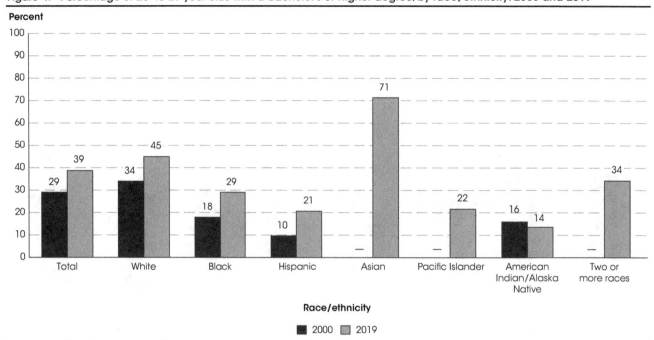

— Not available.
NOTE: Race categories exclude persons of Hispanic ethnicity. Separate data on those who were Asian, Pacific Islander, and of Two or more races were not available in 2000. In 2000, individuals of Two or more races were required to select a single race category. Although rounded numbers are displayed, the figures are based on unrounded data.
SOURCE: U.S. Department of Commerce, Census Bureau, Current Population Survey (CPS), Annual Social and Economic Supplement, 2000 and 2019. See *Digest of Education Statistics 2019*, table 104.20.

In 2019, among 25- to 29-year-olds, the percentages who had attained a bachelor's or higher degree were higher for those who were Asian (71 percent) and White (45 percent) than for those of any other racial/ethnic group. From 2000 to 2019, the percentages of 25- to 29-year-olds who had attained a bachelor's or higher degree increased for those who were White (from 34 to 45 percent), Black (from 18 to 29 percent), and Hispanic (from 10 to 21 percent). Similarly, the percentages of 25- to 29-year-olds who had attained a bachelor's or higher degree increased between 2003 and 2019 for those who were Asian (from 62 to 71 percent) and of Two or more races (from 22 to 34 percent). The percentage of American Indian/Alaska Native 25- to 29-year-olds who had attained a bachelor's or higher degree in 2019 (14 percent) was not measurably different from the percentage in 2000, and the percentage of Pacific Islander 25- to 29-year-olds who had attained a bachelor's or higher degree in 2019 (22 percent) was not measurably different from the percentage in 2003.

The gaps between the percentages of White and Black 25- to 29-year-olds and between the percentages of White and Hispanic 25- to 29-year-olds who had attained a bachelor's or higher degree in 2019 (16 percentage points and 24 percentage points, respectively) were not measurably different from the corresponding gaps in 2000.

Similar to the pattern observed at the bachelor's or higher degree level, the percentage of 25- to 29-year-olds who had attained a master's or higher degree was higher for Asian 25- to 29-year-olds (29 percent) than for those of any other racial/ethnic group in 2019.[4] In addition, the percentage was higher for those who were White (10 percent) than for those who were Black (6 percent) and Hispanic (3 percent). From 2000 to 2019, the percentages who had attained a master's or higher degree increased for those who were White (from 6 to 10 percent), Black (from 4 to 6 percent), and Hispanic (from 2 to 3 percent). In addition, the percentage of Asian 25- to 29-year-olds who had attained a master's or higher degree increased from 2003 to 2019 (from 19 to 29 percent). The percentage of 25- to 29-year-olds of Two or more races with a master's or higher degree in 2019 (10 percent) was also higher than the percentage in 2003 (4 percent).

The gap between the percentages of White and Black 25- to 29-year-olds who had attained a master's or higher degree in 2019 (4 percentage points) was not measurably different from the gap in 2000. However, the White-Hispanic gap at the master's or higher degree level widened during this time, from 4 to 7 percentage points.

Endnotes:

[1] High school completion includes those who graduated from high school with a diploma as well as those who completed high school through equivalency programs, such as a GED program.

[2] American Indian/Alaska Native 25- to 29-year-olds who had attained a master's or higher degree are not included in this comparison because the sample size in 2019 was too small to provide reliable estimates.

[3] In 2019, the sample of male Pacific Islander 25- to 29-year-olds was too small to provide reliable comparisons by gender at any level of educational attainment.

[4] American Indian/Alaska Native and Pacific Islander 25- to 29-year-olds who had attained a master's or higher degree are not included in this comparison because sample sizes in 2019 were too small to provide reliable estimates.

Reference tables: *Digest of Education Statistics 2019,* table 104.20; *Digest of Education Statistics 2016*, table 104.20

Related indicators and resources: Disability Rates and Employment Status by Educational Attainment [*The Condition of Education 2017 Spotlight*]; Educational Attainment [*Status and Trends in the Education of Racial and Ethnic Groups*]; International Educational Attainment; Snapshot: Attainment of a Bachelor's or Higher Degree for Racial/Ethnic Subgroups [*Status and Trends in the Education of Racial and Ethnic Groups*]; Trends in Employment Rates by Educational Attainment [*The Condition of Education 2013 Spotlight*]

Glossary: Associate's degree; Bachelor's degree; Educational attainment (Current Population Survey); Gap; High school completer; High school diploma; Master's degree; Postsecondary education; Racial/ethnic group

Young Adults Neither Enrolled in School nor Working

Overall, the percentage of 18- to 24-year-olds neither enrolled in school nor working was lower in 2018 (13 percent) than shortly before the recession in 2006 (15 percent) and shortly after the recession in 2011 (18 percent). In 2018, the percentage of 20- to 24-year-olds neither enrolled in school nor working was higher for those who had not completed high school (41 percent) than for those who had completed high school (12 percent).

Schooling and working are core activities in the transition from childhood to adulthood. Young adults who are detached from these activities, particularly if they are detached for several years, may have difficulty building a work history that contributes to future employability and higher wages.[1] Young adults who are neither enrolled in school nor working may be detached from these activities for a variety of reasons. For example, they may be seeking educational opportunities or work but are unable to find them, or they may have left school or the workforce temporarily or permanently for personal, family, or financial reasons. This indicator examines rates at which young adults in a variety of age groups are neither enrolled in school nor working. The indicator presents data across three years: 2006, 2011, and 2018. The 2006 data provide information on outcomes prior to the recession experienced by the U.S. economy between December 2007 and June 2009,[2] the 2011 data represent the period shortly after the recession ended, and the 2018 data provide the most recent information available.

Figure 1. Percentage of 18- to 24-year-olds who were neither enrolled in school nor working, by age group: 2006, 2011, and 2018

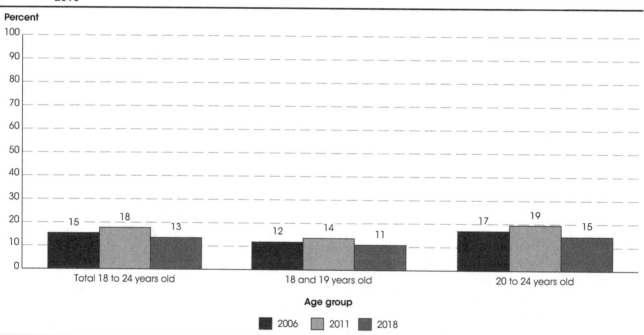

NOTE: Data are based on sample surveys of the entire population in the given age range residing within the United States, including the 50 states, the District of Columbia (D.C.), and Puerto Rico. Both noninstitutionalized persons (e.g., those living in households, college housing, or military housing located within the United States) and institutionalized persons (e.g., those living in prisons, nursing facilities, or other healthcare facilities) are included. Institutionalized persons made up 1 percent of all 18- to 24-year-olds in 2018. Although rounded numbers are displayed, the figures are based on unrounded data.
SOURCE: U.S. Department of Commerce, Census Bureau, American Community Survey (ACS), 2006, 2011, and 2018. See *Digest of Education Statistics 2019*, table 501.30.

Thirteen percent of 18- to 24-year-olds were neither in school nor working in 2018 overall. The percentage was higher for 20- to 24-year-olds (15 percent) than for 18- and 19-year-olds (11 percent).

Overall, the percentage of 18- to 24-year-olds neither in school nor working was lower in 2018 (13 percent) than shortly before the recession in 2006 (15 percent) and

shortly after the recession in 2011 (18 percent). Specifically, among 18- and 19-year-olds, the percentage neither in school nor working was lower in 2018 (11 percent) than in 2006 (12 percent) and 2011 (14 percent). Likewise, the percentage of 20- to 24-year-olds neither in school nor working was also lower in 2018 (15 percent) than in 2006 (17 percent) and 2011 (19 percent).

Figure 2.   Percentage of 18- to 24-year-olds who were neither enrolled in school nor working, by race/ethnicity: 2018

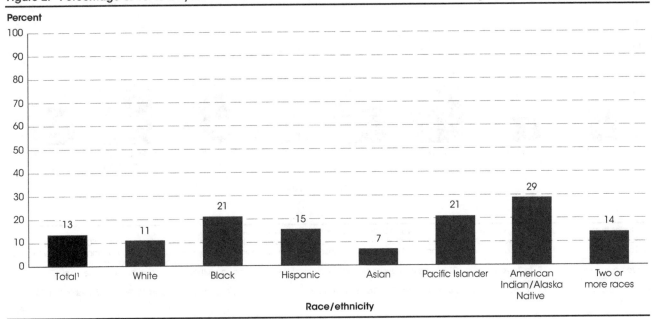

¹ Includes respondents who wrote in some other race that was not included as an option on the questionnaire.
NOTE: Data are based on sample surveys of the entire population in the given age range residing within the United States, including the 50 states, the District of Columbia (D.C.), and Puerto Rico. Both noninstitutionalized persons (e.g., those living in households, college housing, or military housing located within the United States) and institutionalized persons (e.g., those living in prisons, nursing facilities, or other healthcare facilities) are included. Institutionalized persons made up 1 percent of all 18- to 24-year-olds in 2018. Race categories exclude persons of Hispanic ethnicity. Although rounded numbers are displayed, the figures are based on unrounded data.
SOURCE: U.S. Department of Commerce, Census Bureau, American Community Survey (ACS), 2018. See *Digest of Education Statistics 2019*, table 501.30.

In 2018, the percentage of 18- to 24-year-olds neither in school nor working varied by race/ethnicity. The percentage neither in school nor working was higher for those who were American Indian/Alaska Native (29 percent) than for their peers of any other racial/ethnic group. This percentage was lowest for those who were

Asian (7 percent). The percentage was also lower for those who were White (11 percent) than for their peers of any other racial/ethnic group. In addition, the percentage neither in school nor working was lower for those who were of Two or more races (14 percent) and Hispanic (15 percent) than for their Black peers (21 percent).

Figure 3. Percentage of 18- to 24-year-olds who were neither enrolled in school nor working, by race/ethnicity and sex: 2018

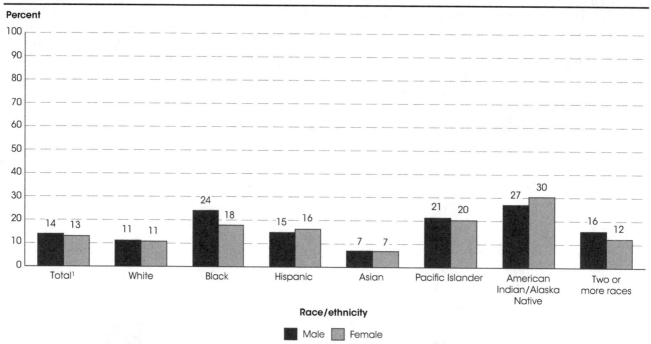

Percent

¹ Includes respondents who wrote in some other race that was not included as an option on the questionnaire.
NOTE: Data are based on sample surveys of the entire population in the given age range residing within the United States, including the 50 states, the District of Columbia (D.C.), and Puerto Rico. Both noninstitutionalized persons (e.g., those living in households, college housing, or military housing located within the United States) and institutionalized persons (e.g., those living in prisons, nursing facilities, or other healthcare facilities) are included. Institutionalized persons made up 1 percent of all 18- to 24-year-olds in 2018. Race categories exclude persons of Hispanic ethnicity. Although rounded numbers are displayed, the figures are based on unrounded data.
SOURCE: U.S. Department of Commerce, Census Bureau, American Community Survey (ACS), 2018. See *Digest of Education Statistics 2019*, table 501.30.

The percentage of 18- to 24-year-olds who were neither in school nor working in 2018 was higher for males than for females overall (14 vs. 13 percent). This pattern was also observed for those who were Black (24 vs. 18 percent) and of Two or more races (16 vs. 12 percent).[3] However, for those who were Hispanic, the percentage neither in school nor working was lower for males than for females (15 vs. 16 percent).[4]

Figure 4. Percentage of 20- to 24-year-olds who were neither enrolled in school nor working, by sex, race/ethnicity, and high school completion status: 2018

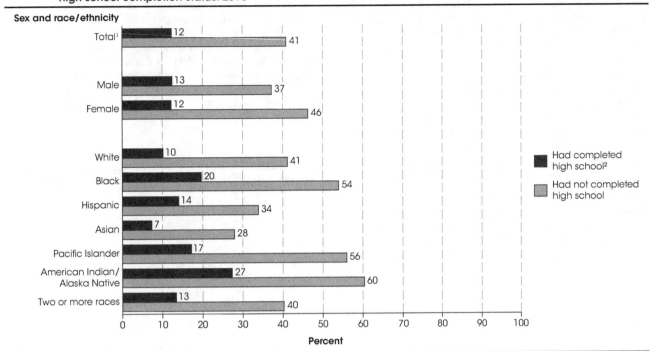

¹ Includes respondents who wrote in some other race that was not included as an option on the questionnaire.
² Includes respondents who completed high school through equivalency programs, such as a GED program.
NOTE: Data are based on sample surveys of the entire population in the given age range residing within the United States, including the 50 states, the District of Columbia (D.C.), and Puerto Rico. Both noninstitutionalized persons (e.g., those living in households, college housing, or military housing located within the United States) and institutionalized persons (e.g., those living in prisons, nursing facilities, or other healthcare facilities) are included. Institutionalized persons made up 1 percent of all 18- to 24-year-olds in 2018. Race categories exclude persons of Hispanic ethnicity. Although rounded numbers are displayed, the figures are based on unrounded data.
SOURCE: U.S. Department of Commerce, Census Bureau, American Community Survey (ACS), 2018. See *Digest of Education Statistics 2019*, table 501.30.

In 2018, the percentage of 20- to 24-year-olds[5] who were neither in school nor working was higher for those who had not completed high school[6] (41 percent) than for those who had completed high school (12 percent). These differences by high school completion status were observed for males and females as well as for all racial/ethnic groups. For example, the percentage who were neither in school nor working was 25 percentage points higher for males who had not completed high school than for males who had completed high school and 34 percentage points higher for females who had not completed high school than for females who had completed high school. The gap by high school completion status was larger for females than for males. In addition, the gap by high school completion status was larger for those who were Black and White (34 and 31 percentage points, respectively) than for their Asian and Hispanic peers (21 and 20 percentage points, respectively).

Endnotes:

[1] Fernandes-Alcantara, A.L. (2015). *Disconnected Youth: A Look at 16 to 24 Year Olds Who Are Not Working or In School* (CRS Report No. R40535). Washington, DC: Congressional Research Service. Retrieved January 3, 2020, from https://fas.org/sgp/crs/misc/R40535.pdf.

[2] National Bureau of Economic Research. (2010). *U.S. Business Cycle Expansions and Contractions.* Retrieved January 3, 2020, from https://www.nber.org/cycles.html.

[3] For White 18- to 24-year-olds, the percentage was also higher for males (11.2 percent) than for females (10.8 percent), though both percentages rounded to 11 percent.

[4] For American Indian/Alaska Native 18- to 24-year-olds, this percentage was not measurably different between males (27 percent) and females (30 percent).

[5] The narrower 20- to 24-year old range was chosen to reduce the number of high school students in this analysis.

[6] High school completion includes those persons who graduated from high school with a diploma as well as those who completed high school through equivalency programs, such as a GED program.

Reference tables: *Digest of Education Statistics 2019*, table 501.30

Related indicators and resources: College Enrollment Rates; Employment and Unemployment Rates by Educational Attainment; Immediate College Enrollment Rate; Youth and Young Adults Neither Enrolled in School nor Working [*Status and Trends in the Education of Racial and Ethnic Groups*]

Glossary: Gap; High school completer; Racial/ethnic group

Annual Earnings

For 25- to 34-year-olds who worked full time, year round in 2018, higher educational attainment was associated with higher median earnings. This pattern was consistent from 2000 through 2018. For example, in 2018 the median earnings of those with a master's or higher degree ($65,000) were 19 percent higher than the earnings of those with a bachelor's degree ($54,700), and the median earnings of those with a bachelor's degree were 57 percent higher than the earnings of high school completers ($34,900).

This indicator examines the annual earnings of 25- to 34-year-olds who worked full time, year round (i.e., worked 35 or more hours per week for 50 or more weeks per year). Many people in this age group recently exited formal education and may be entering the workforce for the first time or transitioning from part-time to full-time work. In 2018, some 74 percent of those who were in the labor force[1] worked full time, year round. This percentage was generally higher for those with higher levels of educational attainment. For example, 80 percent of those with a bachelor's degree worked full time, year round in 2018, compared with 72 percent of high school completers (those with only a high school diploma or an equivalency credential such as a GED) in this age group.

Figure 1. Percentage of 25- to 34-year-olds in the labor force who worked full time, year round, by educational attainment: 2000–2018

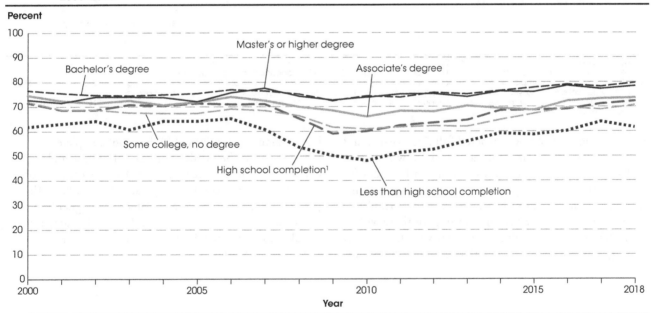

[1] Includes equivalency credentials, such as the GED.
NOTE: Data are based on sample surveys of the noninstitutionalized population, which excludes persons living in institutions (e.g., prisons or nursing facilities) and military barracks. *Full-time, year-round* workers are those who worked 35 or more hours per week for 50 or more weeks per year. The labor force refers to the population who reported working or looking for work in the given year.
SOURCE: U.S. Department of Commerce, Census Bureau, Current Population Survey (CPS), Annual Social and Economic Supplement, 2001–2019; and previously unpublished tabulations. See *Digest of Education Statistics 2019*, table 502.30.

Changes over time in the percentage of 25- to 34-year-olds in the labor force who worked full time, year round varied by level of educational attainment. The percentage of labor force participants who worked full time, year round increased among those with a bachelor's degree (from 77 percent in 2000 to 80 percent in 2018) and those with a master's or higher degree (from 73 percent in 2000 to 78 percent in 2018). At educational attainment levels lower than a bachelor's degree, there was no measurable difference between 2000 and 2018 in the percentage of labor force participants who worked full time, year round: those who did not complete high school (62 percent in 2018), those who completed high school (72 percent in 2018), those with some college but no degree (71 percent in 2018), and those with an associate's degree (73 percent in 2018).

More recently, between 2010 and 2018 the percentages of 25- to 34-year-olds in the labor force who worked full time, year round increased for every level of educational attainment. For example, during this period, the percentage of high school completers who worked full time, year round increased from 60 to 72 percent, and the corresponding percentage of those with a bachelor's degree increased from 74 to 80 percent.

Figure 2. Median annual earnings of full-time, year-round workers ages 25–34, by educational attainment: 2018

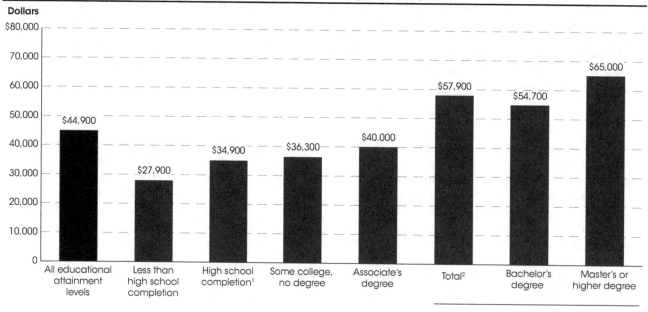

¹ Includes equivalency credentials, such as the GED.
² Represents median annual earnings of full-time, year-round workers ages 25–34 with a bachelor's or higher degree.
NOTE: Data are based on sample surveys of the noninstitutionalized population, which excludes persons living in institutions (e.g., prisons or nursing facilities) and military barracks. *Full-time, year-round* workers are those who worked 35 or more hours per week for 50 or more weeks per year.
SOURCE: U.S. Department of Commerce, Census Bureau, Current Population Survey (CPS), Annual Social and Economic Supplement, 2019. See *Digest of Education Statistics 2019,* table 502.30.

For 25- to 34-year-olds who worked full time, year round, higher educational attainment was associated with higher median earnings; this pattern was consistent from 2000 through 2018. For example, in 2018, the median earnings of those with a master's or higher degree were $65,000, some 19 percent higher than the earnings of those with a bachelor's degree ($54,700). In the same year, the median earnings of those with a bachelor's degree were 57 percent higher than the earnings of high school completers ($34,900), and the median earnings of high school completers were 25 percent higher than the earnings of those who did not complete high school ($27,900). This pattern of higher earnings associated with higher levels of educational attainment also held for both males and females, as well as for those who were White, Black, Hispanic, and Asian.

Figure 3. Median annual earnings of full-time, year-round workers ages 25–34, by educational attainment: 2000–2018

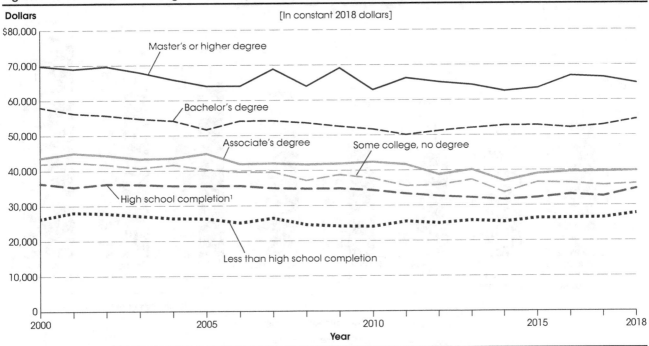

[1] Includes equivalency credentials, such as the GED.
NOTE: Data are based on sample surveys of the noninstitutionalized population, which excludes persons living in institutions (e.g., prisons or nursing facilities) and military barracks. *Full-time, year-round* workers are those who worked 35 or more hours per week for 50 or more weeks per year. Earnings are presented in constant 2018 dollars, based on the Consumer Price Index (CPI), to eliminate inflationary factors and to allow for direct comparison across years.
SOURCE: U.S. Department of Commerce, Census Bureau, Current Population Survey (CPS), Annual Social and Economic Supplement, 2001–2019; and previously unpublished tabulations. See *Digest of Education Statistics 2019*, table 502.30.

The median earnings (in constant 2018 dollars)[2] of 25- to 34-year-olds who worked full time, year round declined from 2000 to 2018 at most educational attainment levels. The exceptions were those who did not complete high school and those with a master's or higher degree: neither of these groups had a measurable change in median earnings between these two years. During this period, the median earnings of high school completers in this age group declined from $36,500 to $34,900 (a 4 percent decrease). The median earnings of those with some college but no degree declined from $42,100 to $36,300 (a 14 percent decrease). Similarly, the median earnings of those with an associate's degree declined from $43,700 to $40,000 (a 9 percent decrease). The median earnings of those with a bachelor's degree declined from $58,200 to $54,700 (a 6 percent decrease).

The difference in median earnings between 25- to 34-year-olds with a bachelor's degree and those who were high school completers was smaller in 2018 than 2000. In 2000, the median earnings of those with a bachelor's degree were $21,800 higher than the median earnings of high school completers; in 2018, this difference was $19,800. The narrower gap in 2018 was primarily due to the decrease in earnings for those with a bachelor's degree. Differences between median earnings of individuals who completed high school and those who did not and between median earnings of individuals with a master's or higher degree and those with a bachelor's degree did not change measurably during this same period.

Figure 4. Median annual earnings of full-time, year-round workers ages 25–34, by educational attainment and sex: 2018

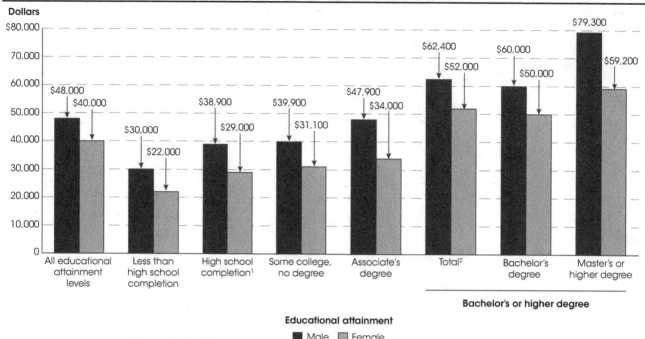

¹ Includes equivalency credentials, such as the GED.
² Represents median annual earnings of full-time, year-round workers ages 25–34 with a bachelor's or higher degree.
NOTE: Data are based on sample surveys of the noninstitutionalized population, which excludes persons living in institutions (e.g., prisons or nursing facilities) and military barracks. *Full-time, year-round* workers are those who worked 35 or more hours per week for 50 or more weeks per year.
SOURCE: U.S. Department of Commerce, Census Bureau, Current Population Survey (CPS), Annual Social and Economic Supplement, 2019. See *Digest of Education Statistics 2019*, table 502.30.

In 2018, the median earnings of 25- to 34-year-old males who worked full time, year round were higher than the corresponding median earnings of their female peers at every level of educational attainment, ranging from 20 percent higher for those with a bachelor's degree to 41 percent higher for those with an associate's degree. For example, the median earnings of males in this age group with a master's or higher degree ($79,300) were 34 percent higher than those of their female peers ($59,200). The median earnings of male high school completers in this age group ($38,900) were 34 percent higher than those of their female peers ($29,000).

In general, the median earnings of White 25- to 34-year-olds who worked full time, year round exceeded the corresponding median earnings of their Black and Hispanic peers at most attainment levels in 2018. For instance, the median earnings for those with a bachelor's degree were $57,700 for those who were White, compared with $45,100 for their Hispanic peers and $40,900 for their Black peers. The exceptions were those with some college and those with a master's or higher degree, where there were no measurable differences in median earnings between those who were White and Hispanic. However, among those with a master's or higher degree, those who were Asian had higher median earnings ($80,100) than their White ($63,600), Hispanic ($59,900), and Black ($53,800) peers.

Endnotes:
¹ The labor force consists of all civilians who are employed or seeking employment.

² Constant dollars based on the Consumer Price Index, prepared by the Bureau of Labor Statistics, U.S. Department of Labor.

Reference tables: *Digest of Education Statistics 2019*, table 502.30.
Related indicators and resources: Earnings and Employment [*Status and Trends in the Education of Racial and Ethnic Groups*]; Employment and Unemployment Rates by Educational Attainment; Employment Outcomes of Bachelor's Degree Holders [*web-only*]; Post-College Employment Outcomes by Field of Study and Race/Ethnicity [*The Condition of Education 2016 Spotlight*]

Glossary: Associate's degree; Bachelor's degree; Constant dollars; Consumer Price Index (CPI); Educational attainment (Current Population Survey); Employment status; High school completer; High school diploma; Master's degree; Median earnings; Racial/ethnic group

Employment and Unemployment Rates by Educational Attainment

In 2019, the employment rate for female 25- to 34-year-olds with a bachelor's or higher degree was 44 percentage points higher than for similar individuals who had not completed high school.

This indicator focuses on 25- to 34-year-olds and examines recent trends in two distinct yet related measures of labor market conditions: the employment rate and the unemployment rate. The *employment rate* (also known as the employment to population ratio) is the percentage of persons in the civilian noninstitutionalized population who are employed.[1] The *unemployment rate* is the percentage of persons in the civilian labor force (i.e., all civilians who are employed or seeking employment) who are not working and who made specific efforts to find employment sometime during the prior 4 weeks.

Figure 1. Employment rates of 25- to 34-year-olds, by sex and educational attainment: 2019

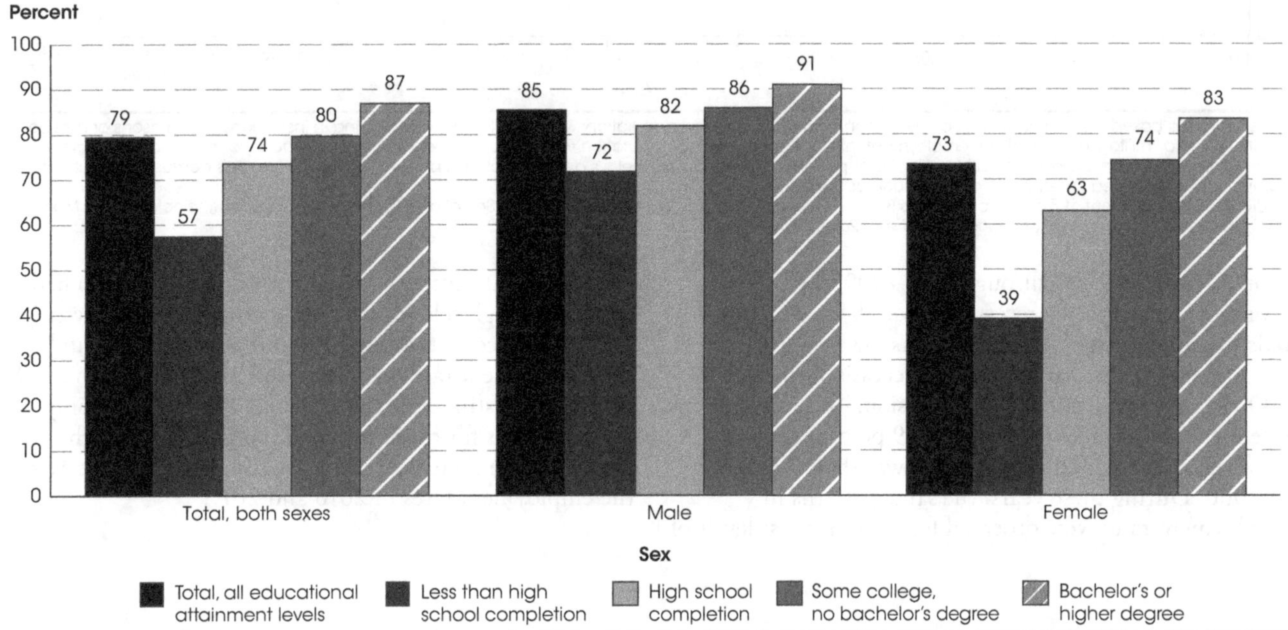

NOTE: Data are based on sample surveys of the civilian noninstitutionalized population, which excludes persons living in institutions (e.g., prisons or nursing facilities) and all military personnel. The employment rate, or employment to population ratio, is the number of persons in each group who are employed as a percentage of the civilian population in that group. "Some college, no bachelor's degree" includes persons with an associate's degree. "High school completion" includes equivalency credentials, such as the GED. Although rounded numbers are displayed, the figures are based on unrounded data. SOURCE: U.S. Department of Commerce, Census Bureau, Current Population Survey (CPS), Annual Social and Economic Supplement, March 2019. See *Digest of Education Statistics 2019*, tables 501.50, 501.60, and 501.70.

In 2019, the employment rate was higher for those with higher levels of educational attainment. For example, the employment rate was highest for 25- to 34-year-olds with a bachelor's or higher degree (87 percent). The employment rate for those with some college[2] (80 percent) was higher than the rate for those who had completed high school[3] (74 percent), which was higher than the employment rate for those who had not completed high school (57 percent). The same pattern was observed among both sexes. For example, the employment rate for females was highest for those with a bachelor's or higher degree (83 percent) and lowest for those who had not completed high school (39 percent).

Employment rates were higher for 25- to 34-year-old males than for their female peers in 2019, overall and at each level of educational attainment. The difference in employment rates between males and females (also referred to in this indicator as the gender gap) was narrower at higher levels of educational attainment. For instance, the gender gap was 7 percentage points for those with a bachelor's or higher degree, while the gender gap was 19 percentage points for those who had completed high school and 33 percentage points for those who had not completed high school.

Figure 2.   Employment rates of 25- to 34-year-olds, by educational attainment: Selected years, 2000 through 2019

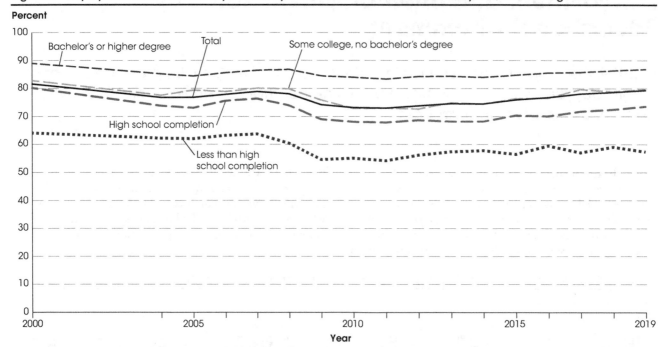

NOTE: Data are based on sample surveys of the civilian noninstitutionalized population, which excludes persons living in institutions (e.g., prisons or nursing facilities) and all military personnel. The employment rate, or employment to population ratio, is the number of persons in each group who are employed as a percentage of the civilian population in that group. "Some college, no bachelor's degree" includes persons with an associate's degree. "High school completion" includes equivalency credentials, such as the GED.
SOURCE: U.S. Department of Commerce, Census Bureau, Current Population Survey (CPS), Annual Social and Economic Supplement, selected years, March 2000 through 2019. See *Digest of Education Statistics 2013, 2014, 2016, 2018,* and *2019,* table 501.50.

From December 2007 through June 2009, the U.S. economy experienced a recession.[4] For 25- to 34-year-olds overall, the employment rate was lower in 2010 (73 percent), immediately after the recession, than in 2000 (82 percent), prior to the recession. The employment rate increased after 2010, reaching 79 percent in 2019; however, the rate in 2019 was still lower than the rate in 2000. During these years, the same patterns in employment rates were observed for those at most levels of educational attainment. For instance, for those who had completed high school, the employment rate was lower in 2010 (68 percent) than in 2000 (80 percent). Although the employment rate then increased to 74 percent in 2019, this rate was still lower than the rate in 2000. The only exception was for those who had not completed high school, where there was no measurable difference between the employment rates in 2010 and 2019.

Figure 3. Unemployment rates of 25- to 34-year-olds, by sex and educational attainment: 2019

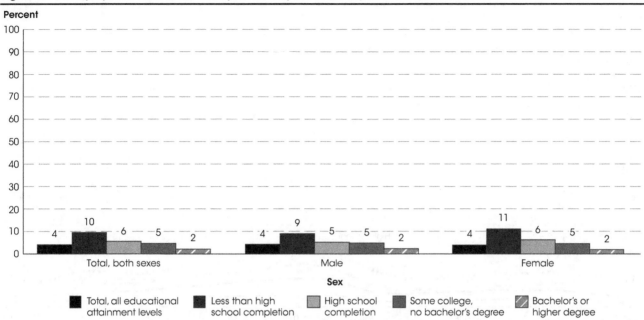

NOTE: Data are based on sample surveys of the noninstitutionalized population, which excludes persons living in institutions (e.g., prisons or nursing facilities); this figure includes data only on the civilian population (excludes all military personnel). The unemployment rate is the percentage of persons in the civilian labor force who are not working and who made specific efforts to find employment sometime during the prior 4 weeks. The civilian labor force consists of all civilians who are employed or seeking employment. "Some college, no bachelor's degree" includes persons with an associate's degree. "High school completion" includes equivalency credentials, such as the GED. Although rounded numbers are displayed, the figures are based on unrounded data.
SOURCE: U.S. Department of Commerce, Census Bureau, Current Population Survey (CPS), Annual Social and Economic Supplement, March 2019. See *Digest of Education Statistics 2019*, tables 501.80, 501.85, and 501.90.

Overall, the unemployment rate in 2019 was lower for 25- to 34-year-olds with higher levels of educational attainment. For example, the unemployment rate was lowest for those with a bachelor's or higher degree (2 percent). The unemployment rate was also lower for individuals with some college (5 percent) and those who had completed high school (6 percent) compared with those who had not completed high school (10 percent). A similar pattern was observed by sex.

There was no measurable difference between the overall unemployment rates for male and female 25- to 34-year-olds in 2019. In addition, there were no measurable differences between the unemployment rates by sex at any level of educational attainment.

Figure 4.   Unemployment rates of 25- to 34-year-olds, by educational attainment: Selected years, 2000 through 2019

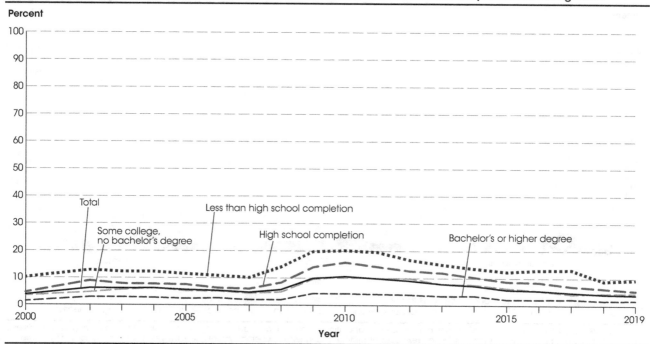

NOTE: Data are based on sample surveys of the noninstitutionalized population, which excludes persons living in institutions (e.g., prisons or nursing facilities); this figure includes data only on the civilian population (excludes all military personnel). The unemployment rate is the percentage of persons in the civilian labor force who are not working and who made specific efforts to find employment sometime during the prior 4 weeks. The civilian labor force consists of all civilians who are employed or seeking employment. "Some college, no bachelor's degree" includes persons with an associate's degree. "High school completion" includes equivalency credentials, such as the GED.
SOURCE: U.S. Department of Commerce, Census Bureau, Current Population Survey (CPS), Annual Social and Economic Supplement, selected years, March 2000 through 2019. See *Digest of Education Statistics 2013, 2017, 2018,* and *2019,* table 501.80.

For 25- to 34-year-olds overall, the unemployment rate was higher in 2010 (11 percent), immediately after the recession, than in 2000 (4 percent), prior to the recession. The unemployment rate decreased after 2010, to 4 percent in 2019, and this rate was not measurably different from the rate in 2000. During these years, the same patterns in unemployment rates were observed at each level of educational attainment.

Endnotes:

[1] Data in this indicator are based on sample surveys of the civilian noninstitutionalized population, which excludes persons living in institutions (e.g., prisons or nursing facilities) and excludes all military personnel.

[2] In this indicator, "some college" includes those with an associate's degree and those who have attended college but have not obtained a bachelor's degree.

[3] Includes equivalency credentials, such as the GED.

[4] National Bureau of Economic Research. (2010). *U.S. Business Cycle Expansions and Contractions.* Retrieved October 22, 2018, from https://www.nber.org/cycles.html.

Reference tables: *Digest of Education Statistics 2019,* tables 501.50, 501.60, 501.70, 501.80, 501.85, and 501.90; *Digest of Education Statistics 2013, 2014, 2016,* and *2018,* table 501.50; and *Digest of Education Statistics 2013, 2017,* and *2018,* table 501.80

Related indicators and resources: Annual Earnings; Disability Rates and Employment Status by Educational Attainment [*The Condition of Education 2017 Spotlight*]; Employment Outcomes of Bachelor's Degree Holders [*web-only*]; Post-College Employment Outcomes by Field of Study and Race/ Ethnicity [*The Condition of Education 2016 Spotlight*]; Trends in Employment Rates by Educational Attainment [*The Condition of Education 2013 Spotlight*]; Unemployment [*Status and Trends in the Education of Racial and Ethnic Groups*]

Glossary: Bachelor's degree; College; Educational attainment (Current Population Survey); Employment status; Gap; High school completer

The indicators in this chapter of *The Condition of Education* compare the United States education system to the education systems in other countries. The indicators examine enrollment rates, educational attainment, education expenditures, and student performance on international assessments in reading, mathematics, and science. The indicators focus on comparison to other countries in the Organization for Economic Cooperation and Development (OECD), and include supplemental data from other countries when available.

This chapter's indicators are available at *The Condition of Education* website: http://nces.ed.gov/programs/coe.

Chapter 4

International Comparisons

International Comparisons: Reading Literacy at Grade 4

In 2016, the United States, along with 15 other education systems, participated in the new ePIRLS assessment of students' comprehension of online information. The average online informational reading score for fourth-grade students in the United States (557) was higher than the ePIRLS scale centerpoint (500). Only three education systems (Singapore, Norway, and Ireland) scored higher than the United States.

The Progress in International Reading Literacy Study (PIRLS) is an international comparative assessment that evaluates reading literacy at grade 4. The assessment is coordinated by the TIMSS[1] and PIRLS International Study Center at Boston College with the support of the International Association for the Evaluation of Educational Achievement (IEA). PIRLS has been administered every 5 years since 2001. In 2016, there were 58 education systems that had PIRLS reading literacy data at grade 4.[2] These 58 education systems included both countries and other benchmarking education systems (portions of a country, nation, kingdom, emirate, or other non-national entity).[3] Sixteen of these education systems, including the United States, also administered ePIRLS, a new computer-based extension of PIRLS designed to assess students' comprehension of online information.

Figure 1.   Average reading scale scores of fourth-grade students on PIRLS, by education system: 2016

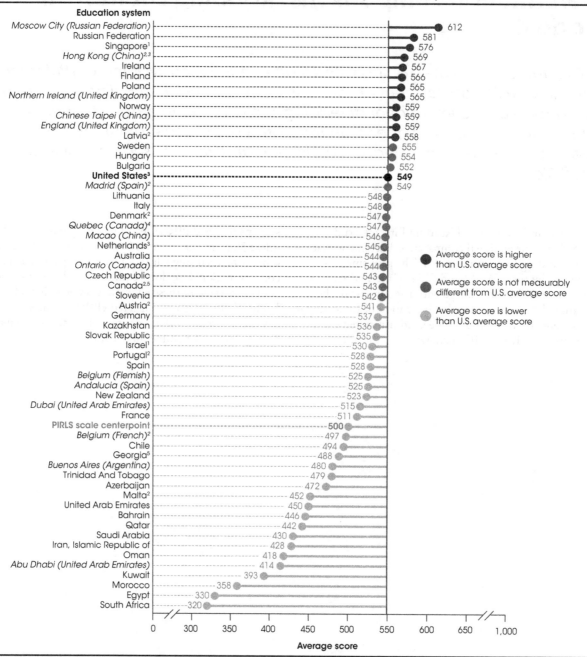

[1] National Defined Population covers less than 90 percent of the National Target Population (but at least 77 percent).
[2] National Defined Population covers 90 to 95 percent of the National Target Population.
[3] Met guidelines for sample participation rates only after replacement schools were included.
[4] Did not satisfy guidelines for sample participation rates.
[5] National Target Population does not include all of the International Target Population.
NOTE: Education systems are ordered by PIRLS average scale score. Italics indicate participants identified as a non-national entity that represents a portion of a country. The PIRLS scores are reported on a scale from 0 to 1,000, with the scale centerpoint set at 500 and the standard deviation set at 100. Education systems that did not administer PIRLS at the target grade are not shown. For more information about individual countries and assessment methodology, please see *Methods and Procedures in PIRLS 2016* (https://timssandpirls.bc.edu/publications/pirls/2016-methods.html).
SOURCE: International Association for the Evaluation of Educational Achievement (IEA), Progress in International Reading Literacy Study (PIRLS), 2016. See *Digest of Education Statistics 2017*, table 602.10.

In 2016, the average reading literacy score for fourth-grade students in the United States (549) was higher than the PIRLS scale centerpoint (500).[4] The U.S. average score was higher than the average scores of 30 education systems (over half of the participating education systems) and not measurably different from the average scores of 15 education systems. The United States scored lower than 12 education systems: Moscow City (Russian Federation), the Russian Federation, Singapore, Hong Kong (China), Ireland, Finland, Poland, Northern Ireland (United Kingdom), Norway, Chinese Taipei (China), England (United Kingdom), and Latvia.

Figure 2. Percentage of fourth-grade students performing at selected PIRLS international benchmarks in reading, by education system: 2016

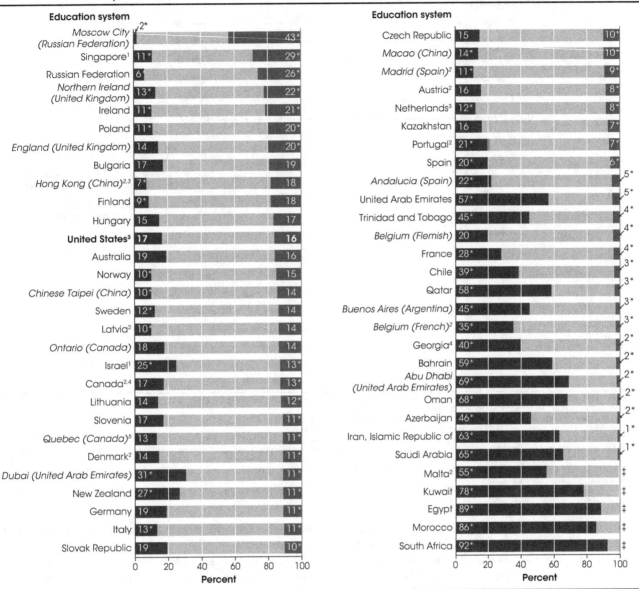

■ Low or below
■ Advanced
* *p* < .05. Significantly different from the U.S. percentage.
‡ Reporting standards not met (too few cases for a reliable estimate).
[1] National Defined Population covers less than 90 percent of the National Target Population (but at least 77 percent).
[2] National Defined Population covers 90 to 95 percent of the National Target Population.
[3] Met guidelines for sample participation rates only after replacement schools were included.
[4] National Target Population does not include all of the International Target Population.
[5] Did not satisfy guidelines for sample participation rates.
NOTE: Education systems are ordered by the percentage of students reaching the *Advanced* international benchmark. Although rounded numbers are displayed, the figures are based on unrounded data. The PIRLS scores are reported on a scale from 0 to 1,000. PIRLS describes achievement at four international benchmarks along the reading achievement scale: *Low* (400), *Intermediate* (475), *High* (550), and *Advanced* (625). The score cut-points were selected to be as close as possible to the 25th, 50th, 75th, and 90th percentiles. Each successive point, or benchmark, is associated with the knowledge and skills that students successfully demonstrate at each level. Italics indicate participants identified as a non-national entity that represents a portion of a country. Education systems that did not administer PIRLS at the target grade are not shown. For more information about individual countries and assessment methodology, please see *Methods and Procedures in PIRLS 2016* (https://timssandpirls.bc.edu/publications/pirls/2016-methods.html).
SOURCE: International Association for the Evaluation of Educational Achievement (IEA), Progress in International Reading Literacy Study (PIRLS), 2016. See *Digest of Education Statistics 2017*, table 602.10.

PIRLS describes achievement at four international benchmarks along the reading achievement scale: *Low* (400), *Intermediate* (475), *High* (550), and *Advanced* (625). In 2016, about 16 percent of U.S. fourth-graders reached the *Advanced* benchmark. The percentages of students reaching this benchmark ranged from 1 percent in Saudi Arabia and in the Islamic Republic of Iran to 43 percent in Moscow City (Russian Federation). Seven education systems (Moscow City [Russian Federation], Singapore, the Russian Federation, Northern Ireland [United Kingdom], Ireland, Poland, and England [United Kingdom]) had a higher percentage of fourth-graders who reached the *Advanced* benchmark than the United States did.

Figure 3. Average online informational reading scale scores of fourth-grade students on ePIRLS, by education system: 2016

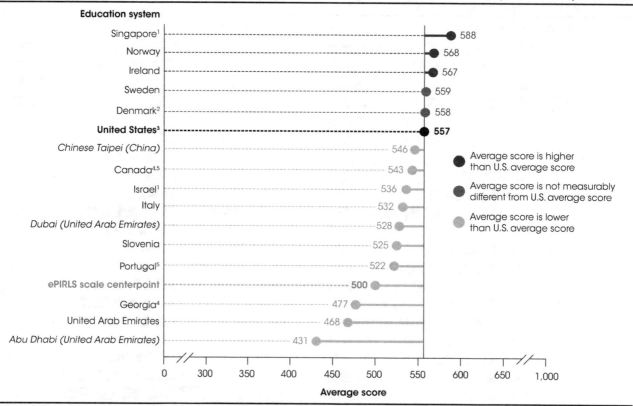

[1] National Defined Population covers less than 90 percent of the National Target Population (but at least 77 percent).
[2] Did not satisfy guidelines for sample participation rates.
[3] Met guidelines for sample participation rates only after replacement schools were included.
[4] National Target Population does not include all of the International Target Population.
[5] National Defined Population covers 90 to 95 percent of the National Target Population.
NOTE: Education systems are ordered by ePIRLS average scale score. Italics indicate participants identified as a non-national entity that represents a portion of a country. The ePIRLS scores are reported on a scale from 0 to 1,000, with the scale centerpoint set at 500 and the standard deviation set at 100. For more information about individual countries and assessment methodology, please see *Methods and Procedures in PIRLS 2016* (https://timssandpirls.bc.edu/publications/pirls/2016-methods.html).
SOURCE: International Association for the Evaluation of Educational Achievement (IEA), Progress in International Reading Literacy Study (PIRLS), 2016. See *Digest of Education Statistics 2017*, table 602.15.

In 2016, the United States, along with 15 other education systems, participated in the new ePIRLS assessment of students' comprehension of online information. The average online informational reading score for fourth-grade students in the United States (557) was higher than the ePIRLS scale centerpoint (500). The U.S. average score was higher than the average scores of 10 education systems and not measurably different from the average scores of 2 education systems. Only three education systems (Singapore, Norway, and Ireland) scored higher than the United States.

Figure 4. Percentage of fourth-grade students performing at selected ePIRLS international benchmarks in online informational reading, by education system: 2016

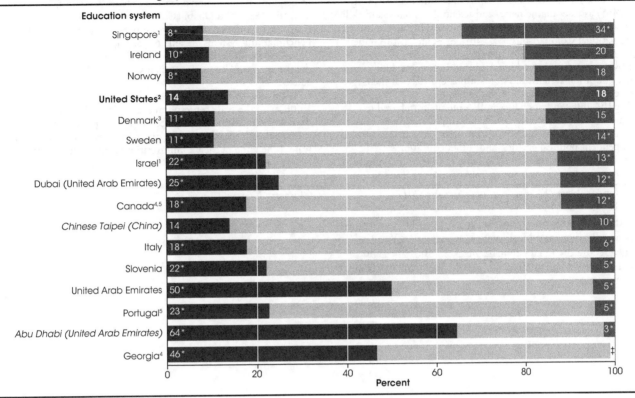

■ Low or below
■ Advanced

* *p* < .05. Significantly different from the U.S. percentage.
‡ Reporting standards not met (too few cases for a reliable estimate).
[1] National Defined Population covers less than 90 percent of the National Target Population (but at least 77 percent).
[2] Met guidelines for sample participation rates only after replacement schools were included.
[3] Did not satisfy guidelines for sample participation rates.
[4] National Target Population does not include all of the International Target Population.
[5] National Defined Population covers 90 to 95 percent of the National Target Population.
NOTE: Education systems are ordered by the percentage of students reaching the *Advanced* international benchmark. Although rounded numbers are displayed, the figures are based on unrounded data. The ePIRLS scores are reported on a scale from 0 to 1,000. ePIRLS describes achievement at four international benchmarks along the reading achievement scale: *Low* (400), *Intermediate* (475), *High* (550), and *Advanced* (625). The score cut-points were selected to be as close as possible to the 25th, 50th, 75th, and 90th percentiles. Each successive point, or benchmark, is associated with the knowledge and skills that students successfully demonstrate at each level. Italics indicate participants identified as a non-national entity that represents a portion of a country. For more information about individual countries and assessment methodology, please see *Methods and Procedures in PIRLS 2016* (https://timssandpirls.bc.edu/publications/pirls/2016-methods.html).
SOURCE: International Association for the Evaluation of Educational Achievement (IEA), Progress in International Reading Literacy Study (PIRLS), 2016. See *Digest of Education Statistics 2017*, table 602.15.

Similar to PIRLS, ePIRLS also describes achievement at four international benchmarks along the reading achievement scale: *Low* (400), *Intermediate* (475), *High* (550), and *Advanced* (625). In 2016, about 18 percent of U.S. fourth-graders reached the *Advanced* benchmark. The percentages of students reaching this benchmark ranged from 3 percent in Abu Dhabi (United Arab Emirates) to 34 percent in Singapore. Singapore was the only education system with a higher percentage of fourth-graders who reached the *Advanced* benchmark than in the United States. Ireland, Norway, and Denmark had percentages of fourth-graders who reached the *Advanced* benchmark that were not measurably different from the percentage in the United States.

Endnotes:

[1] The Trends in International Mathematics and Science Study (TIMSS) assesses mathematics and science knowledge and skills at grades 4 and 8. For more information on TIMSS, see indicator International Comparisons: U.S. 4th-, 8th-, and 12th-Graders' Mathematics and Science Achievement.

[2] PIRLS was administered in 61 education systems. However, three education systems did not administer PIRLS at the target grade and are not included in this indicator.

[3] The IEA differentiates between IEA members, referred to always as "countries," and "benchmarking participants." IEA member countries include both "countries," which are complete, independent political entities, and "other education systems," or non-national entities (e.g., England, the Flemish community of Belgium). Non-national entities that are not IEA member countries (e.g., Abu Dhabi [United Arab Emirates], Ontario [Canada]) are designated as "benchmarking participants." These benchmarking systems are able to participate in PIRLS even though they may not be members of the IEA. For convenience, the generic term "education systems" is used when summarizing across results.

[4] PIRLS and ePIRLS scores are reported on a scale from 0 to 1,000, with the scale centerpoint set at 500 and the standard deviation set at 100. The scale centerpoint represents the mean of the overall PIRLS achievement distribution in 2001. The PIRLS scale is the same in each administration; thus a value of 500 in 2016 equals 500 in 2001.

Reference tables: *Digest of Education Statistics 2017*, tables 602.10 and 602.15

Related indicators and resources: International Comparisons: Science, Reading, and Mathematics Literacy of 15-Year-Old Students; International Comparisons: U.S. 4th-, 8th-, and 12th-Graders' Mathematics and Science Achievement; Reading Performance

Glossary: N/A

International Comparisons: U.S. 4th-, 8th-, and 12th-Graders' Mathematics and Science Achievement

According to the 2015 Trends in International Mathematics and Science Study (TIMSS), the United States was among the top 15 education systems in science (out of 54) at grade 4 and among the top 17 education systems in science (out of 43) at grade 8. In mathematics, the United States was among the top 20 education systems at grade 4 and top 19 education systems at grade 8.

The Trends in International Mathematics and Science Study (TIMSS) is an international comparative assessment that evaluates mathematics and science knowledge and skills at grades 4 and 8. The TIMSS program also includes TIMSS Advanced, an international comparative study that measures the advanced mathematics and physics achievement of students in their final year of secondary school who are taking or have taken advanced courses. These assessments are coordinated by the TIMSS & PIRLS[1] International Study Center at Boston College, under the auspices of the International Association for the Evaluation of Educational Achievement (IEA), an international organization of national research institutions and government agencies.

In 2015, TIMSS mathematics and science data were collected by 54 education systems at 4th grade and 43 education systems at 8th grade.[2] TIMSS Advanced data were also collected by nine education systems from students in the final year of their secondary schools (in the United States, 12th-graders). Education systems include countries (complete, independent, and political entities) and other benchmarking education systems (portions of a country, nation, kingdom, or emirate, and other non-national entities).[3] In addition to participating in the U.S. national sample, Florida participated individually as a state at the 4th and 8th grades.

Figure 1.   Average TIMSS mathematics assessment scale scores of 4th-grade students, by education system: 2015

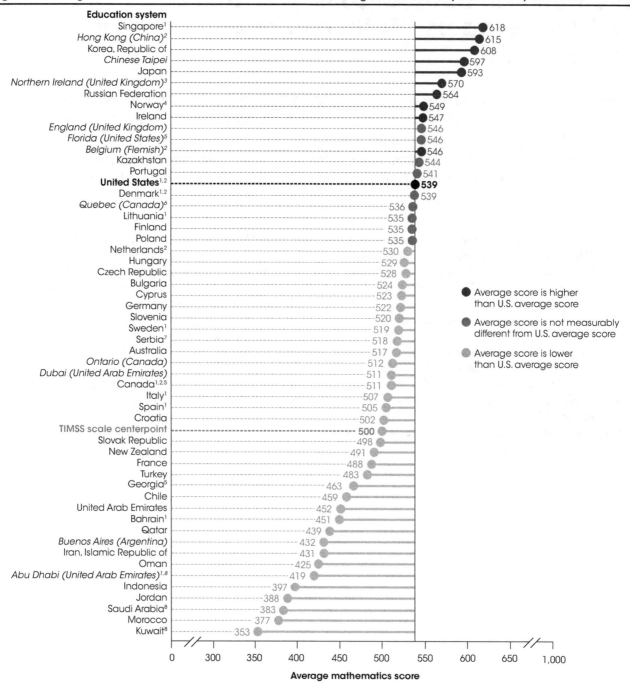

[1] National Defined Population covers 90 to 95 percent of the National Target Population, as defined by TIMSS.
[2] Met guidelines for sample participation rates only after replacement schools were included.
[3] Nearly satisfied guidelines for sample participation rates after replacement schools were included.
[4] Norway collected data from students in their fifth year of schooling rather than in grade 4 because year 1 in Norway is considered the equivalent of kindergarten rather than the first year of primary school.
[5] National Target Population does not include all of the International Target Population, as defined by TIMSS.
[6] Did not satisfy guidelines for sample participation rates.
[7] National Defined Population covers less than 90 percent of the National Target Population (but at least 77 percent), as defined by TIMSS.
[8] Reservations about reliability because the percentage of students with achievement too low for estimation exceeds 15 percent but does not exceed 25 percent.
NOTE: Education systems are ordered by average score. Education systems that are not countries are shown in italics. Participants that did not administer TIMSS at the target grade are not shown; see the international report for their results (http://timssandpirls.bc.edu/timss2015/international-results/). U.S. state data are based on public school students only. The TIMSS scale centerpoint is set at 500 points and represents the mean of the overall achievement distribution in 1995. The TIMSS scale is the same in each administration; thus, a value of 500 in 2015 equals 500 in 1995. For more information on the International and National Target Populations, see https://nces.ed.gov/timss/timss15technotes_intlreqs.asp.
SOURCE: International Association for the Evaluation of Educational Achievement (IEA), Trends in International Mathematics and Science Study (TIMSS), 2015. See *Digest of Education Statistics 2016*, table 602.20.

At grade 4, the U.S. average mathematics score (539) in 2015 was higher than the TIMSS scale centerpoint (500).[4] Ten education systems[5] had higher average mathematics scores than the United States, 9 had scores that were not measurably different, and 34 education systems had lower average scores. The 10 education systems with average mathematics scores above the U.S. score were Belgium (Flemish), Chinese Taipei, Hong Kong (China), Ireland, Japan, Northern Ireland (Great Britain), Norway, the Republic of Korea, the Russian Federation, and Singapore. Florida's average mathematics score was not measurably different from the U.S. national average.

At grade 4, the U.S. average science score (546) in 2015 was also higher than the TIMSS scale centerpoint of 500. Seven education systems had higher average science scores than the United States, 7 had scores that were not measurably different, and 38 education systems had lower average scores. The 7 education systems with average science scores above the U.S. score were Chinese Taipei, Finland, Japan, Hong Kong (China), the Republic of Korea, the Russian Federation, and Singapore. Florida's average science score was not measurably different from the U.S. national average.

Figure 2.   Average TIMSS science assessment scale scores of 4th-grade students, by education system: 2015

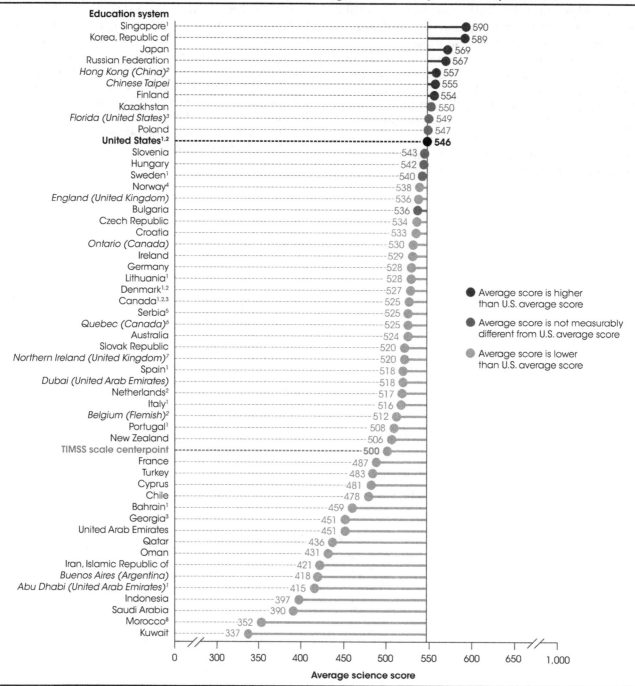

¹ National Defined Population covers 90 to 95 percent of the National Target Population, as defined by TIMSS.
² Met guidelines for sample participation rates only after replacement schools were included.
³ National Target Population does not include all of the International Target Population, as defined by TIMSS.
⁴ Norway collected data from students in their fifth year of schooling rather than in grade 4 because year 1 in Norway is considered the equivalent of kindergarten rather than the first year of primary school.
⁵ National Defined Population covers less than 90 percent of the National Target Population (but at least 77 percent), as defined by TIMSS.
⁶ Did not satisfy guidelines for sample participation rates.
⁷ Nearly satisfied guidelines for sample participation rates after replacement schools were included.
⁸ Reservations about reliability because the percentage of students with achievement too low for estimation exceeds 15 percent but does not exceed 25 percent.
NOTE: Education systems are ordered by average score. Education systems that are not countries are shown in italics. Participants that did not administer TIMSS at the target grade are not shown; see the international report for their results (http://timssandpirls.bc.edu/timss2015/international-results/). U.S. state data are based on public school students only. The TIMSS scale centerpoint is set at 500 points and represents the mean of the overall achievement distribution in 1995. The TIMSS scale is the same in each administration; thus, a value of 500 in 2015 equals 500 in 1995. For more information on the International and National Target Populations, see https://nces.ed.gov/timss/timss15technotes_intlreqs.asp.
SOURCE: International Association for the Evaluation of Educational Achievement (IEA), Trends in International Mathematics and Science Study (TIMSS), 2015.
See *Digest of Education Statistics 2016*, table 602.20.

Figure 3. Average TIMSS mathematics assessment scale scores of 8th-grade students, by education system: 2015

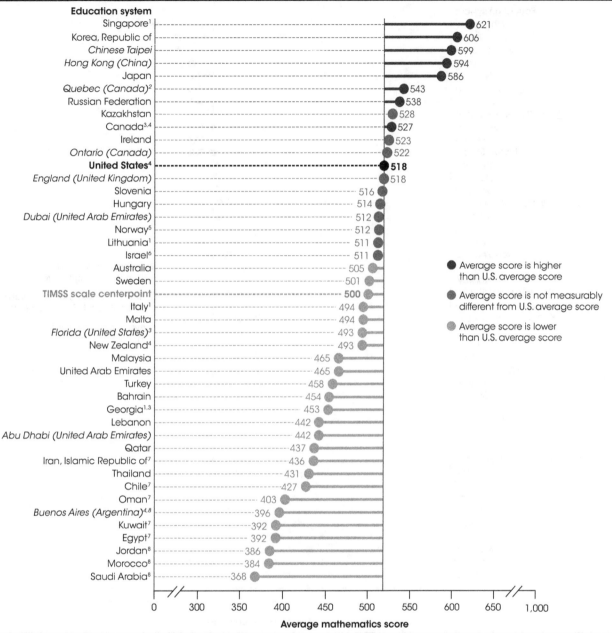

[1] National Defined Population covers 90 to 95 percent of the National Target Population, as defined by TIMSS.
[2] Did not satisfy guidelines for sample participation rates.
[3] National Target Population does not include all of the International Target Population, as defined by TIMSS.
[4] Met guidelines for sample participation rates only after replacement schools were included.
[5] Norway collected data from students in their fifth year of schooling rather than in grade 4 because year 1 in Norway is considered the equivalent of kindergarten rather than the first year of primary school.
[6] National Defined Population covers less than 90 percent of the National Target Population (but at least 77 percent), as defined by TIMSS.
[7] Reservations about reliability because the percentage of students with achievement too low for estimation exceeds 15 percent but does not exceed 25 percent.
[8] Reservations about reliability because the percentage of students with achievement too low for estimation exceeds 25 percent.
NOTE: Education systems are ordered by average score. Education systems that are not countries are shown in italics. Participants that did not administer TIMSS at the target grade are not shown; see the international report for their results (http://timssandpirls.bc.edu/timss2015/international-results/). U.S. state data are based on public school students only. The TIMSS scale centerpoint is set at 500 points and represents the mean of the overall achievement distribution in 1995. The TIMSS scale is the same in each administration; thus, a value of 500 in 2015 equals 500 in 1995. For more information on the International and National Target Populations, see https://nces.ed.gov/timss/timss15technotes_intlreqs.asp.
SOURCE: International Association for the Evaluation of Educational Achievement (IEA), Trends in International Mathematics and Science Study (TIMSS), 2015. See *Digest of Education Statistics 2016*, table 602.30.

At grade 8, the U.S. average mathematics score (518) in 2015 was higher than the TIMSS scale centerpoint of 500. Eight education systems had higher average mathematics scores than the United States, 10 had scores that were not measurably different, and 24 education systems had lower average scores. The 8 education systems with average mathematics scores above the U.S. score were Canada, Chinese Taipei, Hong Kong (China), Japan, Quebec (Canada), the Republic of Korea, the Russian Federation, and Singapore. Florida's average mathematics score was below the U.S. national average.

Figure 4. Average TIMSS science assessment scale scores of 8th-grade students, by education system: 2015

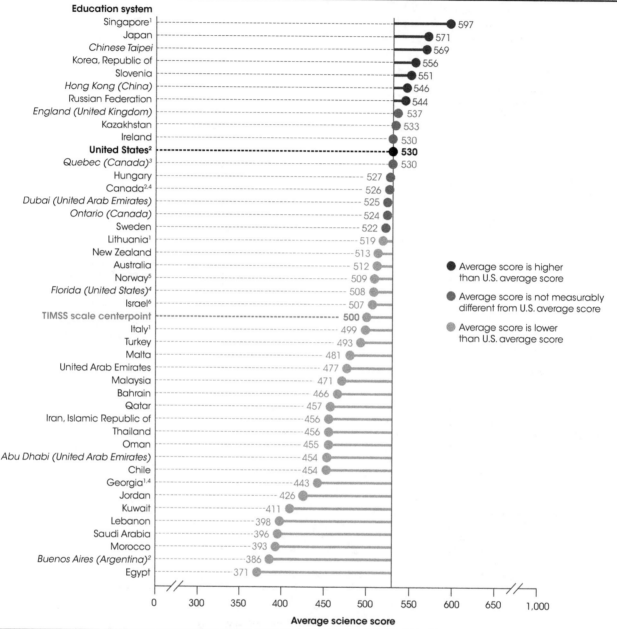

[1] National Defined Population covers 90 to 95 percent of the National Target Population, as defined by TIMSS.
[2] Met guidelines for sample participation rates only after replacement schools were included.
[3] Did not satisfy guidelines for sample participation rates.
[4] National Target Population does not include all of the International Target Population, as defined by TIMSS.
[5] Norway collected data from students in their fifth year of schooling rather than in grade 4 because year 1 in Norway is considered the equivalent of kindergarten rather than the first year of primary school.
[6] National Defined Population covers less than 90 percent of the National Target Population (but at least 77 percent), as defined by TIMSS.
NOTE: Education systems are ordered by average score. Education systems that are not countries are shown in italics. Participants that did not administer TIMSS at the target grade are not shown; see the international report for their results (http://timssandpirls.bc.edu/timss2015/international-results/). U.S. state data are based on public school students only. The TIMSS scale centerpoint is set at 500 points and represents the mean of the overall achievement distribution in 1995. The TIMSS scale is the same in each administration; thus, a value of 500 in 2015 equals 500 in 1995. For more information on the International and National Target Populations, see https://nces.ed.gov/timss/timss15technotes_intlreqs.asp.
SOURCE: International Association for the Evaluation of Educational Achievement (IEA), Trends in International Mathematics and Science Study (TIMSS), 2015. See *Digest of Education Statistics 2016*, table 602.30.

At grade 8, the U.S. average science score (530) in 2015 was higher than the TIMSS scale centerpoint of 500. Seven education systems had higher average science scores than the United States, 9 had scores that were not measurably different, and 26 education systems had lower average scores. The seven education systems with average science scores above the U.S. score were Chinese Taipei, Hong Kong (China), Japan, the Republic of Korea, the Russian Federation, Singapore, and Slovenia. Florida's average science score was below the U.S. national average.

Figure 5. Average advanced mathematics scores and coverage index of TIMSS Advanced students, by education system: 2015

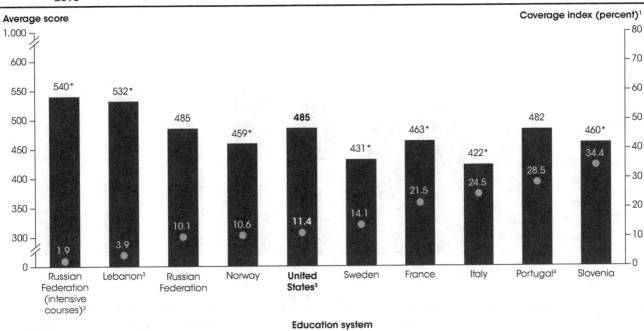

* *p* < .05. Significantly different from the U.S. percentage.
[1] The advanced mathematics coverage index is the percentage of the corresponding age cohort covered by students in their final year of secondary school who have taken or are taking advanced mathematics courses. The corresponding age cohort is determined for education systems individually. In the United States, the corresponding age cohort is considered 18-year-olds. For additional details, see the Technical Notes available at http://nces.ed.gov/timss/timss15technotes.asp.
[2] Intensive courses are advanced mathematics courses that involve 6 or more hours per week. Results for students in these courses are reported separately from the results for other students from the Russian Federation taking courses that involve 4.5 hours per week.
[3] Did not satisfy guidelines for sample participation rates.
[4] Met guidelines for sample participation rates only after replacement schools were included.
NOTE: Education systems are ordered by the advanced mathematics coverage index. The TIMSS Advanced scale centerpoint is set at 500 points and represents the mean of the overall achievement distribution in 1995. The TIMSS Advanced scale is the same in each administration; thus, a value of 500 in 2015 equals 500 in 1995.
SOURCE: International Association for the Evaluation of Educational Achievement (IEA), Trends in International Mathematics and Science Study (TIMSS) Advanced, 2015. See *Digest of Education Statistics 2016*, table 602.35.

The TIMSS Advanced assessment measures the advanced mathematics and physics achievement of students in their final year of secondary school who are taking or have taken advanced courses. In TIMSS Advanced, the U.S. average advanced mathematics score (485) in 2015 was lower than the TIMSS Advanced scale centerpoint (500). Two education systems had higher average advanced mathematics scores than the United States, two (Portugal and the Russian Federation) had scores that were not measurably different, and five education systems had lower average scores. The education systems with higher average advanced mathematics scores than the United States were Lebanon and the Russian Federation's intensive track (i.e., advanced students taking 6 or more hours of advanced mathematics per week).[6] Such comparisons, however, should take into account the "coverage index," which represents the percentage of students eligible to take the advanced mathematics assessment. The advanced mathematics coverage index ranged from 1.9 percent for the Russian Federation's intensive track to 34.4 percent in Slovenia.

Figure 6. Average physics scores and coverage index of TIMSS Advanced students, by education system: 2015

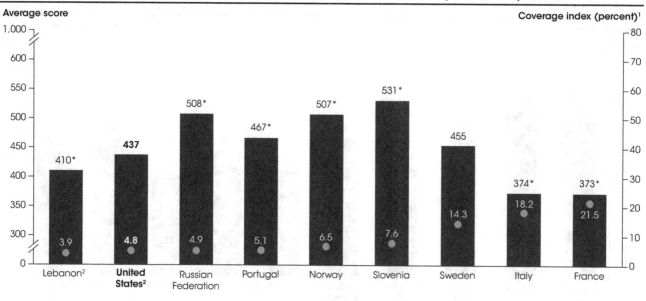

* *p* < .05. Significantly different from the U.S. percentage.
[1] The physics coverage index is the percentage of the corresponding age cohort covered by students in their final year of secondary school who have taken or are taking physics courses. The corresponding age cohort is determined for education systems individually. In the United States, the corresponding age cohort is considered 18-year-olds. For additional details, see the Technical Notes available at http://nces.ed.gov/timss/timss15technotes.asp.
[2] Did not satisfy guidelines for sample participation rates.
NOTE: Education systems are ordered by the advanced physics coverage index. The TIMSS Advanced scale centerpoint is set at 500 points and represents the mean of the overall achievement distribution in 1995. The TIMSS Advanced scale is the same in each administration; thus, a value of 500 in 2015 equals 500 in 1995.
SOURCE: International Association for the Evaluation of Educational Achievement (IEA), Trends in International Mathematics and Science Study (TIMSS) Advanced, 2015. See *Digest of Education Statistics 2016*, table 602.35.

In TIMSS Advanced, the U.S. average physics score (437) in 2015 was lower than the TIMSS Advanced scale centerpoint (500). Four education systems had higher average physics scores than the United States, one (Sweden) had a score that was not measurably different, and three education systems had lower average scores. The education systems with higher average advanced science scores than the United States were Norway, Portugal, the Russian Federation, and Slovenia. The physics coverage index ranged from 3.9 percent in Lebanon to 21.5 percent in France.

Endnotes:

[1] The Progress in International Reading Literacy Study (PIRLS) evaluates reading literacy at grade 4. For more information on PIRLS, see indicator International Comparisons: Reading Literacy at Grade 4.

[2] Armenia, which participated at both grades, is not included in these counts or the results reported in this indicator because their data are not comparable for trend analyses.

[3] Benchmarking systems are able to participate in TIMSS even though they may not be members of the IEA. Participating allows them the opportunity to assess their students' achievement and to evaluate their curricula in an international context.

[4] TIMSS and TIMSS Advanced scores are reported on a scale from 0 to 1,000, with a scale centerpoint set at 500 and the standard deviation set at 100. The TIMSS scale centerpoint represents the mean of the overall achievement distribution in 1995. The TIMSS scale is the same in each administration; thus, a value of 500 in 2015 equals 500 in 1995 when that was the international average.

[5] The IEA differentiates between IEA members, referred to always as "countries" and "benchmarking participants." IEA member countries include both "countries," which are complete, independent political entities and "other education systems," or non-national entities (e.g., England, the Flemish community of Belgium). Non-national entities that are not IEA member countries (i.e., Florida, Abu Dhabi) are designated as "benchmarking participants." For convenience, the generic term "education systems" is used when summarizing across results.

[6] The Russian Federation tested two samples in advanced mathematics in 2015. Results for students in the intensive mathematics courses of 6 or more hours per week are reported separately from the results for the Russian Federation's advanced students taking courses of only 4.5 hours per week.

Reference tables: *Digest of Education Statistics 2016*, tables 602.20, 602.30, and 602.35

Related indicators and resources: International Comparisons: Reading Literacy at Grade 4; International Comparisons: Science, Reading, and Mathematics Literacy of 15-Year-Old Students; Mathematics Performance; Science Performance

Glossary: N/A

Indicator 4.3

International Comparisons: Reading, Mathematics, and Science Literacy of 15-Year-Old Students

In 2018, there were 8 education systems with higher average reading literacy scores for 15-year-olds than the United States, 30 with higher mathematics literacy scores, and 11 with higher science literacy scores.

The Program for International Student Assessment (PISA), coordinated by the Organization for Economic Cooperation and Development (OECD), has measured the performance of 15-year-old students in reading, mathematics, and science literacy every 3 years since 2000. In 2018, PISA was administered in 79[1] countries and education systems,[2] including all 37 member countries of the OECD.

PISA 2018 results are reported by average scale score (from 0 to 1,000) as well as by the percentage of students reaching particular proficiency levels. Proficiency results are presented in terms of the percentages of students reaching proficiency level 5 and above (i.e., top performers) and the percentages of students performing below proficiency level 2 (i.e., low performers). Proficiency level 2 is considered a baseline of proficiency by the OECD.

Table 1. Average scores of 15-year-old students on the Program for International Student Assessment (PISA) reading literacy scale, by education system: 2018

Education system	Average score		Education system	Average score	
OECD average	**487**	▼	*Ukraine*	466	▼
B-S-J-Z (China)[1]	555	⏶	Turkey[2]	466	▼
Singapore	549	⏶	Slovak Republic	458	▼
Macau (China)	525	⏶	Greece	457	▼
Hong Kong (China)	524	⏶	Chile	452	▼
Estonia	523	⏶	*Malta*	448	▼
Canada	520	⏶	*Serbia*	439	▼
Finland	520	⏶	*United Arab Emirates*	432	▼
Ireland	518	⏶	*Romania*[2]	428	▼
Korea, Republic of	514		*Uruguay*	427	▼
Poland	512		*Costa Rica*[2]	426	▼
Sweden	506		*Cyprus*	424	▼
New Zealand	506		*Moldova, Republic of*	424	▼
United States	**505**		*Montenegro, Republic of*	421	▼
United Kingdom	504		*Mexico*[2]	420	▼
Japan	504		*Bulgaria*[2]	420	▼
Australia	503		*Jordan*[2]	419	▼
Chinese Taipei	503		*Malaysia*[2]	415	▼
Denmark	501		*Brazil*[2]	413	▼
Norway	499		*Colombia*[2]	412	▼
Germany	498		*Brunei Darussalam*	408	▼
Slovenia	495	▼	*Qatar*	407	▼
Belgium	493	▼	*Albania*	405	▼
France	493	▼	*Bosnia and Herzegovina*	403	▼
Portugal	492	▼	*Argentina*	402	▼
Czech Republic	490	▼	*Peru*[2]	401	▼
Netherlands	485	▼	*Saudi Arabia*	399	▼
Austria	484	▼	*Thailand*[2]	393	▼
Switzerland	484	▼	*North Macedonia*	393	▼
Croatia	479	▼	*Baku (Azerbaijan)*[3]	389	▼
Latvia	479	▼	*Kazakhstan*	387	▼
Russian Federation	479	▼	*Georgia*	380	▼
Italy	476	▼	*Panama*[2]	377	▼
Hungary	476	▼	*Indonesia*	371	▼
Lithuania	476	▼	*Morocco*[2]	359	▼
Iceland	474	▼	*Lebanon*	353	▼
Belarus	474	▼	*Kosovo*	353	▼
Israel	470	▼	*Dominican Republic*[2]	342	▼
Luxembourg	470	▼	*Philippines*[2]	340	▼

⏶ Average score is higher than U.S. average score at the .05 level of statistical significance.
▼ Average score is lower than U.S. average score at the .05 level of statistical significance.
[1] *B-S-J-Z (China)* refers to the four PISA participating China provinces: Beijing, Shanghai, Jiangsu, and Zhejiang.
[2] At least 50 percent but less than 75 percent of the 15-year-old population is covered by the PISA sample.
[3] Less than 50 percent of the 15-year-old population is covered by the PISA sample.
NOTE: Education systems are ordered by 2018 average score. Scores are reported on a scale from 0 to 1,000. Italics indicate non-OECD countries and education systems. Education systems are marked as OECD countries if they were OECD members in 2018. The OECD average is the average of the national averages of the OECD member countries, with each country weighted equally. In the case of reading literacy, the 2018 OECD average does not include Spain due to issues with its PISA 2018 reading literacy data. Although Spain's PISA 2018 data meet international technical standards, its reading literacy data show unusual student response behavior that prevent them from being reported at this time. Although Vietnam participated in PISA 2018, technical problems with its data prevent results from being discussed in this indicator.
SOURCE: Organization for Economic Cooperation and Development (OECD), Program for International Student Assessment (PISA), 2018. See *Digest of Education Statistics 2019*, table 602.50.

In 2018, average reading literacy scores ranged from 340 in the Philippines to 555 in Beijing, Shanghai, Jiangsu, and Zhejiang (B-S-J-Z) (China). The U.S. average reading score (505) was higher than the OECD average score (487).

Eight education systems had higher average reading scores than did the United States, and 11 education systems had scores that were not measurably different from the U.S. score.

Figure 1. Percentage of 15-year-old students performing on the Program for International Student Assessment (PISA) reading literacy scale, by selected proficiency levels and education system: 2018

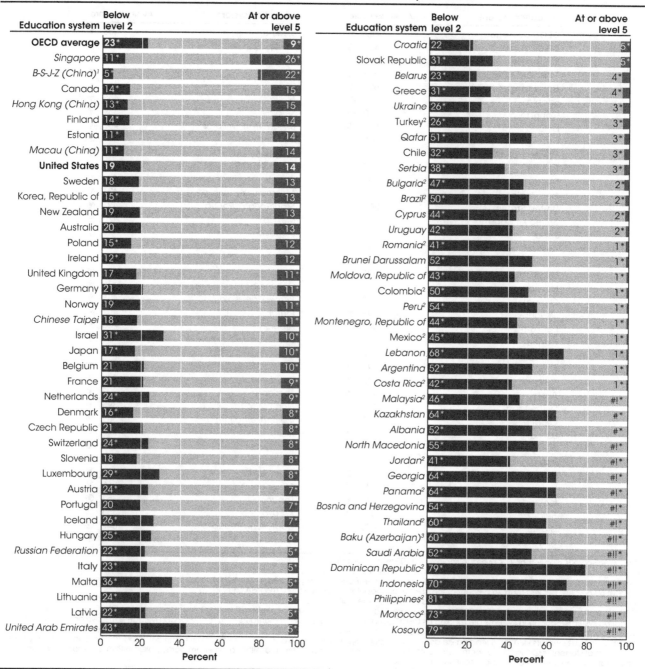

■ Below level 2
■ At or above level 5
\# Rounds to zero.
! Interpret data with caution. Estimate is unstable due to high coefficient of variation (> 30 percent and ≤ 50 percent).
!! Interpret data with caution. Estimate is unstable because the standard error represents more than 50 percent of the estimate.
* $p < .05$. Significantly different from the U.S. percentage.
[1] B-S-J-Z (China) refers to the four PISA participating China provinces: Beijing, Shanghai, Jiangsu, and Zhejiang.
[2] At least 50 percent but less than 75 percent of the 15-year-old population is covered by the PISA sample.
[3] Less than 50 percent of the 15-year-old population is covered by the PISA sample.
NOTE: Education systems are ordered by 2018 percentages of 15-year-olds in levels 5 and above. Descriptions of the skills and knowledge of students at each reading proficiency level are available at https://nces.ed.gov/surveys/pisa/pisa2018/pdf/ReadingProfLevelDescriptionV2.pdf. To reach a particular proficiency level, a student must correctly answer a majority of items at that level. Students were classified into reading proficiency levels according to their scores. Exact cut scores are as follows: below level 2 is a score less than or equal to 407.47; at or above level 5 is a score equal to or greater than 625.61. Scores are reported on a scale from 0 to 1,000. Italics indicate non-OECD countries and education systems. Education systems are marked as OECD countries if they were OECD members in 2018. The OECD average is the average of the national percentages of the OECD member countries, with each country weighted equally. In the case of reading literacy, the 2018 OECD average does not include Spain due to issues with its PISA 2018 reading literacy data. Although Spain's PISA 2018 data meet international technical standards, its reading literacy data show unusual student response behavior that prevent them from being reported at this time. Although Vietnam participated in PISA 2018, technical problems with its data prevent results from being discussed in this indicator.
SOURCE: Organization for Economic Cooperation and Development (OECD), Program for International Student Assessment (PISA), 2018. See *Digest of Education Statistics 2019*, table 602.50.

PISA reports reading literacy in terms of eight proficiency levels, with level 1c being the lowest and level 6 being the highest. Descriptions of the skills and knowledge of students at each reading proficiency level can be found here. Students performing at levels 5 and 6 have mastered the sophisticated reading skills required to interpret and evaluate deeply embedded or abstract text and are considered top performers. The percentage of U.S. students who were top performers in reading literacy (14 percent) was larger than the OECD average percentage (9 percent). Percentages of top performers ranged from nearly 0 percent in 16 education systems to 26 percent in Singapore. Two education systems, Singapore and B-S-J-Z (China), had larger percentages of top performers in reading literacy than did the United States.

The percentage of U.S. students who were low performers in reading literacy (19 percent) was smaller than the OECD average percentage (23 percent). Percentages of low performers ranged from 5 percent in B-S-J-Z (China) to 81 percent in the Philippines. Twelve education systems had smaller percentages of low performers in reading literacy than did the United States.

Table 2. Average scores of 15-year-old students on the Program for International Student Assessment (PISA) mathematics literacy scale, by education system: 2018

Education system	Average score		Education system	Average score	
OECD average	**489**	⬆	Croatia	464	⬇
B-S-J-Z (China)[1]	591	⬆	Israel	463	⬇
Singapore	569	⬆	Turkey[2]	454	⬇
Macau (China)	558	⬆	Ukraine	453	⬇
Hong Kong (China)	551	⬆	Greece	451	⬇
Chinese Taipei	531	⬆	Cyprus	451	⬇
Japan	527	⬆	Serbia	448	⬇
Korea, Republic of	526	⬆	Malaysia[2]	440	⬇
Estonia	523	⬆	Albania	437	⬇
Netherlands	519	⬆	Bulgaria[2]	436	⬇
Poland	516	⬆	United Arab Emirates	435	⬇
Switzerland	515	⬆	Brunei Darussalam	430	⬇
Canada	512	⬆	Romania[2]	430	⬇
Denmark	509	⬆	Montenegro, Republic of	430	⬇
Slovenia	509	⬆	Kazakhstan	423	⬇
Belgium	508	⬆	Moldova, Republic of	421	⬇
Finland	507	⬆	Baku (Azerbaijan)[3]	420	⬇
Sweden	502	⬆	Thailand[2]	419	⬇
United Kingdom	502	⬆	Uruguay	418	⬇
Norway	501	⬆	Chile	417	⬇
Germany	500	⬆	Qatar	414	⬇
Ireland	500	⬆	Mexico[2]	409	⬇
Czech Republic	499	⬆	Bosnia and Herzegovina	406	⬇
Austria	499	⬆	Costa Rica[2]	402	⬇
Latvia	496	⬆	Peru[2]	400	⬇
France	495	⬆	Jordan[2]	400	⬇
Iceland	495	⬆	Georgia	398	⬇
New Zealand	494	⬆	North Macedonia	394	⬇
Portugal	492	⬆	Lebanon	393	⬇
Australia	491	⬆	Colombia[2]	391	⬇
Russian Federation	488	⬆	Brazil[2]	384	⬇
Italy	487		Argentina	379	⬇
Slovak Republic	486		Indonesia	379	⬇
Luxembourg	483		Saudi Arabia	373	⬇
Spain	481		Morocco[2]	368	⬇
Lithuania	481		Kosovo	366	⬇
Hungary	481		Panama[2]	353	⬇
United States	**478**		Philippines[2]	353	⬇
Belarus	472		Dominican Republic[2]	325	⬇
Malta	472				

⬆ Average score is higher than U.S. average score at the .05 level of statistical significance.
⬇ Average score is lower than U.S. average score at the .05 level of statistical significance.
[1] B-S-J-Z (China) refers to the four PISA participating China provinces: Beijing, Shanghai, Jiangsu, and Zhejiang.
[2] At least 50 percent but less than 75 percent of the 15-year-old population is covered by the PISA sample.
[3] Less than 50 percent of the 15-year-old population is covered by the PISA sample.
NOTE: Education systems are ordered by 2018 average score. Scores are reported on a scale from 0 to 1,000. Italics indicate non-OECD countries and education systems. Education systems are marked as OECD countries if they were OECD members in 2018. The OECD average is the average of the national averages of the OECD member countries, with each country weighted equally. Although Vietnam participated in PISA 2018, technical problems with its data prevent results from being discussed in this indicator.
SOURCE: Organization for Economic Cooperation and Development (OECD), Program for International Student Assessment (PISA), 2018. See *Digest of Education Statistics 2019*, table 602.60.

In mathematics literacy, average scores in 2018 ranged from 325 in the Dominican Republic to 591 in B-S-J-Z (China). The U.S. average mathematics score (478) was lower than the OECD average score (489). Thirty education systems had higher average mathematics scores than did the United States, and 8 education systems had scores that were not measurably different from the U.S. score.

Figure 2. Percentage of 15-year-old students performing on the Program for International Student Assessment (PISA) mathematics literacy scale, by selected proficiency levels and education system: 2018

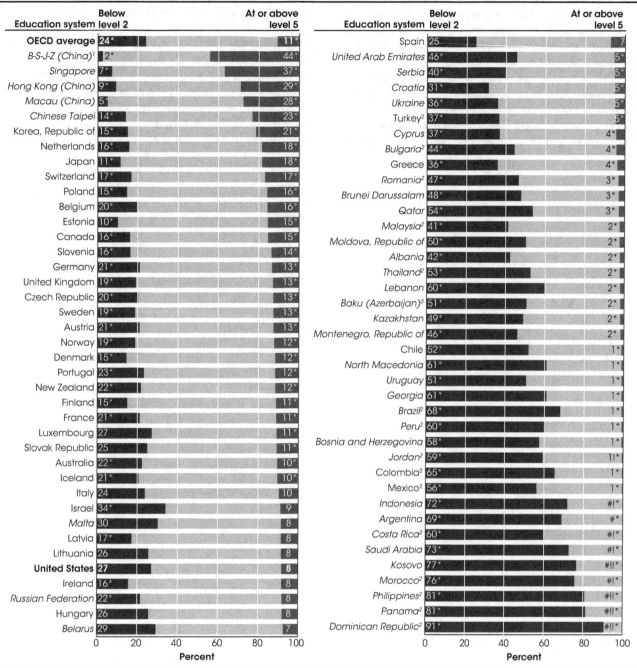

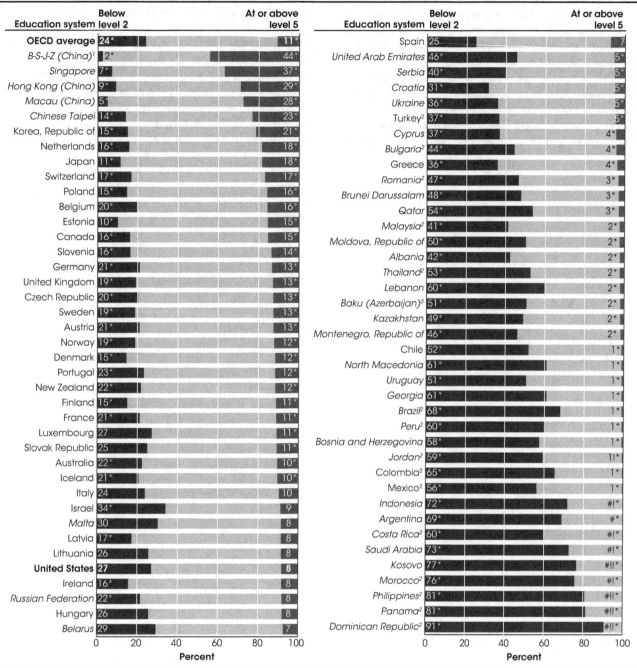
■ Below level 2
■ At or above level 5
Rounds to zero.
! Interpret data with caution. Estimate is unstable due to high coefficient of variation (> 30 percent and ≤ 50 percent).
!! Interpret data with caution. Estimate is unstable because the standard error represents more than 50 percent of the estimate.
* $p < .05$. Significantly different from the U.S. percentage.
[1] B-S-J-Z (China) refers to the four PISA participating China provinces: Beijing, Shanghai, Jiangsu, and Zhejiang.
[2] At least 50 percent but less than 75 percent of the 15-year-old population is covered by the PISA sample.
[3] Less than 50 percent of the 15-year-old population is covered by the PISA sample.
NOTE: Education systems are ordered by 2018 percentages of 15-year-olds in levels 5 and above. Descriptions of the skills and knowledge of students at each mathematics proficiency level are available at https://nces.ed.gov/surveys/pisa/pisa2018/pdf/MathProfLevelDescriptionV2.pdf. To reach a particular proficiency level, a student must correctly answer a majority of items at that level. Students were classified into mathematics proficiency levels according to their scores. Exact cut scores are as follows: Below Level 2 (a score less than 420.07); At or Above Level 5 is a score equal to or greater than 606.99. Scores are reported on a scale from 0 to 1,000. Italics indicate non-OECD countries and education systems. Education systems are marked as OECD countries if they were OECD members in 2018. The OECD average is the average of the national percentages of the OECD member countries, with each country weighted equally. Although Vietnam participated in PISA 2018, technical problems with its data prevent results from being discussed in this indicator.
SOURCE: Organization for Economic Cooperation and Development (OECD), Program for International Student Assessment (PISA), 2018. See *Digest of Education Statistics 2019*, table 602.60.

PISA reports mathematics literacy by six proficiency levels, with level 1 being the lowest and level 6 being the highest. Descriptions of the skills and knowledge of students at each mathematics proficiency level can be found here. At levels 5 and 6, students can demonstrate the advanced mathematical thinking and reasoning skills required to solve problems of greater complexity. The percentage of U.S. students who were top performers on the mathematics literacy scale (8 percent) was smaller than the OECD average percentage (11 percent). Percentages of top performers ranged from nearly 0 percent in nine education systems to 44 percent in B-S-J-Z (China). Twenty-nine education systems had larger percentages of top performers in mathematics literacy than did the United States.

The percentage of U.S. students who were low performers in mathematics literacy (27 percent) was larger than the OECD average percentage (24 percent). Percentages of low performers ranged from 2 percent in B-S-J-Z (China) to 91 percent in the Dominican Republic. Thirty education systems had smaller percentages of low performers in mathematics literacy than did the United States.

Table 3. Average scores of 15-year-old students on the Program for International Student Assessment (PISA) science literacy scale, by education system: 2018

Education system	Average score		Education system	Average score	
OECD average	**489**	▼	Italy	468	▼
B-S-J-Z (China)[1]	590	⬣	Slovak Republic	464	▼
Singapore	551	⬣	Israel	462	▼
Macau (China)	544	⬣	*Malta*	457	▼
Estonia	530	⬣	Greece	452	▼
Japan	529	⬣	Chile	444	▼
Finland	522	⬣	*Serbia*	440	▼
Korea, Republic of	519	⬣	*Cyprus*	439	▼
Canada	518	⬣	*Malaysia*[2]	438	▼
Hong Kong (China)	517	⬣	*United Arab Emirates*	434	▼
Chinese Taipei	516	⬣	*Brunei Darussalam*	431	▼
Poland	511	⬣	*Jordan*[2]	429	▼
New Zealand	508		*Moldova, Republic of*	428	▼
Slovenia	507		*Thailand*[2]	426	▼
United Kingdom	505		Uruguay	426	▼
Netherlands	503		*Romania*[2]	426	▼
Germany	503		*Bulgaria*[2]	424	▼
Australia	503		*Mexico*[2]	419	▼
United States	**502**		*Qatar*	419	▼
Sweden	499		*Albania*	417	▼
Belgium	499		*Costa Rica*[2]	416	▼
Czech Republic	497		*Montenegro, Republic of*	415	▼
Ireland	496		*Colombia*[2]	413	▼
Switzerland	495		*North Macedonia*	413	▼
France	493	▼	*Peru*[2]	404	▼
Denmark	493	▼	*Argentina*	404	▼
Portugal	492	▼	*Brazil*[2]	404	▼
Norway	490	▼	*Bosnia and Herzegovina*	398	▼
Austria	490	▼	*Baku (Azerbaijan)*[3]	398	▼
Latvia	487	▼	*Kazakhstan*	397	▼
Spain	483	▼	*Indonesia*	396	▼
Lithuania	482	▼	*Saudi Arabia*	386	▼
Hungary	481	▼	*Lebanon*	384	▼
Russian Federation	478	▼	*Georgia*	383	▼
Luxembourg	477	▼	*Morocco*[2]	377	▼
Iceland	475	▼	*Kosovo*	365	▼
Croatia	472	▼	*Panama*[2]	365	▼
Belarus	471	▼	*Philippines*[2]	357	▼
Ukraine	469	▼	*Dominican Republic*[2]	336	▼
Turkey[2]	468	▼			

⬣ Average score is higher than U.S. average score at the .05 level of statistical significance.
▼ Average score is lower than U.S. average score at the .05 level of statistical significance.
[1] B-S-J-Z (China) refers to the four PISA participating China provinces: Beijing, Shanghai, Jiangsu, and Zhejiang.
[2] At least 50 percent but less than 75 percent of the 15-year-old population is covered by the PISA sample.
[3] Less than 50 percent of the 15-year-old population is covered by the PISA sample.
NOTE: Education systems are ordered by 2018 average score. Scores are reported on a scale from 0 to 1,000. Italics indicate non-OECD countries and education systems. Education systems are marked as OECD countries if they were OECD members in 2018. The OECD average is the average of the national averages of the OECD member countries, with each country weighted equally. Although Vietnam participated in PISA 2018, technical problems with its data prevent results from being discussed in this indicator.
SOURCE: Organization for Economic Cooperation and Development (OECD), Program for International Student Assessment (PISA), 2018. See *Digest of Education Statistics 2019*, table 602.70.

Average scores in science literacy in 2018 ranged from 336 in the Dominican Republic to 590 in B-S-J-Z (China). The U.S. average science score (502) was higher than the OECD average score (489). Eleven education systems had higher average science scores than did the United States, and eleven education systems had scores that were not measurably different from the U.S. score.

Figure 3. Percentage of 15-year-old students performing on the Program for International Student Assessment (PISA) science literacy scale, by selected proficiency levels and education system: 2018

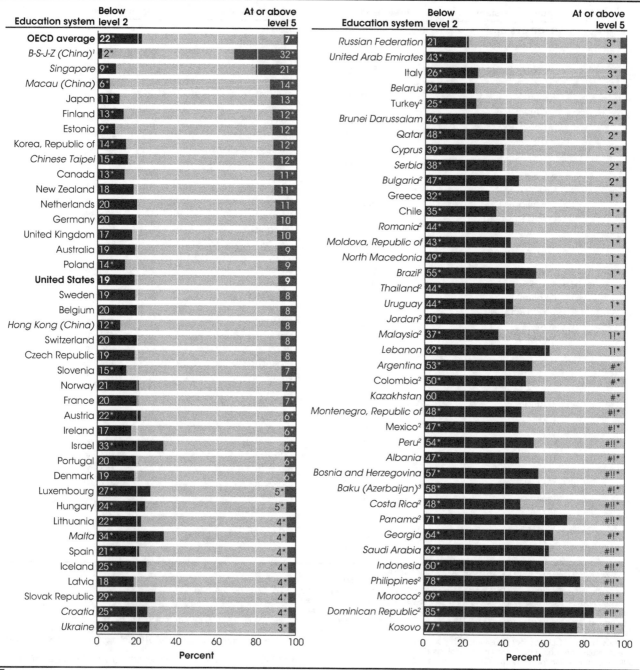

■ Below level 2
■ At or above level 5
\# Rounds to zero.
! Interpret data with caution. Estimate is unstable due to high coefficient of variation (> 30 percent and ≤ 50 percent).
!! Interpret data with caution. Estimate is unstable because the standard error represents more than 50 percent of the estimate.
* $p < .05$. Significantly different from the U.S. percentage.
[1] B-S-J-Z (China) refers to the four PISA participating China provinces: Beijing, Shanghai, Jiangsu, and Zhejiang.
[2] At least 50 percent but less than 75 percent of the 15-year-old population is covered by the PISA sample.
[3] Less than 50 percent of the 15-year-old population is covered by the PISA sample.
NOTE: Education systems are ordered by 2018 percentages of 15-year-olds in levels 5 and above. Descriptions of the skills and knowledge of students at each science proficiency level are available at https://nces.ed.gov/surveys/pisa/pisa2018/pdf/ScienceProfLevelDescriptionV2.pdf. To reach a particular proficiency level, a student must correctly answer a majority of items at that level. Students were classified into science proficiency levels according to their scores. Exact cut scores are as follows: Below Level 2 (a score less than 409.54); At or Above Level 5 is a score equal to or greater than 633.33. Scores are reported on a scale from 0 to 1,000. Italics indicate non-OECD countries and education systems. Education systems are marked as OECD countries if they were OECD members in 2018. The OECD average is the average of the national percentages of the OECD member countries, with each country weighted equally. Although Vietnam participated in PISA 2018, technical problems with its data prevent results from being discussed in this indicator.
SOURCE: Organization for Economic Cooperation and Development (OECD), Program for International Student Assessment (PISA), 2018. See *Digest of Education Statistics 2019*, table 602.70.

PISA reports science literacy in terms of seven proficiency levels, with level 1b being the lowest and level 6 being the highest. Descriptions of the skills and knowledge of students at each science proficiency level can be found here. Students scoring at proficiency levels 5 and 6 can apply scientific knowledge in a variety of complex real-life situations. The percentage of U.S. students who were top performers in science literacy (9 percent) was larger than the OECD average percentage (7 percent). Percentages of top performers ranged from nearly 0 percent in 18 education systems to 32 percent in B-S-J-Z (China).

Ten education systems had larger percentages of top performers in science literacy than did the United States.

The percentage of U.S. students who were low performers in science literacy (19 percent) was smaller than the OECD average percentage (22 percent). Percentages of low performers ranged from 2 percent in B-S-J-Z (China) to 85 percent in the Dominican Republic. Twelve education systems had smaller percentages of low performers in science literacy than did the United States.

Endnotes:

[1] Although Spain's PISA 2018 data meet international technical standards, its reading literacy data show unusual student response behavior that prevent them from being reported at this time. Although Vietnam participated in PISA 2018, technical problems with its data prevent results from being discussed. Therefore, results are presented for 77 education systems for reading literacy and 78 education systems for mathematics and science literacy.
[2] For the purposes of this indicator, "education systems" refer to all entities participating in PISA, including countries as well as subnational entities (e.g., cities or provinces).

Reference tables: *Digest of Education Statistics 2019*, tables 602.50, 602.60, and 602.70
Related indicators and resources: International Comparisons: Reading Literacy at Grade 4; International Comparisons: U.S. 4th-, 8th-, and 12th-Graders' Mathematics and Science Achievement; Mathematics Performance; Reading Performance; Science Performance

Glossary: Organization for Economic Cooperation and Development (OECD)

Enrollment Rates by Country

In contrast to the near universal enrollment of 5- to 14-year-olds in all OECD countries, enrollment rates among 15- to 19-year-olds varied across OECD countries in 2017, ranging from 59 percent in Colombia to 95 percent in Belgium. Some 83 percent of 15- to 19-year-olds in the United States were enrolled in school at any level, which was slightly lower than the average of OECD countries (84 percent).

This indicator uses data from the Organization for Economic Cooperation and Development (OECD) to compare educational enrollment rates by age group across countries. The OECD is a group of 37 countries whose purpose is to promote trade and economic growth. The OECD also collects and publishes an array of data on its member countries.

Across OECD countries, students generally follow a similar pathway through the education system. Before beginning primary (elementary) education, children may be enrolled in an early childhood education program and/or a preprimary education program, such as kindergarten in the United States.[1] Across OECD countries, compulsory education typically begins at the start of primary education.[2,3] Upon completion of primary education, students progress through lower secondary (middle school) and upper secondary (high school) education. Compulsory education typically ends during or at the completion of upper secondary education—around age 17 or 18 in the United States—after which time students may continue into either postsecondary nontertiary education (short career/technical educational programs) or tertiary education (postsecondary degree programs). While the educational pathway is similar across OECD countries, enrollment rates differ across countries and across age groups. Also, if a country enrolls many residents of other countries, the country's total population in the specified age group can be smaller than the total number enrolled, resulting in enrollment estimates exceeding 100 percent.

Figure 1. Percentage of 3- and 4-year-olds enrolled in school, by Organization for Economic Cooperation and Development (OECD) country: 2017

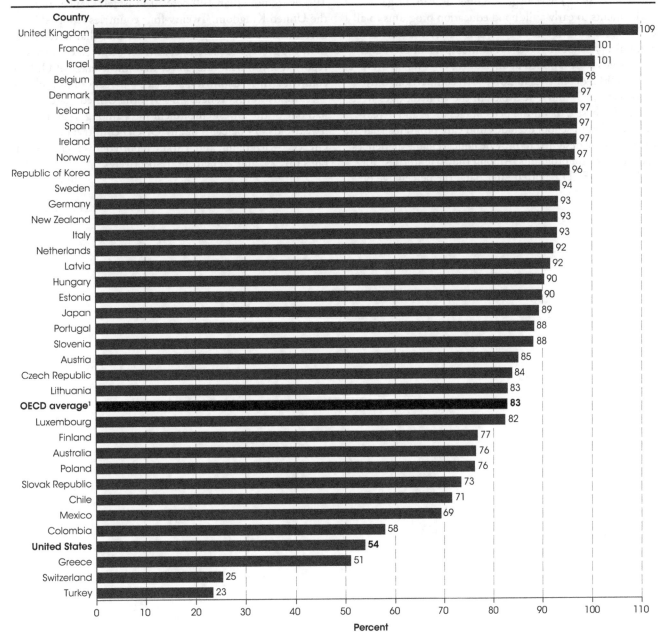

[1] Refers to the mean of the data values for all reporting Organization for Economic Cooperation and Development (OECD) countries, to which each country reporting data contributes equally. The average includes all current OECD countries for which a given year's data are available, even if they were not members of OECD in that year.

NOTE: Of the 37 OECD countries, 36 are included in this figure. Canada is excluded because the 2017 enrollment rate for 3- and 4-year-olds is not available. For each country, this figure shows the number of 3- and 4-year-olds who are enrolled in that country as a percentage of that country's total population of 3- and 4-year-olds. Enrollment rates may be underestimated for countries that are net exporters of students and may be overestimated for countries that are net importers. If a country enrolls many residents of other countries, the total number of students enrolled may be larger than the country's total population of 3- and 4-year-olds, resulting in enrollment estimates exceeding 100 percent. Although rounded numbers are displayed, the figures are based on unrounded data.

SOURCE: Organization for Economic Cooperation and Development (OECD), Online Education Database, retrieved September 16, 2019, from http://stats.oecd.org/Index.aspx. See *Digest of Education Statistics 2019*, table 601.35.

In recent years, many OECD countries (although not the United States) have begun to offer universal legal entitlements to early childhood education programs to all children for at least one or two years before the start of compulsory schooling.[4] As a result, 83 percent of 3- and 4-year-olds were enrolled at any education level on average across OECD countries in 2017.[5,6] In comparison, only 54 percent of 3- and 4-year-olds in the United States were enrolled. These data on the percentages of 3- and 4-year-olds enrolled in school exclude child care programs that are not primarily designed to provide educational experiences, such as day care programs. Among the 36 countries[7] for which the OECD reported 2017 data, the percentage of 3- and 4-year-olds enrolled ranged from 23 percent in Turkey to more than 100 percent in Israel, France, and the United Kingdom. Twenty-four countries reported enrollment rates among 3- and 4-year-olds that were higher than the average of OECD countries, while 12 countries reported enrollment rates lower than the average of OECD countries. In 17 countries, at least 90 percent of 3- and 4-year-olds were enrolled. In 2017, the United States had one of the lowest enrollment rates among 3- and 4-year-olds (54 percent) of any OECD country; only Greece, Switzerland, and Turkey reported lower enrollment rates (51, 25, and 23 percent, respectively).

Figure 2. Percentage of 5- to 14-year-olds enrolled in school, by Organization for Economic Cooperation and Development (OECD) country: 2017

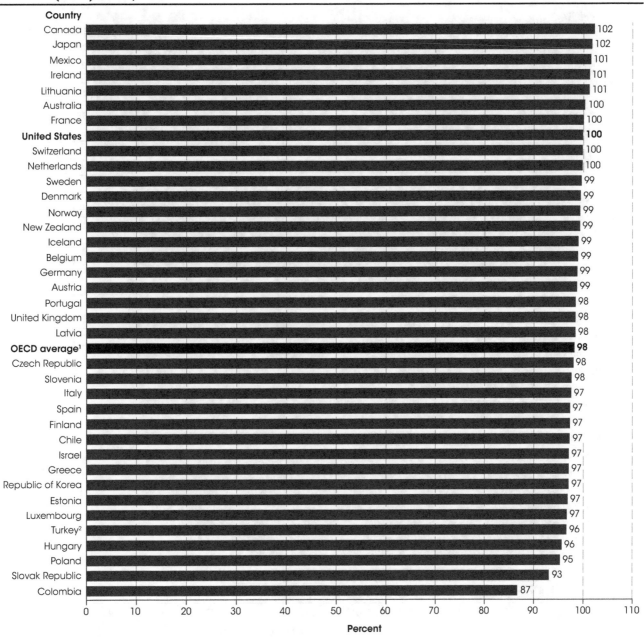

Enrollment rates among 5- to 14-year-olds were similar across OECD countries.[8] In 2017, the percentage of 5- to 14-year-olds enrolled in school varied by 16 percentage points across all 37 OECD countries—ranging from 87 percent in Colombia to 100 percent (or more) in Australia, Lithuania, Ireland, Mexico, Japan, and Canada.[9] Nearly 100 percent (99.8 percent) of 5- to 14-year-olds

in the United States were enrolled in school at any level, compared with the average of OECD countries of 98 percent. Enrollment among 5- to 14-year-olds in OECD countries is nearly universal due to compulsory schooling laws that cover primary and lower secondary education programs in all OECD countries.

Figure 3. Percentage of 15- to 19-year-olds enrolled in school, by Organization for Economic Cooperation and Development (OECD) country and level of education: 2017

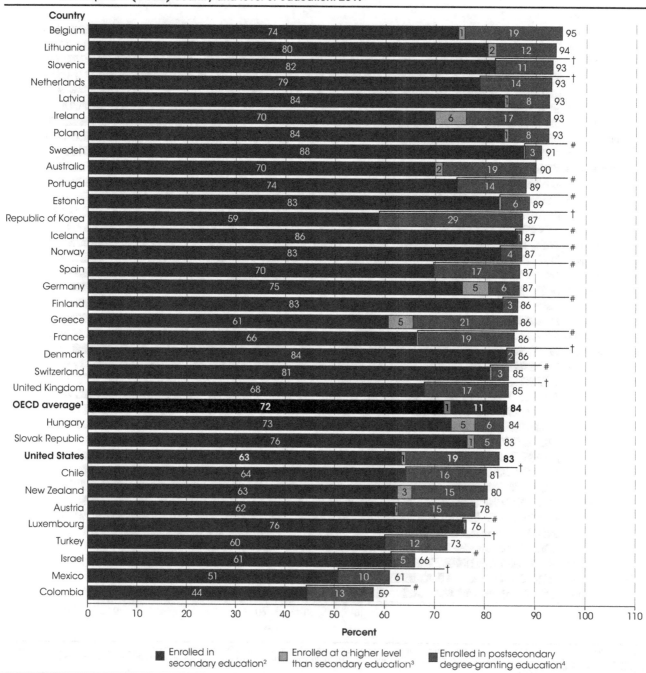

† Not applicable.
# Rounds to zero.
[1] Refers to the mean of the data values for all reporting Organization for Economic Cooperation and Development (OECD) countries, to which each country reporting data contributes equally. The average includes all current OECD countries for which a given year's data are available, even if they were not members of OECD in that year.
[2] Refers to International Standard Classification of Education (ISCED) 2011 level 2 (lower secondary education) and level 3 (upper secondary education). Secondary education generally corresponds to grades 7–12 in the United States.
[3] Refers to programs classified at ISCED 2011 level 4 (postsecondary nontertiary education). Postsecondary nontertiary education generally corresponds to postsecondary vocational programs below the associate's degree level in the United States.
[4] Postsecondary degree-granting programs (tertiary education programs) correspond to all postsecondary programs leading to associate's and higher degrees in the United States. Includes ISCED 2011 level 5 (corresponding to U.S. programs at the associate's degree level), level 6 (bachelor's or equivalent level), level 7 (master's or equivalent level), and level 8 (doctoral or equivalent level). Enrollment rates may not be directly comparable across countries due to differing definitions of tertiary education and the age at which it begins.
NOTE: Of the 37 OECD countries, 33 are included in this figure. Japan, Canada, the Czech Republic, and Italy are excluded because 2017 enrollment rates for 15- to 19-year-olds in these countries are not available for all education levels presented in the figure. For each country, this figure shows the number of 15- to 19-year-olds who are enrolled in that country as a percentage of that country's total population of 15- to 19-year-olds. Enrollment rates may be underestimated for countries that are net exporters of students and may be overestimated for countries that are net importers. If a country enrolls many residents of other countries, the total number of students enrolled may be larger than the country's total population of 15- to 19-year-olds. Enrollment estimates can also be affected if population and enrollment data were collected at different times. In addition to secondary and postsecondary education, total enrollment in all levels of education may include enrollment in ISCED 2011 level 1 (primary or elementary education). Includes both full-time and part-time students. Although rounded numbers are displayed, the figures are based on unrounded data. Detail may not sum to totals because of rounding.
SOURCE: Organization for Economic Cooperation and Development (OECD), Online Education Database, retrieved September 24, 2019, from http://stats.oecd.org/Index.aspx. See *Digest of Education Statistics 2019*, table 601.40.

In contrast to the near universal enrollment of 5- to 14-year-olds in all OECD countries, enrollment rates among 15- to 19-year-olds varied more widely across OECD countries. Among the 36 countries[10] for which the OECD reported 2017 data, the percentage of 15- to 19-year-olds enrolled in school at any level ranged from 59 percent in Colombia to 95 percent in Belgium. Part of this variation can be attributed to the end of compulsory schooling and the transition of some students into the labor market. In 2017, some 83 percent of 15- to 19-year-olds in the United States were enrolled in school at any level, which was slightly lower than the average of OECD countries (84 percent).

The 15- to 19-year-old age group spans the period during which students generally finish secondary education and potentially go on to more advanced schooling.[11] Among 15- to 19-year-olds who remain enrolled in school after completion of secondary education, some transition into postsecondary nondegree education (corresponding to a short career/technical educational program in the United States)[12] while others pursue postsecondary degree-granting education (corresponding to an associate's or higher degree in the United States).[13] On average across OECD countries, 72 percent of 15- to 19-year-olds were enrolled in secondary education in 2017, while 1 percent were enrolled in postsecondary nondegree education programs and 11 percent were enrolled in postsecondary degree-granting education programs.[14] Across OECD countries, there were differences in the share of 15- to 19-year-olds enrolled in secondary school compared with the share enrolled in a higher level of education. For example, the percentage of 15- to 19-year-olds in the United States enrolled in secondary education (63 percent) was lower than the average of OECD countries (72 percent), while the percentage enrolled in postsecondary nondegree education programs (just under 1 percent) was similar to the average of OECD countries (just over 1 percent) and the percentage enrolled in postsecondary degree-granting education programs (19 percent) was higher than the average of OECD countries (11 percent). In all OECD countries for which the 2017 data were available for secondary, postsecondary nondegree, and postsecondary degree-granting education and the education levels were applicable, higher percentages of 15- to 19-year-olds were enrolled in secondary school than in postsecondary nondegree or postsecondary degree-granting education.

In the United States, it is more common for 15- to 19-year-olds to transition into a postsecondary degree-granting program than into a postsecondary nondegree program after completing secondary school. Among the 26 countries[15] for which the OECD reported 2017 data on postsecondary nondegree education programs, the percentages of 15- to 19-year-olds who were enrolled in such programs ranged from less than 1 percent in 17 countries and from 1 to 6 percent in 9 countries. Among the 36 countries[16] for which the OECD reported 2017 data on postsecondary degree-granting education programs, the percentages of 15- to 19-year-olds who were enrolled in such programs ranged from 1 percent in Luxembourg and Iceland to 29 percent in Korea. For all 25 countries[17] for which the OECD reported 2017 data on both postsecondary nondegree and postsecondary degree-granting education, enrollment rates of 15- to 19-year-olds in postsecondary nondegree programs were lower than enrollment rates in postsecondary degree-granting programs.

The specific age at which students make the transition from secondary education to postsecondary education differs by country. In all OECD countries except Colombia, a majority of 15-year-olds, 16-year-olds, and 17-year-olds were enrolled in secondary school in 2017. In addition, 29 out of 36 OECD countries reported that the percentage of 18-year-olds enrolled in secondary school was higher than the percentage enrolled in a postsecondary degree-granting program, and 14 countries reported that the percentage of 19-year-olds enrolled in secondary school was higher than the percentage enrolled in a postsecondary degree-granting program. In the United States, 101 percent of 15-year-olds, 28 percent of 18-year-olds, and 5 percent of 19-year-olds were enrolled in secondary school in 2017.

Figure 4. Percentage of 19-year-olds enrolled in secondary education and postsecondary nondegree and degree-granting programs, by Organization for Economic Cooperation and Development (OECD) country: 2017

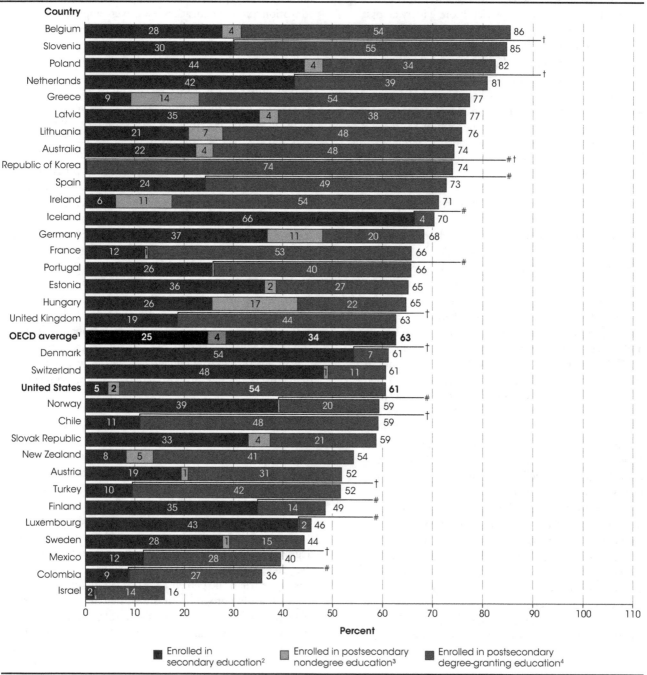

† Not applicable.
# Rounds to zero.
[1] Refers to the mean of the data values for all reporting Organization for Economic Cooperation and Development (OECD) countries, to which each country reporting data contributes equally. The average includes all current OECD countries for which a given year's data are available, even if they were not members of OECD in that year.
[2] Refers to International Standard Classification of Education (ISCED) 2011 level 2 (lower secondary education) and level 3 (upper secondary education). Secondary education generally corresponds to grades 7–12 in the United States.
[3] Refers to programs classified at ISCED 2011 level 4 (postsecondary nontertiary education). Postsecondary nontertiary education generally corresponds to postsecondary vocational programs below the associate's degree level in the United States.
[4] Postsecondary degree-granting programs (tertiary education programs) correspond to all postsecondary programs leading to associate's and higher degrees in the United States. Includes ISCED 2011 level 5 (corresponding to U.S. programs at the associate's degree level), level 6 (bachelor's or equivalent level), level 7 (master's or equivalent level), and level 8 (doctoral or equivalent level). Enrollment rates may not be directly comparable across countries due to differing definitions of postsecondary education and the age at which it begins.
NOTE: Of the 37 OECD countries, 33 are included in this figure. Japan, Canada, the Czech Republic, and Italy are excluded because 2017 enrollment rates for 19-year-olds in these countries are not available for all education levels presented in the figure. For each country, this figure shows the number of 19-year-olds who are enrolled in that country as a percentage of that country's total population of 19-year-olds. Enrollment rates may be underestimated for countries that are net exporters of students and may be overestimated for countries that are net importers. If a country enrolls many residents of other countries, the total number of students enrolled may be larger than the country's total population of 19-year-olds. Enrollment estimates can also be affected if population and enrollment data were collected at different times. Includes both full-time and part-time students. Although rounded numbers are displayed, the figures are based on unrounded data.
SOURCE: Organization for Economic Cooperation and Development (OECD), Online Education Database, retrieved September 24, 2019, from http://stats.oecd.org/Index.aspx. See *Digest of Education Statistics 2019*, table 601.40.

Since enrolling in a postsecondary degree-granting education program is the most prevalent educational pathway in the United States among those who remain enrolled in education after secondary school, the next portion of this indicator examines how the transition from secondary school to a postsecondary degree-granting program in the United States compares with other OECD countries. Examining enrollment rates of 19-year-olds draws out differences in the typical age students transition from secondary school to a postsecondary degree-granting program across countries. As previously noted, 14 out of 36 OECD countries reported that a higher percentage of 19-year-olds were enrolled in secondary school than

in a postsecondary degree-granting program in 2017. In contrast, 22 countries—including the United States—reported having a higher percentage of 19-year-olds enrolled in a postsecondary degree-granting program than in secondary school. In the United States, 54 percent of 19-year-olds were enrolled in a postsecondary degree-granting program, whereas 5 percent were enrolled in secondary school. The percentage of 19-year-olds enrolled in secondary school in the United States was lower than the average of OECD countries (5 vs. 25 percent), but the percentage of 19-year-olds enrolled in a postsecondary degree-granting program in the United States was higher than the average of OECD countries (54 vs. 34 percent).

Figure 5.   Percentage of 20- to 29-year-olds enrolled in school, by Organization for Economic Cooperation and Development (OECD) country and level of education: 2017

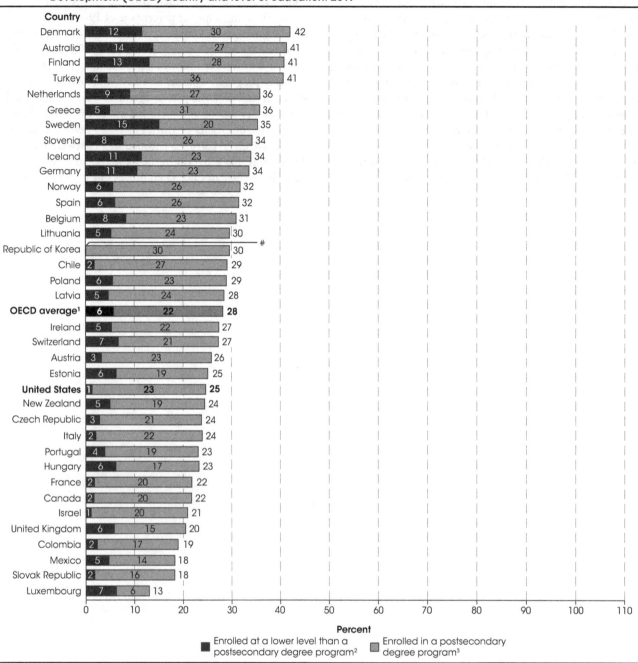

Rounds to zero.

[1] Refers to the mean of the data values for all reporting Organization for Economic Cooperation and Development (OECD) countries, to which each country reporting data contributes equally. The average includes all current OECD countries for which a given year's data are available, even if they were not members of OECD in that year.

[2] In general, 20- to 29-year-olds who are enrolled in school but not in a postsecondary degree-granting program, are enrolled in a postsecondary nondegree program or in secondary education. "Postsecondary nondegree programs" refer to programs classified at International Standard Classification of Education (ISCED) 2011 level 4. ISCED 4 (postsecondary nontertiary education) typically corresponds to postsecondary vocational programs below the associate's degree level in the United States. "Secondary education" refers to ISCED 2011 level 2 (lower secondary education) and level 3 (upper secondary education) and generally corresponds to grades 7–12 in the United States.

[3] Corresponds to all postsecondary degree-granting programs leading to associate's and higher degrees in the United States. Includes ISCED 2011 level 5 (corresponding to U.S. programs at the associate's degree level), level 6 (bachelor's or equivalent level), level 7 (master's or equivalent level), and level 8 (doctoral or equivalent level). Enrollment rates may not be directly comparable across countries due to differing definitions of postsecondary education and the age at which it begins.

NOTE: Of the 37 OECD countries, 36 are included in this figure. Japan is excluded because 2017 enrollment rates for 20- to 29-year-olds are not available. For each country, this figure shows the number of 20- to 29-year-olds enrolled in that country as a percentage of that country's total population of 20- to 29-year-olds. Enrollment rates may be underestimated for countries that are net exporters of students and may be overestimated for countries that are net importers. If a country enrolls many residents of other countries, the total number of students enrolled may be larger than the country's total population of 20- to 29-year-olds. Enrollment estimates can also be affected if population and enrollment data were collected at different times. Includes both full-time and part-time students. Although rounded numbers are displayed, the figures are based on unrounded data. Detail may not sum to totals because of rounding.

SOURCE: Organization for Economic Cooperation and Development (OECD), Online Education Database, retrieved September 24, 2019, from http://stats.oecd.org/Index.aspx. See *Digest of Education Statistics 2019*, table 601.40.

Among the 36 countries[18] for which the OECD reported 2017 data, the percentage of 20- to 29-year-olds enrolled in school ranged from 13 percent in Luxembourg to 42 percent in Denmark. Thirteen countries reported that 30 percent or more of 20- to 29-year-olds were enrolled in school in 2017, of which four countries (Denmark, Australia, Finland, and Turkey) reported that 40 percent or more of 20- to 29-year-olds were enrolled. In 2017, some 25 percent of 20- to 29-year-olds in the United States were enrolled in school at any level, which was lower than the average of OECD countries (28 percent).

The 20- to 29-year-old age group spans the period during which students generally persist through (and potentially complete) a postsecondary degree-granting program. In all OECD countries for which 2017 data were available, higher percentages of 20- to 29-year-olds were enrolled in a postsecondary degree program in 2017 than were enrolled in other levels of education. In the United States, 23 percent of 20- to 29-year-olds were enrolled in postsecondary degree programs in 2017. There were several countries, however, that had relatively large shares of 20- to 29-year-olds enrolled in a lower level of education than a postsecondary degree program. For example, 15 percent of 20- to 29-year-olds in Sweden and 14 percent of 20- to 29-year-olds in Australia were enrolled in a lower level of education than a postsecondary degree program.

Endnotes:

[1] Early childhood educational programs are targeted at children ages 0–2 and preprimary education programs are targeted at children age 3 years until the start of primary education. The upper age limit for preprimary education depends on the theoretical starting age of primary education. (See http://uis.unesco.org/sites/default/files/documents/international-standard-classification-of-education-isced-2011-en.pdf.)

[2] The boundary between preprimary and primary coincides with the transition point in an education system where systematic teaching and learning in reading, writing, and mathematics begins. Although some preprimary programs may already provide some introduction in reading, writing, and mathematics, these programs do not yet give children sound basic skills in these areas, and thus do not sufficiently fulfill the criteria for classification as primary education. The transition from preprimary to primary education is typically marked by entry into nationally designated primary, elementary, or basic educational institutions or programs. (See http://uis.unesco.org/sites/default/files/documents/international-standard-classification-of-education-isced-2011-en.pdf.)

[3] OECD. (2019). Who Participates in Education? In *Education at a Glance 2019: OECD Indicators*. (Indicator B1, pp. 146–159). Paris: OECD Publishing. https://www.oecd-ilibrary.org/education/education-at-a-glance-2019_f8d7880d-en.

[4] OECD. (2019). How Do Early Childhood Education Systems Differ Around the World? In *Education at a Glance 2019: OECD Indicators*. (Indicator B2, pp. 160–178). Paris: OECD Publishing. https://www.oecd-ilibrary.org/education/education-at-a-glance-2019_f8d7880d-en.

[5] While these enrollment rates include 3- and 4-year-olds enrolled in school at any level, 3- and 4-year-olds across OECD countries are generally enrolled in programs classified by the International Standard Classification of Education (ISCED) 2011 as ISCED 0 (early childhood education). In the United States, ISCED 0 programs are commonly referred to as preprimary school, preschool, nursery school, or prekindergarten. Child care programs that are not primarily designed to provide educational experiences, such as day care programs, are not included in ISCED 0.

[6] Throughout this indicator, the "average of OECD countries" refers to the mean of the data values for all reporting Organization for Economic Cooperation and Development (OECD) countries, to which each country reporting data contributes equally. The average includes all current OECD countries for which a given year's data are available, even if they were not members of the OECD in that year. Countries excluded from analyses in this indicator may be included in the average of OECD countries.

[7] Canada is excluded because 2017 data on the enrollment rate of 3- and 4-year-olds are not available.

[8] While enrollment rates include 5- to 14-year-olds enrolled in school at any level, students of this age group across OECD countries are generally enrolled in programs classified as ISCED 1 (primary education or elementary school) or ISCED 2 (lower secondary education or middle school). In the United States, ISCED 1 corresponds to grades 1–6 and ISCED 2 corresponds to grades 7–9.

[9] Some of a country's population may be enrolled in a different country, and some persons enrolled in the country may be residents of a different country. Enrollment rates may be underestimated for countries such as Luxembourg that are net exporters of students and may be overestimated for countries that are net importers. If a country enrolls many residents of other countries, the country's total population in the specified age group can be smaller than the total number enrolled, resulting in enrollment estimates exceeding 100 percent.

[10] Japan is excluded because 2017 data on enrollment rates of 15- to 19-year-olds are not available.

[11] Secondary school includes programs classified as ISCED 2 (lower secondary education or middle school) and ISCED 3 (upper secondary education or high school). Secondary education generally corresponds to grades 7–12 in the United States.

[12] Refers to programs classified at ISCED level 4. ISCED 4 (postsecondary nontertiary education) typically corresponds to postsecondary vocational programs below the associate's degree level in the United States.

[13] Includes all postsecondary programs leading to associate's and higher degrees in the United States. Postsecondary degree programs include ISCED level 5 (corresponding to U.S. programs at the associate's degree level), level 6 (bachelor's or equivalent level), level 7 (master's or equivalent level), and level 8 (doctoral or equivalent level).

[14] The average of OECD countries for the percentage of 15- to 19-year-olds enrolled in postsecondary nondegree education programs excludes Chile, Denmark, Mexico, the Netherlands, the Republic of Korea, Slovenia, Turkey, and the United Kingdom because postsecondary nondegree programs are not applicable in these countries and excludes Canada, the Czech Republic, and Italy because 2017 data on enrollment rates of 15- to 19-year-olds in postsecondary nondegree programs are not available. The average of OECD countries for the percentage of 15- to 19-year-olds enrolled in postsecondary nondegree education programs excludes Japan because 2017 data on enrollment rates of 15- to 19-year-olds in postsecondary degree-granting programs are not available.

[15] Chile, Denmark, Mexico, the Netherlands, the Republic of Korea, Slovenia, Turkey, and the United Kingdom are excluded because postsecondary nondegree programs are not applicable in these countries. Canada, the Czech Republic, and Italy are excluded because 2017 data on enrollment rates of 15- to 19-year-olds in postsecondary nondegree programs are not available.

[16] Japan is excluded because 2017 data on enrollment rates of 15- to 19-year-olds in postsecondary degree-granting programs are not available.

[17] Chile, Denmark, Mexico, the Netherlands, the Republic of Korea, Slovenia, Turkey, and the United Kingdom are excluded because data on postsecondary nondegree programs are not applicable in these countries. Canada, the Czech Republic, and Italy are excluded because 2017 data on enrollment rates of 15- to 19-year-olds in postsecondary nondegree programs are not available. Japan is excluded because 2017 data on enrollment rates of 15- to 19-year-olds in postsecondary degree-granting programs are not available.

[18] Japan is excluded because 2017 data on enrollment rates of 20- to 29-year-olds are not available.

Reference tables: *Digest of Education Statistics 2019*, tables 601.35 and 601.40

Related indicators and resources: International Educational Attainment; Postbaccalaureate Enrollment; Preschool and Kindergarten Enrollment; Private School Enrollment; Public School Enrollment; Undergraduate Enrollment

Glossary: Elementary school; Enrollment; International Standard Classification of Education (ISCED); Organization for Economic Cooperation and Development (OECD); Postsecondary education; Preschool; Secondary school

International Educational Attainment

Across OECD countries, the average percentage of 25- to 64-year-olds with any postsecondary degree was 37 percent in 2018, an increase of 15 percentage points from 2000. During the same period, the percentage of U.S. 25- to 64-year-olds with any postsecondary degree increased 11 percentage points to 47 percent.

The Organization for Economic Cooperation and Development (OECD) is a group of 37 countries whose purpose is to promote trade and economic growth. The OECD also collects and publishes an array of data on its member countries. This indicator uses OECD data to compare educational attainment across countries using two measures: *high school completion* and *attainment of any postsecondary degree*.[1] In the United States, "high school completion" refers to individuals who have been awarded a high school diploma or an equivalent credential, such as the GED. "Attainment of any postsecondary degree" refers to individuals who have been awarded an associate's or higher degree.[2]

Among the 34 countries[3] for which the OECD reported 2018 data on high school completion rates, the percentages of 25- to 64-year-olds who had completed high school ranged from less than 40 percent in Mexico to more than 90 percent in the United States, the Slovak Republic, Canada, Poland, Lithuania, and the Czech Republic.[4] Twenty-one countries reported that more than 80 percent had completed high school as of 2018. Additionally, among the 35 countries[5] for which the OECD reported 2018 data on postsecondary attainment rates, the percentages earning any postsecondary degree ranged from less than 20 percent in Mexico and Italy to more than 50 percent in Japan and Canada. Twenty-six countries reported that more than 30 percent in this age range had earned any postsecondary degree as of 2018.

Figure 1. Percentage of the population 25 to 64 years old who had completed high school in Organization for Economic Cooperation and Development (OECD) countries: 2000 and 2018

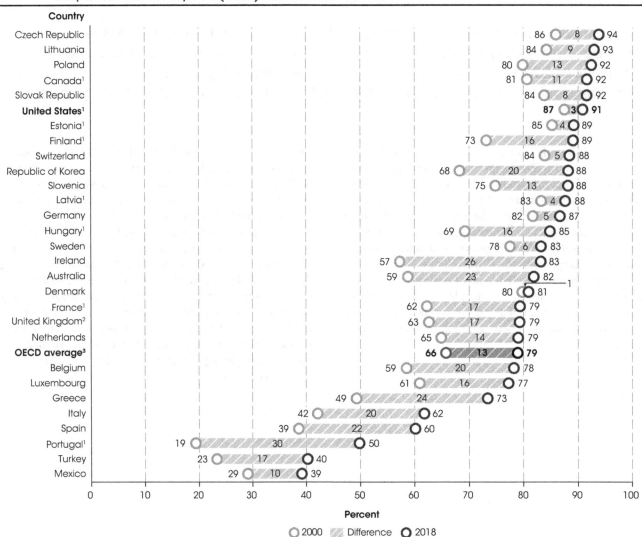

Country	2000	Difference	2018
Czech Republic	86	8	94
Lithuania	84	9	93
Poland	80	13	92
Canada[1]	81	11	92
Slovak Republic	84	8	92
United States[1]	**87**	**3**	**91**
Estonia[1]	85	4	89
Finland[1]	73	16	89
Switzerland	84	5	88
Republic of Korea	68	20	88
Slovenia	75	13	88
Latvia[1]	83	4	88
Germany	82	5	87
Hungary[1]	69	16	85
Sweden	78	6	83
Ireland	57	26	83
Australia	59	23	82 — 1
Denmark	80		81
France[1]	62	17	79
United Kingdom[2]	63	17	79
Netherlands	65	14	79
OECD average[3]	**66**	**13**	**79**
Belgium	59	20	78
Luxembourg	61	16	77
Greece	49	24	73
Italy	42	20	62
Spain	39	22	60
Portugal[1]	19	30	50
Turkey	23	17	40
Mexico	29	10	39

Percent

○ 2000   ▨ Difference   ● 2018

[1] The International Standard Classification of Education (ISCED) was revised in 2011. Although data for 2000 were originally calculated using the 1997 version of ISCED, the footnoted countries revised their 2000 data to align with the 2011 version of ISCED.
[2] Data include some persons who completed a sufficient number of certain types of programs, any one of which individually would be classified as a program that only partially completes the high school (or upper secondary) level of education.
[3] Refers to the mean of the data values for all reporting Organization for Economic Cooperation and Development (OECD) countries, to which each country reporting data contributes equally. The average includes all current OECD countries for which a given year's data are available, even if they were not members of the OECD in that year. Countries not shown in this figure may be included in the OECD average.
NOTE: Of the 37 OECD countries, 29 are included in this figure. Austria, Chile, Colombia, Iceland, Israel, Japan, New Zealand, and Norway are excluded because data are not available for these countries for either 2000 or 2018. Data in this figure refer to degrees classified under ISCED 2011 as completing level 3 (upper secondary education) or to comparable degrees under ISCED 1997. In the United States, "high school completion" refers to individuals who have been awarded a high school diploma or an equivalent credential, such as the GED. ISCED 2011 was used to calculate data for 2018 for all countries. Some data have been revised from previously published figures. Although rounded numbers are displayed, the figures are based on unrounded data.
SOURCE: Organization for Economic Cooperation and Development (OECD), Online Education Database, retrieved September 23, 2019, from https://stats.oecd.org/Index.aspx. See *Digest of Education Statistics 2019*, table 603.10.

In each of the 29 countries[6] for which the OECD reported data on high school completion rates in both 2000 and 2018, the percentage of 25- to 64-year-olds who had completed high school was higher in 2018 than in 2000. The OECD average percentage[7] of those with a high school education rose from 66 percent in 2000 to 79 percent in 2018. Meanwhile, in the United States the percentage who had completed high school rose from 87 to 91 percent during this period.

For 25- to 34-year-olds, the OECD average percentage who had completed high school rose from 76 to 85 percent between 2000 and 2018, while the corresponding percentage for the United States increased from 88 to 92 percent. The high school completion gap between the United States and the OECD average was narrower in 2018 than in 2000 in this age group. In 2018, the rate of high school completion in this age group in the United States was 8 percentage points higher than the OECD average, while the gap in 2000 was 12 percentage points.

Figure 2. Percentage of the population who had completed high school in Organization for Economic Cooperation and Development (OECD) countries, by selected age groups: 2018

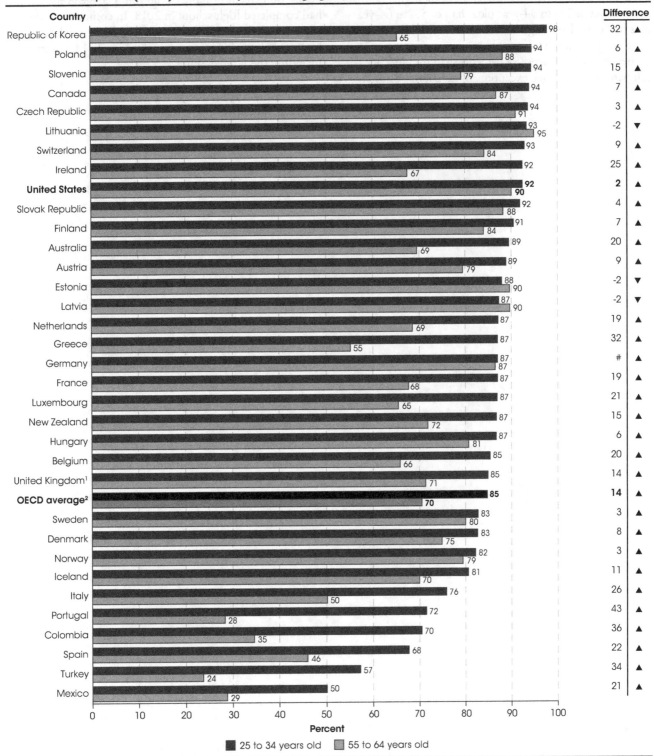

▲ The percentage of 25- to 34-year-olds who had completed high school is higher than the percentage of 55- to 64-year-olds who had completed high school.
▼ The percentage of 25- to 34-year-olds who had completed high school is lower than the percentage of 55- to 64-year-olds who had completed high school.
[1] Data include some persons who completed a sufficient number of certain types of programs, any one of which individually would be classified as a program that only partially completes the high school (or upper secondary) level of education.
[2] Refers to the mean of the data values for all reporting Organization for Economic Cooperation and Development (OECD) countries, to which each country reporting data contributes equally. The average includes all current OECD countries for which a given year's data are available, even if they were not members of the OECD in that year. Countries not shown in this figure may be included in the OECD average.
NOTE: Of the 37 OECD countries, 34 are included in this figure. Chile, Israel, and Japan are excluded because 2018 data are not available for these countries. Data in this figure refer to degrees classified under the International Standard Classification of Education (ISCED) 2011 as completing level 3 (upper secondary education). In the United States, "high school completion" refers to individuals who have been awarded a high school diploma or an equivalent credential, such as the GED. Although rounded numbers are displayed, the figures are based on unrounded data.
SOURCE: Organization for Economic Cooperation and Development (OECD), Online Education Database, retrieved September 23, 2019, from https://stats.oecd.org/Index.aspx. See *Digest of Education Statistics 2019*, table 603.10.

In 31 of the 34 countries for which the OECD reported 2018 data on high school completion rates, higher percentages of 25- to 34-year-olds than of 55- to 64-year-olds had completed high school.[8] Across OECD countries, the average high school completion percentage was higher for younger ages (85 percent) than for older ages (70 percent). The three exceptions were Latvia, Estonia, and Lithuania. In 28 countries, including the United States, 80 percent or more of the younger age group had completed high school in 2018. In comparison, the percentage of the older age group who had completed high school was 80 percent or more in only 13 countries, including the United States.

Figure 3. Percentage of the population 25 to 64 years old who had attained any postsecondary degree in Organization for Economic Cooperation and Development (OECD) countries: 2000 and 2018

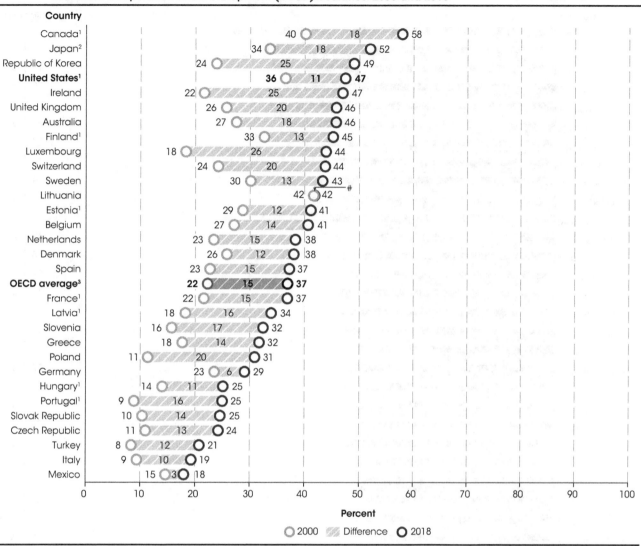

Rounds to zero.
[1] The International Standard Classification of Education (ISCED) was revised in 2011. Although data for 2000 were originally calculated using the 1997 version of ISCED, the footnoted countries revised their 2000 data to align with the 2011 version of ISCED.
[2] Data for both years include some postsecondary nontertiary awards (i.e., awards that are below the associate's degree level).
[3] Refers to the mean of the data values for all reporting Organization for Economic Cooperation and Development (OECD) countries, to which each country reporting data contributes equally. The average includes all current OECD countries for which a given year's data are available, even if they were not members of the OECD in that year. Countries not shown in this figure may be included in the OECD average.
NOTE: Of the 37 OECD countries, 30 are included in this figure. Austria, Chile, Colombia, Iceland, Israel, New Zealand, and Norway are excluded from this figure because data are not available for these countries for either 2000 or 2018. Data in this figure include all tertiary (postsecondary) degrees, which correspond to all degrees at the associate's level and above in the United States. Under ISCED 2011, tertiary degrees are classified at the following levels: level 5 (corresponding to an associate's degree in the United States), level 6 (a bachelor's or equivalent degree), level 7 (a master's or equivalent degree), and level 8 (a doctoral or equivalent degree). ISCED 2011 was used to calculate data for 2018 for all countries. Some data have been revised from previously published figures. Although rounded numbers are displayed, the figures are based on unrounded data.
SOURCE: Organization for Economic Cooperation and Development (OECD), Online Education Database, retrieved September 23, 2019, from https://stats.oecd.org/Index.aspx. See *Digest of Education Statistics 2019*, table 603.20.

In 29 of the 30 countries[9] for which the OECD reported data on postsecondary attainment rates in both 2000 and 2018, the percentage of 25- to 64-year-olds who had earned any postsecondary degree was higher in 2018 than in 2000. Lithuania was the only country that did not follow this pattern. During this period, the OECD average percentage of those with any postsecondary degree increased by 15 percentage points to 37 percent in 2018, while the corresponding percentage for the United States increased by 11 percentage points to 47 percent.

For 25- to 34-year-olds, the OECD average percentage with any postsecondary degree rose from 26 percent

in 2000 to 44 percent in 2018. The corresponding percentage for this age group in the United States rose from 38 to 49 percent. The postsecondary attainment gap between the United States and the OECD average narrowed in this age group between 2000 and 2018 as a result of the relatively larger increases in postsecondary degree attainment across the OECD countries. The postsecondary attainment rate in this age group in the United States was 12 percentage points higher than the OECD average in 2000; by 2018, this gap had decreased to 5 percentage points.

Figure 4. Percentage of the population who had attained any postsecondary degree in Organization for Economic Cooperation and Development (OECD) countries, by selected age groups: 2018

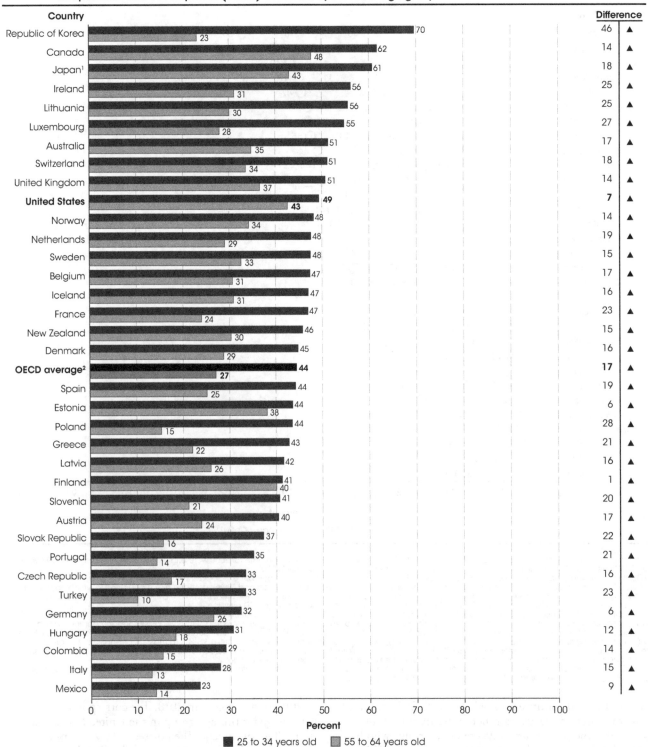

▲ The percentage of 25- to 34-year-olds with any postsecondary degree is higher than the percentage of 55- to 64-year-olds with any postsecondary degree.
[1] Data include some postsecondary nontertiary awards (i.e., awards that are below the associate's degree level).
[2] Refers to the mean of the data values for all reporting Organization for Economic Cooperation and Development (OECD) countries, to which each country reporting data contributes equally. The average includes all current OECD countries for which a given year's data are available, even if they were not members of the OECD in that year. Countries not shown in this figure may be included in the OECD average.
NOTE: Of the 37 OECD countries, 35 are included in this figure. Chile and Israel are excluded from the figure because data are not available for 2018. All data in this figure were calculated using the International Standard Classification of Education (ISCED) 2011 classification of tertiary (postsecondary) degrees. Under ISCED 2011, tertiary degrees are classified at the following levels: level 5 (corresponding to an associate's degree in the United States), level 6 (a bachelor's or equivalent degree), level 7 (a master's or equivalent degree), and level 8 (a doctoral or equivalent degree). Although rounded numbers are displayed, the figures are based on unrounded data.
SOURCE: Organization for Economic Cooperation and Development (OECD), Online Education Database, retrieved September 23, 2019, from https://stats.oecd.org/Index.aspx. See *Digest of Education Statistics 2019*, table 603.20.

Postsecondary attainment rates were higher among 25- to 34-year-olds than among 55- to 64-year-olds in all 35 countries for which the OECD reported 2018 data on postsecondary attainment rates. The OECD average percentage of the younger ages who had earned any postsecondary degree (44 percent) was higher than the corresponding percentage of the older ages (27 percent). In the United States, 49 percent of the younger age group had earned any postsecondary degree compared with 43 percent of the older age group. Finland (40 percent), Japan (43 percent), and Canada (48 percent) were the only other countries where 40 percent or more of the older age group had earned any postsecondary degree. In comparison, there were 24 countries in which 40 percent or more of the younger age group had earned any postsecondary degree.

Figure 5. Percentage of the population 25 to 34 years old who had attained a postsecondary degree in Organization for Economic Cooperation and Development (OECD) countries, by highest degree attained: 2018

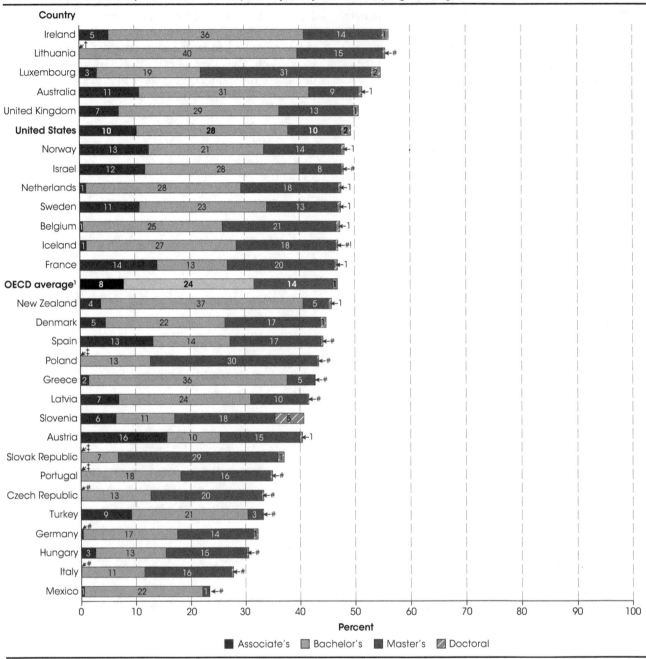

† Not applicable.
# Rounds to zero.
! Interpret data with caution. The coefficient of variation (CV) for this estimate is between 30 and 50 percent.
‡ Reporting standards not met.
[1] Refers to the mean of the data values for all reporting Organization for Economic Cooperation and Development (OECD) countries, to which each country reporting data contributes equally. The average includes all current OECD countries for which a given year's data are available, even if they were not members of the OECD in that year. Countries not shown in this figure may be included in the OECD average.
NOTE: Of the 37 OECD countries, 29 are included in this figure. Data for Canada, Chile, Colombia, Estonia, Finland, Japan, the Republic of Korea, and Switzerland are excluded from the figure because separate data are not available for all attainment levels. All data in this figure were calculated using the International Standard Classification of Education (ISCED) 2011 classification of tertiary (postsecondary) degrees. Under ISCED 2011, tertiary degrees are classified at the following levels: level 5 (corresponding to an associate's degree in the United States), level 6 (a bachelor's or equivalent degree), level 7 (a master's or equivalent degree), and level 8 (a doctoral or equivalent degree). Although rounded numbers are displayed, the figures are based on unrounded data.
SOURCE: Organization for Economic Cooperation and Development (OECD), Online Education Database, retrieved September 23, 2019, from https://stats.oecd.org/Index.aspx. See *Digest of Education Statistics 2019*, table 603.30.

The percentage of 25- to 34-year-olds who had attained specific postsecondary degrees (e.g., associate's degrees, bachelor's degrees, master's degrees, and doctoral degrees) varied across OECD countries in 2018. Among the 29 countries[10] for which the OECD reported 2018 data for all attainment levels, the percentage of those whose highest degree attained was an associate's degree ranged from less than 1 percent in Italy, the Czech Republic, Germany, Mexico, and Belgium to 16 percent in Austria. The percentage of those whose highest degree attained was an associate's degree in the United States (10 percent) was higher than the OECD average (8 percent). The percentage of this age group whose highest degree attained was a bachelor's degree ranged from 7 percent in the Slovak Republic to 40 percent in Lithuania. In the United States, the percentage of those whose highest degree attained was a bachelor's degree (28 percent) was higher than the OECD average (24 percent). The percentage of those whose highest degree attained was a master's degree ranged from 1 percent in Mexico to 31 percent in Luxembourg. The percentage of this age group in the United States whose highest degree attained was a master's degree (10 percent) was lower than the OECD average (14 percent). Finally, the percentage in this age group who attained a doctoral degree did not vary as widely across OECD countries: with the exception of Ireland (just above 1 percent), the United States and Luxembourg (both 2 percent), and Slovenia (5 percent), all countries reported that 1 percent or less of 25- to 34-year-olds had attained this level of education.

Endnotes:

[1] Attainment data in this indicator refer to comparable levels of degrees, as classified by the International Standard Classification of Education (ISCED). ISCED was revised in 2011. The previous version, ISCED 1997, was used to calculate data for all years prior to 2014. ISCED 2011 was used to calculate data for 2014 and later years and may not be directly comparable to ISCED 1997.

[2] Under ISCED 2011, postsecondary degrees are classified at the following levels: level 5 (corresponding to an associate's degree in the United States), level 6 (a bachelor's or equivalent degree), level 7 (a master's or equivalent degree), and level 8 (a doctoral or equivalent degree). The structure of education differs across countries and not all countries have significant numbers of awards at each of these degree levels.

[3] Chile, Israel, and Japan are excluded because 2018 data on high school completion rates are not available for these countries.

[4] Data in this section refer to degrees classified as ISCED 2011 level 3, which generally corresponds to high school completion in the United States, with some exceptions.

[5] Chile and Israel are excluded because 2018 data on postsecondary attainment rates are not available.

[6] Austria, Chile, Colombia, Iceland, Israel, Japan, New Zealand, and Norway are excluded because data are not available for these countries for either 2000 or 2018.

[7] Throughout this indicator, the "OECD average" refers to the mean of the data values for all reporting Organization for Economic Cooperation and Development (OECD) countries, to which each country reporting data contributes equally. The average includes all current OECD countries for which a given year's data are available, even if they were not members of the OECD in that year. Countries excluded from analyses in this indicator may be included in the OECD average.

[8] In Germany, the difference was less than 1 percent.

[9] Austria, Chile, Colombia, Iceland, Israel, New Zealand, and Norway are excluded because data are not available for these countries for either 2000 or 2018.

[10] Canada, Chile, Colombia, Estonia, Finland, Japan, the Republic of Korea, and Switzerland are excluded from this analysis because separate 2018 data are not available for these countries at all attainment levels.

Reference tables: *Digest of Education Statistics 2019*, tables 603.10, 603.20, and 603.30

Related indicators and resources: Educational Attainment of Young Adults; Education Expenditures by Country; International Comparisons: Reading Literacy at Grade 4; International Comparisons: Reading, Mathematics, and Science Literacy of 15 Year Old Students; International Comparisons: U.S. 4th-, 8th-, and 12th-Graders' Mathematics and Science Achievement

Glossary: Associate's degree; Bachelor's degree; Doctoral degree; Educational attainment; Gap; High school completer; International Standard Classification of Education (ISCED); Master's degree; Organization for Economic Cooperation and Development (OECD); Postsecondary education

Education Expenditures by Country

In 2016, the United States spent $13,600 per full-time-equivalent (FTE) student on elementary and secondary education, which was 39 percent higher than the average of Organization for Economic Cooperation and Development (OECD) member countries of $9,800 (in constant 2018 U.S. dollars). At the postsecondary level, the United States spent $31,600 per FTE student, which was 95 percent higher than the average of OECD countries ($16,200).

This indicator uses material from the Organization for Economic Cooperation and Development (OECD) to compare countries' expenditures on education using two measures: *expenditures on public and private education institutions per full-time-equivalent (FTE) student* and *total government and private expenditures on education institutions as a percentage of gross domestic product (GDP).* The OECD is an organization of 37 countries that collects and publishes an array of data on its member countries. Education expenditures are from public revenue sources (governments) and private revenue sources, and they include current and capital expenditures. Private sources include payments from households for school-based expenses such as tuition, transportation fees, book rentals, and food services, as well as public funding via subsidies to households, private fees for education services, and other private spending that goes through the educational institution. The *total government and private expenditures on education institutions as a percentage of GDP* measure allows for a comparison of countries' expenditures relative to their ability to finance education. Purchasing power parity (PPP) indexes are used to convert other currencies into U.S. dollars. Monetary amounts are in constant 2018 dollars based on national Consumer Price Indexes.[1]

Expenditures per FTE student at the elementary/secondary level varied across OECD countries[2] in 2016, ranging from $3,200 in Colombia to $20,400 in Luxembourg. The United States spent $13,600 per FTE student at the elementary/secondary level, which was 39 percent higher than the average of OECD countries[3] reporting data ($9,800).

Expenditures per FTE student at the postsecondary level also varied across OECD countries in 2016, ranging from $6,900 in Colombia to $50,000 in Luxembourg. The United States spent $31,600 per FTE student at the postsecondary level, which was 95 percent higher than the average of OECD countries reporting data ($16,200).

Figure 1. Expenditures and percentage change in expenditures per full-time-equivalent (FTE) student for elementary and secondary education, by Organization for Economic Cooperation and Development (OECD) country: 2005 and 2016

[In constant 2018 U.S. dollars]

OECD country	2005	2016	Percent change, 2005 to 2016
Luxembourg	—	$20,400	†
Switzerland[1]	—	15,700	†
Austria	—	15,300	†
Norway	$12,900	14,400	12
United States	**12,600**	**13,600**	**8**
Belgium	9,700	12,800	33
Iceland	16,700	12,200	-27
Republic of Korea	—	12,200	†
Sweden	9,000	12,000	33
Germany	8,500	11,700	37
United Kingdom	10,300	11,600	13
Netherlands	9,500	11,500	21
Canada[1,2]	—	11,100	†
Australia	9,400	10,900	16
France	8,600	10,500	22
Japan	7,800	10,300	32
Finland	8,100	10,200	26
New Zealand	—	9,800	†
OECD average[3]	**7,900**	**9,800**	**24**
Portugal[4]	6,800	9,200	36
Ireland	7,300	9,100	24
Italy	8,600	8,900	4
Spain	7,800	8,900	14
Slovenia	8,900	8,800	-1
Israel	5,600	8,500	51
Estonia	5,600	7,400	32
Czech Republic	5,300	7,300	39
Hungary	6,000	7,300	20
Poland	4,100	7,200	75
Latvia	4,800	7,000	46
Slovak Republic	3,600	6,900	94
Greece[1,4]	6,400	6,200	-3
Lithuania	—	6,100	†
Turkey	—	5,800	†
Chile	3,300	5,200	57
Mexico	3,400	3,400	#
Colombia	—	3,200	†
Denmark	10,900	—	†

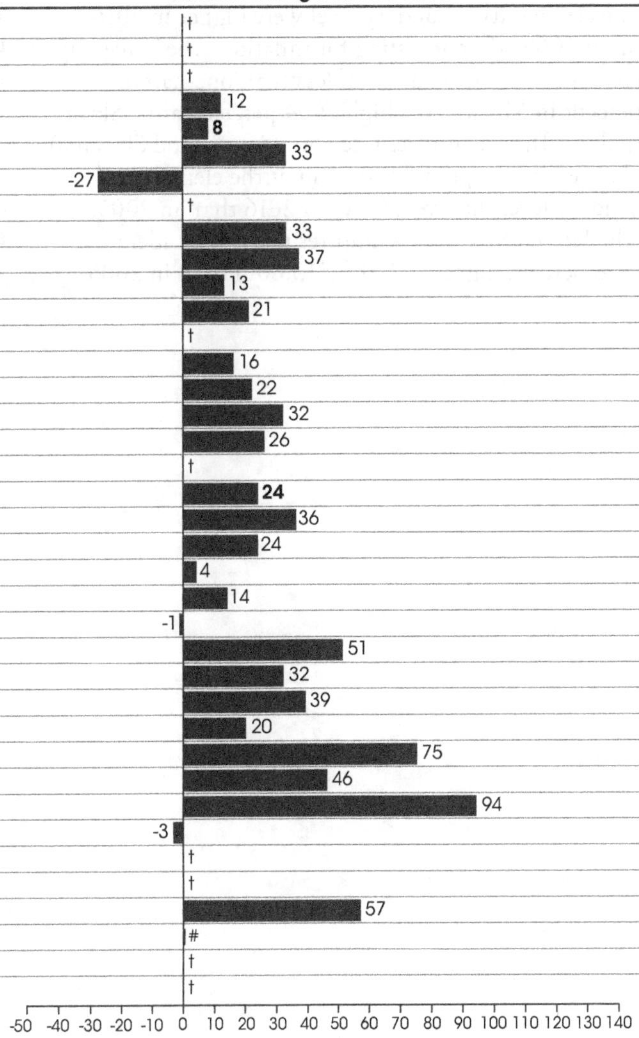

-50 -40 -30 -20 -10 0 10 20 30 40 50 60 70 80 90 100 110 120 130 140

Percent change in expenditures per FTE student

— Not available.
† Not applicable.
# Rounds to zero.
[1] Includes public institutions only.
[2] Education expenditures include preprimary education (for children ages 3 and older).
[3] Refers to the mean of the data values for all reporting Organization for Economic Cooperation and Development (OECD) countries, to which each country reporting data contributes equally. The average includes all current OECD countries for which a given year's data are available, even if they were not members of OECD in that year.
[4] Education expenditures exclude postsecondary non-higher education.
NOTE: Includes both government and private expenditures. Expenditures for International Standard Classification of Education (ISCED) level 4 (postsecondary non-higher education) are included in elementary and secondary education unless otherwise noted. Data adjusted to U.S. dollars using the purchasing power parity (PPP) index. Constant dollars based on national Consumer Price Indexes, available on the OECD database cited in the SOURCE note below. Some data have been revised from previously published figures. Although rounded numbers are displayed, the figures are based on unrounded data.
SOURCE: Organization for Economic Cooperation and Development (OECD), Online Education Database, retrieved November 20, 2019, from https://stats.oecd.org/Index.aspx. See *Digest of Education Statistics 2019*, table 605.10.

In 2016, the average of OECD countries' expenditures per FTE student at the elementary/secondary level was $9,800, compared with $7,900 in 2005. In 24 of the 27 OECD countries with data available for both years, including the United States, expenditures per FTE student at the elementary/secondary level were higher in 2016 than in 2005, after adjusting for inflation. The percentage increases ranged from a low of less than one-half of 1 percent in Mexico to a high of 94 percent in the Slovak Republic. Three countries (Iceland, Greece, and Slovenia) had expenditures per FTE student at the elementary/ secondary level that were lower in 2016 than in 2005. In the United States, expenditures per FTE student were 8 percent higher in 2016 ($13,600) than in 2005

($12,600). Of the 27 countries with data available in both 2005 and 2016, some 21 had higher percentage increases in expenditures than the United States; Italy, Mexico, Slovenia, Greece, and Iceland were lower.

In 2005, the United States had the third highest expenditures per FTE student at the elementary/secondary level of the 27 countries with available data for 2005 and 2016, after Iceland ($16,700) and Norway ($12,900). In 2016, the United States was second behind Norway ($14,400). In addition, the gap between the United States and the country with the highest expenditures per FTE student at the elementary/secondary level decreased from $4,200 in 2005 to $800 in 2016.

Figure 2. Expenditures and percentage change in expenditures per full-time-equivalent (FTE) student for postsecondary education, by Organization for Economic Cooperation and Development (OECD) country: 2005 and 2016

[In constant 2018 U.S. dollars]

OECD country	2005	2016	Percent change, 2005 to 2016
United States	$30,400	$31,600	4
Sweden	18,200	25,300	39
Netherlands	18,800	20,100	7
Japan[1]	14,500	19,500	34
Belgium	15,700	18,900	21
Germany	15,700	18,000	15
Finland	15,000	17,900	19
Australia	19,400	16,800	-13
France	13,200	16,600	26
OECD average[2]	12,700	16,200	27
Iceland[1]	18,000	15,200	-16
Estonia	5,800	13,800	138
Ireland	12,000	13,300	11
Spain	12,300	13,100	6
Hungary	8,500	11,900	41
Italy	8,800	11,900	35
Slovak Republic	7,600	11,900	57
Portugal[1]	11,600	11,300	-3
Israel	12,200	11,300	-7
Czech Republic	8,600	10,500	22
Poland	6,100	9,300	52
Chile	9,200	8,700	-5
Lithuania	6,700	8,200	22
Mexico	10,600	8,200	-23
Latvia	6,700	7,900	17

-50 -40 -30 -20 -10 0 10 20 30 40 50 60 70 80 90 100 110 120 130 140

Percent change in expenditures per FTE student

[1] Postsecondary non-higher education included in both secondary and postsecondary education in one or both data years (2005 and 2016).
[2] Refers to the mean of the data values for all reporting Organization for Economic Cooperation and Development (OECD) countries, to which each country reporting data contributes equally. The average includes all current OECD countries for which a given year's data are available, even if they were not members of OECD in that year.
NOTE: Austria, Canada, Colombia, Denmark, Greece, Luxembourg, New Zealand, Norway, the Republic of Korea, Slovenia, Switzerland, Turkey, and the United Kingdom are excluded from this figure because data on expenditures were unavailable for either 2005 or 2016. Includes both government and private expenditures. Data adjusted to U.S. dollars using the purchasing power parity (PPP) index. Constant dollars based on national Consumer Price Indexes, available on the OECD database cited in the SOURCE note below. Some data have been revised from previously published figures. Although rounded numbers are displayed, the figures are based on unrounded data.
SOURCE: Organization for Economic Cooperation and Development (OECD), Online Education Database, retrieved November 20, 2019, from https://stats. oecd.org/Index.aspx. See *Digest of Education Statistics 2019*, table 605.10.

In 2016, the average of OECD countries' expenditures per FTE student at the postsecondary level was $16,200, compared with $12,700 in 2005. Of the 24 OECD countries with data available in both years, expenditures per FTE student at the postsecondary level were higher in 2016 than in 2005 in 18 countries, including the United States. In the United States, expenditures per FTE student at the postsecondary level were 4 percent higher in 2016 ($31,600) than in 2005 ($30,400). Of the 18 countries with expenditures per FTE student that were higher in 2016 than in 2005, the percentage increase in

expenditures per FTE student at the postsecondary level ranged from a low of 4 percent in the United States to a high of 138 percent in Estonia. While the United States had the smallest percentage increase in expenditures per FTE student at the postsecondary level between 2005 and 2016, it had the highest expenditures per FTE student in both 2005 and 2016 among the OECD countries reporting data in both years. Six countries (Mexico, Iceland, Australia, Israel, Chile, and Portugal) had expenditures per FTE student at the postsecondary level that were lower in 2016 than in 2005.

Figure 3. Expenditures per full-time-equivalent (FTE) student for elementary and secondary education in selected Organization for Economic Cooperation and Development (OECD) countries, by gross domestic product (GDP) per capita: 2016

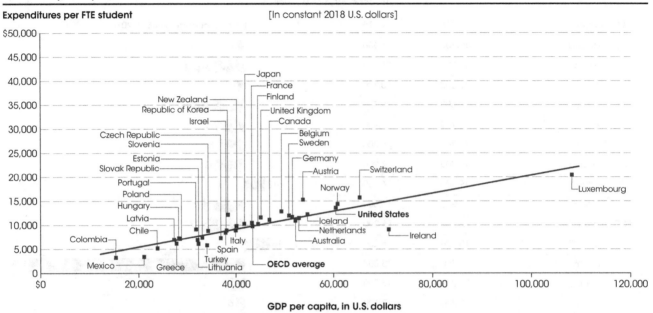

Expenditures per FTE student [In constant 2018 U.S. dollars]

GDP per capita, in U.S. dollars

— Linear relationship between spending and country wealth for 36 OECD countries reporting data (elementary/secondary): r^2 = .78; slope = 0.19; intercept = 1,734. NOTE: Denmark is excluded from this figure because data on expenditures were not available in 2016. Includes both government and private expenditures. GDP per capita data are estimated or provisional for Greece, Mexico, and Spain. Expenditures for International Standard Classification of Education (ISCED) level 4 (postsecondary non-higher education) are included in elementary and secondary education unless otherwise noted. Data on expenditures for Canada, Greece, and Italy do not include postsecondary non-higher education. Data on expenditures for Canada include preprimary education. Data adjusted to U.S. dollars using the purchasing power parity (PPP) index. Constant dollars based on national Consumer Price Indexes, available on the OECD database cited in the SOURCE note below. "OECD average" refers to the mean of the data values for all reporting Organization for Economic Cooperation and Development (OECD) countries, to which each country reporting data contributes equally. The average includes all current OECD countries for which a given year's data are available, even if they were not members of OECD in that year. SOURCE: Organization for Economic Cooperation and Development (OECD), Online Education Database, retrieved November 20, 2019, from https://stats.oecd.org/Index.aspx. See *Digest of Education Statistics 2019*, table 605.10.

A country's wealth (defined as GDP per capita) is positively associated with its education expenditures per FTE student at the elementary/secondary and postsecondary levels. In 2016, of the 15 countries with a GDP per capita greater than the average of OECD countries that also reported data for elementary/secondary education expenditures per FTE student, 14 countries had elementary/secondary education expenditures per FTE student that were higher than the average of OECD countries. These 14 countries were Luxembourg, Switzerland, Norway, the United States, Iceland, Austria, the Netherlands, Australia, Germany, Sweden, Belgium, Canada, the United Kingdom, and Finland. The exception was Ireland, which had lower elementary/secondary expenditures per FTE student than the average of OECD countries ($9,100 vs. $9,800).

Of the 21 countries with a GDP per capita lower than the average of OECD countries that also reported data for elementary/secondary education expenditures per FTE student, 17 countries also had elementary/secondary education expenditures per FTE student that were lower than the average of OECD countries in 2016. These 17 countries were Italy, Spain, Israel, the Czech Republic, Slovenia, Turkey, Estonia, Lithuania, the Slovak Republic, Portugal, Poland, Hungary, Greece, Latvia, Chile, Mexico, and Colombia. The exceptions were New Zealand, France, Japan, and the Republic of Korea, which had expenditures per FTE student at the elementary/secondary level that were higher than the average for OECD countries.

Figure 4. Expenditures per full-time-equivalent (FTE) student for postsecondary education in selected Organization for Economic Cooperation and Development (OECD) countries, by gross domestic product (GDP) per capita: 2016

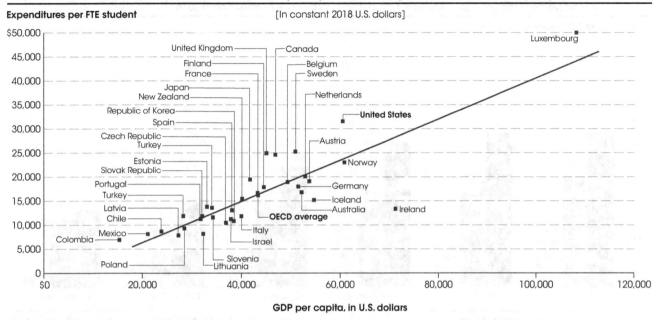

— Linear relationship between spending and country wealth for 34 OECD countries reporting data (postsecondary): r² = .74; slope = 0.43; intercept = -2,176.
NOTE: Denmark, Greece, and Switzerland are excluded from this figure because data on expenditures were not available in 2016. Includes both government and private expenditures. GDP per capita data are estimated or provisional for Mexico and Spain. Data on expenditures for Japan and Portugal include International Standard Classification of Education (ISCED) level 4 (postsecondary non-higher education). Data adjusted to U.S. dollars using the purchasing power parity (PPP) index. Constant dollars based on national Consumer Price Indexes, available on the OECD database cited in the SOURCE note below. "OECD average" refers to the mean of the data values for all reporting Organization for Economic Cooperation and Development (OECD) countries, to which each country reporting data contributes equally. The average includes all current OECD countries for which a given year's data are available, even if they were not members of OECD in that year.
SOURCE: Organization for Economic Cooperation and Development (OECD), Online Education Database, retrieved November 20, 2019, from https://stats.oecd.org/Index.aspx. See *Digest of Education Statistics 2019,* table 605.10.

At the postsecondary level in 2016, of the 14 countries with a GDP per capita that was higher than the average of OECD countries that also reported data for postsecondary education expenditures per FTE student, 12 also had postsecondary education expenditures per FTE student that were higher than the average of OECD countries. The two exceptions were Ireland and Iceland, both of which had lower expenditures per FTE student at the postsecondary level ($13,300 and $15,200, respectively) than the average of OECD countries ($16,200). Of the

20 countries with a lower GDP per capita than the average of OECD countries that also reported data for postsecondary education expenditures per FTE student, 18 countries had education expenditures per FTE student that were lower than the average of OECD countries at the postsecondary level. The two exceptions were Japan and France; both countries reported higher postsecondary expenditures per FTE student ($19,500 and $16,600, respectively) than the average of OECD countries.

Figure 5. Government and private expenditures on education institutions as a percentage of gross domestic product (GDP) for Organization for Economic Cooperation and Development (OECD) countries with the two highest and lowest percentages of expenditures for all institutions, by level of education: 2016

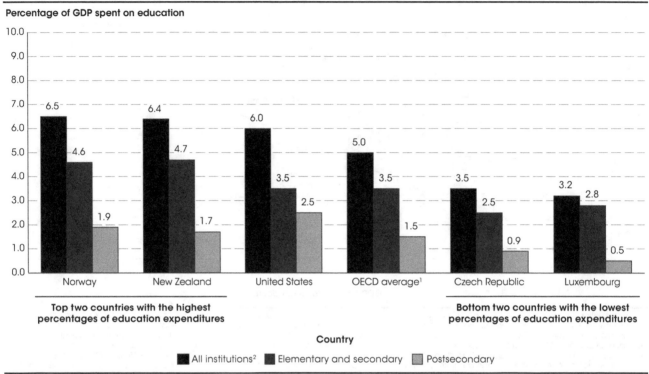

Percentage of GDP spent on education

Top two countries with the highest percentages of education expenditures

Bottom two countries with the lowest percentages of education expenditures

Country

■ All institutions[2] ■ Elementary and secondary ▨ Postsecondary

[1] Refers to the mean of the data values for all reporting Organization for Economic Cooperation and Development (OECD) countries, to which each country reporting data contributes equally. The average includes all current OECD countries for which a given year's data are available, even if they were not members of OECD in that year.
[2] Includes expenditures that could not be reported by level of education.
NOTE: Expenditures for International Standard Classification of Education (ISCED) level 4 (postsecondary non-higher education) are included in elementary and secondary education. Although rounded numbers are displayed, the figures are based on unrounded data. Detail may not sum to totals because of rounding.
SOURCE: Organization for Economic Cooperation and Development (OECD), Online Education Database, retrieved October 14, 2019, from https://stats.oecd.org/Index.aspx. See *Digest of Education Statistics 2019*, table 605.20.

Among the 35 OECD countries reporting data in 2016, there were 19 countries that spent a higher percentage of GDP on total government and private expenditures on education institutions than the average of OECD countries. Norway reported the highest total education expenditures as a percentage of GDP (6.5 percent), followed by New Zealand (6.4 percent), Colombia (6.2 percent), the United Kingdom (6.2 percent), Chile (6.1 percent), and the United States (6.0 percent). Conversely, 16 countries spent a percentage of GDP on total education expenditures that was lower than the average of OECD countries. Luxembourg reported the lowest total education expenditures as a percentage of GDP (3.2 percent), followed by the Czech Republic and Ireland (both 3.5 percent) and Lithuania and Italy (both 3.6 percent).

At the elementary/secondary level, the percentage of GDP that the United States spent on total government and private expenditures in 2016 (3.5 percent) was nearly the same as the average of OECD countries. Nineteen other countries also spent a percentage of GDP on elementary/secondary education that was greater than or equal to the average of OECD countries. Seven of these 20 total countries spent 4.0 percent or more of GDP on elementary/secondary education. In contrast, 15 countries spent a percentage of GDP on elementary/secondary education that was less than the average of OECD countries.

At the postsecondary level, the percentage of GDP that the United States spent on total government and private expenditures (2.5 percent) was higher than the average of OECD countries (1.5 percent) and higher than the percentages of all other OECD countries reporting data, except for Chile (also 2.5 percent). In addition to the United States and Chile, only two other countries spent 2.0 percent or more of GDP on postsecondary education: Canada (2.3 percent) and Colombia (2.2 percent).

Endnotes:

[1] National Consumer Price Indexes are available at the OECD Online Education Database (https://stats.oecd.org/Index.aspx).

[2] Denmark is excluded from all analyses on expenditures on public and private education institutions per FTE student because expenditure data at the elementary/secondary and postsecondary levels were not available in 2016. Greece and Switzerland are excluded from analyses of expenditures per FTE student at the postsecondary level because 2016 expenditure data were not available for this level.

[3] Throughout this indicator, the "average of OECD countries" refers to the simple average of the individual country values for all reporting OECD countries, to which each country reporting data contributes equally. The average includes all current OECD countries for which a given year's data are available, even if they were not members of the OECD in that year. Countries excluded from analyses in this indicator may be included in the OECD average.

Reference tables: *Digest of Education Statistics 2019*, tables 605.10 and 605.20

Related indicators and resources: International Educational Attainment; Public School Expenditures

Glossary: Constant dollars; Consumer Price Index (CPI); Elementary school; Expenditures per pupil; Full-time-equivalent (FTE) enrollment; Gross domestic product (GDP); International Standard Classification of Education (ISCED); Organization for Economic Cooperation and Development (OECD); Postsecondary education; Purchasing Power Parity (PPP) indexes; Secondary school

Guide to Sources

National Center for Education Statistics (NCES)

Common Core of Data

The Common Core of Data (CCD) is NCES's primary database on public elementary and secondary education in the United States. It is a comprehensive, annual, national statistical database of all public elementary and secondary schools and school districts containing data designed to be comparable across all states. This database can be used to select samples for other NCES surveys and provide basic information and descriptive statistics on public elementary and secondary schools and schooling in general.

The CCD collects statistical information annually from approximately 100,000 public elementary and secondary schools and approximately 18,000 public school districts (including supervisory unions and regional education service agencies) in the 50 states, the District of Columbia, the Department of Defense Education Activity (DoDEA), the Bureau of Indian Education (BIE), Puerto Rico, American Samoa, Guam, the Northern Mariana Islands, and the U.S. Virgin Islands. Three categories of information are collected in the CCD survey: general descriptive information on schools and school districts, data on students and staff, and fiscal data. The general school and district descriptive information includes name, address, and phone number; the data on students and staff include selected demographic characteristics; and the fiscal data pertain to revenues and current expenditures.

The EDFacts data collection system is the primary collection tool for the CCD. NCES works collaboratively with the Department of Education's Performance Information Management Service to develop the CCD collection procedures and data definitions. Coordinators from state education agencies (SEAs) submit the CCD data at different levels (school, agency, and state) to the EDFacts collection system. Prior to submitting CCD files to EDFacts, SEAs must collect and compile information from their respective local education agencies (LEAs) through established administrative records systems within their state or jurisdiction.

Once SEAs have completed their submissions, the CCD survey staff analyzes and verifies the data for quality assurance. Even though the CCD is a universe collection and thus not subject to sampling errors, nonsampling errors can occur. The two potential sources of nonsampling errors are nonresponse and inaccurate reporting. NCES attempts to minimize nonsampling errors through the use of annual training of SEA coordinators, extensive quality reviews, and survey editing procedures. In addition, each year SEAs are given the opportunity to revise their state-level aggregates from the previous survey cycle.

The NCES Education Demographic and Geographic Estimate (EDGE) program develops annually updated point locations (latitude and longitude) for public elementary and secondary schools included in the CCD database. The estimated location of schools and agency administrative offices is primarily derived from the physical address reported in the CCD directory files. The NCES EDGE program collaborates with the U.S. Census Bureau's EDGE Branch to develop point locations for schools reported in the annual CCD directory file. For more information about NCES school point data, please see https://nces.ed.gov/programs/edge/Geographic/SchoolLocations.

The CCD survey consists of five components: The Public Elementary/Secondary School Universe Survey, the Local Education Agency (School District) Universe Survey, the State Nonfiscal Survey of Public Elementary/Secondary Education, the National Public Education Financial Survey (NPEFS), and the School District Finance Survey (F-33).

Public Elementary/Secondary School Universe Survey

The Public Elementary/Secondary School Universe Survey includes all U.S. public schools providing education services to prekindergarten, kindergarten, grades 1–13, and ungraded students.

The Public Elementary/Secondary School Universe Survey includes data for variables such as NCES school ID number, state school ID number, name of the school, name of the agency that operates the school, mailing address, physical location address, phone number, school type, operational status, county number, county name, full-time-equivalent (FTE) classroom teacher count, low/high grade span offered, school level, students eligible for free lunch, students eligible for reduced-price lunch, total students eligible for free and reduced-price lunch, and student totals and detail (by grade, by race/ethnicity, and by sex). The survey also contains flags indicating whether a school is Title I eligible, schoolwide Title I eligible, a magnet school, a charter school, a shared-time school, or a BIE school, as well as which grades are offered at the school.

Local Education Agency (School District) Universe Survey

The coverage of the Local Education Agency Universe Survey includes all school districts and administrative units providing education services to prekindergarten, kindergarten, grades 1–13, and ungraded students.

The Local Education Agency Universe Survey includes the following variables: NCES agency ID number, state agency ID number, agency name, phone number, mailing address, physical location address, agency type code, supervisory union number, American National Standards Institute (ANSI) state and county code, county name, core based statistical area (CBSA), metropolitan/micropolitan code, metropolitan status code, locale code, congressional district, operational status code, BIE agency status, low/high grade span offered, agency charter status, number of schools, number of full-time-equivalent teachers, number of ungraded students, number of PK–13 students, number of special education/Individualized Education Program students, number of English language learner students, instructional staff fields, support staff fields, and LEA charter status.

State Nonfiscal Survey of Public Elementary/Secondary Education

The State Nonfiscal Survey of Public Elementary/Secondary Education provides state-level, aggregate information about students and staff in public elementary and secondary education. This survey covers public school student membership by grade, race/ethnicity, and state or jurisdiction and covers number of staff in public schools by category and state or jurisdiction. Beginning with the 2006–07 school year, the number of diploma recipients and other high school completers were no longer included in the State Nonfiscal Survey of Public Elementary/Secondary Education File. These data are now published in the public-use CCD State Dropout and Completion Data File.

National Public Education Financial Survey

The purpose of the National Public Education Financial Survey (NPEFS) is to provide state-level aggregate data on revenues and expenditures for public elementary and secondary education. The data collected are useful to (1) chief officers of state education agencies; (2) policymakers in the executive and legislative branches of federal and state governments; (3) education policy and public policy researchers; (4) the press; and (5) citizens interested in information about education finance.

Data for NPEFS are collected from SEAs in the 50 states, the District of Columbia, Puerto Rico, American Samoa, Guam, the Northern Mariana Islands, and the U.S. Virgin Islands. The data file is organized by state or jurisdiction and contains revenue data by funding source; expenditure data by function (the activity being supported by the expenditure) and object (the category of expenditure); average daily attendance data; and total student membership data from the CCD State Nonfiscal Survey of Public Elementary/Secondary Education.

School District Finance Survey

The purpose of the School District Finance Survey (F-33) is to provide finance data for all LEAs that provide free public elementary and secondary education in the United States. National and state totals are not included (national- and state-level figures are presented, however, in the National Public Education Financial Survey).

NCES partners with the U.S. Census Bureau in the collection of school district finance data. The Census Bureau distributes Census Form F-33, Annual Survey of School System Finances, to all SEAs, and representatives from the SEAs collect and edit data from their LEAs and submit data to the Census Bureau. The Census Bureau then produces two data files: one for distribution and reporting by NCES and the other for distribution and reporting by the Census Bureau. The files include variables for revenues by source, expenditures by function and object, indebtedness, assets, and student membership counts, as well as identification variables.

The coverage of the F-33 survey is different from the coverage of the NPEFS survey, as NPEFS includes special state-run and federal-run school districts that are not included in the F-33. In addition, variances in data availability between the two surveys may occur in cases where some data are available at the state level but not at the district level, and this might result in state-aggregated district totals from F-33 differing from the state totals in NPEFS. When states submit NPEFS and F-33 data in their own financial accounting formats instead of the NCES-requested format, variances in the state procedures may result in variances in the data. In these instances, Census Bureau analysts design and implement a crosswalk system to conform state-formatted data to the format for variables in the F-33. Also, differences between the two surveys in the reporting of expenditures for similar data items can occur when there are differences in the methodology that the state respondents use to crosswalk their NPEFS or F-33 data. Finally, the imputation and editing processes and procedures of the two surveys can vary. For further detail on imputations and data editing in the F-33 and NPEFS surveys, please see the FY 16 NCES F-33 (Cornman, Ampadu, and Hanak 2019 [NCES 2019-304]) and NPEFS (Cornman et al. 2019 [NCES 2019-302]) survey documentation.

Further information on the nonfiscal CCD data may be obtained from

Patrick Keaton
Elementary and Secondary Branch
Administrative Data Division
National Center for Education Statistics
550 12th Street SW
Washington, DC 20202
patrick.keaton@ed.gov
https://nces.ed.gov/ccd

Further information on the fiscal CCD data may be obtained from

Stephen Cornman
Elementary and Secondary Branch
Administrative Data Division
National Center for Education Statistics
550 12th Street SW
Washington, DC 20202
stephen.cornman@ed.gov
https://nces.ed.gov/ccd

ED*Facts*

ED*Facts* is a centralized data collection through which state education agencies (SEAs) submit PK–12 education data to the U.S. Department of Education (ED). All data in ED*Facts* are organized into "data groups" and reported to ED using defined file specifications. Depending on the data group, SEAs may submit aggregate counts for the state as a whole or detailed counts for individual schools or school districts. ED*Facts* does not collect student-level records. The entities that are required to report ED*Facts* data vary by data group but may include the 50 states, the District of Columbia, the Department of Defense Education Activity, the Bureau of Indian Education, Puerto Rico, American Samoa, Guam, the Northern Mariana Islands, and the U.S. Virgin Islands. More information about ED*Facts* file specifications and data groups can be found at https://www2.ed.gov/about/inits/ed/edfacts/index.html.

ED*Facts* is a universe collection and is not subject to sampling error, although nonsampling errors such as nonresponse and inaccurate reporting may occur. The

U.S. Department of Education attempts to minimize nonsampling errors by training data submission coordinators and reviewing the quality of state data submissions. However, anomalies may still be present in the data.

Differences in state data collection systems may limit the comparability of ED*Facts* data across states and across time. To build ED*Facts* files, SEAs rely on data that were reported by their schools and school districts. The systems used to collect these data are evolving rapidly and differ from state to state.

In some cases, ED*Facts* data may not align with data reported on SEA websites. States may update their websites on schedules different from those they use to report data to ED. Furthermore, ED may use methods for protecting the privacy of individuals represented within the data that could be different from the methods used by an individual state.

ED*Facts* data on English language learners enrolled in public schools are collected in data group 678 within file 141. ED*Facts* 4-year adjusted cohort graduation rate (ACGR) data are collected in data group 695 within file 150 and in data group 696 within file 151. ED*Facts* collects these data groups on behalf of the Office of Elementary and Secondary Education.

For more information about ED*Facts*, please contact

ED*Facts*
Elementary/Secondary Branch
Adminstrative Data Division
National Center for Education Statistics
550 12th Street SW
Washington, DC 20202
EDFacts@ed.gov
https://www2.ed.gov/about/inits/ed/edfacts/index.html

Integrated Postsecondary Education Data System

IPEDS consists of 12 interrelated survey components that provide information on postsecondary institutions and academic libraries at these institutions, student enrollment, student financial aid, programs offered, retention and graduation rates, degrees and certificates conferred, and the human and financial resources involved in the provision of institutionally based postsecondary education. Prior to 2000, the IPEDS survey had the following subject-matter components: Institutional Characteristics; Total Institutional Activity (these data were moved to the Institutional Characteristics component in 1990–91, then to the Fall Enrollment component in 2000–01); Fall Enrollment; Fall Staff; Salaries, Tenure, and Fringe Benefits of Full-Time Faculty; Completions; Finance; Academic Libraries (in 2000, the Academic Libraries component separated from the IPEDS collection); and Graduation Rates. Since 2000, IPEDS survey components occurring in a particular collection year have been organized into three seasonal collection periods: fall, winter, and spring. The Institutional Characteristics and Completions components first took place during the fall 2000 collection. The Employees by Assigned Position (EAP); Salaries, Tenure, and Fringe Benefits of Full-Time Faculty; and Fall Staff components first took place during the winter 2001–02 collection. The Fall Enrollment, Student Financial Aid, Finance, and Graduation Rates components first took place during the spring 2001 collection. In the winter 2005–06 data collection, the EAP; Fall Staff; and Salaries, Tenure, and Fringe Benefits of Full-Time Faculty components were merged into the Human Resources component. During the 2007–08 collection year, the Fall Enrollment component was broken into two components: 12-Month Enrollment (taking place in the fall collection) and Fall Enrollment (taking place in the spring collection). In the 2011–12 IPEDS data collection year, the Student Financial Aid component was moved to the winter data collection to aid in the timing of the net price of attendance calculations displayed on the College Navigator (https://nces.ed.gov/collegenavigator/). In the 2012–13 IPEDS data collection year, the Human Resources component was moved from the winter data collection to the spring data collection, and in the 2013–14 data collection year, the Graduation Rates and Graduation Rates 200 Percent components were moved from the spring data collection to the winter data collection. In the 2014–15 data collection year, a new component (Admissions) was added to IPEDS and a former IPEDS component (Academic Libraries) was reintegrated into IPEDS. The Admissions component, created out of admissions data contained in the fall collection's Institutional Characteristics component, was made a part of the winter collection. The Academic Libraries component, after having been conducted as a survey independent of IPEDS between 2000 and 2012, was reintegrated into IPEDS as part of the spring collection. Finally, in the 2015–16 data collection year, the Outcome Measures survey component was added to IPEDS.

Beginning in 2008–09, the first-professional degree category was combined with the doctor's degree category. However, some degrees formerly identified as first-professional that take more than 2 full-time-equivalent academic years to complete, such as those in Theology (M.Div, M.H.L./Rav), are included in the master's degree category. Doctor's degrees were broken out into three distinct categories: research/scholarship, professional practice, and other doctor's degrees.

The collection of race/ethnicity data also changed in 2008–09. IPEDS now collects a count of students who identify as Hispanic and counts of non-Hispanic students who identify with each race category. The "Asian" race category is now separate from the "Native Hawaiian or Other Pacific Islander" category, and a new category of "Two or more races" has been added.

The degree-granting institutions portion of IPEDS is a census of colleges that award associate's or higher degrees and are eligible to participate in Title IV financial aid programs. Prior to 1993, data from technical and vocational institutions were collected through a sample survey. Beginning in 1993, all data are gathered in a census of all postsecondary institutions. Beginning in 1997, the survey was restricted to institutions participating in Title IV programs.

The classification of institutions offering college and university education changed as of 1996. Prior to 1996, institutions that either had courses leading to an associate's or higher degree or that had courses accepted for credit toward those degrees were considered higher education institutions. Higher education institutions were accredited by an agency or association that was recognized by the U.S. Department of Education or were recognized directly by the Secretary of Education. The newer standard includes institutions that award associate's or higher degrees and that are eligible to participate in Title IV federal financial aid programs. Tables that contain any data according to this standard are titled "degree-granting" institutions. Time-series tables may contain data from both series, and they are noted accordingly. The impact of this change on data collected in 1996 was not large. For example, tables on faculty salaries and benefits were only affected to a very small extent. Also, degrees awarded at the bachelor's level or higher were not heavily affected. The largest impact was on private 2-year college enrollment. In contrast, most of the data on public 4-year colleges were affected to a minimal extent. The impact on enrollment in public 2-year colleges was noticeable in certain states, such as Arizona, Arkansas, Georgia, Louisiana, and Washington, but was relatively small at the national level. Overall, total enrollment for all institutions was about one-half of 1 percent higher in 1996 for degree-granting institutions than for higher education institutions.

Prior to the establishment of IPEDS in 1986, the Higher Education General Information Survey (HEGIS) acquired and maintained statistical data on the characteristics and operations of higher education institutions. Implemented in 1966, HEGIS was an annual universe survey of institutions accredited at the college level by an agency recognized by the Secretary of the U.S. Department of Education. These institutions were listed in NCES's *Education Directory, Colleges and Universities.*

HEGIS surveys collected information on institutional characteristics, faculty salaries, finances, libraries, fall enrollment, student residence and migration, and earned degrees. Since these surveys, like IPEDS, were distributed to all higher education institutions, the data presented are not subject to sampling error. However, they are subject to nonsampling error, the sources of which varied with the survey instrument.

The NCES Taskforce for IPEDS Redesign recognized that there were issues related to the consistency of data definitions as well as the accuracy, reliability, and validity of other quality measures within and across surveys. The IPEDS redesign in 2000 provided institution-specific web-based data forms. While the new system shortened data processing time and provided better data consistency, it did not address the accuracy of the data provided by institutions.

Beginning in 2003–04 with the Prior Year Data Revision System, prior-year data have been available to institutions entering current data. This allows institutions to make changes to their prior-year entries either by adjusting the data or by providing missing data. These revisions allow the evaluation of the data's accuracy by looking at the changes made.

NCES conducted a study (NCES 2005-175) of the 2002–03 data that were revised in 2003–04 to determine the accuracy of the imputations, track the institutions that submitted revised data, and analyze the revised data they submitted. When institutions made changes to their data, NCES accepted that the revised data were the most accurate, correct, and "true" data. The data were analyzed for the number and type of institutions making changes, the type of changes, the magnitude of the changes, and the impact on published data.

Because NCES imputes for missing data, imputation procedures were also addressed by the Redesign Taskforce. For the 2003–04 assessment, differences between revised values and values that were imputed in the original files were compared (i.e., revised value minus imputed value). These differences were then used to provide an assessment of the effectiveness of imputation procedures. The size of the differences also provides an indication of the accuracy

of imputation procedures. To assess the overall impact of changes on aggregate IPEDS estimates, published tables for each component were reconstructed using the revised 2002–03 data. These reconstructed tables were then compared to the published tables to determine the magnitude of aggregate bias and the direction of this bias.

Since the 2000–01 data collection year, IPEDS data collections have been web based. Data have been provided by "keyholders," institutional representatives appointed by campus chief executives, who are responsible for ensuring that survey data submitted by the institution are correct and complete. Because Title IV institutions are the primary focus of IPEDS and because these institutions are required to respond to IPEDS, response rates for Title IV institutions have been high (data on specific components are cited below). More details on the accuracy and reliability of IPEDS data can be found in the *Integrated Postsecondary Education Data System Data Quality Study* (NCES 2005-175).

Further information on IPEDS may be obtained from

Samuel Barbett
Postsecondary Branch
Administrative Data Division
National Center for Education Statistics
550 12th Street SW
Washington, DC 20202
samuel.barbett@ed.gov
https://nces.ed.gov/ipeds/

Fall (12-Month Enrollment)

The 12-month period during which data are collected is July 1 through June 30. Data are collected by race/ethnicity, gender, and level of study (undergraduate or postbaccalaureate) and include unduplicated headcounts and instructional activity (contact or credit hours). These data are also used to calculate a full-time-equivalent (FTE) enrollment based on instructional activity. FTE enrollment is useful for gauging the size of the educational enterprise at the institution. Prior to the 2007–08 IPEDS data collection, the data collected in the 12-Month Enrollment component were part of the Fall Enrollment component, which is conducted during the spring data collection period. However, to improve the timeliness of the data, a separate 12-Month Enrollment survey component was developed in 2007. These data are now collected in the fall for the previous academic year. The response rate for the 12-Month Enrollment component of the fall 2018 data collection was nearly 100 percent. Data from 2 of the 6,274 Title

IV institutions that were expected to respond to this component were imputed due to unit nonresponse.

Further information on the IPEDS 12-Month Enrollment component may be obtained from

Tara Lawley
Postsecondary Branch
Administrative Data Division
National Center for Education Statistics
550 12th Street SW
Washington, DC 20202
tara.lawley@ed.gov
https://nces.ed.gov/ipeds/

Fall (Completions)

The Completions component collects data on the number of students who complete a postsecondary education program (completers) and the number of postsecondary awards earned (completions). This component was part of the HEGIS series throughout its existence. However, the degree classification taxonomy was revised in 1970–71, 1982–83, 1991–92, 2002–03, and 2009–10. Collection of degree data has been maintained through IPEDS.

The nonresponse rate does not appear to be a significant source of nonsampling error for this component. The response rate over the years has been high; for the fall 2018 Completions component, it rounded to 100 percent. Data from 1 of the 6,281 Title IV institutions that were expected to respond to this component were imputed due to unit nonresponse.

Further information on the IPEDS Completions component may be obtained from

Tara Lawley
Postsecondary Branch
Administrative Data Division
National Center for Education Statistics
550 12th Street SW
Washington, DC 20202
tara.lawley@ed.gov
https://nces.ed.gov/ipeds/

Fall (Institutional Characteristics)

This survey collects the basic information necessary to classify institutions, including control, level, and types of programs offered, as well as information on tuition, fees, and room and board charges. Beginning in 2000, the survey collected institutional pricing data from institutions with first-time, full-time, degree/certificate-seeking undergraduate students. Unduplicated full-year enrollment

counts and instructional activity are now collected in the 12-Month Enrollment survey. Beginning in 2008–09, the student financial aid data collected include greater detail.

In the fall 2018 data collection, the response rate for Title IV entities on the Institutional Characteristics component was 100 percent. Of the 6,353 Title IV entities that were expected to respond to this component, all provided data.

Further information on the IPEDS Institutional Characteristics component may be obtained from

Moussa Ezzeddine
Postsecondary Branch
Administrative Data Division
National Center for Education Statistics
550 12th Street SW
Washington, DC 20202
moussa.ezzeddine@ed.gov
https://nces.ed.gov/ipeds/

Winter (Student Financial Aid)

This component was part of the spring data collection from IPEDS data collection years 2000–01 to 2010–11, but it moved to the winter data collection starting with the 2011–12 IPEDS data collection year. This move assists with the timing of the net price of attendance calculations displayed on College Navigator (https://nces.ed.gov/collegenavigator/).

Financial aid data are collected for undergraduate students. Data are collected regarding federal grants, state and local government grants, institutional grants, and loans. The collected data include the number of students receiving each type of financial assistance and the average amount of aid received by type of aid. Beginning in 2008–09, student financial aid data collected includes greater detail on types of aid offered.

In the winter 2018–19 data collection, the Student Financial Aid component collected data about financial aid awarded to undergraduate students, with particular emphasis on full-time, first-time degree/certificate-seeking undergraduate students awarded financial aid for the 2017–18 academic year. In addition, the component collected data on undergraduate and graduate students receiving benefits for veterans and members of the military service. Finally, student counts and awarded aid amounts were collected to calculate the net price of attendance for two subsets of full-time, first-time degree/certificate-seeking undergraduate students: those awarded any grant aid, and those awarded Title IV aid.

The response rate for the Student Financial Aid component in 2018–19 was nearly 100 percent. Of the 6,202 Title IV institutions that were expected to respond, responses were missing for 8 institutions, and these missing data were imputed.

Further information on the IPEDS Student Financial Aid component may be obtained from

Tara Lawley
Postsecondary Branch
Administrative Data Division
National Center for Education Statistics
550 12th Street SW
Washington, DC 20202
tara.lawley@ed.gov
https://nces.ed.gov/ipeds/

Winter (Graduation Rates and Graduation Rates 200 Percent)

In IPEDS data collection years 2012–13 and earlier, the Graduation Rates and Graduation Rates 200 Percent components were collected during the spring collection. In the IPEDS 2013–14 data collection year, however, the Graduation Rates and Graduation Rates 200 Percent collections were moved to the winter data collection.

The 2018–19 Graduation Rates component collected counts of full-time, first-time degree/certificate-seeking undergraduate students beginning their postsecondary education in the specified cohort year and their completion status as of 150 percent of normal program completion time at the same institution where the students started. If 150 percent of normal program completion time extended beyond August 31, 2018, the counts as of that date were collected. Four-year institutions used 2012 as the cohort year, while less-than-4-year institutions used 2015 as the cohort year. Four-year institutions also report for full-time, first-time bachelor's degree-seeking undergraduate students.

Starting with the 2016–17 Graduation Rates component, two new subcohort groups—students who received Pell Grants and students who received a subsidized Direct loan and did not receive Pell Grants—were added.

Of the 5,596 institutions that were expected to respond to the Graduation Rates component, responses were missing for 7 institutions, and these missing data were imputed.

The 2018–19 Graduation Rates 200 Percent component was designed to combine information reported in a prior collection via the Graduation Rates component with current information about the same cohort of students. From previously collected data, the following counts were obtained: the number of students entering the institution as full-time, first-time degree/certificate-seeking students in a cohort year; the number of students in this cohort completing within 100 and 150 percent of normal program completion time; and the number of cohort exclusions (such as students who left for military service). Then the number of additional cohort exclusions and additional program completers between 151 and 200 percent of normal program completion time was collected. Four-year institutions reported on bachelor's or equivalent degree-seeking students and used cohort year 2010 as the reference period, while less-than-4-year institutions reported on all students in the cohort and used cohort year 2014 as the reference period. Of the 5,203 institutions that were expected to respond to the Graduation Rates 200 Percent component, responses were missing for 4 institutions, and these missing data were imputed.

Further information on the IPEDS Graduation Rates and Graduation Rates 200 Percent components may be obtained from

Andrew Mary
Postsecondary Branch
Administrative Data Division
National Center for Education Statistics
550 12th Street SW
Washington, DC 20202
andrew.mary@ed.gov
https://nces.ed.gov/ipeds/

Winter (Admissions)

In the 2014–15 survey year, an Admissions component was added to the winter data collection. This component was created out of the admissions data that had previously been a part of the fall Institutional Characteristics component. Situating these data in a new component in the winter collection enables all institutions to report data for the most recent fall period.

The Admissions component collects information about the selection process for entering first-time degree/certificate-seeking undergraduate students. Data obtained from institutions include admissions considerations (e.g., secondary school records, admission test scores), the number of first-time degree/certificate-seeking undergraduate students who applied, the number admitted, and the number enrolled. Admissions data were collected only from institutions that do not have an open admissions policy for entering first-time students.

Data collected for the IPEDS winter 2018–19 Admissions component relate to individuals applying to be admitted during the fall of the 2018–19 academic year (the fall 2018 reporting period). Of the 2,021 Title IV institutions that were expected to respond to the Admissions component, all responded.

Further information on the IPEDS Admissions component may be obtained from

Moussa Ezzeddine
Postsecondary Branch
Administrative Data Division
National Center for Education Statistics
550 12th Street SW
Washington, DC 20202
moussa.ezzeddine@ed.gov
https://nces.ed.gov/ipeds/

Spring (Fall Enrollment)

This survey has been part of the HEGIS and IPEDS series since 1966. Response rates have been relatively high, generally exceeding 85 percent. Beginning in 2000, with web-based data collection, higher response rates were attained. In the spring 2019 data collection, in which the Fall Enrollment component covered student enrollment in fall 2018, the response rate was greater than 99 percent. Of the 6,267 institutions that were expected to respond, 6 institutions did not respond, and these data were imputed.

Beginning with the fall 1986 survey and the introduction of IPEDS (see above), a redesign of the survey resulted in the collection of data by race/ethnicity, gender, level of study (i.e., undergraduate and graduate), and attendance status (i.e., full-time and part-time). Other aspects of the survey include allowing (in alternating years) for the collection of age and residence data. The Fall Enrollment component also collects data on first-time retention rates, student-to-faculty ratios, and student enrollment in distance education courses. Finally, in even-numbered years, 4-year institutions provide enrollment data by level of study, race/ethnicity, and gender for nine selected fields of study or Classification of Instructional Programs (CIP) codes. (The CIP is a taxonomic coding scheme that contains titles and descriptions of primarily postsecondary instructional programs.)

Beginning in 2000, the survey collected instructional activity and unduplicated headcount data, which are needed to compute a standardized, full-time-equivalent (FTE) enrollment statistic for the entire academic year. As of 2007–08, the timeliness of the instructional activity data has been improved by collecting these data in the fall as part of the 12-Month Enrollment component instead of in the spring as part of the Fall Enrollment component.

Further information on the IPEDS Fall Enrollment component may be obtained from

Tara Lawley
Postsecondary Branch
Administrative Data Division
National Center for Education Statistics
550 12th Street SW
Washington, DC 20202
tara.lawley@ed.gov
https://nces.ed.gov/ipeds/

Spring (Finance)

This survey was part of the HEGIS series and has been continued under IPEDS. Substantial changes were made in the financial survey instruments in fiscal year (FY) 1976, FY 1982, FY 1987, FY 1997, and FY 2002. While these changes were significant, a considerable effort has been made to present only comparable information on trends and to note inconsistencies. The FY 1976 survey instrument contained numerous revisions to earlier survey forms, which made direct comparisons of line items very difficult. Beginning in FY 1982, Pell Grant data were collected in the categories of federal restricted grant and contract revenues and restricted scholarship and fellowship expenditures. The introduction of IPEDS in the FY 1987 survey included several important changes to the survey instrument and data processing procedures. Beginning in FY 1997, data for private institutions were collected using new financial concepts consistent with Financial Accounting Standards Board (FASB) reporting standards, which provide a more comprehensive view of college finance activities. The data for public institutions continued to be collected using the older survey form. The data for public and private institutions were no longer comparable and, as a result, no longer presented together in analysis tables. In FY 2001, public institutions had the option of either continuing to report using Government Accounting Standards Board (GASB) standards or using the new FASB reporting standards. Beginning in FY 2002, public institutions could use either the original GASB standards, the FASB standards, or the new GASB Statement 35 standards (GASB35). Beginning in FY 2004, public institutions could no longer submit survey forms based on the original GASB standards. Beginning in FY 2008, public institutions could submit their GASB survey forms using a revised structure that was modified for better comparability with the IPEDS FASB finance forms, or the institutions could use the structure of the prior forms used from FY 2004 to FY 2007. Similarly, in FY 2008, private nonprofit institutions and public institutions using the FASB form were given an opportunity to report using the forms that had been modified to improve comparability with the GASB forms, or they could use forms with a structure that was consistent with the prior years. In FY 2010, the use of the forms with the older structure was discontinued, and all institutions used either the GASB and FASB forms that had been modified for comparability. Also, in FY 2010, a new series of forms was introduced for non-degree-granting institutions that included versions for for-profit, FASB, and GASB reporting institutions. From FY 2000 through FY 2013, private for-profit institutions used a version of the FASB form with much less detail than the FASB form used by private nonprofit institutions. As of FY 2014, however, private for-profit institutions have been required to report the same level of detail as private nonprofit institutions.

Possible sources of nonsampling error in the financial statistics include nonresponse, imputation, and misclassification. The unweighted response rate has been about 85 to 90 percent for most of the years these data appeared in NCES reports; however, in more recent years, response rates have been much higher because Title IV institutions are required to respond. Since 2002, the IPEDS data collection has been a full-scale web-based collection, which has improved the quality and timeliness of the data. For example, the ability of IPEDS to tailor online data entry forms for each institution based on characteristics such as institutional control, level of institution, and calendar system and the institutions' ability to submit their data online are aspects of full-scale web-based collections that have improved response.

The response rate for the FY 2018 Finance component was greater than 99 percent: Of the 6,341 institutions and administrative offices that were expected to respond, 10 did not respond, and these missing data were imputed.

Further information on the IPEDS Finance component may be obtained from

Samuel Barbett
Postsecondary Branch
Administrative Data Division
National Center for Education Statistics
550 12th Street SW
Washington, DC 20202
samuel.barbett@ed.gov
https://nces.ed.gov/ipeds/

Spring (Human Resources)

The Human Resources component was part of the IPEDS winter data collection from data collection years 2000–01 to 2011–12. For the 2012–13 data collection year, the Human Resources component was moved to the spring 2013 data collection in order to give institutions more time to prepare their survey responses.

IPEDS Collection Years, 2012–13 to Present

In 2012–13, new occupational categories replaced the primary function/occupational activity categories previously used in the IPEDS Human Resources component. This change was required in order to align the IPEDS Human Resources categories with the 2010 Standard Occupational Classification (SOC) system. In tandem with the change in 2012–13 from using primary function/occupational activity categories to using the new occupational categories, the sections making up the IPEDS Human Resources component (which previously had been Employees by Assigned Position, Fall Staff, and Salaries) were changed to Full-Time Instructional Staff, Full-time Noninstructional Staff, Salaries, Part-Time Staff, and New Hires.

The web pages "Archived Changes—Changes to IPEDS Data Collections, 2012–13" (https://nces.ed.gov/ipeds/InsidePages/ArchivedChanges?year=2012-13) and "2012–13 IPEDS Human Resources (HR) Occupational Categories Compared with 2011–12 IPEDS HR Primary Function/Occupational Activity Categories" (https://nces.ed.gov/ipeds/resource/download/IPEDS_HR_2012-13_compared_to_IPEDS_HR_2011-12.pdf) provide information on the redesign of the IPEDS Human Resources component initiated in the 2012–13 data collection year.

In 2018, an update to the Standard Occupational Classification (SOC) system was released. As a consequence, revisions were made to the occupational categories in the Human Resources component in the IPEDS spring 2019 data collection. These revisions are described on the web page "Resources for Implementing Changes to the IPEDS Human Resources (HR) Survey Component Due to Updated 2018 Standard Occupational Classification (SOC) System" (https://nces.ed.gov/ipeds/report-your-data/taxonomies-standard-occupational-classification-soc-codes).

In the IPEDS spring 2019 data collection, the response rate for the Human Resources component was greater than 99 percent. Of the 6,339 institutions and administrative offices that were expected to respond, 7 institutions did not respond, and these missing data were imputed.

IPEDS Collection Years Prior to 2012–13

In collection years before 2001–02, IPEDS conducted a Fall Staff survey and a Salaries survey; in the 2001–02 collection year, the Employees by Assigned Position (EAP) survey was added to IPEDS. In the 2005–06 collection year, these three surveys became sections of the IPEDS "Human Resources" component.

Data gathered by the EAP section categorized all employees by full- or part-time status, faculty status, and primary function/occupational activity. Institutions with M.D. or D.O. programs were required to report their medical school employees separately. A response to the EAP was required of all 6,858 Title IV institutions and administrative offices in the United States and other jurisdictions for winter 2008–09, and 6,845, or 99.8 percent unweighted, responded. Of the 6,970 Title IV institutions and administrative offices required to respond to the winter 2009–10 EAP, 6,964, or 99.9 percent, responded. Of the 7,256 Title IV institutions and administrative offices required to respond to the EAP for winter 2010–11, about 99.9 percent responded. In the original winter 2010–11 data collection, 7,252 responded to the EAP and data for the 4 nonrespondents were imputed; the next year, 1 of the nonrespondents whose data were imputed submitted a revision.

The main functions/occupational activities of the EAP section were primarily instruction, instruction combined with research and/or public service, primarily research, primarily public service, executive/administrative/managerial, other professionals (support/service), graduate assistants, technical and paraprofessionals, clerical and secretarial, skilled crafts, and service/maintenance.

All full-time instructional faculty classified in the EAP full-time nonmedical school part as either (1) primarily instruction or (2) instruction combined with research and/or public service were included in the Salaries section, unless they were exempt.

The Fall Staff section categorized all staff on the institution's payroll as of November 1 of the collection year by employment status (full time or part time), primary function/occupational activity, gender, and race/ethnicity. Title IV institutions and administrative offices were only required to respond to the Fall Staff section in odd-numbered reporting years, so they were not required to respond during the 2008–09 Human Resources data collection. However, of the 6,858 Title IV institutions and administrative offices in the United States and other jurisdictions, 3,295, or 48.0 percent unweighted, did provide data in the Fall Staff section that year. During the 2009–10 Human Resources data collection, when all 6,970 Title IV institutions and administrative offices were required to respond to the Fall Staff section, 6,964, or 99.9 percent, did so. A response to the Fall Staff section of the 2010–11 Human Resources collection was optional, and 3,364 Title IV institutions and administrative offices responded that year (a response rate of 46.3 percent).

The Salaries section collected data for full-time instructional faculty (except those in medical schools in the EAP section, described above) on the institution's payroll as of November 1 of the collection year by contract length/teaching period, gender, and academic rank. The reporting of data by faculty status in the Salaries section was required from 4-year degree-granting institutions and above only. Salary outlays and fringe benefits were also collected for full-time instructional staff on 9/10- and 11/12-month contracts/teaching periods. This section was applicable to degree-granting institutions unless exempt.

Between 1966–67 and 1985–86, this survey differed from other HEGIS surveys in that imputations were not made for nonrespondents. Thus, there is some possibility that the salary averages presented in this report may differ from the results of a complete enumeration of all colleges and universities. Beginning with the surveys for 1987–88, the IPEDS data tabulation procedures included imputations for survey nonrespondents. The unweighted response rate for the 2008–09 Salaries survey section was 99.9 percent. The response rate for the 2009–10 Salaries section was 100.0 percent (4,453 of the 4,455 required institutions responded), and the response rate for 2010–11 was 99.9 percent (4,561 of the 4,565 required institutions responded). Imputation methods for the 2010–11 Salaries survey section are discussed in *Employees in Postsecondary Institutions, Fall 2010, and Salaries of Full-Time Instructional Staff, 2010–11* (NCES 2012-276).

Further information on the Human Resources component may be obtained from

Samuel Barbett
Postsecondary Branch
Administrative Data Division
National Center for Education Statistics
550 12th Street SW
Washington, DC 20202
samuel.barbett@ed.gov
https://nces.ed.gov/ipeds/

National Assessment of Educational Progress

The National Assessment of Educational Progress (NAEP) is a series of cross-sectional studies initially implemented in 1969 to assess the educational achievement of U.S. students and monitor changes in those achievements. In the main national NAEP, a nationally representative sample of students is assessed at grades 4, 8, and 12 in various academic subjects. The assessment is based on frameworks developed by the National Assessment Governing Board (NAGB). It includes both multiple-choice items and constructed-response items (those requiring written answers). Results are reported in two ways: by average score and by achievement level. Average scores are reported for the nation, for participating states and jurisdictions, and for subgroups of the population. Percentages of students performing at or above three achievement levels (*Basic*, *Proficient*, and *Advanced*) are also reported for these groups.

Main NAEP Assessments

From 1990 until 2001, main NAEP was conducted for states and other jurisdictions that chose to participate. In 2002, under the provisions of the No Child Left Behind Act of 2001, all states began to participate in main NAEP, and an aggregate of all state samples replaced the separate national sample. (School district-level assessments—under the Trial Urban District Assessment [TUDA] program—also began in 2002.)

Results are available for the mathematics assessments administered in 2000, 2003, 2005, 2007, 2009, 2011, 2013, 2015, and 2017. In 2005, NAGB called for the development of a new mathematics framework. The revisions made to the mathematics framework for the 2005 assessment were intended to reflect recent curricular emphases and better assess the specific objectives for students at each grade level.

The revised mathematics framework focuses on two dimensions: mathematical content and cognitive demand. By considering these two dimensions for each item in the assessment, the framework ensures that NAEP assesses an appropriate balance of content, as well as a variety of ways of knowing and doing mathematics.

Since the 2005 changes to the mathematics framework were minimal for grades 4 and 8, comparisons over time can be made between assessments conducted before and after the framework's implementation for these grades. The changes that the 2005 framework made to the grade 12 assessment, however, were too drastic to allow grade 12 results from before and after implementation to be directly compared. These changes included adding more questions on algebra, data analysis, and probability to reflect changes in high school mathematics standards and coursework; merging the measurement and geometry content areas; and changing the reporting scale from 0–500 to 0–300. For more information regarding the 2005 mathematics framework revisions, see https://nces.ed.gov/nationsreportcard/mathematics/frameworkcomparison.asp.

Results are available for the reading assessments administered in 2000, 2002, 2003, 2005, 2007, 2009, 2011, 2013, 2015, and 2017. In 2009, a new framework was developed for the 4th-, 8th-, and 12th-grade NAEP reading assessments.

Both a content alignment study and a reading trend, or bridge, study were conducted to determine whether the new reading assessment was comparable to the prior assessment. Overall, the results of the special analyses suggested that the assessments were similar in terms of their item and scale characteristics and the results they produced for important demographic groups of students. Thus, it was determined that the results of the 2009 reading assessment could still be compared to those from earlier assessment years, thereby maintaining the trend lines first established in 1992. For more information regarding the 2009 reading framework revisions, see https://nces.ed.gov/nationsreportcard/reading/whatmeasure.asp.

In spring 2013, NAEP released results from the NAEP 2012 economics assessment in *The Nation's Report Card: Economics 2012* (NCES 2013-453). First administered in 2006, the NAEP economics assessment measures 12th-graders' understanding of a wide range of topics in three main content areas: market economy, national economy, and international economy. The 2012 assessment is based on a nationally representative sample of nearly 11,000 students in the 12th grade.

In *The Nation's Report Card: A First Look—2013 Mathematics and Reading* (NCES 2014-451), NAEP released the results of the 2013 mathematics and reading assessments. Results can also be accessed using the interactive graphics and downloadable data available at the online Nation's Report Card website (https://nationsreportcard.gov/reading_math_2013/).

The Nation's Report Card: A First Look—2013 Mathematics and Reading Trial Urban District Assessment (NCES 2014-466) provides the results of the 2013 mathematics and reading TUDA, which measured the reading and mathematics progress of 4th- and 8th-graders from 21 urban school districts. Results from the 2013 mathematics and reading TUDA can also be accessed using the interactive graphics and downloadable data available at the online TUDA website (https://nationsreportcard.gov/reading_math_tuda_2013/).

The online interactive report *The Nation's Report Card: 2014 U.S. History, Geography, and Civics at Grade 8* (NCES 2015-112) provides grade 8 results for the 2014 NAEP U.S. history, geography, and civics assessments. Trend results for previous assessment years in these three subjects, as well as information on school and student participation rates and sample tasks and student responses, are also presented.

In 2014, the first administration of the NAEP Technology and Engineering Literacy (TEL) Assessment asked 8th-graders to respond to questions aimed at assessing their knowledge and skill in understanding technological principles, solving technology and engineering-related problems, and using technology to communicate and collaborate. The online report *The Nation's Report Card: Technology and Engineering Literacy* (NCES 2016-119) presents national results for 8th-graders on the TEL assessment.

The Nation's Report Card: 2015 Mathematics and Reading Assessments (NCES 2015-136) is an online interactive report that presents national and state results for 4th- and 8th-graders on the NAEP 2015 mathematics and reading assessments. The report also presents TUDA results in mathematics and reading for 4th- and 8th-graders. The online interactive report *The Nation's Report Card: 2015 Mathematics and Reading at Grade 12* (NCES 2016-018) presents grade 12 results from the NAEP 2015 mathematics and reading assessments.

Results from the 2015 NAEP science assessment are presented in the online report *The Nation's Report Card: 2015 Science at Grades 4, 8, and 12* (NCES 2016-162). The assessment measures the knowledge of 4th-, 8th-, and 12th-graders in the content areas of physical science, life science, and Earth and space sciences, as well as their understanding of four science practices (identifying science principles, using science principles, using scientific inquiry, and using technological design). National results are reported for grades 4, 8, and 12, and results from 46 participating states and one jurisdiction are reported for grades 4 and 8. Since a new NAEP science framework was introduced in 2009, results from the 2015 science assessment can be compared to results from the 2009 and 2011 science assessments, but cannot be compared to the science assessments conducted prior to 2009.

As a consequence of NAEP's transition from paper-based assessments to technology-based assessments, data were needed regarding students' access to and familiarity with technology, at home and at school. The Computer Access and Familiarity Study (CAFS) was designed to fulfill this need. CAFS was conducted as part of the main administration of the 2015 NAEP. A subset of the grade 4, 8, and 12 students who took the main NAEP were chosen to take the additional CAFS questionnaire. The main 2015 NAEP was administered in a paper-and-pencil format to some students and a digital-based format to others, and CAFS participants were given questionnaires in the same format as their NAEP questionnaires.

The online Highlights report *2017 NAEP Mathematics and Reading Assessments: Highlighted Results at Grades 4 and 8 for the Nation, States, and Districts* (NCES 2018-037) presents an overview of results from the NAEP 2017 mathematics and reading reports. Highlighted results include key findings for the nation, states/jurisdictions, and

27 districts that participated in the Trial Urban District Assessment (TUDA) in mathematics and reading at grades 4 and 8.

Results from the NAEP 2018 TEL Assessment are contained in the online report *The Nation's Report Card: Highlighted Results for the 2018 Technology and Engineering Literacy (TEL) Assessment at Grade 8* (NCES 2019-068). The digitally based assessment (participants took the assessment via laptop) was taken by approximately 15,400 eighth-graders from about 600 schools across the nation. Results were reported in terms of average scale scores (on a 0 to 300 scale) and in relation to the NAEP achievement levels *NAEP Basic*, *NAEP Proficient*, and *NAEP Advanced*.

The online reports *2019 NAEP Reading Assessment: Highlighted Results at Grades 4 and 8 for the Nation, States, and Districts* and *2019 NAEP Mathematics Assessment: Highlighted Results at Grades 4 and 8 for the Nation, States, and Districts* (NCES 2020-012) present overviews of results from the NAEP 2019 reading and mathematics reports. Highlighted results include key findings for the nation, states/jurisdictions, and 27 districts that participated in the Trial Urban District Assessment (TUDA) in mathematics and reading at grades 4 and 8.

NAEP Long-Term Trend Assessments

In addition to conducting the main assessments, NAEP also conducts the long-term trend assessments. Long-term trend assessments provide an opportunity to observe educational progress in reading and mathematics of 9-, 13-, and 17-year-olds since the early 1970s. The long-term trend reading assessment measures students' reading comprehension skills using an array of passages that vary by text types and length. The assessment was designed to measure students' ability to locate specific information in the text provided; make inferences across a passage to provide an explanation; and identify the main idea in the text.

The NAEP long-term trend assessment in mathematics measures knowledge of mathematical facts; ability to carry out computations using paper and pencil; knowledge of basic formulas, such as those applied in geometric settings; and ability to apply mathematics to skills of daily life, such as those involving time and money.

The Nation's Report Card: Trends in Academic Progress 2012 (NCES 2013-456) provides the results of 12 long-term trend reading assessments dating back to 1971 and 11 long-term trend mathematics assessments dating back to 1973.

Further information on NAEP may be obtained from

Daniel McGrath
Reporting and Dissemination Branch
Assessments Division
National Center for Education Statistics
550 12th Street SW
Washington, DC 20202
daniel.mcgrath@ed.gov
https://nces.ed.gov/nationsreportcard

National Postsecondary Student Aid Study

The National Postsecondary Student Aid Study
(NPSAS) is a comprehensive nationwide study of how
students and their families pay for postsecondary
education. Data gathered from the study are used to
help guide future federal student financial aid policy.
The study covers nationally representative samples of
undergraduates, graduates, and first-professional students
in the 50 states, the District of Columbia, and Puerto
Rico, including students attending less-than-2-year
institutions, community colleges, and 4-year colleges
and universities. Participants include students who do
not receive aid and those who do receive financial aid.
Since NPSAS identifies nationally representative samples
of student subpopulations of interest to policymakers
and obtains baseline data for longitudinal study of these
subpopulations, data from the study provide the base-year
sample for the Beginning Postsecondary Students (BPS)
longitudinal study and the Baccalaureate and Beyond
(B&B) longitudinal study.

Originally, NPSAS was conducted every 3 years.
Beginning with the 1999–2000 study (NPSAS:2000),
NPSAS has been conducted every 4 years. NPSAS:08
included a new set of instrument items to obtain baseline
measures of the awareness of two new federal grants
introduced in 2006: the Academic Competitiveness Grant
(ACG) and the National Science and Mathematics Access
to Retain Talent (SMART) grant.

The first NPSAS (NPSAS:87) was conducted during the
1986–87 school year. Data were gathered from about
1,100 colleges, universities, and other postsecondary
institutions; 60,000 students; and 14,000 parents. These
data provided information on the cost of postsecondary
education, the distribution of financial aid, and the
characteristics of both aided and nonaided students and
their families.

For NPSAS:93, information on 77,000 undergraduates
and graduate students enrolled during the school year was
collected at 1,000 postsecondary institutions. The sample

included students who were enrolled at any time between
July 1, 1992, and June 30, 1993. About 66,000 students
and a subsample of their parents were interviewed by
telephone. NPSAS:96 contained information on more
than 48,000 undergraduate and graduate students
from about 1,000 postsecondary institutions who were
enrolled at any time during the 1995–96 school year.
NPSAS:2000 included nearly 62,000 students (50,000
undergraduates and almost 12,000 graduate students)
from 1,000 postsecondary institutions. NPSAS:04
collected data on about 80,000 undergraduates and
11,000 graduate students from 1,400 postsecondary
institutions. For NPSAS:08, about 114,000 undergraduate
students and 14,000 graduate students who were enrolled
in postsecondary education during the 2007–08 school
year were selected from more than 1,730 postsecondary
institutions.

NPSAS:12 sampled about 95,000 undergraduates and
16,000 graduate students from approximately 1,500
postsecondary institutions. Public access to the data is
available online through PowerStats (https://nces.ed.gov/
datalab/).

NPSAS:16 sampled about 89,000 undergraduate and
24,000 graduate students attending approximately
1,800 Title IV eligible postsecondary institutions in the
50 states, the District of Columbia, and Puerto Rico. The
sample represents approximately 20 million undergraduate
and 4 million graduate students enrolled in postsecondary
education at Title IV eligible institutions at any time
between July 1, 2015, and June 30, 2016.

Further information on NPSAS may be obtained from

Aurora D'Amico
Tracy Hunt-White
Longitudinal Surveys Branch
Sample Surveys Division
National Center for Education Statistics
550 12th Street SW
Washington, DC 20202
aurora.damico@ed.gov
tracy.hunt-white@ed.gov
https://nces.ed.gov/npsas

National Teacher and Principal Survey (NTPS)

The National Teacher and Principal Survey is a set of
related questionnaires that collect descriptive data on the
context of elementary and secondary education. Data
reported by schools, principals, and teachers provide a
variety of statistics on the condition of education in the
United States that may be used by policymakers and the

general public. The NTPS system covers a wide range of topics, including teacher demand, teacher and principal characteristics, teachers' and principals' perceptions of school climate and problems in their schools, teacher and principal compensation, district hiring and retention practices, general conditions in schools, and basic characteristics of the student population.

The NTPS is a redesign of the Schools and Staffing Survey (SASS), which was conducted from the 1987–88 school year to the 2011–12 school year. Although the NTPS maintains the SASS survey's focus on schools, teachers, and administrators, the NTPS has a different structure and sample than SASS. In addition, whereas SASS operated on a 4-year survey cycle, the NTPS operates on a 2-year survey cycle. The NTPS universe of schools is confined to the 50 states plus the District of Columbia. It excludes the Department of Defense dependents schools overseas, schools in U.S. territories overseas, and CCD schools that do not offer teacher-provided classroom instruction in grades 1–12 or the ungraded equivalent. Bureau of Indian Education schools are included in the NTPS universe, but these schools were not oversampled and the data do not support separate BIE estimates.

The NTPS includes three key components: school questionnaires, principal questionnaires, and teacher questionnaires. NTPS data are collected by the U.S. Census Bureau through mail and online questionnaires with telephone and in-person field follow-up. The school and principal questionnaires were sent to sampled schools, and the teacher questionnaire was sent to a sample of teachers working at sampled schools.

The school questionnaire asks knowledgeable school staff members about grades offered, student attendance and enrollment, staffing patterns, teaching vacancies, programs and services offered, curriculum, and community service requirements. In addition, basic information is collected about the school year, including the beginning time of students' school days and the length of the school year.

The principal questionnaire collects information about principal/school head demographic characteristics, training, experience, salary, goals for the school, and judgments about school working conditions and climate. Information is also obtained on professional development opportunities for teachers and principals, teacher performance, barriers to dismissal of underperforming teachers, school climate and safety, parent/guardian participation in school events, and attitudes about educational goals and school governance.

The teacher questionnaire collects data from teachers about their current teaching assignment, workload, education history, and perceptions and attitudes about teaching. Questions are also asked about teacher preparation, induction, organization of classes, computers, and professional development.

The NTPS was first conducted during the 2015–16 school year. The school sample for the 2015–16 NTPS was based on an adjusted public school universe file from the 2013–14 Common Core of Data (CCD), a database of all the nation's public school districts and public schools. (The NTPS definition of a school is the same as the SASS definition of a school—an institution or part of an institution that provides classroom instruction to students, has one or more teachers to provide instruction, serves students in one or more of grades 1–12 or the ungraded equivalent, and is located in one or more buildings apart from a private home.)

In the 2015–16 NTPS, the school sample consisted of about 8,300 public schools; the principal sample consisted of about 8,300 public school principals; and the teacher sample consisted of about 50,000 public school teachers. Weighted unit response rates were 72.5 percent for the school survey, 71.8 percent for the principal survey, and 67.8 percent for the teacher survey.

Whereas the 2015–16 NTPS covered only schools, teachers, and principals in the public sector, the 2017–18 NTPS covered schools, teachers, and principals in both the public and private sectors. In the 2017–18 NTPS, all principals associated with sampled public and private schools were also included in the sample. Teachers associated with a selected school were sampled from a list of teachers that was provided by the school, collected from school websites, or purchased from a vendor. The selected samples included about 10,600 traditional and charter public schools and their principals, 60,000 public school teachers, 4,000 private schools and their principals, and 9,600 private school teachers.

Weighted unit response rates for the 2017–18 NTPS were 72.5 percent for the public school survey and 64.5 percent for the private school survey, 70.2 percent for the public school principal survey and 62.6 percent for the private school principal survey, and 76.9 percent for the public school teacher survey and 75.9 percent for the private school teacher survey.

General information on NTPS and electronic copies of the questionnaires are available at the NTPS home page (https://nces.ed.gov/surveys/ntps).

For additional information about the NTPS program, please contact

Maura Spiegelman
Cross-Sectional Surveys Branch
Sample Surveys Division
National Center for Education Statistics
550 12th Street SW
Washington, DC 20202
maura.spiegelman@ed.gov
https://nces.ed.gov/surveys/ntps

Private School Universe Survey

The purposes of the Private School Universe Survey (PSS) data collection activities are (1) to build an accurate and complete list of private schools to serve as a sampling frame for NCES sample surveys of private schools and (2) to report data on the total number of private schools, teachers, and students in the survey universe. Since its inception in 1989, the survey has been conducted every 2 years. Selected findings from the 2015–16 PSS are presented in the First Look report *Characteristics of Private Schools in the United States: Results From the 2017–18 Private School Universe Survey* (NCES 2019-071).

The PSS produces data similar to that of the Common Core of Data for public schools, and can be used for public-private comparisons. The data are useful for a variety of policy- and research-relevant issues, such as the growth of religiously affiliated schools, the number of private high school graduates, the length of the school year for various private schools, and the number of private school students and teachers.

The target population for this universe survey is all private schools in the United States that meet the PSS criteria of a private school (i.e., the private school is an institution that provides instruction for any of grades K through 12, has one or more teachers to give instruction, is not administered by a public agency, and is not operated in a private home).

The survey universe is composed of schools identified from a variety of sources. The main source is a list frame initially developed for the 1989–90 PSS. The list is updated regularly by matching it with lists provided by nationwide private school associations, state departments of education, and other national guides and sources that list private schools. The other source is an area frame search in approximately 124 geographic areas, conducted by the U.S. Census Bureau.

Of the 40,302 schools included in the 2009–10 sample, 10,229 were found ineligible for the survey. Those not responding numbered 1,856, and those responding numbered 28,217. The unweighted response rate for the 2009–10 PSS survey was 93.8 percent.

Of the 39,325 schools included in the 2011–12 sample, 10,030 cases were considered as out-of-scope (not eligible for the PSS). A total of 26,983 private schools completed a PSS interview (15.8 percent completed online), while 2,312 schools refused to participate, resulting in an unweighted response rate of 92.1 percent.

There were 40,298 schools in the 2013–14 sample; of these, 10,659 were considered as out-of-scope (not eligible for the PSS). A total of 24,566 private schools completed a PSS interview (34.1 percent completed online), while 5,073 schools refused to participate, resulting in an unweighted response rate of 82.9 percent.

The 2015–16 PSS included 42,389 schools, of which 12,754 were considered as out-of-scope (not eligible for the PSS). A total of 22,428 private schools completed a PSS interview and 7,207 schools failed to respond, which resulted in an unweighted response rate of 75.7 percent.

Of the 43,384 schools included in the 2017–18 sample, 15,272 cases were considered as out-of-scope (not eligible for the PSS). A total of 22,895 private schools completed a PSS interview, while 5,217 schools refused to participate, resulting in an unweighted response rate of 81.4 percent.

Further information on the PFS may be obtained from

Steve Broughman
Cross-Sectional Surveys Branch
Sample Surveys Division
National Center for Education Statistics
550 12th Street SW
Washington, DC 20202
stephen.broughman@ed.gov
https://nces.ed.gov/surveys/pss

Projections of Education Statistics

Since 1964, NCES has published projections of key statistics for elementary and secondary schools and higher education institutions. The latest report is *Projections of Education Statistics to 2028* (NCES 2020-024). The *Projections of Education Statistics* series provides national data for elementary and secondary enrollment, high school graduates, elementary and secondary teachers, expenditures for public elementary and secondary education, enrollment in postsecondary degree-granting institutions, and postsecondary degrees conferred. The report also provides state-level projections for public elementary and secondary enrollment and public high school graduates. These models are described in the report's appendix on projection methodology.

Differences between the reported and projected values are, of course, almost inevitable. In *Projections of Education Statistics to 2028*, an evaluation of past projections revealed that, at the elementary and secondary levels, projections of public school enrollments have been quite accurate: mean absolute percentage differences for enrollment in public schools ranged from 0.3 to 1.2 percent for projections from 1 to 5 years in the future, while those for teachers in public schools were 3.0 percent or less. At the higher education level, projections of enrollment have been fairly accurate: mean absolute percentage differences were reported as 5.9 percent or less for projections from 1 to 5 years into the future in *Projections of Education Statistics to 2026* (NCES 2018-019). (*Projections of Education Statistics to 2027* and *Projections of Education Statistics to 2028* did not report mean absolute percentage errors for institutions at the higher educational level because enrollment projections were calculated using a new model.)

Further information on *Projections of Education Statistics* may be obtained from

William Hussar
Annual Reports and Information Staff
National Center for Education Statistics
550 12th Street SW
Washington, DC 20202
william.hussar@ed.gov
https://nces.ed.gov/pubs2020/2020024.pdf

School Survey on Crime and Safety

The School Survey on Crime and Safety (SSOCS) is the only recurring federal survey that collects detailed information on the incidence, frequency, seriousness, and nature of violence affecting students and school personnel, as well as other indicators of school safety from the schools' perspective. SSOCS is conducted by the National Center for Education Statistics (NCES) within the U.S. Department of Education and collected by the U.S. Census Bureau. Data from this collection can be used to examine the relationship between school characteristics and violent and serious violent crimes in primary, middle, high, and combined schools. In addition, data from SSOCS can be used to assess what crime prevention programs, practices, and policies are used by schools. SSOCS has been conducted in school years 1999–2000,

2003–04, 2005–06, 2007–08, 2009–10, 2015–16, and 2017–18.

The sampling frame for SSOCS:2018 was constructed using the 2014–15 CCD Public Elementary/Secondary School Universe data file. The sampling frame was restricted to regular public schools, charter schools, and schools with partial or total magnet programs in the 50 states and the District of Columbia. It excluded special education schools, vocational schools, alternative schools, virtual schools, newly closed schools, home schools, ungraded schools, schools with a highest grade of kindergarten or lower, Department of Defense Education Activity schools, and Bureau of Indian Education schools, as well as schools in Puerto Rico, American Samoa, the Northern Marianas, Guam, and the U.S. Virgin Islands.

The SSOCS:2018 universe totaled 82,300 schools. The SSOCS:2018 findings were based on a nationally representative, stratified, random sample of 4,803 U.S. public schools. Data collection for SSOCS:2018 began on February 20, 2018, and continued through July 18, 2018. Although SSOCS has historically been conducted by mail with telephone and e-mail follow-up, the 2018 survey administration experimented with an online questionnaire. The survey also experimented with offering a $10 cash incentive to a subset of sampled schools. A total of 2,762 primary, middle, high, and combined schools provided complete SSOCS:2018 questionnaires, yielding a weighted response rate of 62 percent.

Further information about SSOCS may be obtained from

Rachel Hansen
Cross-Sectional Surveys Branch
Sample Surveys Division
National Center for Education Statistics
550 12th Street SW
Washington, DC 20202
rachel.hansen@ed.gov
https://nces.ed.gov/surveys/ssocs/

Other Department of Education Agencies

Office of Special Education Programs

Annual Report to Congress on the Implementation of the Individuals with Disabilities Education Act

The Individuals with Disabilities Education Act (IDEA) is a law ensuring services to children with disabilities throughout the nation. IDEA governs how states and public agencies provide early intervention, special education, and related services to more than 6.9 million eligible infants, toddlers, children, and youths (when paired with specific number) with disabilities.

IDEA, formerly the Education of the Handicapped Act (EHA), requires the Secretary of Education to transmit, on an annual basis, a report to Congress describing the progress made in serving the nation's children with disabilities. This annual report contains information on children served by public schools under the provisions of Part B of IDEA and on children served in state-operated programs for persons with disabilities under Chapter I of the Elementary and Secondary Education Act.

Statistics on children receiving special education and related services in various settings and school personnel providing such services are reported in an annual submission of data to the Office of Special Education Programs (OSEP) by the 50 states, the District of Columbia, the Bureau of Indian Education schools, Puerto Rico, American Samoa, Guam, the Northern Mariana Islands, the U.S. Virgin Islands, the Federated States of Micronesia, Palau, and the Marshall Islands. The child count information is based on the number of children with disabilities receiving special education and related services on December 1 of each year. Count information is available from https://ideadata.org/.

Since all participants in programs for persons with disabilities are reported to OSEP, the data are not subject to sampling error. However, nonsampling error can arise from a variety of sources. Some states only produce counts of students receiving special education services by disability category because Part B of the EHA requires it. In those states that typically produce counts of students receiving special education services by disability category without regard to EHA requirements, definitions and labeling practices vary.

Further information on this annual report to Congress may be obtained from

Office of Special Education Programs
Office of Special Education and Rehabilitative Services
U.S. Department of Education
400 Maryland Avenue SW
Washington, DC 20202
https://www2.ed.gov/about/reports/annual/osep/index.
   html
https://sites.ed.gov/idea/
https://ideadata.org/

Other Governmental Agencies and Programs

Bureau of Labor Statistics

Consumer Price Indexes

The Consumer Price Index (CPI) represents changes in prices of all goods and services purchased for consumption by urban households. Indexes are available for two population groups: a CPI for All Urban Consumers (CPI-U) and a CPI for Urban Wage Earners and Clerical Workers (CPI-W). Unless otherwise specified, data in this report are adjusted for inflation using the CPI-U. These values are generally adjusted to a school-year basis by averaging the July through June figures. Price indexes are available for the United States, the 4 Census regions, 9 Census divisions, 2 size of city classes, 8 cross-classifications of regions and size-classes, and 23 local areas. The major uses of the CPI include as an economic indicator, as a deflator of other economic series, and as a means of adjusting income.

Also available is the Consumer Price Index research series using current methods (CPI-U-RS), which presents an estimate of the CPI-U from 1978 to the present that incorporates most of the improvements that the Bureau of Labor Statistics has made over that time span into the entire series. The historical price index series of the CPI-U does not reflect these changes, though these changes do make the present and future CPI more accurate. The limitations of the CPI-U-RS include considerable uncertainty surrounding the magnitude of the adjustments and the several improvements in the CPI that have not been incorporated into the CPI-U-RS for various reasons. Nonetheless, the CPI-U-RS can serve as a valuable proxy for researchers needing a historical estimate of inflation using current methods. This series has not been used in NCES tables.

Further information on consumer price indexes may be obtained from

Bureau of Labor Statistics
U.S. Department of Labor
2 Massachusetts Avenue NE
Washington, DC 20212
https://www.bls.gov/cpi/

Employment and Unemployment Surveys

Statistics on the employment and unemployment status of the population and related data are compiled by the Bureau of Labor Statistics (BLS) using data from the

Current Population Survey (CPS) and other surveys. The CPS, a monthly household survey conducted by the U.S. Census Bureau for the Bureau of Labor Statistics, provides a comprehensive body of information on the employment and unemployment experience of the nation's population, classified by age, sex, race, and various other characteristics.

Further information on unemployment surveys may be obtained from

Bureau of Labor Statistics
U.S. Department of Labor
2 Massachusetts Avenue NE
Washington, DC 20212
cpsinfo@bls.gov
https://www.bls.gov/bls/employment.htm

Census Bureau

American Community Survey

The Census Bureau introduced the American Community Survey (ACS) in 1996. Fully implemented in 2005, it provides a large monthly sample of demographic, socioeconomic, and housing data comparable in content to the Long Forms of the Decennial Census up to and including the 2000 long form. Aggregated over time, these data serve as a replacement for the Long Form of the Decennial Census. The survey includes questions mandated by federal law, federal regulations, and court decisions.

Since 2011, the survey has been mailed to approximately 295,000 addresses in the United States and Puerto Rico each month, or about 3.5 million addresses annually. A larger proportion of addresses in small governmental units (e.g., American Indian reservations, small counties, and towns) also receive the survey. The monthly sample size is designed to approximate the ratio used in the 2000 Census, which requires more intensive distribution in these areas. The ACS covers the U.S. resident population, which includes the entire civilian, noninstitutionalized population; incarcerated persons; institutionalized persons; and the active duty military who are in the United States. In 2006, the ACS began collecting data from the population living in group quarters. Institutionalized group quarters include adult and juvenile correctional facilities, nursing facilities, and other health care facilities. Noninstitutionalized group quarters include college and university housing, military barracks, and other noninstitutional facilities such as workers and religious group quarters and temporary shelters for the homeless.

National-level data from the ACS are available from 2000 onward. The ACS produces 1-year estimates for jurisdictions with populations of 65,000 and over and 5-year estimates for jurisdictions with smaller populations. The 1-year estimates for 2018 used data collected between January 1, 2018, and December 31, 2018, and the 5-year estimates for 2014–2018 used data collected between January 1, 2014, and December 31, 2018. The ACS produced 3-year estimates (for jurisdictions with populations of 20,000 or over) for the periods 2005–2007, 2006–2008, 2007–2009, 2008–2010, 2009–2011, 2010–2012, and 2011–2013. Three-year estimates for these periods will continue to be available to data users, but no further 3-year estimates will be produced.

Further information about the ACS is available at https://www.census.gov/programs-surveys/acs/.

Census of Population—Education in the United States

Some NCES tables are based on a part of the decennial census that consisted of questions asked of a 1 in 6 sample of people and housing units in the United States. This sample was asked more detailed questions about income, occupation, and housing costs, as well as questions about general demographic information. This decennial census "long form" is no longer used; it has been replaced by the American Community Survey (ACS).

School enrollment. People classified as enrolled in school reported attending a "regular" public or private school or college. They were asked whether the institution they attended was public or private and what level of school they were enrolled in.

Educational attainment. Data for educational attainment were tabulated for people ages 15 and over and classified according to the highest grade completed or the highest degree received. Instructions were also given to include the level of the previous grade attended or the highest degree received for people currently enrolled in school.

Poverty status. To determine poverty status, answers to income questions were used to make comparisons to the appropriate poverty threshold. All people except those who were institutionalized, people in military group quarters and college dormitories, and unrelated people under age 15 were considered. If the total income of each family or unrelated individual in the sample was below the corresponding cutoff, that family or individual was classified as "below the poverty level."

Further information on the 1990 and 2000 Census of Population may be obtained from

Population Division
Census Bureau
U.S. Department of Commerce
4600 Silver Hill Road
Washington, DC 20233
https://www.census.gov/main/www/cen1990.html
https://www.census.gov/main/www/cen2000.html

Current Population Survey

The Current Population Survey (CPS) is a monthly survey of about 50,000 households conducted by the U.S. Census Bureau for the Bureau of Labor Statistics. The CPS is the primary source of labor force statistics on the U.S. population. In addition, supplemental questionnaires are used to provide further information about the U.S. population. The March supplement (also known as the Annual Social and Economic [ASEC] supplement) contains detailed questions on topics such as income, employment, and educational attainment; additional questions, such as items on disabilities, have also been included. In the July supplement, items on computer and internet use are the principal focus. The October supplement also contains some questions about computer and internet use, but most of its questions relate to school enrollment and school characteristics.

CPS samples are initially selected based on results from the decennial census and are periodically updated to reflect new housing construction. The current sample design for the main CPS, last revised in July 2015, includes about 70,000 households. Each month, about 50,000 of the 70,000 households are interviewed. Information is obtained each month from those in the household who are 15 years of age and over, and demographic data are collected for children 0–14 years of age. In addition, supplemental questions regarding school enrollment are asked about eligible household members age 3 and over in the October CPS supplement.

In January 1992, the CPS educational attainment variable was changed. The "Highest grade attended" and "Year completed" questions were replaced by the question "What is the highest level of school . . . has completed or the highest degree . . . has received?" Thus, for example, while the old questions elicited data for those who completed more than 4 years of high school, the new question elicited data for those who were high school completers, i.e., those who graduated from high school with a diploma as well as those who completed high school through equivalency programs, such as a GED program.

A major redesign of the CPS was implemented in January 1994 to improve the quality of the data collected. Survey questions were revised, new questions were added, and computer-assisted interviewing methods were used for the survey data collection. Further information about the redesign is available in *Current Population Survey, October 1995: (School Enrollment Supplement) Technical Documentation* at https://www.census.gov/prod/techdoc/cps/cpsoct95.pdf.

Caution should be used when comparing data from 2011 through 2018 (which reflect 2010 Census-based controls) with data from 2002 through 2011 (which reflect 2000 Census-based controls and with data from 2001 and earlier (which reflect population controls based on the 1990 and earlier Censuses). Changes in population controls generally have relatively little impact on summary measures such as means, medians, and percentage distributions; they can, however, have a significant impact on population counts. For example, use of the 1990 census-based population controls resulted in about a 1 percent increase in the civilian noninstitutional population and in the number of families and households. Thus, estimates of levels for data collected in 1994 and later years will differ from those for earlier years by more than what could be attributed to actual changes in the population. These differences could be disproportionately greater for certain subpopulation groups than for the total population.

Beginning in 2003, the race/ethnicity questions were expanded. Information on people of Two or more races were included, and the Asian and Pacific Islander race category was split into two categories—Asian and Native Hawaiian or Other Pacific Islander. In addition, questions were reworded to make it clear that self-reported data on race/ethnicity should reflect the race/ethnicity with which the responder identifies, rather than what may be written in official documentation.

The estimation procedure employed for monthly CPS data involves inflating weighted sample results to independent estimates of characteristics of the civilian noninstitutional population in the United States by age, sex, and race. These independent estimates are based on statistics from decennial censuses; statistics on births, deaths, immigration, and emigration; and statistics on the population in the armed services. Generalized standard error tables are provided in the Current Population Reports; methods for deriving standard errors can be found within the CPS technical documentation at https://www.census.gov/programs-surveys/cps/technical-documentation/complete.html. The CPS data are subject to both nonsampling and sampling errors.

Standard errors were estimated using the generalized variance function prior to 2005 for March CPS data and prior to 2010 for October CPS data. The generalized variance function is a simple model that expresses the variance as a function of the expected value of a survey estimate. Standard errors were estimated using replicate weight methodology beginning in 2005 for March CPS data and beginning in 2010 for October CPS data. Those interested in using CPS household-level supplement replicate weights to calculate variances may refer to *Estimating Current Population Survey (CPS) Household-Level Supplement Variances Using Replicate Weights* at https://thedataweb.rm.census.gov/pub/cps/supps/HH-level_Use_of_the_Public_Use_Replicate_Weight_File.doc.

Further information on the CPS may be obtained from

Associate Directorate for Demographic Programs—
  Survey Operations
Census Bureau
U.S. Department of Commerce
4600 Silver Hill Road
Washington, DC 20233
301-763-3806
dsd.cps@census.gov
https://www.census.gov/programs-surveys/cps.html

Computer and Internet Use

The Current Population Survey (CPS) has been conducting supplemental data collections regarding computer use since 1984. In 1997, these supplemental data collections were expanded to include data on internet access. More recently, data regarding computer and internet use were collected in October 2010, July 2011, October 2012, July 2013, July 2015, and November 2017.

In the July 2011, 2013, and 2015 supplements, as well as in the November 2017 supplement, the sole focus was on computer and internet use. In the October 2010 and 2012 supplements questions on school enrollment were the principal focus, and questions on computer and internet use were less prominent. Measurable differences in estimates taken from these supplements across years could reflect actual changes in the population; however, differences could also reflect any unknown bias from major changes in the questionnaire over time due to rapidly changing technology. In addition, data may vary slightly due to seasonal variations in data collection between the July, October, and November supplements. Therefore, caution should be used when making year-to-year comparisons of CPS computer and internet use estimates.

The most recent computer and internet use supplement, conducted in November 2017, collected household information from all eligible CPS households, as well as information from individual household members age 3 and over. Information was collected about the household's computer and internet use and the household member's use of the Internet from any location in the past year. Additionally, information was gathered regarding a randomly selected household respondent's use of the Internet.

For the November 2017 basic CPS, the household-level nonresponse rate was 14.3 percent. The person-level nonresponse rate for the computer and internet use supplement was an additional 23.0 percent. Since one rate is a person-level rate and the other a household-level rate, the rates cannot be combined to derive an overall rate.

Further information on the CPS Computer and Internet Use Supplement may be obtained from

Associate Directorate for Demographic Programs—
  Survey Operations
Census Bureau
U.S. Department of Commerce
4600 Silver Hill Road
Washington, DC 20233
301-763-3806
dsd.cps@census.gov
https://www.census.gov/programs-surveys/cps.html

Educational Attainment

Reports documenting educational attainment are produced by the Census Bureau using the March Current Population Survey (CPS) supplement (Annual Social and Economic supplement [ASEC]). Currently, the ASEC supplement consists of approximately 68,300 interviewed households. Both recent and earlier editions of *Educational Attainment in the United States* may be downloaded at https://www.census.gov/topics/education/educational-attainment/data/tables.All.html.

In 2014, the CPS ASEC included redesigned questions on income (specifically retirement income) and health insurance coverage, which were followed, in the 2015 CPS ASEC, by changes to allow spouses and unmarried partners to specifically identify as opposite- or same-sex. Beginning with the 2019 CPS ASEC, the Census Bureau used a modified processing system that improved procedures for imputing income and health insurance variables. The Census Bureau analyzed the impact of the use of the new processing system by comparing its use with the use of the legacy processing system on income, poverty, and health insurance coverage data from 2017 ASEC files. The Census Bureau found that differences in the overall poverty rate and household income resulting from the use of the new processing system compared to the legacy processing system were not statistically significant, although there were differences for some demographic groups. Use of the new processing system caused the supplemental poverty rate (https://www.census.gov/topics/income-poverty/supplemental-poverty-measure.html) to decrease overall and for most demographic groups. The Census Bureau attributed the decrease to improvements in the new processing system's imputation of medical-out-of-pocket expenses, housing subsidies, and school lunch receipts. More information on these changes can be found at https://www.census.gov/newsroom/blogs/research-matters/2019/09/cps-asec.html.

In addition to the general constraints of CPS, some data indicate that the respondents have a tendency to overestimate the educational level of members of their household. Some inaccuracy is due to a lack of the respondent's knowledge of the exact educational attainment of each household member and the hesitancy to acknowledge anything less than a high school education.

Further information on educational attainment data from CPS may be obtained from

Associate Directorate for Demographic Programs—
  Survey Operations
Census Bureau
U.S. Department of Commerce
4600 Silver Hill Road
Washington, DC 20233
301-763-3806
dsd.cps@census.gov
https://www.census.gov/programs-surveys/cps.html

School Enrollment

Each October, the Current Population Survey (CPS) includes supplemental questions on the enrollment status of the population age 3 years and over. Currently, the October supplement consists of approximately 50,000 interviewed households, the same households interviewed in the basic Current Population Survey. The primary sources of nonsampling variability in the responses to the supplement are those inherent in the main survey instrument. The question of current enrollment may not be answered accurately for various reasons. Some respondents may not know current grade information for every student in the household, a problem especially prevalent for

households with members in college or in nursery school. Confusion over college credits or hours taken by a student may make it difficult to determine the year in which the student is enrolled. Problems may occur with the definition of nursery school (a group or class organized to provide educational experiences for children) where respondents' interpretations of "educational experiences" vary.

For the October 2018 basic CPS, the household-level nonresponse rate was 15.2 percent. The person-level nonresponse rate for the school enrollment supplement was an additional 9.2 percent. Since the basic CPS nonresponse rate is a household-level rate and the school enrollment supplement nonresponse rate is a person-level rate, these rates cannot be combined to derive an overall nonresponse rate. Nonresponding households may have fewer persons than interviewed ones, so combining these rates may lead to an overestimate of the true overall nonresponse rate for persons for the school enrollment supplement.

Although the principal focus of the October supplement is school enrollment, in some years the supplement has included additional questions on other topics. In 2010 and 2012, for example, the October supplement included additional questions on computer and internet use.

Further information on CPS methodology may be obtained from https://www.census.gov/programs-surveys/cps.html.

Further information on the CPS School Enrollment Supplement may be obtained from

Associate Directorate for Demographic Programs—
  Survey Operations
Census Bureau
U.S. Department of Commerce
4600 Silver Hill Road
Washington, DC 20233
301-763-3806
dsd.cps@census.gov
https://www.census.gov/programs-surveys/cps.html

Decennial Census, Population Estimates, and Population Projections

The decennial census is a universe survey mandated by the U.S. Constitution. It is a questionnaire sent to every household in the country, and it is composed of seven questions about the household and its members (name, sex, age, relationship, Hispanic origin, race, and whether the housing unit is owned or rented). The Census Bureau also produces annual estimates of the resident population by demographic characteristics (age, sex, race, and Hispanic origin) for the nation, states, and counties, as well as national and state projections for the resident population. The reference date for population estimates is July 1 of the given year. With each new issue of July 1 estimates, the Census Bureau revises estimates for each year back to the last census. Previously published estimates are superseded and archived.

Census respondents self-report race and ethnicity. The race questions on the 1990 and 2000 censuses differed in some significant ways. In 1990, the respondent was instructed to select the one race "that the respondent considers himself/herself to be," whereas in 2000, the respondent could select one or more races that the person considered himself or herself to be. American Indian, Eskimo, and Aleut were three separate race categories in 1990; in 2000, the American Indian and Alaska Native categories were combined, with an option to write in a tribal affiliation. This write-in option was provided only for the American Indian category in 1990. There was a combined Asian and Pacific Islander race category in 1990, but the groups were separated into two categories in 2000.

The census question on ethnicity asks whether the respondent is of Hispanic origin, regardless of the race option(s) selected; thus, persons of Hispanic origin may be of any race. In the 2000 census, respondents were first asked, "Is this person Spanish/Hispanic/Latino?" and then given the following options: No, not Spanish/Hispanic/Latino; Yes, Puerto Rican; Yes, Mexican, Mexican American, Chicano; Yes, Cuban; and Yes, other Spanish/Hispanic/Latino (with space to print the specific group). In the 2010 census, respondents were asked "Is this person of Hispanic, Latino, or Spanish origin?" The options given were No, not of Hispanic, Latino, or Spanish origin; Yes, Mexican, Mexican Am., Chicano; Yes, Puerto Rican; Yes, Cuban; and Yes, another Hispanic, Latino, or Spanish origin—along with instructions to print "Argentinean, Colombian, Dominican, Nicaraguan, Salvadoran, Spaniard, and so on" in a specific box.

The 2000 and 2010 censuses each asked the respondent "What is this person's race?" and allowed the respondent to select one or more options. The options provided were largely the same in both the 2000 and 2010 censuses: White; Black, African American, or Negro; American Indian or Alaska Native (with space to print the name of enrolled or principal tribe); Asian Indian; Japanese; Native Hawaiian; Chinese; Korean; Guamanian or Chamorro; Filipino; Vietnamese; Samoan; Other Asian; Other Pacific Islander; and Some other race. The last three options included space to print the specific race. Two significant differences between the 2000 and 2010 census questions

on race were that no race examples were provided for the "Other Asian" and "Other Pacific Islander" responses in 2000, whereas the race examples of "Hmong, Laotian, Thai, Pakistani, Cambodian, and so on" and "Fijian, Tongan, and so on," were provided for the "Other Asian" and "Other Pacific Islander" responses, respectively, in 2010.

The census population estimates program modified the enumerated population from the 2010 census to produce the population estimates base for 2010 and onward. As part of the modification, the Census Bureau recoded the "Some other race" responses from the 2010 census to one or more of the five OMB race categories used in the estimates program (for more information, see https://www.census.gov/programs-surveys/popest/technical-documentation/methodology.html).

Further information on the decennial census may be obtained from https://www.census.gov.

Department of Justice

Bureau of Justice Statistics

A division of the U.S. Department of Justice Office of Justice Programs, the Bureau of Justice Statistics (BJS) collects, analyzes, publishes, and disseminates statistical information on crime, criminal offenders, victims of crime, and the operations of the justice system at all levels of government and internationally. It also provides technical and financial support to state governments for development of criminal justice statistics and information systems on crime and justice.

For information on the BJS, see https://www.bjs.gov/.

National Crime Victimization Survey

The National Crime Victimization Survey (NCVS), administered for the U.S. Bureau of Justice Statistics (BJS) by the U.S. Census Bureau, is the nation's primary source of information on crime and the victims of crime. Initiated in 1972 and redesigned in 1992 and 2016, the NCVS collects detailed information on the frequency and nature of the crimes of rape, sexual assault, robbery, aggravated and simple assault, theft, household burglary, and motor vehicle theft experienced by Americans and American households each year. The survey measures both crimes reported to the police and crimes not reported to the police.

NCVS estimates presented may differ from those in previous published reports. This is because a small number of victimizations, referred to as series victimizations, are included using a new counting strategy. High-frequency repeat victimizations, or series victimizations, are six or more similar but separate victimizations that occur with such frequency that the victim is unable to recall each individual event or describe each event in detail. As part of ongoing research efforts associated with the redesign of the NCVS, BJS investigated ways to include high-frequency repeat victimizations, or series victimizations, in estimates of criminal victimization. Including series victimizations results in more accurate estimates of victimization. BJS has decided to include series victimizations using the victim's estimates of the number of times the victimizations occurred over the past 6 months, capping the number of victimizations within each series at a maximum of 10. This strategy for counting series victimizations balances the desire to estimate national rates and account for the experiences of persons who have been subjected to repeat victimizations against the desire to minimize the estimation errors that can occur when repeat victimizations are reported. Including series victimizations in national rates results in rather large increases in the level of violent victimization; however, trends in violence are generally similar regardless of whether series victimizations are included. For more information on the new counting strategy and supporting research, see *Methods for Counting High-Frequency Repeat Victimizations in the National Crime Victimization Survey* at https://www.bjs.gov/content/pub/pdf/mchfrv.pdf.

Readers should note that in 2003, in accordance with changes to the Office of Management and Budget's standards for the classification of federal data on race and ethnicity, the NCVS item on race/ethnicity was modified. A question on Hispanic origin is now followed by a new question on race. The new question about race allows the respondent to choose more than one race and delineates Asian as a separate category from Native Hawaiian or Other Pacific Islander. An analysis conducted by the Demographic Surveys Division at the U.S. Census Bureau showed that the new race question had very little impact on the aggregate racial distribution of the NCVS respondents, with one exception: There was a 1.6 percentage point decrease in the percentage of respondents who reported themselves as White. Due to changes in race/ethnicity categories, comparisons of race/ethnicity across years should be made with caution.

Every 10 years, the NCVS sample is redesigned to reflect changes in the population. In the 2006 NCVS, changes in the sample design and survey methodology affected the survey's estimates. Caution should be used when comparing the 2006 estimates to estimates of other years. For more information on the 2006 NCVS data, see *Criminal Victimization, 2006*, at https://www.bjs.gov/content/pub/pdf/cv06.pdf; the NCVS 2006 technical

notes, at https://bjs.ojp.usdoj.gov/content/pub/pdf/cv06tn.pdf; and *Criminal Victimization, 2007*, at https://bjs.ojp.usdoj.gov/content/pub/pdf/cv07.pdf. Due to a sample increase and redesign in 2016, victimization estimates among youth were not comparable to estimates for other years and are not available in this report. For more information on the redesign, see https://www.bjs.gov/content/pub/pdf/cv16re.pdf.

The number of NCVS-eligible households in the 2018 sample was approximately 208,000. Households were selected using a stratified, multistage cluster design. In the first stage, the primary sampling units (PSUs), consisting of counties or groups of counties, were selected. In the second stage, smaller areas, called Enumeration Districts (EDs), were selected from each sampled PSU. Finally, from selected EDs, clusters of four households, called segments, were selected for interview. At each stage, the selection was done proportionate to population size in order to create a self-weighting sample. The final sample was augmented to account for households constructed after the decennial census. Within each sampled household, the U.S. Census Bureau interviewer attempts to interview all household members age 12 and over to determine whether they had been victimized by the measured crimes during the 6 months preceding the interview.

The first NCVS interview with a housing unit is conducted in person. Subsequent interviews are conducted by telephone, if possible. All persons age 12 and older are interviewed every 6 months. Households remain in the sample for 3 years and are interviewed seven times at 6-month intervals. Since the survey's inception, the initial interview at each sample unit has been used only to bound future interviews to establish a time frame to avoid duplication of crimes uncovered in these subsequent interviews. Beginning in 2006, data from the initial interview have been adjusted to account for the effects of bounding and have been included in the survey estimates. After a household has been interviewed its seventh time, it is replaced by a new sample household. In 2018, the household response rate was about 73 percent, and the completion rate for persons within households was about 82 percent. Weights were developed to permit estimates for the total U.S. population 12 years and older. For more information on the 2018 NCVS, see https://www.bjs.gov/content/pub/pdf/cv18.pdf.

Further information on the NCVS may be obtained from

Barbara A. Oudekerk
Victimization Statistics Branch
Bureau of Justice Statistics
barbara.a.oudekerk@usdoj.gov
https://www.bjs.gov/

School Crime Supplement

Created as a supplement to the NCVS and codesigned by the National Center for Education Statistics and Bureau of Justice Statistics, the School Crime Supplement (SCS) survey has been conducted in 1989, 1995, and biennially since 1999 to collect additional information about school-related victimizations on a national level. This report includes data from the 1995, 1999, 2001, 2003, 2005, 2007, 2009, 2011, 2013, 2015, and 2017 collections. The 1989 data are not included in this report as a result of methodological changes to the NCVS and SCS. The SCS was designed to assist policymakers, as well as academic researchers and practitioners at federal, state, and local levels, to make informed decisions concerning crime in schools. The survey asks students a number of key questions about their experiences with and perceptions of crime and violence that occurred inside their school, on school grounds, on the school bus, or on the way to or from school. Students are asked additional questions about security measures used by their school, students' participation in after-school activities, students' perceptions of school rules, the presence of weapons and gangs in school, the presence of hate-related words and graffiti in school, student reports of bullying and reports of rejection at school, and the availability of drugs and alcohol in school. Students are also asked attitudinal questions relating to fear of victimization and avoidance behavior at school.

The SCS survey was conducted for a 6-month period from January through June in all households selected for the NCVS (see discussion above for information about the NCVS sampling design and changes to the race/ethnicity variable beginning in 2003). Within these households, the eligible respondents for the SCS were those household members who had attended school at any time during the 6 months preceding the interview, were enrolled in grades 6–12, and were not homeschooled. In 2007, the questionnaire was changed and household members who attended school sometime during the school year of the interview were included. The age range of students covered in this report is 12–18 years of age. Eligible respondents were asked the supplemental questions in the SCS only after completing their entire NCVS interview. It should be noted that the first or unbounded NCVS interview has always been included in analysis of the SCS data and may result in the reporting of events outside of the requested reference period.

The prevalence of victimization for 1995, 1999, 2001, 2003, 2005, 2007, 2009, 2011, 2013, 2015, and 2017 was calculated by using NCVS incident variables appended to the SCS data files of the same year. The NCVS type of crime variable was used in the SCS to classify student victimizations into the categories "serious violent," "violent," and "theft." The NCVS variables asking where the incident happened (at school) and what the victim was doing when it happened (attending school or on the way to or from school) were used to ascertain whether the incident happened at school. Only incidents that occurred inside the United States are included.

In 2001, the SCS survey instrument was modified. In 1995 and 1999, "at school" had been defined for respondents as meaning in the school building, on the school grounds, or on a school bus. In 2001, the definition of at "school" was changed to mean in the school building, on school property, on a school bus, or going to and from school. The change to the definition of "at school" in the 2001 questionnaire was made in order to render the definition there consistent with the definition as it is constructed in the NCVS. This change to the definition of "at school" has been retained in subsequent SCS collections. Cognitive interviews conducted by the U.S. Census Bureau on the 1999 SCS suggested that modifications to the definition of "at school" would not have a substantial impact on the estimates.

A total of about 9,700 students participated in the 1995 SCS, and 8,400 students participated in both the 1999 and 2001 SCS. In 2003, 2005, 2007, 2009, 2011, 2013, 2015, and 2017, the numbers of students participating were 7,200, 6,300, 5,600, 5,000, 6,500, 5,700, 5,500, and 7,100, respectively. In the 2017 SCS, the household completion rate was 76 percent.

In the 1995, 1999, 2001, 2003, 2005, 2007, 2009, 2011, 2013, 2015, and 2017 SCS collections, the household completion rates were 95 percent, 94 percent, 93 percent, 92 percent, 91 percent, 90 percent, 92 percent, 91 percent, 86 percent, 82 percent, and 76 percent, respectively, and the student completion rates were 78 percent, 78 percent, 77 percent, 70 percent, 62 percent, 58 percent, 56 percent, 63 percent, 60 percent, 58 percent, and 52 percent, respectively. The overall SCS unit response rate (calculated by multiplying the household completion rate by the student completion rate) was about 74 percent in 1995, 73 percent in 1999, 72 percent in 2001, 64 percent in 2003, 56 percent in 2005, 53 percent in 2007, 51 percent in 2009, 57 percent in 2011, 51 percent in 2013, 48 percent in 2015, and 40 percent in 2017. (Prior to 2011, overall SCS unit response rates were unweighted; starting in 2011, overall SCS unit response rates are weighted.)

There are two types of nonresponse: unit and item nonresponse. NCES requires that any stage of data collection within a survey that has a unit base-weighted response rate of less than 85 percent be evaluated for the potential magnitude of unit nonresponse bias before the data or any analysis using the data may be released (NCES Statistical Standards, 2002, at https://nces.ed.gov/statprog/2002/std4_4.asp). Due to the low unit response rate in 2005, 2007, 2009, 2011, 2013, 2015, and 2017, a unit nonresponse bias analysis was done. Unit response rates indicate how many sampled units have completed interviews. Because interviews with students could only be completed after households had responded to the NCVS, the unit completion rate for the SCS reflects both the household interview completion rate and the student interview completion rate. Nonresponse can greatly affect the strength and application of survey data by leading to an increase in variance as a result of a reduction in the actual size of the sample and can produce bias if the nonrespondents have characteristics of interest that are different from the respondents. In order for response bias to occur, respondents must have different response rates and responses to particular survey variables. The magnitude of unit nonresponse bias is determined by the response rate and the differences between respondents and nonrespondents on key survey variables. Although the bias analysis cannot measure response bias since the SCS is a sample survey and it is not known how the population would have responded, the SCS sampling frame has several key student or school characteristic variables for which data are known for respondents and nonrespondents: sex, age, race/ethnicity, household income, region, and urbanicity, all of which are associated with student victimization. To the extent that there are differential responses by respondents in these groups, nonresponse bias is a concern.

In 2005, the analysis of unit nonresponse bias found evidence of bias for the race, household income, and urbanicity variables. White (non-Hispanic) and Other (non-Hispanic) respondents had higher response rates than Black (non-Hispanic) and Hispanic respondents. Respondents from households with an income of $35,000–$49,999 and $50,000 or more had higher response rates than those from households with incomes of less than $7,500, $7,500–$14,999, $15,000–$24,999, and $25,000–$34,999. Respondents who live in urban areas had lower response rates than those who live in rural or suburban areas. Although the extent of nonresponse bias cannot be determined, weighting adjustments, which corrected for differential response rates, should have reduced the problem.

In 2007, the analysis of unit nonresponse bias found evidence of bias by the race/ethnicity and household income variables. Hispanic respondents had lower response rates than respondents of other races/ethnicities. Respondents from households with an income of $25,000 or more had higher response rates than those from households with incomes of less than $25,000. However,

when responding students are compared to the eligible NCVS sample, there were no measurable differences between the responding students and the eligible students, suggesting that the nonresponse bias has little impact on the overall estimates.

In 2009, the analysis of unit nonresponse bias found evidence of potential bias for the race/ethnicity and urbanicity variables. White students and students of other races/ethnicities had higher response rates than did Black and Hispanic respondents. Respondents from households located in rural areas had higher response rates than those from households located in urban areas. However, when responding students are compared to the eligible NCVS sample, there were no measurable differences between the responding students and the eligible students, suggesting that the nonresponse bias has little impact on the overall estimates.

In 2011, the analysis of unit nonresponse bias found evidence of potential bias for the age variable. Respondents 12 to 17 years old had higher response rates than did 18-year-old respondents in the NCVS and SCS interviews. Weighting the data adjusts for unequal selection probabilities and for the effects of nonresponse. The weighting adjustments that correct for differential response rates are created by region, age, race, and sex, and should have reduced the effect of nonresponse.

In 2013, the analysis of unit nonresponse bias found evidence of potential bias for the age, region, and Hispanic origin variables in the NCVS interview response. Within the SCS portion of the data, only the age and region variables showed significant unit nonresponse bias. Further analysis indicated that only the age 14 and the west region categories showed positive response biases that were significantly different from some of the other categories within the age and region variables. Based on the analysis, nonresponse bias seems to have little impact on the SCS results. In 2015, the analysis of unit nonresponse bias found evidence of potential bias for age, race, Hispanic origin, urbanicity, and region in the NCVS interview response. For the SCS interview, the age, race, urbanicity, and region variables showed significant unit nonresponse bias. The age 14 group and rural areas showed positive response biases that were significantly different from other categories within the age and urbanicity variables. The northeast region and Asian race group showed negative response biases that were significantly different from other categories within the region and race variables. These results provide evidence that these subgroups may have a nonresponse bias associated with them. In 2017, the analysis of unit nonresponse bias found that the race/ethnicity and census region variables showed significant differences in response rates between different race/ethnicity and census region subgroups. Respondent and nonrespondent distributions were significantly different for the race/ethnicity subgroup only. However, after using weights adjusted for person nonresponse, there was no evidence that these response differences introduced nonresponse bias in the final victimization estimates. Response rates for SCS survey items in all survey years were high—typically over 95 percent of all eligible respondents, meaning there is little potential for item nonresponse bias for most items in the survey. The weighted data permit inferences about the eligible student population who were enrolled in schools in all SCS data years.

Further information about the SCS may be obtained from

Rachel Hansen
Cross-Sectional Surveys Branch
Sample Surveys Division
National Center for Education Statistics
550 12th Street SW
Washington, DC 20202
rachel.hansen@ed.gov
https://nces.ed.gov/programs/crime/

Other Organization Sources

International Association for the Evaluation of Educational Achievement

The International Association for the Evaluation of Educational Achievement (IEA) is composed of governmental research centers and national research institutions around the world whose aim is to investigate education problems common among countries. Since its inception in 1958, the IEA has conducted more than 30 research studies of cross-national achievement. The regular cycle of studies encompasses learning in basic school subjects. Examples are the Trends in International Mathematics and Science Study (TIMSS) and the Progress in International Reading Literacy Study (PIRLS). IEA projects also include studies of particular interest to IEA members, such as the TIMSS 1999 Video Study of Mathematics and Science Teaching, the Civic Education Study, and studies on information technology in education.

The international bodies that coordinate international assessments vary in the labels they apply to participating education systems, most of which are countries. IEA differentiates between IEA members, which IEA refers to as "countries" in all cases, and "benchmarking participants." IEA members include countries such as the United States and Ireland, as well as subnational entities such as England and Scotland (which are both part of the United Kingdom), the Flemish community of Belgium, and Hong Kong (a Special Administrative Region of China). IEA benchmarking participants are all subnational entities and include Canadian provinces, U.S. states, and Dubai in the United Arab Emirates (among others). Benchmarking participants, like the participating countries, are given the opportunity to assess the comparative international standing of their students' achievement and to view their curriculum and instruction in an international context.

Some IEA studies, such as TIMSS and PIRLS, include an assessment portion, as well as contextual questionnaires for collecting information about students' home and school experiences. The TIMSS and PIRLS scales, including the scale averages and standard deviations, are designed to remain constant from assessment to assessment so that education systems (including countries and subnational education systems) can compare their scores over time as well as compare their scores directly with the scores of other education systems. Although each scale was created to have a mean of 500 and a standard deviation of 100, the subject matter and the level of difficulty of items necessarily differ by grade, subject, and domain/dimension. Therefore, direct comparisons between scores across grades, subjects, and different domain/dimension types should not be made.

Further information on the International Association for the Evaluation of Educational Achievement may be obtained from https://www.iea.nl/.

Trends in International Mathematics and Science Study

The Trends in International Mathematics and Science Study (TIMSS, formerly known as the Third International Mathematics and Science Study) provides data on the mathematics and science achievement of U.S. 4th- and 8th-graders compared with that of their peers in other countries. TIMSS collects information through mathematics and science assessments and questionnaires. The questionnaires request information to help provide a context for student performance. They focus on such topics as students' attitudes and beliefs about learning mathematics and science, what students do as part of their mathematics and science lessons, students' completion of homework, and their lives both in and outside of school; teachers' perceptions of their preparedness for teaching mathematics and science, teaching assignments, class size and organization, instructional content and practices, collaboration with other teachers, and participation in professional development activities; and principals' viewpoints on policy and budget responsibilities, curriculum and instruction issues, and student behavior. The questionnaires also elicit information on the organization of schools and courses. The assessments and questionnaires are designed to specifications in a guiding framework. The TIMSS framework describes the mathematics and science content to be assessed and provides grade-specific objectives, an overview of the assessment design, and guidelines for item development.

TIMSS is on a 4-year cycle. Data collections occurred in 1995, 1999 (8th grade only), 2003, 2007, 2011, and 2015. TIMSS 2015 consisted of assessments in 4th-grade mathematics; numeracy (a less difficult version of 4th-grade mathematics, newly developed for 2015); 8th-grade mathematics; 4th-grade science; and 8th-grade science. In addition, TIMSS 2015 included the third administration of TIMSS Advanced since 1995. TIMSS Advanced is an international comparative study that measures the advanced mathematics and physics achievement of students in their final year of secondary school (the equivalent of 12th grade in the United States) who are taking or have taken advanced courses. The TIMSS 2015 survey also collected policy-relevant information about students, curriculum emphasis, technology use, and teacher preparation and training.

Progress in International Reading Literacy Study

The Progress in International Reading Literacy Study (PIRLS) provides data on the reading literacy of U.S. 4th-graders compared with that of their peers in other countries. PIRLS is on a 5-year cycle: PIRLS data collections have been conducted in 2001, 2006, 2011, and 2016. In 2016, a total of 58 education systems, including both IEA members and IEA benchmarking participants, participated in the survey. Sixteen of the education systems participating in PIRLS also participated in ePIRLS, an innovative, computer-based assessment of online reading designed to measure students' approaches to informational reading in an online environment.

PIRLS collects information through a reading literacy assessment and questionnaires that help to provide a context for student performance. Questionnaires are administered to collect information about students' home and school experiences in learning to read. A student questionnaire addresses students' attitudes toward reading and their reading habits. In addition, questionnaires are given to students' teachers and school principals in order to gather information about students' school experiences in developing reading literacy. In countries other than the United States, a parent questionnaire is also administered. The assessments and questionnaires are designed to

specifications in a guiding framework. The PIRLS framework describes the reading content to be assessed and provides objectives specific to 4th grade, an overview of the assessment design, and guidelines for item development.

TIMSS and PIRLS Sampling and Response Rates

2016 PIRLS

As is done in all participating countries and other education systems, representative samples of students in the United States are selected. The sample design that was employed by PIRLS in 2016 is generally referred to as a two-stage stratified cluster sample. In the first stage of sampling, individual schools were selected with a probability proportionate to size (PPS) approach, which means that the probability is proportional to the estimated number of students enrolled in the target grade. In the second stage of sampling, intact classrooms were selected within sampled schools.

PIRLS guidelines call for a minimum of 150 schools to be sampled, with a minimum of 4,000 students assessed. The basic sample design of one classroom per school was designed to yield a total sample of approximately 4,500 students per population. About 4,400 U.S. students participated in PIRLS in 2016, joining 319,000 other student participants around the world. Accommodations were not provided for students with disabilities or students who were unable to read or speak the language of the test. These students were excluded from the sample. The IEA requirement is that the overall exclusion rate, which includes exclusions of schools and students, should not exceed more than 5 percent of the national desired target population.

In order to minimize the potential for response biases, the IEA developed participation or response rate standards that apply to all participating education systems and govern whether or not an education system's data are included in the TIMSS or PIRLS international datasets and the way in which its statistics are presented in the international reports. These standards were set using composites of response rates at the school, classroom, and student and teacher levels. Response rates were calculated with and without the inclusion of substitute schools that were selected to replace schools refusing to participate. In the 2016 PIRLS administered in the United States, the unweighted school response rate was 76 percent, and the weighted school response rate was 75 percent. All schools selected for PIRLS were also asked to participate in ePIRLS. The unweighted school response rate for ePIRLS in the final sample with replacement schools was 89.0 percent and the weighted response rate was 89.1 percent. The weighted and unweighted student response rates for PIRLS were both 94 percent. The weighted and unweighted student response rates for ePIRLS were both 90 percent.

2015 TIMSS and TIMSS Advanced

TIMSS 2015 was administered between March and May of 2015 in the United States. The U.S. sample was randomly selected and weighted to be representative of the nation. In order to reliably and accurately represent the performance of each country, international guidelines required that countries sample at least 150 schools and at least 4,000 students per grade (countries with small class sizes of fewer than 30 students per school were directed to consider sampling more schools, more classrooms per school, or both, to meet the minimum target of 4,000 tested students). In the United States, a total of 250 schools and 10,029 students participated in the grade 4 TIMSS survey, and 246 schools and 10,221 students participated in the grade 8 TIMSS (these figures do not include the participation of the state of Florida as a subnational education system, which was separate from and additional to its participation in the U.S. national sample).

TIMSS Advanced, also administered between March and May of 2015 in the United States, required participating countries and other education systems to draw probability samples of students in their final year of secondary school—ISCED Level 3—who were taking or had taken courses in advanced mathematics or who were taking or had taken courses in physics. International guidelines for TIMSS Advanced called for a minimum of 120 schools to be sampled, with a minimum of 3,600 students assessed per subject. In the United States, a total of 241 schools and 2,954 students participated in advanced mathematics, and 165 schools and 2,932 students participated in physics.

In TIMSS 2015, the weighted school response rate for the United States was 77 percent for grade 4 before the use of substitute schools (schools substituted for originally sampled schools that refused to participate) and 85 percent with the inclusion of substitute schools. For grade 8, the weighted school response rate before the use of substitute schools was 78 percent, and it was 84 percent with the inclusion of substitute schools. The weighted student response rate was 96 percent for grade 4 and 94 percent for grade 8.

In TIMSS Advanced 2015, the weighted school response rate for the United States for advanced mathematics was 72 percent before the use of substitute schools and 76 percent with the inclusion of substitute schools. The

weighted school response rate for the United States for physics was 65 percent before the use of substitute schools and 68 percent with the inclusion of substitute schools. The weighted student response rate was 87 percent for advanced mathematics and 85 percent for physics. Student response rates are based on a combined total of students from both sampled and substitute schools.

Further information on the TIMSS study may be obtained from

Stephen Provasnik
International Assessment Branch
Assessments Division
National Center for Education Statistics
550 12th Street SW
Washington, DC 20202
(202) 245-6442
stephen.provasnik@ed.gov
https://nces.ed.gov/timss
https://www.iea.nl/timss

Further information on the PIRLS study may be obtained from

Sheila Thompson
International Assessment Branch
Assessments Division
National Center for Education Statistics
550 12th Street SW
Washington, DC 20202
(202) 245-8330
sheila.thompson@ed.gov
https://nces.ed.gov/surveys/pirls/
https://www.iea.nl/pirls

Organization for Economic Cooperation and Development

The Organization for Economic Cooperation and Development (OECD) publishes analyses of national policies and survey data in education, training, and economics in OECD and partner countries. Newer studies include student survey data on financial literacy and on digital literacy.

Online Education Database (OECD.Stat)

The statistical online platform of the OECD, OECD.Stat, allows users to access OECD's databases for OECD member countries and selected nonmember economies. A user can build tables using selected variables and customizable table layouts, extract and download data, and view metadata on methodology and sources.

Data for educational attainment in this report are pulled directly from OECD.Stat. (Information on these data can be found in chapter A, indicator A1 of annex 3 in *Education at a Glance 2018* and accessed at https://www.oecd-ilibrary.org/education/education-at-a-glance-2018/sources-methods-and-technical-notes_eag-2018-36-en.) However, to support statistical testing for NCES publications, standard errors for some countries had to be estimated and therefore may not be included on OECD.Stat. Standard errors for 2017 and 2018 for Poland, Turkey, and the Republic of Korea; for 2017 for the Netherlands and Slovenia; and for the 2017 and 2018 postsecondary data for Japan were estimated by NCES using a simple random sample assumption. These standard errors are likely to be lower than standard errors that take into account complex sample designs. Lastly, NCES estimated the standard errors for the OECD average using the sum of squares technique.

OECD.Stat can be accessed at https://stats.oecd.org/. A user's guide for OECD.Stat can be accessed at https://stats.oecd.org/Content/themes/OECD/static/help/WBOS%20User%20Guide%20(EN).pdf.

Program for International Student Assessment

The Program for International Student Assessment (PISA) is a system of international assessments organized by the Organization for Economic Cooperation and Development (OECD), an intergovernmental organization of industrialized countries, that focuses on 15-year-olds' capabilities in reading literacy, mathematics literacy, and science literacy. PISA also includes measures of general, or cross-curricular, competencies such as learning strategies. PISA emphasizes functional skills that students have acquired as they near the end of compulsory schooling.

PISA is a 2-hour exam. Assessment items include a combination of multiple-choice questions and open-ended questions that require students to develop their own response. PISA scores are reported on a scale that ranges from 0 to 1,000, with the OECD mean set at 500 and a standard deviation set at 100. In each education system, the assessment is translated into the primary language of instruction; in the United States, all materials are written in English.

Forty-three education systems participated in the 2000 PISA; 41 education systems participated in 2003; 57 (30 OECD member countries and 27 nonmember countries or education systems) participated in 2006; and 65 (34 OECD member countries and 31 nonmember countries or education systems) participated in 2009. (An additional nine education systems administered the 2009 PISA in 2010.) In PISA 2012, 65 education systems (34 OECD member countries and 31 nonmember countries or education systems), as well as the states of Connecticut, Florida, and Massachusetts, participated. In the 2015 PISA, 70 education systems (35 OECD member countries and 35 nonmember countries or education systems), as well as the states of Massachusetts and North Carolina and the territory of Puerto Rico, participated. In PISA 2018, 79 education systems (37 OECD member countries and 42 nonmember countries or education systems) participated.

To implement PISA, each of the participating education systems scientifically draws a nationally representative sample of 15-year-olds, regardless of grade level. In the 2018 PISA, there were 162 participating schools and 4,811 participating students. The overall weighted school response rate was 76 percent, and the overall weighted student response rate was 85 percent.

The intent of PISA reporting is to provide an overall description of performance in reading literacy, mathematics literacy, and science literacy every 3 years, and to provide a more detailed look at each domain in the years when it is the major focus. These cycles will allow education systems to compare changes in trends for each of the three subject areas over time. In the first cycle, PISA 2000, reading literacy was the major focus, occupying roughly two-thirds of assessment time. For 2003, PISA focused on mathematics literacy as well as the ability of students to solve problems in real-life settings. In 2006, PISA focused on science literacy; in 2009, it focused on reading literacy again; and in 2012, it focused on mathematics literacy. PISA 2015 focused on science, as it did in 2006. PISA 2018 focused on reading, as it did in 2009; it also offered an optional assessment of financial literacy, administered by the United States.

Further information on PISA may be obtained from

Patrick Gonzales
International Assessment Branch
Assessments Division
National Center for Education Statistics
550 12th Street SW
Washington, DC 20202
patrick.gonzales@ed.gov
https://nces.ed.gov/surveys/pisa

Glossary

A

Achievement gap See Gap.

Achievement levels, NAEP Specific achievement levels for each subject area and grade to provide a context for interpreting student performance. At this time they are being used on a trial basis.

> ***NAEP Basic***—denotes partial mastery of the knowledge and skills that are fundamental for *proficient* work at a given grade.

> ***NAEP Proficient***—represents solid academic performance. Students reaching this level have demonstrated competency over challenging subject matter.

> ***NAEP Advanced***—signifies superior performance.

Adjusted Cohort Graduation Rate (ACGR) The number of students who graduate in 4 years with a regular high school diploma divided by the number of students who form the adjusted cohort for the graduating class. From the beginning of 9th grade (or the earliest high school grade), students who are entering that grade for the first time form a cohort that is "adjusted" by adding any students who subsequently transfer into the cohort and subtracting any students who subsequently transfer out, emigrate to another country, or die.

Associate's degree A degree granted for the successful completion of a sub-baccalaureate program of studies, usually requiring at least 2 years (or equivalent) of full-time college-level study. This includes degrees granted in a cooperative or work-study program.

B

Bachelor's degree A degree granted for the successful completion of a baccalaureate program of studies, usually requiring at least 4 years (or equivalent) of full-time college-level study. This includes degrees granted in a cooperative or work-study program.

C

Capital outlay Funds for the acquisition of land and buildings; building construction, remodeling, and additions; the initial installation or extension of service systems and other built-in equipment; and site improvement. The category also encompasses architectural and engineering services including the development of blueprints.

Catholic school A private school over which a Roman Catholic church group exercises some control or provides some form of subsidy. Catholic schools for the most part include those operated or supported by a parish, a group of parishes, a diocese, or a Catholic religious order.

Certificate A formal award certifying the satisfactory completion of a postsecondary education program. Certificates can be awarded at any level of postsecondary education and include awards below the associate's degree level.

Charter school See Public charter school.

Classification of Instructional Programs (CIP) A taxonomic coding scheme that contains titles and descriptions of primarily postsecondary instructional programs. It was developed to facilitate NCES collection and reporting of postsecondary degree completions by major field of study using standard classifications that capture the majority of reportable program activity. It was originally published in 1980 and was revised in 1985, 1990, 2000, and 2010.

College A postsecondary school that offers general or liberal arts education, usually leading to an associate's, bachelor's, master's, or doctor's degree. Junior colleges and community colleges are included under this terminology.

Combined school A school that encompasses instruction at both the elementary and the secondary levels; includes schools starting with grade 6 or below and ending with grade 9 or above.

Constant dollars Dollar amounts that have been adjusted by means of price and cost indexes to eliminate inflationary factors and allow direct comparison across years.

Consumer Price Index (CPI) A price index that measures the average change in the cost of a fixed market basket of goods and services purchased by consumers. Indexes vary for specific areas or regions, periods of time, major groups of consumer expenditures, and population groups. The CPI reflects spending patterns for two population groups: (1) all urban consumers and urban wage earners and (2) clerical workers. CPIs are calculated for both the calendar year and the school year using the U.S. All Items CPI for All Urban Consumers (CPI-U). The calendar year CPI is the same as the annual CPI-U. The school year CPI is calculated by adding the monthly CPI-U figures, beginning with July of the first year and ending with June of the following year, and then dividing that figure by 12.

Control of institutions A classification of institutions of elementary/secondary or postsecondary education by whether the institution is operated by publicly elected or appointed officials and derives its primary support from public funds (public control) or is operated by privately elected or appointed officials and derives its major source of funds from private sources (private control).

Current expenditures (elementary/secondary) The expenditures for operating local public schools, excluding capital outlay and interest on school debt. These expenditures include such items as salaries for school personnel, benefits, student transportation, school books and materials, and energy costs. Beginning in 1980–81, expenditures for state administration are excluded.

Instruction expenditures Include expenditures for activities related to the interaction between teacher and students. Include salaries and benefits for teachers and instructional aides, textbooks, supplies, and purchased services such as instruction via television, webinars, and other online instruction. Also included are tuition expenditures to other local education agencies.

Administration expenditures Include expenditures for school administration (i.e., the office of the principal, full-time department chairpersons, and graduation expenses), general administration (the superintendent and board of education and their immediate staff), and other support services expenditures.

Transportation Includes expenditures for vehicle operation, monitoring, and vehicle servicing and maintenance.

Food services Include all expenditures associated with providing food to students and staff in a school or school district. The services include preparing and serving regular and incidental meals or snacks in connection with school activities, as well as the delivery of food to schools.

Enterprise operations Include expenditures for activities that are financed, at least in part, by user charges, similar to a private business. These include operations funded by sales of products or services, together with amounts for direct program support made by state education agencies for local school districts.

D

Degree-granting institutions Postsecondary institutions that are eligible for Title IV federal financial aid programs and grant an associate's or higher degree. For an institution to be eligible to participate in Title IV financial aid programs it must offer a program of at least 300 clock hours in length, have accreditation recognized by the U.S. Department of Education, have been in business for at least 2 years, and have signed a participation agreement with the Department.

Direct Loan Program The William D. Ford Federal Direct Loan (Direct Loan) Program, established in 2010, is the largest federal student loan program. Direct Loans can be awarded to undergraduate students, with the either interest subsidized (based on need) or unsubsidized; to parents of undergraduate students; or to graduate students. The U.S. Department of Education is the lender for these loans.

Disabilities, children with Those children evaluated as having any of the following impairments and who, by reason thereof, receive special education and related services under the Individuals with Disabilities Education Act (IDEA) according to an Individualized Education Program (IEP), Individualized Family Service Plan (IFSP), or a services plan. There are local variations in the determination of disability conditions, and not all states use all reporting categories.

Autism Having a developmental disability significantly affecting verbal and nonverbal communication and social interaction, generally evident before age 3, that adversely affects educational performance. Other characteristics often associated with autism are engagement in repetitive activities and stereotyped movements, resistance to environmental change or change in daily routines, and unusual responses to sensory experiences. A child is not considered autistic if the child's educational performance is adversely affected primarily because of an emotional disturbance.

Deaf-blindness Having concomitant hearing and visual impairments that cause such severe communication and other developmental and educational problems that the student cannot be accommodated in special education programs solely for deaf or blind students.

Developmental delay Having developmental delays, as defined at the state level, and as measured by appropriate diagnostic instruments and procedures in one or more of the following cognitive areas: physical development, cognitive development, communication development, social or emotional development, or adaptive development. Applies only to 3- through 9-year-old children.

Emotional disturbance Exhibiting one or more of the following characteristics over a long period of time, to a marked degree, and adversely affecting educational performance: an inability to learn that cannot be explained by intellectual, sensory, or health factors; an inability to build or maintain satisfactory interpersonal relationships with peers and teachers; inappropriate types of behavior or feelings under normal circumstances; a general pervasive mood of unhappiness or depression; or a tendency to develop physical symptoms or fears associated with personal or school problems. This term does not include children who are socially maladjusted, unless they also display one or more of the listed characteristics.

Hearing impairment Having a hearing impairment, whether permanent or fluctuating, which adversely affects the student's educational performance, but which is not included under the definition of "deaf" in this section.

Intellectual disability Having significantly subaverage general intellectual functioning, existing concurrently with defects in adaptive behavior and manifested during the developmental period, which adversely affects the child's educational performance.

Multiple disabilities Having concomitant impairments (such as intellectually disabled-blind, intellectually disabled-orthopedically impaired, etc.), the combination of which causes such severe educational problems that the student cannot be accommodated in special education programs solely for one of the impairments. Term does not include deaf-blind students.

Orthopedic impairment Having a severe orthopedic impairment that adversely affects a student's educational performance. The term includes impairment resulting from congenital anomaly, disease, or other causes.

Other health impairment Having limited strength, vitality, or alertness due to chronic or acute health problems, such as a heart condition, tuberculosis, rheumatic fever, nephritis, asthma, sickle cell anemia, hemophilia, epilepsy, lead poisoning, leukemia, or diabetes, which adversely affect the student's educational performance.

Specific learning disability Having a disorder in one or more of the basic psychological processes involved in understanding or in using spoken or written language, which may manifest itself in an imperfect ability to listen, think, speak, read, write, spell, or do mathematical calculations. The term includes such conditions as perceptual disabilities, brain injury, minimal brain dysfunction, dyslexia, and developmental aphasia. The term does not include children who have learning problems which are primarily the result of visual, hearing, motor, or intellectual disabilities, or of environmental, cultural, or economic disadvantage.

Speech or language impairment Having a communication disorder, such as stuttering, impaired articulation, language impairment, or voice impairment, that adversely affects the student's educational performance.

Traumatic brain injury Having an acquired injury to the brain caused by an external physical force, resulting in total or partial functional disability or psychosocial impairment or both, that adversely affects the student's educational performance. The term applies to open or closed head injuries resulting in impairments in one or more areas, such as cognition; language; memory; attention; reasoning; abstract thinking; judgment; problem-solving; sensory, perceptual, and motor abilities; psychosocial behavior; physical functions; information processing; and speech. The term does not apply to brain injuries that are congenital or degenerative or to brain injuries induced by birth trauma.

Visual impairment Having a visual impairment that, even with correction, adversely affects the student's educational performance. The term includes partially seeing and blind children.

Distance education Education that uses one or more technologies to deliver instruction to students who are separated from the instructor and to support regular and substantive interaction between the students and the instructor synchronously or asynchronously. Technologies used for instruction may include the following: Internet; one-way and two-way transmissions through open broadcasts, closed circuit, cable, microwave, broadband lines, fiber optics, and satellite or wireless communication devices; audio conferencing; and DVDs and CD-ROMs, if used in a course in conjunction with the technologies listed above.

Doctor's degree (also referred to as doctoral degree) The highest award a student can earn for graduate study. Includes such degrees as the Doctor of Education (Ed.D.); the Doctor of Juridical Science (S.J.D.); the Doctor of Public Health (Dr.P.H.); and the Doctor of Philosophy (Ph.D.) in any field, such as agronomy, food technology, education, engineering, public administration, ophthalmology, or radiology. The doctor's degree classification encompasses three main subcategories—research/scholarship degrees, professional practice degrees, and other degrees—which are described below.

Doctor's degree—research/scholarship A Ph.D. or other doctor's degree that requires advanced work beyond the master's level, including the preparation and defense of a dissertation based on original research, or the planning and execution of an original project demonstrating substantial artistic or scholarly achievement. Examples of this type of degree may include the following and others, as designated by the awarding institution: the Ed.D. (in education), D.M.A. (in musical arts), D.B.A. (in business administration), D.Sc. (in science), D.A. (in arts), or D.M (in medicine).

Doctor's degree—professional practice A doctor's degree that is conferred upon completion of a program providing the knowledge and skills for the recognition, credential, or license required for professional practice. The degree is typically awarded after a period of study such that the total time to the degree, including both preprofessional and professional preparation, equals at least 6 full-time-equivalent academic years. Some doctor's degrees of this type were formerly classified as first-professional degrees. Examples of this type of degree may include the following and others, as designated by the awarding institution: the D.C. or D.C.M. (in chiropractic); D.D.S. or D.M.D. (in dentistry); L.L.B. or J.D. (in law); M.D. (in medicine); O.D. (in optometry); D.O. (in osteopathic medicine); Pharm.D. (in pharmacy); D.P.M., Pod.D., or D.P. (in podiatry); or D.V.M. (in veterinary medicine).

Doctor's degree—other A doctor's degree that does not meet the definition of either a research/scholarship doctor's degree or a professional practice doctor's degree.

E

Education specialist/professional diploma A certificate of advanced graduate studies that further educators in their instructional and leadership skills beyond a master's degree level of competence.

Educational attainment The highest grade of regular school attended and completed.

Educational attainment (Current Population Survey) A measure that uses March CPS data to estimate the percentage of civilian, noninstitutionalized people who have achieved certain levels of educational attainment. Estimates of educational attainment do not differentiate between those who graduated from public schools, those who graduated from private schools, and those who earned a GED; these estimates also include individuals who earned their credential or completed their highest level of education outside of the United States.

1972–1991 During this period, an individual's educational attainment was considered to be his or her last fully completed year of school. Individuals who completed 12 years of schooling were deemed to be high school graduates, as were those who began but did not complete the first year of college. Individuals who completed 16 or more years of schooling were counted as college graduates.

1992–present Beginning in 1992, CPS asked respondents to report their highest level of school completed or their highest degree received. This change means that some data collected before 1992 are not strictly comparable with data collected from 1992 onward and that care must be taken when making comparisons across years. The revised survey question emphasizes credentials received rather than the last grade level attended or completed. The new categories include the following:

- High school graduate, high school diploma, or the equivalent (e.g., GED)

- Some college but no degree

- Associate's degree in college, occupational/vocational program

- Associate's degree in college, academic program (e.g., A.A., A.S., A.A.S.)

- Bachelor's degree (e.g., B.A., A.B., B.S.)

- Master's degree (e.g., M.A., M.S., M.Eng., M.Ed., M.S.W., M.B.A.)

- Professional school degree (e.g., M.D., D.D.S., D.V.M., LL.B., J.D.)

- Doctor's degree (e.g., Ph.D., Ed.D.)

Elementary school A school classified as elementary by state and local practice and composed of any span of grades not above grade 8.

Employment status A classification of individuals as employed (either full or part time), unemployed (looking for work or on layoff), or not in the labor force (due to retirement, unpaid employment, or some other reason).

English language learner (ELL) An individual who, due to any of the reasons listed below, has sufficient difficulty speaking, reading, writing, or understanding the English language to be denied the opportunity to learn successfully in classrooms where the language of instruction is English or to participate fully in the larger U.S. society. Such an individual (1) was not born in the United States or has a native language other than English; (2) comes from environments where a language other than English is dominant; or (3) is an American Indian or Alaska Native and comes from environments where a language other than English has had a significant impact on the individual's level of English language proficiency.

Enrollment The total number of students registered in a given school unit at a given time, generally in the fall of a year. At the postsecondary level, separate counts are also available for full-time and part-time students, as well as full-time-equivalent enrollment. See also Full-time enrollment, Full-time-equivalent (FTE) enrollment, and Part-time enrollment.

Expenditures per pupil Charges incurred for a particular period of time divided by a student unit of measure, such as average daily attendance or fall enrollment.

Expenditures, total For elementary/secondary schools, these include all charges for current outlays plus capital outlays and interest on school debt. For degree-granting institutions, these include current outlays plus capital outlays. For government, these include charges net of recoveries and other correcting transactions other than for retirement of debt, investment in securities, extension of credit, or as agency transactions. Government expenditures include only external transactions, such as the provision of perquisites or other payments in kind. Aggregates for groups of governments exclude intergovernmental transactions among the governments.

F

Financial aid Grants, loans, assistantships, scholarships, fellowships, tuition waivers, tuition discounts, veteran's benefits, employer aid (tuition reimbursement), and other monies (other than from relatives or friends) provided to students to help them meet expenses. Except where designated, includes Title IV subsidized and unsubsidized loans made directly to students.

For-profit institution See Private institution.

Free or reduced-price lunch See National School Lunch Program.

Full-time enrollment The number of students enrolled in postsecondary education courses with total credit load equal to at least 75 percent of the normal full-time course load. At the undergraduate level, full-time enrollment typically includes students who have a credit load of 12 or more semester or quarter credits. At the postbaccalaureate level, full-time enrollment includes students who typically have a credit load of 9 or more semester or quarter credits, as well as other students who are considered full time by their institutions.

Full-time-equivalent (FTE) enrollment For postsecondary institutions, enrollment of full-time students, plus the full-time equivalent of part-time students. The full-time equivalent of the part-time students is estimated using different factors depending on the type and control of institution and level of student.

G

Gap Occurs when an outcome—for example, average test score or level of educational attainment—is higher for one group than for another group and when the difference between the two groups' outcomes is statistically significant.

Geographic region One of the four regions of the United States used by the U.S. Census Bureau, as follows:

Northeast	Midwest
Connecticut (CT)	Illinois (IL)
Maine (ME)	Indiana (IN)
Massachusetts (MA)	Iowa (IA)
New Hampshire (NH)	Kansas (KS)
New Jersey (NJ)	Michigan (MI)
New York (NY)	Minnesota (MN)
Pennsylvania (PA)	Missouri (MO)
Rhode Island (RI)	Nebraska (NE)
Vermont (VT)	North Dakota (ND)
	Ohio (OH)
	South Dakota (SD)
	Wisconsin (WI)

South	West
Alabama (AL)	Alaska (AK)
Arkansas (AR)	Arizona (AZ)
Delaware (DE)	California (CA)
District of Columbia (DC)	Colorado (CO)
Florida (FL)	Hawaii (HI)
Georgia (GA)	Idaho (ID)
Kentucky (KY)	Montana (MT)
Louisiana (LA)	Nevada (NV)
Maryland (MD)	New Mexico (NM)
Mississippi (MS)	Oregon (OR)
North Carolina (NC)	Utah (UT)
Oklahoma (OK)	Washington (WA)
South Carolina (SC)	Wyoming (WY)
Tennessee (TN)	
Texas (TX)	
Virginia (VA)	
West Virginia (WV)	

Gross domestic product (GDP) The total national output of goods and services valued at market prices. GDP can be viewed in terms of expenditure categories which include purchases of goods and services by consumers and government, gross private domestic investment, and net exports of goods and services. The goods and services included are largely those bought for final use (excluding illegal transactions) in the market economy. A number of inclusions, however, represent imputed values, the most important of which is rental value of owner-occupied housing.

H

High school completer An individual who has been awarded a high school diploma or an equivalent credential, including a GED certificate.

High school diploma A formal document regulated by the state certifying the successful completion of a prescribed secondary school program of studies. In some states or communities, high school diplomas are differentiated by type, such as an academic diploma, a general diploma, or a vocational diploma.

Historically black colleges and universities (HBCUs) Accredited higher education institutions established prior to 1964 with the principal mission of educating black Americans. Federal regulations (20 USC 1061 (2)) allow for certain exceptions of the founding date.

Household All the people who occupy a housing unit. A house, an apartment, a mobile home, a group of rooms, or a single room is regarded as a housing unit when it is occupied or intended for occupancy as separate living quarters, that is, when the occupants do not live and eat with any other people in the structure, and there is direct access from the outside or through a common hall.

I

Individuals with Disabilities Education Act (IDEA) A federal law enacted in 1990 and reauthorized in 1997 and 2004. IDEA requires services to children with disabilities throughout the nation. IDEA governs how states and public agencies provide early intervention, special education, and related services to eligible infants, toddlers, children, and youth with disabilities. Infants and toddlers with disabilities (birth–age 2) and their families receive early intervention services under IDEA, Part C. Children and youth (ages 3–21) receive special education and related services under IDEA, Part B.

Interest on debt Includes expenditures for long-term debt service interest payments (i.e., those longer than 1 year).

International Standard Classification of Education (ISCED) Used to compare educational systems in different countries. ISCED is the standard used by many countries to report education statistics to the United Nations Educational, Scientific, and Cultural Organization (UNESCO) and the Organization for Economic Cooperation and Development (OECD). ISCED was revised in 2011.

ISCED 2011 ISCED 2011 divides educational systems into the following nine categories, based on eight levels of education.

ISCED Level 0 Education preceding the first level (early childhood education) includes early childhood programs that target children below the age of entry into primary education.

ISCED Level 01 Early childhood educational development programs are generally designed for children younger than 3 years.

ISCED Level 02 Pre-primary education preceding the first level usually begins at age 3, 4, or 5 (sometimes earlier) and lasts from 1 to 3 years, when it is provided. In the United States, this level includes nursery school and kindergarten.

ISCED Level 1 Education at the first level (primary or elementary education) usually begins at age 5, 6, or 7 and continues for about 4 to 6 years. For the United States, the first level starts with 1st grade and ends with 6th grade.

ISCED Level 2 Education at the second level (lower secondary education) typically begins at about age 11 or 12 and continues for about 2 to 6 years. For the United States, the second level starts with 7th grade and typically ends with 9th grade. Education at the lower secondary level continues the basic programs of the first level, although teaching is typically more subject focused, often using more specialized teachers who conduct classes in their field of specialization. This subject-oriented coursework is the main criterion for distinguishing lower secondary education from primary education. If there is no clear breakpoint for this organizational change, lower secondary education is considered to begin at the end of 6 years of primary education. In countries with no clear division between lower secondary and upper secondary education, and where lower secondary education lasts for more than 3 years, only the first 3 years following primary education are counted as lower secondary education.

ISCED Level 3 Education at the third level (upper secondary education) typically begins at age 15 or 16 and lasts for approximately 3 years. In the United States, the third level starts with 10th grade and ends with 12th grade. Upper secondary education is the final stage of secondary education in most OECD countries. Instruction is often organized along subject-matter lines, in contrast to the lower secondary level, and teachers typically must have a higher-level, or more subject-specific, qualification. There are substantial differences in the typical duration of programs both across and between countries, ranging from 2 to 5 years of schooling. The main criteria for classifications are (1) national boundaries between lower and upper secondary education and (2) admission into educational programs, which usually requires the completion of lower secondary education or a combination of basic education and life experience that demonstrates the ability to handle the subject matter in upper secondary schools. Includes programs designed to review the content of third level programs, such as preparatory courses for tertiary education entrance examinations, and programs leading to a qualification equivalent to upper secondary general education.

ISCED Level 4 Education at the fourth level (postsecondary non-tertiary education) straddles the boundary between secondary and postsecondary education. This program of study, which is primarily vocational in nature, is generally taken after the completion of secondary school and typically lasts from 6 months to 2 years. Although the content of these programs may not be significantly more advanced than upper secondary programs, these programs serve to broaden the knowledge of participants who have already gained an upper secondary qualification.

ISCED Level 5 Education at the fifth level (short-cycle tertiary education) is noticeably more complex than in upper secondary programs giving access to this level. Content at the fifth level is usually practically based and occupationally specific, and it prepares students to enter the labor market. However, the fifth level may also provide a pathway to other tertiary education programs (the sixth or seventh level). Short cycle-tertiary programs last for at least 2 years, and usually for no more than 3. In the United States, this level includes associate's degrees.

ISCED Level 6 Education at the sixth level (bachelor's or equivalent level) is longer and usually more theoretically oriented than programs at the fifth level, but may include practical components. Entry into these programs normally requires the completion of a third or fourth level program. They typically have a duration of 3 to 4 years of full-time study. Programs at the sixth level do not necessarily require the preparation of a substantive thesis or dissertation.

ISCED Level 7 Education at the seventh level (master's or equivalent level) has significantly more complex and specialized content than programs at the sixth level. The content at the seventh level is often designed to provide participants with advanced academic and/or professional knowledge, skills, and competencies, leading to a second degree or equivalent qualification. Programs at this level may have a substantial research component but do not yet lead to the award of a doctoral qualification. In the United States, this level includes professional degrees such as J.D., M.D., and D.D.S., as well as master's degrees.

ISCED Level 8 Education at the eighth level (doctoral or equivalent level) is provided in graduate and professional schools that generally require a university degree or diploma as a minimum condition for admission. Programs at this level lead to the award of an advanced, postgraduate degree, such as a Ph.D. The theoretical duration of these programs is 3 years of full-time enrollment in most countries (for a cumulative total of at least 7 years at the tertiary level), although the length of the actual enrollment is often longer. Programs at this level are devoted to advanced study and original research.

ISCED 1997 ISCED 1997 divides educational systems into the following seven categories, based on six levels of education.

ISCED Level 0 Education preceding the first level (early childhood education) usually begins at age 3, 4, or 5 (sometimes earlier) and lasts from 1 to 3 years, when it is provided. In the United States, this level includes nursery school and kindergarten.

ISCED Level 1 Education at the first level (primary or elementary education) usually begins at age 5, 6, or 7 and continues for about 4 to 6 years. For the United States, the first level starts with 1st grade and ends with 6th grade.

ISCED Level 2 Education at the second level (lower secondary education) typically begins at about age 11 or 12 and continues for about 2 to 6 years. For the United States, the second level starts with 7th grade and typically ends with 9th grade. Education at the lower secondary level continues the basic programs of the first level, although teaching is typically more subject focused, often using more specialized teachers who conduct classes in their field of specialization. This subject-oriented coursework is the main criterion for distinguishing lower secondary education from primary education. If there is no clear breakpoint for this organizational change, lower secondary education is considered to begin at the end of 6 years of primary education. In countries with no clear division between lower secondary and upper secondary education, and where lower secondary education lasts for more than 3 years, only the first 3 years following primary education are counted as lower secondary education.

ISCED Level 3 Education at the third level (upper secondary education) typically begins at age 15 or 16 and lasts for approximately 3 years. In the United States, the third level starts with 10th grade and ends with 12th grade. Upper secondary education is the final stage of secondary education in most OECD countries. Instruction is often organized along subject-matter lines, in contrast to the lower secondary level, and teachers typically must have a higher-level, or more subject-specific, qualification. There are substantial differences in the typical duration of programs both across and between countries, ranging from 2 to 5 years of schooling. The main criteria for classifications are (1) national boundaries between lower and upper secondary

education and (2) admission into educational programs, which usually requires the completion of lower secondary education or a combination of basic education and life experience that demonstrates the ability to handle the subject matter in upper secondary schools.

ISCED Level 4 Education at the fourth level (postsecondary non-tertiary education) straddles the boundary between secondary and postsecondary education. This program of study, which is primarily vocational in nature, is generally taken after the completion of secondary school and typically lasts from 6 months to 2 years. Although the content of these programs may not be significantly more advanced than upper secondary programs, these programs serve to broaden the knowledge of participants who have already gained an upper secondary qualification.

ISCED Level 5 Education at the fifth level (first stage of tertiary education) includes programs with more advanced content than those offered at the two previous levels. Entry into programs at the fifth level normally requires successful completion of either of the two previous levels.

ISCED Level 5A Tertiary-type A programs provide an education that is largely theoretical and is intended to provide sufficient qualifications for gaining entry into advanced research programs and professions with high skill requirements. Entry into these programs normally requires the successful completion of an upper secondary education; admission is competitive in most cases. The minimum cumulative theoretical duration at this level is 3 years of full-time enrollment. In the United States, tertiary-type A programs include first university programs that last approximately 4 years and lead to the award of a bachelor's degree and second university programs that lead to a master's degree or a first-professional degree such as an M.D., a J.D., or a D.V.M.

ISCED Level 5B Tertiary-type B programs are typically shorter than tertiary-type A programs and focus on practical, technical, or occupational skills for direct entry into the labor market, although they may cover some theoretical foundations in the respective programs. They have a minimum duration of 2 years of full-time enrollment at the tertiary level. In the United States, such programs are often provided at community colleges and lead to an associate's degree.

ISCED Level 6 Education at the sixth level (advanced research qualification) is provided in graduate and professional schools that generally require a university degree or diploma as a minimum condition for admission. Programs at this level lead to the award of an advanced, postgraduate degree, such as a Ph.D. The theoretical duration of these programs is 3 years of full-time enrollment in most countries (for a cumulative total of at least 7 years at levels five and six), although the length of the actual enrollment is often longer. Programs at this level are devoted to advanced study and original research.

L

Locale codes A classification system to describe a type of location. The "Metro-Centric" locale codes, developed in the 1980s, classified all schools and school districts based on their county's proximity to a Metropolitan Statistical Area (MSA) and their specific location's population size and density. In 2006, the "Urban-Centric" locale codes were introduced. These locale codes are based on an address's proximity to an urbanized area. For more information see https://nces.ed.gov/programs/edge/docs/ EDGE_NCES_LOCALE_2015.pdf.

Pre-2006 Metro-Centric Locale Codes

Large City: A central city of a consolidated metropolitan statistical area (CMSA) or MSA, with the city having a population greater than or equal to 250,000.

Mid-size City: A central city of a CMSA or MSA, with the city having a population less than 250,000.

Urban Fringe of a Large City: Any territory within a CMSA or MSA of a Large City and defined as urban by the Census Bureau.

Urban Fringe of a Mid-size City: Any territory within a CMSA or MSA of a Mid-size City and defined as urban by the Census Bureau.

Large Town: An incorporated place or Census-designated place with a population greater than or equal to 25,000 and located outside a CMSA or MSA.

Small Town: An incorporated place or Census-designated place with a population less than 25,000 and greater than or equal to 2,500 and located outside a CMSA or MSA.

Rural, Outside MSA: Any territory designated as rural by the Census Bureau that is outside a CMSA or MSA of a Large or Mid-size City.

Rural, Inside MSA: Any territory designated as rural by the Census Bureau that is within a CMSA or MSA of a Large or Mid-size City.

2006 Urban-Centric Locale Codes

City, Large: Territory inside an urbanized area and inside a principal city with a population of 250,000 or more.

City, Midsize: Territory inside an urbanized area and inside a principal city with a population less than 250,000 and greater than or equal to 100,000.

City, Small: Territory inside an urbanized area and inside a principal city with a population less than 100,000.

Suburb, Large: Territory outside a principal city and inside an urbanized area with a population of 250,000 or more.

Suburb, Midsize: Territory outside a principal city and inside an urbanized area with a population less than 250,000 and greater than or equal to 100,000.

Suburb, Small: Territory outside a principal city and inside an urbanized area with a population less than 100,000.

Town, Fringe: Territory inside an urban cluster that is less than or equal to 10 miles from an urbanized area.

Town, Distant: Territory inside an urban cluster that is more than 10 miles and less than or equal to 35 miles from an urbanized area.

Town, Remote: Territory inside an urban cluster that is more than 35 miles from an urbanized area.

Rural, Fringe: Census-defined rural territory that is less than or equal to 5 miles from an urbanized area, as well as rural territory that is less than or equal to 2.5 miles from an urban cluster.

Rural, Distant: Census-defined rural territory that is more than 5 miles but less than or equal to 25 miles from an urbanized area, as well as rural territory that is more than 2.5 miles but less than or equal to 10 miles from an urban cluster.

Rural, Remote: Census-defined rural territory that is more than 25 miles from an urbanized area and is also more than 10 miles from an urban cluster.

M

Master's degree A degree awarded for successful completion of a program generally requiring 1 or 2 years of full-time college-level study beyond the bachelor's degree. One type of master's degree, including the Master of Arts degree, or M.A., and the Master of Science degree, or M.S., is awarded in the liberal arts and sciences for advanced scholarship in a subject field or discipline and demonstrated ability to perform scholarly research. A second type of master's degree is awarded for the completion of a professionally oriented program, for example, an M.Ed. in education, an M.B.A. in business administration, an M.F.A. in fine arts, an M.M. in music, an M.S.W. in social work, and an M.P.A. in public administration. Some master's degrees—such as divinity degrees (M.Div. or M.H.L./Rav), which were formerly classified as "first-professional"—may require more than 2 years of full-time study beyond the bachelor's degree.

Median earnings The amount which divides the income distribution into two equal groups, half having income above that amount and half having income below that amount. Earnings include all wage and salary income. Unlike mean earnings, median earnings either do not change or change very little in response to extreme observations.

N

National School Lunch Program A federally assisted meal program that was established by President Truman in 1946 and that is operated in public and private nonprofit schools and residential child care centers. To be eligible for free lunch, a student must be from a household with an income at or below 130 percent of the federal poverty guideline; to be eligible for reduced-price lunch, a student must be from a household with an income between 130 percent and 185 percent of the federal poverty guideline.

Nonprofit institution See Private institution.

Nonresident alien A person who is not a citizen or national of the United States and who is in this country on a visa or temporary basis and does not have the right to remain indefinitely.

Nonsectarian school Nonsectarian schools do not have a religious orientation or purpose and are categorized as regular, special program emphasis, or special education schools. See also Regular school.

O

Organization for Economic Cooperation and Development (OECD) An intergovernmental organization of industrialized countries that serves as a forum for member countries to cooperate in research and policy development on social and economic topics of common interest. In addition to member countries, partner countries contribute to the OECD's work in a sustained and comprehensive manner.

Open admissions Admission policy whereby the school will accept any student who applies.

Other religious school Other religious schools have a religious orientation or purpose, but are not Roman Catholic. Other religious schools are categorized according to religious association membership as Conservative Christian, other affiliated, or unaffiliated.

P

Part-time enrollment The number of students enrolled in postsecondary education courses with a total credit load

less than 75 percent of the normal full-time credit load. At the undergraduate level, part-time enrollment typically includes students who have a credit load of less than 12 semester or quarter credits. At the postbaccalaureate level, part-time enrollment typically includes students who have a credit load of less than 9 semester or quarter credits.

Postbaccalaureate certificate An award that requires completion of an organized program of study beyond a bachelor's degree. It is designed for persons who have completed a baccalaureate degree, but does not meet the requirements of a master's degree. Even though teacher preparation certificate programs may require a bachelor's degree for admission, they are considered sub-baccalaureate undergraduate programs, and students in these programs are undergraduate students.

Postbaccalaureate enrollment The number of students working toward advanced degrees and of students enrolled in graduate-level classes but not enrolled in degree programs.

Postsecondary education The provision of formal instructional programs with a curriculum designed primarily for students who have completed the requirements for a high school diploma or equivalent. This includes programs of an academic, vocational, and continuing professional education purpose, and excludes avocational and adult basic education programs.

Postsecondary institutions (basic classification by level)

4-year institution An institution offering at least a 4-year program of college-level studies wholly or principally creditable toward a baccalaureate degree.

2-year institution An institution offering at least a 2-year program of college-level studies which terminates in an associate degree or is principally creditable toward a baccalaureate degree. Data prior to 1996 include some institutions that have a less-than-2-year program, but were designated as institutions of higher education in the Higher Education General Information Survey.

Less-than-2-year institution An institution that offers programs of less than 2 years' duration below the baccalaureate level. Includes occupational and vocational schools with programs that do not exceed 1,800 contact hours.

Poverty (official measure) The U.S. Census Bureau uses a set of money income thresholds that vary by family size and composition. A family, along with each individual in it, is considered poor if the family's total income is less than that family's threshold. The poverty thresholds do not vary geographically and are adjusted annually for inflation using the Consumer Price Index. The official poverty definition counts money income before taxes and does not include capital gains and noncash benefits (such as public housing, Medicaid, and food stamps).

Prekindergarten Preprimary education for children typically ages 3–4 who have not yet entered kindergarten. It may offer a program of general education or special education and may be part of a collaborative effort with Head Start.

Preschool An instructional program enrolling children generally younger than 5 years of age and organized to provide children with educational experiences under professionally qualified teachers during the year or years immediately preceding kindergarten (or prior to entry into elementary school when there is no kindergarten). See also Prekindergarten.

Private institution An institution that is controlled by an individual or agency other than a state, a subdivision of a state, or the federal government, which is usually supported primarily by other than public funds, and the operation of whose program rests with other than publicly elected or appointed officials.

    Private nonprofit institution An institution in which the individual(s) or agency in control receives no compensation other than wages, rent, or other expenses for the assumption of risk. These include both independent nonprofit institutions and those affiliated with a religious organization.

    Private for-profit institution An institution in which the individual(s) or agency in control receives compensation other than wages, rent, or other expenses for the assumption of risk (e.g., proprietary schools).

Private school Private elementary/secondary schools surveyed by the Private School Universe Survey (PSS) are assigned to one of three major categories of religious orientation (Catholic, other religious, or nonsectarian) and, within each major category, one of three subcategories based on the school's religious affiliation provided by respondents.

    Catholic Schools categorized according to governance, provided by Roman Catholic school respondents, into (i) parochial, (ii) diocesan, and (iii) private Catholic schools.

    Other religious Schools that have a religious orientation or purpose but are not Catholic. Other religious schools are categorized according to religious association membership, provided by respondents, into (i) Conservative Christian, (ii) other affiliated, and (iii) unaffiliated schools. Conservative Christian schools are those "Other religious" schools with membership in at least one of four associations: Accelerated Christian Education, American Association of Christian Schools, Association of Christian Schools International, and Oral Roberts University Education Fellowship. Affiliated schools are those "Other religious" schools not classified as Conservative Christian with membership in at least 1 of 11 associations—Association of

Christian Teachers and Schools, Christian Schools International, Evangelical Lutheran Education Association, Friends Council on Education, General Conference of the Seventh-Day Adventist Church, Islamic School League of America, National Association of Episcopal Schools, National Christian School Association, National Society for Hebrew Day Schools, Solomon Schechter Day Schools, and Southern Baptist Association of Christian Schools—or indicating membership in "other religious school associations." Unaffiliated schools are those "Other religious" schools that have a religious orientation or purpose but are not classified as Conservative Christian or affiliated.

    Nonsectarian Schools that do not have a religious orientation or purpose and are categorized according to program emphasis, provided by respondents, into (i) regular, (ii) special emphasis, and (iii) special education schools. Regular schools are those that have a regular elementary/secondary or early childhood program emphasis. Special emphasis schools are those that have a Montessori, vocational/technical, alternative, or special program emphasis. Special education schools are those that have a special education program emphasis.

Property tax The sum of money collected from a tax levied against the value of property.

Public charter school A school providing free public elementary and/or secondary education to eligible students under a specific charter granted by the state legislature or other authority, and designated by such authority to be a charter school.

Public school or institution A school or institution controlled and operated by publicly elected or appointed officials and deriving its primary support from public funds.

Purchasing Power Parity (PPP) indexes PPP exchange rates, or indexes, are the currency exchange rates that equalize the purchasing power of different currencies, meaning that when a given sum of money is converted into different currencies at the PPP exchange rates, it will buy the same basket of goods and services in all countries. PPP indexes are the rates of currency conversion that eliminate the difference in price levels among countries. Thus, when expenditures on gross domestic product (GDP) for different countries are converted into a common currency by means of PPP indexes, they are expressed at the same set of international prices, so that comparisons among countries reflect only differences in the volume of goods and services purchased.

R

Racial/ethnic group Classification indicating general racial or ethnic heritage. Race/ethnicity data are based on the Hispanic ethnic category and the race categories listed below (five single-race categories, plus the Two or more races category). Race categories exclude persons of Hispanic ethnicity unless otherwise noted.

White A person having origins in any of the original peoples of Europe, the Middle East, or North Africa.

Black or African American A person having origins in any of the black racial groups of Africa. Used interchangeably with the shortened term *Black*.

Hispanic or Latino A person of Cuban, Mexican, Puerto Rican, South or Central American, or other Spanish culture or origin, regardless of race. Used interchangeably with the shortened term *Hispanic*.

Asian A person having origins in any of the original peoples of the Far East, Southeast Asia, or the Indian subcontinent, including, for example, Cambodia, China, India, Japan, Korea, Malaysia, Pakistan, the Philippine Islands, Thailand, and Vietnam. Prior to 2010–11, the Common Core of Data (CCD) combined Asian and Pacific Islander categories.

Native Hawaiian or Other Pacific Islander A person having origins in any of the original peoples of Hawaii, Guam, Samoa, or other Pacific Islands. Prior to 2010–11, the Common Core of Data (CCD) combined Asian and Pacific Islander categories. Used interchangeably with the shortened term *Pacific Islander*.

American Indian or Alaska Native A person having origins in any of the original peoples of North and South America (including Central America), and who maintains tribal affiliation or community attachment.

Two or more races A person identifying himself or herself as of two or more of the following race groups: White, Black, Asian, Native Hawaiian or Other Pacific Islander, or American Indian or Alaska Native. Some, but not all, reporting districts use this category. "Two or more races" was introduced in the 2000 Census and became a regular category for data collection in the Current Population Survey in 2003. The category is sometimes excluded from a historical series of data with constant categories. It is sometimes included within the category "Other."

Regular school An elementary/secondary or charter school providing instruction and education services that does not focus primarily on special education, vocational/technical education, or alternative education.

Retention rate A measure of the rate at which students persist in their educational program at an institution, expressed as a percentage. For four-year institutions, this is the percentage of first-time bachelor's (or equivalent) degree-seeking undergraduates from the previous fall who are again enrolled in the current fall. For all other institutions, this is the percentage of first-time degree/certificate-seeking students from the previous fall who either re-enrolled or successfully completed their program by the current fall.

Revenue All funds received from external sources, net of refunds, and correcting transactions. Noncash transactions, such as receipt of services, commodities, or other receipts in kind are excluded, as are funds received from the issuance of debt, liquidation of investments, and nonroutine sale of property.

S

Salary The total amount regularly paid or stipulated to be paid to an individual, before deductions, for personal services rendered while on the payroll of a business or organization.

School district An education agency at the local level that exists primarily to operate public schools or to contract for public school services. Synonyms are "local basic administrative unit" and "local education agency."

Secondary school A school comprising any span of grades beginning with the next grade following an elementary or middle school (usually 7, 8, or 9) and ending with or below grade 12. Both junior high schools and senior high schools are included.

Status dropout rate (American Community Survey) Similar to the status dropout rate (Current Population Survey), except that institutionalized persons, incarcerated persons, and active duty military personnel living in barracks in the United States may be included in this calculation.

Status dropout rate (Current Population Survey) The percentage of civilian, noninstitutionalized young people ages 16–24 who are not in school and have not earned a high school credential (either a diploma or equivalency credential such as a GED certificate). The numerator of the status dropout rate for a given year is the number of individuals ages 16–24 who, as of October of that year, have not completed a high school credential and are not currently enrolled in school. The denominator is the total number of individuals ages 16–24 in the United States in October of that year. Status dropout rates count the following individuals as dropouts: those who never attended school and immigrants who did not complete the equivalent of a high school education in their home country.

STEM fields Science, Technology, Engineering, and Mathematics (STEM) fields of study that are considered to be of particular relevance to advanced societies. For the purposes of *The Condition of Education*, STEM fields include biological and biomedical sciences, computer and information sciences, engineering and engineering technologies, mathematics and statistics, and physical sciences and science technologies.

Student membership An annual headcount of students enrolled in school on October 1 or the school day closest to that date. The Common Core of Data (CCD) allows a student to be reported for only a single school or agency.

For example, a vocational school (identified as a "shared time" school) may provide classes for students from a number of districts and show no membership.

T

Title IV eligible institution A postsecondary institution that meets the criteria for participating in federal student financial aid programs. An eligible institution must be any of the following: (1) an institution of higher education (with public or private, nonprofit control), (2) a proprietary institution (with private for-profit control), and (3) a postsecondary vocational institution (with public or private, nonprofit control). In addition, it must have acceptable legal authorization, acceptable accreditation and admission standards, eligible academic program(s), administrative capability, and financial responsibility.

Traditional public school Publicly funded schools other than public charter schools. See also Public charter school and Public school or institution.

Tribal colleges and universities An institutional classification developed by the Andrew W. Carnegie Foundation for the Advancement of Teaching. Tribal colleges and universities, with few exceptions, are tribally controlled and located on reservations. They are all members of the American Indian Higher Education Consortium.

Tuition and fees A payment or charge for instruction or compensation for services, privileges, or the use of equipment, books, or other goods. Tuition may be charged per term, per course, or per credit.

U

Undergraduate students Students registered at an institution of postsecondary education who are working in a baccalaureate degree program or other formal program below the baccalaureate, such as an associate's degree, vocational, or technical program.

U.S. resident A citizen or national, or a person who has been admitted as a legal immigrant for the purpose of obtaining permanent resident alien status.

W

Women's colleges Colleges or universities identified by the Women's College Coalition as women's colleges.